Hexagon Series on Human and Environmental Security and Peace **Vol. 6**

Series Editor: Hans Günter Brauch

Thanh-Dam Truong • Des Gasper
Editors

Transnational Migration and Human Security

The Migration–Development–Security Nexus

With 6 Figures, 18 Tables and 2 Boxes

Springer

ISS International Institute of Social Studies Erasmus

Editors
Dr. Thanh-Dam Truong, International Institute of Social Studies, Erasmus University Rotterdam, Kortenaerkade 12, The Hague, NL-2502 LT Netherlands, truong@iss.nl

Prof. Dr. Des Gasper, International Institute of Social Studies, Erasmus University Rotterdam, Kortenaerkade 12, The Hague, NL-2502 LT Netherlands, gasper@iss.nl

ISSN 1865-5793 e-ISSN 1865-5807
ISBN 978-3-642-12756-4 e-ISBN 978-3-642-12757-1
DOI 10.1007/978-3-642-12757-1
Springer Heidelberg Dordrecht London New York

Library of Congress Control Number: 2011926527

Cover design: deblik, Berlin

Cover illustration: The first photo of a truck loaded with people was taken by Julien Brachet (University of Paris), the second photo by Pascal Meunier (France) shows a building site of boats in South Oman.
Both photographers granted the copyright.

Typesetting and layout: Thomas Bast, AFES-PRESS e.V., Mosbach, Germany

Printed on acid-free paper

Springer is part of Springer Science+Business Media (www.springer.com)

Contents

Preface

The book has grown out of collaborative research endeavours of migration experts and development practitioners in the *International Institute of Social Studies* (IISS) of Erasmus University Rotterdam in The Hague, The Netherlands and the Centre on Human Security at Chubu University, Japan. Most of the chapters in the book are extensively revised versions of a selection from 54 papers presented at a conference held in The Hague in August 2007. Others are additional papers that extend and complement the conference papers. A separate set of papers from the conference has appeared as a special issue of the journal *Gender, Technology and Development*, 12,3 (2008), with the title "Trans-local Livelihoods and Connections: Embedding a Gender Perspective into Migration Studies" (co-edited by Thanh-Dam Truong and Des Gasper). A volume co-edited by Kinhide Mushakoji and Mustapha Kamal Pasha on "Human (In)Security in the Networks of Global Cities" was published in 2008 (Kasugai City, Japan: Chubu University, Centre for Human Security Studies).

The network of scholars and practitioners engaged in this volume approach the study of migration with a focal understanding that the social divisions and legal ambiguities brought about by transnational migration cannot be resolved by piecemeal and one-off policies. Often, these policies are de-contextualized from broader processes of neoliberal globalization, and in turn, produce stopgap solutions. Challenging and changing a globally unsustainable system promoted, and/or supported, by neoliberal forms of thought and practices requires the cooperation of academics from a variety of fields and bridging of the divides between professionals (advocates, activists, practitioners and academics) involved directly or indirectly in decision-making processes.

This collection of chapters strives to enhance the quality of debates on the 'migration-development-security' nexus by clarifying their factual premises and theoretical terms and by asking new questions from a transnational perspective. All contributions to this volume have been anonymously peer-reviewed.

The volume brings together concerns that drive practical action as well as those that are set more in theoretical discourses that bear particular values and agendas. The essays seek to speak across the domains of practice and theory and to orient the messages towards public concerns for human dignity, rights and security. Through this collection of chapters, we hope to stimulate our readers towards engaging in a more rigorous study of transnational migration, as well as taking stock of its historically situated meanings.

The Hague, July 2010 Thanh-Dam Truong and Des Gasper

Acknowledgements

The direct and indirect contributions of many individuals and organizations to this book are sincerely acknowledged. Through the generous support received from Japan (the Japanese Ministry of Education and Chubu University) and the Netherlands (the International Institute of Asian Studies at Leiden University, the Municipality of the Hague and Oxfam-NOVIB), the Conference entitled "International Migration, Multi-local Livelihoods and Human Security" took place on 30–31 August 2007. During the conference and in the subsequent production of this publication, the editors were fortunate to have received intellectual support from members of the research cluster on "International Migration and Human Security" at the *International Institute of Social Studies* (ISS) of Erasmus University Rotterdam, in The Hague, The Netherlands. Professor Kinhide Mushakoji, of Osaka University, Japan, is warmly acknowledged for his friendship and for having stimulated our thinking on development ethics and human security through his profound contributions.

We wish to thank all persons who took part in this conference and shared their insights with us. Our appreciation is also extended to the support of several ISS-EUR alumni in conference logistics and the documentation of the deliberations of the conference, especially to Phaedra Veenendaal, Emily Hillenbrand, Doris Anna Hilber, Patricia Fortin, David Jean-Laniel, My-Linh Nguyen, Fanny Petitbon, Malika Basu, and Jiraporn Laocharoenwong.

The collaboration of individuals from diverse fields of study and disciplines as peer reviewers has, in many ways, enriched the contributions to this publication. We wish to thank the following persons: Laura Maria Agustin, Takeshi Akiba, Alexis Aronowitz, Peter van Bergeijk, Sylvia Bergh, Annette Brunovskis, Supang Chantavanich, Nigel Dower, Michael Flynn, Thomas Gammeltoft-Hansen, Andrew Geddes, Arjan de Haan, Jeff Handmaker, Linda Herrera, Vegard Iversen, Amarjit Kaur, Jonathan Klaaren, Robert Koulish, Wendy Larner, Stephanie Limoncelli, Mahmood Messkoub, Paulien Muller, Jan Nederveen Pieterse, Bridget O'Laughlin, Mustapha Kamal Pasha, Peter Penz, John Pilgrim, Irudaya Rajan, Fridus Steijlen, Liliana Suarez, Keiko Yamanaka and Roger Zetter.

To cite all the contributions made by colleagues, students and friends listed in this section is almost impossible. As editors of this publication, we are humbled by everyone's contribution. In acknowledging your support, we apologize for any incompleteness and inadequacy of this presentation.

The process of preparing the book has benefitted throughout from the advice of Prof. Dr. Hans Günter Brauch, Editor of the Hexagon Series on Human and Environmental Security and Peace. His collegial support and commitment is a model for cross-disciplinary and cross-cultural cooperation. Christian Witschel, Agata Oelschlaeger and Almas Schimmel, Springer Publishers, Heidelberg, are especially thanked for having enabled the creation of this platform to articulate our thoughts and for their flexibility. Thomas Bast is warmly acknowledged for his typesetting and indexing work. Anjani Abella of Plexus Development Initiative has assisted us diligently throughout the entire process of preparation of the manuscript. We are indebted to her for her professionalism in combination with a personal commitment and interest in the thematic scope of this publication. Leslie O'Brien and Erik Hoff are thanked for their editorial support. We also thank a British editor who has given much time and expertise in the last phase of the production process. In the process of preparing this book, we are fortunate to have been supported by a wonderful team.

The Hague, July 2010 Thanh-Dam Truong and Des Gasper

Part I Introduction

1 Transnational Migration, Development and Human Security

Thanh-Dam Truong and Des Gasper

1.1 Introductory Remarks

Driven by diverse forces – economic pressures and opportunities, climate change, war, conquest, and transformation of political regimes – human migration has been central to circulation of knowledge and values, goods and labour. Yet it has been subject to mainly disciplinary inquiries and the existing body of studies has lacked a comprehensive perspective. This volume precisely attempts such a comprehensive historical and experiential perspective, and as a result leads us to reconsider the meanings of 'human', 'movement', and 'borders.'

The 'migration-development-security' nexus has deep historical roots set in the construction of the modern state, but has only recently emerged as subject of a self-conscious discursive field. It has been influenced by the changing modalities of governing, with processes of neoliberal globalization contributing to the intensification of the existing forms and the creation of new transnational forms of migration. The acceleration of globalization has produced unprecedented transnational flows (of finance, goods, ideas, people, small weapons and substances), changed the organizational frameworks that facilitate them, and altered the workings of the modern nation-state in dramatic ways. A host of complex questions have been raised regarding how the organization of these cross-border flows undermines, or alters, state authority over national security and people's security in daily lives. The sociological, political and economic drivers behind these flows, the multifaceted identities of their actors, and the permeability of territorial, cultural and political borders reveal the limits of the traditional conception of the 'nation-state' and the need to rethink its dynamic construction beyond a self-identified and fixed entity.

The ongoing reconfiguration of borders manifests attempts to revise this centuries-old concept which has sought to integrate the meaning of a geopolitical entity with a cultural and/or ethnic entity. 'Re-bundling' of economic, social and cultural affinities at regional levels is one way to provide more effectiveness in the management of resources and human flows, given the lack of consensus at the global level. The management of human flows remains particularly problematic due to the tension between legal approaches that judge the legitimacy of border crossing according to a codification system of singular reasons for movement (business, tourism, employment, education, asylum-seeking, or family reunion) and the sociological realities that involve intermeshing motives and evolving human relationships within and across borders. Although migrants' choices are conditioned by legislation, their actions also transform the legal space. For this and other reasons, the migration policy domain is essentially interactive and can be torn between competing goals and rationalities.

Foucault's insights into the mechanisms of societal control and the delimitation of scientific discourses are suggestive for exploring the 'migration-development-security' nexus. He emphasizes the need for attentiveness to the institutional context of an emergence of mechanisms and discourses, and to how different ideas have been brought into a field of intervention and become enacted in particular directions (Gutting 1994). Questioning the fundamental epistemological and ontological assumptions that are prevalent and exploring their biases and how they drive the dynamics of practice are fundamental to understanding current social tensions and finding possible ways of transformation.

This volume tries to bridge the divides in social thought between explanation and justification, and between philosophical and substantive concerns. In doing so it is part of a wider search for new pathways for change. Approaching the subject of migration by way of revisiting presuppositions that have been taken as givens, and exploring their role in shaping rules and institutions governing the movements of people across borders, have helped to reveal the mentalities

T.-D. Truong and D. Gasper (eds.), *Transnational Migration and Human Security*, Hexagon Series on Human and Environmental Security and Peace 6, DOI 10.1007/978-3-642-12757-1_1, © Springer-Verlag Berlin Heidelberg 2011

and rationalities that made up, and continue to make up, the reality of today.

The essays contained here reveal aspects of power and privilege set within 'international migration' as a discursive field and at its intersection with two related fields: 'development' and 'security' - with attention to the human implications. The essays bring to the fore areas that require more systematic assessment of the knowledge claims that inform migration policy regulation, penalties and incentives, and the modalities of intervention, in order to draw lessons for theory and practice. Time-bound and historically-situated meanings ascribed to human movement across borders vary greatly. Territoriality, sovereignty and their reconfigurations play a central role in shaping such social meanings which affect the lives and experiences of the subjects of migration themselves. The volume attempts a cross-disciplinary way forward in contemporary understanding of international migration and its links with both development and human security as research fields and policy domains.

Collins' (2000) concept of matrix of domination - inspired by Foucault's knowledge/power apparatus and Weber's insights on bureaucracy - addresses interlocking systems of oppression and disempowerment (race, class and gender) by shifting social thought away from the conventional additive approach to relations of dominance. She reveals how different systems of domination may operate through reliance (in varying degrees) on mechanisms that can acquire simultaneously a systemic and interpersonal nature. Her matrix of domination is relevant to migration as a field of intervention and its intersections with the two associated fields of security and development. An adjusted version of this matrix for our purposes contains the following:

1. *A hegemonic dimension*: how ideology, culture, knowledge and consciousness can lend legitimacy to the workings of power in the delimitations of human movement as a subject of study and field of intervention.
2. *An institutional dimension*: how dominant values, norms and beliefs produce and reproduce practices that define 'security' in relation to forms of human movement in particular ways.
3. *A disciplinary dimension*: how bureaucracy and surveillance practices that use these values play an important role in hiding the effects of structural inequality among the migrant populations.
4. *An interpersonal and inter-group dimension*: how the first three dimensions are played out in everyday life situations and affect people on the move under specific circumstances.

The next two sections in this introductory chapter sketch the domains of migration, security and development, and suggest their interconnections in terms of the dimensions mentioned above. We highlight key dividing issues, and identify areas for reflection, conversation and action on different ethical frameworks in relation to migration, within a core concern for the improvement of the position of groups subjected to various forms of disempowerment.

1.2 The 'Migration-Security-Development' Nexus: Danger and Opportunity

1.2.1 Migration and Security

The term 'migration' stems from the Latin root *migrare*, meaning to move from one place to another. It first appeared in the English language in the 1610's, referring to persons; and in the 1640's referring to animals.[1] Today the term also refers to a variety of movements, amongst them the processes of transferring data between storage types, formats or computer systems; or the movement of microorganisms between people, animals and plants. It is clear that migration of diverse kinds is essential to life in all aspects and that, for humans, migration involves organization, change and adjustment.

Surveillance of human movement has been a core activity for modern nation-states since their inception in the 16th and 17th centuries in Europe. Foucault (1975) traced the historical transformation of discipline and punishment associated with the rise of the modern state and provided insights into why and how human migration became an issue for state surveillance. Begun as a system of permanent registration of the population in a given locality in order to control the plague, systems of registration became extended to the documentation of growing floating populations in urban areas. With population dislocation and pauperization growing as the capitalist system took hold, anti-nomadic techniques - such as workhouses, schools and induction to the military - were adopted to neutralize dangers, fix those people seen as 'useless or disturbed populations', and avoid the inconven-

1 See at: <http://www.etymonline.com/index.phip?term=migration> (30 January 2010).

iences and perceived threat of over-large assemblies. The function of these techniques of power was gradually adapted to take up a more positive role in the society – notably to increase the possible utility of the individuals subjected to these techniques of surveillance – in other words, to make them 'productive'. This inversion of the functionality of power – from repressive to 'enabling' – initiated the formation of a disciplinary society, connected to the broader historical processes of economic, juridico-political and scientific reform in the search for progress.[2]

Viewed from this vantage point, human movement between different localities within modern Europe was originally framed in the negative terms of a *danger* to society.[3] But with transformations of production relations and the recognition of migration as a structural and durable phenomenon with far-reaching economic, social and political consequences, the notion of 'danger/threat' began to be juxtaposed with that of 'opportunity'.

Torpey's (2000) analysis of the gradual emergence of the passport over the past three centuries extends Foucault's insights on state surveillance of population movements and complements two key perspectives in historical analyses of the state. These are Marx's concept of appropriation of the means of production by the capitalist classes, and Weber's concept of appropriation of the means of violence and the control of their legitimate use by the state. Torpey emphasizes a third dimension of processes of appropriation and monopoly: that of "the legitimate means of movement" (2000: 1).

Torpey shows that the passport was not an invention of the early 20th century, but of a much earlier era. Monopolization of the right to authorize and regulate movements has been intrinsic to the state, even in its early modern form. The progressive advance of the use of the passport as a means of controlling population movements today expresses the 'stateness' of states and their power to provide an 'identity' – a national identity – for citizens, which is not independent of the documents that 'prove' it. It distinguishes the 'national/citizen' from the 'alien' and from the undocumented. Without this passport as a document of national identity, not only is identity unknowable, it is non-existent from a legal perspective. Although a national identity gives access to rights, and can be therefore crucial to livelihood, people can only enter it on stringent conditions and escape from it with difficulty. This monopolization has the effect of reinforcing an interlinked set of processes. They include:

> the (gradual) definition of states everywhere – at least from the point of view of the international system – as 'national' (i.e., as 'nation-states' comprised of members understood as nationals); the codification of laws establishing which types of persons may move within or across their borders, and determining how, when and where they may do so; the stimulation of the worldwide development of techniques for uniquely and unambiguously identifying each and every person on the face of the globe, from birth to death; the construction of bureaucracies designed to implement this regime of identification and to scrutinize persons and documents in order to verify identities; and the creation of a body of legal norms designed to adjudicate claims by individuals to enter into particular spaces and territories (Torpey 2000: 7).

A product of incremental juridico-political reform, the passport conjoined the repressive side of state discipline with its enabling side. State-security and the security of its citizens or nationals were connected through this means. The question of states accepting aliens from other countries arose as an issue during the two World Wars, owing to rising concerns for institutional accountability for the massive movements of refugees across the continents. Ambivalence about state accountability was evident (O'Brien 2003) and has persisted until today. Nevertheless, the legacy of inter-state collaboration did provide a certain degree of institutional accountability for international labour migrants as guest workers (Cholewinski 1994) and for refugees, most of whom would be today termed 'forced migrants' or 'asylum seekers'. For many countries today, the economic utility of aliens has become the prime criterion by which to assess the impact of in-migration.

Cross-border migration patterns since the end of the Cold War show complex characteristics that pose new challenges to established notions of identity and security. Attempts to address problems arising from cross border migration have given birth to several different (through logically interconnected) policy agendas on migration in development cooperation:

---

2 See at: <http://foucault.info/documents/disciplineAndPunish/foucault.disciplineAndPunish.panOpticism.html> (14 September 2009).

3 According to Bader (2005), in the Western world, membership regimes in the city-states of classical Greece were severely restrictive. Aristotle who initiated a long tradition of republican exclusionism declared them legitimate. The subsequent decline of the city-states and the rise of the Roman Empire saw unprecedented freedom of movement and multiple-citizenship, supported by the idea of cosmopolitanism and moral inclusiveness.

1. Post-conflict reconstruction, durable solutions for refugees, and co-development to stem the outflows of economic migrants;
2. Control over movements facilitated by privately organized networks that challenge state surveillance and undermine state security;[4]
3. Economic costs and benefits of migration to sending and receiving countries;
4. Globalization, the knowledge economy and the supply of talents.

Government control is compartmentalized into these separate policy agendas and remains also within the dualistic frame of 'danger' (to be contained) and 'opportunity' (to be promoted). Taking into account the mixed forces that often drive the migration processes remains a challenge for policymakers.

From a developmental and North-South perspective, although the volumes of the flows of people and remittances are often referred to as a key concern, there is reason to think that the politics of human migration and its relationship with the nation-state are really the core issues. In 2003 the United Nations estimated that the total number of international migrants in the world stood at 175 million in 2000, up from 154 million in 1990, or about three per cent of the total world population.[5] Today the estimated stock of people living outside their country of birth is 214 million in 2010, or 3.1 per cent of the total world population of 6,900 million. The statistical picture shows gravitation from low to high-income areas, suggesting that cross-border labour migration is to a great extent an issue of security of livelihood and economic advancement.[6] By contrast, refugees and internally displaced persons are primarily located in the developing world, reflecting pervasive conflicts in the development process. The UNHCR database shows that there were some 42 million forcibly displaced people worldwide at the end of 2008, including 15.2 million refugees, 827,000 asylum-seekers (pending cases) and 26 million internally displaced persons. Developing countries are host to 80 per cent of the world's refugees.[7]

Unlike cross-border movements of goods – which can be stored, destroyed or sold cheaply when in excess – the movements of people involve human lives, which are inevitably interwoven with each other in intricate ways. States' handling of migrants affects both the individuals concerned and the lives of those connected to them, and therefore human rights and dignity have always been a primary issue. Beyond the questions of economic efficiency and effective border control, migration policy of all types has broader implications for social ethics and the morality of a given polity.

Attempts to make social ethics more prominent in international relations have brought the link between international migration and human security to the fore (Graham/Poku 2000; Truong 2005, 2006; Gasper/Truong 2010a). The concept of human security entails that states are responsible not only for national security but also for protecting the basic rights of citizens and residents. The concept challenges the orthodox approach to international security which

4 For example, in the case of Canada, Bear (1999) illustrates seven distinct categories of migrants based on their entry status and long-term status, being: 1) legal-legal (legal entry and legal immigration); 2) illegal-legal (illegal entry under false or undocumented methods with the goal to change status after arrival); 3) legal-illegal (legal entry with time-specific visas and overstay); 4) illegal-illegal (by independent means such as own-account or through friends); 5) illegal-illegal (by indentured means such as through the service of organized crime networks who prepay migration costs to be repaid after successful entry, sometimes even when entry is unsuccessful); 6) 'indentured' legal-legal (through similar indentured means as under 5, but with a legal status); 7) internal migration (mobility within the same national jurisdiction during intermediary status prior to integration).

5 See at: <http://www.iom.int/jahia/webdav/shared/shared/mainsite/policy_and_research/un/58/A_58_98_en.pdf>.

6 See at: <http://migration.ucdavis.edu/mn/more.php?id=3585_0_5_0> (16 February 2010). This source indicates that the countries with the greatest numbers of international migrants are: US (43 million); Russia (12 million); Germany (11 million); Saudi Arabia, Canada, and France (about seven million each). Forty per cent of the total population of migrants are found in these six countries. Oil exporter states in the Gulf of the Middle East have the highest population proportions of international migrants. In Qatar more than 85 per cent of residents are migrants, and in UAE and Kuwait the figure is 70 per cent. The countries with the lowest international migrant shares of residents include China, Indonesia, Vietnam, Peru and Cuba where the figure is less than one-tenth of one per cent of current residents.

7 See at: <http://www.unhcr.org/4A375c426.html> (30 March 2010). Open conflicts in Iraq, Afghanistan, Sudan, Democratic Republic of Congo and Georgia have contributed to the growing number of refugees, though localized conflicts are also responsible. It is doubtful if UNHCR figures on internally displaced persons also cover those affected by large-scale development projects, such as the construction of dams and infrastructure.

marginalizes concerns for security of the daily lives of ordinary people. The international security policy agenda has similarly tended to marginalize issues of human displacement and migration – both as a cause and a consequence of conflict (Newman/van Selm 2003; Fagan/Munck 2009). The concept of human security further helps to draw out the connections of migration issues in a continuum of events, from conflict to failures both in development efforts and development-related global governance frameworks (Commission on Human Security 2003; Truong 2009a; Gasper 2010). The concept respects the personal dimensions of security, and those factors of oppression and exploitation derived from the specific nature of migrants' entry to circuits of cross-border movement. Migrants are often placed in a situation of liminality, suspended at a threshold, straddling between different administrative and juridical systems, cultures and identities. Apart from social and economic vulnerabilities, this situation generates new types of risks for migrants owing to the perceptions held by society about the legitimacy of their presence and to a process of identity construction based on fear and distrust for the 'Other'.

Since 9/11, the 'War on Terror' has re-asserted the orthodox approach to international security, thwarting the concept of human security. Security now acquires communitarian meanings. For example 'homeland security' in the US; 'societal security' (which involves the security of a collective identity) in the EU. Law and policy in many parts of the world today reflect the tendency to approach migration management in a narrowly instrumental way. Emphasis is placed on economic expediency, exclusionary communitarian principles, and technological fixes in surveillance aimed at discouraging particular types of migration.

The legal space around international migrants is hierarchical, conditioned by state preferences and admission policies that define the relation between the alien and the state in specific ways. Those in the lower strata are the least protected groups under international law. The race, class and gender effects of migration restrictions are visible through societal discourses characterized by polarizations between 'cultural diversity' versus 'homogeneity', economic 'gains' versus 'losses', or 'social cohesion' versus 'disintegration'. These framings of 'opportunity' and 'danger' can translate into discriminatory practices that impose great financial, social and physical costs, especially upon the weakest groups.

1.2.2 Migration and Development: Integrating Perspectives From Across a Fragmented Field

Migration became a subject of scientific interest in the late 19th century with the work of Ernest Georg Ravenstein, an English geographer of German origin who sought to demonstrate that migration occurs according to specific laws rather than erratically.[8] In the last few decades, the subject has proliferated across many disciplines: economics, legal studies, sociology, anthropology, history, political science and international relations. Until recently the field of study has largely concentrated on deepening some of Ravenstein's ideas with the intention of providing answers to the following questions: Why do people migrate, through which pathways, how and with what consequences for sending and receiving areas? Traditional pursuits on the behaviour of migrants and states continue to dominate the field. Recently questions regarding cultural identities and associational life, assimilation and resistance have been added.

Massey and colleagues note that the field consists of "a fragmented set of theories that have developed largely in isolation from one another, sometimes but not always segmented by disciplinary boundaries" (Massey/Arango/Hugo/Kouaouci/Pellegrino/Taylor 1998: 17). Given that migration has accelerated in the last centuries, with distinct cycles correlated with changes in the world economy and transformations of polities, there is now consensus on the need to study this phenomenon as part of the globalizing processes driven by the emergence and growth of capitalist economies. Close reference to the perspectives of social ethics in migration, the meanings given to 'economic efficacy', and the consequences for polities and cultural systems in the long term become vital.

The field is currently subdivided into separate study areas. Forced migration covers displacement and cross-border refugees. International migration is

8 Using census data from the United Kingdom, Ravenstein (1885 and 1889) developed his 'Laws of Migration' which included 1) 'push-pull' process, or a gravitation from unfavourable conditions in one location – such as oppressive laws, and heavy taxation – towards another location with more favourable conditions; 2) each main current of migration produces a compensating counter current; 3) the decrease in volume of migration as distance increases; 4) migration takes place in stages rather than one long move; 5) social differentials (e.g., gender, social class, age) influence a person's experience and pattern of mobility.

sub-divided into different foci (labour, education, marriage formation, retirement, assimilation, ethnic relationships) and overlaps with transnational migration research. The latter examines a variety of practices, including plural civic memberships, economic involvements, social networks and cultural identities linking people and institutions together across two or more nation-states in diverse and multi-layered patterns (Levitt/Glick-Schiller 2004).

An emerging area of research on transmigration examines the phenomenon of migrants-in-transit in one or more countries while on the way to their planned destination of settlement. Exploring the movements and adaptations of transiting groups (the routes chosen, the use of multiple locales, and the livelihoods they pursue), this area of research looks at 'transitivity' as a social condition within the continuum of a migratory trajectory. There are some important implications for understanding 'temporality', 'permanence', and the notion of country of origin and transit. The traditional understanding of migration trajectories based on a linear and bidirectional move – from a country of origin to a recipient country and return – no longer holds. Instead, multi-directional patterns have emerged among those passing through one or more countries while on the way to their preferred destination. Their trajectories are not comparable with the conventional definition of international (or transnational migrants) who usually cross borders, settle in a recipient country and maintain ties with their home countries. Labour migrants can enter a recipient country legally, but may consider it an in-between station on the way to somewhere else, rather than a final destination.

In research on human trafficking the term 'transitivity' is used to bring to light the complexity of this process, which may start in a different country from the country of origin, or occur in distinct phases. Diverse forms of transitivity have been found: people migrating legally from one country to another who find themselves at risk because of poverty, discrimination and marginalization and become trapped in a trafficking network; people trafficked from one country to another for a particular purpose who are later trafficked to a third country for a different purpose; and people trafficked internally, from a rural area to an urban area, who are later trafficked to another country for a different purpose (UNICEF 2003: 13).

Driven primarily by policy concerns, migration research has been influenced mainly by behaviourism, in varying forms and degrees. It draws largely from the body of thought in, or strongly influenced by, neoclassical microeconomics and macro-sociology (Arango 2000). These traditions have considered only observable behaviour as relevant, and place issues of 'mind' or 'consciousness' in the subjective domain outside the area of focus of objective social science.

Attempts to overcome the limits of the dominant frameworks in international migration studies have now produced a rich body of literature on transnational migration, most of it recent, concerned with migrants' agency and the formation of their social identities. Scholars have borrowed insights from recent social constructivist theories in international relations that analyse the relations between nation-states in light of the activities of transnational corporations and civil society organizations that pierce through borders. Such studies use the term 'transnationalism' to refer to the multifaceted and multi-local processes of cross-border migration (Smith/Guarnizo 1998). The transnational approach aims to expose the deceptive binary constructs – such as national-international and local-global – found in dominant discourses on migration, and to reveal and explore the locations of transnational interactions, including villages and townships, borders and bureaucracies.

Built on an actor-oriented approach to the study of the 'missing middle', or the meso level of interaction, this approach offers valuable alternative methods to analyse how rights, security and livelihoods are affected by migration, at multiple sites, thus uncovering the broader significance of 'transnationalism' for sending and receiving societies. Faist (2000) introduces the concept of 'transnational social spaces' as virtual as well as real spaces – made up of practices adopted by migrants and stay-behinds – that connect both worlds as well as the activities of institutions such as nation-states that try to control these spaces. Activities in such spaces also influence the dynamics of mobility and immobility (e.g. providing resources and information for those wishing to move, and supporting the stay-behinds).

Migrants' social identities, subject positions and agency are formed by a convergence of diverse social forces which can involve complex intersections between different structures of social inequality (legal status, gender, class, age, race and sexuality) and social consciousness. Representation, boundary marking and the construction of social and political space in relation to migrants as subjects reflect this complexity and pose great challenges to deliberative democracy and access to rights. Far from being uniform, diverse power relationships control these transnational social spaces. For those who migrate through 'irregular means' today, information asymmetry and cognitive conflicts about the rights and obligations of the involved actors prevail. Information asymmetry can lead to unjust economic redistribution, and cognitive conflicts add to the denial of rights on grounds of 'culture'. [9]

Today transnational migration often occurs in cross-cultural contexts, implying an encounter between different frames of reference about rights and obligations. Cognitive conflicts about rights and obligations that arise at different moments in the entire migration process (decision-making, transit, job placement, return) typically leave those who are voiceless with no support, at best, and with fatal consequences at worst. The fluidity of migrants' social identities may often obstruct the kind of consciousness required to overcome social divisions, and hence may undermine resistance to oppression, or exacerbate competition where there are opportunities.

More analysis is required of the transnational social spaces through which migrants can assert their sense of being and belonging in order to claim rights. The nation-state, its polity, territorial and cultural boundaries pose significant barriers to the deliberative agency of footloose transnational migrants and transmigrants, with or without an approved formal legal identity. Thus, as useful as it is, the transnational migration paradigm must accord greater significance to structures of state, local configurations of administrative power, and the glaring imbalances in power relations between different transnational actors.

Recent studies of the migration industry as a loosely formed entity, comprised of private employment agencies, migrant networks and state agencies, have helped to reveal the working of social hierarchies within transnational spaces. Despite our having only fragmented knowledge which frequently lacks an evaluative and comparative dimension, existing studies show that states' practices and political norms do mould the conditions under which migration brokers can operate (Lucas 2005). Migration policy regimes and recruitment practices therefore bear specific regional geopolitical and cultural features. Particular macro-economic and institutional linkages also play an important role in selectively channelling certain types of migrant labour to particular sectors within a country or region. These linkages also influence the behaviour of recruiting networks, which not only provide services passively but also actively mobilize labour and shape migration patterns.

The emerging architecture of the migration brokerage industry formed by interactions between different actors - the state through its administrative laws, service providers and migrants through market mechanisms - now involves a plethora of activities (recruitment, provision of loans, arrangement of legal documents and travel, job placement and so forth) and operates across different national jurisdictions (Kuptsch 2006). In a neoliberal environment which advocates free movement of factors of production but imposes selective restrictions on the movement of people, the operation of this industry generates intermeshing practices that need to be scrutinized from a human rights perspective.[10] Studies have shown a wide range of rights violations in the low-skill sectors; many of the violations are not formally classifiable.[11]

One widespread practice is to tie migrants to their employers or 'sponsors'. They withhold travel documents and identity papers or impose excessive charges for food and accommodation. This not only reduces migrants' earnings but also prevents them from finding alternatives. Excessive fees charged upon arrival for non-transparent purposes, failure to fulfil placement obligations, contract substitution and disappearance of agents after collection of fees, have also been widely reported (Kuptsch 2006). Practices in the migration industry also contribute to the shaping of the conditions of migrants' entry to the labour market indirectly, such as becoming 'structurally embedded' in 'temporary' arrangements, meaning: circular labour migration on short-term visas without the possibility for extension (Tsuda 1999), and 'Just-in-Time' labour delivery to support the 'flexible staffing' system adopted by employers to operate in highly fluctuating markets (Higuchi/Tanno 2003).

---

9 For example domestic workers perform household tasks that historically have been assigned a diminished value due to the culture of gender, a problem further exacerbated by their association with particular groups (women, minorities, migrants). Workers are often forbidden from leaving the house. See at:<http://www.globalrights.org/site/DocServer/Domestic_Workers_report-_FINAL.pdf?docID=5503> (25 February 2010).

10 Goldstein (2006) describes the 'sweating system' or labour recruitment practices prevalent in the 18th, 19th and early 20th centuries in low-skilled work, in which workers' bargaining power was weakened and improvements in wages and working conditions suppressed. Today's realities, he suggests, may well mean a return to this system, which is an outcome of the dysfunctionality of law and democratic deliberation at several levels.

11 National legislations often do not recognize some of the abuses experienced by migrant workers as violation of their rights.

Maltreatment of migrant workers can lead receiving states to encourage direct recruitment in order to eliminate brokers' fees and malpractices. However, direct hiring has failed due to 'kickback' arrangements involving employers, brokers and state officials (Tierney 2007). Close cooperation between recruiters and state agents in sending countries can lead to the formation of an alliance of interests which can be detrimental to migrant workers' rights (Wee/Sim 2004). The scope for justice-seeking actions in migration is often limited by the monopoly of the state over the means of movement, since this monopoly can be abused. Governments are the only actors who can provide legal papers, but government officials can collude with recruiters by receiving 'kickbacks' to grant permissions without having checked the true nature of the work contract. These problems, reflecting information asymmetry between recruiting agents and the migrants, then spill over to the domains of workplace entitlements and remittances.

The return to a systems approach in migration studies as discussed above recognizes the mutual interplay between 'structure' and 'agency', and how migration systems evolve from interactions between regulations and the (potentially transformative) actions of those involved: the migrants, employers, social networks, civic organizations and law enforcement agents. Understanding these interactions can contribute to new theoretical insights which may then extend to the domain of intersecting inequalities, shaping security-seeking actions of particular groups of migrants and the challenges these pose to justice-seeking actions.

Feminist scholarship on migration investigates the relationships between gender, worlds of work and culture. It has explored the emotional and social as well as economic values of female niches of migration for work – such as domestic and care work, commercial sex work, or cross-cultural family formation (Truong 1996; Ehrenreich/Hochschild 2003; Palriwala/Uberoi 2008). The cultural representation of 'women' and 'gender' has become a site for competing understandings of many different migration-related controversies (such as prostitution and trafficking; migration for marriage formation through brokers; global care chains which outsource care, thus creating deficit and crisis in the sending countries). These analyses reveal rival ethical-political rationalities which establish the 'objects' of protection in opposed ways – in terms of asserted public morality and general societal well-being versus concern for specific categories of migrants.[12] Analyses of gender dynamics in the socio-cultural contexts of migration decisions further show how state ideology and policy shape the social environment in which networks operate and form their distinctive spatial arrangements and pathways of movements (Tyner 2000; Oishi 2005).

Feminist scholarship in migration studies has furthered our understanding by bringing the significance of 'gender' and distinct epistemological and methodological values to bear in research and interpretation. Besides gender-differentiated patterns of mobility, identified by Ravenstein more than 100 years ago, scholarship shows how gender moulds thinking, reasoning and understanding of human movements and the identities of those on the move. Now seen as a multifaceted process, transnational migration is analysed as something that profoundly influences a variety of domains in social lives – sexuality, gender, work, organization of caring practices, institutional life, as well as domination and resistance. In this respect feminist scholarship has deepened the meaning of the term 'feminization of migration' far beyond just one of Ravenstein's laws of migration.

Practices of control of migration in most countries today are born out of shifting modes of power, the declining commitment to welfare provision or assurance, and the ascendancy of a new logic dominated by public fiscal concerns. Today's new forms of debt-financed migration[13] undertaken by individuals for the sake of private household survival and growth are being stimulated by a migration industry that extends itself in the nebulous zone of services. The new forms reflect a complex web of inequalities co-constituted by neoliberal doctrines and pre-existing hierarchical relations between knowledge forms, people and their societies. Despite processes which enhance the interdependence – between reproductive, productive and virtual economies – and weave human lives together,

12 For example, the focus on the care sector has exposed the chains of negative externalities by which an enhancement of care provision through labour import in some country can lead to the denial of the entitlement to care of others who stay behind (Parreñas 2002). In many countries this has led to a moral outcry about the care crisis that places the blame on women migrants (for neglecting their children and families) rather than examining state policy and the organization of care as a domain. See: Perera (2009).

13 Debt-financed migration is characterized by the central role of intermediaries (mostly private) in financing the costs of migration for resource-constrained migrants, who may enter servitude contracts on a temporary basis to pay back the debt before they can retain their full earnings.

people remain divided by unequal structural relations based on race, gender, class and nation (Peterson 2003). A cognitive frame that insists on sharply distinct social entities, rather than acknowledging their interconnectedness and interlocking nature, serves to reinforce these structures.

1.3 Overview of the Chapters

The book contains twenty two chapters, grouped in five parts.

1.3.1 Part I: Introduction

The two chapters in Part I address the main themes of the book. This introductory chapter presents the field of discussion and gives synopses of the chapters. It is followed by a keynote chapter by Thanh-Dam Truong on "The Governmentality of Transnational Migration and Security: The Making of a New Subaltern". It provides a historical and factual survey setting the scene and presenting interpretive themes relevant to the whole book. By tracing the main lines in the framing of 'security', Truong identifies the historical junctures where its specific meanings have merged with those of 'migration' and 'development', involving the use of particular ethical norms and modes of conceptualization. A core issue today is the gradual practical and conceptual erosion of the legal boundaries set in the Westphalian framework of inter-state relations and the emergence of fragmented modes of regulation. By exploring the meanings of human mobility in the four extant frameworks of international legislation, Truong shows how the differentiation of meanings reflects an 'art' of governing migration, which seeks to maintain a hierarchical global society supported by a logic of triage moulded by politics within nation-states rather than to secure human rights in the migration process. She argues that this 'art' of governing has been bolstered by a neoliberal perspective on 'being human', centred on a restricted notion of 'autonomy' that contains a serious ontological and epistemological bias. It also carries important ethical implications because it promotes excessive individualism at the expense of relations of care and reciprocity in mutual recognition and respect. This perspective cannot be expected to deliver human security outcomes. The challenge ahead is for critical thought to engage with, and learn from, the experiences of insecurity endured by the new 'subalterns' - those who have no line of social mobility although their existence may involve constant physical re-location. Learning from these experiences can help expose the currently fragmented vision of human movement across borders and the narrow utilitarian and nationalist logics that underpin it. Such an engagement - combined with learning from practices of reflexivity within and across cultures - can help to introduce an alternative conception of security-oriented collective agency by building on an ontology of care and deepening the notion of caring in social thought and action.

1.3.2 Part II: Neoliberal Governmentality and Transnational Migration: The Interplay of Business Forces and Security Fears

Governments frequently select migration policy positions which privilege security, trade and finance considerations over more people-centred concerns. The chapters in Part II show how giving priority to business concerns can lead to support for forms of migration considered 'desirable' and 'profitable' for business while retaining tight restrictions on those forms labelled as 'undesirable' and 'costly' to the state. Mirroring the wider construction of a 'neoliberal subject', migration management policy is biased towards the entrepreneurial aspects of 'being' and 'moving'. The chapters show the entrenched instrumental reasoning that sees people overwhelmingly as tools for economic gain rather than integrally as whole human beings. At the same time the wish to keep out some categories of migrants means that immigration and asylum issues often become conflated, leading to the framing of their presence as potential cause for disintegration of social and public 'security'. Use of the vocabulary of 'security' and 'threat' in discourses on immigration conflicts with and can override routine economic concerns.

Mexico is one of the top handful of countries as a source of out-migration and is a major transit country for aspirants from further south who seek to enter the United States or to return from there and travel home. Responding to demands for labour, and seeking to support or join their families, these travellers and work-seekers are often harassed, legally victimized and culturally denigrated within both Mexico and the US. Chapter 3 on "Migration from Mexico and Central America to the United States: Human Insecurities and Paths for Change", by Gustavo Verduzco and María Isabel de Lozano, looks at the experiences of those who attempt to cross Mexico, both Mexican and non-Mexican nationals. It draws on secondary data and a survey of migrants in two Mexican cities on the US border and interviews with migrants, officials, priests and representatives of human rights groups. The chapter illustrates how, located at the intersection of the two universes along the Mexico-US border, the cities on the Mexican side have become extraordinary containers of mobile populations: those expelled from the US, those seeking to get in or get back in, and those returning home and becoming stranded.

The Mexican government has come under great pressure from the US to seal both its northern and southern borders against migrants and drug smugglers. While on paper Mexico's internal surveillance of migration has been relatively humane (protecting transit migrants from abuse, not treating them as criminals), policy practices have hardened in recent years. Intensive border patrols and increased roadside checks within Mexico have led to use of more dangerous routes, and to higher prices charged by person-smugglers (*polleros*), which suggests that it is the migration-facilitating networks who benefit most from the surveillance. Some *polleros* dupe migrants and channel them into sex-work, or kidnap them in order to demand a ransom from family members in the US. In turn, the US border police avoid paperwork and expense, by placing all captured illegal migrants in one category and repatriating all to Mexico, including third country nationals, without the consent of the Mexican government. Many of those dumped in this fashion by the US police are minors. One result is homelessness among transmigrants. Verduzco and Lozano underline the irony that in the land of opportunity and the market economy where many citizens wish to hire the services of these willing potential immigrant workers, the 'huddled masses' face such difficulties. They also show a further irony, for as wage-earning migrants face greater difficulties now in crossing borders to revisit their country of origin, the motivation increases for their dependants to join them there in the US.

In chapter 4 on "The Blind Spot of Repression: Migration Policies and Human Survival in the Central Sahara", Julien Brachet examines the growth of measures by European Union (EU) countries to block trans-Sahara and trans-Mediterranean migratory flows. Labour migration from the Sahel countries into North African countries includes long established migratory patterns connected with livelihood systems. Most of those involved in newer patterns of movement northwards into and across the Sahara also seek to go no further than the North African countries. However, fears of massive inflows of sub-Saharan migrants into Europe seem now to drive policy in EU states and they have taken what appear to be disproportionate actions, including several recent bilateral agreements with North African states to curb the flows. Libya – a country that seeks to re-establish its international respectability – agreed to increase border controls and to accept illegal migrants deported from Italy who had purportedly entered via Libya, in exchange for considerable development aid. Brachet finds that for the EU virtually all sub-Saharans travelling in the Sahara are now redefined as intercontinental economic migrants. The rhetoric of fear and control contributes to a misinterpretation of all trans-Saharan migration as trans-Mediterranean migration. Based on several years of research in Niger – the one country with which Nigeria (by far the most populous country in Africa) shares its northern border – Brachet estimates that only 10 to 20 per cent of the migrants travelling to North Africa through Niger every year continue on to Europe. This would be a modest figure compared to official estimates.

The new policies and practices in North and West African countries towards migrants, under pressure from the EU, have doubtful impact in curbing the number of migrants reaching Europe, yet they carry broader consequences for the region: they disrupt patterns of movement, within this region of Africa and endanger the livelihoods of large populations, they drive them into more dangerous routes and channels; and detention and deportations of migrants into North Africa become increasingly frequent – often in deplorable conditions that trample basic principles of human rights whose defender the European Union claims to be. Brachet concludes that the new policies put ordinary inhabitants of the sub-Saharan region "under house arrest", and contravene the guarantee in the Universal Declaration of Human Rights that everyone has the right to leave any country, including their own.

Chapter 5 on "Europeanization and the Right to Seek Refugee Status: Reflections on Frontex", by Wies Maas and Thanh-Dam Truong, looks at EU border and asylum policies and practices. The effects of the abolition of internal borders through the implementation of the Schengen Agreement since 1995, amplified also by unanticipated external pressures, led to the creation of Frontex in 2005 by the European Council of Ministers, with the aim of strengthening the EU's external borders. Placed at the junction between migration and security politics, Frontex's formation and trajectory reflect both the flaws in the process of European integration and the limited success in putting the Common Asylum Policy into effect. A more restrictive interpretation of the right to seek asylum and a higher degree of control without agreement on adequate human rights standards for border and pre-border control means that member states run the risk of violating the European Convention on Human Rights and are vulnerable to the criticism of state-led group-profiling and racism. Given that asylum seekers are now almost forced to enter illegally, a netherworld of illegality has emerged - which is considered further in the chapters by Skilbei and Tveit and by Hintjens, Kumar and Pouri. Overseeing a hybrid policy system with blurred competences and various opt-outs, Frontex's effectiveness now requires public scrutiny. With the European Parliament only marginally involved, and national parliaments of member states not being part of controlling Frontex operations, a 'democratic deficit' has arisen. Together with a surveillance approach that is obsessed with danger and crime, all this has dangerous implications for basic liberties within the EU itself.

The sheer scale of Europe's demographic imbalance - a fast aging population, and reproduction by the indigenous population at far below replacement levels - brings both strong demands for immigrant workforces and major resistance to them. In chapter 6 on "Fortress Europe and the Dutch Donjon: Securitization, Internal Migration Policy and Irregular Migrants' Counter Moves", Godfried Engbersen and Dennis Broeders discuss the measures in the EU to identify and penalize those migrants who still gain unauthorized entry, with special reference to the Netherlands – one of the countries where resistance to immigrants has become intense. They present in particular the measures to prevent unauthorized ('irregular') migrants from having access to formal employment and social services, and evidence on the various intended and unintended effects.

Recognizing that the Union's external borders are inevitably somewhat porous, EU leaders and officials have instituted an array of internal 'gates' by which to capture irregular migrants or exclude them from important goods. The Netherlands is at the forefront here. First, there is identity control: to prevent irregulars from acquiring the documents required to access vital goods; and to acquire information on excluded individuals in order to identify and continue to exclude them, including expel them after due process. Identity control measures include database projects at the EU level, including biometric data. People unable to provide legally satisfactory documents are held in a greatly expanded system of detention centres while they are investigated prior to possible expulsion. 'Irregulars' sometimes resist by destroying their original legal identity markers – individuals with no confirmed legal identity are difficult to expel since other countries are unwilling to accept them – and/or by acquiring new ones. Inevitably the situation has generated a market in 'legal' identities. Second, there are increased inspections and penalties imposed on employers of irregular migrants, although various adaptive responses exist for employers and migrants including use of subcontractors and intermediary recruitment agencies who are skilled in operating the system. Irregular migrants are being driven out of formal sector work into informal employment, as in hotels and restaurants, and more than before into criminal activities. The mega database projects have a similar perverse effect: the more that those who have overstayed – after an original legal entry on a visitor's visa or as an asylum applicant – become at risk of detection, the more that latecomers instead enter illegally via smuggling organizations.

The next step in the migration control chain, after seeking to block and discourage entry, and to detect, discourage and expel illegal migrants, is to encourage return to the country of origin and to reduce the pressures for others to come. The expectation among Northern policymakers has been that economic development in sender countries will reduce migrant outflow. Various studies suggest instead that economic development increases the ability to move and perhaps also the aspiration to move. It also increases the need to move in the case of people who are physically displaced by new infrastructure or economically displaced by restructuring.

Chapter 7 by Alejandra Boni and Joan Lacomba on "The New Co-Development Agenda: Official and Non-Official Initiatives between Morocco and Spain" looks at how the idea of 'co-development' emerged in negotiations between the European Union and especially its immediate southern neighbours during the 1990s, and how it has grown since then. They show how advocates of co-development in Europe express the need to consider a migrant population as a vector or agent of development between its 'host' country and its 'sending' country, establishing a central role to be played by migrants by becoming a development link on both sides. Yet EU policy on co-development has in practice been subordinate to measures of direct migration control and prevention. The authors observe that the reference to positive links between migration and development is absent at the level of the relationship between the EU and Morocco, where a view of migration centred on illegal immigration and migratory flow control prevails. Similarly, Spain's migration policies perceive co-development as linked to economic development in the countries of origin and to the return of migrants. Yet Spain's multi-level polity allows for independent initiatives from Autonomous Communities, as well as from NGOs and migrant groups, and these agents have been more flexible and imaginative than Madrid. Referring to Ramón (2005: 51), Boni and Lacomba emphasize that the agents of co-development are not just governments in their bilateral relationships, but primarily migrants themselves and secondarily the social agents of both societies (labour unions, companies, educational institutions, citizen organizations, NGOs). A large gap typically exists between migrant associations and official co-development programmes: the former lack recognition and resources and distrust the very term 'co-development' as officially used, owing to its strong connotations of migration control and encouragement to return. Official co-development policies, Boni and Lacomba reveal, are characterized by a remarkable distance between discussions and actions, and between the statements that present migrations as positive for development and the attempts to prevent them. A less contradictory and better scientifically grounded conception of co-development, they suggest, may be found in Malgesini (2007: 31) who defines it "as the set of positive effects of immigration for the development of the origin and hosting society generated by the contact and exchange between people from different backgrounds".

The major recent focus of attention regarding relations between international migration and economic development has been the rapidly increasing and impressive volume of migrants' financial remittances to low- and middle-income countries of origin. This has been matched by ambitious schemes to facilitate, channel and regulate the remittances through formal banking channels. At present half or more of remittances are still handled through informal providers, who offer a flexible, non-bureaucratic, door-to-door service - which is also anonymous: a vital consideration for migrants with irregular legal status. Chapter 8 on "Financial Globalization and the Mechanisms of Migrants' Remittance Institutions: Formed by Supply or Demand?" by Amrita Sharma and Karim Knio, examines the motives involved in creating a new assemblage of financial institutions, with attention to the cases of India, Indonesia and the Philippines. Financial sector agencies have become keen to control what are seen as substantial and fast growing money flows, and to weave around them new financial products which can be traded, as part of the realms of speculation that eventually crashed in 2008–2009. In addition, some governments of migrant sending countries have been keen to compensate for actual or expected declines or fluctuations in foreign aid or foreign private investment; and governments of many countries have feared that informal remittance channels are or can be used to fund terrorist organizations. Reviewing the evidence, the authors suggest that the current drive to formalize remittance channels, and the mechanisms thus set up, come more from commercial interest than from concerns for migrants' well-being. Financial system regulators should seek to understand and serve migrants' needs rather than drive their monies into the circuits of speculative financial capitalism.

Spanning all these concerns – recruitment, legal and illegal; prevention and repatriation; remittances and other lines for 'co-development' - is the largest specialist organization in the field: the International Organization for Migration (IOM), an intergovernmental giant with more than 7,000 employees. Originally the Intergovernmental Committee for European Migration, it continues to be dominated in funding and orientation by its high-income member states. It produces the largest periodic survey, the *World Migration Report*, a series that started appearing from 2000 as high-income countries began to realize that a stance of exclude-and-restrict, while domestically politically popular, could not meet their economic and social demands. Elaboration of the 'migration management' agenda has involved two broad thrusts. First, arguments to persuade low-income country governments that while high control and selectivity with respect to migration into high-income countries would prevail, there would be large potential profit from cooperation with the governments of these countries to prepare and supply various categories of skilled and semi-skilled labour, typically through temporary but often recurrent migration. Second, efforts to quietly persuade the populations of high-income countries that continuing inflows on a large-scale are unavoidable and that it is better to handle these through legally controlled channels. In effect, the model low-income country becomes the Philippines. Since the 1970's this country has done as recommended above and built an enormous bureaucracy that helps place Filipino workers in high-income countries around the world. More than ten per cent of its population are at any given moment abroad, sending remittances which comprise around ten per cent of GDP, although, as many scholars judge, with little long-term benefit for its economy, society or polity: remittances have become a substitute for internal reform.

Chapter 9 on "Managing Migration in the IOM's World Migration Report 2008", by Beatriz Campillo Carrete and Des Gasper, looks at the most recent of the *World Migration Reports*. The chapter illustrates the use of methods of discourse analysis to identify the principles of selection, interpretation, prioritization and argumentation that structure such a report. It gives particular attention to the choices and use of key terms, like 'mobility', 'needs' and 'globalization', and of key metaphors that guide the discussion, notably the metaphor of 'flows'. Dominated by the model of thinking and reasoning in neoclassical and neoliberal economics and the policy preoccupations of high-income countries, the central policy claims in the Report concern the 'need' for international cooperation to match labour demand and supply within a global framework (as a concomitant of economic globalization in other respects), and that such cooperation will support economic development worldwide. It proposes in great detail methods for managed labour migration. A human rights stance makes occasional appearances, represented by uses of the term 'human mobility' rather than 'labour mobility' or 'mobility for economic purposes', but it remains firmly subordinated to economic priorities based on market power. Migrants' opinions and agency receive little attention. Even so, the *World Migration Report 2008* represents efforts towards a more open global economic order and an attempt to shift from an agenda overwhelmingly focused on restriction, by building public acceptance of substantial immigration to match labour demand. Low-skilled migrants, however, will remain largely excluded formally, since the informal supply of such migrants is expected to be ample, and formal exclusion helps to keep their labour low-cost.

1.3.3 Part III: Migration as Life Experiences: Agency in the Grey Zone

The chapters in Part II were largely discussions at the macro-level, examining also the perspectives of officials in governmental or intergovernmental organizations or associations of employers or bankers, with only occasional references to the life experiences of individuals who seek a livelihood or family reunion through migration. In contrast, the focus in Part III is on migration as life experiences, to consider the unintended or intended effects of the migration management regimes which combine formal restriction and controlled entry with large-scale informal reliance on immigrant labour. Policies shaped by global market expansion under a cloud of security fears create 'grey zones' for specific groups of migrants, with little concern for their welfare. The panoply of legal controls creates a series of ambiguous spaces in interpreting and applying the laws, in balancing the wishes of employers and potential employees against the fears and objections of others, and in living outside the law. Part III examines the effects and side effects, the resulting lived experiences, in a series of locales: foreign women working as street prostitutes in Norway; young women in South East Asia on the move in order to seek work; youth moving likewise between European countries; and students from low-income countries who combine studies in Australia with paid work while also aiming for longer-term residence. The essays show how migrants negotiate their way in pursuit of economic and personal goals while facing the risk of falling into exploitative traps, and the importance for policy formulation of taking cognisance of this insiders' knowledge and experience.

The population of women in street prostitution in Norway rapidly transformed in just a few years, between 2003 and 2008, to become predominantly composed of women from Nigeria. A high proportion of these have been trafficked – brought in illegally and with elements of deception or even duress by organizations that typically continue to control and to some degree exploit them. Chapter 10 on "Mission Impossible? Voluntary and Dignified Repatriation of Nigerian Victims of Trafficking", by May-Len Skilbrei and Marianne Tveit, builds on interviews with 150 Nigerian women in street prostitution, representing one-third of that group in Norway in 2006, to cast light on the possibilities for repatriation of identified victims of trafficking who request assistance. Driven by poverty and deteriorating family circumstances, and in consultation with their families in Nigeria, these women sought entry into Europe to earn and send money back home. To gain entry they used the services of smugglers (for amounts between US $13,000 and $80,000, often closer to the higher figure) leaving themselves with large debts in addition to their targets for earning in order to save and remit. In many cases deception was involved: women were promised a job and residence permit, but subsequently received no such document and were forced into commercial sex work. Most of the interviewed women had spent some years already in other European countries before beginning to work in Norway, and often were not permanently resident there but periodically flew in to take advantage of the higher prices paid for sexual services. Uninterested in the option of assisted return made available by the Norwegian government, most interviewed women felt strong needs to make something out of their huge investments of money and personal suffering, rather than return 'home' merely older, empty-handed and humiliated. Many also indicated fear of punishment by their pimp or madam if they were to return to Nigeria, and expressed dissatisfaction at the male dominance and relative frequency of violence there. Fear of arrest and detention upon return – the alternative being to bribe the responsible state officials – was also prevalent. Returning home in such circumstances would make sex work in some other part of Nigeria the only viable 'home' option for many of them. Taking up new debts and re-entering the stream of trafficked and smuggled persons returning to Europe was a more likely outcome.

The Norwegian-Nigerian case study shows limitations of the assumption that victims of trafficking want, or will benefit from, repatriation. Chapter 11 on "Migrant Women and Their Vulnerability in the Trafficking-Migration Continuum: Evidence from Asia", by Yu Kojima, shows how a policy approach built on a dichotomous contrast between human trafficking and legal routes of migration is misguided. She examines the full spectrum of the migration process of female migrant workers in some parts of Asia who are involved in private care and commercial sexual services. Many are drawn into illegal work after an initial period in legal activity. From the experiences of these young women Kojima shows how the scope of present legal measures does not fully reflect the complex process and context of migration in which these women are involved. Kojima argues for greater attention to the various intersecting aspects of inequality and vulnerability. Understanding the intricate and dynamic nature of the material and subjective conditions associated with the migration-trafficking continuum and the importance of the intersecting processes of discrimination against migrant women and youth could significantly improve policy and human rights protection.

Chapter 12 on "The EU's Ambiguous Position on Migrant Underage Workers", by Roy Huijsmans, examines the European Union's possible circumvention of human rights policy on children by adoption of the conceptual category of 'youth'. Huijsmans explores the (in)compatibility of the dominant concept of children (those under the age of 18, according to the Convention on the Rights of the Child) and the phenomenon of adolescent migrant workers (between the ages of 15 and 18) within the EU, for example under the 'Youth in Action' programme that promotes inter-EU cultural exchange and labour movement. Besides, among young people who move for purposes of work, a majority combine study, 'volunteering', 'traineeship' and 'exchange' with paid work. The 1994 EU Directive on the Protection of Young People at Work in fact allows that children be employed from the age of 13, if it will not be "detrimental to regular school attendance or prevent children benefitting fully from their education".[14] Full-time work by 13 and 14 year olds during school vacations and by 15–17 year olds throughout the year and in any part of the EU appears permissible. Seeing the positive in the possibilities opened up for children to express agency and independence, Huijsmans examines also the risks to children's rights. The introduction of the term 'youth' (understood as from 13 to 30 by the 'Youth in Action' programme) may be seen as an attempt by the EU to free itself from some of the constraints set by the rights-based and human trafficking discourses. Huijsmans considers the data on migrant teenage workers, and notes the risks that the introduction of the 'youth' terminology within the EU entails, including for temporary seasonal work under harsh conditions and possibly even for trafficking into sex work. He concludes however that adolescents of 15, 16 and 17 are not infants. The chances that they make high-risk choices are no greater than those for adults in comparable situations. While some migrants classified under the category of 'youth' may become subject to abusive practices, the alternative should not be to condemn their migration for work but to find a framework for safe migration. Overall, he suggests that, by endorsing migrant work under the age of 18 but making it subject to labour law at the national level, the EU provisions for free movement of workers can make involvement by minors in migrant work safer, targeting exploitation and abuse rather than migration itself.

The following essay (chapter 13) on "Learning how to Work the Grey Zone: Issues of Legality and Illegality among Indian Students in Australia", by Michiel Baas, takes us from teenage workers to international university students who also become involved in paid work. Baas examines the aggressively marketed tertiary education industry in Australia, which plays a sig-

14 EU Council Directive 94/33/EC of 22 June 1994 on the protection of young people at work, consulted on 24 May 2010 at: http://eur-lex.europa.eu/smartapi/cgi/sga_doc?smartapi!celexapi!prod!CELEXnumdoc&lg=EN&numdoc=31994L0033&model=guichett.

nificant role in facilitating the entry of migrants. Indeed chapter 4 of the 2008 *World Migration Report* is devoted to this type of migration. In 2006, almost two per cent of Australia's population consisted of foreign students, and there are now close to 100,000 students from India alone. Many of the Indian students whom Baas interviewed spoke of a problematic quality of education and of current poor conditions of living and working, but said that they planned to apply for permanent residence. Many had this intention in advance of applying for a study programme. Almost half of foreign students come through private agencies, which channel them to particular educational institutions from which the agencies receive a commission, and to particular courses that favour the students' qualification for permanent residence. To obtain this qualification and pay off educational debts, they work long hours in paid employment alongside their studies – often beyond the legally permitted 20 hours per week and with 'cash-in-hand' payment to avoid any paper trail. Baas indicates that the motivation of Indians to study in Australia has increasingly become to acquire permanent residence rights. An 'Overseas Students Act' and an associated 'National Code' in Australia regulate the international marketing of educational services. Recruitment with a primary purpose to provide an immigration route is prohibited, but many tertiary education organizations and immigration businesses are critically dependent on income from foreign students. Economic analysis is insufficient however - at least for the prospective migrants. It cannot explain why still relatively so few people try to migrate, and why emigrants are concentrated among particular social groups and localities. So Baas explores also the imaginative dimension of transnational migration: how large numbers of middle class young Indians have become able to not just imagine but also act on a vision of an alternative life based far away in Australia. The gains reaped by the providers have led the Australian state and universities to ignore the grey zone that has emerged, and the lifestyles envisaged by the students inure them to endure it.

1.3.4 Part IV: Transnational Identities and Issues of Citizenship

The meanings ascribed to citizenship are under intense pressure from globalization. Migration in particular leads to the reconstruction of social identities and worldviews, for both migrants and non-migrants. The chapters in Part IV illustrate how identities, belongingness and relationships are re-positioned by the effects of globalization, the political and policy environments and the predominance of market imperatives. Several chapters examine migrants' transnational identities and multi-local politics, to explain tensions and dilemmas arising around state obligations to citizens and migrants. The chapters attend to the life realities of the subjects themselves - whether migrants, 'indigenous' citizens, or state-less nationals. The authors reveal a need to re-conceptualize citizenship and re-cast state obligations in ways that are more ethically inclusive and appropriate for societies that are increasingly heterogeneous and multicultural - themes taken further in Part V.

Chapter 14 on "Gender, Technology and Migration in Export-Production of Shrimps: Identity Formation and Labour Practices in Surat Thani Province, Thailand", by Bernadette P. Resurreccion and Edsel E. Sajor, illuminates how migrants seek to make sense of and in their lives, in their specific geographical, social and legal setting. Their identities are formed and re-formed in daily interactions and discourses in their work 'habitus'. In particular, the identity-markers of 'gender', 'migrant' and 'worker' interact to produce specific labour control practices affecting wage levels and migrant workers' well-being. The chapter draws from research on the use of migrant labour from Northeast Thailand, Laos and Myanmar in the production for export of genetically engineered shrimp in Southern Thailand. Whereas large-scale enterprises employ Thai migrant workers coming from the North, medium and small farms employ mainly migrant husband-wife couples from neighbouring countries. Migrant couples are often together with their pre-school children but the school age children have to be sent back to the home area. Owners consider couples more reliable and more productive: the wife is available to support in the round-the-clock tasks of shrimp farming as well as to keep the male worker stable and responsible. The couples are usually paid a 'family wage' far less than a double wage; typically the wife is not classified as a 'real' worker. The family wage system is applied much less to Thai workers. Most Thai female workers receive a separate wage, and although they too fulfil supplementary and lower status roles, they are able to engage in additional income generating activities locally in combination with childcare. Burmese workers in particular have much less latitude to engage in supplementary paid work, though their 'wife' role is comparable with their Thai counterparts. Resurreccion and Sajor show how a particular set of life-world niches has emerged around shrimp farming, and how, through migration, different gender and ethnic identities are formed and solidified – partly according to the scale of production; and how they sustain different systems of rights and entitlements.

Chapter 15 on "Changing Identities, Multi-local Politics and Citizenship: Reflections on the Agency of Migrants from Indonesia and their Descendants in the Netherlands", by Ton van Naerssen, looks at the dialectics of migrant identity formation and transnational practices among people from the former Dutch East Indies who moved to the Netherlands, concentrating on the two largest groups: the Nederlands-Indisch (mixed-race 'Dutch-Indonesians' or in this chapter, 'Indisch-Dutch') and the Moluccans (from what are now two provinces in the east of Indonesia). The case has particular interest since it extends over several generations, has been much studied, shows both continuing evolution of identities and continuing distinctive group identities, and provides a sharp contrast between these two groups. The differences are understood within a transnational perspective, including reference to factors in both the host country and the migrant-sending country as well as to their mutual relations. For example, Moluccan identity and citizenship in the Netherlands have critically depended on the Moluccan struggle for independence from Indonesia. Historically classified as temporary residents in the Netherlands by the Dutch state, the Moluccans' failure to realize an independent Moluccan Republic pushed them into a grey zone owing to their inability to identify as either 'Dutch' or 'Indonesian'. The chapter asks how this identification may change if and as meanings ascribed to citizenship undergo fundamental changes. Second, van Naerssen explores how the increasing economic linkages between Indonesia and the Netherlands in the various strands of the 'migration-development nexus' are at the same time a cultural space which gives new dimensions to the identities of some of the migrants and their families, and to the meaning of their citizenship. For both groups, the Moluccans and the Indisch-Dutch, ties to Indonesia seem not to wither over time: instead, the number of transnational community organizations grows. The chapter casts implicit light on the 'host' community of white Dutch and on their Netherlands-specific official concept of *allochtoon*, whereby the grandchildren and great-grandchildren of immigrants sixty years ago from 'the Indies' remain conceptually separated from the white Dutch, whether or not they are Dutch citizens and regardless of how they identify themselves.

Chapter 16 on "Pro-asylum Advocacy in the EU: Challenging the 'State of Exception'", by Helen Hintjens, Richa Kumar and Ahmed Pouri, looks at the motivations and practices of activists and advocates who seek to protect the rights of asylum seekers and refugees in Western Europe. It looks in particular at the felt identities of the activists, and how these are affected by their resistance to the '3-Ds' that have become central instruments in EU policy towards asylum seekers – destitution, detention and deportation. As seen earlier in Maas and Truong's chapter on Frontex, people claiming asylum in the European Union are now virtually forced to enter illegally. If they reach Europe they face the battery of deterrence policies illustrated in the chapter by Engbersen and Broeders, that seek to exclude asylum seekers from all access to a legal existence and thus to dissuade them through destitution. Hintjens, Kumar and Pouri describe not only the policies but also the practices of how asylum-seekers' rights are routinely suspended by officialdom and decision-makers whenever they see fit, within the 'state of exception' that now operates across the EU Detention camps, often run by private companies, are operated as instruments of deterrence. Similarly, the lessons learned by destitute asylum seekers are intended for a wider audience of transmigrants or potential asylum seekers as well; and private companies and corporatized public agencies have quotas and targets for deportations.

In the context of the felt threat of 'terrorism', the rise of a 'surveillance state', and the progressive erosion of the rights of asylum seekers, those who seek to assist or defend them are themselves increasingly liable to surveillance and harassment. What motivates them to enter and persist in such work? The cases from the Netherlands and UK presented by Hintjens, Kumar and Pouri show people who stumbled by chance onto the harsh realities of current-day practice of the 3-Ds in the EU. The experiences of the activists, including of these authors, lead them to reflect on the nature of the world system and the possible parallels (now at a global level) with the elaborate system of privilege, exclusions and deportations that was practised in apartheid-era South Africa. Advocates across Europe converge on a perception of the 3-Ds as part of a system of global injustice.

Chapter 17 on "Human or Public? The Referents of Security in Discourses on Migrants in Japan", by Tatsuo Harada (with Kenji Kimura), shows how Japanese government policy documents on development cooperation and international relations use the discourse of 'human security' to stress the security of the individual human being, worldwide. In stark contrast, much internal discourse about those 'distant others' who have arrived as labour migrants in Japan identifies them as threats to 'public security' whose 'dangerous' character justifies their exclusion from mainstream society. They are excluded even from the public education system. The 'human' seen at a distance becomes the dangerous 'other' when viewed at close quarters in the homeland. Strikingly, this exclusion, which relates in part to the Japanese self-image of being ethnically homogeneous, has occurred also for groups who had been identified as preferred immigrants after Japan's domestic 'reserve armies' of rural labour and women were exhausted: the *Nikkeijin* – the ethnic Japanese from Brazil and Peru whose entry was permitted by the immigration law of 1990 based on *jus sanguinis*. Understanding of the real and felt insecurities of people in Japan, both migrants and indigenes, becomes an essential but neglected task for the voluminous Japanese work on 'human security'. The chapter takes up this challenge with special reference to the Chubu region, one of Japan's manufacturing heartlands, to which many *Nikkeijin* workers were drawn. It looks first at Brazilian *Nikkeijin*. Their children speak Portuguese at home and often cannot cope in Japanese schools; those rejected by the school system have no access to other state-supported education (indeed foreigners in Japan have no legal right to education at all) and become adrift, rendering them almost unemployable except in illicit activities. The chapter reports also the experiences of overstayers from South Asia who work in factories under exploitative terms. Rather than requesting approval to hire foreigners the factories prefer to use 'illegals' – who can be paid less, lack medical care rights, and can be easily dismissed. Given trends that undermine local communities, such as local government expenditure cuts and closure of local hospitals and small shops, the immigrants become targets of reactions that express locally felt insecurity. Harada advises that responding to these negative cycles of social exclusion requires that domestic policymakers absorb the principle of pervasive interconnection which has justified adoption of a 'human security' perspective in international relations.

The themes of mutual interconnection, inclusion and mutual benefit, and preservation or building of community all appear again but in special forms in the final chapter in Part IV, "The Global Forum on Migration and Development: 'All Talk and No Action' or 'A Chance to Frame the Issues in a Way that Allows You to Move Forward Together?'", by Bernice Roldan and Des Gasper. It explores the proposed rationale of the Global Forum launched by Kofi Annan in 2006 as UN Secretary General, as an informal inter-governmental discussion space rather than as part of the UN system. The first part analyses Annan's advocacy of the Forum, through close textual analysis of his speech to the High-Level Dialogue that he convened in New York. His position involved a series of claims: 1) migration must be managed; 2) to proceed from the present entrenched disagreements and mistrust requires constructive structured communication; 3) the Global Forum can provide this and is a feasible way forward, unlike proposals for binding international conventions; 4) through processes of growing mutual education and mutual acceptance the Forum can be fruitful. Annan's hypotheses could appear to be rather optimistic when the implied notions of building trust and community (amongst those referred to in the chapter as 'migro-crats', the managers and policymakers in the global networks of migration) are unpacked, and the validity of the assumptions (about how regular channels and fora of systematic but relatively informal communication can affect attitudes and in turn affect choices) is tested.

The second part of the chapter monitors how these hypotheses had fared by the time of the second GFMD conference, held in Manila in 2008, using other methods of discourse analysis to dissect its concluding report. The Manila meeting's declaration of a 'focus on the person' appeared in reality to mean a focus on the 'migro-crats' and their interactive processes of mutual education and teambuilding aimed at producing practical cooperation. The report is relatively silent on migrants themselves, but claims that the Forum process is "changing the way the world looks at migration and development" and, "more importantly...changing the way we deal with each other on [migration and development]" (paragraphs 2 and 3 of the conference's final report: Conejos 2008). To clarify this whole strategy and draw out its mindset and assumptions, the chapter presents a series of accessible tools of discourse analysis that may be more widely useful in migration studies and for participation in migration policy debate.

1.3.5 Part V: Ethics of Modern-day Transnational Migration: A Human Security Perspective

Transnationalism involves the intensive routine interconnection of what were previously largely separate national spaces. We see diverse competing global models of reasoning for ordering this emergent global space. One model envisions a world of separate national homes in which international migrants are felt as a troublesome complication – useful but also a threat. Another is the model of the global market in which migrants are considered as a mobile factor of production with few rights. Thirdly is the vision of a world of international human rights in which migrants share and belong, and which includes instituted accountability for protecting their rights and well-being. The final section of this volume consolidates a framework for description, explanation, evaluation and response: a version of human security thinking which seeks to ground human rights values both in a critique of the predominant forms of liberal and neoliberal thought, as well in the search for alternatives which are sensitive to contextual differences. Intra-nationally we must move beyond a Rawlsian liberal justice framework and conception of a social contract, which continues to conceive of people only as autonomous legal units. Focussing only on the individuality of people narrows the potential for fellowship with others. Internationally, a human security framework goes beyond the Westphalian conception of states and citizenship and responds to a transnational and interpenetrated system. It offers a suitably pluralist approach, setting universal human rights thinking within humanly richer and more conflict-aware perspectives.

Chapter 19 on "International Migration, Well-being and Transnational Ethics", by Des Gasper, gives a perspective for considering the well-being of migrants – of people in the 'sender' society and people in the 'receiver' society – integrating human rights thinking with care ethics and a sensitivity to subjectivities. Active respect for each person worldwide relies on some informed awareness of the contents of their lives. In reaction to much philosophical literature in international relations, the chapter seeks a better empirical grounding for the stage of philosophical argument. Starting by looking at the contents of migrant lives, it moves to consider their evaluation, in terms of well- and ill-being and the justice and injustice of their generation and distribution, including reference to criteria of fair process, fair deserts and fair opportunity. The relevant empirical background includes awareness of the historical record of dispossession, domination and discrimination over the past five centuries. Linking to the chapters in Part IV, Gasper notes how migration jumbles up the contents of the national 'societies' that are assumed to be discrete units by 'realist' international relations and nationalist ethics theorists. Migration creates new liminal zones and increases the plurality within identity, building a world system of a myriad of overlapping communities, not of self-contained nation-states. These more complex liminal identities can help to counter the 'othering' processes that often render identities crude and mutually antagonistic. Nevertheless, any rethinking of the contents of the 'self' and of one's 'interests' is a long-term process which may depend on a prior phase of respectful coexistence motivated by enlightened self-interest. Human security thinking thus centrally emphasizes the theme of 'common security': that in an interconnected world to disrespect the security of others will undermine your own security. Cooperative co-existence motivated by awareness of interdependence can gradually foster acceptance of plurality among and within identities, and of sharing across identities, and the perception that one's identity can be enriched rather than threatened by that of others.

Chapter 20 on "Migration, Morality and Finance", by Amiya Kumar Bagchi, further investigates the assumptions used in philosophical discussions of the ethics of migration. Bagchi challenges the lack of attention to macro-structures and systems that reproduce and exacerbate inequality and poverty, including those financial and trade structures which contribute strongly to injustice in most societies, and the assumption that dramatic socio-economic inequality is inevitable. He posits gross international inequality and poverty as the root causes of streams of 'illegal' migrants. Here he removes the 'veil of ignorance' placed over the historical record, and identifies several recent major shifts that have in his view aggravated international inequality and fed pressures to emigrate: the movement since the 1970s against granting predominant roles to the state in developing countries in long-term economic development strategy and in provision of social services; the transfer instead of sovereign authority to financial markets; and the decline and fall of the Soviet bloc. The nature and widespread failure of the associated economic structural adjustment programmes implemented in the 1980s and 90s fed new waves of migration. So too has unlimited and unregulated capital mobility across international borders, including the acceptance of funds by many international banks without asking any questions, which permits continuous capital flight from poor economies. Yet the countries which receive these funds impose the strictest restrictions on inflows of labour. Bagchi suggests that the required reforms must start from principles of universal human rights. They should include regulation of the export and import of capital in all countries, with prohibition of trading in derivatives; compensation to low-income countries for acquisition by high-income countries of their highly skilled personnel, balancing the right of freedom of movement against the obligations arising from sponsored education; and granting citizenship to willing immigrants after a brief period.

Not only are national boundaries and systems of migration control associated with different treatment of those inside and those outside a national border, they can lead to different treatment of groups within a nation's borders. In the case of South Africa during *apartheid*, its rulers insisted that there was nothing peculiar about their arrangements but that they merely reproduced within one country the set of principles used globally. They then aimed to make the arrangements more defensible by declaring a few pockets of South Africa to be separate countries. These pockets, being the historic 'reserves' or 'homelands', were where low-income workers would be born and bred. They would be transferred to the 'white' areas when ready to work, periodically returned to the 'reserves' at the end of each contract and permanently returned when old, ill or otherwise no longer wanted. While the more skilled types of black labour were permitted to settle permanently in South Africa's cities, the less skilled were admitted only as workers without families for fixed-period contracts.

In Chapter 21 on "Migration Regimes and the Politics of Insiders/Outsiders: Japan and South Africa as Distant Mirrors", Yoichi Mine sees parallels between this system of exploitation and the currently practised and promoted arrangements in high-income countries. The system of 'reserves' was used in many colonial situations, for it allowed employers to avoid contributing, or to pay much less, towards the reproduction costs of workers' families. When formal influx control in South Africa was abolished in the 1990s, the expected massive influx from the reserves did not happen; if poorly educated rural dwellers have access to some resources in the 'reserves' they do not necessarily abandon this, and their homeplace and loved ones, in order to take their chances in urban shantytowns. What has happened instead in South Africa is an influx of perhaps three million illegal migrants from other African countries, who are cheaper and more compliant because they are illegal and thus more attractive to businesses that now face global competition. Continuation of strong segmentation in the workforce plays the same roles as under apartheid: to divide and rule, and to exploit more intensively particular groups. Mine suggests that these principles are at play also in modern-day Japan, and elsewhere. In Japan as in most high-income countries, global competition increases employers' interest in cheap labour; and jobs that are nowadays considered demanding, dirty, dangerous, or otherwise undesirable, are left for immigrants. The Immigration Control Act was amended in 1990 to allow corresponding supply, including from communities of *Nikkeijin* in Latin America. As discussed in the chapters by Harada and Mushakoji, these groups remain largely socially excluded. In addition, a 'trainees' system has been established to bring in unskilled foreign labour on fixed-term contracts, allocated to specific employers and often without protection of labour legislation. Such migration regimes in Japan and elsewhere have the same rationale as in the apartheid system: to benefit from the labour of groups who are kept socially marginal and excluded from most of the benefits that they help to produce, and who will have to bear most of their own costs of social reproduction. South African history suggests that institutionalization of such divisive exploitative systems, with dichotomization of insiders and outsiders, jeopardizes social morality and, eventually, social peace.

Chapter 22 on "State and Immigrant Diaspora Identity in Contemporary Japan: From a Developmentalist National Ethic towards a Multicultural Development Ethic of Common Human Security", by Kinhide Mushakoji, offers thoughts on how to inspire and guide moves towards more moral and sustainable systems. Mushakoji goes beyond Bagchi, to argue that human rights thinking alone will not suffice. He outlines an approach to synthesis of collective and individual rights and norms. Without such a synthesis, positive Enlightenment values will continue to be perceived in many societies as exogenous and criticised as an imposition of cultural colonialism. Universalist and individualist ethics in the tradition of the Western Enlightenment must be adapted to allow different identity communities to each have an acknowledged and respected right to identity reproduction. The right to identity reproduction applies to states but cannot be limited to these. The Japanese state enforces this right when it comes to the reproduction of the identity of Japanese people and the nation. When it comes to diaspora communities, this right is ignored. Like many countries, Japan emphasizes a proud and unified national identity as a key value (to be reproduced through the education system) that provides a basis for preservation and advancement of the nation-state. Such an ethic was articulated in the late 19th century Meiji construction of the modern

Japanese state, which emphasized loyalty to family, superiors and the nation, rather than starting from individual rights. Under the American occupation in 1947 a new Law on Education emphasized instead the formation of responsible individuals. It was replaced in 2006 by a new Law that reaffirms the reproduction of a homogeneous unified Japanese nation. Like the previous Laws it covers only Japanese nationals, ignoring non-nationals residing in Japan. For them the state accepts no responsibility in education. In principle, immigrants are expected either to go 'home' once they have made their economic contribution, or to assimilate and become 'completely Japanese'. In Mushakoji's view, this dichotomous approach creates marginalized, unprotected and partly 'illegal' immigrant communities operating within a large informal sector. It not only undermines the well-being of the immigrants, it undermines also the security of the Japanese state and people.

Premised on a Westphalian notion of competing nation-states based on single identities, the Japanese state views immigrant communities that have not been homogenized into the Japanese mainstream as problems, rather than as assets who, thanks to their more complex identities provide creative bridges between Japan and the rest of the world. In reality, security is only attainable as common security, based on respect for assuring each other's security. It is necessary to extend the Bandung Principles, of 'peaceful coexistence' and 'equal mutual benefit', to relations between all identity communities, non-state-based as well as state-based. Mushakoji argues that a human security approach recognises this need to empower non-state identity communities rather than only those based on the nation-state, since identity production and reproduction form the basis for practices of caring and for every ethical framework. He sets this proposal within a larger perspective, of movement towards transcendence of all exclusionary identities and towards cross-cultural as well as multi-cultural democracies.

1.4 Conclusion

This volume examines the historical experience of cross-border migration in recent decades as co-constituted by the enactment of economic cosmopolitanism under neoliberal doctrines and pre-existing hierarchical relations between societies and peoples. Processes of structural reform on a global scale in the last three decades have stimulated multi-scale transformations and social re-ordering that generate insecurity and drive migration. To help societies find adaptations to the complex realities of migration that are integral to globalizing processes, we argue for alternative ethical modes of reasoning about the 'migration-development-security nexus', and for ways of thinking that can transcend dualisms and dichotomies and emphasize the relational and processual nature of being. Peoples and societies have become inextricably linked through the interconnected processes of globalization. It is no longer acceptable to use a perspective limited to cultural or territorial boundaries to define morally relevant identities. At the same time, ethical reflection here requires understanding the diverse relations between different forms of deprivation and responsibility, and the range of emergent subjectivities and practices not easily captured by extant frameworks of cosmopolitanism and universal rights. For these reasons we have found the human security approach as a helpful base for further dialogues on migration in a peaceful world order.

2 The Governmentality of Transnational Migration and Security: The Making of a New Subaltern

Thanh-Dam Truong

2.1 Introduction

Historical and comparative studies have demonstrated that migration (as human mobility across geographical areas and regions) is a dynamic process, interacting with livelihood systems, regulatory norms and security-enhancing institutions, both materially and subjectively (Hoerder 2002; Schrover/van der Leun/Lucassen/Quispel 2008). Migration cannot be understood in truncated ways, in parts and fragments of reality rather than the totality of the universe in which the phenomenon rose, became institutionalized and transformed at different historical moments. A core issue today is the gradual practical and conceptual erosion of the legal boundaries set in the Westphalian framework of inter-state relations and the emergence of fragmented modes of regulation of the movement of people across border of nation-states. This reflects the inability of governments to reconcile the tension within global capitalism, which on the one hand prises national economies open and on the other remains unaccountable for the adverse human consequences of this openness. The architecture of global governance of migration today shows how diverse rationalities have played out one against another to produce a situation in which growth-driven norms are taking over from rights norms based on human dignity enshrined in the Universal Declaration of Human Rights. This calls for a reconsideration of migration and security as two key areas of state prerogative, in light of their transnational and trans-local implications.

The vast body of literature on migration studies shows diversity of perspectives, disciplinary orientations and mandates (Brettell/Hollifield 2000). The underlying ethos has so far rarely been made explicit. Such mandates span what Buroway (2005) refers to as a 'problem-solving approach' (or instrumental knowledge) at one end of the spectrum and an approach to 'reflexive knowledge' or critical knowledge for emancipation at the other. Although Buroway's binary distinction has been subject to criticism (Morrow 2008), it is useful to distinguish the approaches taken in the studies on migration and show how they interact and transform one another as global migration unfolds.

The problem-solving approach draws its principles from the ethos of the nation-state and its sub-components to evaluate processes by which an institution or a set of social relations operates in a given domain of migration policy – labour import and export, welfare, remittances, cultural assimilation and humanitarian concerns. The critical knowledge approach draws its principles from transnational studies, seeking to expose deceptive binary constructs, such as state/society and global/local. The approach of transnational migration studies begins from the lives of migrants, placing migration within a larger perspective that rejects the long-held notion that society is one and the nation and state are the same. It seeks to reformulate the concept of 'society' within the framework of a transnational arena, inspired by Bourdieu's concept of social field to grasp the full spectrum of diverse social transactions and their implications for state and migrants' strategic choices (Basch/Glick-Schiller/Szanton Blanc 1994; Smith/Guarnizo 1998; Levitt/Glick Schiller 2004).

The Copenhagen school of thought in international relations, built on a critical knowledge approach, provides new ideas to analyse the mutual constitution of security and migration (Buzan/Wæver/De Wilde 1998). This school creates openings to investigate 'security' in the transnational field by extending the focus on traditional state-centred meanings to social realms, viewing 'state security' (primarily concerned with the protection of territorial sovereignty) and 'societal security' (concerned with the formation of a collective identity and the connection between such an identity and common interests) as mutually informing and influencing one another. A three-dimensional method to analyse securitization as a process

T.-D. Truong and D. Gasper (eds.), *Transnational Migration and Human Security*, Hexagon Series on Human and Environmental Security and Peace 6, DOI 10.1007/978-3-642-12757-1_2, © Springer-Verlag Berlin Heidelberg 2011

set in a historical moment is proposed: 1) the identification of an existential threat (or security move); 2) emergency action; 3) their effects on inter-unit relations regarding rule breaking (meaning the justification of a range of policies that would otherwise not have been considered legitimate). Thus the basic questions are: who can make a security move and how; what issues are included in the referent of security in this move; what are the enabling conditions of this move and its outcomes.

Followers of this school of thought applied the concept of securitization critically to show how the discursive interactions between public and private actors have produced a framing of security that depicts 'migration' as an 'existential threat' to host societies, with implications for the institutionalization of new conduct and practices towards the population of non-citizens (Huysmans 2000, 2006; Abrahamsen 2005; Curley/Wong 2008). While the focus of these studies is regional, their broader relevance lies in their attempt to bring into focus the ethical-political dimensions in the relationship between security and migration. In other words, ethical norms about security and migration are not to be taken as pre-givens but as constituted through discursive practices by a variety of private and public actors and strategies of governments.

This chapter draws on these ideas to trace the main lines in the framing of 'security' to show the historical junctions where specific meanings of 'security' intersected with 'migration' and 'development'. 'Security framing' is useful to reveal the technologies of power that link these three domains in a triadic way – by appealing to particular ethical norms and modes of conceptualization about 'security' (intra-, inter-state security, trade) at given times. Tensions in this triadic relationship appear at a deeper level of the ontology of the nation-state as a normative vision of political order. This ontology sits uneasily with the global evolution of capitalism and has been modified in various ways.[1] Understanding security, migration and development as a triadic and interactive relationship within a particular context of re-configuring the global political economy is essential in order to develop new ideas for transformations towards harmonious and peaceful co-existence.

1 Security moves today are tapping into collective historical memories with particular significance about the state (theocratic, humanist liberal and market-based communist).

First, we provide a synthesis on the ontology of the nation-state, its original meanings of security and how privileges have been built into particular forms of human mobility across and between geographical areas and regions. Second, we illustrate how the modification of the ontology of the nation-state for the purpose of cooperation between groups of states has also affected the naming, framing and regulation of mobility. Third, we show how the meanings of human mobility in the four extant bodies of international legislation (the Refugee Convention, Mode 4 of the General Agreement of Trade and Services, the United Nations Convention on Transnational Organized Crime and its Protocols and the International Convention on the Protection of the Rights of All Migrant Workers and Members of Their Families) reflect the politics of re-assertion of the authority of the state under pressures of market-driven globalisation processes, and how the differentiation of meanings and inconsistency in application reveal the desire of the power holders to maintain a hierarchical global society supported by particular politics within nation-states. Failure to deal with migration holistically – as outcomes of economic transformations and re-ordering societies – has led to the formation of a new subaltern class labelled as 'irregular migrants' in the EU and 'criminal aliens' in the US and Japan, labels that are now being circulated more widely. The fourth section introduces a different notion of the unity of 'being human', in an appeal to a different approach to politics. We draw on the voices of plain truth (*parrhesia*) regarding 'mobility', 'temporal ability' and 'vulnerability' as pre-conceptual realities of humankind. This alternative mode of understanding 'being human' seeks to direct attention to the ontology of care, for social thought on caring relations lies at the heart of justice (Engster 2007). This may help provide more balance to an overwhelming emphasis on the autonomy and reason of the individual.

2.2 The Ontology of the Nation-State: Apprehending Security, Rights and Migration

An ontology – as depicted by Bourdieu in his writings on *habitus* and symbolic violence (1990), Galtung (1990) on cultural violence and Foucault (1984a) on the history of systems of thought – refers to a phenomenon of *longue durée*. The term conveys the notions of the silent behaviour, habits and practices drawn from a repository of meanings in religious, spiritual, mythological symbols and philosophy. Concerned with long-term processes of structuring social relations, these authors posit the view that an ontology does not exist only in an abstract form; it also has significance through the directing of thinking in the organization of social relationships and institutions.

Foucault's concept of the ethos and art of governing (*governmentality*) helps us to discern the ontology of the nation-state and its transformations. The genealogical method he uses to investigate the epistemic shifts in human sciences in the 17th and 18th centuries treats ontology as a historical formation, lending support to the key assumptions on which a particular system of knowledge/practices is based. Thus the method of genealogy does not take the question of 'human essence' as datum, but as a manifestation of a given ontology. An ontology conveys, through the language of religion or science and philosophy, particular notions about human nature from which an understanding of human freedom and individuality are derived.

Debate about natural law, rights and sovereignty makes deliberate use of a particular concept of 'human nature' in order to distinguish itself from other types of discourse, such as theology or biology (Foucault 1984b). The language of human nature is intimately linked with the creation of a political community, its institutions and societal knowledge. For the analyst, the term 'human nature' may be apprehended as an epistemic indicator to assess the strategies of truth-claiming in a history of veridiction (Foucault 1984b). Tracing how 'human nature' is defined, codified and regulated, in conjunction with a particular model of citizenship, is important for understanding the art of government (Foucault 1991a, 1991b). Governmentality can thus be understood in a more simplified meaning of governmental rationality and the knowledge system that supports it.

The theme of *governmentality* was one of Foucault's working hypotheses on the reciprocal constitution of forms of knowledge and power techniques, regimes of representation and modes of intervention (Foucault 1991a, 1991b; Lemke 2007). Modes of government intervention are viewed as historically sited in discourses where concepts are formed; objects and borders are specified; and arguments for (or against) a given exercise of power are justified. Government seeks to gain legitimacy *per pro* a given field and thus the ability to address a problem. This simultaneously triggers a process of subject identity formation. Political struggles can bring changes in modes of governing, but aspirations for emancipation can be co-opted, discernable by way of examining the reformulations of rationale, categorization, object and subject of control that are immanent in what he calls a *dispositif* of power (Foucault 1991a).

Foucault (2007) discerned three inter-related meanings of security: 1) sovereignty confirmed through the enactment of law on a multiplicity of subjects (as people or the populace) within a territory; 2) discipline consisting of techniques of individualization directed at making individual subjects docile, conformists and governable; 3) security as an abstraction of the diversity within a population that can be statistically conceived and managed through the guidance of the human sciences (demographics, economics, the science of finance and administration). The key issue is not state domination or increasing control of the state over its populace, but the shifting emphasis in the 'ethos' and 'art' of governing. For example, the shift from the administrative state (police and discipline) to one in which governmental power is dispersed through society by way of professional power at different sites (education, health, correction systems, etc).

The Treaty of Westphalia in 1648 marked a turning point in the governmental rationality in which the view on a 'system of security' was adopted (Foucault 2007: 291, 297). Due to the tendency of states to expand the boundaries of their economic activities they ended up competing with one another, making international strife a primary source of threat to state security. Maintaining security within territorial boundaries thus became insufficient. States, as they then existed, were apprehended as a field of forces; and in the new governmental rationality, the preservation of the state within a general order was no longer perceived as being as significant as the balancing of power in the management of the relations of force between them (population movement and circulation of goods) (Foucault 2007: 296).

From the start this model of security carried seeds of conflict based on culture, ethnicity and gender as subject identities. The model conflated 'nation' with 'sovereignty' and territoriality and thereby the interests of the state with those of the people living under its jurisdiction. The notion of 'citizenship', with its rights, was therefore built on an elitist definition of natural and legal persons and effectively became binding for the whole society under the 'social contract'. The model largely obscured the reality of society as comprising social agents with a plurality of beliefs, actions, statures and strategic interests. It also promoted a centripetal move of power whereby the 'citizenry' traded off some of their communal rights in return for state protection (Held 1983). Just as issues of diversity in belonging came under the 'nation' as an asserted common referent suppressing diversity of history and language within a territory, so too were the specific concerns of women as social subjects (Fraser in Agosin 2001). Practices of the management of natural resources based on a bio-centric worldview (taking into account the cyclical need for renewal) were sidelined, and a new framing of 'nature' as comprising inert matters for conquest became normalized (Merchant 1980, 2003). A spread of this model across different regions of the world through colonization reproduced similar structures of state and societal relations, and squeezed highly heterogeneous social groups into newly created bounds (variously defined as protectorate, colony and dependent territory).

Movement across borders grew as economies expanded. Forced trans-Atlantic movements through slave trading practices, and indentured modes of movement within and between colonies were based on such conceptions about the human (and its nature) that natural rights were considered inapplicable to those forced and indentured (Behrendt 1999; Grant 2005; Cohen 1987). In parallel, unrestricted and state-subsidized immigration enabled the movement of an estimated 50 million people from Europe to the New World during the 19th and through the first half of the 20th century.[2] By the late 1920's, policy restrictions had been introduced in the United States and later in South Africa, Brazil, Australia, New Zealand and Canada specifically directed at non-European ethnic groups.[3] McKeown (2004) reveals that there were also movements from Europe to Northern Asia and from East and South Asia to Southeastern Asia that were comparable in size and demographic impact to the transatlantic flows.

Such movements contributed to the formation of heterogeneous and hybrid identities, which generally have been overwritten by the construct of the nation-state as a homogeneous entity. The main problem for the nation-state has been the fuzziness of the boundaries of its cultural identity. The aggregation of communities with diverse bases in secular beliefs, religious faiths, ethnicity and race into one signifier of the nation, posed new questions: where does a national identity begin and where does its protection end; what are the responsibilities of the various actors; to whom are they accountable; which mechanisms of protection matter most to whom?

Security as social order (achieved at the expense of the suppression of the meanings of *difference* within a territory) and a territory's protection (the principal rationale for war between states) turned against empires in moments of political turmoil. World War I erupted over meanings of 'nation' and escalated over the matter of boundaries of colonial territories, an issue that carried over into post-colonial contexts. The pursuit of security and justice that followed was directed at preventing war and the persecution of minority groups. Gains made by the League of Nations created under the Treaty of Versailles in 1919 were the established parameters of justifiable intervention by the international community in the internal affairs of states based on human rights abuse (against minorities). The moment provided an opportunity for anti-slavery activism movements to bring into focus the 'new slaveries' of European imperialism. These included coercive systems of labour taxation, indentured servitude, and evidence of atrocities including the trafficking of women and girls for the purpose of prostitution. The 1926 Slavery Convention endorses the definition of slavery in international law as well as the obligation to secure and just treatment of native populations in territories under the control of the signatories, and specifically to both ensure fair and humane conditions for women and children's labour and halt the trafficking in women and minors. The mechanisms established to monitor and control the forced migration of women and minors for the purpose of prostitution were in many ways ineffective given the conditions imposed by the nation-states – respect for sovereign decision-making and immunity of military camps from external inspection (Truong 1990). Although the creation of the International Labour Organization in 1929 explicitly linked individual rights to economic security, issues concerning the links between economic vulnerability and the trafficking of women and children for prostitution remained unattended. More importantly, the effect of a stigmatized sexual identity on the everyday security of

2 The United States, Canada, South America, Australasia and southern Africa were the main recipient areas. Britain was a dominant source of migrants but also prominent were Germany, Scandinavia and other parts of Northwestern Europe; then, later, other European areas: parts of the Austro-Hungarian Empire, Italy, Spain, Portugal, Poland and Russia (Hatton and Williamson 2005).

3 Hatton and Williamson (2005: 7) cite a variety of legal mechanisms of restriction – notably contract labour laws, (Chinese) exclusion acts, excludable classes and head taxes.

women involved in commercial sexual services was not recognized as a significant issue.

Viewed from this perspective, the specific discourse regarding human rights and their links to the system of nation-states as political communities had been connected with the idea of controlling war, and promoting religious toleration and respect for minorities to ensure effective interactions between states. The meaning of rights shows a fluctuation between an aspiration for all people as members of humanity, and a reduction of the meaning of humanity to specific groups based on their subjective identities defined by states. The pursuit of justice as key condition for security was incomplete for those whose subjective identities occupy a position of minor significance to the state. Teitel (2003) shows how this transitional period built up towards a full inclusion, then turned away from it to the point of a mere preservation of a minimalist rule of law identified chiefly with maintaining order. In other words, the nation-state was to be preserved by disciplinary means rather than by ensuring rights to all.

2.3 From Bipolarity to Trilateralism: The Security, Migration and Development Triad

The multilateral system put in place in the post-World War II period marked a new turn in governmental rationality. World order and the state system of security acquired an additional dimension. The Westphalian notion of balance of power was supplemented with the concepts of 'decolonization' and 'cooperation between states' for peace. In a bipolar world dominated by the Soviet Union and the United States, security was divided into two administrative domains: 1) control over weapons of mass destruction and 2) development (which was narrowly conceived as modernization and poverty alleviation to prevent war). In this predictive and prescriptive universe of bipolarity, the social construct of the free world versus the communist world was based on competition for a reigning position in the world order and the diverse cultural and social meanings of 'being human' became suppressed. In the modernization model the 'modern' is counter-poised with 'tradition' – the latter being treated as a residue of history expected to vanish gradually in a linear progression towards an ideal democratic system of the free world. In the communist model 'collective interests' are counter-poised with 'individual interests', which are treated as a historical feature of capitalism and therefore expected to disappear in a linear progression towards a classless society as an ideal of democracy. Both systems adopted a mechanical worldview in which the human subject is treated as a fairly fixed and stable entity whose desire and identity can be moulded for the greater good of their respective social designs. Human mobility between the two global camps was framed as defection and state treason. Within each of them, it was planned and regulated at varying degrees of stringency.

By the 1960's new challenges had begun to transform this system: 1) transnationalism became recognized as a phenomenon, evidenced by the operations of multinational corporations piercing through borders; 2) internal social revolts; 3) the widening of the sphere of Soviet influence and Third-World nationalist allies. The initial mapping of a new order may be found in Crozier, Huntington and Watanuki's treatise entitled *The Crisis of Democracy* (1975). A joint product of three elite scholars representing the trilateral global capitalist elite blocs (Western Europe, US, and Japan), the treatise discerned the problem of *governability of democracy* prevalent in the free world – and offered recommendations to address it. An intrinsic threat to democracy was seen to have grown out of the economic expansion of the 1960s in the trilateral regions, which led to the upsurge of social movements asserting their "disgust with the corruption, materialism, and inefficiency of democracy and with the subservience of democratic government to monopoly capitalism" (Crozier/Huntington/Watanuki 1975: 6). These authors characterized social movements as being driven by new values no longer grounded on materialistic, work-oriented and public-spirited ethics, and saw their actions as attempts to de-legitimize political, and other forms of, authority given that they tended to consider all civil institutions (family, church, trade union, universities and even the military) to be undemocratic. Democratic politics became anomic, transforming the public sphere into an arena for asserting conflicting interests rather than a platform from which to build common purposes (Crozier/Huntington/Watanuki 1975: 161). Demands on governments to meet the needs of specific groups – coupled with an escalation of those needs – led to a financial overload on governments, which spilled over to the economy and society (Crozier/Huntington/Watanuki 1975: 164). One solution was to separate a political system from its society to allow: 1) society to return to its own (autonomously formed) authority, and 2) the state to restore its authority over a restricted public sphere. The authors prescribed a more confined vertical relationship between the state and its citizenry and a multiplication of horizontal relations between civil organizations to address intrinsic challenges. They perceived extrinsic threat as coming from the then Soviet Union and its Third World allies, particularly with the introduction in the 1970s of the notion of 'socialist economic integration' under the Council for Mutual Economic Assistance (CMEA) linking three continents - Europe, Asia and the Western hemisphere (Bloed 1988).

The Trilateral Commission, which these authors represented, identified the key limits for democratic change as being derived from the inability of the public and its leaders to understand global interdependence in terms of relations that pierce through borders of nation-states (Sklar 1980: 3). The main idea behind 'trilateralism' was the nurturing of "the habits and practices of working together among the trilateral regions [USA, Europe, Japan] in order to promote a healthy (i.e. mutually beneficial and not mutually suicidal) level of competition between the capitalist powers; forge a common front against the Third World and the Soviet Union; 'renovate' international political economy in the interest of global business and finance; and make trilateral democracy more 'governable'" Sklar (1980: 8). Harmonizing trade and social well-being between member countries to create *trilateral unity* was a key objective to stabilize democracy at home. Anticipated social costs associated with this objective were to be deflected onto non-members rather than laterally shared between the members (Sklar 1980). An undemocratic element was built into this vision of governance through the idea of externalizing costs of renovating the 'Self' (trilateral unity) to 'Others' (the rest of the world).

The reconfigurations of inter-state systems of security that flowed from this vision saw unprecedented patterns and levels of migration, partly triggered by civil strife, conflicts and regime changes and partly by the growing mobility of finance and flexibility of labour. In the immediate post-Cold War era the discursive construct of cross border migration hinged on two main categories (labour migrants and refugees) with distinctive principles. Labour migration was viewed as a new form of 'transnationalism', which was seen as potentially benefitting both the recipient countries and the countries of origins. A combination of factors, which included on the one hand the decline of Official Development Assistance (ODA) and the rise in migrants' remittances, and on the other hand the looming demographic crisis in the trilateral regions, made the temporary arrangements for migrant workers an attractive option for these regions. The key issue to be addressed was *effective* management. Likewise, effective directing of remittance flows to social infrastructure (rather than personal consumption) was seen as the condition for the development of migrants sending societies. Humanitarian principle would be applied to the refugee situation (Meissner/Hormats/Walker/Ogata 1993).

In brief, the vision of migration in the post-Cold War world order resided initially - and uncomfortably - between an instrumental logic and a humanitarian one, as if migrant workers do not actually need welfare rights and refugees do not actually need work. Setting these categories apart, while necessary for states to regulate and manage human flows across border, also creates differences in subject identities among those on the move, and in disciplinary measures regarding entry, entitlements and rights. These differences can obscure the hegemonic vision of trilateral democracy and its exclusionary ethics.

2.4 Governance of Global Migration: A Contested Order

Unsettled differences between governments gave rise to new measures of global migration control having conflicting rationalities. In addition to the 1951 Refugee Convention, three pieces of international legislation have been created to govern cross border movement. These are the 1995 Mode 4 of the General Agreement on Trade in Services (GATS) of the World Trade Organization (WTO); the 2000 United Nations Convention Against Transnational Organized Crime and its supplements commonly referred to as the Palermo Protocols,[4] and the 2003 International Convention on the Protection of the Rights of All Migrant Workers and Members of their Families.

The 1951 UN Convention related to the Status of Refugees[5] initially covered displacement within Eu-

4 The supplements are the Protocol to Prevent, Suppress and Punish Trafficking in Persons, especially women and children and, the Protocol against the Smuggling of Migrants by Land, Sea and Air.

5 The Convention defines a refugee as a person who "owing to a well-founded fear of being persecuted for reasons of race, religion, nationality, membership of a particular social group or political opinion, is outside the country of his (*sic*) nationality and is unable or, owing to such fear, is unwilling to avail himself (*sic*) of the protection of that country" (Article 1, A2).

rope immediately following the end of World War II and migration resulting from political persecution during the Cold War.[6] The 1967 Protocol extended its validity to similar situations in other parts of the world owing to tension arising from decolonization and nation-state building. The principle of *non-refoulement* is fundamental to the protection of refugees.[7] A major turning point in refugee legislation occurred in the *Comprehensive Plan of Action* (CPA) for Indo-Chinese Refugees in 1989 with the introduction of the concept of 'voluntary repatriation'. This concept was first applied to those Vietnamese 'Boat People' in Hong Kong who had been unsuccessful in 'passing' the refugee screening procedures. The persons concerned had the single option to return voluntarily. Those who did not seize the offer would face detention, then subsequent 'orderly return' or 'orderly repatriation' - which just meant deportation (Zieck 1997: 463-468). The concept was later adopted in several Southeast Asian countries, and applied also to Laotian and Cambodian nationals.

Although voluntary return is drawn from the 'right of return', some analysts view this turn as both driven by geopolitical interests and a step in the direction of hardening the guidelines for refugee determination (Chimni 2004). From a humanitarian perspective, the scale and complexity of population displacement during the 1980s made the application of the refugee status to displaced persons (due to armed conflicts, generalized violence and foreign aggression) mandatory. From a managerial perspective, critics argue that the original mandate of the 1951 Convention could not accommodate these new forms of displacement given that the forms of 'political persecution' which emerged in post-war Europe and in the bipolar world that followed were different (Collinson 1993). In practice the concept of the 'refugee' as defined in the Convention was neither able to accommodate all the movements induced by complex social tensions prevalent in many parts of the developing and the post-Soviet worlds (UNHCR 2006), nor was it able to account for emerging movements induced by natural disasters or famine situations.

These new complexities in population displacement have become prolonged features. Displaced persons unable to return home for reasons not sanctioned by the Refugee Convention must rely on the discretion of the host government to confer on them a humanitarian status - inferior to that of a refugee in terms of both rights and length of stay. Only a minority of them obtain this status. Cases of refugees compelled to move on from their first country of asylum due to lack of protection have become common. A continuum has evolved between repeated displacement and the crossing of borders due to the lack of protection, creating a new phenomenon called 'transitivity' (UNICEF 2003: 13). This continuum has enabled an intermeshing of practices formally defined as asylum seeking, human smuggling, human trafficking and migration (UNHCR 1995, 2006). In respect of the majority of displaced persons, voluntary repatriation, reintegration, rehabilitation and post-conflict reconstruction have become the key words in efforts to find durable solutions (UNHCR 2003). Handling population displacements within the humanitarian assistance agenda contributed, in turn, to the human security agenda. This agenda seeks to integrate human development and human rights to build a comprehensive redistributive framework premised on human dignity as a core referent (Commission on Human Security 2003; Truong, 2005; Gasper/Truong 2010a, 2010b).

Receptivity to the human security agenda has been obstructed by a general climate of reluctance compounded by an anxiety for the 'Other', amplified since 9/11 2001. The understanding of the term human security as common security can take on a communitarian rather than a universal meaning. Common security, articulated for example in discourses on the enlargement of Europe, or cooperation in Asia and the Pacific, has been translated into a policy of deterrence-of-entry through legislation that enforces more restrictive interpretation of categories of migrants (Morris-Suzuki 2007b), and a spread of the partial privatization of security globally (Koulish 2009; Flynn/Cannon 2009). The introduction of new 'non-entrée' mechanisms, externalized measures of control (interception, offshore refugee determination, control of ports of entry) and visas (in the name of efficiency and security at the expense of accuracy) reflect a generalized abdication of responsibility to protect the right to seek asylum.

The outcome is the formation of concentric circles of security, centred on an ontology of the nation constructed as the collective self, with surrounding protective layers to fend off attacks by the 'Others' (including both known and unpredictable forces). In the case of Europe, these concentric circles are composed of: 1) territorial control by policing land, sea and air; and 2) an organizational control that restricts

6 Hungary in 1956 and Czechoslovakia in 1968.

7 As spelled out in Article 33 of the Convention, no person should be forcibly returned to a country where his/her life or freedom would be at risk.

migrants' entitlements and informal space for survival (access to work, social security, associations) in order to ensure that, while entry may be possible, social protection is not claimable (Geddes 2005). Externalizing protective layers also occurs by way of erecting barriers against entry through bilateral treaties and by extra-territorialization of border control (Dover 2008).

The second piece of international legislation dealing with people's movement across borders is Mode 4 of the General Agreement on Trade in Services (GATS) of the World Trade Organization (WTO). This organization came into being in 1995 as an outcome of the 1986–94 Uruguay Round of negotiations after earlier negotiations under the General Agreement on Tariffs and Trade (GATT), with the mandate to ensure "that trade flows as smoothly, predictably and freely as possible".[8] This General Agreement distinguishes between four modes of supplying services.[9]

Mode 4 covers the legal requirements for the presence of "natural persons" of one Member in the territory of another Member to supply a service. Although the text GATS suggests that Mode 4 can include service suppliers at all skill levels, in practice WTO members' current commitments are generally limited to the high skilled 'natural persons' (managers, executives, specialists), although these terms are generally not clearly defined.[10] Annex 10 specifies that the agreement does not apply to people seeking permanent employment or to conditions for obtaining citizenship, permanent residence or permanent employment.[11] These matters are left to the discretion of member countries.

The Mode is thus practiced within the regulatory frameworks of national policies on trade and migration. But since the definition of 'natural persons' does not clearly define the subsets of temporary labour migration, the Mode is subject to bilateral negotiations by which regulations are contextually defined under the authority of governmental migration managers operating under the auspices of national security. Thus a vertical link between migration, trade and national security (as fields of intervention) is formed, drawing a clear dividing line between free movement of 'natural persons' and other types. Highly qualified professionals belong to the permissive order; semi-skilled and unskilled labourers belong to the zone of contestation over meanings and codification of skills. Forced migration falls outside the framework of the Mode, irrespective of the fact that forced migrants may be skilled people. What seems to matter is the relationship with business which defines the mode of entry, rather than who the people are.

Mode 4 raised considerable debate among both high-income and lower-income countries about the implications for labour migration, immigration policy and border controls. High-income countries are concerned that full liberalization of Mode 4 will facilitate permanent migration and unauthorized migration, or open their borders to an overwhelming number of unskilled and semi-skilled migrants with the anticipated problems of cultural assimilation. Lower-income countries are concerned that the Mode will facilitate 'brain drain' or, in reverse, the presence of significantly large numbers of highly paid consultants who would be in competition with their nationals on an unlevel playing field.

As a result of these concerns, and combined with the failure of the Doha round of negotiations in 2008 to reach a compromise on agricultural import rules, new attempts are being made to move the discussions forward by re-orienting WTO discussions towards development and aid issues. There is growing acceptance for recognizing trade and migration policies jointly within Mode 4 and for recognizing trade and migration as complements rather than substitutes (IOM 2008). The emerging approach is to pressure WTO into adjusting its terms in effective response to emerging global challenges.

---

8 See at: <http://www.wto.org/english/res_e/doload_e/inbr_e.pdf> (9 July 2009).

9 Mode 1 on cross-border supply covers service flows from the territory of one Member into the territory of another Member - such banking or architectural services transmitted via telecommunications or mail. Mode 2 on consumption abroad refers to situations where a service consumer moves into another Member's territory to obtain a service (tourism, health care, education). Mode 3 on commercial presence refers to a service supplier of one Member establishes a territorial presence - through ownership or lease of premises - in another Member's territory to provide a service as in the case of domestic subsidiaries of companies in insurance, tourism, health or education.

10 For example in bilateral negotiations service suppliers now cover migrant labour in selected sector such as health and education rather than exclusively intra-corporate transfer of personnel.

11 See at: <http://www.wto.org/english/thewto_e/whatis_e/tif_e/agrm6_e.htm#oblig> (20 March, 2010).

By 2006 development objectives had been brought back into the agenda of trade liberalization; and in this regard policy coherence required what Pascal Lamy has described as "navigating through the archipelago of global governance" - referring to human rights, health, trade, finance, and social rights.[12] Mode 4 has since been opened to discussion about migration - under the rubric of trade and development cooperation. This would involve extending the legal provision regarding movement of 'natural persons' to apply to low-skilled labour through temporary arrangements and greater coherence in development policy (Kategekwa 2006). Arrangements for temporary and circular migration are coming into practice, although the issue of migrants' rights protection remains problematic. In high-income countries such arrangements can include an accretion of low-skilled labourers who may temporarily buffer deficits due to demographic changes (Mattoo/Carzaniga 2003); they nonetheless remain socially contentious and politically unpredictable (for the safety of migrant workers) given the periodic increase of xenophobic sentiment in domestic politics.

Kaur and Metcalfe (2007) note that states in Pacific Asia continued through the last three decades to classify and separate out migrants from 'expatriates', and skilled workers from the 'lower skilled' (unskilled) tier of labour, despite significant changes in financial capital flows, structural changes in modes of economic production and demographic transformations. Particularly in Malaysia and Japan, extension of citizenship or residency to migrants is highly exclusionary and selective. In Malaysia and Singapore, migrant women workers are forbidden from marrying citizens or permanent residents and are subjected to a pregnancy test every six months; if found pregnant they face deportation (Garcés-Mascareñas 2008; Cheah 2009). Governments, so its seems, deal with migrant labour only as an abstract category, a factor of production, not with the integral being of a human person.

The third piece of legislation - the United Nations Convention Against Transnational Organized Crime signed by 117 states in 2000 and ratified by 110 of those states in 2003 - emerged as a major response to the growing influence of transnational organized crime. The Palermo Protocols (the Trafficking Protocol and the Migrants Smuggling Protocol) supplement the Convention. The near total ratification in only two years after its proposal reflects the growing intolerance of all forms of irregular migration. After the Convention came into force, human rights lawyers and activists point out that at the level of implementation crime control has become the driving force behind the two protocols, overwriting victims' rights to protection.

The Migrant Smuggling Protocol aims at the eradication of a crime involving the profit-driven procurement of illegal entry of a person into a state of which that person is not a national or resident, because this crime undermines the integrity of states and communities and costs many human lives.[13] Yet Cheah (2009) shows that its broader objective seems to be the control of unauthorized entry, given that practices on human rights protection are less apparent than those controlling crime when the protocol is translated into national legislation. The overlap between smuggling and trafficking also remains unaddressed.

The implementation of the Trafficking Protocol - built on the three tiers of prevention, protection, and prosecution - has been criticized for being driven by criminal investigation and prosecution. Prevention measures remain highly debated as they do not pay attention to structural causes, and often result in the surveillance and restriction of the mobility of those identified as vulnerable groups. Protection measures in many countries are conditional on cooperation by the victims with an authority in charge of criminal investigation. Non-cooperation by the victims, due to fear of retaliation by traffickers, can result in repatriation with, or without, a modest sum of money for income-generation and eventual resettlement back home. Many trafficked persons are simply arrested as criminals for having entered a country by illegal means, and deported.[14]

Gallagher (2008: 830) notes: "Even where strong laws and institutions are in place, the attitudinal shifts required to deliver justice, protection, and support to those who have been exploited are often frustratingly slow"; and when there is a state interest in striving for economic competitiveness by maintaining a large and disempowered sector of the labour market, this con-

---

12 See at: <http://www.wto.org/english/news_e/sppl_e/sppl20_e.htm>, 11 July 2009; Pacal Lamy: "The WTO in the Archipelago of Global Governance". Speech delivered at Institute of International Studies, Geneva, 14 March 2006.

13 See at: <http://www.unodc.org/unodc/en/human-trafficking/smuggling-of-migrants.html> (28 March 2010)

14 See at: <http://content.undp.org/go/newsroom/updates/hiv-www-news/south-east-asias-first-womens-court-on-trafficking-and-hiv-.en> (5 March, 2010).

flicts with the taking of effective action. A United Nations agency mandated to implement the Convention against Transnational Organized Crime observed: "the trafficking network improves each day whereas the system to fight the phenomenon remains unquestionably fragile and sometimes disconcertingly inconsistent" (UNODC 2006: 102). Overall, the fight against human smuggling and trafficking has shown counter-productive tendencies given that the need to protect the trafficked individuals is often overwritten by the agenda of crime control, leading to a phenomenon labelled as "collateral damage" (Pollock 2007). A structural tension exists between a policy that seeks to restrict entry and a reality whereby many of those people who seek to migrate in search of a better life do not have the legal means to do so. If left unresolved, this tension is bound to foster an environment that will only further benefit profit-seeking criminals given that the lack of security experienced by one group has become a business opportunity for another (Truong 2003).

The fourth piece of legislation, the International Convention on the Protection of the Rights of All Migrant Workers and Members of their Families (ICRMW), went through 12 years of debate and negotiation before its enactment in July 2003 after reaching the minimum 20 countries required for ratification in addition to the ten that originally signed the Convention. The Convention endorses the principle of indivisibility of rights: civil, political, socioeconomic and cultural. Articles 10 and 11 make provision for the prevention of, and the imposition of penalties on, human trafficking. After what was nearly 20 years of campaigning, 42 UN member states had ratified and 16 signed the Convention by December 2009.[15] Most ratifying countries belong to the low-income group where the majority of migrant workers originate. They currently account for roughly three per cent of the global work force of more than three billion (IOM 2008). Low-income countries also are the host to a substantial number of migrants in transit. Major migrant-receiving countries belong to high-income regions – Western Europe, North America, Pacific Asia (Japan, Singapore, Malaysia), Australia and the Gulf States. These countries have not ratified the Convention although they are host to the majority of international migrant workers. India and Russia as important receiving countries have followed a similar option.

A report on the *Treaty Monitoring Bodies* (TMB) from January 1994 to January 2004 – giving an update in 2007 – sets out to ascertain whether countries that have not signed the ICRMW (nor have shown any intention to) have actually used relevant provisions in other core human rights treaties to protect the rights of migrants (Guimont/Silvestri/Proli 2008)[16]. Findings show that they have, but there is a tendency to aggregate the migrant population and conflate the different 'unwanted' categories: refugees, asylum-seekers, unaccompanied minors and trafficked persons. The terminology used by treaty bodies sometimes suffers from incoherence and there is no consistent handling of migrant concerns. Deportation and detention emerged as key concerns. This finding concurs with other micro studies revealing inaccuracies and lack of coherence when interpreting the status of migrants in transit zones by categories (Lyons/Ford 2007).

Centrally placed in this arena is the International Organization for Migration (IOM), which emerged from the post-World War II Intergovernmental Committee for Migration (ICM) to become in 1989 a migration management agency. It now plays a central role in promoting orderly migration. In IOM's view, "orderly migration" is understood as upholding human dignity and the well-being of migrants while ascertaining the benefits brought about by migration to society.[17] Antiracist groups, migrant organizations and human rights defenders take issue with the meaning used for "orderly and humane migration", and the nature of the decision-making processes, which only recognize in/justice (in the management of migration) by their own definition of 'order'.[18]

Despite the proliferation of consultative processes – notably the High Level Dialogue on Migration and Development organized by the UN General Assembly in September 2006 and the subsequent Global Forums on Migration and Development in July 2007 (Brussels), October 2008 (Manila) and November 2009 (Athens) – the question of the human rights of migrants has not gained much ground on the global agenda. These annual meetings are voluntary and decisions arising from these forums are mostly non-binding; they merely provide a venue for exploring meth-

15 See at: <http://www.december18.net/category/work-field/migrant-workers-convention> (16 December 2006).

16 See at: <http://www.december18.net/sites/default/files/The_UN_Treaty_Monitoring_Bodies_and_Migrant_Workers_a_Samizdat.pdf> .

17 See at: <http://www.iom.int/jahia/jsp/index.jsp> (28 March 2010).

18 See at: <http://www.noborder.org/> (23 November 2009).

ods through which migration may contribute towards development goals. So long as instrumentalist and utilitarian values continue to govern the triadic relationship of security, migration and development, then the fundamental rights and security of many migrants in the lower occupational tiers and those bound up in trafficking and smuggling networks will remain at risk. The extant disjunction between the right to free movement and the right of nation-states to defend borders and control access to their territory can be a matter of life and death for those seeking to cross borders by means that are not sanctioned by institutional rules (Cornelius 2001; Carling 2007).

To this end, new questions are being raised about the meaning of 'good governance' in migration. Pascal Lamy points out that prior to the attachment of the concepts of rights and security to the Westphalian notion of nation-state and citizenship, in medieval continental Europe, the concept of 'governance' designated the method of organising feudal power to provide coherence among adjacent suzerainties.

> There was no central power as such, but a body, ***primus inter pares***, whose purpose was to settle disputes peacefully and see that any conflicting interests were reconciled in consultation with those involved.... The concept thus focused on ***unity*** [author's emphasis] - not uniqueness - of interests.[19]

This concept disappeared with the formation of the nation-state in the 16th century, but re-emerged in the 1980's to mean a decision-making process that enables continual negotiations between stakeholders. Negotiations among stakeholders appear consistent with Habermas' (1984) model of 'deliberative democracy', or achieving consensus in the public arena through communicative actions. A missing element in the translation of deliberative democracy into consensus-building among stakeholders is notably the notion of 'inter-subjectivity', to which Habermas had attached the meaning of mutual understanding and communication free of ideological domination. Observing the standards of discourse ethics is necessary for affirming the validity of principles emerging from dialogues (Flyvbjerg 1998).

What Lamy does not bring out is the fact that since the 'crisis of democracy' was identified in the 1970s, the state has set limits on its own action by way of introducing the concept of private-public partnership according to which civil society is expected to democratize itself autonomously. The questions of who has the authority to set up which discourse ethics and in what domain, and which discourse ethics should be considered paramount, remain problematic. Having abstained from moral leadership the state has now become a strategic site for co-optation by dominant groups in civil society in order to steer the course in their interest, under the cloak of public interest. Political decisions are now derived from the presentation of certain supposedly 'neutral facts' along with certain lines of reasoning which are rational from the perspective of the strategic options of the power holders.

The source of power has actually, during the last decades, irrevocably shifted away from governments towards global finance, which is able to direct and pre-empt deliberations. Bernard Lietaer in an interview with Sarah van Gelder remarked (1997: 4)[20]:

> When a government does something not to the liking of the market - like the British in '91, the French in '94 or the Mexicans in '95 - nobody sits down at the table and says 'you shouldn't do this'. A monetary crisis simply manifests in that currency. So a few hundred people [the financiers], who are not elected by anybody and have no collective responsibility whatsoever, decide what your pension fund is worth - among other things.

A return to the medieval concept of governance - as distinct from government - and its underlying principle of unity can no longer adequately overcome the double crisis of democracy today: recognition and legitimacy.

Financial liberalization policy is based on a special interest agenda rather than designed on the basis of the best available economic theory and evidence (Stiglitz 2000). Decision-making devoid of accountability and representativeness now turns the problem of 'governability of democracy' on its head. Rather than the upsurge of social movements as in the 1960s (which were feared to have politicized and destabilized all civil institutions) it is now the enormous upsurge of global finance (which has greatly realigned its relationship with the state) that is putting the ethos of democracy itself in danger.

There is as yet no holistic theory and morality for trans-border movement (of people or goods or of finance). The tendency is to consider financial crises as deriving naturally from a given human temperament.

19 Pascal Lamy: "The WTO in the Archipelago of Global Governance". Speech delivered at Institute of International Studies, Geneva, 14 March 2006. See at: <http://www.wto.org/english/news_e/sppl_e/sppl20_e.htm> (11 July 2009).

20 See at: <http://www.yesmagazine.org/issues/money-print-your-own/beyond-greed-and-scarcity/Bernard Lietaer> (30 March 2010).

In point of fact, this temperament is being continuously created and amplified (Lietaer 1997). Likewise, the 'human temperament' in migration continues to nest comfortably in the construct of preferences in the push-pull dynamics. Administrative procedures on trans-border human mobility continue to hold on to an ontology that posits the human being as having rigid identity and the nation-state as being a discrete entity in respect of international relations. An emerging contradiction for which no solution is yet in sight is the reality by which business and finance [as well as the impacts of their fluctuations] has actually gone global while justice remains operational primarily within the confines of the nation-state (Caron 2007). Deliberations in a global arena - pre-structured by hierarchies of nation, class, gender and ethnicity, and conducted without the standards of discourse ethics - can ignore the need for transformation (inclusive of the ontological and epistemological dimensions) in order to achieve social justice. Dominant groups continue to downplay significant aspects of transformation and support a form of pragmatism serving their interests.

The enactment of the four international pieces of legislation on human movements across borders discussed above reflects a hegemonic perspective which restricts the legitimacy of movement to those associated with capital. The 'perverse' behaviour of capital in the domain of human smuggling and trafficking is yet to be addressed effectively. The disunity and fragmentation of these pieces of legislation are something that Lamy's metaphor of the 'archipelago of governance' has captured only partly: these islands of contention are the tips of a unified landmass but separated by a sea of misrecognition. A perspective that selectively deals only with the emerged and not the submerged misses the progressive and cumulative transformations of movement (of people, finances or goods) across borders.

Expulsion of segments of populations on the move by a collective alliance of containment is a sign of a deepening and intensifying crisis within liberal democracies. Militarization, an extension of militaristic rules to civilian spheres (Enloe 1989) and the emergence of new 'zones of interdiction' (or the militarized surveillance both along borders and extraterritorially) to contain attempts to cross borders in search for security (as a secure life space) affirm what Foucault calls the 'heterotopias' of crisis and of deviation - referring to the spheres into which particular behaviours are placed and categorized (Foucault 1984c). These concepts are helpful to make sense of the current handling of persons whose behaviour is seen as resulting from a crisis situation. Victims of trafficking are placed in the category of a moral crisis and hence deserve protection and assistance. They are to be distinguished from 'irregular migrants' or 'criminal aliens' who are placed in the category of 'deviant' behaviour defined in relation to the required means and norms of migration. As fence breakers, they deserve detention and punishment rather than public assistance. The confusing semantics of trafficking and smuggling at the level of policy implementation serve to legitimize the detention of all forms of 'deviancy'.

Davidson (2003) makes mention of Foucault's heterotopias, citing them as grey areas with blurred accountabilities, and drawing parallels with the practice of 'territorial excision'. By such means governments can discipline migrants' movement, simultaneously freeing the state from responsibility towards non-citizens in its territory. In his view, present-day statehood has developed a way to commandeer, manage and condition these 'spaces' - keeping within national and international law to varying degrees - thus showing the continued relevance of the nation-state to persons (citizens and non-citizens) at the most basic level: that of physical movement. The exigencies of such confinement under ill-defined areas of legality depict an ongoing transformation of statehood: one driven by a market-centric logic that creates a 'borderless world' which may be a reality for some types of movement but remains a mirage for others. The line between the order (utopia) of democracy and human rights, and the disorder (heterotopias) of crisis and 'deviancy' reflects a communitarian vision within states [or a community of states] and the logic of 'triage' - the selection of people on a basis of economic expediency rather than moral principles - on a global scale.

A world of global integration ruled by triage is possible in the absence of moral leadership and the prevalence of imprudent speculations. A narrow understanding of the economy separated from the social life that sustains it re-enforces structures of a governance that continues to fragment understanding of social change and refuses to accept differences in forms of human movement across borders as different manifestations of the same process of re-forming the world order under a hegemonic understanding of security.

2.5 Reframing Security: The *Parrhesia* of the Subaltern

The dysfunctions of the ethical-political principles of neo-liberalism manifest what de Sousa Santos (2007) called "cognitive injustice" or an epistemological relationship in which the 'self' is incapable of recognizing the 'other': something crucial for reciprocity in active human relationships. Reality is codified into "this side of the line" and "the other side of the line" and operates such that "the other side of the line" vanishes, which is to say it no longer exists in any relevant or comprehensible way of being (Santos 2007: 45, 46). Deep understanding requires reflexivity in ontological framings of security to apprehend an emerging global structure of physical (im)mobility defined according to permitted modes of entry, time frame, skills, labour needs, crime and social burdens. Such reflexivity must take note of the nexus of security and mobility from the perspective of the ongoing transformations of international political economy and their implications for judicial systems and moral reasoning about global inequality.

Referring to a specific group for whom cognitive injustice matters significantly, Spivak calls attention to the meaning of the "Subaltern" in Antonio Gramsci's work, recorded by Ranajit Guha. She defines subalternity as the space of difference where the "social lines of mobility...do not permit the formation of a recognizable basis of action" (Spivak 2005: 476), emphasizing a kind of class without agency. Those who move within modes that are not legally sanctioned may well be conceived as a new global subaltern class defined by their subject relationship with the state, a relationship that restrict their physical and social mobility and provides no basis for their collective action. To claim the legitimacy of their presence, a different notion of the unity of being human can be helpful to encourage the recognition of human traits that have been bypassed.

Two statements - one by an undocumented migrant and the other by two scholars on disability on the perennial aspects of being human - may serve here as an entry point to the *parrhesia* of this new class of subaltern.

> I do not understand much about states and borders: I only know that the earth is round and that - unlike trees which have roots - human beings have feet to walk with.[21]

> No one emerges self-sufficient from the womb, no able-bodied person can be sure that she will continue to be able-bodied throughout her later years, and there is no guarantee that any of us will escape disabling encounters with the world. In this sense, no one is ever more than temporarily able-bodied. The designation temporarily able-bodied invites us to consider different sorts of vulnerability, different points of frailty, as features of our common lot and accordingly to shift our understandings of flourishing, social justice, and embodiment (Breckenridge/Volger 2001: 346).

These messages tell of 'movement', 'temporal ability' and 'vulnerability' as pre-conceptual realities of humankind. They highlight the limits of those historical definitions of 'human nature', which accord a duality between emotion and reason, body and intellect. They direct attention to the need for shifting practices of knowing towards the perennial aspects of being human, to promote a more humble epistemology that is inclusive of different modes of being and moral reasoning. They may be considered the *parrhesia* of those who occupy the hemisphere of cognition occluded by the hegemonic understanding of 'human nature' and its 'security'.

The disorientation from what is real in a pre-conceptual sense is caused by a certain line of ideation that has produced cultural universes encapsulating the notion of 'being' through particular registers of meanings (biology, theology, or reason), attaching a particular identity and set of rights accordingly (sex, skin colour, biological fitness, faith). Reason being a signifier for maturity and autonomy rules in the current forms of deliberative democracy.

The meanings of *parrhesia,* translated as "free speech in democracy",[22] are revealed in Foucault's work (2001) as frankness, truth, danger, criticism and obligation. Foucault uses the concept of *parrhesia* as a mode of discourse by which one speaks openly and truthfully about one's opinions and ideas without the use of rhetoric, manipulation or generalization. Modern scientific reasoning based on the necessity for valid evidence makes the use of *parrhesia* problematic given that speech, when not examined or criticized, cannot be considered as necessarily having a valid re-

21 See at: <http://nooneisillegal-montreal.blogspot.com/> (10 July 2009).

22 The Ancient Greeks used the term to refer to the care for oneself, which requires first achieving mastery over oneself, and facing one's weaknesses in an honest way. Truth telling in this context involved exact coincidence between belief and truth. Classical Greece merged the concept with rhetoric to mean a way of speaking truth in spite of danger (for example when speaking to a tyrant about the incompatibility between tyranny and justice).

lation to truth. In other words, the nexus of knowledge/power and scientific disciplines can obstruct the practice of *parrhesia*.

For social scientists today, the two statements cited above may serve to assert the unity of being human by claiming mobility, temporary ability and vulnerability as equally valid with other ruling qualities. These perennial human traits require, indeed, no special validation. Encountering the *parrhesia* on the perennial aspects of being human may allow truth back in its place for re-thinking the ontological premises of 'being human'. The belief in being human as an individual reality characterized by autonomy, cherished by liberalism, and its recent permutation into self-care under neo-liberalism (Truong 2009a) is not only biased at the ontological and epistemological level, but also has profound ethical implications as it underscores individualism (and therefore competition) and overwrites relations of reciprocity and caring for others. It is important that it be revealed how a cherished notion of human nature can represent interests and strategic options of particular humans rather than expressing the texture of being human in the elementary sense of the word. This *parrhesia* should invite scholars to engage in practices of learning from trans-disciplinary, trans-philosophical and trans-group communications whereby to rethink and recast human nature in terms that express the perennial traits of 'temporality', 'vulnerability' 'mobility' supported a web of caring relationships in order to flourish, rather only in terms of some selected favoured qualities.

There is a definite and pressing need to transcend the limits of the technocratic-utilitarian understanding of migration as either flows of labour or social burdens. To restore the right of being mobile, of returning to or staying in one's place peacefully, requires the re-visioning of the ontology of the nation-state and its position in international relations. This re-visioning should give validity to the diversity of forms of human mobility within and across geographical areas today as part of the transformation in structures of international political economy and their transnational and trans-local linkages. Shifting understandings of flourishing, social justice and embodiment from the Kantian's view of abstract reason and maturity can help accommodate other ways of 'being' through the ontology of care, and recognize what too narrow a view of human nature can do to society.

2.6 Conclusion

This chapter has pointed to the moments of dislocation and relocation of particular representations of 'human nature' in the fields of migration, security and development. Each of them is framed according to time-bound and group-bound understandings of mobility, safety and flourishing. Contemporary attempts to achieve justice as the universality of rights have encountered the obstruction of positivism, which regards justice as a technical and managerial problem and a matter of consistent application of rules set by free choice in a polity. This has fostered a segmented approach to achieving rights in the domain of the international, separating out the 'feasible' and 'non-feasible' for the exercise of free choice. The current model of security with its fragmented vision of movement across borders reflects the utilitarian logic of triage as a ruling principle. The liberal state and economy in the latter half of the last century evidently succeeded in realigning interests in civil society towards corporatism, paving the way for the global market. No adequate attention was given to the historical reality that human movements across borders have always accompanied global trade expansion.

Questions of 'securitization of development' (Duffield 2002; Abrahamsen 2005) on the one hand, and those of 'intersections of development and security' under the concept of human security on the other (Thomas 2000; McRae/Hubert 2001; Sachs/McArthur 2005) are now pressing issues. The choice is between 1) the use of security-oriented measures to ensure full compliance with a growth-driven and trade-led path of development; and 2) the promotion of a development path based on principles of social justice to address grievances of various kinds, taking into account state and human security as mutually supportive. The contrast between the two options is to make security institutions (army, police, private security organizations) work for the elite as opposed to making the law work for common people in a process of development which involves a societal transformation towards peace and well-being. Maintenance of the balance lies within civil society and its critical knowledge. Shifting the ethos and art of governing away from the current neo-liberal pragmatism (which is devoid of ethical principles, scientific law or principled inclusive discourse ethics) is a major task ahead. Counter-movements of critical knowledge through self-reflection can help extend the intention for well-being beyond the mere construct of the 'self' as bounded by the nation-state (or a group of states) so as to grasp the full sense of human unity.

In this respect it is helpful to approach the meaning of 'security', as being the aspiration for order and well-being through justice, in a double sense: a contextual phenomenon and a process of transformation. As a contextual phenomenon different subjectivities (defended by communitarian politics of different types and at different levels) influence this notion. As a process of transformation oriented towards universal human well-being, this notion has encountered continuous and self-reflexive moments. Engagement with the voice of plain truth about the perennial traits of 'being human' can be helpful both to transform ways of understanding 'flourishing', and acknowledge how 'caring' in social thought can bring about a more holistic view on security.

Part II Neoliberal Governmentality and Transnational Migration: the Interplay of Security Fears and Business Forces

3 Migration from Mexico and Central America to the United States: Human Insecurities and Paths for Change

Gustavo Verduzco and María Isabel de Lozano

3.1 Introduction[1]

Globalization has created new service activities, novel technologies and consumption preferences. In the most economically advanced countries labour demands have shifted patterns and opened up new opportunities for less privileged inhabitants in regions of the South. The necessary legal, social and political instruments to protect migrant workers' rights nonetheless do not (yet) exist. This has led to an increase in human insecurity, especially among those who have dared to take the chance and emigrate from one country to another outside institutional frameworks. The main dilemma that potential migrants confront is between scarcity or low quality of jobs at home and better opportunities in a foreign country but with unknown or unforeseen danger, insecurities and exploitation. How and why have these contradictions come about? How has a protection system for people become a menace and even a dangerous element for many of them? What processes or changes have been taking place in some countries to offset these trends?

This chapter takes a more hermeneutical note and asks: how is it that geographical mobility leads some groups of migrants to illegality while other groups remain protected by law? Could one say that a system for protecting people has become a selective one? Why is it that a protection system seems undemocratic? Answering some aspects these questions would require looking into the several specific changes which have taken place in Mexico, Central America and the United States towards the end of the last century. Still, a Gramscian perspective would also suggest that a protection system is not necessarily planned for or suited to subaltern groups. To provide a reading of the situation that combines both perspectives, the specific circumstance that both Mexicans and Central American migrants experience when travelling to the US will be sketched, and some related policy dimensions more fully discussed. The focus here is on how policy affects the situations of 'in-transit' migrants, or the hundreds of thousands of Mexicans and Central Americans travelling every year towards the border between the US and Mexico with the intent of crossing it.

To gain insight on the important aspects of their experiences as 'in-transit' migrants a survey was made of migrant minors and adult women in two Mexican cities on the country's northern border (Nogales and Ciudad Juárez) at the end of 2006. A series of in-depth interviews were also conducted with a variety of those involved: migrants of various age groups; public officials in charge of border control in Mexico; priests, and representatives of human rights groups. The interviews took place in the two border cities cited and in Mexico City. The idea was to reveal new dimensions of the phenomenon of 'transmigration' characterized by mixed flows, using two lenses: 1) the intensification of South-North emigrations, and 2) restrictive migration policies in the US and Mexico. The main objective is to bring to light the dimensions and degree of human insecurity experienced by migrants who cross through Mexico and arrive at the northern border. This is contrasted with government and civic responses to their difficulties.[2]

1 Part of this chapter was rewritten while on a sabbatical at the Instituto Tecnológico de Estudios Superiores in EGAP, Monterrey, México. The authors are grateful for the collaboration of Nadia Nehls and they appreciate the translation by Susan Beth Kapilian. The chapter was written prior to introduction of the new immigration law in Arizona at the end of April 2010, which would make the failure to carry immigration documents a crime and give the police broad power to detain anyone suspected of being in the country illegally.

T.-D. Truong and D. Gasper (eds.), *Transnational Migration and Human Security*, Hexagon Series on Human and Environmental Security and Peace 6, DOI 10.1007/978-3-642-12757-1_3, © Springer-Verlag Berlin Heidelberg 2011

3.2 US Immigration Policy and Migratory Flows from Mexico

Hundreds of thousands of Mexicans now travel each year to the US in search of better job opportunities. This has turned Mexico into one of the countries with the highest emigration rates. More than 11 million people born in Mexico currently reside in the US and of these roughly six million live there illegally (Passel/D'Vera 2009). Alongside Mexican emigrants there are many people from Central and South America (especially the former) who cross this country to reach the border with the US. Thus, every year, besides the Mexicans who try to enter the US hundreds of thousands of non-Mexican nationals also enter Mexico and travel the entire length of the country in their journey to the US. A majority of these migrants lack the documentation required to enter either Mexico or the US. The position of Mexico as country of origin and transit, and the large number of Mexican and in-transit migrants, affect the social, economic and political conditions of the places from which people move, as well as those places where they 'manage' their 'in-transit' existence.

During the past 15 years the US government has allocated a considerable amount of public funds both for surveillance along its border with Mexico and for constructing barriers along the most highly trafficked areas of this border.[3] In addition, US cities have enacted legislation to curtail provision of social services to undocumented migrants, in spite of the reality that many of them have been working for more than the last two decades in the US without adequate channels for becoming legalized. While measures for fighting what is termed as unauthorized migration failed to reduce the flow significantly, the US demand for workers rose. Especially from 1990 through to 2000 there was an intensification of migration flows from Mexico, reaching an average net entry into the US of 500,000 to 600,000 people per year, most of them undocumented (Passel 2003; Passel/D'Vera 2009).

Although these legislative measures have effectively slowed down the mechanisms of Mexican circular migration,[4] they also led to an increase of the duration of stay among undocumented migrants in the US. In other words, undocumented migrants have become essentially trapped in the US for long periods. One of the consequences has been an increase of the emigration rate of the family members of undocumented migrants, who had remained in their place of origin thus far. First, the women migrated then later one could observe the presence of minors who travelled to reunite with their parents.[5]

Increased border control mechanisms in the fight against unauthorized migration along the US southern border meant a growth in the number of Border Patrol agents. The US Border Patrol had 4,026 agents in 1992; by 2005 there were 11,106, nearly 90 per cent of them patrolling the US southern border.[6] After the attack on the US on 11 September 2001 the Government introduced new policy measures. In 2002 Congress approved the Homeland Security Act to restructure the *Immigration and Naturalization Service* (INS). With this restructuring the Border Patrol became part of the US *Customs and Border Protection* (CBP)[7] under the Department of Homeland Security. In late 2006 Congress approved the Secure Fence Act, authorizing the construction of another 700 miles (1,125 kilometres) of fence along the border with Mexico. In July 2007 the Congress also approved the Homeland Security Appropriations Act for the recruiting and training of 23,000 agents for the US Border Patrol, the installation of fences along another 400-plus miles (more than 700 km) and 105 radar equipment and photographic towers along a roughly

2 This work was done partly with the support of the project "Human (In)Security in the Networks of Global Cities," directed by Prof. Kinhide Mushakoji and coordinated by the Centre for Human Security Studies of the University of Chubu, Japan, with the support of the Japanese Ministry of Culture. This project has been coordinated by Prof. Yoichi Mine and Prof. Tatsuo Harada with the support of Kenji Kimura.

3 Wayne Cornelius (2006) reveals that the United States government spent more than 20 billion dollars during the 1993–2006 periods to reinforce control and surveillance of its border with Mexico.

4 See at: <http://deepblue.lib.umich.edu/bitstream/2027.42/50920/1/145.pdf>, (21 April 2010). The term is defined as follows: "Circular migration takes a social unit to a destination set of arrangements, which returns it to the origin after a well-defined interval" (Tilly 1976: 7). Mexican 'circular migration' to the US fits this definition (particularly undocumented seasonal work, a phenomenon that had existed until the early 1990's when control measures were introduced).

5 See at: López/Villaseñor (2001); at: <http://www.comminit.com/es/node/170290> (2 April 2010).

6 See at: <http://trac.syr.edu/immigration/reports/143> (26 May 2010).

7 CBP [United States Customs and Border Protection], 2008: "Securing America's Borders"; at: <www.cbp.gov/xp/cgov/about/mission> (2 April 2010).

190 mile stretch (some 300 km) of the border (DHS 2008).

It is hard to ascertain the number of people who cross the border without documentation; only indirect sources of information exist. The most important sources are: 1) the Border Patrol records on the detention of migrants; 2) records of the Mexican *Instituto Nacional de Migración* (INM) [National Immigration Institute] on repatriation of undocumented Mexicans detained in the US; 3) Mexico's "Survey on Migration along the Northern Border" (*Encuesta sobre Migración de la Frontera Norte*, or EMIF). Although none of these records report the total number of crossings of undocumented persons they give an idea of the amount of movement across the border, as well as trends through the years.

The Department of Homeland Security reported that, during the period from 1986 to 2006, the US authorities had detained an average of 1.3 million migrants having no valid documentation per year (DHS 2006: 91). Mexican migrants represent a very large proportion of those detained by the US Border Patrol. In 2006 was reported that 1,057,253 undocumented Mexicans were detained,[8] which is a little more than 80 per cent of the total number of detainees that year. El Salvadoran migrants are the next numerous among the migrants detained in the US: 46,329 in 2006. 33,365 Hondurans and 25,135 Guatemalans were also detained (DHS 2006: 92).

The information from Mexico's Survey on Migration along the Northern Border (COLEF 2006) tells something about the mobility strategies that migrants use in the face of the stricter control measures at the border. In 1993 the crossing points preferred by undocumented migrants were located in the area of the coastal city Tijuana, at the extreme north-west point of Mexico; approximately half of all undocumented migrants reportedly crossed there. After Tijuana were the crossing points close to the cities of Nogales (on the border with Arizona), Ciudad Juárez (across the border-river from El Paso, Texas), and then Matamoros (the city closest to the Gulf of Mexico on the Rio Grande estuary).

US policies have also stimulated a shift in the routes of illegal traffic across its border with Mexico, from traditional urban zones to less populated and more rural and barren areas, an assumption being that this would discourage undocumented migration (Núñez-Neto 2005: 10). Anguiano and Trejo's analysis (2007) noted that migrants' strategies varied according to their particular migration experiences. In 1993 the less experienced migrants from new emigration regions preferred to cross the border at Matamoros. By 2003 they had also started to cross the Sonora Desert into Arizona. Migrants from populations with a migratory tradition rejected the Sonoran route and preferred the urban alternatives (Ciudad Juárez, Tijuana and Matamoros). In other words the more experienced migrants continued using traditional sites while newcomers to the venture chose the more difficult and less trodden paths because their perceptions of risk differed (Anguiano/Trejo 2007: 8–9). The knowledge and experience of individual migrants (regarding not only the difficulties in crossing the border but also the means of contact with people who can facilitate such crossings) are dissimilar. Crossing at traditional points requires less help from *polleros* – people who aid migrants for a fee. During fieldwork conducted at the border zones close to Nogales and Ciudad Juárez it was observed that in these new regions, where a greater number cross over, migrants are continually finding and using new crossing points. Once US authorities become aware of a new crossing point surveillance of that place is reinforced, obliging migrants to look again for an alternative. Statistics collected by the Beta Groups confirm an increase in the number of crossings far from Ciudad Juárez – such as Anapra (nearly 20 miles distant) and Palomas (84 miles distant).[9]

Although the social and economic conditions prevailing in Central America and Mexico help explain the increase in their movement, the recent border control policies also appears to have played a significant role. A rise in women and minors in migration flows in the first two years this decade has been reported (COLEF 2002). Stricter border control measures mean that migrants encounter greater difficulties in returning to their country of origin, therefore wives and children seek to reunite with their husbands/fathers. Data on Mexican women repatriated from 2004 to 2007 show an annual average of 82,000 – accounting for between 15 per cent and 16 per cent of all repatriation (INM 2007: 5).

Interviews conducted along Mexico's northern border reveal that the increase of migrant minors

8 This figure does not necessarily coincide with the number of repatriated Mexicans reported by the Mexican National Immigration Institute.

9 The Beta Groups were founded by the INM in 1990 to provide protection for migrants' safety (physical well-being and property) when they travel along the Mexican borders.

through Mexico's northern border zone became apparent in the mid-1980's and numbers rose further during the 1990's. It is impossible to obtain reliable figures for those years because the INM did not begin to distinguish repatriated migrants by age until 2003. Available data in the period 2003 to 2007 show an average of 38,000 minors were repatriated every year, being between seven and nine per cent of all cases of repatriation (INM 2009). It is important to note here that migration is generally not an individual affair. The method of 'headcount' and control of individual entry fails to account for the fact that migrants and their movements are often linked to their communal and social responsibilities. Seeing the individuals within the particular communal and familial structures can provide better understanding and improve policy for migrants and their families.

3.3 Mexico's Policies and 'In-Transit' Migrants

Like other countries with in-transit migrants which pursue a mixture of control practices, either due to their proximity to the destination country or to their function as a place from which these migrants hope to reach their intended destination, Mexico's geopolitical situation plays an important additional role. Located next to the US, a hegemonic country in this region, Mexico is one of the members of the *North American Free Trade Agreement* (NAFTA) since 1994 (including Canada and the U.S). Mexico has generally implemented measures for controlling the entrance of foreigners directly in line with requirements of the US government.

Prior to NAFTA Mexico already initiated migration policy measures on its southern border in the 1980's. As the situation was then, neither the Mexican government nor the inhabitants of Mexico's southern region were concerned with clarifying territorial limits or taking border control measures. The Southern border was a 'forgotten frontier' (as it was called for many years). People travelled and crossed freely without much requirement regarding identification. The armed conflicts that arose between some Central American countries in the late 1970's had repercussions in Mexico and began to change the situation. During the early years of these hostilities between 380,000 and 500,000 persons from El Salvador, Honduras and Guatemala became displaced from their communities.[10] The Mexican Government, through the Mexican *Commission for Aid to Refugees* (COMAR) in coordination with the *United Nations High Commissioner for Refugees* (UNHCR), granted refuge and material aid to foreigners who requested it - being mainly those from Guatemala. Those conflicts and the migrations they caused had other effects in the region.

Two additional factors particularly affected the situation on Mexico's southern border. On more than one occasion the Guatemalan army conducted raids into Mexican territory with the excuse that they were chasing Guatemalan guerrillas, and in the framework of the Cold War the US was concerned that such guerrilla movement would spread into Mexico. The Mexican Government therefore set in motion operations on its southern border imposing military and public security forces there to control movements across the border. Those events imprinted something of a military character on the way the Mexican government originally conceived its actions in respect of migrants, something that may also explain the current abuse of the undocumented population (Casillas 2006: 58). Militarization of Mexico's southern region intensified further because of the Zapatista uprising in the Chiapas state in 1994. In addition, measures undertaken to control drug trafficking have also influenced migration policy. In the 1980's the US requested Mexico's cooperation to combat drug trafficking. This intensified in the 1990's and then became a strategic problem of national security. In 1999 the Mexican government established the 'Sealing the Borders' programme by means of which a military-police blockade was established to detect, pursue and confiscate drug shipments from South America (Casillas 2006: 58). During the Mexican President Vicente Fox's Administration (2000-2006) funds were increased for border control measures aimed at stopping unauthorized migration from Central America, drug trafficking, and other types of smuggling. The Mexican government signed bilateral agreements with Guatemala, Belize, El Salvador and Honduras to this effect.

Following the anti-terrorist paranoia of the G.W. Bush Administration in 2002, bilateral agreements between the US, Canada and Mexico concerning 'Smart Borders' were signed. The agreement with Mexico included commitments for cooperation among defence, security, intelligence, migration, and judicial institutions. In June of that year Mexico and Guatemala

10 See at: Tirado (2005) <http://www.inm.gob.mx/estudios/foros/documentos%20basicos/4%20frontera%20sur%20y%20seguridad%20nacional.pdf> (23 April 2010).

signed the Agreement for the Creation of the High-Level Group for Border Security (GASEF).[11] In 2003 a project was begun in Mexico called "Strengthening of the Regional Delegations of the Southern Border" which would increase the number of migration stations[12] from 25 to 52 through the country. In addition, the governments of Mexico, Canada, and the US signed the Security and Prosperity Partnership of North America (SPPNA) on 23 March 2005.[13] This proposed developing and implementing compatible migration security measures including requirements for admission and duration of stay, policy standards for persons with visas and surveillance standards. All three governments pledged to develop mechanisms for exchanging information on programmes for monitoring travellers lacking a visa and to conduct joint assessments of border crossings. SPPNA proposals include strengthening cooperation protocols and creating new mechanisms to secure common borders while facilitating legitimate travel and trade in the North American region. One proposed mechanism is 'pre-clearance' - which has long been in place at airports but is now extended to the land border. Under this inspection scheme US officials would be stationed in a NAFTA member state to intercept illegitimate cargos (including possibly human cargo) before they reach the US border.[14]

The Mexican General Population Law (*Ley General de la Población*) regulates migration affairs but does not deal with current situations in a satisfactory way; there are contradictions and gaps. The Law makes no mention of the rights of migrants. It does, however, contain rules in the realm of criminal law - specifying human trafficking and use of false documents as crimes, sanctioning inquisitive conduct on the part of authorities, and laying down penalties for unauthorized entry and residence.[15] The Law stipulates that the Mexican *National Migration Institute* (INM) is charged with the control of migration and empowers the *Federal Preventive Police* (PFP) to support the Institute in surveillance activities. In 2005 the National Institute of Migration became integrated into the *Sistema de Seguridad Nacional de Mexico* or the National Security System of Mexico (Diario Oficial de la Federación, 2005). The focus on security by policing measures buttresses a policy of repression and containment of migration through Mexico, especially via its southern border. This limits Mexico's policy to the apprehension, detention and deportation of those without valid documents, reinforcing the representation of migrants as a threat to national security.

Under these regulations the Mexican government treats Central Americans entering the country (legally and with documentation) far worse than how any of the Central American governments treat Mexicans entering their countries. Migrants from Central America and some South American countries face requirements similar to those set by the US government to enter its territory: visas have become more expensive, processing times longer and bureaucracy more hindering. These actions are in line with the commitment Mexico took through the SPPNA with the US and Canada to create programmes for monitoring travellers lacking a visa (Kimball 2007: 13, 16).

According to Kimball, one result of the Mexican policies towards movements of migrants from the south was to intensify control mechanisms in-land which has led to a paradoxical situation: while the border with Guatemala and Belize continues to be relatively free from controls, checkpoints have appeared along Mexico's major highways. An agent of the INM interviewed by Kimball summed it up as follows, "Crossing the border is no problem; the problem is trying to cross through Mexico" (Kimball 2007: 64). In August 2005 there was a daily average of 32 INM officials patrolling the entire southern border and another 226 INM officials assigned to inland highways in the southern region (Kimball 2007: 83). The mission of the International Federation of Human Rights (IFHR) told of "the porosity of the borderline and the ease with which undocumented workers cross the

11 In Mexico the *Centre for Research and National Security* (CISEN) serves as Technical Secretary for this agreement.

12 A migration station is responsible for recording arrival and departure at the various ports of entry to Mexico. The different categories used in classifying the data correspond largely to those identified explicitly in Mexican legislation (Ley General de Populacion, 1974); some categories lack definitions.

13 See at: SPPNA (2005); at: <http://www.spp.gov/report_to_leaders/index.asp?dName=report_to_leaders> (29 April 2010).

14 See at: <http://www.fas.org/sgp/crs/row/RS22701.pdf>, (5 April, 2010).

15 Sanctions stipulated in Articles 117, 118, 119, 120, 122, 123, 124, 125, 126, and 127 of the General Law on Population. See at: <http://www2.ohchr.org/english/bodies/cmw/docs/fmigraciones_en.pdf> (21 April 2010). Foreigners who violate the terms of their visa may be sentenced to up to six years in prison (Articles 119, 120 and 121). Foreigners who misrepresent the terms of their visa while in Mexico (such as working with out a permit) can also be imprisoned.

border between Guatemala and Mexico" and added, "The numerous interceptions of migrants are, in fact, made inland in Mexican territory and not at the border" (IFHR 2008: 19). The persistence of corruption and human rights violations against migrants in transit through Mexico seems actually to serve as a means of dissuasion similar to the walls the US constructed along its own southern border. "While it is true that our country has not built barriers to stop Central American migration, another invisible, painful wall has been erected in our country: that of the abuses and violations committed against the fundamental rights of migrants whose status is irregular" (IFHR 2008: 15).

Criticism directed at the gap between the Mexican government's efforts to promote and protect the human rights of its citizens living abroad, and the absence of corresponding domestic actions to protect the human rights of migrant workers in its territory has led to some change.[16] The INM had formulated, and presented, a Proposal for a Comprehensive Migration Policy regarding Mexico's Southern Border in 2005. It included a strategy for the protection of migrants' human rights and was a significant step forward (INM 2005c). Other items included the suggestions to disseminate knowledge on migrants' human rights, to supervise procedures involved in non-criminal apprehensions, to promote a culture for reporting abuses, and to widen cooperation networks among government entities, civic organizations and international agencies in order to protect migrants. The INM also proposed to extend the documentation to Guatemalan temporary workers who come annually to the southern part of the country. This policy of documenting and registering temporary workers from Guatemala is new; it is not applicable to all temporary migrant workers in the region. Visas would also be granted to visitors coming from neighbouring countries to the south.

Acknowledging that a migrant status should not affect the inalienability of the human rights of a person is important for promoting further change. Progress in this direction included an initiative in April 2007 by Mexico's Chamber of Deputies seeking to modify certain articles of the General Population Law towards the decriminalization of undocumented migration, in particular Articles 119 and 120.[17] A year later the Mexican Senate ratified that reform. The expectation is that this will ameliorate the situation for in-transit migrants.

3.4 Confluence at the Borders: Risks and Migrants' Vulnerability

Mexico's southern border is one of the most dynamic on the continent. "[I]t acts as a port of communication with Central and South America, as an artery that joins the rest of the continent to its northern section. In the past five years there has been spectacular growth of irregular migration flows across this border, particularly of Central Americans" (Artola 2005: 2). It is known that every year thousands of Central American migrants attempt to enter the US through Mexico without any documentation - only to be detained by the US Border Patrol; and that in some places the number of foreign migrants staying in the shelters for migrants is greater than the recorded number detained by Mexican authorities.

The INM estimates that in 2004 more than 1.8 million persons entered the country by the southern border; approximately 17 percent of them did not carry proper documentation. The number of persons entering the country without proper documentation had nearly tripled between 2001 and 2004 (INM 2007). Data on foreigners detained and deported to their countries of origin because they lack the valid documents can be obtained from the INM and the Survey on Migration along the Guatemala-Mexico Border (COLEF 2004). The INM figures refer to the number of non-criminal apprehensions and actual deportations, not to the number of times an individual person is apprehended and/or deported; some migrants may be deported several times over the course of a single year. The official figures therefore must be treated critically. During the 1990s the authorities conducted an annual average of 115,000 deportations of foreigners without valid documentation. From 2000 to 2007 the average annual number of such deportations rose to 189,084.[18] Whether the increase in detentions is the result of a strengthening of opera-

16 Partido de la Revolución Democrática (PRD), 2006: "Parliamentary Group of the Chamber of Deputies", in: *Press Conference* No. *0445*, Mexico (September 3).

17 Partido de la Revolución Democrática (PRD), 2006: "Parliamentary Group of the Chamber of Deputies", in: *Press Conference* No. *0445*, Mexico (September 3).

18 See at: <http://www.migrationinformation.org/feature/display.cfm?ID=389> (10 April 2010). This number is an indirect measurement, recording those who failed to cross on their way to the United States. Since Mexico records apprehension and deportation events, it is possible that the same person was deported multiple times.

tional capabilities - with more material and human resources assigned to the control and expulsion of foreigners - or the result of a rise in number of (attempted) border crossings cannot be discerned from these figures (Casillas 2007). There is no actual figure of the average frequency a given migrant is deported but Casillas' research (2007) indicates that most migrants make several attempts. Other indicators show that despite the intensification of policing operations thousands of migrants manage to elude controls.

Arámbula and Santos (2007) compare data from the INM's state delegation in Veracruz during the year 2004 with records from the "Father Ricardo Zapata's Migrants' Home" in Río Blanco. The delegation detained 14,000 migrants; the Migrants' Home reported having attended to more than 31,000 migrants that same year. Most foreigners detained in Mexico for having entered the country without the proper documentation (90 per cent) come from Central American countries. Of those, Guatemalans still represent the majority (between 44 per cent and 51 per cent) but in the early 2000's the influx of Hondurans increased, while of El Salvadorans decreased. The number of migrants from other countries (mainly Cuba and Ecuador) also rose.

The foreign workers entering Mexico via the country's southern border for temporary jobs are mostly Guatemalans who travel to work in the coffee plantations in the region of Soconusco, in southern Chiapas. Mexico initially attempted to control this movement by granting collective permits to employers to use Guatemalan workers. In the 1970's the number of foreign workers began to surpass that of the native Mexican population in that region. Increasing occurrence of labour conflicts led to the introduction of the Agricultural Visitor's Migration Form in 1997, as a first step in a procedure to document all Guatemalan workers employed in the plantations of Chiapas. Some 40,000 temporary permits are now granted each year to foreign workers. This figure underestimates the actual number of people arriving and leaving. When workers' family members are included estimates of increase are put at something like 100,000 per year.[19] This number of migrant workers also covers foreigners currently working in Quintana Roo, a tourist area on the Caribbean Sea (INM 2005b: 3; ICHR 2003).

The dynamic nature of the populace of Mexico's southern border region has stimulated the growth of cities such as Tapachula, Ciudad Hidalgo and Tuxtla Gutiérrez in Chiapas. It has also increased demand for foreign workers (Guatemalans, Hondurans and El Salvadorans) in the sectors of construction and services - particularly for women in domestic service and the hotel industry (INM 2005b). Temporary labour migration in Mexico is not necessarily circular as is the case in Quintana Roo; foreigners find opportunities for more permanent work in the service sector and the informal economy, and also it is generally the case that Central American migrants working in southern Mexico are doing so with the intention of saving enough money to continue migrating north to the US rather than returning home (INM 2005b: 12).

In areas near the US-Mexican border there now is a confluence of Mexican and non-Mexican migrants trying to enter the US. Aside from persons of diverse nationalities travelling through Mexico to its northern border to enter the US there are also the Mexican migrants doing the same from different places within Mexico. Undocumented migrants are more vulnerable to all kinds of risk and abuse than are Mexican nationals and foreigners with a legal status. There are situations and persons that threaten completion of their migration projects.[20] One convincing conclusion derived from the extensive research in Mexico is that border control strategies have had a bearing on the increase in risks for migrants. Father Ademar Barilli reports on how Central American migrants face a series of threats (extortion, assault, theft, rape, murder) by gangs and individuals and quite often by those in uniform (police, soldiers, immigration officers and security guards), plus accidents which cause loss of life or physical damage. In his words: "To arrive at the southern border of Mexico is to arrive at the beginning of the nightmare of the American dream."[21]

3.4.1 Risky Routes and Death

The intensification of surveillance has made the trip to the north more expensive, traffic of undocumented migrants has increased, and migrants are therefore looking for alternative paths to reach their goal; some

19 Castillo (2001); at: <http://alhim.revues.org/index603.html> (2 April 2010).

20 Ruiz, Olivia, 2003: *La migración centroamericana en la frontera sur: Un perfil del riesgo en la migración indocumentada internacional* (USA: Center for US-Mexican Studies, 10 June); at: <http://repositories. cdlib. org/usmex/ruiz> (10 April 2010).

21 See "Migration Through Mexico: The Perils Facing Central Americans", in: *Mesoamerica*, 25,6 (June 2006); at: <http://www.mesoamericaonline.net/MES0_ARCHIVES/Features/FEAJUN06.pdf> (1 April 2010).

of these involve major risks. Along Mexico's southern border migration points and routes have also shifted towards places more dangerous for migrants. New routes have opened up through mountainous and relatively unpopulated wooded areas. Transit by sea – previously ruled out because of the dangers posed – is now increasingly common as migrants try to avoid checkpoints. Migrants make the sea crossing in unsafe boats overloaded with passengers. At the northern border the greatest flow of migrants is now recorded as passing through the Altar Desert in Sonora.

The growing number of migrants who die while attempting to cross Mexico's borders is the most serious result of stringent border control. Any effort to document the cases of accidents and deaths of migrants faces a systematic lack of information; but the impression gained is that more attention has been paid to documenting deaths of migrants at the country's northern border – particularly on the US side – than at Mexico's southern border.

The non-governmental organization California Rural Legal Assistance Foundation (CRLAF) has been registering the deaths of migrants in the US border zone since 1995.[22] Apparently every border control implemented by the US government is correlated with an increase in the number of migrant deaths. The data provided by the Foundation tallies with other research which estimates that between 1993 and 2006 approximately 4,000 people died attempting to cross into the US (Anguiano/Trejo 2007: 4). The principal causes of migrant deaths in the region are hypothermia/sunstroke and drowning. On the Mexican side of the border from 1999 to 2003, reportedly 159 migrants died (Pérez 2005: 157). Between 2004 and 2007 143 migrants died while in that region of the country.[23]

In recent years it is Mexico's southern border that has become the most difficult and dangerous crossing area for undocumented migrants. Records of deaths of migrants in this region and in their transit through Mexican territory are deficient, according to INM. It is known that 67 migrants died during 2004, 72 during 2005, 54 in 2006, and 34 in 2007.[24] Other sources provide information which contrasts with that put out by the INM. The Rapporteurship of the ICHR mentions learning from human rights organizations that 120 Central Americans perished in the vicinity of Mexico's southern border during the year 2000 (ICHR 2003). The IFHR report notes that the Honduran Government informed it that 168 migrants from their country died in Mexico's southern border region during 2006, and that in the first quarter of 2007 ninety-one Hondurans had met their death (IFHR 2008: 22).

Accidents among migrants in the border zones of Guatemala, Mexico and the US are practically a daily occurrence, according to reports. In the three-year period from 2005 to 2007 in Mexico alone, members of the Beta Groups rescued 20,105 migrants (mostly Mexicans and Central Americans) – the majority in the areas of Mexico's northern border. During the same period the Beta Groups attended to 2,807 wounded or injured migrants. On the southern border the cause of most serious accidents involving migrants (primarily Central Americans) was the so-called 'train of death'. The Beta Groups reported that 96 migrants were physically damaged in 2005, 74 in 2006, and 39 in 2007; three of those cases occurred in the Coahuila northern Mexico – the rest took place in the country's south-eastern region, very possibly associated with train accidents (INM 2009). In April 2000, two hundred Central American migrants were rescued after being trapped in a railcar near Palenque in Chiapas. Five of them died.[25]

3.4.2 Abuse by State Agents and Third Parties

Lack of legal protection for unregistered migrants leaves this population vulnerable to abuses and human rights violations by the authorities and third parties. Yet, due to their status, undocumented migrants rarely seek support services. Despite the near total lack of formal complaints lodged by the affected migrants, human rights violations against migrants in Mexico have been widely documented and denounced by Special Rapporteurs of the United Nations, the Organization of American States, the Mexican National Human Rights Commission, and civil society organizations.

Numerous research studies, news articles and documentaries have been published on the subject. These show that rather than protecting migrants, policies focusing on security and border control have favoured a climate in which the source of insecurity of one group becomes a gainful opportunity for another. In-transit

22 California Rural Legal Assistance Foundation, at: <www.stopgatekeeper.org> (10 April 2010).

23 Data provided by the Director of Information of the National Immigration Institute in a telephone interview in March 2008.

24 Data provided verbally over the telephone by the Director of Information of the National Immigration Institute.

25 *La Jornada*, 13 April 2001.

migrants are unfamiliar with the social and cultural aspects of the areas through which they travel; they are ignorant of local legislation and cannot identify the authorities or distinguish their jurisdictions; but they do make every effort to remain inconspicuous and to be seen as natives. "From the time migrants leave their places of origin, there are people who seek them out to take advantage of them in one way or another" (testimony of the Coordinator of the Southern Tapachula Beta Group, cited by Ruiz 2003: 13).[26] As foreseen in a document of the IOM (International Organization for Migration) presented in 1997:

> Although regulatory measures clearly constitute a key component of national migration strategies, those measures per se cannot achieve lasting, humanitarian solutions to the problems of irregular migration and trafficking. In fact, in an unexpected way, they may contribute to the growth of such practices (IOM 1997: 3).

In Mexico it is difficult to determine whether authorities or private parties abuse migrants most frequently; studies come up with numerous incidents of both. The migrants themselves tell of municipal, state and federal authorities as well as traffickers and gangs of common criminals. The kinds of abuses they suffer are robbery, extortion, criminal deception, arbitrary detention, physical and sexual assault (Castilla 2006, 2007). The migrants do not file formal complaints against these abuses; very few cases are presented to the Mexican National Human Rights Commission (*Comisión Nacional de los Derechos Humanos*, or CNDH) - the agency to which private parties may reports abuses by authorities. In 2005 the Commission passed on 391 complaints to the INM and in 2006, 278. Records kept by civic organizations attending to migrants and involved in human rights protection are an essential source of information.

In 2004 the Centre for Migrants' Human Rights in Ciudad Juárez on the northern border attended to more than 350 injured persons, 56 per cent of whom reported having been a victim of crime and violation of their human rights. From a sample of 1,000 Central Americans interviewed by the civic association *Frontera con Justicia* (Justice at the Border) in Saltillo in northern Mexico, between April 2005 and March 2006, came report of 1,558 incidents of aggression: beatings, assaults, threats, gunshots fired into the air, and pursuit were the most frequent. Guatamala's Federal Attorney General's Office for Human Rights reported that 25 per cent of the Guatemalan migrants deported back to their country stated they had been victims of abuse. Roughly one in four of those abuses had occurred in Guatemala; three out of four in Mexico. Close on half the cases occurring in Mexico were allegedly perpetrated by agents of the National Immigration Institute - the Mexican governmental agency in charge of migration control.

One of the main reasons for the increase in abuse by authorities is the plain fact that the amount of migrant movement has reached a level beyond the capacity of authorities to handle the situation according to established minimal standards to be observed for migrants' physical well being and the protection of their property. Despite the increased number of migration stations across the country, some states in Mexico have no facilities for holding migrants, or the capacity they have is insufficient. Mexico's human rights organizations are constantly denouncing the practice of taking detained foreigners (including minors) to municipal jails - in most cases facing charges of petty crimes.[27] The detention may continue for many months without explanation or legal justification. In some cases military officials also become involved along with the police (Díaz/Kuhner 2007).

In February 2008 the press reported a riot at the migration station in Tenosique, Tabasco (southern Mexico); 159 foreigners apprehended by the INM were living in a space for only 80 persons.[28] The same source tells that in some stations conditions are unhygienic, there is a lack of drinking water or food and local officials abuse the migrants verbally and physically. In 2006, as a result of 73 complaints filed by the Mexican National Human Rights Commission against the Mexican National Immigration Institute, 187 civil servants were reprimanded for violating the human rights of Central American migrants through physical maltreatment, lack of provision of food and the generally poor conditions in which they were held.

When representatives of the IFHR visited the southern Mexican states they left with the impression that detention is rarely pursued to the point of extraditing the migrants to their countries of origin, but is rather just the means for subjecting them to extortion. Nearly all the Central American migrants without valid travel documents interviewed in Mexico had been subject to extortion at least once by municipal,

26 See Ruiz (2003); at: <http://repositories.cdlib.org/ usmex/ ruiz>; (14 June 2009).

27 Entre Redes (ER), 2000: *Informative bulletin of civil organizations in Central America and Mexico on aspects related to migration*, No. 2.

28 López, René Alberto, 2008: "Deportan a migrantes amotinados en Tabasco", in: *La Jornada*, 24 February.

state or federal officials, as well as by criminals. Threats, beatings, sexual harassment or rape of women and, in some cases, extrajudicial executions, have been reported. Both police and private security forces commonly use violence to a disproportionate degree (IFHR 2008).

Violations by private parties are common for those hiring the services of a *pollero*. The migrants who hire *polleros* do so either because of their unfamiliarity with the situation involved in crossing a border, or because they want to reduce the degree of insecurity along the route and ensure success in arriving at their destination. To save money, some migrants do not use the services of a *pollero*; they cross the border on their own, or in small groups accompanied by experienced migrants. As new obstacles to migration arise migrants must implement different strategies and forge new paths. This generates increased demand for people traffickers, greater specialization of their networks, and higher costs for their services. In 1994 *polleros* charged between US $500 and 1,500 dollars for crossing the northern border from one city to another.[29] The fee to be smuggled across the border into California had risen to between US $2,000 and US $2,500 in 2004.[30] Today to cross over from some place in Sonora to Phoenix, Arizona *polleros* charge US $3,000.[31] Along Mexico's southern border *polleros* offer to take migrants to US territory for between US $7,000 and $14,000 dollars per person (Casillas 2006; Anguiano/Trejo 2007).

Some *polleros* still work independently, practising what they call 'ant trafficking' because it is less expensive, but individuals are increasingly hiring out to larger trafficking networks (Casillas 2006). These networks are more likely to succeed because of their collaborative structure based on the direct and indirect participation of public agents and private parties. In the research that Casillas conducted in Tapachula on Mexico's southern border, *polleros* are the only visible agent in a broad, diverse, multi-sectoral participation structure with different types of complicity from private parties linked to the goods and services sector (sales clerks, prostitutes, waitresses, domestic workers, nightclub staff, vendors, hotel employees, transportation workers, and lawyers) to public agents (municipal police, military, local judicial and migration agents), to name a few (Casillas 2006: 26). The clandestine nature of migrant trafficking allows *polleros* the room for manoeuvre to abuse migrants: they fail to provide agreed upon services; they abandon migrants in transit; they cheat, trick, rob and abuse them sexually. In both border regions trafficking networks sometimes use underage persons as *polleros* because the authorities are less likely to arrest and charge them.

3.4.3 Women and Minors

The research done by Díaz and Kuhner (2007) among foreign women detained at the migration-station in Mexico City illustrates the delicate situation of women migrants in transit through Mexico's southern border region. They interviewed 90 foreign women in Mexico City who had been detained by immigration authorities and who showed some of the characteristics of migrants traversing Mexico on their way to the US. More than eighty were from a Latin American country: mostly Guatemala, Honduras and El Salvador. A majority were young, aged 18 to 24; fourteen of them were minors. Two out of five of them had extant husbands, the other three were either single, divorced or widows. Most had children, only twelve of whom had them with them; the rest had left them in their places of origins. Most of the women were employed before they migrated; but wanted to find a better-paying job. "Although the migrants interviewed were reluctant to speak about physical or sexual violence experienced during the journey, 26 per cent (of a total of 90 women interviewed) acknowledged having suffered such violence" (Díaz/Kuhner 2007). In the majority of cases the person who perpetrated the violence was an official, although the women also identified traffickers, railroad guards and other civilians. Sexual violence often occurred as 'payment' for transport or in exchange for not being detained by the authorities. Some women, aware of the high probability of rape, had gone so far as to receive contraceptive injections prior to making the trip.

No fewer that 2 out of 5 women interviewed by Díaz and Kuhner (2007) said they had been the victims of extortion in Mexico; they could be the object

---

29 See Gustavo LoÏpez Castro, 1998: "Factors that Influence Migration: Coyotes and Alien Smuggling"; at: <http://www.utexas.edu/lbj/uscir/binpapers/v3a-6lopez.pdf> (16 April, 2010)

30 Ewing, Walter A., no date: *Sabotaging National Security: The Paradox of US Border-Enforcement and Immigration Policies* (New York: Immigration Policy Center); at: <www.immigrationpolicy.org>; and at: <http://research.utep.edu/Portals/379/035.pdf> (16 April, 2010).

31 Apostolopoulos, Sonmez, Kronenfeld, Castillo, McLendon, and Smith, (2008: 292); at: <http://www.uncg.edu/phe/STI%20HIV%20Risks%20for%20Migrant%20Mexican%20Laborers.pdf> (16 April 2010).

of such abuse up to even twenty times as part of the process of being detained. The principal perpetrators of these acts were highway patrol officers, municipal police and INM agents; among the private agents taxi and bus drivers were also cited. Aside from violence these agents threaten denouncement to the authorities. When money is the currency instead of sex, the sums demanded from women migrants range from US $10 to $100 per incident (Díaz/Kuhner 2007).

The help of a trafficker may mean greater probability of success in crossing the border, but it involves significant risk for women migrant. Substantial risks are: travelling in unsafe conditions in boats, trucks, trailers and train compartments; being abandoned in unpopulated areas; being detained in some unidentified place while the traffickers extort more money from the migrants' family in the US. Some women reported that during the attempts to avoid checkpoints while they tried to cross the borders the traffickers separated them from their children.

Fieldwork conducted by the authors in two border regions between Mexico and the US gained information on migrant minors. Of seventy minors (both male and female) interviewed two out of five had already begun to work in their places of origin (despite being underage). Thirty-three of them were intending to look for a job in the US. Two out of five of the interviewees travelled with a relative; others went with a friend or acquaintance but no fewer than one in five travelled alone and did not know any of the people they met along the way. Some migrants face a long and hazardous trip to reach Mexico's northern border: six out of seventy minors interviewed had left their place of origin no more than 30 days before the day on which they were interviewed; eleven of the seventy reported they had started their journey more than a year previously.

3.4.4 Migration and Crime: Impact of a Conflation

In Mexico's southern border region a situation prevails favouring the execution and cover-up of many illicit activities affecting migrants. Trafficking in people is not an isolated phenomenon, and as it becomes more specialized it relies on structures using drug traffickers and people dealing in other illegal merchandise (Artola 2005: 2). The increased presence of women and children in the migration flow instigated an increase in illegal trafficking for the purposes of involuntary exploitation, trickery and deception. In his report on the study of Tapachula and some neighbouring localities, Casillas tells of small groups in charge of migrant trafficking having links with trade in people for the purpose of sexual exploitation (Casillas 2005). He found indications of the operation of both national and trans-national networks dealing in this illegal trade. Although it is undeniable that borders are gateways not only for migrants but also for illegal trade in trafficking people, drugs, vehicles and other products[32], media coverage has combined with a paucity of objective studies on crime and its relation to migration to confuse (or/and exaggerate) some aspects; this hinders a comprehensive analysis of the human insecurity of migrants.

After the criminal gangs, known as the *Mara Salvatrucha 13* (MS13) and *Barrio 18*, had entered Mexico's southern border region at the end of 2004, "this topic became front-page news; it brought about several statements by decision-makers regarding its dimensions, as well as the implementation of programs that pointed to the *Maras* as a threat to the country's public security" (Balmaceda 2007: 14). These gangs emerged during the 1980's in certain California cities with large Central American refugee communities. Trained by El Salvadorans and Guatemalans who had some military experience these criminal gangs adopted guerrilla-style tactics. When the armed conflicts in Guatemala and El Salvador had ended in the 1990s the US deported the *MS13* and *Barrio 18* members to their countries of origin – thereby transporting their criminal enterprises to Central America and eventually Mexico. By 2005 Mexican youths were taking part in these gangs who operated in 15 of Mexico's states but with greater influence in the southeastern region, especially Chiapas.

The violent nature of these gangs and their organization created an attitude of apprehension towards them in the media, and Government departments now tend to associate these gangs with all sorts of criminal activities – not only the trafficking of people and drugs but also, even, terrorism. Some scholars associate these groups with "transnational criminal organizations" (Iñiguez 2005); others argue that the transnational nature of the *Maras* is limited to the reproduction of their identity and the dynamics of violence at the local level (Balmaceda 2007: 103). The point of greatest agreement is that this type of juvenile delinquency cannot be considered a problem of national security (Valenzuela 2005). In some places,

32 Artola (2005: 3) contends that "the routes used for the people trafficking are the same as those utilized in the traffic of other goods and services, be they legal or not".

though, it may represent a problem of public security that affects migrants in transit – particularly those who travel on the freight trains through Chiapas.

Along the US Mexican border national security discourse created an especially anti-migrant sentiment after 9/11. A disturbing increase in paramilitary groups patrolling to stop Latino workers from entering the country unauthorized has been observed. These often racist and xenophobic vigilantes detain the migrants they find and hand them over to the border patrol. Some migrants testify of rough and sometimes threatening treatment by these groups. Within Mexico members of non-governmental organizations have reported in the media that they have been victims of harassment and anonymous threats because they have taken steps to defend the migrants. The press has indeed reported a series of accusations, regarding detention and harassment of, and threatening behaviour against, persons who offer food, medical attention and lodging to Central American migrants by officials of the Federal Bureau of Investigation and the Immigration authority – accusing them of being people traffickers. Cases of such criminalization of humanitarian aid have been filed in the states of Chiapas, Querétaro, Oaxaca and Veracruz.[33]

Summing up, border control strategies have serious consequences for the safety of in-transit undocumented migrants, both in terms of the crossing points along the border (southern as well as northern) and the routes taken. Lack of legal protection plus the clandestine nature of movements also leave this population vulnerable to abuses and human rights violations by the authorities and third parties without recourse to justice.

3.5 Support for In-Transit Migrants

The increase in border control by the US during the 1990's brought about numerous programmes and institutions supporting migrants. Early efforts to address the problems migrants experience while in transit concentrated on places with the greatest flow and the greatest risks. Thus, these initiatives concentrated in the area of Tijuana. Subsequently, programmes and institutions for attending to migrants extended to other border cities and have adjusted their orientation owing to changes in the composition and behaviour of migrants. This research has identified different institutionalized patterns for attending to migrants in transit in Mexico: 1) Government institutions and programmes; 2) civil society organizations, many of them linked to the Roman Catholic Church or to other churches; 3) Sin Fronteras (No Borders), a civil society organization headquartered in Mexico City and which, due to its nature, stands out among social organizations.

3.5.1 Government Programmes

Prior to 1993 the Mexican and US governments had no defined guidelines for conducting repatriation processes. Repatriation was often carried out without the US government notifying the Mexican authorities *a priori*, nor even with any assurance that the repatriated persons were Mexican citizens. In 1993 the Collaboration Agreement on the Problem of Minors at the Border came into effect (INM 2009). From then on both governments established further agreements on procedures to effect sure and orderly repatriation of Mexican citizens – having respect for the migrants' human rights and, especially, the protection of minors.

The INM is the Mexican authority in charge of receiving Mexicans repatriated from the US but the Mexican consulates (there in the US) must also participate. US migration authorities are required to notify the staff at Mexican consulates of border cities in the US at least two hours in advance of making the repatriation, whereupon Consular staff should arrive and identify the Mexicans and notify INM agents (who should also come there to get declarations of nationality from the migrants). US Border Patrol agents should then, finally, hand over the repatriated persons to the Mexican authorities (Secretaría de Relaciones Exteriores 2004).

A fieldwork visit by the authors to Nogales ascertained that the US immigration authorities do not always comply with its agreement with Mexico as regards the repatriation of minors. Border patrol agents often separate minors from their adult relatives as a tactic for discouraging future border crossings. The only thing they actually achieve is to oblige those parents to visit all the region's shelters to find their children who must remain in those shelters until claimed by a family member. It was also noted that the repatriation of minors sometimes takes place without the presence of a representative of the Mexican consulate – although the corresponding INM authority is present in effect. In Chihuahua and Sonora, in the north, repatriations of adults often occur without no-

33 CDHMAP (2006); at: <http://centroprodh.org.mx/2008> (26 May 2010).

tifying any Mexican authority: the border police simply take the detainees to the borderline and make them cross over to the Mexican side.

In addition, to avoid further paperwork and expense, the US border police commonly ignore the fact that some migrants are citizens of a Central American country. Citizens from countries other than Mexico who are without documents often end up on the streets in northern Mexico because the US Border Patrol agents have repatriated them into Mexico and not to their home country, and without the consent of the Mexican authorities. Some legal provisions on repatriation have not functioned perfectly, but there is progress towards establishing better-regulated, increasingly reliable conduct from both authorities. For the process of deportation of foreign migrants detained in Mexican territory, the Mexican government has signed bilateral repatriation agreements with the governments of Guatemala, Honduras and El Salvador. These agreements are essentially logistical: they set the schedule and locations at which deportations will be effected, plus the schedule and places for reception of the migrants. Some social organizations have nonetheless denounced the fact that the Mexican government continues to conduct massive deportations, which violate the terms set down in international legal instruments. These require every detainee to be identified and registered during the deportation process, and each case to be investigated to ensure that the deported migrants are not in danger for their life or physical well-being when returned to their country of origin.

For deportation of Central American minors travelling alone there are no clear regulations in force for conducting repatriations such as shall guarantee their safety, security and respect for their human rights. The IFHR mission report expresses concern for unaccompanied Central American minors detained in Mexico and deported to their countries of origin. They are handed over at border sites to agents of their home government; but in many instances there are no clear measures for delivering them to their parents or other relatives. Minors from Honduras and El Salvador are sometimes taken to their places of origin along with adults (IFHR 2008: 39).

The initiative for creating Beta Groups for the protection of migrants in Mexico was a government response to complaints made by civic organizations regarding increased abuse against migrants in Mexico. These were founded within the INM to protect migrants' physical well-being and property. The first Beta Group was set up in Tijuana in 1990. In 1994 the Beta Group of Nogales was established, and in 1995 those of Tecate (in the State of Baja California) and Matamoros (in the State of Tamaulipas) began operations. At present there are sixteen groups along both Mexico's borders. These Beta Groups attend to migrants in transit regardless of their nationality and document status. The groups perform many tasks. They offer guidance to migrants about dangers involved (through signs and distribution of pamphlets); patrol areas representing risks for migrants; effect rescue operations and provide first aid; protect migrants against criminals; channel migrants to shelters where they can receive social assistance, and channel complaints of abuses committed by either government agents or by private parties. These groups recently gained in strength with more members and better training. This work is important to help generate a more favourable climate towards undocumented migrants and to offer them security while in transit. The IFHR acknowledged that they are "a public entity of humanitarian aid that is unique in the world" (IFHR 2008: 20).

In 1996 the Inter-Institutional Programme for Attention to Border Minors began to function within the Mexican Government's programme of cooperation with the United Nations Children's Fund (UNICEF). The DIF (Mexican National System for Integral Family Development) coordinates the programme; the INM (National Migration Institute of the Ministry of the Interior) and the Ministry of Foreign Affairs participate. Under this programme "temporary shelter is provided to repatriated minors and to minors undergoing migration processes towards the US without the protection of any family member" (Aranda 2004: 61). In both cases they remain under the protection of the DIF while procedures are being conducted for reuniting them with their family or, when necessary, transferring them to their place of origin.

This inter-institutional programme currently has a network of twenty temporary shelters in six border states – all five of the states along Mexico's northern border and one of the four along its southern border (in Tapachula, Chiapas). The state and municipal systems of the DIF operate eight shelters; NGOs run 12 others (INM 2009). In 1998, the first year for which information was recorded, the programme's network attended to 8,560 minors. In the early years of the programme Sonora and Baja California states had the largest number of minors passing through the system. In 2007 the programme helped 21,366 boys and girls. The exact number of minors who travel alone or who are repatriated without family members being involved is unclear.

Table 3.1: Boys and girls attended to by the Inter-institutional Program's network of shelters. **Source:** DIF; Deputy Director's Office for Sectoral and Regional Programs; *Statistical Yearbooks.*

	Total	Boys	Girls
1998	8 560		
1999	8 045		
2000	8 768		
2001	7 620		
2002	6 708	4 688	2 020
2003	7 194	5 173	2 021
2004	10 920	7 735	3 185
2005	18 392	13 262	5 130
2006	20 516	16 101	4 405
2007	21 366	16 997	4 369

Nearly all migrant minors attended to by this programme have been repatriated by the US authority (97.6 per cent) and only 2.4 per cent are not repatriated.[34] Almost all of them are Mexicans. 372 non-Mexican minors were sheltered in 2005. The 2005 records also show that of those who were sheltered 883 were between one and five years of age (4.8 per cent); 2,429 between six and twelve years of age (13.2 per cent); 15,069 between 13 and 17 years of age (81.9 per cent of the total) (DIF 2007). Individual shelters have a small operating budget; they are unable to pay for transport and living conditions have their shortcomings. The INM supports the state and municipal DIF offices in the transfer of minors to shelters - given available staff and vehicles at the disposal of the INM delegation. The INM also covers the costs of transporting these minors to their home areas. Some of the shelters participating in the network are civic associations with limited funds.

In 2005 the National Employment Service (or SNE in Spanish) of the Ministry of Labour and Social Welfare (or STPS in Spanish) began a "Repatriates Working" programme in various northern border cities. Repatriated adult Mexicans received by the INM are channelled, upon request, to the offices of the SNE. There they receive two types of support: 1) funds to stay in the city and either look for a job or apply for a possible scholarship for necessary training; 2) money (2,000 Mexican pesos) to cover transport, food and lodging to return to their place of origin. The governments of some border municipalities have also implemented measures to provide economic support to repatriated persons - either to pay for a shelter run by a civic association or for travel and food expenses covering return to their places of residence. In some border states the INM has made agreements with companies rendering services such as out-of-town transport so that repatriated persons who desire to return to their place of origin may obtain a 50 per cent discount on their tickets (INM 2009).

In April 2008 the Ministry of the Interior had begun a pilot programme called "Human Repatriation" to provide Mexicans who are repatriated via Tijuana with shelter and food for up to two weeks, opportunities to contact their families and support to find temporary work in Tijuana or to return home. It is possible that this programme will eventually replace the STPS programme and include town council-run programmes; intentions are similar to those of the Inter-Institutional Programme for Attention to Border Minors, which involves federal, state and municipal agencies and civic organizations.

The Mexican National Human Rights Commission and the State Commissions of that agency have place on the Advisory Board of the Inter-Institutional Programme for Attention to Border Minors and are the official channel for migrants to lodge complaints about abuse by authorities. Staffs from these commissions visit areas where migrants congregate - such as crossing points, shelters, bus stations or migration stations, to offer their services. In cases where Mexican migrants claim abuse on the part of the US authorities they may receive repatriation support through the Mexican consulate; in cases where private parties in Mexican territory perpetrate the abuse the migrants need to go to the Federal Attorney General's Office of Mexico to lodge a complaint. A major challenge is how to inform the migrants effectively about these procedures and channels for their access to rights.

3.5.2 Civic Organizations

Pioneers in the work of setting up shelters for migrants were the Scalabrinian Missionaries - a Catholic religious congregation which since the 19th century had become expert in handling this problem throughout the world. In the early 1990's the Missionaries of

34 Outgoing migrants, who have not yet crossed the border, usually do not require this service because they prefer not to call attention to themselves.

San Carlos Scalabriniani had opened a Migrants' Home in Ciudad Juárez; Dominican priests took the home over in 2006. In 1993 a Migrants' Home was set up in Guatemala City; in 1995 one was established in Tecún Umán, Guatemala; another in 1997 at Tapachula, Chiapas, and in Agua Prieta, Sonora. The last Scalabriniani Home was set up in Nuevo Laredo, Tamaulipas in 2003. Since then migrants' homes have opened in locations far from the border - places such as Arriaga, Chiapas and Río Blanco, Veracruz. These shelters offer food, lodging, spiritual support, guidance, first-level medical care, and the defence and promotion of migrants' human rights - including for deported migrants and refugees.

In 1999 the Network of Scalabrinian Migrants' Homes established an organizational structure of the homes enabling joint effort with other non-governmental organizations or churches, promoting human, cultural, social and spiritual aspects among the migrant population. This project was established as a Civic Association with a Board of Patrons through which the necessary funds for operation are obtained and the volunteer work is coordinated. The tasks performed by this network go beyond providing direct services to migrants in the shelters; it has also planned and carried out actions aimed at creating awareness among the citizenry through marches, celebrations, commemorations, calls to solidarity and similar motions. Although this is only the beginning, the network, with the support of human rights organizations, has begun programmes for protecting migrants' human rights specifically in education and promotion of awareness, legal advice and social benefit.

In line with the work done by the Scalabrinians, other humanitarian organizations are involved in providing services to migrants while in transit. These efforts have expanded and diversified according to migrants' movement. At first they concentrated their attention near the northern border, and then later some shelters were opened in the southern border region. At first they were only for men since males were in the greater majority, but subsequently places opened up for women and minors. In recent years some shelters have adapted areas to receive women, but the scarcity of funds is a hindrance and there remain few shelters for women. In Ciudad Juárez there is no women's shelter. In Nogales the DIF maintains the Women Migrants Home.

In the case of minors, prior to the operation of the government's Inter-Institutional Programme, the Young Men's/Women's Christian Association (YM/WCA) of Mexico and the US created the YMCA Border Initiative to establish a chain of shelters called YMCA Homes for Migrant Minors in cities with large numbers in transit in Mexico's northern border region. The first YMCA shelter for minors in Tijuana was set up in 1992; in 1995 it opened another one in Ciudad Juárez; then one in Piedras Negras, Coahuila; and then Agua Prieta, Sonora. Before the Inter-Institutional Programme began INM agents in those cities took repatriated minors to the YMCA Homes who took over responsibility for them. These homes have now become part of the network of shelters run by the Inter-Institutional Programme and continue to offer migrant minors of both sexes a free provisional home; the difference is that the minors are now under the guardianship of the Mexican government through the DIF.

The efforts made by different organizations to attend to the problems of these in-transit migrants are invaluable, yet are still insufficient to meet all the needs. In the case of minors the DIF with the support of non-governmental organizations manage to provide food and lodging to all those minors repatriated by the US; the major task of attending to the minors who travel in Mexico's southern border region is still pending to date. Lodging provisions for adults come mainly from civic organizations, but there are indications that this is still insufficient - especially for women migrants.

Finally, among civic organizations active in providing support to migrants, *Sin Fronteras* (No Border) plays a unique role. A non-profit organization located in Mexico City and founded in December 1995 by a group of social activists and academics, *Sin Fronteras* is legally constituted as a Private Assistance Institution and attends to migrants and refugees from any country in the world - though they are mainly from other Latin American countries - transiting Mexico on their journey to the US. Support from Mexican volunteers has been fundamental; in 2005 *Sin Fronteras* had 800 volunteers from churches, civil society networks and university students doing their period of social service. Its orientation is very different from the organizations mentioned in the previous section in that it also participated actively in the establishment of more suitable migration policies and programmes. *Sin Fronteras* is practically the only non-governmental organization dealing with migration policy and defence of migrants' rights in Mexico. Its work is so relevant that, at present, organizations such as the COMAR and the INM refer numerous migrants to it.

3.6 Concluding Remarks

The data presented in this chapter show the complexity of migration processes from Mexico and Central America towards the US. This movement increased during the latter decades of the 20th century when the global and regional economies began to restructure. One of the effects has been the division of workers into two new categories: those organized institutionally - at least as regards documentation for employment - and those not covered or protected by any institution, despite the fact that both types of workers respond to the same forces of global demand. This contradiction occurs to a heightened extent in contexts of greater (economic) contact between countries, such as is the case with the *North American Free Trade Agreement* (NAFTA) between Canada, the US and Mexico. In this region all the factors of production are subject to free exchange - except labour.

The people who are referred to as 'migrants' from Mexico and Central America have often stated (both when interviewed individually and through spokespersons of their organizations) that they should not have to be treated as criminals but rather, what they are, simple workers seeking to earn an honest living. Nevertheless, lately they have also endured harassment (by local officials) at their workplaces far from Mexico's border. It is now become common for Mexican and Central American workers who have been living with their families in the US for many years to be thrown out of the country all of a sudden - no account being taken of their family situation. At present there are nearly 5.5 million children in the US whose parents are unauthorized migrants (Fortuny/Capps/Simms/Chaudry 2009). This has contributed to the tension sometimes felt among unauthorized migrants in the US but also in the Mexican border cities which have become the places where these exiled workers come together 'out of necessity' along with those waiting for an opportunity to enter the US.

Over the years the Mexican authorities have come to wield control over migrants from Central American countries - not so much through investments in technology as in the US but rather by extorting money from the migrants they are sworn to safeguard within their jurisdictions. The new security policies of the US have pressured the Mexican government to change its foreign policies with sister countries in Latin America. This casts a shadow over the positive actions conducted by the Mexican government not only for Guatemalan refugees in the 1980's but for refugees from Spain, Argentina, Chile and Brazil in different periods of the 20th century. Mexico was previously always an example of solidarity in its practices towards the citizens of other countries; now the government has had to forget its 'good practice'. This is only one example of how a hegemonic country exercises power over less powerful and dependent countries.

This chapter also endeavoured to present some positive efforts made by civil society and church congregations to help protect migrants in their journey northwards. These actions restore human solidarity because groups and persons of all kinds and national origins take part in them. It is evident that society is undergoing an unresolved transition between the local and the global, between standardization and diversity. Perhaps this is a prelude to the rise of a new universal citizenry only now being forged thanks to the drive of these migrants - women and men, boys and girls - who resolutely face the conditions of a world they want to improve.

4 The Blind Spot of Repression: Migration Policies and Human Survival in the Central Sahara

Julien Brachet

4.1 Introduction

The central Sahara region has a long-standing history of migratory movements as a mode of livelihoods. Movements from the Sahel to Algeria and Libya for seasonal employment emerged in the 1950's, and by the early 1990's concerns over migratory movements in this region translated into the important arena of competing interests over livelihood and security. Despite human-made obstacles constituted by the predatory practices of local representatives of the Nigerien state on the one hand and the hardening of North African migration policies on the other, tens of thousands of migrants from sub-Saharan Africa travel each year to North Africa via the city of Agadez in northern Niger. These migratory movements have become an important factor in international relations in multiple directions: between sub-Saharan governments and between North African and European governments.

The emphasis placed by the media and by European and North African governments on migrants who intend to travel on to Europe has meant that virtually all sub-Saharans travelling in the Sahara are redefined as intercontinental economic migrants. In a context of hardening identity politics and xenophobia, such emphasis strengthens the fear of an illusory 'threat of migration' to the northern shore of the Mediterranean, while obscuring the complexity and diversity of people's movements within the Sahara itself. This emphasis works in conjunction with the idea of 'common' management of migration flows between Africa and Europe as expressed in the re-launch of the '5 plus 5 dialogue' in Lisbon in 2001 and the recurrent declaration by European governments that they intend to "step up and make more efficient the fight against illegal migration, both in transit and in sending countries".[1] The notion of 'common management' focuses primarily on security measures and border protection, leading to the externalization of border control, by moving security checks southward from Europe's territorial borders to the Mediterranean Sea, North African countries and the Sahara (Carling 2007; De Haas 2007; Fischer-Lescano/Löhr/Tohidipur 2009). Through bilateral or multilateral agreements, European governments have gradually encouraged their North African counterparts to increase the surveillance of their borders, both land and sea, in an attempt to detect all kinds of trans-Saharan migration as early as possible. Rhetoric of fear and control contributes to a misinterpretation of all trans-Saharan migration as trans-Mediterranean migration, built on an inaccurate and superficial appreciation of reality.

This chapter offers a local perspective on the dynamic nature and recent transformations of the Saharan migration system, drawing on information gathered during fieldwork undertaken between 2003 and 2007[2] to show how such policies affect those who live or travel through these areas. An illustration of the historical significance of intra-African migration systems for the economic development of Northwest Africa is followed by an analysis of new patterns of migrations that have emerged since the 1990's throughout the Central Sahara, and by a critical appraisal of media and government fears about human trafficking and smuggling in the region. A brief outline of the externally driven legal and institutional frameworks that govern the movements of people in this area is provided, followed by a discussion of how people succeed in crossing the borders between Niger, Algeria and Libya, highlighting how state representatives deal with (and partake in) local migration systems. The

1 Ministerial Conference on migration in the Western Mediterranean, Tunis, 16–17 October 2002.

2 I am grateful to Judith Scheele for helping me to translate this text. I would also like to thank Thanh-Dam Truong for her comments on earlier versions of this paper.

T.-D. Truong and D. Gasper (eds.), *Transnational Migration and Human Security*, Hexagon Series on Human and Environmental Security and Peace 6, DOI 10.1007/978-3-642-12757-1_4, © Springer-Verlag Berlin Heidelberg 2011

various strategies adopted by migrants and facilitating agents to cope with hardened migration policies are presented in light of their possible local impacts in the Central Sahara.

4.2 Intra-African Migration Systems as an Important Factor of Economic Development in Northwest Africa: The Case of the Central Sahara

Trade and travel within and across the Sahara goes back to the dawn of history. In the Central Sahara, however, economic migration as it is today began largely at the end of the 1950's with the arrival of low-skilled Sahelian workers at *In Ekker* and *Reggane* in southern Algeria, where the French had nuclear bases. During the 1960's, following Algeria's independence (1962) and Libya's sudden wealth due to the discovery and exploitation of oil, the leaders of these two states set up development policies for the Saharan regions of their countries. The large-scale development projects that followed created high demand for low-skilled labour - notably in the agricultural sector which could not be met locally or even nationally; and then serious droughts in the Sahel (1960 to 1973) led to famine and a severe crisis within pastoral economies. This accelerated and indeed instigated migration to the Algerian and Libyan Sahara. At first it mostly involved relatively young men from the Sahelian and Saharan zones of the states of the Sahel belt, and their numbers and organization only changed gradually through until the 1980's. During the 1990's, however, migrations increased, bringing more migrants from a wider range of countries (Bredeloup/ Pliez 2005).

Owing to unreliable record keeping at checkpoints, and the clandestine nature of some journeys, it is difficult to evaluate the volume of these migratory flows. In the case of Niger - a known transit country - the figures produced by official state services, especially border police, are only approximate and often incomplete. The conditions in which checks occur at the border posts of Assamaka (between Niger and Algeria) and Dirkou (between Niger and Libya) together with the widespread corruption render official statistics unreliable; but the main problem with the statistics is the significance of 'irregular'[3] migration, which by definition, cannot be assessed. Although it is clearly important to have exact figures on migration between sub-Saharan Africa, the Maghreb and Europe, the relevant authorities show no interest in producing them; nor in fact do they have the professional means so to do. Politicians rarely wait for social scientists to put forward numbers before they make decisions. Despite the unreliability of the figures produced the media make sensational news of them, befitting the political aims of the relevant authorities.

To deal with the deficiencies of national statistics researchers may come up their own figures in an attempt to quantify flows as they are observed. They produce estimates derived from various sources: the media, official statistics and - more importantly - field observations plus information provided by fellow researchers and reports produced by NGOs, local associations and international agencies. This method becomes more effective the more time the researcher spends in the specified terrain. In this way, the researcher can assess the magnitude in such a way that enables him to counter claims that have been made without the support of scientific research. After several years of research in Niger it is possible to estimate that there are approximately 50,000 to 100,000 migrants travelling to North Africa through Niger every year; judging by numbers of returnees by land, only 10 to 20 per cent seem to continue their journey to Europe (Brachet 2009b). Such a numerical range might seem too broad to be useful for policymakers. Nevertheless, calculations by other researchers show that the illegal migratory flows from sub-Saharan Africa to Europe are minimal compared with overall migration within the region, even according to the highest estimates (De Haas 2007). These alternative calculations are vital as they provide a reading different from the official ones, which are often based on extrapolations not backed up by actual observations. Such figures can be manipulated.

Imprecise head counts apart, statistics cannot reveal the exchange that occurs during and because of these migrations. On their way to the Maghreb, sub-Saharan migrants spend different amounts of time in the villages and towns through which they travel. For several decades, therefore, these migrants have participated in the economic vitality of the Sahara. Foreign migrants have shaped such cities as Sebha in Libya and Tamanrasset in Algeria as much with respect to urban development and economic activities as to socio-cultural practices (Nadi 2007; Pliez 2003; Spiga 2005). These transformations are less noticeable in

3 The term *irregular migration* refers to crossing a border without a valid document and/or authorisation (Ghosh 1998).

Figure 4.1: International migration routes to and through the Sahara. **Source:** Brachet 2009.

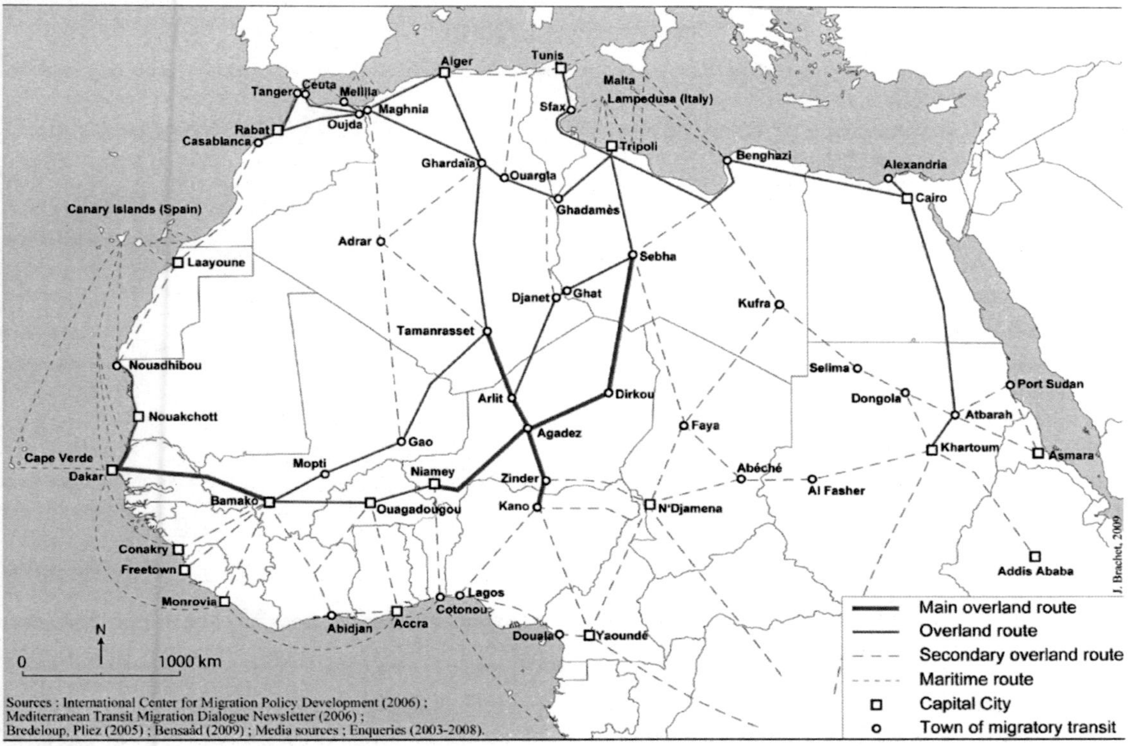

Agadez - a Nigerien town of comparable size (with a population of about 100,000 inhabitants). Changes are mainly visible in the development of transport companies, the construction or refurbishment of temporary lodgings and, especially, in the injection of ready money into the local economy.

As shown elsewhere (Brachet 2009a) migrants annually contribute several billion francs CFA to the local economy by their participation in the official economy and through the taxes they are obliged to pay to local officials. In a village such as Dirkou, with less than 10,000 inhabitants, changes are even more visible. Being a contact point between the Nigerien and Libyan migration networks, this oasis has grown considerably over the last few years. A new district named *Sabon Gari* ('new village') has developed where most activities are concentrated on the transport of people and goods between Niger and Libya; it is more densely populated today than the old village.

The resulting international road traffic has become indispensable both for the export of salt and dates from the oases of North-Eastern Niger to the south, and for the import of basic supplies. Caravan trade is now secondary in most oases near the main tracks. Trade and exchange on various levels are interwoven: trans-Saharan migrants and their demand for transport have revitalized the regional and cross-border trade supplying people in northern Niger with foodstuffs and some manufactured goods. Many freight carriers supplement their earnings by escorting migrants on all or part of their journey. The practice of combining transport services for people and goods reflects the long-standing and profitable interdependence of trade and migration in the Sahara, but has now become less common because of tougher migration policies.

4.3 Overlapping Institutional Frameworks: Abstruseness and Patchiness Regarding Migrants' Rights

Analysis of legislation and policies on international migration reveals a tension between the concepts of state sovereignty and migrants' rights (Dauvergne 2008). At one level principles and norms deriving from the notion of state sovereignty - such as the right to protect national borders, to admit or refuse entry to foreign nationals - can be explained in terms of the

Figure 4.2: CEN-SAD and ECOWAS member states. **Source:** Brachet 2009.

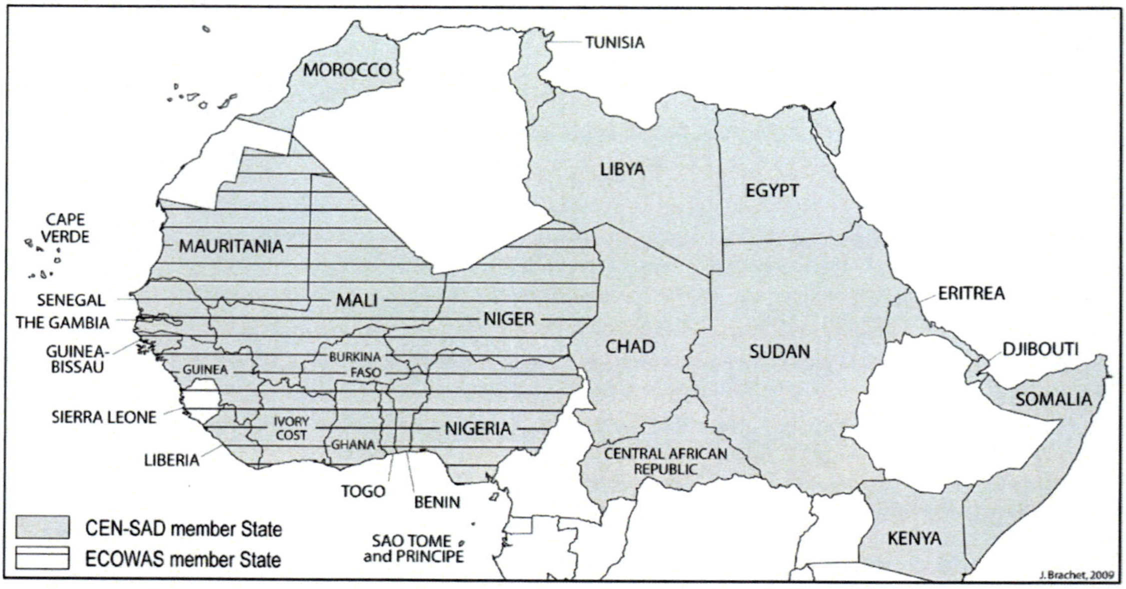

relations between states. At another level various international conventions recognize the rights of people who move across borders, yet the specific right to work and take residence, and other rights, are specified by a particular state according to the relationship it establishes with the migrant. The diversity of texts (laws or non-binding conventions) and the various levels of their applicability (national, bilateral or international) make interpretation of the rights of migrants extremely complex. This is certainly the case with the Central Saharan migration system, where various institutional and legal frameworks which protect migrants and govern international migration overlap.[4]

4.3.1 The Limited Efficiency of International Commitments

In addition to ratified UN conventions, Central Saharan governments have obligations in several supranational institutional frameworks concerned with migration. Being in the heartland of Saharan migration, Niger belongs to various inter-governmental organizations which aim to encourage free movement for nationals of member states, such as the Community of Sahel-Saharan States (CEN-SAD) and the Economic Community of West African States (ECOWAS).

Since first cited in the 1998 constitutional charter drafted in Syrte (birthplace of the Libyan president Mu'ammar Ghaddafi), the principle of free movement between CEN-SAD member states has been emphasized regularly. In 2000 the Libyan government temporarily abolished all visa requirements for nationals of member states who were employed in Libya. In 2007, however, visa requirements were re-established, with the exception of nationals from the Maghreb countries.[5] Even in times when migration from sub-Saharan Africa was tolerated or even encouraged, migrants were generally denied full legal status since Libyan authorities rarely legalized their arrival on Libyan territory. In this way the Libyan government attempted to maintain a minimum of legitimacy vis-à-vis its African partners, while deporting other foreigners by force. This fools no one however. After the deportation of several hundreds of his co-nationals, a Nigerien journalist noted "This radical deportation of sub-Saharans seriously questions Ghaddafi's interpretation of the African Union (UA) and the Community of Sahelo-Saharan countries".[6]

When the UN embargo against Libya was lifted in 1999 the Libyan government, in need of international respectability, found that the issue of migration could

4 For the UN and ILO conventions, see Truong (2007).

5 See at: <http://terra.rezo.net/article770.html> (30 March 2010); Delphne Perrin, 2008: "L'étranger rendu visible au Maghreb. La voie ouverte à la transposition des politiques juridiques migratoires européennes", in: *Asylon(s)*: 4.

6 See at: <www.republicain-niger.com>, in: *Le Républicain*, 7–13 October 2004 (30 March 2010).

Figure 4.3: Advertisement for the ECOWAS travel certificate. **Source:** <http://regionswatch.blogspot.com/2007_09_01_archive.html> (28 April 2010).

constitute an important stake in international negotiations. Border control and the deportation of illegal migrants have since become central elements in the relationship between Libya and the European Union. By agreeing to increase its border controls and to accept illegal migrants caught in Italy (who purportedly had travelled via Libya) Colonel Ghaddafi has officially recognized Libya as a transit country for sub-Saharan African migrants on their way to Europe, in exchange for considerable development aid. But, along with Morocco and Algeria, Libya refused to sign an agreement of re-admission proposed by the European Union in the name of all CEN-SAD member states.[7]

> We don't need a visa in Africa, we are at home here, we can travel just like that, like you in Europe, you can go from one country to the next with the Schengen visa (Congolese migrant, interviewed in Agadez, 15 April 2003).

Adepoju (2002) notes that while the principle of free movement proposed by the CEN-SAD remains an intention and not much else, the ECOWAS has implemented a protocol of free movement ratified by all its member states since 1979. This means that migrants can travel to and then through Niger all the way to the southern borders of Algeria and Libya without any administrative problems. However, irrespective of migrants' nationalities (ECOWAS member-states or non-member-states) and affiliated travel documents, the conditions of travel are the same for all: they can travel throughout Niger, but are illegally 'taxed' at every security checkpoint (Brachet 2009a). Thus, although all migrants state that it is *easy to travel without a visa* as there is no need for official papers to cross borders, they inevitably have to pay a 'tip' to get through the checkpoints. In other words, instead of paying a visa fee to the state, they pay a fee to border controllers. ECOWAS would like to see this reality change and has initiated, and advertised, a travel certificate (see figure 4.3).

In January 2008 the heads of ECOWAS states adopted a 'common approach to migration' to improve their management of migratory movements within and between regions. Largely inspired by the 2006 Euro-African meetings on migration and development held in Rabat and Tripoli and therefore influenced by the European representations of West African migrations, this text states that the fight against "illegal migration" is one of its main objectives.[8] Legal condemnation of individuals - based on their alleged intention - to pre-empt their actions is not only absurd but also overrides article 13.2 of the Universal Declaration of Human Rights stipulating that everyone has the right to leave any country, including their own. States apparently respect human rights only when they feel like it.

The combating of 'illegal migration' has since brought profound changes to ECOWAS policy on free movement, despite criticism of the notion used. ECOWAS no longer merely aims to facilitate free movement of people within its territory, but it now at-

7 See at: <www.panapress.com>, in: *Panapress*, 11 March 2009 (30 March 2010).

8 See at: <http://www.oecd.org/dataoecd/17/2/41400366.pdf> (30 March 2010).

tempts to control migration directed beyond this territory. West African elites have adopted European rhetoric and fear of migrants, thus no longer considering migration primarily as a means of development. They have instead agreed to participate in the fight against 'illegal migration' to Europe.

4.3.2 National Legal Frameworks and the Bilateral Links with EU Member States

National legal frameworks do not necessarily reflect the *de facto* migration policies of Saharan states; the gap between political discourses, international commitments, a nation's legislation and the active engagement of state representatives can be considerable. Recent legal reforms in Algeria and Libya reflect changed perceptions of, and reaction to, migration that are clearly different from the situation in Niger.

For several years legal changes in the Maghreb have been the result of a 'transposition' of European migration laws, and seem to correspond to Euro-Mediterranean agreements rather than to Sahelo-Saharan realities. Algeria, which is not part of the international organizations mentioned above, has long seen itself as exclusively a sending country. Foreigners can enter the national territory and travel freely after obtaining a standard consular visa. Although Algeria has, in reality, been battling illegal migration for several decades, the Algerian government established an official migration policy only in 2008 – drafting a convention that fixes the conditions of entry, stay and travel of foreign nationals, based on an ordinance from 1966 (Perrin 2009). This new legislation increases sanctions against illegal migrants and those who have helped them enter the country, live there, or leave it (Zeghbib 2009). A similar law was enacted in Libya in 2005 and was followed in 2007 by the obligation for all foreign nationals, apart from specific Arab countries, to obtain a visa. As a founding country and driving force of the CEN-SAD and an erstwhile proponent of Pan-African solidarity and free movement, Libya now takes active part in the general toughening of North African migration policies.

In Niger international migration is not considered a problem that needs to be solved, and no explicit policy on migration has developed. Legally, beyond the international agreements ratified by the government and implemented more or less successfully, only one law on the status of refugees deals with the presence of foreign nationals on the national territory (law 97-17 promulgated on 20 June 1997). There is, in fact, a lack of any migration policy or official guidelines, and a resistance of pressures exerted by the IOM and the EU to co-opt West African states in the fight against 'illegal migration' (allegedly towards Europe) in the way they successfully have co-opted North African governments (Brachet 2009b).

Yet the impact of state involvement in migration depends less on official policy than on the ways policy translates into practice. Thus, although Niger has no real migration policy (apart from specific interstate agreements on free movement), travel within the country depends on the good will of state security agents. In addition, the recent tightening of Algerian and Libyan migration policies hampers migration networks. These developments have changed the ways migrants can travel in the Sahara, especially across the southern borders of Algeria and Libya; 'illegal migration' has become more dangerous and risky there than in the southern Sahara.

4.4 Crossing Saharan Borders: From Unofficial to Clandestine Modes

4.4.1 Getting from Niger into Algeria: State Control, Migrants' Movements and Spatial Transformation

For many decades Algeria has been a country of seasonal migration for many people from the Sahel looking for employment in agriculture and construction – increasingly also now in other sectors. To a lesser number of sub-Saharans today, Algeria is nothing more than a station for on their way to Europe, but one which can easily become a country of retention for those who do not have the means or possibilities to continue further north. In their different forms, migrations to and through Algeria are a vital part of the current transformation of this country, and especially of the economic development of its Saharan regions, although unemployment is on the rise throughout the country and unskilled labour in little demand.[9]

Unofficial immigration, long limited to the south and hence of little concern to most Algerians, has attracted government attention since the early 1990's, leading to an inquiry by the National Bureau of Statistics – the results of which have remained unpublished (Spiga 2005: 88). When migrants started to travel and settle throughout the territory, the matter began to at-

9 Fargues, Philippe (Ed.), 2005: *Migrations méditerranéennes. Rapport 2005* (Florence: Institut Universitaire Européen, unpublished)

tract public attention, as to be seen in the national press (which often represents sub-Saharan migrants as the source of all evils). The reports indirectly led to outbursts of xenophobic violence, such as in Oran in September 2005 when local residents "took over the hotels used by Black Africans to 'send them home'. Their personal belongings were thrown out into the street and burned."[10]

Such outbursts of violence against foreigners by civilians fortunately remain exceptional. At the national level the Algerian government has had to cope for several years now with European pressures concerning the management of migratory flows. As a result, today the Algerian government approaches the question of migration as a problem and publicly states its readiness to fight against unofficial migration towards and through its territory.[11] Yet increased border controls and checks within the country have not stopped migration towards Algeria; it has merely changed the ways migrants attempt to cross the border.

For nationals of countries south of the Sahara, to obtain a visa in one of the Algerian consulates in those countries is virtually impossible. Those who attempt to do so in their country of origin or in the Algerian consulate in Agadez are questioned about the reasons for their journey, and have to show documents that are generally impossible to obtain (an official letter of sponsorship, or a hotel reservation, a bank statement, insurance and so forth). Further, if their application is successful, the visa granted only allows a short stay in Algerian territory. At the border post of *In Guezzam* generally only two kinds of migrants enter Algeria legally: students or professional athletes hosted by an Algerian university or club, and nationals of countries who have an agreement of free movement with Algeria, such as Guinea and Mali.

It is therefore the case that most migrants enter Algeria illegally. Until recently Algerian smugglers could bribe Algerian police officers in *In Guezzam* to take illegal migrants through on the official route. Today this is no longer possible. All illegal migrants have to cross the border secretly, relying on migration networks that take them directly from Agadez and Arlit to Tamanrasset or Djanet. It takes one or two days to reach Tamanrasset from Niger, depending on the place of departure and the route chosen. During the journey the migrants (who may be as many as 30 packed on each four-wheel-drive pick-up) hardly ever get off it. As the ground is flat for most of the way these trucks are easily seen even from far away, hence drivers prefer to avoid stopping even for food and/or rest. Trucks stop several kilometres before reaching their destination to unload their passengers who continue on foot.

The journey to Djanet takes longer, three to five days, and is more dangerous. Efforts by the Algerian government to stop illegal border crossings are concentrated in this region[12] and have been indirectly supported by the US as part of their fight against international terrorism in general but in particular against organizations present in the Central Sahara (such as Al-Qâ'ida in the Islamic Maghreb). There is a constant risk of breakdown, which can be lethal if the truck cannot be repaired immediately. As drivers rarely take the same route twice they cannot rely on another truck coming by, and they each only carry water for a few days. Hence most journeys on this route are undertaken in convoys.

> To go to Djanet, you never go on your own: you go through the desert and if a truck on its own breaks down there you are going to die. You need two or three cars...sometimes even ten Toyotas, loaded with foreigners (Tuareg people smuggler, Agadez, November 2004, author's interview).

Robbery and abandonment are other dangers specific to this route. Local robbers know that each day groups made of at least ten migrants of will travel through the area with enough money to finance their trip. All the robbers need do is wait at certain key points such as one of the few wells in the area. Robbers and smugglers sometimes collude in robbing the migrants at a predetermined place and share the loot. In these attacks passengers are robbed of all their money and objects of value (watches, jewellery), and sometimes are faced with violence. Yet most migrants finally do arrive at their destination. Their greatest danger is abandonment by their drivers in the desert. In fact certain drivers leave their passengers between the Aïr, the Ahaggar and the Tassilin Ajjer, telling them that within a couple of hours of walking they will reach Djanet. Although everyone involved in migration networks publicly condemned such behaviour, abandonment by drivers is not an exceptional occurrence.

10 *Le Quotidien d'Oran*, 6 September 2005.

11 Labdelaoui, Hocine, 2005: "Algérie: dimension politique et sociale des migrations", in: Fargues (see above).

12 *El Watan*, 20 April 2006.

4.4.2 Niger to Libya: Variations on the Theme of Illegality

Sub-Saharan migrants cross the border between Libya and Niger in ever-changing ways, depending on variations in Libyan migration policies. At times it is open, at times partly or totally closed. The Libyan authorities constantly modify the status of the border, to the point where transporters in the border area base their activities on concrete practical possibilities rather than on official decrees. Closure of the border between Libya and the Sudan in 2003 put an end to trans-border movement there (Drozdz/Pliez 2005). This is not the case for the Nigero-Libyan connection, where traffic has never stopped, even when the border was ostensibly closed.

There are few migrants who travel legally - that is to say those who own a passport with a Libyan visa. Most people who travel do not have the necessary documents. The Saharan migration networks have developed two ways of crossing the border that cope with the vacillations in Libyan migration policy. One is to bring migrants across the border on the official route, relying on the tolerance of the Libyan government and the possibility to corrupt border police in the Libyan border post at Tumo. The other is to bring them into Libya secretly, away from all official control points, until the intended destination. The human smuggling networks use one or the other way depending on whether the Libyan authorities declare the border closed or open. The status of the border does not alter the fact that illegal crossings do occur; it just alters the way they occur. Until the early 2000s closures never lasted long and most trans-border networks could rely on their social capital to function efficiently. At the times of prohibition during the later years, personal ties with border police can facilitate a crossing.

Since 2002 the Libyan government has decided to control its borders effectively, at first in exchange for Italian support when negotiating the end of the European arms embargo (hence allowing Libya sufficient weaponry to survey its borders), then more generally as part of Libya's return to international diplomacy. While it remains at times possible to negotiate with border police, their tolerance and readiness to 'be persuaded' has, however, clearly diminished. Fewer smugglers seem able to negotiate unofficial entry into Libya. Hence secrecy has become the cheapest and the most efficient way to carry out their lucrative business, but this is now riskier. In the absence of an agreement with the Libyan border police, any arrest results in imprisonment for drivers and passengers, with seizure of the truck and all the goods carried. As a result, many traders who used to carry both passengers and goods between Agadez and Sebha now concentrate on the haulage of goods from Niger to Libya. They rarely carry migrants, and then only those who have obtained the necessary paperwork, which they carefully check before departure. Passenger transport thus has become the domain of underground networks whose drivers know the terrain and its smuggling routes extremely well.

Libya, with its wealth derived from oil, needs foreign labour in order to carry out the large-scale development projects planned by the government, and also to staff various sectors of its economy (agriculture and construction in particular). Hence, while Libya negotiated its comeback to international diplomacy by accepting funds for increased border controls and retention camps for illegal migrants, the Libyan government had no qualms about openly encouraging labour migration from sub-Saharan Africa (Pliez 2004). Further signs of openness towards sub-Saharans include the publicity for the Libyan company Afriqiyah Airways, which links Tripoli and Benghazi with several African capitals, and the development of Pan-African organizations such as CEN-SAD. These contradictions in Libyan rhetoric and its practical application reveal Ghaddafi's ambiguous position towards migration, and the difficulty in defining an African policy after the embargo, independently of other geopolitical concerns.

In Morocco, Algeria, Tunisia and Libya the tightening of migration policies has led to a change in national legislation and stricter border controls and internal security checks; these make travel and life for sub-Saharan migrants more and more dangerous and expensive. Detention and deportation of migrants has become increasingly frequent, often in conditions so deplorable that they quash all basic principles of human rights whose advocate the European Union so passionately claims to be. The impact of these policies on curbing the number of migrants nonetheless remains rather limited. An analysis of migrations between Niger, Algeria and Libya shows rather that the routes and means chosen are adapted to the new circumstances, indicating the adaptability and dynamic nature of migration networks. Migrants continue to enter Libya and Algeria illegally, but increasingly also clandestinely. Local forms of tolerance - while diminishing in is varying degrees in both countries - indicate the need to take into account, in addition to the question of the necessary means for border surveillance, the willingness and interest displayed by local actors (political elites, state representatives, local residents) concerning the control and the restriction of trans-Saharan migrations.

Under pressure from their European neighbours, Libya and Algeria have accepted several types of aid in exchange for collaboration. Sporadic arrests and collective deportations seem to correspond to ways of 'managing' foreigners in their countries, despite various international conventions, rather than to an attempt to end migration altogether. In Libya even more than in Algeria, the flagrant contradictions in official rhetoric on migration (according to the moment and the interlocutor) show the country's ambiguous position vis-à-vis trans-Saharan migrations. They also indicate the difficulty Libya experiences in trying to reconcile international pressures with incompatible local histories, nationalist with Pan-African logics, economic with political interests, and a Euro-Mediterranean partnership based on the control of migrations with the construction of an African Union and areas of free movement within one continent.

4.5 The Central Sahara and the European Union: Security for Whom?

Recent Euro-African meetings dealing with unofficial migration between the two continents - involving at times representatives from dozens of countries and international organizations - have declared the Sahara a priority zone in the fight against unofficial African immigration. While it is true that some of the migrants arriving illegally in Spain, France or Italy have first crossed the Sahara, only a minority of those who travel through the Sahara continue all the way to Europe, and most move within this region for reasons related to their livelihoods. Regional migration has long been a way of dealing with economic and climatic insecurity in the region, while seasonal labour migration is central to the region's economy. Further, as we have seen, contemporary migrations are indispensable in local transport, trade and supply networks, and 'transit' migrants have, by the cheap labour they provide, become an important element in local economic growth. There is also the benefit of remittances to the communities of origins. The severe crisis that Niger experienced in 2005, for example, could be met locally by an enhanced regional seasonal labour migration that generated remittances, while decreasing temporarily the demand on local food resources (Oumarou 2008). While mobility has always been part of life in the area, migration within the Sahara is increasingly one of the many strategies of diversification necessary for survival in the Sahel belt. It has become the more significant since the political crises and subsequent economic breakdown in the Ivory Coast, the former regional pole of attraction.

The European and increasingly North African tendency to conflate all forms of human movement in the Sahara with migration aimed at Europe has a potentially devastating effect on the local economies, yet the control of unofficial immigration into Europe continues to be ineffective. Media and government reports or statistics of uncertain origins reinforce this tendency, thereby constructing an illusory 'threat of migration' which acts as a justification for restrictive migration policies and security measures, often under pressure from the EU. Foreigners from southern countries are construed as a problem, a risk or a menace. This is why Europe, to fight against illegal migration from sub-Saharan Africa, encourages the countries of North Africa - and, recently those of the Sahel - firmly to control or even put a stop to all migration in the region.[13] The EU position towards Saharan migrations contradicts its own principle of mobility within its own territory, by which the circulation of people is seen as a positive factor in its own process of cultural integration and economic development. By intervening beyond its own borders to control migratory movements into its territory the EU is disrupting entire intra-African migration systems: ones which have long been an important factor of economic development in Northwest Africa while historically of little concern to Europe.

4.6 Conclusion

Approaches to Saharan migration not based on careful empirical studies in the field can obscure both the infinite variation of migratory practices in the area as well as the role they play in human survival and livelihoods. Migration systems are inherently sensitive to political changes on all levels and require understanding the conjunction of international pressures, poli-

13 Comparing my own results with those of other researchers, and with official reports and media sources, we can estimate the total number of sub-Saharan Africans who enter Europe by maritime routes illegally in the low tens of thousands each year, at the most. This figure is very low in comparison with other migratory flows to Europe.

cies, local realities and contingencies, using an inductive method. In the Sahara regions of Niger migrations have led to the establishment of very active transport companies which function within internationalized networks. They are managed on the one hand by transport agents who might still be linked to trading elites who control modern forms of commerce, and on the other hand by people of nomadic tradition drawing on their technical expertise as travellers to act as guides or drivers. These movements revitalize both legal and illegal trade; they also give new life to other kinds of activities such as accommodation and telecommunications, and transform local labour markets with a supply of cheap labour. Through these economic activities, both formal and informal, and through the fees migrants pay to local state representatives, migrants import hard currency into the regional economy of Agadez, to an amount which has been estimated at several billion francs CFA annually (Brachet 2009a). It is vital to understand migration as an essential and constitutive part of local economies. Should migratory flows change direction, or borders be definitively closed, these positive effects could cease. Intensification of migrations within the Sahara in recent years has, though, been accompanied by toughened migration policies in North Africa and by an increase in the number of checkpoints on Saharan routes. The representation of the open and unlimited space of free men of the desert constructed by travel agencies does not reflect the current reality. The Sahara is actually becoming increasingly 'broken up', finely combed by the various surveillance systems which hinder free movement, making it more expensive and dangerous, slowing it down and even sometimes putting a stop to it. The 'breaking up' of Saharan space is the result of a remodelling and the multiplication of actively-controlled borders; these may be stable or temporary, mere points or lines or whole zones, and fixed in a 'space' which is mobile. Borders that are now being opened to let through material and immaterial goods are increasingly being closed to inhabitants of the poorest countries, thereby officially putting most inhabitants of the sub-Saharan region 'under house arrest'.

5 Europeanization and the Right to Seek Refugee Status: Reflections on Frontex

Wies Maas and Thanh-Dam Truong

5.1 Introduction

Since the end of the Cold War, relations between immigration politics and national security have undermined the continuing validity of the 1951 Refugee Convention in different parts of the world.[1] In the European Union (EU), the effects of the abolishment of internal borders since the Schengen Agreement in 1985 have fostered a linkage between migration and security politics, amplified also by unanticipated external pressures. Efforts to harmonize policy in the domain of migration and asylum within an enlarged EU have produced a hybrid system with blurred competences, opt-outs, and a different status for new member states. Furthermore, the creation of Frontex in 2005 has raised concerns about the legitimacy of extra-territorial border control, amongst many other issues.[2]

Frontex may be seen as the outcome of a re-balancing of powers between the member states, the Council and the Commission that has shifted the coordination of operational activity from an intergovernmental approach under the authority of the Council to that of the Community or a supranationalist approach (Neal 2009). Frontex seems to embody the persistent tension between these approaches to EU integration. At the time of writing, Frontex lacks its own operational power and relies on the consent of member states for all its activities.

The lack of consensus on adequate standards for border and pre-border controls - such as identifying asylum-seekers along EU borders and ensuring access to asylum procedures, deciding on where asylum-seekers should be disembarked when intercepted, and who should be responsible for the examination of asylum claims - means that border control operations are inevitably controversial from a human rights perspective. Frontex joint interception operations at sea since 2006 in the Atlantic (Hera), the central Mediterranean region (Nautilus) and the Western Mediterranean area (Poseidon) remain the most contentious tasks. Apart from the principle of *non-refoulement* that obliges states not to divert ships carrying people who seek asylum, international maritime rules also forbid a ship's captain from ignoring calls for rescue. The failure to agree on adequate human right standards for border and pre-border control modalities means that member states run the risk of violating the European Convention on Human Rights (Weinzierl 2008) and can also be vulnerable to critique of state-led group profiling and racism (Bunyan 2010).

This chapter places Frontex within the broader process of Europeanization and illustrates how its emergence manifests the evolution of thinking and manoeuvres behind EU policies on immigration that gradually undermines the validity of the Refugee Convention despite formal commitments by all member states. Frontex may be symptomatic of this wider process and in many ways has taken on the flaws inherent in the process of European integration itself. We will first explain how the right to seek refugee status has been compromised in the process of Europeanization. Next we will illustrate the process through which this compromise has emerged, was negotiated and enacted, giving birth to Frontex as an institutional reality. The remainder of the chapter will offer a perspective on the nature of Europeanization as a process and its outcome, drawing particularly upon Philippe Schmitter's identification of the dichotomy between transformative and reproductive approaches to Euro-

---

1 The 1951 United Nations Convention Relating to the Status of Refugees, is commonly known as the Refugee Convention. The recent EU documents concerning this Convention use the term, Geneva Convention.

2 Frontex is the European Agency for the Management of Operational Cooperation at the External Borders of the member states of the EU, by Council Regulation (EC) 2007/2004 (26.10.2004, OJL 349/25.11.2004).

T.-D. Truong and D. Gasper (eds.), *Transnational Migration and Human Security*, Hexagon Series on Human and Environmental Security and Peace 6, DOI 10.1007/978-3-642-12757-1_5, pean integration to explain the emergence of Frontex as an unfolding reality.

5.2 Europeanization of Immigration Policy and its Effects on the Right to Seek Refugee Status

The concept of Europeanization is used by scholars seeking to move beyond the one-dimensional concept of European integration as 'communitarization' or harmonization. Despite its popularity the definition of 'Europeanization' remains contested. Originally, the term was adopted to analyse the influence of EU Community Laws and supranational directives[3] on the institutional structures and policies of the various member states. Although this perspective is still the dominant approach in the literature (Faist/Ette 2007; Olsen 2002), the breadth of the term has been extended to denote a variety of changes within European politics, describing a multi-facetted process that is "variously affecting actors and institutions, ideas and interests" (Featherstone 2003: 3) across and beyond the EU. The meaning of Europeanization in its most minimalist sense is the responses to, and effects of, European integration and policies developed at the level of the European Community (Featherstone 2003). This definition appears appropriate for our analysis, which focuses mainly on the change of rules in governmental attempts to harmonize immigration policy at EU level and how they affect refugee and asylum policy.

The right to seek refugee status (or to claim asylum) itself can be inferred from the 1951 Refugee Convention to which all EU member states are party. To prevent *refoulement* as a core principle of the Convention, this right entails that anyone presenting him or herself at, or within, the borders of a particular country as someone seeking asylum due to political persecution should be granted a fair procedure of determination on an individual basis without the threat of return, or rejection before entry. Asylum seekers might however be transferred to a safe third country provided they will be granted the possibility to lodge a claim for asylum in that third country (Goodwin-Gill 1985; Rijpma/Cremona 2007).

The application of the Refugee Convention in the EU territory was far from uniform, embedded as it has been in member states' particular histories and politics, plus the fact that it is also bound by the principle of national sovereignty. A wide variance has existed insofar as the interpretation of the definition of a refugee is concerned. Harmonizing its application implies the major challenge of reducing disparities between member states' legislation and practices. A driving force behind the harmonization of migration and refugee policies has been the removal of systematic border controls between member states, while simultaneously strengthening them with non-members. The process of border removal and the subsequent harmonization of asylum and migration polices has gone through several stages of modification, moving gradually from an intergovernmental mode of cooperation, to attempts to create a Common European Asylum System at the supranational level. The different stages of Europeanization in the area of asylum and migration revealed the ongoing tension between state sovereignty and European integration, reflecting a fractured process.

The first stage of harmonization began with the Schengen Agreement signed in 1985;[4] the transformative stage with the Treaty of Amsterdam in 1997 and beyond. The first step of implementation of the Agreement was the Gradual Abolition of Checks at the Common Borders of signatory countries. In parallel, an Ad Hoc Working Group on Immigration was formed in 1986 and created the 1990 Dublin Convention in an attempt to harmonize asylum policies in the EU, beyond the signatories of the 1985 Agreement. This convention seeks to avoid two types of situations: the shuttling of refugees from one member state to another, and multiple or simultaneous applications. It ensures that every application for asylum is examined by a member state and requires in principle that individuals make their application for asylum in the first EU country they enter. Although the Schengen area has come to represent a territory with common application of some rules and procedures with regards to visas, asylum requests and border controls, not all countries cooperating in Schengen are parties, either because they do not wish to eliminate border controls or because they do not yet fulfil the required conditions.[5]

3 EU Community Law is also known as *Acquis communautaire*. This includes all the treaties, regulations and directives passed by the European institutions as well as the rulings of the Court of Justice.

4 Five of the then ten member states of the European Community (Belgium, France, Luxembourg, the Netherlands and West Germany) signed this Agreement.

The introduction of a number of Treaties (Maastricht 1992, Amsterdam 1997, Nice 2001, Lisbon 2009) gradually altered the decision making structure within the EU. The Treaty of Maastricht (1992) created a single market with free movement of goods, persons, services and capital, under a three-pillar structure of decision-making. The first pillar - the European Community - is the only supranational one. It deals mainly with economic integration and related social and environmental policies. The second pillar deals with EU's external relations under the name of Common Foreign and Security Policy. The third pillar focuses on *Justice and Home Affairs* (JHA) where asylum and immigration reside. The Treaty excluded one category from the free-movement-mantra: refugees. "Thus an exception to the logic of territorial integration [was] created out of the bodies of refugees" (Guild 2006: 637).

Under the Treaty of Amsterdam (1997) mandated to create an area of "freedom, security and justice" for citizens of member states, decision-making on the movements of third-country nationals into, and within, EU territory shifted from the third to the first pillar under Title IV on Visas, Asylum and Immigration. In this shift, the two pre-existing initiatives at European level in this field - the Schengen Agreement and the Dublin Convention - became Community Laws.[6] The third pillar received a new name: Police and Justice Cooperation in Criminal matters.

The difference between the first and the other two pillars lies primarily in the mode of decision-making. The first pillar is characterized by the supranational principle, according to which member states partly transferred their sovereignty in decision-making to the Community level, whereas decisions in the other two pillars are predominantly intergovernmental and enacted based on voting by unanimity. The powers of the European Parliament, the Commission and the European Court of Justice in these two pillars are limited. The 1999 Tampere Programme set out policy guidelines and practical objectives for the progressive implementation of the Treaty, including agreements on minimum standards to be decided upon by unanimity.

5 The Schengen area now covers nearly all EU member-states, with the exception of the United Kingdom and Ireland, Bulgaria, Cyprus and Romania, see at: <http://ec.europa.eu/youreurope/nav/en/citizens/travelling/schengen-area/index_en.html> (30 March 2010).

6 In practice, this shift makes Asylum and Immigration a cross-pillar issue since member states increasingly turn to third country solutions.

Despite the repeated reaffirmation of the commitments to the protection of refugees in documents of EU institutions, human rights organizations are accusing "European governments and institutions [...to] continue to scale back rights protections for asylum seekers and migrants" (McKleever/Schultz/Swithern 2005: 14). Scholars have extensively covered the scaling back of protection as permeated through EU policy developments (Lavenex 2004; Lavenex/Uçarer 2004; Da Lomba 2004; Guild 2006; Rijpma/Cremona 2007; van Selm 2005). They have noted three key trends: 1) impeding access to EU territory, 2) impeding access to the process of fair determination, and 3) externalization of border control.

An examination of some key directives of the European Council that affect the right to seek asylum shows that major compromises had been made at the EU level.[7] The Visa-Regulation ((EC) 539/2001), for example, lists the countries whose nationals must be in possession of visas when crossing the external borders, and those whose nationals are exempted from that requirement. It is a case-by-case approach to the assessment of a variety of criteria relating inter alia to illegal immigration, public policy and security, and to the European Union's external relations with third countries. Article 1, Clause 7 on stateless persons and recognized refugees allows member states to decide whether these categories of persons shall be subject to the visa requirement or not; exemption should be based on the third country in which these persons reside and which issued their travel documents. Persons in need of international protection are in the worst position for obtaining these kinds of documents (Tekofsky 2006: 11). Visa requirements are not a breach of international refugee law per se, but do make it more difficult for those trying to seek protection.

7 This chapter examined treaties, policies, conclusions and other EU documents published up till October 2009. In 2008–2009, several relevant developments have taken place that require further analysis such as: Judgment of the European Court of Justice, 6 May 2008, C-133/06. European Parliament v. Council of the European Union; Return Directive (Directive 2008/115/EC, 16 December 2008); European Pact on Immigration and Asylum (adopted by the European Council, 15–16 October 2008, document 13440/08); Stockholm Programme (adopted by the Council, 10–11 December 2009); Treaty of Lisbon (entered into force 1 December 2009); Frontex External Evaluation of the European Agency for the Management of Operational Cooperation at the External Borders of the Member States of the European Union, by COWI, January 2009.

In addition to visa requirements, the Schengen Agreement already imposed penalties on carriers that bring in aliens without proper identification papers and are refused entry by obliging them to assume responsibility by returning the individuals concerned either to the home country or to a third country. To supplement this provision, the Council adopted a directive (2001/51/EC) that lays down provisions for obligations on carriers transporting passengers into the territory of member states. The directive also sought to harmonize financial penalties currently provided for by member states in cases where carriers fail to meet their obligations (e.g. when the carrier refuses to take the alien back on board or the state of destination refuses entry and has the alien sent back). Taking into account the differences in legal systems and practices between member states, the fines for failure to control the validity of travel documents and visas adequately now vary between Euros 3,000 and Euros 5,000 per person, or a single fine of 500,000 € without taking into account the number of persons carried.[8]

In effect, this regulation implies the devolving of responsibility of border control to private agents, although the directive mentions that its application is without prejudice to the obligations resulting from the 1951 Convention and that fines shall not be imposed if third country nationals seek international protection. McKleever and colleagues (2005: 38) point out that carriers' personnel are "unlikely to be trained in refugee law, and are certainly unaccountable for their actions under international law". Thus, while the intention of the penalty rule may be a mechanism to pre-empt entries without valid documents, it can have the effect of violating the principle of non-refoulement, particularly when carriers are returning third country persons in need of protection without them having had access to procedures for asylum application.

Although individual EU member states already started to introduce both visa policies and carrier sanction practices in the 1980's and early 1990's, it was through the process of Europeanization that these practices became binding upon all Member States, and therefore limited room for more liberal practices at national levels with regards to visa systems or the non-application of fines for carriers (Da Lomba 2004). The combined effect of visa requirements and carrier sanctions make it difficult for asylum seekers to enter the EU through regular channels, forcing them to resort to dangerous and illegal forms of travel.[9]

In addition to restricted access to EU territory, other policies can jeopardize access to a fair determination procedure. For instance, Article 7 (1(b)) in the Qualification Directive (2004/83/EC) - on the minimum standards for the qualification and status [of third country nationals or stateless persons as refugees or as persons who otherwise need international protection] and the content of the protection granted - refers to "parties or organisations, including international organisations, controlling the State or a substantial part of the territory of the State" as potential actors for protection. Given that "quasi-state entities controlling part of a territory are often, by their very nature, temporary and unstable" (McKleever/Schultz/Swithern 2005: 22), to recognize them as "potential actors for protection" can imply sending asylum seekers back to such places under the safe-third country principle. Furthermore, the two positive additions in the directive [persecution of a gender-specific nature (art.9.2(f)) and non-state actors as possible agents of persecution (art.6(c)] contain no specification on fair procedures of determination of persecution or on guarantees of access to a territory within the EU once such determination is established. These are left to national legislatures.

The Council Directive 2005/85/EC of 1 December 2005 [on Minimum Standards on Procedures in member states for Granting and Withdrawing Refugee Status] introduces the safe third country, which entails that an asylum seeker is denied a substantive determination procedure if the person in question has travelled through a country deemed 'safe', where he could have applied for refugee protection. The application of the safe third country concept is not in breach with refugee law, as long as a proper assessment is undertaken as to whether the third country concerned is indeed safe. The directive goes further by granting member states the possibility *not to examine an application at all* in case of a *super-safe third country*. The idea that a country can be deemed safe for anyone is contentious, and safe places might become unsafe overnight. The directive does not provide for the obligation to conduct regular updates on the safety of a third country. More importantly, the principle of a 'safe third country' also leads to the 'externalization'

8 See at: <http://www.statewatch.org/news/2003/jun/03spain.htm> (30 January 2010).

9 See at: <http://www.statewatch.org/analyses/crimes-of-arrival.pdf > (15 Oct 2009); Webber, Frances, 1996/2000: "Crimes of Arrival: Immigrants and Asylum-seekers in the New Europe".

of migratory pressure on neighbouring countries with limited resources and less developed asylum systems (Post/Niemann 2007).

Perhaps the most significant development has been the creation of Frontex, which reflects the externalization of refugee protection on the one hand (by impeding access to EU-territory and/or procedures), and a democratic deficit on the other (given the limited role of the European Court of Justice, the European Parliament and national parliaments of individual Member States). Frontex website describes its raison d'être as the integration of "national border security systems of member states against all kinds of threats that could happen at, or through, the external borders of the member states". The agency carries out risk analysis and research, and is responsible for both establishing common training standards for national border guards and providing support to joint return operations. All joint-operations are based on risk assessments, which describe (among other issues) "the roots, routes, modus operandi, patterns of irregular movements, conditions of the countries of transit, statistics of irregular flows and displacement" (Carrera 2007: 14). Yet the substance of those assessments remains hidden from the public (for reasons related to the risk of being adversely used by human smuggling and trafficking networks, not to mention other actors).

These joint return operations as well as the (interception) operations at sea[10] in particular pose problems for the protection of the right to seek refugee status. The joint-return competence, through which Frontex provides assistance in the transfer of presumably illegal immigrants back to their country of origin or a transit country, "is the most widely discussed assignment of the Agency, especially as regards human rights, the increasing number of expulsions and the lack of common EU policy in immigration and asylum" (Jorry 2007: 17–18). The lack of a Common European Asylum System (CEAS)[11] makes joint-return operations controversial because there is no possibility for verifying: 1) whether there are asylum seekers among these 'illegal migrants'; 2) if there were, whether asylum seekers have been put through a fair process; 3) whether some authority has determined the status of a safe country.

Interception operations at sea, which Frontex coordinates, have been most visible. These operations can occur either in the territorial waters of a member state of the EU, in the open sea, or in the territorial waters of a third state. Their purpose is to discourage immigrants from setting off in the first place. In the case of vessels having already set out to sea, the joint forces of Frontex attempt to intercept them in the territorial waters of a third country in cooperation with that state, and transport them back; mostly to African shores. Only if vessels have already passed the 24-mile zone and find themselves in international waters, are they guided to the nearest EU territory to grant asylum seekers the ability to make an asylum claim (Carrera 2007; Jorry 2007). These interceptions in the territorial waters of third states can be regarded as preemptive action in the domain of migration, and in effect, they can also prevent people in need of asylum from leaving a country.

Bilateral agreements between the main countries involved are required for these joint operations to take place in territorial waters of third countries. The actual substance of these bilateral agreements remains closed to the public (Carrera 2007; Rijpma/Cremona 2007), making these operations appear dubious. For example, a UNHCR official commented, "difficult situations may arise out on the high seas and it is difficult to tell what is going on in interception operations"[12] (see also Kopp 2007; Jorry 2007). When asked about the fate of refugees who might be targeted by these kinds of operations, the director of Frontex, Mr. Laitinen, responded: "Refugees? They aren't refugees, they're illegal immigrants".[13] Frontex reports mainly on how many people are intercepted, diverted or sent back. No information is released on the identity of those who have not been sent back. Until recently, asylum-seekers were simply non-existent in its vocabulary.

It is remarkable that an organization that deals with border management - thus inevitably also with those fleeing political persecution, violence and conflict - until recently made no reference to asylum seekers, refugees or member states' obligations under the Refugee Convention. Until very recently its regula-

10 Frontex tasks are not limited to operations at sea, but include any area of border protection including airports and land-borders.

11 For more information on CEAS see: Ferguson Sidorenko, Olga, 2007: *The Common European Asylum System* (The Hague: T.M.C Asser Press).

12 See at: <http://www.europeanvoice.com/archive/article.asp?id=27753>, 2 November 2009; Crosbie, Judith, 2007: "Frontier Agency Keeps Migrants in its Sights", in: *European Voice*, 13, 13 (4 April 2007).

13 See at: <http://www.goethe.de/ins/sn/dak/ges/en2081562.htm>, 2 Nov 2009; Kopp, Karl, 2007: "Rights on the Edge - The EU's Common Asylum Policy".

tions, website and the evaluation of the joint operations reflected this gap. As Rijpma and Cremona (2007: 20) note, the EU appears to be "erecting a 'Berlin wall on water' to control its border while removing it from public scrutiny". An external evaluation of Frontex conducted by a European consulting firm (registered as COWI) reveals that the budget of the agency has increased remarkably in its relatively short existence – from more than 6.2 million in 2005 to more than 70.4 million Euros in 2008. The total budget for 2008 was about twice that of 2007 and four times that of 2006, the first full operational year. Controlling at sea absorbed about 62 per cent of the total.[14] In an attempt to prevent unauthorised immigration to the EU, the movement of those in need of asylum is also being curbed.

Public pressure led to gradual changes. In 2007, Frontex invited UNHCR to establish an institutional form of cooperation for the training of border guards (UNHCR 2007b). In addition, the original Frontex Regulation was amended by the RABIT-Regulation ((EC) 853/2007). Article 1 of this Regulation establishes Rapid Border Intervention Teams (RABIT) to provide operational assistance to a member state in urgent cases, such as the arrival of large numbers of third-country nationals. Notwithstanding the implications of such RABIT-teams, Article 2 includes that it "shall apply without prejudice to the rights of refugees and persons requesting international protection". However, Frontex has not made clear anywhere how the protection of refugees is to be made operational and has restricted the amount of public information available. It is difficult, therefore, to check whether safeguards for asylum-seekers are really in place (ECRE 2007; ILPA 2007). The European Council meetings of 18/19 June and of 29/30 October 2009, underlined the need to strengthen Frontex's coordination of operations and the need for clear rules of engagement for joint patrolling, including rules on disembarkation of rescued persons. The meetings also stressed that when conducting a border surveillance operation, member states are obliged to observe specifically cited international laws.[15]

In sum, EU policymaking – through visa requirements, carrier sanctions, the embedding of the safe-third country rule and in particular the creation of Frontex – has raised fundamental questions for the protection of the right to seek refugee status to which all member states have expressed commitment. Understanding the process leading up to the creation of Frontex is important to develop new insights on the nature of Europeanization itself.

5.3 The Making of Frontex in the Europeanization of Immigration Policy

Da Lomba (2004: 36) suggests that, in principle, there are three reasons why the transfer of competences regarding matters of immigration to the first pillar might help facilitate the adoption of appropriate measures and ensure their application in line with international refugee and human rights law. First, being supranational this pillar provides a larger role for bodies that have expressed concern about the protection of the right to seek refugee status: the European Commission and the European Parliament. Second, the supranational role of the Community can ensure a more effective system as it can impose more stringent obligations and constraints on the member states, provided that European Union standards in the field of asylum comply with international refugee and human rights law. Third, the European Court of Justice – entrusted under this pillar with the competence to check member states on their implementation and interpretation of legislation adopted by the European Council – reinforces the stringent nature of legislation.

Yet, the process of Europeanization in the field of migration asylum seems to have worked to the detriment of refugee protection. This requires an explanation for underlying forces that have driven the process of Europeanization in this particular field. Scholars have identified various dynamics in this process of Europeanization of immigration policy that may help shed some light on the detrimental outcome of the process in terms of refugee protection. These are: voting by unanimity; downward harmonizing; the lack of public scrutiny; the accession of new member-states; and externalization.

14 See at: <http://www.statewatch.org/news/2009/may/Frontex-eval-report-2009.pdf>, 26–27, 29 January 2010.

15 The United Nations Convention on the Law of the Sea, the International Convention for the Safety of Life at Sea, the International Convention on Maritime Search and Rescue, the United Nations Convention against Transnational Organized Crime and its Protocol against the Smuggling of Migrants by Land, Sea and Air, the Convention relating to the Status of Refugees, the European Convention on Human Rights and other relevant international instruments. See: Council of the European Union, 5323/1/10 REV 1, Brussels, 21 January 2010.

Qualified Majority Voting (QMV)[16] is the normal method of decision-making by the European Council under the first pillar, which, in principle, should minimize the need for compromise and thus often speeds up the decision-making process at the intergovernmental level. However, the transfer of asylum and immigration policies to the first pillar, the supranational level, has involved a transitional period. Notwithstanding the fact that transitional periods are relatively common in the European integration process, it is important to note that for the first time unanimity prevailed in the first pillar and that the shift to QMV was conditional on the prior adoption of minimum standards at the supranational level (Lavenex 2001). The role of both the Commission and the European Parliament in human rights enhancement was therefore temporarily sidelined. The fact that national ministers, who approve decisions in Council, have to be accountable to their national parliaments counterbalanced this lack of democratic control at the supranational level.

The shift to QMV took place in December 2005, one year after the creation of Frontex by Council Regulation (EC) 2007/2004 (26.10.2004, OJL 349/25.11.2004) and six years after the introduction of the Tampere Programme, and during the first year of European enlargement. The conservation of the voting by unanimity rule carried the risk that "the foundations of a common European asylum system [would] endorse the lowest standards in force in the Union, thus threatening compliance with international law" (Da Lomba 2004: 43). This mode of decision-making is often said to have led to the adoption of the lowest common denominator, because all states need to accept the proposed legislation (Van Selm 2005; Lavenex 2001). Indeed many authors have commented that the adoption of such standards "has helped limit liberal regimes in traditional refugee receiving countries" (Lavenex 2001: 861).

No systematic analysis exists on the development of national asylum and immigration policies in member states since the abolition of internal borders. Available evidence seems to support the claim of downward harmonization. For example, France and Germany, arguably the driving forces behind cooperation in asylum matters, and certainly the most influential states, both made amendments to their constitution restricting their asylum system during the 1990's (Faist/Ette 2007; Post/Niemann 2007).[17] The disappearance of internal borders has been cited as a factor leading to de facto harmonization, as states begin to emulate each other's practices (Da Lomba 2004; Guild 2006; McKleever/Schultz/Swithern 2005; Post/Niemann 2007). In both countries "the advocates of restrictive reforms managed to reframe the domestic asylum problem into one of negative redistribution in a 'porous' *Europe passoire*" (Lavenex 2001: 862).

With the creation of Frontex a democratic deficit arose: national parliaments of most member states are not involved in decision-making and the European Parliament is left out in all matters except the approval on its budget (Rijpma/Cremona 2007). The matter of different status being assigned to the new EU-member states is also an issue. The ten new states that acceded to the Union in 2004[18] and the two in 2007[19] were obliged to adopt the full *Acquis* and to participate in Frontex, whereas others had had the opportunity to opt-out.[20] Central and Eastern European Countries (CEEC) had never been major refugee receiving countries, and did not have well-developed asylum systems; but they were seen as important transit countries for asylum seekers trying to make their way to Western Europe. For some of the EU-15 it was therefore critical that the new member states adhere to the same restrictive standards they did in order to prevent immigrants and refugees penetrating the EU through porous Eastern borders (Jorry 2007; Webber 1996). In one respect the accession of these new member states was positive, because they were required to sign the Refugee Convention and the European Convention on Human Rights. Given that most of the policies adopted at a European level were of a

16 *Qualified majority voting* (QMV) is a system of voting in the Council, which requires a decision to receive a set number of votes (each member state has a certain number of votes, weighted broadly based on population). The decision must be agreed by a majority of members.

17 For case studies on the domestic impact of Europeanization on immigration and asylum systems, see Faist and Ette (2007), e.g. on Germany, Poland and the UK. The proposition of downwards harmonization calls for further inquiry.

18 Malta, Cyprus, Slovenia, Estonia, Latvia, Lithuania, Poland, Czech Republic, Slovakia, Hungary

19 Romania and Bulgaria

20 Another anomaly of the communitarization process is the opt-outs of the UK, Ireland and Denmark. These opt-outs are not absolute. The UK and Ireland can decide to opt-in into immigration and asylum measures. Ireland and Denmark can also unilaterally decide to renounce the Protocol. The effect of these opt-outs on refugee protection is not self-evident.

restrictive nature the asylum systems in the new member states could likewise not be other than restrictive.[21]

As we have seen, the enlargement of the EU eastward was accompanied by a shift in Visas, Asylum and Immigration policies from an inter-governmentalist approach to EU level in 2005 given that decisions are now made through QMV. Although this mode could minimize the need for compromises at the lowest common denominator, it is not a guarantee by itself for higher standards of refugee protection. QMV could well work to the detriment of refugee protection if the preferences of larger member states are in favour of stringent asylum policies; unanimity can also be used to prevent stricter collective action. According to Antoniou, QMV "will only facilitate the adoption of acts satisfying the majority of the bigger states like Germany, France, Spain and UK. What would help is efficient judicial control on policies of the EU and a role for the European Parliament".[22]

Furthermore since the process of Europeanization has also led to the framing of asylum and migration as external relations issues, member states have tried to deal with such issues through third-country channels by using the inter-governmental second pillar. Several authors note that these practices have rapidly developed into a shift of responsibility for asylum seekers to third countries (even within the EU) as the most important aspect of a "common refugee policy" (Rijpma/Cremona 2007; Lavenex/Uçarer 2004). This externalization of asylum and migration issues is particularly apparent in the set-up of Frontex and its responsibilities. The interception operations in the waters of third countries coordinated by the agency can be seen as symptomatic for the externalization of the responsibility over asylum seekers, as these operations curb the mobility of asylum seekers and place a burden on these third states (Carrera 2007).

Incomplete Europeanization appears to have led not only to the introduction of restrictive asylum systems in new members states, but also to instances that could be called de-Europeanization, "where the preferences of the national government are in contradiction to the development of European immigration policy" (Faist/Ette 2007: 18). The Dublin system is a case in point. The Dublin Regulation ((EC) 343/2003) provides for rules to determine which state is responsible for dealing with an asylum application, while simultaneously preventing multiple applications in several member states. Article 10 of Regulation states that the member state through which the asylum seeker entered the territory irregularly will be responsible for its application. As asylum seekers have hardly any possibility to obtain access to the EU legally, entry into the EU will usually be irregular. Thus, these provisions place a disproportionate responsibility on states at the external borders of the Union, leading to a redistribution of asylum seekers by default (Lavenex 2001). "What Italy and Malta call a 'European' problem has, thanks to this regulation, reverted to being clearly their national problem [...] in some senses this is a paradoxical and counter-intuitive result of deepening European integration" (Van Selm/Cooper 2006: 47, 59).

In the absence of European burden-sharing mechanisms, border-states have started to make their own arrangements to relieve their disproportionate burden. A case in point is Italy. This country has independently sought to sign readmission agreements with various Maghreb states, most strikingly with Libya, a non-party country to the Refugee Convention without a functioning asylum system (Baldwin-Edwards 2006). Sending back to Libya people categorized as 'illegal' immigrants prior to the process of determination could result in *refoulement,* as evidenced by the case of Lampedusa in October 2004 when "Italy returned 1.000 people, without allowing them to claim asylum, to Libya, which in turn deported them to Egypt and Nigeria" (Schuster 2005: 12). Similar reports surfaced in Spain and Malta (see van Selm/Cooper 2006[23]; McKleever/Schultz/Swithern 2005).

Since December 2005 the European Parliament (upon initiatives of the Commission) has enjoyed the right of co-decision; but does not have the right to initiate new legislation. The right of the European Court of Justice remains circumscribed, given that it can only make a ruling when a case is pending before a court of a member state against whose decisions there is no judicial appeal under its national law. As the historical institutionalist school asserts, an institution and "its" decisions are "sticky" (Pollack 2005: 20-

21 A case in point is Poland, where the amendments of the Alien Act in 2001 and 2003 enshrined European immigration policies, like temporary residence permits, carrier sanctions and the safe third country concept. For analysis, see Faist and Ette (2007).

22 See Theofania Antoniou: "The Communitarisation of the Asylum Policy: a Ticket to Enhanced Human Rights Protection?", 30 June 2003; at: <http://www.cafebabel.co.uk/article/484/the-communitarisation-of-the-asylum-policy-a-ticket-to-enhanced-human-rights-protection.html > (5 November 2009).

23 See at: <http://www.migrationpolicy.org/pubs/Boat_People_Report.pdf> (1 April 2010).

21). In this regard it might be difficult to overcome the minimal standards set in the years of unanimity voting in general and the foundations of Frontex in particular.

Nevertheless, European Parliament involvement in Frontex has already had some effect. The RABIT Regulation in July 2007 was one of the first pieces of co-decision legislation to be adopted under Title IV and positively specifies that the agency's operations should take into account refugee protection (Carrera 2007: 4). Yet democratic control remains limited: The European Parliament only has a say on the agency when the regulation needs to be amended, and in terms of the budget. It is therefore difficult to scrutinize the actions of the agency on behalf of member states. The Lisbon Treaty, which came into force in December 2009, increases the legislative power of the European Parliament and places it on an equal footing with the Council in the co-decision procedure, which has been extended to cover areas such as immigration.[24] Article 18 of the Charter of Fundamental Rights of the European Union (2007/C 303/01) guarantees the right to asylum 'with due respect for the rules of the Geneva Convention of 28 July 1951 and the Protocol of 31 January 1967 relating to the status of refugees and in accordance with the Treaty on European Union and the Treaty on the Functioning of the European Union'.[25]

5.4 Europeanization and Restrictive Asylum Policy: A Theoretical Reflection

The traditional debate on European integration has been between neo-functional spillover theories and intergovernmental state-centred explanations. A more recent debate focuses on policies rather than on the process of integration and sets social constructivist interpretations against rational choice theories. An even newer generation of EU integration theories argue that the intergovernmental state-centred perspective, especially, has neglected both the institutional setting and its (unintended) consequences. In an attempt to map various approaches to European integration, Philippe Schmitter clusters these theoretical orientations along the lines of a dichotomy between transformative and reproductive approaches. There are two defining dimensions that set neo-functionalism together with sociological institutionalism against (liberal) inter-governmentalism coupled with rational choice institutionalism; the former group being characterized as 'constructivist' and 'transformative', the latter as described as 'rationalist' and 'reproductive' (figure 5.1).[26]

Within the transformative group, both neo-functionalist and sociological institutionalist approaches presume that both "actors and the 'games they play' will change significantly in the course of the integration process" (Schmitter 2004: 47). The starting point of the neo-functionalist position is different from that of the constructivist in that the former starts from the rationalist assumption of utility-maximizing elites as the initial drive for integration, whereas the constructivist does not adhere to this. However, once integration has been set into motion, political spillover leads to convergence of socially constructed identities to the supranational level, leading to "some constitutive effect of European integration on the various societal and political actors" (Risse 2004: 162). Thus, both neo-functionalist and sociological institutionalist explanations revolve around the transformation and construction of European norms, beliefs and identities. Alternatively, they could also be branded actor-based approaches, as the driving forces for integration are the identities of the *actors* involved. One critique is that these actor-based approaches offer no explanation as to which or whose interests are involved in shaping and modifying this identity. These approaches lack a perspective on power.

In contrast, liberal inter-governmentalism and rational choice institutionalism start from the premise that integration "reproduces the existing characteristics of its member-state as participants and the inter-state system of which they are part" (Schmitter 2004: 47). In these approaches sovereign states remain the central actors, whose preferences determine the pace and outcome of the integration process. Obviously not every member state is in an equal position to determine this pace and outcome. Existing unequal power relations within the EU as a system of states mean that the integration process will be – by and large – determined by the interests of bigger and more powerful member states. From a rational institutionalist perspective, these existing power disparities be-

24 See at: <http://europa.eu/lisbon_treaty/glance/index_en.htm> (21 March 2010).

25 See at: <http://www.europarl.europa.eu/charter/pdf/text_en.pdf> (30 March 2010).

26 The diagram has been considerably simplified; for a full depiction and a thorough explanation see Schmitter (2004).

Figure 5.1: Theories of regional integration. **Source:** Schmitter (2004: 48).

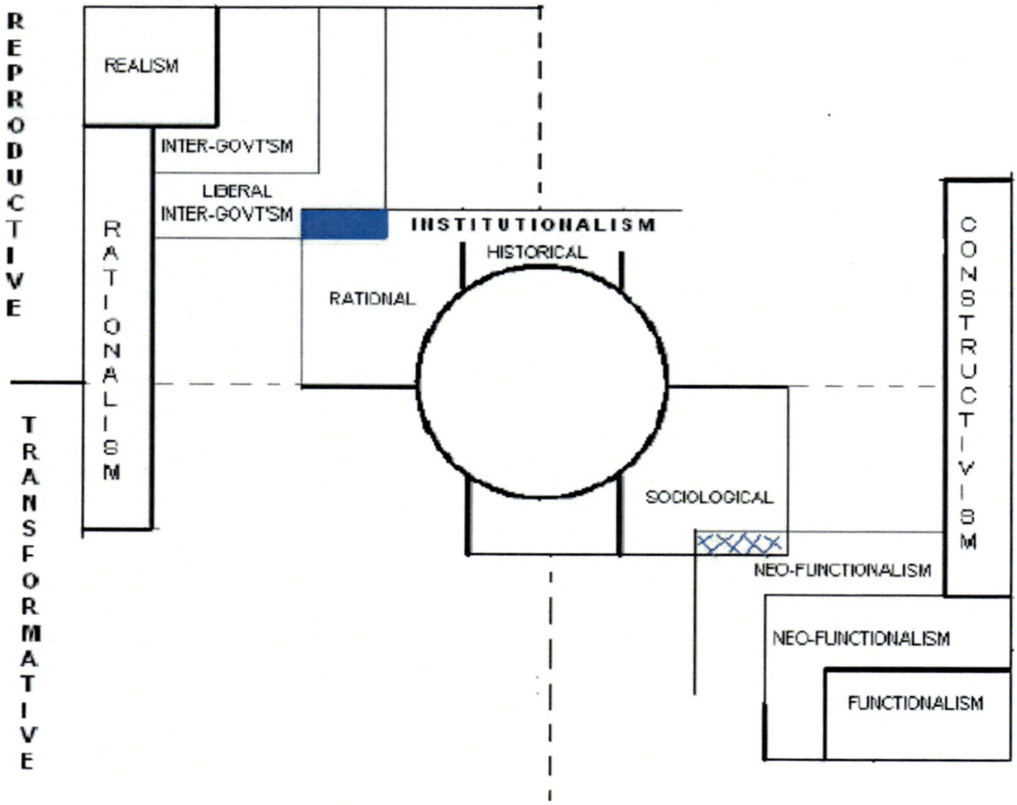

tween member states also tend to be reproduced in the institutions created at the European level, for example apparent in the relative weight that is given to each vote in the Council. In contrast to the actor-based approaches, this reproductive perspective is derived from a 'structuralist' point of view, in "that it takes as its object of investigation a 'system', that is, the reciprocal relations among parts of a whole, rather than the study of the different parts in isolation" (Palma 1989 in Cypher/Dietsz 1997: 171). Hence the relationship of member states vis-à-vis each other is determined by their position in the state-system as a whole. [27]

How can these reproductive versus transformative approaches help to explain the reasons behind the partiality in the European integration process in terms of the outcomes of asylum and immigration policy? The EU does not develop in a vacuum, and thus pressures exogenous to the integration process can play a pivotal role in the drive for integration. Both reproductive and transformative approaches account for exogenous pressures and their spillovers, although assigning a different explanatory value to them. For neo-functionalists in an "increasingly global world, states seek international solutions to domestic problems" (Faist/Ette 2007: 7–8). Due to exogenous spillovers, states decide to transfer sovereignty to a supranational level, because issues go beyond their national ability to solve. Conversely from a liberal inter-governmentalist position, it would be argued that exogenous pressures lead "to the convergence of national preferences and therefore establish a precondition for cooperation" (Faist/Ette 2007: 8).

In the case of immigration and asylum policies, exogenous pressures that led to the 'Europeanization' of the policy field of migration were manifold and multi-layered. The end of the Cold War accelerated economic globalization. The breakup of the former So-

27 In all of these approaches there seems to be a lack of attention to power relations beyond the state level, such as companies or classes that could be shaping the integration process, which would be interesting for further inquiry.

viet Union (plus the loss of its grip on Central and Eastern Europe) together with the unification of Germany meant a tremendous destabilization of previous ways of life and subsequently a remarkable upsurge in asylum seekers crossing European borders during the 1990's. This upsurge coincided with rising levels of unemployment throughout Western Europe, leading to civil unrest, rising xenophobia and consequently an increase in right-wing governments who introduced restrictive national legislation. Given the interdependent nature of the refugee protection regime, and perhaps also as a result of a *functional* spillover effect of the Schengen Agreement and the subsequent dismantling of internal borders, liberal governments felt the need to follow the course adopted by right-wing governments. Furthermore, advancing globalization resulted in increased cross-border crime and organized acts of terrorism. Hence, 'measures towards harmonizing the treatment of asylum seekers arriving in the EU have become confused with issues of security'.[28] The 9/11 acts of terrorism only intensified securitization of immigration and asylum issues.

The neo-functional approach saw functional spillovers as an important drive for deeper European integration. The most important functional pressure was the abolition of internal border controls, meaning that once an asylum seeker crossed any EU-border they could practically apply for asylum in any or even a multitude of member states. In order to contain this increased risk of 'asylum shopping', mechanisms were created for determining which member state be responsible for processing an application; but these mechanisms in turn created their own functional pressures to harmonize asylum systems (Post/Niemann 2007).

An additional functional pressure at this stage was the looming enlargement in 2004: the EU borders were expanding to eastward frontiers that were 'porous'. It became essential that the old member states at the eastern border of the EU be secured from large inflows of immigrants. These functional pressures have been a prime incentive for European cooperation in the field of asylum and immigration, seemingly favouring a transformative explanation of EU integration. Yet these pressures cannot of themselves explain why Europeanization took the course it did. Functional pressures are also factors in a liberal inter-governmentalist argument where these pressures build up to a national convergence of preference. To ascertain whether the character of Europeanization can indeed be explained from a transformative perspective, the role of the Commission, plus political spillover effects, and the role of other interest groups need to be analysed.

Because migration and asylum issues became defined within the security framework, analytical approaches have not paid sufficient attention to economic interest groups and multinational corporations as having any major role in shaping policy. In general, 'immigration politics...are usually regarded as elite-dominated and characterized as a policy sector with strong executive dominance and only minor access by the legislatures, political parties and interest groups' (Faist/Ette 2007: 24). It is unlikely that elite-convergence of loyalties occurred before the communitarization, because national ministries of the interior prevailing in the field of immigration had hardly been involved in the European integration process (Lavenex 2001: 867). There is 'sparse evidence for socialization of national officials into European preferences or identities' (Pollack 2004: 25). Had it been the Commission that called the tune for further integration, the question to be asked is: why was a transitional period of five years included, and why were some states allowed to opt out? In addition, decision-making processes during those transitional years have been characterized as cumbersome negotiations with 'the tendency of the Council to water down the most liberal proposals'[29] coming from the Commission. If indeed there had been a transformation of the loyalties of the political elites, why then were member states so reluctant to hand over sovereignty, and thereby create such a hybrid system? It seems that a transformed identity does not come in as a helpful explanatory tool for the 'turn to Europe'.

Although it is impossible to deny that functional pressures have been a driving force behind European cooperation in immigration and asylum issues, it is important to recall that EU member states were reluctant to give up sovereignty, as exemplified by the incorporation of decision-making by unanimity in the first pillar and the conditional shift to QMV. In addition many asylum issues were only dealt with in the second pillar. Moreover, the fact that three member states could opt out all together seems to hint at the persistence of the primacy of member states in con-

28 See at: <http://www.aieu.be/static/documents/Tampere_AI_June_2004.doc>, 28 Aug 2007; Amnesty International, 2004: 'Threatening Refugee Protection: Amnesty International's Overall Assessment of the Tampere Asylum Agenda, June 1999-May 2004', p. 1.

29 Antoniou 2003 see above.

gruence with reproductive approaches to European integration. With immigration and asylum framed as security issues the liberal assumption that national preferences reflect the balance of economic interests does not seem to hold true.[30] It seems more likely that national preferences were themselves largely shaped by the exogenous pressures described above - being chiefly the large influx of asylum seekers following the abolition of internal borders. This could then have shaped electoral preferences for more stringent asylum policies, which in its turn led to a convergence of national preferences of several member states, setting the stage for further cooperation in the field of immigration.

Some countries have taken in many more asylum seekers, proving that exogenous pressures do not affect member states in similar ways. Moravcsik and Nicolaïdis analysed how and why "Germany [was] the government most vulnerable for external interdependence, since it [took] a disproportionate share of EU immigrants and was [thus] the most adamant promoter of greater EU involvement" (Moravcsik/Nicolaïdis 1999: 63). Germany also shares the largest border with the new member states, making it particularly vulnerable for asylum seekers coming from the East; hence, it was important for Germany that functioning and restrictive asylum policies were put in place before the new member states would accede and that accession was made conditional upon the adoption of these policies. Germany in particular sought to have the EU endorse its bilateral agreements with the soon-to-be-member-states on policies of returning immigrants to transit countries (Moravcsik/Nicolaïdis 1999: 63), and through the Treaty of Amsterdam the EU received the competence to conclude readmission agreements alongside member states. Germany, facilitated by unanimity voting, was also able to export its 'super-safe-third-country' concept to the European level (Post/Niemann 2007).

By contrast, countries like Britain and Ireland, being islands with stronger natural borders, opposed EU involvement. Britain even threatened to use a veto but was eventually allowed to opt out of Title IV, together with Ireland and Denmark. The third member state with significant bargaining power was France, which was hesitant to put more power into the hands of the Commission and would only go along with the communitarization if a transitional period was included (Moravcsik/Nicolaïdis 1999: 78-79). It seems that the outcomes of negotiations in Amsterdam were indeed a reflection of the relative bargaining power of member states: Germany setting the stage, France determining the pace and the UK being allowed to go its own way. 'The primary lesson of Amsterdam for bargaining theory is that no amount of institutional facilitation or political entrepreneurship, supranational or otherwise, can overcome underlying divergence or ambivalence in national interests' (Moravcsik/Nicolaïdis 1999: 83).

The reproductive approach seems to hold some validity with respect to the role of strong member states and the persistence of inter-governmentalism, but how then can we explain the shift away from unanimity voting and the choice for supra-nationalism by the rest of the member states after the transitional period? A rational choice theory inclined towards institutionalism maintains that states pool sovereignty through QMV in order to enhance the credibility of their agreements. In this case it made particular sense in light of the (then) forthcoming enlargement. Restrictive immigration and asylum policies and thus tight border controls would not be desirable for the new member states as they 'could notably endanger local economies' (Jorry 2007: 4) and would entail a higher asylum burden on them. The dilemma for the old member states was that they were reluctant to give up sovereignty in the field of asylum and migration, while at the same time they needed to be sure that especially the new member states would not defect. The five-year transitional period allowed them to agree on minimum standards by unanimity that the new member states would have to comply with. An additional institutional logic is that institutions and their decisions are 'sticky', and therefore once those minimal standards had been accomplished, QMV became a major barrier to any attempt to rescind past choices (Pollack 2005).

5.5 Conclusion

This chapter has sought to explain the evolution of migration and asylum policy within the wider process of Europeanization by highlighting how member states have manoeuvred the key tensions arising from the desire to create a community without borders between member states but with strong borders between the Community and non-member states. Migration has continued to touch the heart of the sovereign nation-state. The "reproductive approach" to Euro-

30 To what extent economic interests did play a role in shaping the process of Europeanization regarding migration would be interesting for further research.

pean integration and the logic of consequentialism can explain how some member states apparently have been careful to transfer a minimal amount of sovereignty, whereas powerful member states seem to have been able to push through preferences in their own interest, placing a larger burden on weaker members and turning those situated at the enlarged EU borders into larger recipient countries of asylum seekers (van Selm/Cooper 2006).

This logic of consequentialism has led to a process of partial or incomplete Europeanization characterized by unanimity voting and a lack of public scrutiny or judicial control. This process has led to the adoption of policies that raise questions concerning the fundamental right to seek refugee status. The process may have concurrently led to a downward harmonization of asylum systems among member states and the emulation of each other's restrictive practices, although further research and a systematic analysis of national asylum systems would be required to verify this. Particularly evident is that the process of Europeanization has led to the externalization of international responsibility over refugees.

The creation of Frontex in 2005 can be seen as the embodiment of this externalization in the field of asylum and migration, as many of its tasks are enacted outside the territory of the EU, in particular the interception operations in the waters of third countries. From this perspective the creation of Frontex can be understood in the same "logic of consequentialism" as opposed to a "logic of appropriateness" applied to the wider process of Europeanization. The decision to create this agency was based on unanimity, with some member states opting-out, the new member states being obliged to join, and without the involvement of the European Parliament. In other words, Frontex is a direct result of the partial Europeanization process. Frontex also came about because of exogenous and functional spillover, such as the increase in cross-border crime, the abolishment of internal borders and above all the looming enlargement of the EU. Member states have been reluctant to relinquish sovereignty in the field of border protection, which can be seen in the reliance by Frontex on the consent of member states for all its activities. One democratic deficit may be noted in that the European Parliament is only marginally involved in deciding on the budget; national parliaments of most member states are not involved.

The creation of a Common European Asylum System and migration policy are works in progress. It was only at the end of 2005 that unanimity voting was abandoned, and the Commission was granted the exclusive right of initiative and the European Parliament the right to co-decision. This came at the moment of the European crisis when the Dutch and French voted 'No' against the Constitutional Treaty, a crisis which was resolved only towards the end of 2009. The 2007 Frontex Regulation has shown the positive impact of co-decision since it includes explicitly the protection of refugees. Yet the institutional structure of decision-making remains 'hybrid', reflecting the continuous tension between state sovereignty and European integration (Post/Niemann 2007).[31] The European Court of Justice still does not have full competences, and many issues concerning migration and asylum are dealt with in the second pillar, given the fact that a Common European Asylum System is yet to be created. Thus "the implementation of a 'securitarian', state-centred policy frame..., paradoxically, poses severe constraints on the EU's capacity to develop a [true] common refugee policy' (Lavenex 2001: 855).[32]

As an agency of the first pillar, Frontex is assuming tasks across the second pillar of foreign policy and security policy and the third pillar of surveillance and crime control inside and outside the EU. A broadened mandate of this agency is emerging, which will involve the coordination of national surveillance systems and foster their interconnection into a functioning network. This turning point poses new questions about the relationship between public security and civil liberty, which require efficacious scrutiny by researchers and human rights practitioners.

31 With enforcement of the Lisbon Treaty (December 2009) competences will change, which calls for a renewed analysis.

32 The Council of Europe Commissioner for Human Rights - Thomas Hammarberg - has raised his concern in September 2008 about the trend in criminalizing the irregular entry and presence of migrants in Europe; and how this corrodes established international law principles and causes many human tragedies without achieving its purpose of genuine control; at: <http://www.coe.int/t/commissioner/Viewpoints/080929_en.asp> (6 February 2010).

6 Fortress Europe and the Dutch Donjon: Securitization, Internal Migration Policy and Irregular Migrants' Counter Moves

Godfried Engbersen and Dennis Broeders

6.1 Introduction

Since '9/11', immigration and security policy have increasingly intertwined. Political elites have taken the view that immigration policy can contribute to combating and preventing terrorism (Guild 2009; Huysmans 2006; Boswell 2007; ACVZ 2003), adding to the longer standing view that flows of unwanted migrants are a security threat to a welfare state if these groups obtain straightforward access to public provisions. In the more comprehensive welfare states there is a paradox of solidarity and exclusion (Freeman 1995). Maintenance of national, comprehensive forms of internal solidarity (in the fields of health care, social security, education, public housing) for the benefit of native citizens and legal foreign residents implies the exclusion of outsiders from the welfare state's social entitlements. As Christian Joppke (1999: 6) concisely put it: "Because rights are costly, they cannot be for everybody". Aside from this, irregular migrants are assumed to undermine the labour market position of citizens and established residents through job displacement and unfair wage competition. This argument recently gained more importance in the Mediterranean countries due to the 2009 economic crisis and increasing unemployment.

This chapter focuses on irregular migrants, a category of migrants who do not have a legal residence status in the Netherlands. This is not to say that they illegally crossed the external borders of the EU. Many of them migrated legally on a (tourist) visa or had applied for asylum. They crossed into 'irregularity' at a later stage when their visa expired, or when their asylum application was rejected. By remaining in the country, they become 'irregular'.[1] Governments have responded in several ways to the presence of irregular migrants. One strategy is to accept and tolerate it for economic and humanitarian reasons. This policy characterized most West European countries in the 1970–1990 period (Cornelius/Tsuda/Martin/Hollifield 2004). A second strategy, followed primarily by South European countries, is to assign a legal status to some of these persons through regularization programmes (Levinson 2005). A third strategy is to combat illegality. Termed as 'Fortress Europe' this strategy has been the principal line taken in most continental European welfare states since the early 1990's (Engbersen/Van der Leun 2001), and is now taking hold in other European countries, topping the European public agenda and gaining acceptance even in the United States (Jencks 2007; NCSL 2009). The 'combat' strategy has led to a stronger focus on 'internal border control', which includes various measures for excluding irregular migrants from the formal labour market and public provisions. Emphasis on controls led to increasing involvement on the part of employers and public housing corporations, welfare agencies, schools and health care bodies (Van der Leun 2003). The shift 'inward' also entails the tracing, identification and detention of unwanted migrants found residing in the territory in spite of external border control, as well as their exclusion from the formal labour market and the welfare state. Large EU databases now enable states to monitor migrant movements and to expel unwanted migrants more effectively. Furthermore, detention capacity has been increased to facilitate the identification and expulsion of apprehended irregular migrants (Broeders 2007, 2009a).

This chapter describes the current EU and Dutch policies for 'combating' irregular migration. The Netherlands is presented as a crucial case of the For-

1 The term 'irregular migrants' is used here in order not to criminalize or de-legitimize *a priori* specific groups of migrants. The term 'illegal migrants' is often used in EU documents ("The fight against illegal migration") and will be used only when it is used in EU documents, or in other government documentation quoted in this chapter. The legal term 'illegal alien' denotes an alien who does not have a legal residence status.

T.-D. Truong and D. Gasper (eds.), *Transnational Migration and Human Security*, Hexagon Series on Human and Environmental Security and Peace 6, DOI 10.1007/978-3-642-12757-1_6, © Springer-Verlag Berlin Heidelberg 2011

tress Europe strategy of internal migration control. Second, we analyse the counter strategies of irregular migrants in reaction to the new restrictive policies. Irregular immigrants are not passive agents; they react to changing options and create new solutions for their problems (Broeders/Engbersen 2007). Analysis of these various positions enables assessment of the extent to which the new restrictive policies are generating new security problems. There are definite indications that the new systems of internal border control have led to unintended negative consequences – such as rising crime levels among irregular migrants and increasing dependence on the informal economy (Engbersen/Van der Leun 2001). The outline of this chapter is as follows. There is first a brief overview of the current Dutch and partly EU-policies for fighting irregular migration. Then we discuss the implications of these immigration policies for the residence strategies of irregular immigrants. Residence strategies are strategies that enable irregular immigrants to make ends meet and remain in the Netherlands. We will then analyse three important strategies: labour market participation, criminal behaviour and manipulation of identity to prevent expulsion. The final section examines the complexity of policies dealing with irregular migration, their unintended consequences, and their implications for security issues.

6.2 Fortress Europe and the Dutch Donjon

If the European Union can be characterized as a 'fortress', then the Netherlands can be seen as its donjon. A donjon, or a keep, is the fortified central tower that forms the heart of a fortress. It contains the most valuable supplies and the most important living quarters of the castle.[2] Translated into immigration policies, the Netherlands represents an important example of a 'keep' in the EU to shield from 'irregular' migrants. The donjon is the welfare state, the labour market and, in essence, the right of residence plus all the other rights and privileges which that entails. Obviously, modern donjons and fortresses do not rely solely, or even predominantly, on walls, gates and a moat. Actual 'fortifications' are to be found at the fringes of Europe where some of the external Schengen borders have been strengthened with fences, surveillance equipment, guards and watchtowers; but the truth is that the external borders of the EU are too long to patrol effectively (Groenendijk 2002; Carling 2007). States have gradually realized that 'keeping them out' is only part of a possible answer to unwanted migration.

One important policy shift in recent years has been the growing importance of internal control on irregular migrants in the Netherlands, but also in countries such as Germany and Denmark. This comprises an array of measures including legislation, documentation and registration, exclusion from public services, employer sanctions and police control (Cornelius/Tsuda/Martin/Hollifield 2004; Van der Leun 2006), plus new forms of (digital) surveillance.

6.2.1 Strategies of Exclusion

One of the prime struggles between irregular migrants and the Dutch state apparatus is control over identity and identification. In matters of immigration, control over identity (passport, visa) has always been one key to inclusion and exclusion (cf. Torpey 2000); but in the age of computerization, database technology and cross-referencing identity control occupies centre stage. Moreover, in a constitutional state, such as the Netherlands, identification of irregular migrants is key to any policy of exclusion. Guarding the Dutch donjon is these days a matter of an internal migration control revolving around three main concepts: exclusion, surveillance and identification. The link between exclusion and surveillance can follow two separate, and essentially contradictory, logics (Broeders/Engbersen 2007; Broeders 2009b). The first logic is 'exclusion from documentation' and the second is 'exclusion through documentation and registration'.

Exclusion from documentation and registration deploys surveillance to exclude irregular immigrants from key institutions of society, such as labour and housing markets and even informal networks of family and people from their home countries. Under this logic, irregular migrants are (formally) excluded from legal documentation and registration, and are thus excluded from the institutions themselves as they lack the proper 'tickets' to gain entry. This strategy of exclusion covers also the de-legitimization and criminalization of all those who may be employing, housing and aiding irregular immigrants. These strategies are prominent in the Netherlands and other North-Western EU member states where registration is routinely

2 'Donjon' should not be confused with the *dungeons* – the prison cells – which all medieval castles would have, generally built in below the basic ground-level of the 'keep'.

used to exclude irregular migrants from (semi-) public institutions and the labour market.

Exclusion through documentation and registration involves practices that aim to document irregular immigrants themselves through a strategy of recently developed detection and identification tools. Identifying and documenting irregular migrants is necessary for detection, but also for expulsion, as states have gradually found that "unidentifiable immigrants are constitutionally rather invulnerable to expulsion" (Van der Leun 2003: 108). The expulsion of irregular migrants can only function when one can establish identity, nationality and (preferably) migration history of individuals. If not, expulsion is likely to be resisted from within (lawyers and judges) and from abroad (countries of transit and origin) in addition to resistance from the persons themselves. It is therefore vital for the state to connect 'irregulars' with their 'true' legal identities.

Policies operating under this logic of exclusion aim to document and register the individual as an irregular migrant. Documentation and registration are to establish: 1) the irregular status of the person and 2) establish and (re) connect them with their individual 'true' legal identity. In other words, registration is used to identify or even re-identify 'irregulars' (Broeders 2007). This helps to facilitate exclusion in the ultimate sense: expulsion from the state. Investment in this strategy is much more recent than in the first, and has become dominant in advanced welfare states of Northern Europe.

6.2.2 Exclusion in the Netherlands

Since the end of the guest worker era, successive Dutch governments have enacted policies to address the issue of unwanted migrants. As in most countries, the labour market was the first target. The initial measures to curb (irregular) labour migration took effect in the late 1970's in the area of employer sanctions. The primary aim then was to 'demagnetize' the labour market (Martin/Miller 2000; Martin 2004) . In other words, sanctions and policy were directed primarily at domestic employers; the irregular migrants themselves were less affected. Resident irregular migrants did not become an explicit policy or public problem until the early 1990's. The period up to the early 1990's can be characterized as one of increasingly strict regulation of entry through immigration law and policy along with a simultaneous lax approach towards irregular residence and irregular work. Irregulars, once established were able to find work even in the formal labour market. They could then still obtain a Social-Fiscal number (henceforth Sofi-number) which allows a person to hold jobs with tax-paying wages. The enforcement regime on informal labour was lax and in a number of sectors such as agriculture and horticulture, where in spite of high unemployment figures employers find it difficult to fill vacancies, the authorities often turned a blind eye.

In the early 1990's, this informal policy of toleration changed drastically. In 1991, the government tied the sofi number to a legal residence requirement, thus barring the route to legal participation in the labour market. Other measures followed, such as the Marriages of Convenience Act in 1994 and the compulsory Identification Act of the same year. Also in 1994 the Aliens Act was amended in order to introduce new policies in the field of asylum policy. The centrepiece of the new policy of internal migration control was the Linkage Act of 1998, intended to exclude irregular migrants from the benefits of the welfare state. This Act amended the Aliens Act plus some 25 other legislative items (dealing with social security, housing, education and health care) and made entitlements in these fields dependent on residence status (Pluymen/Minderhoud 2002). Parallel to these legal innovations the Dutch government also invested heavily in database systems able to identify, register and track resident migrants.

Ten years on, in 2004, the Dutch Government published a White Paper on Irregular Migrants (*Illegalennota*). In this White Paper the regulations and policies of exclusion from institutions were supplemented with procedures aimed at the detection and identification of irregular migrants. Priorities in this white paper included: 1) cutting off access to employment and housing by intensifying controls, 2) intensifying the fight against identity fraud through increasing controls by the police, 3) increasing the detention capacity for irregular migrants, and 4) expelling more apprehended migrants through the expulsion policy programme. The growing importance of the second logic of exclusion is evident from the emphasis placed on identification and detection of identity fraud, use of detention and importance of expulsion policies. Other EU member states share some of the Dutch policy priorities. Many (northern) EU members have also been increasing their detention capacity for irregular migrants and rejecting asylum seekers with the aim of facilitating expulsion (Welch/Schuster 2005; Van Kalmthout/Hofstee/Van der Meulen/Frieder 2007; Jesuit Refugee Service, 2005).

Recently Fortress Europe came to the aid of its Dutch donjon in matters of *internal* migration control. The EU Ministers for Justice and Home Affairs eventually realized that that the outer walls of the fortress lack sufficient deterrence, given that migrants who pass the hurdle of border controls (legally or illegally) are nevertheless able to live unimpeded in irregular residence in one of the member states (Lahav/ Guiraudon 2006; Lavenex 2006). The European Commission's Return Action Plan of 2002, which states that the message should get across that "immigration must take place within a clear legal procedural framework and that illegal entry and residence will not lead to the desired stable form of residence" (Samers 2004: 41) expresses this most clearly. The most important instrument under development at the EU level is the emergent network of EU migration databases, consisting of the Schengen Information System (SIS), the Eurodac database and the Visa Information System (VIS). These may become important tools for the (re-) identification of irregular migrants. These databases will store massive amounts of data, including biometric identifiers, on potential irregular migrants. They will register as many immigrants as possible from 'suspect' legal categories (asylum seekers are registered in Eurodac) and 'suspect' countries of origin (visa-applicants will be registered in the VIS to get the percentage of immigrants that cross into irregularity at a later stage). These systems can re-identify irregular migrants who try to conceal their identity to avoid expulsion.[3] In matters of migration management, organizing and equipping data exchange at the European level has value for a country's domestic policies. The Netherlands and Germany are the leading advocates for such European data exchange.[4]

6.3 Shifts in Strategies of Irregular Immigrants

The realization that 'keeping them out' (border control) has to be supplemented with policies of 'getting them out' (internal migration control and expulsion) is but a first step. Putting such policies into practice requires political determination, budget resources and delegating the task of exclusion to private and public agencies, but especially to public service employees working in agencies who interact directly with citizens by providing public goods like education, health, welfare or public housing (Lipsky 1980). In addition there is a layer of 'street-level bureaucracies' which involve police officers, labour inspectors and other law enforcement personnel.

During the 'toleration years' there was a big gap between national legislation and its actual implementation by municipalities and street-level bureaucracies. Professionals, public service workers and local officials used their discretionary and political powers to mitigate the social consequences of anti-irregular immigration or asylum policies for specific groups, thus enabling some groups to gain access to public services after all (Rusinovic/Van der Leun/Chessa/Engbersen/Vos 2002; Van der Leun 2003). With the introduction of stricter policies that gap has apparently narrowed (in the Netherlands) because new legislation and new technological equipment which makes effective control of immigrants possible now intersects with the discretion these professionals apply in their work. Of course, both employers and irregular immigrants still develop strategies to get around exclusionary policies by making use of quasi-legitimate and illegitimate means. Public service workers, professionals and local authorities also play a role in this respect (Jordan/Düvell 2002; Anderson 2005); but the margins between which irregular migrants can be supported are getting closer.

A crucial question is, how do irregular immigrants react to these new policies of exclusion and identification? Irregulars have shown remarkable creativity and inventiveness, developing strategies and informal institutions, enabling them to continue residing in the Netherlands. In response to changes in policy they change tactics, look for ways of circumvention and move to other spheres and contexts. Both the irregular immigrants and the institutional surroundings in which they exist, and are active, have a stake in resisting the state's efforts to make society legible and thus more controllable (Scott 1998). Their means to do this are less sophisticated than are those of the state but that is not to say that they are ineffective.[5]

3 For an analysis of these data systems see Broeders (2007).

4 See at: <http://www.sussex.ac.uk/sei/documents/wp72.pdf>; see Aus (2003, 2006).

5 Scott (1985) refers to everyday popular resistance to state policies in situations of extreme inequality as the "weapons of the weak": hardly impressive, but nonetheless effective in certain contexts.

6.4 From Formal to Informal Work

The first line of action governments took against irregular (migrant) labour was the introduction of employer sanctions. The penalization of employers (and irregular employees themselves) varies in severity from country to country; in some fines are high; employers can be imprisoned, licences revoked (Robin/Barros 2000). The consensus is that the effectiveness of employer sanctions to deter irregular entry and employment was declining by the turn of the century. Martin and Miller (2000: 2) assert that the effectiveness of employer sanctions has been undermined by a variety of practices, involving the spread of false documents, the rise of subcontractors plus intermediaries, together with inadequate labour and migration law, insufficient enforcement budgets and deficient cooperation between agencies. Shifting strategies of irregular migrants combined with inadequate means of implementing policies lie at the root of this ineffectiveness. Boswell and Straubhaar (2004: 5) suggest, however, that the Netherlands and some other governments are increasingly taking the "combat of illegal foreign labour" seriously. "Germany, the Netherlands and France all have tough legislation, and have stepped up efforts at enforcement since the early 1990's."

As stated earlier, the Dutch government laid a protective ring of documents and documentary requirements around the formal labour market from the early 1990's onwards to block access to stable tax-paid jobs, with the intention to cut off any possibilities for people without valid documents to build up a quasi-legal position through the labour market (Van der Leun 2003; Engbersen 2003). With the easy venues into the labour market being cut off, irregular migrants have been seeking new ways to become employable. Assuming, borrowing or buying a 'legal identity' has been one main way to regain access. Many countries have seen the emergence of an illegal 'paper market' (Vesta 2008) producing and selling false papers. In addition there is a widespread practice of lending legitimate documents (passports, social security numbers, etc.) to irregular migrants, either freely or for money (Engbersen 2001).

Intermediary organizations also gained ground as it became more difficult for an individual irregular alien to gain access to the labour market. Subcontracting and temporary employment agencies have become important institutions to facilitate a match between the demand and the supply of irregular workers. Interestingly, often, official economic policies of deregulation and creating labour markets are more flexible and offer opportunities for these intermediary structures. It is through these that the irregulars could find their niche. Yet, as Martin and Miller (2000: 16) remark, the general trend towards deregulation and greater flexibility in labour markets undercuts governmental policies aimed at curbing irregular entry and employment. The boom of legal, semi-legal and shady temp agencies in the Netherlands was clearly a direct result of the Government's deregulation of temp agencies (Van der Leun/Kloosterman 2006). Portes and Haller (2005: 409) point to a paradox of state control: "... official efforts to obliterate unregulated activities through the proliferation of rules and controls often expand the very conditions that give rise to these activities". This does not mean that regulations create informality, but they do seem to enhance opportunities for engaging in irregular activities. It has been suggested that a too repressive and authoritarian surveillance of informal activities drives them further underground, depriving authorities of information and control over them. "The systematic withdrawal of information from government agents has proven by far the most effective tool in the hands of civil society to resist authoritarian rule" (Portes/Haller 2005: 420).

During the 1990's and into the 2000's the Dutch government did try to get a firmer grip on irregularity in the labour market. To begin with there were legal initiatives such as the extension of the Dutch Act on Chain Liability to the garment sector in 1994 which made retailers formally responsible for the illegal practices of their contractors. Then labour market controls were intensified, inspections became more targeted (based on risk analysis) and in certain sectors and industries the government organized 'crackdowns'. The introduction of a Clothing Intervention Team which organized raids on Turkish sewing shops and specifically targeted violations of the Foreign Nationals Employment Act (*Wet Arbeid Vreemdelingen* or WAV), was one of the main reasons for the nearly complete disappearance of the garment industry in Amsterdam (Raes/Rath/Dreef/ Kumcu/Reil/ Zorlu 2002). Comparable teams, in which all the relevant government agencies cooperate, were introduced for horticulture (Westland Intervention Team), and the new Social Security Inspectorate (*Sociale Inlichtingen en Opsporingsdienst* or SIOD) targeted temporary work agencies in the Netherlands. During the 2000's, the Labour Inspectorate saw its ranks growing in size. Political priorities finally converted into extra funds, more personnel (the number of inspectors grew from 80 in 1999 to 180 in 2006) and a new legal basis for the system of giving fines. Since 2005 the Labour Inspectorate can make use of an administrative fine, instead of going the lengthy and cumbersome route through the Public Prosecutors office; this has resulted in many more, and higher fines (*Arbeidsinspectie* 2006).

Another trend in labour market inspections is the growing use of computerized and networked checks on identities and other documentary requirements on site. Although these efforts to improve the state's grip on the labour market are certainly not without flaws, they do seem to have some effect. During 1992, 3170 irregular immigrants were interviewed in the city of Rotterdam. One-third of them were unemployed. In 2001, 156 irregular immigrants were interviewed throughout the country. Again, one in three proved to be unemployed; but a remarkable shift from the formal to the informal economy had taken place. While in the early 1990's 30 percent of the irregular immigrants had worked within the formal labour market, almost none of them still did so ten years later (see Engbersen/Staring/Van der Leun 2002; Van der Leun/Kloosterman 2006).[6] It is also striking that many of them were moving towards the restaurant and catering sector and into the domain of personal services. Irregular labour is more difficult to control in these sectors as compared with traditional sectors such as construction, agriculture and horticulture.

6.5 Rise in Subsistence Crime

Apart from the shift from formal to informal employment there is also a shift from legal economic activities to illicit ones. There are serious indications that under the influence of stricter policies irregular immigrants are more likely to become involved in specific forms of crime, such as theft and possession of false documents. These indications derive from a number of studies conducted in different periods on the possible interrelation between irregular migration and crime. The empirical basis of these studies is police data concerning the apprehension of irregular immigrants in Rotterdam between 1989 and 1994 and country-wide police data on the apprehension of irregular immigrants between 1997 and 2004. These studies support the 'marginalization thesis' that a restrictive policy marginalizes irregular migrants by excluding them from the labour market and public provisions, and contributes to forms of subsistence crime. It is through criminal activities that some groups of irregular immigrants manage to continue to reside in the Netherlands (Broeders/Engbersen 2007). In other words, Government's legal construction of illegality, plus the measures taken to combat illicit activities more effectively, have tended to stimulate the involvement in criminal activities by specific groups of irregular immigrants. The 'marginalization' thesis builds on the premise that the exclusion of irregular immigrants from formal employment and public services has a criminalizing effect on those who find themselves excluded. Empirical data suggests that the intensification of restrictions against illegal aliens after 1997 was co-related with the rise in the number of crime suspects among irregulars. 31 percent of the apprehensions of irregular immigrants were found to be criminal offences in 1997 (Engbersen/Staring/Van der Leun, 2002). This had reached 45 percent by 2003 (Leerkes 2009) and 49 percent in 2004 (Boekhoorn/Speller/Trees/Kruijssen 2004: 156). These studies revealed that the majority of offences by irregular immigrants were theft and burglary. The relatively high increase in offences such as shoplifting, theft and burglary fits the marginalization thesis. It would seem that it has become more difficult for irregular immigrants to support themselves in a legitimate manner. The validity of the marginalization thesis was recently put to a critical test (Leerkes 2009). It turned out that the significant increase in crime could well be partly ascribed to other factors, especially the rise in cross border crime or 'criminal migration' owing to open borders and stronger focus on detection and monitoring. Yet, this analysis did not refute the marginalization thesis. Even when Leerkes (2009) cross-checked for other explanations, marginalization affects appeared responsible for at least one-third of the total increase in crime.[7]

These theoretical and empirical findings were confirmed in a research project on asylum migration and crime in the Netherlands (De Boom/Engbersen/

6 There are also 'legal shifts' that have great impact on irregular migrant labour in the Netherlands. For example, with the extension of the free movement of people to some of the new EU member states (including Poland) the number of irregular migrants in sectors such as construction dropped hugely overnight.

7 Leerkes (2009) took five alternative interpretations into consideration. The increase in crime could also be due to 1) practices of status reclassification by the state, 2) an increase in criminal migration, 3) a rise in crime detection and reporting, 4) a simultaneous rise in crime among regular immigrants, or 5) demographic changes with regards to the composition or size of the irregular population.

Leerkes 2006). This research was based on an analysis of all persons who applied for asylum in the Netherlands between 1995 and 2004 (N=235,000). A distinction was made between 1) asylum migrants who were in the Netherlands legitimately (their requests having been granted); 2) asylum migrants still awaiting the final verdict on their applications; and 3) asylum migrants whose requests had been refused but who remained illegally in the Netherlands. There are significant differences in the legal and social position of these three categories. Asylum seekers who have been granted a refugee status have full access to the labour market and the right to public services such as social housing, health care, education and social security. The position of migrants whose application for asylum is still in process is restricted; they cannot live where they choose and they have limited employment opportunities. They are in fact restricted to seasonal work because they are allowed to work only 12 weeks per year. Their financial position is poor.[8] The weakest legal and social position is, of course, that of asylum-seekers whose cases have rejected and who then remain as 'irregulars'. Empirical results have shown a positive correlation between the weakness of legal status and the involvement in (subsistence) crime. The relative number of (crime) suspects among failed asylum migrants remaining illegally in the Netherlands is much higher (9.9 per cent) compared with those asylum-seekers whose applications are pending (5.4 per cent) or with asylum migrants possessing a legal residence permit (3.4 per cent). Analysis has also revealed that the majority of offences (of which failed asylum migrants are suspected) concern theft and burglary. These economic offences are often merely a means by which to gain sufficient income to stay in the Netherlands. The rise in subsistence crime is a typical example of an unintended consequence of internal immigration control. The body of international literature mostly pays attention to the unintended consequences of *external* border control, such as the rise of human smuggling organizations and migrants deaths along the borders (Kyle/Koslowski 2001; Carter/Merrill 2007; Carling 2007). Our analysis shows, however, that *internal* border control is generating specific forms of subsistence crime.

8 The allowance for food, clothing and spending money is far from generous: adults receive an amount (around €40 per week in 2006), far below the statutory minimum income in the Netherlands .

6.6 Detention, Expulsion and the Importance of Not Being Earnest

Yet another expedient is the shift from being identifiable to unidentifiable. Until the early 1990's those irregular immigrants who could actually obtain a Sofi number became classified as 'white illegals' (irregular, but doing regular work). In the early 1990's the Dutch government closed this legal loophole, making it more and more important for irregular immigrants to be unidentifiable in order to shield themselves from state control. When the risk of detention, apprehension and deportation looms large on the lives of irregular migrants they develop various strategies to change and mask their personal identity and illegal status. Three major ones have been identified (Engbersen 2001). One is the structural or situational adoption of a false identity through the acquisition of false papers, or the use of legitimate documents (such as passports, sofi numbers and medical insurance cards) from legitimate others. Another is the destruction of their identity documents which amounts to the obliteration of their legal identity; this is done in order to prevent and obstruct deportation by the authorities. Unidentifiable irregular migrants are cases immigration authorities have the most difficulty coping with and they are seldom actually deported. A final course of action is the concealment of their irregular status not only from employers and public officials but also from members of their own ethnic community in order to avoid repercussion from within (Staring 1998).

A number of countries have recently developed more serious expulsion policies for irregular migrants. An important instrument in executing these expulsion policies has been increased use of incarceration in detention centres, which, in turn, has prompted (effective) perpetration of falsehoods and hidden identities among irregular migrants. These centres focus both on the organization of forced return programmes, and on establishing the identity and nationality of the apprehended unidentifiable immigrants. Identification of the unwilling is a struggle between the state and the person. Migrants who do not want to leave the territory refuse to cooperate and frustrate procedures. For example, by stating a false name or incorrect country of origin they force the authorities to enter into a complicated bureaucratic process of determination of the nationality of the alien and presentation to embassies for the purpose of obtaining a travel document (e.g a *laissez passer*).

The use of administrative detention is a general European trend justified by, and based on, the assumption that a prison regime will encourage a person to reveal his or her identity. Detention is also considered a deterrent to prevent immigrants coming to Europe through irregular channels. There are now nearly 200 detention centres in the EU located at strategic sites: traditional prisons, islands, airports and detention boats in large seaports (Jesuit Refugee Service, 2005). These detention centres are now used to accommodate apprehended irregular migrants who are difficult to remove; given that the practice of putting them back out on the streets has been discontinued (Van der Leun 2003). In 2006, the Netherlands had nine penitentiary centres with a capacity of 2,100 beds for irregular immigrants. In 2007 there was an additional use of more three 'detention boats' (in addition to the two other detention boats already in operation) and the opening of a new penitentiary centre with place for 1,300 beds. This means that in 2007 approximately 13 percent of total Dutch penitentiary capacity was for the detention of irregular immigrants (Van Kalmthout 2007: 103). Studies reveal, however, that less than half of the irregular migrants apprehended and detained in the Netherlands are expelled from the country and that contrary to what political rhetoric suggests the proportion of effective expulsions has been decreasing (Engbersen/Staring/Van der Leun 2002; Van Kalmthout/Hofstee/Van der Meulen/Dünkel 2007). According to Van Kalmthout and colleagues (2007: 123) who studied the detention of aliens in two Dutch prisons for the period 1994–2003, the percentage of those expelled is less than 35 percent of the total number detained. The ineffectiveness of the policy of expulsion is partly owing to reluctance of countries of origin to cooperate in taking back their irregular migrants (Noll 1999; Lavenex 2006; Ellermann 2008), but also to the difficult identification of irregular migrants. Non-cooperation and the hiding of the truth are very effective and many immigrants are still able to frustrate the administrative processing of return programmes.

Governments are obviously aware of the effectiveness of these simple non-cooperation strategies and have been working on an answer for quite some time. EU member states have been investing heavily in new methods of identification, both domestically and at the EU-level. Given that the struggle over identity is in essence a struggle over documents (since only a documented legal identity facilitates expulsion) states have turned their attention towards the traces left by the irregular migrants themselves in official administrations and registers during the course of their journey into Europe. On the whole there are three possible 'migration histories': 1) the border was crossed illegally (with or without help); 2) the person was an asylum seeker who stayed after the application was rejected; 3) entry was with a legal visa but there was overstay beyond its validity. The two latter categories leave traces in the administrations of the immigration authorities.

In a Europe without internal borders, effective use of such data has to be organized at the level of the EU. In recent years European governments have been developing a network of immigration databases at the EU-level aimed at documenting these migration histories in order to re-identify irregular migrants found in the member states (Broeders 2007). These European databases seek to register as many immigrants as possible from 'suspect' legal categories (e.g. asylum) and 'suspect' countries of origin (visa), in order to discern what percentage of immigrants cross the line into irregularity at a later stage. The Eurodac system registers all asylum applications in the EU and, when it becomes operational, the Visa Information System will register all visa applications for entry. Any irregular migrant apprehended in one of the EU member states can be registered in the Schengen Information System (II). All the entries into these systems consist of both the application data and the fingerprints of the applicant, making the link between a dossier and an irregular migrant a matter of cross-referencing. These systems potentially undermine the most effective strategy – that of being untruthful. A potential side effect of this new policy approach that closes off the identity routes of asylum and a visa may be an increasing dependence on smuggling and trafficking organizations in order to gain access to a direct route of illegal entry.

6.7 Discussion: Security and Internal Migration Control

Through the first decade of this century the Dutch state initiated a number of measures to make the strategies of immigrants more visible in order to exclude, or apprehend and expel, illegal migrants more effectively. Policies have become more restrictive, more legalistic and more embedded in the logic of security; and the scope for irregular immigrants to manoeuvre within the legitimate social institutions is increasingly limited. The stricter policies and enforcement are pushing irregular migrants towards the fringes of legality and beyond. This is a serious side effect of these control policies. Stricter interpretation of the law plus stricter enforcement create new security problems. Other European countries are also investing in policy programmes to strengthen their internal control of migration and are stepping up implementation. Three shifts in the residence strategies of irregular immigrants have been documented: 1) from formal to informal work; 2) from legitimate to criminal behaviour; 3) from identifiable to unidentifiable. In reaction to these strategies the state is countering again with new measures with special instruments to (re-)identify immigrants who do not reveal their identity.

The state is also trying to dismantle those illegitimate organizations (such as illegitimate temporary work agencies, and markets for false documents) which have been established in reaction to restrictive policies and were sometimes aided by the introduction of liberalization policies. There is a constant struggle in the migration arena, in which individual and collective actors involved respond to each other with different strategies (Black 2003; Vesta 2008). But the state is clearly the most powerful party and in the end may gain and keep the upper hand.

There is, nonetheless, empirical evidence that attempts by the state to fight irregular migration are pushing irregular immigrants further underground. The same mechanisms that play a role in external border control are being replicated through the internal border controls. Both forms of control are creating incentives for illegitimate actors to organize illegal entry and residence (including illegal employment, false documents) resulting in greater victimization of aliens. "The result is sometimes", writes Miller (2001: 329), "that the medicine makes the illness worse". Security-oriented discourses and policies aiming to end informal toleration practices are directed at internal control over the migrant population. The matter of there being too many 'white' irregulars having regular jobs has raised serious questions of displacement of workers who are citizens in an era of serious unemployment. Also the view that too many irregular immigrants have gained access to public services has contributed to the image of them as 'welfare abusers', and therefore provides a legitimate base on which to put the onus of the crisis of the welfare state on them. Yet, Dutch citizens are increasingly distrustful of a state that is unable to enforce the law. Nonetheless, the current restrictive policies also produce negative side effects of which subsistence crime is one. Putting people, who are determined to stay, up against the wall will inevitably lead to new avoidance strategies. Their involvement with new (illegitimate) actors and institutions will carry new security risks. The challenge of immigration control will be to find the *right balance* between 'closedness' and openness, and between effective law enforcement and practical toleration policies, capable of dealing with the economic and social ambiguities of advanced immigration societies.

7 The New Co-Development Agenda: Official and Non-Official Initiatives between Morocco and Spain

Alejandra Boni and Joan Lacomba

7.1 Introduction

A search for approaches that can positively connect migration with development in migrants' countries of origin has begun in Europe along with a new perception of the phenomenon of migration and a response to change in the cycle of movement. Pressure has intensified in the last few years during which Europe has set up higher barriers against the arrival of new migrants, and the living conditions for those already settled have become more harsh. Awareness of the intensification of (northward) migration - which is not always in answer to the labour market's needs - has shifted the search for 'solutions' towards the countries of origin.

This chapter traces the meanings of 'co-development' in European policies and their enactment in the relationship between Spain and Morocco. Morocco has become an entry gate to Europe not only for sub-Saharan Africans but also Asian immigrants. Border control between Morocco and Spain has strengthened, and the former has also become a priority country for 'co-development' actions initiated not just by Spain, but also by France, Belgium and Italy. A great deal of public debate in Spain has centred on the Maghrebi country which is separated from it, at its closest point, by less than nine nautical miles.

A distinction is made between state-promoted 'official co-development' (which is characterized by top-down directives and guidelines) and 'non-official co-development' initiatives which are promoted especially by non-governmental organizations and immigrants' associations using a 'bottom-up' approach. The approach by local public administrations (Autonomous Communities and municipalities) is referred to as 'medium' co-development. The aim of this paper is to show that 'co-development' - as conceived at the EU level as well as national level - has become more intertwined with security and trade issues, and remains primarily Eurocentric in that insufficient attention is accorded to local needs in the source countries. Civil society initiatives, in contrast, are directing attention to local issues. Beyond the concern for managing or curbing the flows of migrants, some of these initiatives are seeking to create a positive link between 'migration' and 'development' so as to achieve more equitable human development.

A review of official lines of action and the institutional mechanisms used, suggests that 'co-development' requires firmer commitment by the state (or the EU) to the agenda of democratization and respect for human rights (internationally) rather than allowing security and trade issues to drive action. Initiatives led by civic organizations appear more promising, but are institutionally weak and budget-dependent on governments. A critical understanding of the limits and possibilities of both official and non-official actions on co-development is needed.

7.2 Co-development Policy at the European Union Level

The term 'co-development' has been framed in terms of a restrictive immigration policy - usually in line both with EU security concerns and free trade with countries which in fact are also migrant-senders. The gradual inclusion of 'co-development' in EU policies manifests this trend.

The first reference to the idea of 'co-development' within the scope of migration policy was at the Euro-Mediterranean Conference held in Barcelona in 1995. This Conference laid the foundation for a process intended to build a multilateral framework for dialogue and cooperation between the EU and its Mediterranean partners, bringing together economic and security aspects of cooperation. It also emphasized the social, human and cultural dimensions significant to such cooperation. The Barcelona declaration considered the contribution of civil society essential to the

T.-D. Truong and D. Gasper (eds.), *Transnational Migration and Human Security*, Hexagon Series on Human and Environmental Security and Peace 6, DOI 10.1007/978-3-642-12757-1_7, © Springer-Verlag Berlin Heidelberg 2011

Euro-Mediterranean partnership, and recognized the need to strengthen the channels for decentralized co-operation to encourage exchanges between those who are active in the field of development (Lacomba/ Boni 2008). The term 'co-development' was not explicitly used at that time, nor was the link between migration and development actually articulated. But the declaration did prompt action on the side of civil society. The conclusions of a Euro-Mediterranean Civil Forum meeting held practically in parallel with the official summit did include a clause (Section 10) on the need to consider the migrant populations as a potential agency of development acting between a host country and a sending country, thus establishing a central role which migrants can play in the development link between Europe and its Mediterranean neighbours.[1]

The first formal EU reference to 'co-development' came at the European Council meeting held in Tampere in 1999, where the need for a common migration and asylum policy was brought to the fore (Geddes 2005). The reference to co-development was set out as follows:

> The European Union needs a comprehensive approach to migration addressing political, human rights and development issues in countries and regions of origin and transit. This requires combating poverty, improving living conditions and job opportunities, preventing conflicts, consolidating democratic states, and ensuring respect for human rights, in particular rights of minorities, women and children. To that end, the Union as well as Member States are invited to contribute, within their respective competence under the Treaties, to a greater coherence of internal and external policies of the Union. Partnership with third countries concerned will also be a key element for the success of such a policy, with a view to promoting *co-development* [emphasis added].[2]

A High Level Working Group on Asylum and Migration was set up by the European Council within the Tampere framework and produced different draft action plans for countries considered of special interest: Afghanistan, Albania, Iraq, Morocco, Somalia and Sri Lanka.

Spain was mandated to prepare the Morocco Report, whose Action Plan should focus on the creation of permanent dialogue on immigration between the EU and Morocco. This plan viewed Morocco as an important external border south of the EU, a 'buffer' zone in respect of the migratory pressures. The main guidelines of the Spanish policy towards Morocco, according to the Action Plan, were stipulated as: co-operation to facilitate the socio-economic development of the country; the signing of agreements to implement the mechanisms allowing readmission into Morocco of migrants who have illegally entered the EU through Moroccan territory; and development of temporary migration schemes.[3] Commenting on this Action Plan, Terrón (2004: 14) noted that despite explicit concerns to combat illegal trafficking networks and the emphasis on economic development cooperation initiatives to reduce migratory pressure, the plan nonetheless also included aspects inherent in European immigration policy – such as integration of the (Moroccan) nationals who live in the European Union, their equal treatment along with family reunification and respect for a diversity of cultural identities. No clear reference to 'co-development' was made.

The notion of 'co-development' became explicit at the European Council meeting in Santa Maria da Feira held in 2000 to re-launch the idea of a Euro-Mediterranean partnership under the framework of a 'Common Strategy of the European Union on the Mediterranean Region'. This Strategy highlights the participation of migrants in promoting development in their communities of origin, and aims to: 1) promote transparency and greater predictability of legal systems in partner countries and 2) encourage foreign investment and lawful migrants to pursue activities in favour of co-development with their countries of origin.[4]

Particularly relevant for current European migration policy is the explicit inclusion of the issue of security. Migration issues have shifted rapidly from a focus on labour and finance to the domain of security due to the 9/11 attack and other considerations in respect of EU enlargement.[5] In December 2003 the Commission introduced a new formula with the title 'A Secure Europe in a Better World'.[6] The European Neighbourhood Policy followed in May 2004.[7] The

1 See at: <http://www.medea.be/index.html?page=2&lang=en&doc=1632> (13 April 2010).

2 See at: <http://www.consilium.europa.eu/ueDocs/cms_Data/docs/pressData/en/ec/00200-r1.en9.htm> (27 May 2009).

3 See at: <http://www.mmo.gr/pdf/library/Spain/ECPR_fuentes.pdf> (12 April, 2010).

4 See at: <http://www.consilium.europa.eu/ueDocs/cms_Data/docs/pressData/en/ec/00200-r1.en0.htm> (27 May 2009).

5 See at: <http://www.ucm.es/info/unisci/Marqselim.pdf> (3 November 2009).

6 See at: <http://ue.eu.int/uedocs/cmsUpload/78367.pdf> (27 May 2009).

2003 document made no specific reference to migration, but explicit reference was made to the need to create a ring of well-governed countries to the east of the European Union and on the borders of the Mediterranean with whom the EU could enjoy close and cooperative relations. The 2004 document brought forward clearer ideas of reform in several areas of concern (for example political, security, trade and economic development) and underscored the need to prepare Action Plans with partner countries as part of regional cooperation.[8]

In addition to concerns for regional cooperation to fight illegal immigration, to reduce migration pressure and enhance judicial and police cooperation, four items of the Action Plans present migration in different guises: 1) commitment to shared values; 2) equal treatment in living and working conditions of migrant workers; 3) enhancing the connections between the people in the EU and its neighbours to promote mutual understanding of each other's culture, history, attitude and values; 4) elimination of distorted perceptions. The section on regional cooperation with the EU's Mediterranean neighbours follows the same line, reiterating the commitment to fight illegal immigration, enable legal migration and support specific activities.[9]

In 2005 the European Commission prepared a communication to the Council, the European Parliament, the European Economic and Social Committee and the Committee of the Regions, entitled 'Migration and Development: Some concrete orientations'. This Communication mentions 'co-development' only on its second page when referring to the recommendations of the 1999 Tampere Summit; but it does list a series of new measures aimed at improving the effects of migration upon sender-country development. These are identified as: 1) migrants' remittances; 2) the role of diasporas in home country development; 3) circular migration and 'brain circulation'; 4) the mitigation of adverse 'brain drain' effects.[10] This communication, thus, treats migration on its own merits rather than conflating it with crime and public security. In this line of reasoning migration is viewed as a significant potential for furthering the Millennium Development Goals (MDGs) through remittances, without being a substitute for any increase of Official Development Assistance (ODA). The European Consensus on Development also takes this line and includes numerous references to synergies between migration and development, making migration a positive force for development.[11]

Regarding European policies towards Morocco within the framework of the EU Neighbourhood Policy, the EU/Morocco Action Plan was implemented for a three to five year term.[12] This Plan does not mention 'co-development'; most of the actions related to migration have been developed within the scope of flow control and the fight against illegal migrants. A document dated 23 April 2009 makes a first assessment of the Action Plan, mentioning migration solely when dealing with judicial cooperation and illegal immigration, without any reference to 'co-development'.[13] Aubarell and Aragall's analysis of the EU 2000 to 2006 migration programmes for Morocco (which are charged to the external aid budget) shows that 38 per cent of the EU budget allocated to scheduled action linked to migration flows from Morocco relates to the fight against clandestine migrations (Aubarell/Aragall 2004: 37).

At the level of the relationship between the EU and Morocco, references to positive links between migration and development are absent; a view of migration linked to illegal immigration and control prevails. Consuelo Ramón points out that, "if we speak about the EU, we can hardly use the co-development policies formula properly" (Ramón 2005: 55–60). Yet there are initiatives of regional and local governments, as well as those of civil society, which are more grounded in actual contexts of daily life.

7 See at: <http://ec.europa.eu/world/enp/pdf/strategy/strategy_paper_en.pdf> (27 May 2009).

8 Reference to the Plan prepared by the High Level Group for Morocco is made later.

9 People-to-people projects; promotion of intercultural dialogue through educational and youth exchanges; human resource mobility and transparency of qualifications. See at: <http://www.consilium.europa.eu/ueDocs/cms_Data/docs/pressdata/EN/reports/104630.pdf> (24 June 2009)

10 See at: <http://europa.eu/legislation_summaries/development/sectoral_development_policies/l14166_en.htm> (25 June 2009).

11 See at: <http://europa.eu/legislation_summaries/development/general_development_framework/r12544_en.htm> (25 June 2009).

12 See at: <http://ec.europa.eu/world/enp/pdf/action_plans/morocco_enp_ap_final_en.pdf> (25 June 2009).

13 See at: <http://ec.europa.eu/world/enp/pdf/progress2009/sec09_520_fr.pdf> (25 June 2009).

7.3 Co-development in the Spanish Policy Agenda

In Spain, after the turn of this century, the notion of incorporating migrants' eventual return into the official concept of 'co-development' became established in Government's plan for cooperation and immigration. A more precise focus for co-development was then required and this has been guided towards development cooperation in emigration areas where decentralized cooperation agents play a major role; there is a lower emphasis on the issue of returning. Yet while the national focus on co-development is not based on security concerns as much as it is in the EU, the idea of promoting development in the areas of origin as a means to decrease migration retains a relevant place.

The first mention of co-development in Spanish Government policy came in 2000, within the context of the so-called GRECO[14] Plan (Programa Global de Regulación y Coordinación de la Extranjería e Inmigración or the Global Programme to Regulate and Coordinate Foreign Residents' Affairs and Immigration in Spain). This short-lived Plan (2001-2004) specifically highlighted the need to link policies regarding development cooperation with migration policies, and also the idea that 'co-development' in countries of origin must involve investment in their regions having high rates of emigration. Promoting the possible return of the migrants to their country of origin is built on the assumption that once the migrants have received professional training in Spain and acquired work experience, they will then make a valuable contribution to the development and growth of their countries of origin upon return.

The inclusion of return migration in the Spanish Plan would seem to follow the line of argumentation of a 1997 French report on co-development (Lacomba/Boni 2008). Although Spanish International Cooperation Law does not refer to migration, the Master Plan 2001/04 states that the stability of Morocco makes a joint-development strategy, including solutions to migration, indispensable. However, official Spanish foreign aid to Morocco hardly considers migration issues, and makes few claims beyond the general hypothesis that advancing economic development will make it less likely that people feel a need to leave their place of origin.

In 2005 a Task Force on Co-development was formed, commissioned by the Spanish State Council on Development Cooperation. This Task Force, made up of civil society actors and experts, prepared a consensus document to lay the foundations of official Spanish policy on co-development seeing it as a mode of development cooperation. The Task Group stated that:

> The purpose of co-development is to promote human development and integration within a context of welfare, with the following features: its scenario is the transnational space defined by the relationship between significant areas of origin and settlement of migrants in the countries of origin and destination, considering intermediate or transit countries; it lies within the space shared between cooperation and migration policy; co-development projects work in all the transnational space, in both countries, at least in two of the action areas; it mobilizes a variety of stakeholders connected in the transnational space, among which migrants play a major role as subjects transferring tangible and intangible resources; due to the variety of intervening stakeholders, efficient coordination of networks is the only way to carry out common tasks; the whole set of simultaneous actions integrated in transnational space is articulated via the feedback of processes, with the 'origin group' affecting the 'destination group' in its goals and actions (and *vice versa*); the flow of exchanges in transnational space is bi-directional and comprises people, capital, goods, services and virtual forms of interaction (Task Force on Co-development 2005: 8).

The view of the Task Force is reflected in the contents of the Master Plan for Spanish Cooperation 2005-2008,[15] which stipulates that co-development policy be implemented in line with the policies defined by the Ministry of Labour and Social Affairs and, specifically, by the State Secretariat for Immigration and Emigration - in coordination with other administrations and cooperation agents. Objective number eight of the Strategic Plan for Citizenship and Integration (2007-2010) prepared by the Ministry of Labour and Immigration (MTIN) seeks to foster co-development policies and experiences in migrant countries of origin using a variety of measures. A strong emphasis is placed on participation of migrants themselves in coordination with their associations and Spanish development cooperation agencies.[16]

The Master Plan for Spanish Cooperation considered migration as a source of wealth for both origin and destination countries; and co-development as being an arena for multicultural and transnational activ-

14 The text of this plan is no longer available online but can be found in the State Official Gazette *(Boletín Oficial del Estado)* dated 8 January 2001.

15 See at: <http://www.aecid.es/web/es/publicaciones/Documentos/Plan_director/> (29 May 2009): 171, 172.

ity. It set forth the priority countries for Spanish cooperation in co-development - notably Morocco and Ecuador, due to the high volume of nationals of these countries in Spain as migrant workers.[17] The first official initiative for co-development in Morocco[18] came into operation at the end of 2008 through a call by the Spanish Agency for International Development Cooperation (AECID) for bids to prepare research (and a seminar) to identify and evaluate means for official cooperation with Morocco. Such activities would be expected to lay the foundations of a co-development strategy between Spain and Morocco, providing the guidelines for support of Moroccan immigrants engaged in development projects in their regions of origin.

The presence of co-development in policy became manifest in the recent and ambitious Master Plan for Spanish Cooperation 2009-2012. The Plan reaffirms the importance of protecting the human rights of migrant workers during the whole migration cycle plus the need to preserve coherence between the articulated migration policy and the cooperation policy. The Plan lists several measures which may represent a relative change in the way of understanding co-development from an official standpoint. These are: 1) Effective migration management frameworks; 2) Social protection of migrant workers by ensuring full rights during their temporary stay and throughout their migration cycle; protection of victims of trafficking, particularly for sexual exploitation, with special attention to women and minors; 3) Provision of support to diasporas and migrants' associations to strengthen their skills in organizing and implementing co-development initiatives; 4) Solutions in respect of the brain drain; 5) Consultative mode for design and implementation of policy through multi-stake-holders participation.[19] Apart from the Cooperation Plans with Morocco and Ecuador, cooperation with Senegal - a country with considerable experience in the field of co-development - is also included.

It must be noted that the scope of action by organizations in civil society is already circumscribed given that 'co-development' has been officially framed as economic development through return migration. Nevertheless the presence of multiple actors below state level (Autonomous Communities and Municipalities, civil society organizations of different orientations) suggests multiple interpretations of 'co-development' in line with the values these various actors hold and in response to what affects them most. Given that both Autonomous Communities and regional governments have wide jurisdiction over development cooperation, conforming to the provisions of the State Master Plan as well as accommodating to regional and local variations remain a great challenge.

In keeping with the large number of Moroccan migrants living in Catalonia (the greatest concentration in Spain) and considering the prevalent Catalonian 'outsourcing' to, and investment and commercial interests in, Morocco, Catalonia has made the most progress in affecting co-development. The Catalonian government has its own offices in Morocco and arranges work contracts for Moroccans willing to work in Catalonia, despite the friction this created with the Popular Party which previously held power in Spain. Morocco became a priority target in the Catalonian Autonomous Cooperation Law,[20] under which the Master Plans for Development Cooperation 2003-2006 and 2007-2010[21] specifically refer to promoting co-development as well as providing incentives for projects that stimulate migrant involvement in Catalonia (Lacomba/Boni 2008).

The General Plan for Development Cooperation 2001-2004 for the Autonomous Region of Madrid also treats Morocco as a high priority. In Madrid's Master Plan 2005-2008, the term co-development is for the first time explicitly referred to as a strategic measure, treating both migrant organizations and migrants as 'partners' in the cooperation projects with Madrid.[22] In the Autonomous Community of Valen-

16 See at: <http://ec.europa.eu/ewsi/UDRW/images/items/docl_1314_739898301.pdf> (2 May 2010). On page 45 a budget of € 56,769,825 for the 2007-2010 term, € 16,985,756 is envisaged, with contributions from the Ministry of Labour and Immigration and an amount of € 39,784,069 from the Ministry of Foreign Affairs and Cooperation. In the Executive Summary of the Plan, Premise 1 defines 'integration' as a two-way process of mutual adaptation.

17 According to the data of the National Statistics Institute, at the beginning of 2009 the number of migrants from Morocco in Spain amounted to 683,102, and to 458,437 from Ecuador.

18 As regards Ecuador, the identification tasks of the Pilot Co-Development Project Cañar (Ecuador) - Murcia Region (Spain), promoted by the AECID, started in 2004.

19 See at: <http://www.aecid.es/web/es/publicaciones/Documentos/Plan_director/> (29 May 2009).

20 See at: <http://www.gencat.cat/diari_c/3551/01361125.htm> (5 May 2009). Act 26/2001, dated 31 December 2001 on Development Cooperation.

21 See at: <http://www.gencat.cat/cooperacioexterior/cooperacio/castellano/plan_director_07_10.htm> (29 May 2009)

cia co-development is included in the Master Plans for Valencian Development Cooperation 2004–2007 and 2008–2011.[23] The proposed measures include: consciousness-raising in the countries of origin concerning potential of the migrants; supporting the possibility of repatriation; recruiting active participants from the migrant residents in Valencia to promote development projects in their home countries; and establishing co-development agencies with town councils in towns with high proportions of migrants.

In the Basque Country's Strategic and Master Plan on Development Cooperation 2008–2011 migration is framed as a multi-dimensional phenomenon intimately linked to poverty, which has changed the sociological composition of different territories and the financial dynamics in many countries owing to remittances. Migration should be dealt with from the universal citizenship standpoint – advocating the rights of all human beings by virtue of simply being part of the world. Co-development should thus join the fight against poverty.[24]

The growing use of the term co-development by the different Autonomous Communities is proof of their interest in a field which has become part of the Spanish regional cooperation agenda. Given that immigration policy is a matter for the central government, adherence to EU principles is expected; yet the Autonomous Communities can make proposals which are more ambitious in establishing a relationship between migrant mobility and co-development. This special feature of the Spanish cooperation system is part of the de-centralized character of the Spanish administrative model, and an essential component of the Spanish political system within its constitutional framework (Montiel 2007). The system has been criticized for disregarding the principles of alignment and harmonization proposed by the Paris Declaration 2005 (Acebillo/Boni/McGee/Peris/ Calabuig/Hueso 2009; Burall/Maxwell 2006). Although it is somewhat premature to evaluate the initiatives of actors operating below state level, it is important to note that the approach adopted towards migration by Autonomous Communities appears far less instrumental than that of the central government. In the Autonomous Communities' agenda migrant associations are seen as being vital to co-development, and thus as important for building a bi-directional approach which connects and strengthens the localities involved in each country.

7.4 Non-Official Co-development in Morocco

Pioneer actions of co-development in Spain among non-official actors came from a convergence of two factors: the wish to support the migrant populations and the related opportunity for NGOs to gain experience in the development field (Aubarell/Aragall 2004: 50). In the context of Spanish-Moroccan cooperation the growing prominence of Morocco's civil society[25] has provided an enabling environment for non-official co-development. So far this has included initiatives by the organizations of Moroccan immigrants and those promoted by Morocco-based NGOs, in collaboration with foreign NGOs working in the development field.

In the last few years these have received the support of official channels and have therefore spread in the EU context. For example, Morocco's cooperation with Italy has been developed through local entities such as the *Cooperazione Internazionale* (International Cooperation)[26] and the European Committee for Training and Agriculture.[27] Cooperation with the Netherlands is mediated through the Euro-Mediterranean Centre on Migration and Development (EMCEMO) - an association formed by immigrants.[28] In France, *Migrations et Développement* (Migration and Development)[29] and the Immigration, Development and Democracy Network[30] (formed and led by immigrants) play an important role. It should be noted that both the concentration of Moroccan immigrants in

22 See at: <http://www.madrid.org/cs/Satellite?blobcol=urldata&blobheader=application%2Fpdf&blobheadername1=Content-Disposition&blobheadervalue1=filename%3Dplananual_Maquetaci%C3%B3n+1web.pdf&blobkey=id&blobtable=MungoBlobs&blobwhere=1220442533819&ssbinary=true> (29 May 2009).

23 See at: <http://www.cic.gva.es/index.php?Itemid=46&id=54&option=com_content&task=view> (29 May 2009).

24 See at: <http://www.lankidetza.info/DefinitivoPlanDirectorEstrategico2008-2011.pdf> (29 May 2009).

25 See in this regard the book by Fátima Mernissi (2004) where she describes the contributions by some of the civil leaders of development in Morocco; or the books by Maria-Àngels Roque (2003) and Jesús Núñez (2004) on associativeness and the emergence of civil society in Morocco.

26 See at: <www.cefa.bo.it> (15 June 2009) for information on project activities.

27 See at: <www.coopi.org> (15 June 2009) for information on project activities.

28 See at: <www.emcemo.nl> (16 June 2009) for information on project activities.

29 See at: <www.idd-reseau.org> (15 June 2009).

30 Projects available at: <www.migdev.org> (15 June 2009).

these countries and extant funding lines for projects in Morocco have contributed to forming this pattern of cooperation. The main innovation is the attempt by such organizations to make the cooperation contain an explicit link between migration issues and development concerns.[31]

Spain has only brief and recent experience with civil-society-led co-development initiatives promoted by the weak and highly fragmented Moroccan migrants' associations and ones put through by Spanish development associations (which are stronger than the migrant associations originating in Spain). One example of what was defined in this chapter's introduction as non-official bottom-up co-development is ATIME (the *Asociación Trabajadores Inmigrantes Marroquíes en España* or Association of Moroccan Migrant Workers in Spain). In addition to its well-known fight for the rights of Moroccan workers in Spain, the association has recently established a foundation devoted to international cooperation: the *Red Euromediterránea de Cooperación al Desarrollo* (REMCODE). Its projects are currently located in the north of Morocco, and range from infrastructure improvements and constructing basic facilities to the promotion and strengthening of civic associations. For this purpose, REMCODE benefits from its own field-based technical staff and the cooperation of many local associations.[32]

Another organization of Moroccan migrants in Spain involved in co-development is Development Cooperation in Northern Africa (CODENAF), which was created at the initiative of a group of Moroccan migrants settled in Andalusia. Its profile matches perfectly the concept coined in France of "international solidarity organisations arising from migrations" (Daum 2000). It is a development cooperation organization, which stands out from others precisely because of the leading role played by migrants. Their projects in Morocco are still in an embryonic stage, currently focussing on promoting a network linking the actions of different associations of Moroccan migrants in Spain and that may actively involve them in the development of their country of origin. CODENAF is also part of the Euro-Mediterranean Migration and Development network, of which the organizations EMCEMO (Netherlands) and *Migrations et Développement* (France)[33] are members.

There are also initiatives promoted by other associations of Moroccan migrants, such as the Cultural Association *Ibn Batuta* (ASCIB), with the project, "Reinforcing local abilities and governance in the rural community of *Ouneine* in *Taroudant*". The Association of Moroccan Immigrants in the Balearic Islands, the Association Amazon for Development and Socio-Cultural Promotion in Catalonia, and the Association Al-Amal of Moroccan Immigrants in the Autonomous Community of Valencia, all work in partnership with different Spanish NGOs in development projects in Morocco.

The projects promoted by immigrant associations are mostly low-scale, and they rarely continue or evolve into something more significant. In this respect they reflect the separation that usually exists between official co-development and the associative movement of migrants, both as regards the distrust generated by the very term 'co-development' and as regards their lack of recognition and resources to manage projects. Thus, in the first two cases (ATIME and CODENAF), we find two old associations of immigrants that combine vindication activities in Spain with development actions in Morocco, and are clearly separated from official pronouncements on 'co-development'. As regards the association *Ibn Batuta*, we observe a greater accommodation to the space and logic of the administration, particularly within the regional framework.

Spanish NGOs devoted to development cooperation in Morocco tend to adopt a de-centralized approach that usually counterbalances top-down official co-development. Depending on the history and experience of these civil organizations in development cooperation, some give more space to the initiatives of migrants' organizations, while others operate on a low-scale and usually design projects for cooperation.

The oldest organization is the Catalonian Agricultural Union, *Unió de Pagesos*, one of the organizations channelling Moroccan labour to work in Spanish agriculture by means of recruitment at the source. Based on this experience, this Union has taken a qualitative leap by becoming involved in promoting development actions in Morocco, through the *Fundación Pagesos Solidaris* (Farmer Solidarity Foundation), by training and by raising awareness among temporary workers in their capacity as agents of development in their communities of origin. Its project in *Sidi Yamani* (in northern Morocco) is a symbol of their desire to make migratory flows have positive effects for development on both sides.[34]

31 An extensive analysis of the Moroccan case is in a book by Lacomba (2004a) and another by Fernández/et al. (2008), which devotes specific chapters to Morocco.

32 See at: <www.atime.es/cooperacion.html> (15 June 2009).

33 See at: <www.codenaf.org> (15 June 2009).

The Valencian Refugee Aid Association (AVAR) has been developing a project to create employment for young people in the Tendrara (Morocco) region locally. The idea is to provide alternatives to hold back the migration of minors from this area into Spain by providing financial support to their families to help them remain in the school system with a grant for children under 16 years of age. In addition, training courses are offered for those over 16 years of age in consultation with the Local Council of Associations and with the cooperation of the Association of Moroccan Immigrants of Tendrara in the Valencian Autonomous Community and AVAR.[35]

The organization Cooperation for Peace Assembly in Valencia also undertakes a project to improve the production, distribution, marketing and sustainability conditions of the fishing industry in various communities in the North of Morocco, and to strengthen the relationship between Valencian and Moroccan societies within coastal municipalities. The objectives are to contribute towards creating a 'co-development' culture among Northern and Southern organizations and to improve the conditions of the artisanal fishing industry. Another project by the Cooperation for Peace Assembly aims at preventing illegal migration from Morocco and violation of Moroccan migrants' human rights, with the participation of town councils and institutions in northern Morocco and of the Moroccan community in Madrid, by raising awareness, training, and providing information in Spain and Morocco. The project also envisages the involvement of migrants in identifying and supporting development cooperation projects in the Rif, the mountainous region of Northern Morocco.[36]

In Murcia, the *Asociación para la Cooperación con el Sur - Las Segovias* (ACSUR-Las Segovias or the Association for Cooperation with the South-Las Segovias) initiated a project that seeks to promote networking among migrant women from the Maghreb region, and to coordinate links between these and organizations involving women and young people in Algeria and Morocco. The organization works in the areas of solidarity action, awareness and education from the perspective of human rights, premised on the principle of grass-root participation and the development of local powers. Through exchange of information and dialogues, the project seeks to promote respect for the human rights of migrants as people (men and women) both at their place of origin and destination.[37]

The Spanish Refugee Aid Committee (CEAR) developed the project 'Creating Associative Bases to Undertake Co-development Actions with Morocco', intended to promote a culture of 'association' between northern Morocco and the city of Madrid by creating and reinforcing networks that are already in contact with one another. The Transnational Centre for Rifian Initiatives first started in Madrid, followed by several sessions and meetings held between associations of Madrid, Valencia, Alhucemas, Nador and Oujda in addition to training and micro-credit promotion campaigns.[38]

Finally, the Movement for Peace, Disarmament and Freedom (MPDL) implemented the project "Comprehensive co-development proposal in the province of Alhucemas by training at source potential migrants" intended to contribute towards improving migratory flows between Morocco and Spain by providing concerted action on information, legal and socio-labour advice and support for those travelling between their country of origin and host country. The aim is to support the training of young workers at the source in the hotel and restaurant industry, for which there is a local supply and, eventually, in other places. MPDL also has in place the project "Co-development and Dynamization of the co-operation between Moroccan associative networks in Spain and Morocco", organized by the *Association Marocaine de Solidarité et Développement* (AMSED). This programme lies within the framework of the "Co-development Integral Programme for Morocco, Mali, Niger and bordering countries", implemented by the Movement for Peace and funded by the Spanish Agency for International Development Cooperation (AECID).[39]

Our review of the recent initiatives show that Spanish NGOs have been responding to the call to 'co-development', taking advantage of their prior experience in development cooperation and making both arenas compatible. However, given that the support came mainly from grants of regional governments, these projects must therefore follow the priority lines set and concentrate in areas pre-determined by the calls. Indeed, the bulk of the aforementioned projects share a mission to strengthen the associative movement and a geographical location in northern

34 See at: <www.pagesossolidaris.org> (14 June 2009).

35 See at: <http://dev.webonet.no-ip.com:8001/avar> (15 June 2009).

36 See at: <www.acpp.org> (16 June 2009).

37 See at: <www.acsur.org> (15 June 2009).

38 See at: <www.fundacioncear.org> (15 June 2009).

39 See at: <www.mpdl.org> (15 June 2009).

Morocco. They include the participation of immigrant associations in Spain and their local counterparts in Morocco, and create a new three-pronged relationship, which is inevitably a source for conflict.

7.5 Dawning Co-development: Light and Shadow

At present, co-development usually appears as an opportunity for development in emigration countries. The idea that migration may operate to promote development, and not necessarily to hamper it, has gathered strength, both in the official and unofficial arenas. According to this premise, international bodies and states have recently implemented policies and actions intended to promote the positive effects of migration in the development of the countries of origin. However, they have also often disguised the objective of using development aid for control of migration flows or even their prevention In this sense, official co-development policies contain multiple contradictions, with a remarkable distance between discussions and actions, or between the statements that present migrations as positive for development and the attempts to prevent them. Furthermore, much of the field remains in the stage of discourse and proposals for future projects and to date, many official policies remain unimplemented. Therefore, in spite of the expectation created by the use of the term 'co-development', many doubts and unanswered questions remain. In any event, the challenges for development are so colossal that the actions scheduled may have little consequence.

This kind of contradiction is particularly noticeable at the official level, where co-development remains linked to security concerns and to the return of migrants, forgetting that "promoting the return of migrants without guaranteeing basic living conditions and expectations for the future means a return to sedentarism without a horizon and thus is incompatible with the retention of their function as agents of development" (Gómez 2005: 10). As proven through the texts drafted by different European bodies, official policies repeat a concept of co-development primarily as an instrument to regulate migration. As Jean-François Bayart pointed out, although "initially addressed as associating the civil society and migrants with public development aid, co-development has gradually become a counter-migratory device" (Bayart 2007: 26). Cristophe Daum goes deeper, highlighting the ambiguity between development in the countries of origin and the management of migration flows and arguing that official co-development is more oriented towards organizing cooperation of the States of origin in the control of immigration through a repressive orientation (Daum 2008: 58). Sharing this view, Thomas Lacroix writes:

> The initial definition of co-development has evolved under the pressure exerted by the actors: for public powers, it is a policy of flow management through development in the regions of origin; on this basis, migrants are just development vectors, instruments invested with transnational circulatory capabilities. The re-appropriation of this notion by associative actors and territorial collectives has led to reinvestment in centres of co-development interest. Migrants have become the main topic: their integration in the transnational space, re-appropriation of circulation and the promotion of a statute of mediators have become the main goals of this decentralised co-development (Lacroix 2005: 231–232).

It is in the field of unofficial co-development where we may rebuild our hopes for this idea that some authors have qualified as hardly realizable wishful thinking.[40] Along the lines of attributing the feasibility and leading role in co-development to civil society, Ramón states that "the agents of co-development are not basically Governments in their bilateral relationship, but firstly migrants themselves and, secondly, the social agents of both societies: unions, companies, teaching institutions, citizen organisations, NGOs" (Ramón 2005: 51). She adds that co-development is inspired by two fundamental principles.

> First, the leading role played by migrants as co-development agents. This requires providing migrants and their associations (which need to be promoted) with a decisive role when projecting measures and action lines, and not to perceive them as mere executors of plans drafted from the respective Governments. In addition, this also requires acknowledging the relevance of the initiatives and actions by civil society agents and subordinate State administrations, also in the societies receiving immigration (Ramón 2005: 50).

Certainly, co-development promoted by migrants themselves from the scope of civil society enjoys greater legitimacy than actions by states, and a considerable number of experiences that account for the involvement of migrants in the development of their communities of origin reinforce this view (Lacomba 2004b). By implementing transnational organizational strategies, migrants have proven their dynamism and

40 Expression used by Joaquín Arango in the Sessions on Co-development and Immigration organized in 2003 by the AECI Planning and Evaluation Bureau in Madrid.

capability to operate numerous changes. In fact, with their example, migrants opened the path for state action to follow, forcing them to compete to occupy local and international solidarity spaces.

Hence, some authors underline the importance of the natural role played by migrants in the development of their communities of origin, with or without their states. Malgesini (2007: 31) speaks of "spontaneous co-development", as the set of positive effects of immigration for the development of the origin and hosting societies generated by the contact and exchange between people from different backgrounds. Gómez Gil highlights:

> Historically, people form spontaneous solidarity networks of an extraordinary impact, as a basic component of group sociability and solidarity. Migrants also weave extremely powerful networks from the privacy of their relationships and the historic commitments built in their communities and families, something which at present we call 'co-development' but which merely is a spontaneous expression of sociability and solidarity that people develop.... Precisely, the strength of co-development as an idea is founded on its component of reciprocity, on the pronouncement of common commitment it contains, on the active and participative attitude to contribute towards the improvement of others (Gómez Gil 2005: 7).

Nonetheless, in addition to their own resources and strategies, migrants have also increasingly benefited from the support of development organizations present in host countries (Faist 2006). This global phenomenon is manifest in Morocco, where cooperation between civil society (including migrant associations) and the State is gradually becoming more frequent, but is subject to numerous tensions and contradictions (Lacroix 2005; Lacomba 2005).

Regarding limits, we may first refer to diverse meanings and interpretations of co-development held by the multiplicity of stakeholders. Thus, while public administrations consider co-development mainly as a mode of development cooperation, for NGOs it would be more of a methodology than a strategy, and for migrant associations co-development stands as a vehicle for their own vindication and an opportunity to increase their visibility and participation (Giménez/Martinez/Fernandez/Cortes 2006: 102–105). In this sense, and to illustrate further the diversity of approaches to co-development by the stakeholders, we should highlight that public administrations continue to use the term 'co-development' with great caution, NGOs have largely included it in their vocabulary and projects, and many immigrant associations view it with distrust.

Criticism of the work done by NGOs sometimes come from a too technical idea of co-development, linked to the performance of projects, which considers political transformations only within a context of economic development or of the search for actual synergies between migration and economic development. In contrast, in the work carried out by the organizations created by migrants, they do not disassociate themselves from the demand for rights.[41]

The barriers also include the lack of coordination between the entities that promote co-development actions, with scarce participation of migrant associations, to the detriment of the leading role granted by the original concept of co-development. Grillo and Riccio also argue:

> Problems of control, of misunderstandings due to naïve expectations, of idealisation of partners, of mutual disillusionment, as well as the importance of transnational social networks, and individual and collective social capital (or lack of it). Participants may have to deal with the inexperience, unreliability and self-interest of colleagues, and the demands of relatives (and venal politicians) anxious to share any success. Yet at the very least, co-development is no better or worse than more conventional forms of development (Grillo/Riccio 2004: 109).

7.6 Conclusion

This chapter has offered some reflection on co-development as a new term in European policy seeking to link migration with development goals. We have noted that at the EU level, the meaning of co-development is restricted to immigration control and security concerns. Co-development here appears torn between two different policy objectives: 1) security for the EU, which emphasizes the curb on illegal migration and 2) free trade, which promotes free movement of factors of production, except labour. A key assumption is that migration pressures in sending countries are the outcomes of development failure, which could be solved by using the contributions of migrants and diasporas. The increasing number of declarations posits the idea of migrants' participation in the field of co-development in EU policies being instrumental to curb migration flows.

In Spain, the particular initiatives of certain regional and local governments and, above all, of civil society agents, emphasize their role as transformation

41 This would be the case of the network Immigration, Development and Democracy in France, or the RedCo (Network for Co-Development) in Spain.

agents in their societies of origins. However, despite the growing cooperation on co-development between civil society (including migrant associations) and the state, numerous tensions and contradictions exist, particularly regarding return migration and the lack of a clear vision after return. Other major issues that operate against civil society-based co-development initiatives include the streamlining of the budgets for official development aid, and the high expectations placed on migrants' remittances. Frontier control and national security issues have overshadowed the optimistic perspective on the transnational spaces in which migrants are expected to contribute to 'co-development'.

8 Financial Globalization and the Mechanisms of Migrants' Remittance: Formed by Supply or Demand?

Amrita Sharma and Karim Knio

8.1 Introduction

Governments began to give fuller attention to remittances in the 1990's when their sum total topped the level of Official Development Assistance (ODA) and Foreign Direct Investment (FDI) (Meissner 1993). A decade later remittances had become a new development 'mantra' in global policy frameworks. Following the Post G-8 summit of 2004 in Sea Island there was sudden worldwide activity to improve the infrastructure for remittances and ensure swift safe transfers. In 2007 the World Bank's Committee on Payment and Settlement Systems (CPSS) brought out the General Principles for International Remittance Services which were later endorsed by the G-8, the G-20 and the Financial Stability Forum. Supported by a mix of international financial institutions, NGOs and sending states, this emerging financial infrastructure is comprised of norms, standards and agencies dedicated to manage migrants' remittances for development. Its underlying rationale is that greater inclusion of migrants into financial institutions would enhance the effectiveness of remittances. These initiatives intend to improve the functioning of existing remittance industry by instituting standards, improving transparency, encouraging competition, and easing some of the stifling regulations which otherwise hamper its functioning. Formalization is expected to reduce the costs of remittance transfer, hence increasing the average flows into developing countries. Fuller use of formal banking structures and securitization of future flow was expected to address capital scarcity, promote financial inclusion of the poor and boost financial sector development in countries of origin. Superseded by the unfolding global financial crisis since 2008, this rationale is now subject to criticism. The concerns about reduced remittances due to job losses and return migration to countries of origin in the South[1], raise two main issues: one is the scientific validity of the much touted role assigned to migrants' remittances in development, and the other is the claim that formalization has an advantage over the informal systems of service provision which are characterized by personal connections, a low level of bureaucratic formality and a wider coverage compared with banks.[2] These two issues have broad economic, social and ethical implications and urge a more critical understanding of the relationships between financialization, migrants' remittance and 'development' in the South.

Mainstream theory describes the rise of remittance institutions as evolutionary, correcting market failures and removing possible hurdles in free flow of capital (Fajnzylber/López 2008). This chapter, however, takes the perspective developed by Hudson (2008: 317) who views the financialization process as being built on a continuous search "to find new income streams that can be securitized".[3] Migrants' remittances constitute one of these new income streams. By reviewing the discourses on, and practices of, governance of remittances the chapter discerns a deeper convergence of different lines of interests underpinning the design of financial services for migrant

1 World Bank estimates projected a drop of 5–8 per cent in global remittances in 2009. *The Economic Times*, 3 June 2009; and even countries such as India, which claimed resilience in remittance flows, are experiencing return of migrants. Press Trust of India, 2009: "About 150,000 Indians Return from UAE Due to Recession" See at: <http://www.ndtv.com/news/india/about_15_lakh_indians_return_from_uae_due_to_recession.php> (8 July 2009).

2 Some examples include the Hundi and Hawala system prevalent in South Asia, Fei Ch'ien (flying money) in China, Guanxi in China, Phone Kuan in Thailand, 'door-to-door' in Philippines (Passas 2004).

3 Securitization is a process that involves the isolation of a pool of assets or rights to a set of cash flows and the repackaging of the asset or cash flows into securities as instruments representing either ownership (stocks), a debt agreement (bonds) or the right to ownership (derivatives), which are traded in capital markets.

T.-D. Truong and D. Gasper (eds.), *Transnational Migration and Human Security*, Hexagon Series on Human and Environmental Security and Peace 6, DOI 10.1007/978-3-642-12757-1_8, © Springer-Verlag Berlin Heidelberg 2011

workers. Apart from the interests of banks, the formalization of these services also meets two strategic objectives of states: 1) declining ODA and FDI volumes which have exacerbated the need of some labour-exporting countries to secure migrants' remittances to finance development; and 2) the post-9/11 fear of 'terror-linked' financial flows which make it vital that remittances be included in the formal banking systems to pre-empt any use for destructive purposes.

Examination of the experience of three countries (India, Philippines and Indonesia) shows a political-economic dimension behind this process. The emergence of new architecture for migrants' remittances appears more supply-driven, stimulated by political interests which dominate the agenda of migrants' remittances but are weakly supported by evidence in real life. To the majority of migrant workers who are undocumented/illegal migrants, the formal financial system has little to offer. The focus of the international financial system should be more on adapting to migrants' interests to devise better remittance systems rather than drawing the migrant workers into the ambit of financial capitalism based on unfounded optimism.

8.2 Financialization and Securitization: Migrants' Remittances in the New International Political Economy

Financialization has been one of the key aspects of globalization. Frieden (1995) offers a working definition of financialization as a process wherein the volume of capital movement surpasses that of trade in goods and services. It has meant increasing integration of financial markets across the globe, triggered and emboldened by changes in technology and deregulation. This process creates a need for multiple institutions and since the 1970's there have been significant institutional changes furthering the dominance of finance capital over industrial or commercial capital (Pineault 2001).[4] One clear characteristic of this process is a constant lookout for newer sources of finance. Leyshon and Thrift (2008: 97) write: "Financial capitalism is dependent on the constant searching out, or the construction of, new asset streams, usually through a process of aggregation, which then - and only then - allows speculation to take place".

Hudson (2008: 315) argues that the financialization of remittances is driven by similar needs to acquire previously untouched capital and thus the need to "bring them into the global development architecture". He regards it as yet another attempt to surmount the drop in development finance and, perhaps, find newer sources to fund the Millennium Development Goals. Raghuram (2009) in her study "Which migration, what development" also calls remittances the 'lodestar' around which a whole remittance development industry is being formed. This process involves a large number of non-state actors such as NGOs and international organizations all working to strengthen and perpetuate the process in their unique capacities. One notable aspect of the financialization of remittances is creation of a rhetoric eulogizing remittances as a source of development finance, with with a magnitude surpassing FDI and allegedly being counter-cyclical and well targeted. The international institutions have played a leading role in creating and popularizing this view.

Until the first years of this decade efforts to manage remittances were limited to major migrant sending countries such as Mexico, Philippines, Colombia, Turkey and India. Since then the formalization drive has gained greater momentum and spread out to untouched quarters. For instance, a number of foreign banks moved into the untapped markets of Eastern Europe. Karafolas and Sariannidis (2008) present the case of Albania where a number of Greek and Italian banks moved in to manage remittance flows. These authors argue that the increase of remittances flowing through formal channels (according to figures given) relates to the proliferation of Greek and Italian bank branches within the country.

According to Hudson (2008) the current formalization effort by banks may be divided into two broad categories: one aimed at expanding retail outreach to cover more remittances and bring them into the financial mainstream; another to leverage cash flows and generate more capital through securitization.

Under the first category the key intervention has been the reduction of remittances transfer costs, given

4 Pineault (2001) reviews the scholarship on financialization to show how it has moved from the orthodox Marxian theory of money and the relations between bank and industrial capital adopted by Rudolph Hilferding (1981) to the study of the economic institutions dealing with finance capital, increasingly drawing from the ideas of heterodox economists. Regulation school theorists such as Robert Boyer and David Harvey have been leading contributors to recent institutional analysis of financial systems highlighting the politics behind them. See at: <https://depot.erudit.org/bitstream/002332dd/1/document-2002-01-pineault.pdf> (30 April 2010).

that they constitute a major disadvantage for formal vis-à-vis informal financial institutions. Transfers via official bank channels are often administratively burdensome and remain a closed option for migrants who are unable to open accounts in their countries of residence owing to their temporary situation or (often) illegal/undocumented status. Private companies generally charge high fees with the average cost of official transfer being between 13 and 20 per cent of the total. Informal channels, while cheaper, can incur costs due to risks such as fraud and theft.[5]

The cost of transfer is the key criterion in the choice of a remittance service provider (World Bank 2007). Most non-governmental organizations, international organizations and financial institutions have focused on bringing these costs down to attract remitters by making the prevailing rates offered by different remittance service providers (RSPs) available on the web and allowing consumers to compare prices. These efforts help in increasing transparency, encouraging competition and better choice. Extending the retail outreach, requires forging links with Micro Finance Institutions (MFIs) and making them serve as complement banks: they are often present in places that banks fail to reach and have the expertise of pooling and leveraging small amounts of money (Fritz/Ambrosius/Stiegler 2008). Many MFIs are not authorised to deal with foreign exchange and so a link-up with authorised dealers helps them actively engage in international transfers (Fritz/Ambrosius/Stiegler 2008). This line of connection between the financial institutions, migrants and MFIs is proposed as the win-win solution where the financial institutions (FIs) gain from greater access to hard cash and more clients, and migrants benefit from their financial aptitude and astute money management abilities.

Under the second category, the leveraging of remittances and enhancing their growth potential, banks also placed in a better position than the money transfer operators (MTOs) or the informal service providers. Specialists argue that banks are able to attach a broad portfolio of financial services to remittance transfer services (Alberloa/Salvado 2006; Avila/Schlarb 2008). One of the ways banks offer to increase the benefits from remittances is through securitization of future flow receivables. Ketkar/Ratha (2001: 1) explains this operation as follows:

> In a typical future flow transaction, the borrowing entity (originator) in a developing country sells its future products (receivables) directly or indirectly to an offshore *Special Purpose Vehicle* (SPV), which issues the debt instrument. Designated international customers (obligors) are directed to pay for the goods they import from the originator directly into an offshore collection account managed by a trustee. The collection agent makes principal and interest payments to lenders. Any funds left over are forwarded to the originator.

The authors point out that securitizing remittances helps banks overcome the 'sovereign risk' or what Hudson (2008: 327) term as the fear of "governments defaulting on their loans unilaterally". Because the remittances never actually enter a country once they are pledged to the SPV, these instruments often get a relatively high rating or investment grade even when the rating of that country is at "sub-investment grade" (Hudson 2008: 327). As a result, the issuers of remittance-securities are able to raise more money in the international capital markets. Mexico was the first country to implement securitization in 1994. The value of securities issued using remittances as collateral reportedly then increased more than 40 times during the following ten years (World Bank 2006: 103).

At international level remittance management presents a smarter option vis-à-vis promoting or curtailing migration openly as it is more politically palatable (López-Cordova 2006: 37). There is a fresh impetus for research on better utilization of remittances funded by government-backed development agencies and international funding agencies in the major migrant receiving countries. For labour importing countries by focusing on appropriate utilization of the remittances in the local economy of migrants' origin remittance management appears more politically correct than blatant anti-migration policy. For labour-exporting countries the motivation is clear: effective remittance management helps them service foreign debts, maintain a healthy trade balance and improve their credit rating in international markets. Rupert and Solomon (2005: 83) note the following: "Temporary migration, far from being inconsequential because of the eventual return of the migrant, is transforming the boundaries of sending states, altering the calculus of state policy makers, and serving as a vital source of the external finance necessary for servicing debt and imported oil."

---

5 See at: <http://www.iom.int/jahia/webdav/site/myjahiasite/shared/shared/mainsite/microsites/IDM/workshops/Trade_2003_12141103/issue_day2.pdf>. Passas (2004: 21) reveals that remitters paid 0–1.5 per cent of the remitted amount using the informal system, or a tiny fraction of the sum as compared with the charges made by private companies. It is important to note that there is lack of consensus on the informal systems and methods used in assessment of costs.

Table 8.1: Formal vs. informal methods of transfer. **Source:** Passas (2004: 21).

Formal	Informal
10-20 per cent cost	0-1.5 per cent cost
Service to main cities	Service to remote areas
Detailed records kept	Minimal/no records
Receipt to sender	No receipts to sender
Currency Transaction Report (CTR), Suspicious Activity Report (SAR) filed	No reporting to authority
Collection and delivery at agency premises	At home pick-up and delivery service
Transfer in days/weeks	Transfer in hours
Agency specialised in money services	IVTS mixed with other business

Another important explanation for the wave of formalization lies in the security concerns that arose after the 9/11 attacks on the US. De Goede (2005) points out that in the US Patriot Act 2001 some of the most drastic and important provisions were in the area of financial regulation. 'Data mining' of financial transactions using sophisticated information technology became an important part of the risk management and prediction of terrorist activities, and this rather hit the informal remittance industry.[6] Given that informal service providers account for more than 50 per cent of the remittance industry (Passas 2004), the post-9/11 practices hit the informal networks of money transfers particularly hard. What makes them susceptible to crackdown under the war on terrorism is their poor compliance with formal regulations as a way of keeping operational costs low. Passas (2004) terms them "informal value transfer systems". Characterized by personal connections, these traditional transfers cater to the large section of undocumented migrant workers and neither issue transaction receipts nor maintain records of transactions. Many have existed for centuries, pre-date the formal banking system and are legitimate. They have a much wider coverage compared with banks, and consumers find it much more convenient given that money is collected from and delivered at home. Unskilled migrant workers who would be intimidated by the formalities of banks find it much easier doing business with informal service providers.

De Goede (2005: 38) points out how "the move towards computerized data mining aims to reduce terrorist danger while presenting a commercial opportunity". Heavy emphasis on bringing these informal networks under mainstream financial structures (so that suspicious transactions could be identified and terrorist behaviour predicted) is neither backed by evidence nor shown to be effective (Passas 2004: 36). Contrary to popular belief, much of the money used by 9/11 terrorists was transferred using formal channels (Passas 2003). The 9/11 Commission report by Roth, Greenberg and Willie (2003)[7] also confirms that no amount of surveillance would have helped differentiate the transactions made by 9/11 terrorists from routine transfers. It is possible to argue that the current drive to regulate the informal remittance industry comes more from commercial interests than is formally acknowledged. In its attempt to reconcile the need for new financial regulation with the continuance of de-regulated financial markets the deregulation drive shows its incoherence.

In the wake of the current economic crisis efforts for managing remittances have found fresh credibility in what is termed an 'innovative financing strategy' for the global South. Analysts claim that halving the costs of transfer could result in an extra 12 to 15 billion USD for development in the global south (*The Economic Times*, 12 June 2009).[8] When examined in depth, much of what is written or said about remittance management – efficiency, transparency, competition, accountability – is a reflection of the dominant neoliberal development paradigm. Remittance management is now helping and being helped by financial liberalization around the world: it addresses the inconsisten-

6 Especially the *Hawala* system prevalent in South Asia came under heavy surveillance as being possible clandestine webs of money laundering and terrorism financing.

7 See at: <http://www.9-11commission.gov/staff_statements/911_TerrFin_Monograph.pdf> (1 May 2010).

8 *The Economic Times* 2009: "G8 Eyes Halving Remittances Transfer Costs: Italy", 12 June 2009, See at: <http://economictimes.indiatimes.com/News/International-Business/G8-eyes-halving-remittances-transfer-costs-Italy/articleshow/4650143.cms> (1 May 2010)

cies and hurdles that might obstruct the smooth flow of capital across borders. The way the logic is presented, the activity of the financial markets and the international response to possible sources of market failure appear as instances of self-organization where the markets – being 'complex adaptive systems' – are only heeding the demands made by the remittance industry. The current order in remittance markets is presented as "spontaneous or emergent and is a result of human action and not execution of human design" (Markose 2003: 2). The role the international organizations play is only to correct market failures and enable the smooth functioning of the industry. There are, however, other aspects indicating that this depiction is far from fair and complete. For instance, the current bailout packages offered by governments to save sinking banks makes the magnitude of remittances (337 billion USD annually[9]) seem insignificant. This comparison is helpful in putting these issues in perspective and when examining the broader global development finance dynamics.

8.3 The Science behind Remittance Management

At the global level there are essentially four emerging elements of formalization of remittances: 1) concerted efforts to channel remittances through formal financial institutions; 2) construction of regulatory mechanisms around the transfer of remittances; 3) incorporation of remittance multipliers such as securitization into formal banking channels; and 4) efforts to improve data on remittance flows. Each of these elements has been defended by orthodox economists with nuanced differences about the impact of remittances but generally supportive of formalization. Heterodox perspectives emphasise power relations in a political-economic context and caution against a purely instrumental approach.

8.3.1 Remittances in Orthodox Economic Theory

The standard macroeconomic approach has dealt with remittances as part of international transfers and treated their impact on aggregate expenditure, domestic savings and national output accordingly. When remittances flow into an economy both expenditure and savings are expected to increase. Higher savings are expected to cause increased availability of resources, which leads further to reduced domestic interest rates, inducing investment. This, however, is the most stereotyped model of how remittances work.

In more recent analyses the impact of remittances on the economy is divided into short- and long-term ones. Short-term studies focus on the impact of remittances on exchange rates, domestic interest rates and domestic savings. One debate that has occupied this field is whether remittances have a 'Dutch disease'[10] effect on the economy or lend growth stimulus to capital-starved economies (Loser/Lockwood/Minson/Balcazar 2006).[11] A bulk inflow of remittances, like other sources of international capital flow, causes appreciation of the real exchange rate and reduces its competitiveness in the international arena. López-Cordova and Olmedo (2005: 23) point out that this is similar to the classic 'transfer problem' where a sudden inflow of remittances may initially improve the terms of trade and overall welfare but affect the export competitiveness of the country adversely.

Remittances held in banks in foreign currency can be a further cause of concern. Fritz, Ambrosius and Stiegler (2008) point out that in many developing countries citizens often prefer an international currency because of little faith in the local currency, and that once a foreign currency gains weight in local monetary transactions the trend becomes difficult to reverse. This phenomenon called dollarization, first noted in Latin American countries, has serious adverse consequences. Because of dollarization central banks do not have the same hold on their money in circulation and can lose control of an important macroeconomic instrument, that is: monetary policy. For lack of faith in their domestic currency individual migrant workers prefer to keep their savings in foreign currency. Macroeconomic management would require otherwise and thus such preference has become a policy concern (Fritz/Ambrosius/Stiegler 2008).

In the long-term models the impact of remittances is analysed in terms of their impact on productivity

9 IOM 2008. See at: <http://www.iom.int/jahia/Jahia/op/edit/cache/offonce/pid/1674?entryId=20275> (1 May 2010)

10 The phenomenon refers to appreciation in local currency because of new influxes of large amounts. The term draws its name from the effect a sudden discovery of gas reserves in the North Sea had on the Dutch economy some decades ago. Increase in gas exports caused an appreciation in the local currency affecting other exports and competing imports adversely. The term has since been used to describe similar effects elsewhere.

11 See at: <http://www.g24.org/lose0906.pdf> (1 May 2010).

and inequality in the economies of origin countries. A study by Chami, Jahjah and Fullenkamp (2003) shows that under asymmetric information remittances are likely to have a negative impact on growth in some of the labour-exporting countries; however, the impact on inequality is ambiguous. While some empirical studies show that remittances have a trickle down impact and stimulate local economies (Mendola 2006),[12] others show that benefits from remittances are limited to the few receivers and thus exacerbate inequalities within a region (Hoddinott 1994; Saith 2001). Most policy studies focus on the short-term dynamics of remittances with the aim of designing adequate monetary and fiscal policies to lessen the adverse impact and strengthen the positive effects. When highlighting the impact of formalization, the remittance-enthusiasts largely limit themselves to short-term dynamics.

The migration literature is replete with critiques of remittance-led growth mostly focusing on its non-sustainable nature. There is limited evidence of positive impact of migration on sustained economic development. Castles (2007)[13] for instance, points out the case of Mexico to show how both remittances and *maquiladoras* only deepened the dependence of the country on the US without bringing about any genuine development. Among the major migrant sending countries Turkey is the only one to have achieved a sound level of economic development but scholars doubt that this development was due to better remittance or migration management. Castles (2007) also points out that failure of Turkey to harness remittances during the 1970's and 1980's for industrial growth casts serious doubts on the efficacy of the remittance-led growth discourse.

The above discussion shows the imperfect science of remittance management. The drive to create institutions for the management of remittances chooses to remain ignorant of the past and the lessons it has to offer. The public-policy driven accounts focus on learning from successful initiatives what they term as 'best practices' and replicating them globally. It becomes imperative to understand the reasons behind the political insularity of the current techno-managerial discourse on governance of remittances.

8.3.2 Political Insularity of the Formalization Discourse

Since the beginning of the 1990's governance literature has increasingly gained importance among development practitioners and academics (Smith 2007). Many reasons account for this ascendancy. The end of the Cold War, the proliferation of NGOs and the emergence of relatively new concepts and practices plus the human rights agenda, illustrate some of the driving forces behind this phenomenon (Weiss 2000). These developments have also elicited new forms of conceptualization whereby the term 'governance' is no longer associated just with the state and the machinery of governments but now with all sorts of networks and informal institutions which co-exist and interact with the public sector in any organised polity. The shift from government to something beyond the realm of actual governments has significantly altered the manner in which we conceptualise governance. As Kjaer (2004) points out, if governance is understood as the setting, application and enforcement of the rules of the game, then the institutional grounding of the term is unavoidable.

Hout and Robison (2009) point out that two distinctive approaches to governance can be detected across all fields. World Bank publications, major international donors/organizations and national developmental agencies tend to define and analytically treat governance as a technocratic construction exhibiting research and policy concerns about the design, sequencing, implementation and enforcement of institutional reforms. As such, governance epitomises a 'techno-managerial' fix aimed at the institutional engineering of many areas – such as anti-corruption, decentralization, accountability, transparency and rule of law – which complement and strengthen the efficiency of market institutions. This instrumental view of governance, as they argued, seems to facilitate a notion of insularity where the governance agenda provides a platform to circumvent direct political issues in societies.

The second approach to governance is a perspective that emphasises the significance of asymmetrical relations. The concept denotes an acute understanding of "conflicts over power and wealth underpinning the establishment of authority in market societies" (Hout/Robison 2009: 5). Problems encountered within processes of institutional reform cannot be simply attributed to capacity-building considerations or to prevailing weak institutions. They reflect power dynamics embedded in a particular context. Govern-

12 See at: <http://www.sussex.ac.uk/migration/documents/mwp40.pdf> (1 May 2010).

13 See at: <www.imi.ox.ac.uk/pdfs/WP7%20Comparing%205%20countries.pdf> (1 May 2010).

ance in this analysis therefore implies a direct engagement with the politically contentious issues existing in any polity.

The insights drawn from the literature on the New Institutional Economics (NIE) and its equivalent in the field of political science or Rational Choice Institutionalism (RCI) are, arguably, the theoretical underpinnings of the 'techno-managerial' account of governance. As per NIE/RCI, changes in formal institutions are expected to be achieved more easily than in informal ones, given the time lag associated with adjusting 'mental models' (Denzau/North 1994). Institutional change in these approaches is not only gradual but also conscious. The complex interplay between institutions and organizations explains the approaches of NIE and RCI to change, continuity and economic performance, and contributes to the techno-managerial understanding of governance.

Underlying and triggering these processes is the analytical separation and the concomitant interaction between institutions (which set the rules of the game) and organizations (the players, agencies, etc.). Following North's (1994) seminal contribution to the literature, an important distinction is to be made between formal and informal institutions - seen as aggregations of rules that define how the game (human interaction) is played–and organizations, which consist of groups of individuals guided by the pursuit of common objectives in different spheres (political, economic, social, educational). This analytical distinction is almost balanced by an argument along the lines of Giddens' perspective on structure and agency[14] whereby institutions shape and condition the type of organizations created, while organizations - investing in skills, knowledge and technology for their own survival - are the source and motor of institutional change. For North:

> The organisations that come into existence will reflect the opportunities provided by the institutional matrix. That is, if the institutional framework rewards piracy then piratical organisations will come into existence; and if the institutional framework rewards productive activities then organisations or firms will come into existence to engage in productive activities (North 1994: 361).

Hence, if the process of change is attributed to the synchronization between organizations and institutions, then the institutional anchoring of incentives which protect and safeguard property rights lies at the heart of the approach of NIE/RCI towards medium- and long-term economic performance. Since the institutional framework comprises opportunities and constraints where the organizations or players are rationally bounded, one gets efficient institutions by a polity that has built-in incentives to create and enforce efficient property rights (North 1990). From this perspective, property rights constitute the core economic institutions in a society (Acemoglu/Johnson 2005). The concept as used here is not restricted to the economic sphere but also applies within the political system and among the co-existing norms.

In relation to the political system the techno-managerial conception of governance emphasizes how incremental, yet conscious, institutional engineering can make the rules of those formal institutions (which enforce property rights) more transparent, accountable, predictable and streamlined (Williamson 2000). In parallel it addresses the structure of incentives which, if followed by rationally-bound actors, means that new rules are desirable. Therefore, if it is more rational for players to stick to these property rights-sensitive rules of the game, the process will yield better economic performance in the end (Ostrom 1990). These themes have inspired many World Bank publications (World Bank 1991, 1997) on good governance, anti-corruption, decentralization policies and lately the financial inclusion initiatives under governance of remittances.

The major emphasis of the international organizations involved in remittance market creation is on developing the 'payment system aspects' of remittances (World Bank 2008). According to the current diagnosis several factors hinder the efficient flow of remittances. Ill-developed financial systems in countries of origin, high transaction costs, long processing periods and stifling regulations deter migrants from accessing formal remittance services (World Bank 2008). In the last 12 years the World Bank has helped more than 100 countries institute payment-system reforms in their financial systems. Financial sector development is expected to have a positive effect on the economy by helping overcome credit market failures, fostering growth and reducing poverty (Agarwal/Demirgüç-Kunt/Martinez-Peria 2006).[15] Arguably, developing economies suffer from poorly developed financial markets and a low degree of monetization, and a sig-

14 Giddens' dialectical understanding of the mutual constitutiveness of binary oppositions is evident in his attempt to 'solve' the structure/agency conundrum through his structuration theory (Giddens 1984: 376).

15 See at: <http://econ.worldbank.org/resource.php?type=5> (1 May 2010)

nificant portion of the population that works outside the sphere of the financial system which is unable to access credit and suffers from low productivity (Fritz/Ambrosius/Stiegler 2008). Terry and Wilson (2005: 391) suggest that remittances can be the 'point of entry' into the formal financial system for the poor giving them a plethora of financial products such as loans for housing, mortgages, insurance and pension plans.

The leading assumption behind formalization is that it would increase the savings available in an economy for investment and help stimulate remittance multipliers for economic growth.[16] The remittances-savings line of argument emphasizes that money will be accessible to entrepreneurs and used where it earns highest possible returns. In many developing countries most migrant savings go into purchase of land and houses, which is not considered the best way to mobilize savings (Ratha 2004).[17] In the standard neoclassical format an increase in savings is equated with better prospects for growth and higher per capita income (Fritz/Ambrosius/Stiegler 2008). This assumption has been challenged on several grounds. One striking case is that of Kerala, India where a large amount of remittances in savings accounts remain under-utilized. The economy thus faces the problem of how to convert its high level of savings into productive investment and employment (Kannan/Hari 2002). State level public sector enterprises have failed to attract remitted funds because of low efficiency and poor credibility. Saith (1991) showed that the Kerala economy failed to capitalize the boom in the construction sector and remittance money flew out of the state. Mobilizing these savings has been a problem for policymakers. Evidently there is a gap between the influx of remittances and its growth-inducing utilization, and it is not clear how the formalization efforts would help correct it.

To recapitulate, the academic challenge of NIE/RCI perceptibly revolves more around the *mechanics of institutional analysis*, than the fundamental *formation and post formation questions that surround the genesis of these institutions*. The mechanics of institutional analysis – the analytical and methodological lenses through which institutions have been defined and studied as regards how they operate and how political behaviour confronts or contributes to institutional continuity, change and performance – need to be subject to greater scrutiny. Nonetheless, all these variations, including the institutional tinkering patterns of NIE/RCI, are silent about where these institutions come from, how they are formed, to which perceived interests they relate, and how they are legitimized. In a similar spirit, there are more nuances to the ingredients and drivers of the formalization process than visible in the World Bank type techno-managerial call for governance. Our next contention is that there is a need to investigate more deeply the processes that have led to the creation and then perpetuation of migrant flows, and by extension the remittance flows. We do so by examining the experiences of three countries to show how the political often dominates the economic.

8.4 Different Folks, Different Strokes: The Philippines, India and Indonesia

One of the notable features of the global remittance market is the high variance in the degree of formalization of remittances; there can be stark differences even within a region. While remittance management is fairly advanced in the Latin American and Caribbean region, it is at a nascent stage in Central and Eastern Europe and many countries in Africa. In the Southeast Asian region, the formal banking system channels more than 80 per cent of remittance flows to the Philippines whereas in Indonesia the informal remittance service providers (RSPs) dominate the market (IOM 2008). The immediate question that follows is what determines the level of formalization of remittance transfers?

In this section the systems of three countries are analyzed as regards their levels of formalization and measure of success: the Philippines, India and Indonesia. Philippines is considered to be very advanced in management of remittances. India is known to be a late formalizer with a moderate level of success while Indonesia is known for the speed with which it has gone back to the informal methods of remittance service provision. The different levels of formalization in these countries provide a good contrast and help highlight important determinants of formalization

16 One notable and positive aspect of remittances as a source of foreign finance is that the multiplier effects are more pronounced compared to other sources of foreign exchange. The reason being that the money goes to the lowest strata of society, which generally has a higher than average propensity to consume.

17 See at: <http://www.migrationinformation.org/Feature/display.cfm?ID=256> (1 May 2010). Ratha and Dilip (2004): "Understanding the Importance of Remittances", *Feature Story* Migration Policy Institute, October.

and its success or failure. Analysis shows that migration and remittance management has largely been a state-driven process, determined more by the financial and political needs of the ruling government than by the needs of the market, let alone the migrant workers. The case of the Philippines, the earliest among the formalizers, is particularly illustrative in showing the limitations of remittance-led development.

8.4.1 The Philippines

The Philippines are the fourth largest remittance receiver – after India, China and Mexico. The migrant population accounts for 10 per cent of the total population and remittances now make up nearly 12 per cent of national GDP (IOM 2008). It is also the pet-case of remittance-enthusiasts as a "paradigmatic example of state-driven policy of generating remittance finance through a determined state policy"; "no other country comes close to the same level of state involvement" (Rupert/Solomon 2005: 87). Once dominated by private RSPs, now more than 80 per cent of the remittances coming to the Philippines flow through formal channels (Siracusa/Acacio 2004). This money has been crucial to maintenance of the macroeconomic health of the economy. Nonetheless there is considerable dissent about the impact formalization has had on economic development in the Philippines.

In the early 1970's the Philippines' government established a comprehensive institutional arrangement for the management of migration. This scheme led to the creation of the OWWA (Overseas Workers Welfare Association), CFO (Commission on Filipino Overseas) and later the POEA (Philippine Overseas Employment Administration). The OWWA was for the welfare of the families of migrants and received contributions from the migrants themselves and from the government. The CFO was to ensure the welfare of the migrant workers. In 1982 the POEA evolved as a comprehensive programme bringing a number of activities under one umbrella. Under the programme migrants received induction services – help with documentation and pre-migration orientation courses – all under the supervision of the Ministry of Labour. A number of laws and policies were formulated to ensure the safety of migrants abroad, and also to streamline and leverage remittance flows. The Philippines was one of the first countries to honour its Diaspora by: organizing 'migrant worker days'; calling them 'national heroes'; providing them special rights such as a reduction in import duties; and even organizing beauty contests meant specially for the Diaspora namely 'Miss Overseas Philippines' (Castles 2007).

The trigger for this systematic labour-export infrastructure came during the Marcos regime. Scholars such as Castles (2007) argue that the process began as a measure to cushion the impact of a mismanaged economy during the Marcos years. There was no or little capital investment, debts were mounting and high levels of government corruption made it more difficult for the regime to command legitimacy. Motivated by fear of social unrest and the need to curb political opposition, Marcos declared martial law and started on the path of rapid market liberalization by adopting a wide range of structural adjustment plans under the guidance of the IMF and World Bank.

Before state-level involvement migration had been a vibrant informal sector. By introducing a major programme on systematic export of labour the Marcos regime literally took over the trade in contract labour from private migration merchants using it as instruments for economic and political viability (Siracusa/Acacio 2004). Through the years there have been significant modifications in state policy and private partners have been reinstated with the state playing a supervisory role.

Has this high level of organization and formalization achieved the expected goals? The evidence on this front is predominantly negative. Initially the labour export programme did help the Philippines gain credibility as a global economic actor and improve its credit-worthiness in the global market (Siracusa/Acacio 2004), but this advantage was not sustained. Saith (2001) shows how, having been at the point of economic take-off, the country then suffered from rising unemployment levels, increasing poverty and weak macroeconomic fundamentals. Many years of neglect of agriculture and undervaluation of capital in the Philippines had reduced the economic capacity to absorb the growing labour force. Low rates of domestic savings, combined with excessive dependence on remittances, is one of the serious shortcomings of the Philippines' growth model which makes it particularly vulnerable to external shocks. Bayangos and Jansen (2009) point out that fluctuations in remittance flows are significant, and that the impact of any recession in the US becomes pronounced once endogeneity and pro-cyclicality of remittances are considered. The benefits of migration have also accrued largely to the rich regions and higher income classes, thereby increasing inequality though the authors also argue that growth in the Philippines will be heavily dependent on remittance flows for years to come and that the poor could be worse off without them (Castles 2007).

The Philippines serves as an example of how dependence on remittances can drive attention away from more important structural issues, such as economic land reforms in rural areas, which would challenge deep-rooted bases of inequality and under-development (Castles 2007). Quick-fix measures ignore more important needs of development. Rupert and Solomon (2005: 100) note that migrants neither see these measures as helpful nor remittances as fulfilling any developmental task. Some even mock state actions, such as bestowing 'heroes of the nation' titles, as mere gimmicks to attract more remittance money. After approximately four decades of concerted formalization efforts, the Philippine economy continues to stagger under many, if not more, of the same problems.

8.4.2 India

In 2005-06 India received the highest amount of remittances (24.6 billion USD) followed by China and Mexico (Sasikumar/Hussain 2007). Forty-four per cent of these remittances originated from the US, 24 per cent from the Persian Gulf and 13 per cent from European countries (Chishti 2007).[18] Compared with other major labour-exporting economies (particularly the Philippines, Mexico and Turkey) institutionalization of the process in India started late; gaining import only after the much-known balance of payments (BoP) crisis of 1991. India has been relatively slow and cautious in its approach. On average, however, the efforts have been a success. The use of formal banking channels for the transfer of remittances has increased and the remittance market has grown more competitive with a large number of new RSPs entering the market. In the fiscal year 1990-91 the Reserve Bank of India reported remittances worth 2.1 billion USD (Chisti 2007). In less than 15 years the amount has risen more than ten times. Compared with 1991, when remittances made up 0.7 per cent of GDP, they had grown to three per cent of GDP by 2006 (Chishti 2007).

The Indian governments have long neglected the contribution of remittances to the economy. The 1991 balance of payment (BoP) crisis faced by India came as a turning point.[19] The Indian foreign exchange reserve dropped to record lows and India started on a massive liberalization exercise. Some scholars also call 1991 'India's second independence' (Chishti 2007). In an attempt to shore up all possible sources of foreign exchange, remittances received special attention because of the realization that they made up a large part of India's foreign exchange earnings.

During this period a number of steps to attract contributions from the Diaspora were taken to streamline the remittances flowing into the country. The initiative started under the Congress regime and gained force when the National Democratic Alliance (NDA) came to power. Under the NDA government India celebrated *Pravasi Bharatiya Divas* (Non-resident Indian Day) for the first time. It was an important part of the 'India Shining' campaign of the NDA: Indian growth rate was at its peak and the contributions from the Diaspora were thereby acknowledged and further encouraged. When Congress came back to power in 2004 and retracted numerous policies of the previous government, they maintained special treatment of the Diaspora.

Sasikumar and Hussain (2007) point out that before the 1990's there were hardly any policies to maintain or increase remittance flows. After liberalization migrants received a number of incentives. Among them were higher interest rates (vis-à-vis international market rates) and exchange rate guarantees for foreign-currency denominated accounts (FCNR (B), higher interest rates to rupee-denominated accounts compared with the ordinary citizen (NR (E) RA deposits), arrangements for repatriation of deposits and exemption from wealth and income tax both on deposits and the interest earned on it (Sasikumar/Hussain 2007: 19). "These incentives were provided mainly with a view to augment the foreign exchange reserves of the country, especially in the context of the difficult times the Indian economy had in the sphere of external finance" (Sasikumar/Hussain 2007: 19). There is agreement among scholars that exchange rate liberalization was the key policy move attracting large numbers of migrant workers to the formal banking infrastructure.[20]

18 Chishti, M., 2007: "The Rise in Remittances to India: A Closer Look", in: Migration Policy Institute: "Feature Story", 1 February 2007; at: <http://www.migrationinformation.org/Feature/display.cfm?id=577> (1 May 2010).

19 Attention to remittances was rising long before the 1991 BoP crisis, in the 1970's. For example, creation of the NRI deposit accounts was also to attract foreign capital and shore up the declining foreign exchange reserves (Chisti 2007). This, however, is part of the debate among scholars about whether the Indian economy began to liberalize in the 1970's or 90's.

India is one of the countries where the informal sector for remittances has been particularly strong. Passas (2003) notes that the *Hawala* system of remittance transfer dates back before paper money and formal banking in the Indian subcontinent. Apart from attributes such as trust and convenience, one of the basic attractions of the informal RSPs was that they offered the market exchange rate to migrants - being higher than the rate offered by banks. When India chose to let the Indian currency float and banks started to offer rates determined by the market, there was a significant shift from the informal methods to the banks. From fiscal year 1991 to fiscal year 2006 remittances grew from 2.1 billion USD to 8.5 billion USD (from 0.7 per cent to 3.22 per cent of the GDP) (Chishti 2007). Although there is, to date, no systematic study on the factors leading to the increase in remittances, certain factors - apart from exchange rate liberalization - could better account for that increase. For example, successful IT professionals who had migrated to the US were then motivated by bullish sentiments about the Indian economy after the 1991 reforms to make investment back home. Accepting that national interests motivated the onset of formalization, the success of formalization may also be owing to the critical mass of high-skilled migrant workers then preferring the formal banking channels. But it is important to keep in mind that a large part of the Indian Diaspora from the unskilled/semi-skilled category continues to prefer informal agents (DFID 2005).[21]

There is one aspect of the Indian remittance formalization experience that deserves particular attention. Compared with the case of the Philippines where there was rapid involvement of state agencies, Indian governments have been less active; and entrepreneurial private financial institutions are more in the driving seat - capitalizing on the opportunities opened by liberalization. Despite initial success, use of financial instruments such as securitization has been low vis-à-vis the Philippines and many Latin American countries, making the process slow. There are recurrent demands on the state by banks to raise ceilings on the amount that can be freely remitted by non-residents, and to extend the facility of special FCNR (B) (Foreign Currency Non-Resident) and NR (E) RA (Non-resident External Rupee Account) deposits to Indian nationals living in the country (Mohan 2008). More studies are necessary to be able to comment on this relatively cautious approach.

At the aggregate level only two per cent of the Indian population migrates abroad. There are certain regions, however, such as Kerala, which send large numbers of migrants (mainly to the Gulf countries) and are heavily dependent on remittance income. More than 25 per cent of the state GDP of Kerala comes from remittances; yet the remittance-development link remains elusive. As mentioned earlier, high amounts of savings have failed to translate into economic growth in the state (Kannan/Hari 2002). Castles (2007) also points out that migration has led to 'ostentatious consumption' and displays of wealth in Kerala.

8.4.3 Indonesia

The case of Indonesia is an interesting departure from the principles behind formalization. After the initial steps of formalization were taken the country rapidly returned to the informal methods, and aggressively so. A study of the Indonesia-Malaysia remittance corridor points out that remittance flows through formal channels from Malaysia dropped by a massive 30 per cent between 2002 (0.4 billion USD) and 2006 (0.26 billion USD) and this was despite a significant increase in the number of migrants leaving for Malaysia (Hernandez-Coss/Brown/Buchori/Endo/Todoroki/Naovalitha/Noor/Mar 2008). The authors point out the need for the government to pay attention to the unique characteristics of the Indonesian remittance economy and design measures accordingly.

Indonesia is the fourth most populated country in the world and has recently come to enjoy the reputation as one of the world's largest labour exporters. According to statistics for the year 2006 roughly 4.3 million Indonesians work and live abroad, and remit 5.6 billion USD to the country - of which only 10 per cent flows through formal channels (Hernandez-Coss/Brown/Buchori/Endo/Todoroki/Naovalitha/Noor/Mar 2008). At the beginning of the decade a partnership had developed between the Financial Market Integrity Unit of the World Bank and the East Asia Social Development Unit to streamline remittances flowing into Indonesia.

Hernandez-Coss and co-authors [2008] identify several factors that determine the migrant's choice of transfer channels - cost, physical access, institutional access, regulatory access, competition and financial literacy. Most migration from Indonesia consists of

---

20 See also Chishti, M., 2007: "The Rise in Remittances to India: A Closer Look", in: Migration Policy Institute, "Feature Story", 1 February 2007, at: <http://www.migrationinformation.org/Feature/display.cfm?id=577>.

21 See at: <www.dfid.gov.uk/pubs/files/uk-remittances-report.pdf> (1 May 2010)

unskilled/semi-skilled labour and 80 per cent of the migrant population are women who work in the informal sector. The biggest Indonesian bank (Pos) has only 50 branches that can dispense remittances immediately. By contrast, the informal service providers collect and deliver money door-to-door and have a much wider outreach. Women migrants feel more at ease with the informal agents who speak their language and are less intimidating than the formal bureaucratic banking system (Hernandez-Coss/ Brown/Buchori/Endo/Todoroki/Naovalitha/Noor/ Mar 2008). They note that:

> [d]espite the disadvantages of the informal sector, the formal sector has little to offer the migrant workers in its current state. It is less competitive in terms of accessibility and provides little added value in terms of access to the much needed pre-departure credit or other instruments that might appeal to the migrant workers, especially women and the undocumented (Hernandez-Coss/ Brown/Buchori/Endo/Todoroki/Naovalitha/Noor/ Mar 2008: 14).

Passas (2003) argues that attempts to over-regulate the traditional systems of remittance transfers may be counterproductive. It might push them underground making them more vulnerable to criminal activities. The significant drop in remittances through formal channels in Indonesia discussed above coincided with the introduction of anti-money laundering and anti-terrorism regulations – integral parts of the formalization drive. This suggests that the risk of driving migrants to greater informality through attempts to over-regulate the informal sector is high.

There is also a political dimension behind migration from Indonesia that remains under-researched. Tirtosudamo (2000) brings this out by highlighting the role of the ruling elite and internal politics in stimulating migration from densely populated Java. The author points out that politics in Indonesia is driven by the need to reinforce geographical clusters based on race, religion, tribe and language and that this always involves rooting out dissidents and removing any possible source of challenge or social unrest. These political processes constitute an important motor for international migration from Java and deserve greater attention than is currently given.

Analysis of the available evidence shows that the choice of formalization has a strong political dimension along with the economic – in most cases the political surpassing the economic. In both India and the Philippines state interest for economic survival was explicit. In the Philippines the fear of political turmoil added greater exigency. In the case of Indonesia, even though the migrant streams were shown to be triggered by internal politics by Tirtosudamo [2000], the formalization of remittances was pioneered by the international organizations. In the Philippines there was overzealous state machinery and the formalization process remained state-engineered and state-run, while in India – after the initial exchange rate liberalization – the process was largely steered by private financial institutions. Even today the Indian state continues to follow a cautious approach in raising limits of accounts and extending benefits to larger non-resident populations. The two countries mark two different approaches to formalization. In the absence of primary research there can be no conclusion on which of the two approaches is better. Further primary studies are required to answer this question. The third case of Indonesia where formalization was steered by external agents shows that understanding the nature of migration from a region is important. At places where undocumented migration is high, formalization attempts need to be cautious. Indonesia's reaction to the drive for formalization illustrates the inadequacies of the formal system vis-à-vis the informal and serves as a warning that rash attempts to formalize may drive migrants to riskier options.

8.5 Conclusion

The positive contribution of the remittance-enthusiasts is the lessening of apathy and a negative outlook on international migration. A decade ago migration was considered a symptom of failed development and all interventions aimed at stopping or reducing migration from any given region. The new paradigm creates greater acceptance of migration as a pervasive phenomenon and addresses what De Haan (2002) termed the 'sedentary bias' in public policy. This is a welcome change, especially in contexts where migrants are vulnerable to unscrupulous remittance service providers and, given the lack of information on better options, have to pay more. Yet, to eulogize remittances as the 'new development mantra', or the solution to third world under-development, is to go beyond what can be inferred from the evidence.

The liberal view sees the role of international financial institutions and the states as facilitating market operations by removing possible hurdles against efficient functioning through the creation of norms, regulations and dissemination of information. There is, however, well-founded evidence that remittance markets have been created by dedicated agencies through a web of international organisations, banks and states. There seems to be a much stronger agency aspect in the current drive for formalization than is being admitted. The remittance phenomenon is strikingly similar to the micro-finance story; both drawing credence in the name of financial inclusion of the poor and the leveraging of small savings. Micro-finance has already become a global business sustaining a giant body of rating agencies, banks and NGOs. Remittances are set to join their ranks, putting too great a burden on the shoulders of the poor. More studies are needed to draw connections between the histories of micro-finance and remittances - for it would seem the micro-finance experience has sobering lessons to offer remittance-enthusiasts.

Both the theoretical and the empirical evidence for remittance-led development seem questionable. The much-hyped counter-cyclicality of remittances is only in relation to other sources of development finance and has only recently been put to the test of financial crisis. As such, remittances may have a pro-cyclical nature, vulnerable to the economic booms and busts of the labour-importing countries. A high share of remittances in a gross national product makes that economy particularly vulnerable. The tendency of migrants to hold remittances in foreign currency also poses the risk of dollarization and central banks therefore losing their control on monetary policy. The impact of remittances on growth depends on a wide variety of factors many of which do not lie in the control of policymakers. There is limited evidence that concerted remittance management has led to sustainable economic growth in any region.

Further, there is agreement among scholars that while micro-level impact of remittances has been and continues to be extensively studied, studies on the macroeconomics of remittances are relatively scarce. Recent attention to remittances by global policymakers creates the right platform to undertake more studies on formalization of remittances and their impact on macro-economies. State involvement to leverage greater amounts of remittances should be subject to further research to compare and draw lessons on which approach is more conducive to stimulating growth and under which conditions.

The proposed superiority of formal methods over informal ones is debatable and should be scrutinized from the perspective of migrants' needs. Thoughtless drives to formalization and regulation of the informal remittance industry may lead to migrants resorting to riskier options, thus the impetus towards formalization needs to be driven more by the needs of migrants and not by those of the financial sector. It is not so important which medium is chosen (formal or informal); what is important is whether the given medium delivers. It makes much more sense to invest in the informal system if the informal sector has greater outreach and/or delivers more cost-efficiently (Hernandez-Coss/Brown/Buchori/Endo/Todoroki/Naovalitha/Noor/Mar 2008). More studies will be needed to understand the requirements of migrants in different remittance 'corridors', and suitably to adapt all attempts to manage remittance. Without this, the new 'mantra' on remittance as contributing to development is anything but responsible, for it puts undue pressure on migration to finance development.

9 Managing Migration in the IOM's *World Migration Report 2008*

Beatriz Campillo Carrete and Des Gasper

"Labour migration is now acknowledged as an integral part of the global economic landscape" (IOM 2008: 4).

9.1 Introduction[1]

The International Organization for Migration (IOM)[2] was founded in 1951, originally as the Intergovernmental Committee for European Migration (ICEM) to deal with resettlement of displaced persons, refugees and migrants in the aftermath of the Second World War (Olsen 2002; Wennerholm/Zillen 2003). It acquired its current structure and profile in 1989 and now has more than 125 member countries and almost 7,000 staff worldwide, led from a headquarters in Geneva. IOM's website describes it as "the leading intergovernmental organization in the field of migration", concerned with cooperation to promote international migration law, migration policy debate and guidance, migrants' rights, and attention to health and gender dimensions of migration. What are the assumptions, values and beliefs about migration seen in IOM's current research and proposals?

IOM's emergence as a key actor in world migration management is epitomized by its production in recent years of a flagship publication, the *World Migration Report* (WMR), which first appeared in 2000 and has appeared every two or three years since then.[3] Its arrival in 2000 coincided with a shift in emphasis in rich countries from only restriction of immigration to also controlled promotion. The WMR is one of the many global reports produced by international organizations, such as the World Bank's annual *World Development Report*. Apart from a role in seeking to justify the presence of the organization concerned and to safeguard its budget, such reports are key communicative mechanisms in setting the agenda of negotiations in the international system. They are major reference points for many governments and non-governmental actors, including academia and international and local non-government organizations, for whom they frame the issues and select, process and interpret the data. This chapter analyses the most recent WMR, the *World Migration Report 2008: Managing Labour Mobility in the Evolving Global Economy*, a massive volume of 560 double-columned pages. We investigate the Introduction and Conclusion, for they provide the summary and main messages, and are the chapters that receive by far the most public attention. Such chapters are correspondingly prepared with special care. What are the principles of selection, organization and weighting that guide their argumentation?

We explore the two chapters using a series of tools of policy discourse analysis, within an overall methodology from Teun van Dijk (2001, 2009). First, to situate the texts in socio-political context, the next section introduces the sponsoring organization and its operations. This is followed by an outline of the 2008 Report as a whole, including indication of its authors and focus, to provide the textual context for the two highlighted chapters. Section 4 identifies their macro-structures and key overall meanings, with special attention to the conceptualization of 'migration' and 'mobility' and their relation to trade and economic development. Section 5 investigates selected local meanings and rhetorical choices in the chapters, including the orientating metaphors, and the key roles played by the much-used terms 'flows', 'needs' and 'globalization'. Section 6 summarizes the approach to migration that the Report presents. It contrasts the respect for

1 We are indebted to two referees for detailed suggestions.
2 In French, Spanish and Portuguese, the acronym is OIM.
3 See at: <http://www.iom.int/jahia/Jahia/pid/2>. (10 December 2009).

T.-D. Truong and D. Gasper (eds.), *Transnational Migration and Human Security*, Hexagon Series on Human and Environmental Security and Peace 6, DOI 10.1007/978-3-642-12757-1_9, © Springer-Verlag Berlin Heidelberg 2011

human rights that is declared in the text and the economic notions that it mainly applies to migration. It underlines at the same time the significant shift in emphasis from restriction to permanent 'management' of large-scale migration flows that the Report expresses.

9.2 The International Organization for Migration

The IOM's activities include providing a forum for exchange of information and study of international migration, and promotion of cooperation and coordination (IOM Constitution, 1987, Article 1.1). Its self-presentation–including the very presence, title and bulk of the *World Migration Reports*–can sometimes give an impression that it holds a status virtually equivalent to the member organizations of the United Nations.[4] In reality, IOM is deliberately not part of the UN system. Its mandate is tied to the will of its member states and not to an international convention. Acceptance of new member states is conditional on approval by two-thirds of existing member states (Article 2b). "The Organization shall recognize the fact that control of standards of admission and the number of immigrants to be admitted are matters within the domestic jurisdiction of States, and, in carrying out its functions, shall conform to the laws, regulations and policies of the States concerned" (Article 1.3). No international convention is mentioned in the text of the IOM Constitution. Its starting premises are notions of state-sovereignty and 'orderly migration'.

IOM's internal balance of power and patterns of accountability are inevitably influenced by finance. Its largest funders are the EU and the US. Besides IOM's administrative budget, to which all members contribute, the separate operational budget (Article 25) is derived from donations, including from non-members, and is devoted to three functions in addition to those already mentioned: 1) assistance to migrants, displaced persons and refugees; 2) assistance to labour recruitment needs of member states; and 3) voluntary return migration petitions, as "requested by States or in cooperation with other interested international organizations" (Article 1.1(d)). Thus, IOM operations in return-migration and recruiting are open to special requests by member states and depend on financial capacities and interests of sponsors.

The IOM faces criticism regarding its transparency, accountability and commitment to human rights. The former ICEM was created in the year of adoption of the United Nations Convention Relating to the Status of Refugees for protection of basic rights of refugees.[5] Some migrant rights organizations believe ICEM was created to counter the UN High Commissioner for Refugees.[6] IOM's role in international migration may be more complex than this, but for Geiger (2005) the root issue is that it lacks a mandate that would allow a more humanitarian approach and counteract its dependence on nation-state financial sponsors who are driven by fears of flooding by immigrants. IOM plays, for example, a major role in processes, not always transparent, that allow European states to transfer border enforcement to transit and sending states by means of intergovernmental agreements that make access to EU assistance and to possible partner/member status conditional on cooperation in such enforcement.

> Especially the inter-governmental organisation of IOM has developed into a regional (as well a global) key actor in the new 'management' approach..., and has somehow become not only an 'assistant' for its member states but rather as well a 'managing director' in providing expertise and facilitating sometimes rather questionable formal and informal agreements (Geiger 2005: 25).

While IOM's official mission relates to all major issues related to migration, including refugees and displacement, for more than two decades its focus has been migration management. In a world of nation-states where globalization is now considered unavoid-

4 Its website declares: "The International Organization for Migration has a long standing and intense working relationship with the United Nations (UN) at several levels. Today, there are three formal elements on which IOM's overall relationship with the United Nations is based. The first is the observer status in the UN General Assembly, which IOM obtained in 1992 (GA resolution A/RES/47/4). The second is IOM's inclusion by the General Assembly as a 'standing invitee' in the Inter-Agency Standing Committee (IASC) mechanism, which also started in 1992. The third element is the Cooperation Agreement between IOM and the UN, which was signed in 1996 and provides a formal basis for a closer collaboration between the two secretariats."

5 See at: <http://www.unhcr.org/cgi-bin/texis/vtx/news/opendoc.htm?tbl=NEWS&id=3b6027264> (11 October 2009); UNHCR (2001), "UNHCR Marks 50th Anniversary of U.N. Refugee Convention", *press release,* July 26.

6 See at: <www.noborder.org/iom/index.php> (11 October 2009); Noborder Network: "The IOM, Spies and Migrant Hunters", Communiqué of the Campaign to Combat Global Migration Management, 3 October 2009.

able, states seek to manage their perceived needs for both labour movement and restriction of labour movement. IOM holds that it works in four areas of migration management: facilitating migration; regulating migration; migration and development; and forced migration. Of these, the first three appear in the 2008 World Migration Report. Forced migration is omitted, despite the indirect contributions of the international economic system to its causation. Currently, predominant perspectives do not see the international economic system as threatened by forced migrants. One enormous cloud, though, is beginning to be noted on the horizon: climate change's possible unleashing of massive additional migratory flows - a topic ignored in the 2008 Report until the final pages of its Conclusion.

9.3 Overview of the *World Migration Report 2008*

The introductory chapter of the *World Migration Report* (pp. 1-20) has three parts. The first gives a perspective on the nature of international migration, especially labour migration, and the factors causing it (pp. 1-5). The second part introduces three "clusters of policy challenges...of central interest to this Report" (p. 5): the vast and vague but reassuringly titled area of "effective strategies for the management of international labour mobility" (p. 5); "the relationship between migration and trade" (p. 5); and "the complex relationship between migration and development", by which it essentially refers to the effects of migration on economic growth in low-income countries (p. 7). It also notes five "very significant and sensitive cross-cutting issues" (p. 9): "the human and labour rights and status of migrant workers", "the interface between migrants and the host community", "the management of security issues" and illegal migrants (all on p. 9), the treatment of women migrants, and the way that global migration means that now "health risks and benefits are to a certain degree shared" (p. 11). These cross-cutting issues are problematic aspects or criteria in terms of which pure market-led migration is recognized to be unsatisfactory, and indicate areas where migration should therefore be managed. The Introduction's third section (pp. 12-18) provides the equivalent of an Executive Summary of the volume, including a summary of the concluding chapter.

The Conclusion chapter (pp. 393-401) functions thus not as the summary of the volume, but as a restatement and extension of main messages. It concentrates on underlining needs for policy coordination to connect successfully labour supplies and demands. Illustrative of the internal battles over emphasis and interpretation that are common in such reports, not all of its messages are chosen for mention in the Introduction's overview, including not least its message on climate change. Those messages from the Conclusion which are selected for the Introduction's summary will be reproduced as Box 3.1 below, and provide one overview of the Report.

In between these two chapters come 13 thematic chapters, in two parts. The Report's more descriptive Part A is entitled "The Worlds of Contemporary Mobility for Economic Purposes". Later we examine this choice of terms ('mobility' rather than 'migration'), and the declared restriction to 'economic purposes'. Chapter 1 explains how the growth of global-wide labour markets has been induced by other features of economic globalization. Chapter 2 looks at movements of highly-skilled migrants, implicitly with main attention to movements from low-income to high-income countries, and chapter 3 at the "re-emergence" (p. 13) of large-scale movements of low and semi-skilled migrants, with explicit focus on movements from low-income to high-income countries. Such movements had in fact continued on a large scale in various parts of the world, such as to the Gulf States and in East Asia (for example to Thailand and Malaysia), so talk of 're-emergence' suggests a Northern perspective in the report. Chapters 4 and 5 follow up chapter 2 on highly-skilled migrants, reflecting new driving concerns in rich countries' 'migration management'. Chapter 4 is about movements of students and the deliberate policies in rich countries to retain the most talented foreign students; and chapter 5 examines the relation between tourist movements and migration. Chapter 6 looks at migration of family members who follow an earlier migrant. Chapter 7 considers migration within national boundaries, which is oddly declared a "relatively new sector of migration management" (p. 14), presumably meaning new in terms of attention given by IOM and similar bodies, who have now become aware of its significance as sometimes a prelude to international migration. Chapter 8 treats illegal migration.

Both the scope and the language of coverage in Part A's survey thus suggest a high-income country perspective. At the same time, they reflect how that perspective is evolving. The Introduction begins with reference to "much reduced levels of distrust between developed and developing countries" (p. 1) and "the current and welcome inclination to acknowledge the potentially beneficial outcomes of migratory phenomena" (p. 2). This reflects, for the moment and in some quarters, a relative shift towards an outlook that migration is "a process through which nations are built and strengthened...rather [than] divided and weakened" (p. 2).

The policy-centred Part B of the Report is entitled "Managing Labour Mobility in the Evolving Global Economy". 'Mobility' and 'Economy' remain the declared parameters, with 'Managing' and 'Global' as the chosen emphases. Chapter 9 calls for investment and coordination in research to build required knowledge. Chapter 10 looks at (international) migration management by labour exporting countries, and chapter 11 at management by countries of destination. Chapter 12 turns to "the migration and development relationship", under which heading it discusses the impacts of labour exports on low-income countries' economic growth. Chapter 13 considers options for international cooperation.

The Report is a collective document, written by personnel from IOM, other inter-governmental organizations and researchers from influential universities. All the institutions, with one exception, are based in the North.[7] The editors-in-chief were Gervais Appave, then Director of Migration Policy and Research at the IOM, and Ryszard Cholewinski, a professor at the University of Leicester in Britain. Appave had a career in the Australian civil service from the 1970s, mainly in the Department of Immigration, and worked for IOM from 2001. He is listed as responsible for the Introduction. Cholewinski is a leading researcher on migration, specialized in human rights, employment rights and the international protection of refugees. The Editorial Board of the Report was headed by an American lawyer, Michele Klein Solomon, IOM's incoming Director of Migration Policy, Research and Communications, who previously worked for the US Department of State as a refugee and migration lawyer (1989-2000). Appave, Cholewinski and Solomon are listed as co-responsible for the concluding chapter.

Our focus on the first and last chapters of the Report reflects their special status as overview chapters. Their authors are the senior editors chosen by IOM. The chapters are written as self-standing statements meant for wide audiences. Requests for the other chapters via the IOM website lead to requirements for payment, suggesting that they are intended for specialist organizations and professionals.[8] In contrast, the Introduction and Conclusion are readily accessible and downloadable free of charge.

The profiles of our two chapters' authors, of the researchers in the Report, and of the organization that sponsors the exercise all indicate a predominance of elite circles in high-income countries. We will ask how far the Report is structured by economic ideas derived and institutionalized in the North, and how far that is balanced by other visions of migration and by concern for human rights.

9.4 Overall Themes and Structure: The Logic of Legitimacy Accorded to Labour Mobility

"Language users are unable to memorize and manage all meaning details of a discourse, and hence mentally organize these meanings by global meanings or topics" (van Dijk 2001: 102). In van Dijk's terms, 'global meanings' are the 'semantic macrostructures', the overall leading themes that an author has in mind and that a reader is likely to take away from a complex text: the gist. Often authors approximate at least some of these global meanings through the titles, summaries, conclusion sections and so on.

Here we explore the 2008 Report's global meanings through, first, exploration of its key choices of terminology: a concept of 'mobility' rather than 'migration', and a declared focus on 'labour mobility' and on economic concerns; and second, through examination of titles, themes and structure in the two overview chapters, to identify macro structures of meaning: the basic argument and general principles that guide the content.

7 The chapter authors worked in the following institutions based in high income countries: the Overseas Development Institute (ODI, United Kingdom), International Migration Institute (Italy), Organization for Economic Cooperation and Development (OECD), International Labour Organization (ILO); and a series of influential universities, all but one in the North: Georgetown University and the University of California in the US; the Australian National University; Middlesex University and the Institute of Education, from the UK. One chapter was written by a researcher from the University of the Philippines.

8 However, the chapters can be reached directly via Internet search by title and pdf file type.

9.4.1 'Labour Mobility' Rather Than 'Human Mobility' – Priority to Economic Concerns

The predominant language in the Report is seen in its title, which is also the title of Part B: "Managing Labour Mobility in the Evolving Global Economy". It adopts the wider concept of 'mobility' rather than 'migration'; but concentrates on 'labour mobility' rather than the broader alternative of 'human mobility', and seeks to limit discussion to 'economic' concerns. Let us begin by examining these three choices, as prelude to characterizing the overall argumentative structure and thrust.

First, 'mobility' is chosen rather than 'migration' because, we are told, the latter "has been predominantly linked to a type of movement leading to a permanent change of residence [to] another country" (p. 1). 'Mobility' is better at "incorporating a wider set of migratory behaviours" (p. 11), including temporary movement, multi-stage movement and divided residence. Related to that, it sounds natural and less threatening. Nevertheless, the Report in fact still largely speaks of 'migration', even in the opening section called "Globalization and Mobility" (p. 2 ff) where it declares that it is adopting a focus on mobility. The popular construct of (international) migration as a threat is tamed by presenting a more comforting alternative: mobility; this seems to allow the authors to continue largely using the now tamed term.

Second, although the Conclusion begins with a description of 'human mobility', a 'labour mobility' perspective predominates in the Report. While limiting itself to a focus on mobility for purposes of labour, the Report's references to 'human mobility' have a function. The Introduction notes an ongoing disagreement whether "migration [should] be considered an entirely 'natural' part of human behaviour that has occurred throughout history, or rather as 'unnatural'..." (p. 2). If we see human mobility as natural and indeed as an important part of human societies' evolution and adaptation, then that carries over to its component of labour mobility too.

Third, we saw that Part A's title insists that its focus is "Contemporary Mobility for Economic Purposes" only. Yet the Introduction cites studies (in Box 3, on pp. 10–11) that show how many other purposes are important for migrants. Hew's (2003) research, for example, shows how a major motivation for women in Sarawak to move to cities was to live a 'modern' life, including more independence, despite being in unsatisfying and arduous jobs, and not solely or primarily to have more income (IOM 2008: 10). Similar findings recur in other research (e.g. Kabeer 2000).[9] Educated young people worldwide, similarly, are far less willing to undertake agricultural and other heavy manual work than were their forebears, and often prefer types of work (or even unemployment) which give significantly lower monetary rewards. Further, as we noted, chapters 4, 5 and 6 of the Report are on types of movement that are not primarily for economic purposes - movements of students, tourists, and family members - although the chapters consider the connections of these movements to seeking and taking up work.

The attempt to give priority to economic motives recurs periodically. We see it in the reduction of the discussion of development to just economic growth in poor countries, something narrower than the human development spoken of in the UN system. This narrow concept may match an idea of 'development' as one specialist corner in the system of international organizations. Similarly, the Introduction declares that: "Broad academic, political, cultural and development goals of an essentially humanitarian nature have not completely disappeared [from rich country support for foreign students], but they are now overshadowed by sharper-edged economic objectives" (p. 13). The adjectives and adjectival phrases deserve attention—for example, the brazen use of 'completely'—for they are all optional yet chosen. The phrase, 'essentially humanitarian' marginalizes concerns other than economic profit for a rich country's own enterprises.

The choices seen above - in sum to use the concept of labour mobility rather than that of human migration - appear consistent with a Northern migration manager perspective. Such a view seeks to maintain Northern growth and competitiveness, manoeuvre around deeply suspicious groups in Northern societies, and make progress on specified areas of cooperation with a South that it increasingly respects, sometimes fears as a competitor, and sees itself as increasingly entangled and interdependent with. The language is often grudging or cautious, given the origin and the continuing threats for such a discourse. While demand for highly skilled migrants is "strong, and officially recognized", the numerically greater demand for low and semi-skilled migrants is described only as "noticeable, but often officially ignored" (p. 12). The Report also represents an opening to some previously taboo issues. It sometimes uses the reassur-

9 See at: <http://www.gcim.org/mm/File/ GMP%20No%20 5. pdf> (3 December 2009).

ing, authoritative word 'managing' in such a way as to permit a more pro-human stance.

> The word 'management' has occasionally been criticized as a euphemism for 'restriction' or 'control' and for giving insufficient attention to human rights concerns. As used in *World Migration 2008*, it refers to a planned and thoughtful approach to policy development; and to the careful selection and implementation of appropriate policy responses to the key questions confronting the international community (p. 1).

Behind this veil of vagueness, the message becomes: managed migration, management of large-scale ongoing migration, and not only the 1990s themes of restriction and control. Substantial flows are to be expected.

9.4.2 Macrostructures of the Text

We next identify the main topics of the two chapters. The Introduction uses the following section headings:

1. The Challenge of Migration Management
2. Globalization and Mobility
3. Labour Migration, a Key Aspect of Human Mobility and the Global Economy
4. Major Policy Issues and Challenges
5. Textbox Int. 1 The State of Progress in GATS Mode 4 Negotiations
6. Textbox Int. 2 Global Forum on Migration and Development (GFMD)
7. Textbox Int. 3. Female Labour Migration and Gender Issues
8. Structure of the Report
9. Part A: The Worlds of Contemporary Mobility for Economic Purposes
10. Part B: Managing Labour Mobility in the Evolving Global Economy

The Conclusion does not use section headings. Therefore, Box 9.1 below gives instead the Introduction's summary (pp. 17–18) of the Conclusion chapter, in order to convey the character of that chapter and of the book as a whole.

Interestingly, in a number of respects the Conclusion chapter goes beyond what the Introduction reports about it. It contains, for example, a large text box on "Climate Change and Labour Mobility" (pp. 398–400); but that issue is not mentioned in the Introduction's summary, nor discussed elsewhere in the Introduction other than in a single phrase on page 3. It could have readily been alluded to in Point 8 of the summary. Similarly, Point 6 omits an important concluding phrase used in the corresponding sentence in the Conclusion: "while also ensuring that benefits continue to accrue to migrant workers and their families" (p. 395). Point 7 omits the Conclusion's recognition of down sides to the relation between emigration and economic development, including the brain drain from low-income countries (pp. 396–398). However, the summary still indicates the main intellectual structure of the Report, so we will refer to its points as themes, around which we can make additional remarks.

Points 1 to 3 of the summary sketch the present global situation with respect to human mobility. They reflect how both chapters characterize and explain contemporary international migration: intense labour mobility has emerged, with growing diversity of migration types, now that labour markets connect across countries. (See in particular the Introduction's section on *Globalization and Mobility*.) This is presented as in large part a result of the choice of trade- and capital-liberalization policies by the international community, and thus as agreed for all countries.

The pivotal points, 4 to 6, declare the consequent necessity to manage rather than repress mobility, and sketch an orientation for policy response; points 7 to 10 mention a series of required activities. Points 4 and 5 suggest that proactive policy, migration management, is necessary to reap the significant potential gains from human mobility, via matching demand and supply in an acceptable manner, rather than, as explained elsewhere, relying either on unguided markets that will generate social tensions and political backlash or on crude restrictions that will lead to black markets. Point 6 is central in suggesting a win-win solution to these problems via policy coordination between labour exporting and importing countries, including a variety of temporary labour-importation arrangements. It proposes that developed countries should identify labour market needs and recruitment tasks, and developing countries should prepare nationals to work abroad. "Optimal outcomes will be achieved when the two sets of policies are envisaged as complementary elements of a coherent whole, directed towards the achievement of shared development goals while also ensuring that benefits continue to accrue to migrant workers and their families" (p. 395).

The subsequent points address the policy triangle migration-trade-development. Point 7, as presented more fully in the Conclusion, recognizes potential downsides to migration, but presents them as increasing the case for cooperation in both trade and migration. Point 8 adds reference to human rights consider-

Box 9.1: The Introduction's Summary of the Conclusion. **Source**: WMR: 16-18

...Finally, Chapter 14 **[the Conclusion]** offers a number of observations on the essential features of the contemporary migratory landscape surveyed in this Report, and of the broad policy strategies that could contribute to international efforts to realize the social and economic potential of international labour mobility. These can be summarized in ten brief points:

1. In its many and varied forms, human mobility within and across borders is one of the characteristic and perhaps even defining features of our contemporary world. To a large extent, it is both part and consequence of the complex and interacting social and economic processes involved in the phenomenon of globalization.
2. People seek to move for a large number of personal, family, social, business or work reasons, often in varying combinations,[a)] but the opportunities to move are frequently limited, particularly for low and semi-skilled workers.
3. In view of the choices made by the international community to facilitate the movement of capital, goods and services, human mobility or, more specifically, the movement of human resources, at all skill levels, is now being increasingly factored into the equations intended to yield new economic gains. In other words, labour market dynamics are increasingly operating across international borders.
4. The policy implications of this steadily evolving situation are yet to be fully understood, but it is already apparent that avoiding the issue, ignoring this trend or a passive laissez-faire approach are unlikely to lead to the policy stances needed to realize the social and economic potential of mobility.
5. What is required, therefore, are planned and predictable ways of matching demand with supply in a safe, legal, humane and orderly manner. Given the diversity of labour market needs and of available skills, policies and procedures will have to display commensurate flexibility and adaptability to enable modes of labour mobility that may be short-term, circular, long-term or permanent.
6. Countries of origin and destination are increasingly engaged in the formulation of policies to meet their particular labour mobility objectives, namely, to train and prepare migrant workers for employment abroad on the one hand, and to identify labour market needs and seek recruitment of appropriate personnel on the other. Optimal outcomes will be achieved when the two sets of policies are complementary and mutually supportive elements of a coherent whole, directed towards the achievement of mutual development goals. To be successful, more cooperative approaches to human resource development are needed to meet national, regional and global objectives. Policies and appropriate means are needed as well to secure the participation in this shared endeavour of non-state stakeholders, including employers, recruitment agencies, trade unions, migrant and diaspora associations, and relevant inter-governmental organizations.
7. This pleads for the identification and development of clear linkages between the domains of migration proper and those of development, employment and trade within the broader framework of established global economic interests.
8. To reach that objective, the international community requires a common and accurate understanding of the many important issues at stake, including economic growth, managing social change while maintaining cohesion, upholding social justice and the protection of the human rights of the workers concerned, the pursuit of which amply justify the maintenance and further development of consultations and cooperation at regional and global levels.
9. A closely related need is the enhancement of global, regional and national knowledge of labour market trends, labour force profiles and labour migration trends through the establishment of appropriate databases and analytical work.
10. Of relevance to all of the above is the recognition of capacity-building requirements of all governments, in particular those of developing countries, to assess the levels of need, formulate policy and legislation, improve labour migration and related human resource development programmes through experimentation and innovation, and to monitor and evaluate outcomes.

A new spirit of partnership in outlook and action is both possible and essential to realizing beneficial outcomes for the international community as a whole, including countries of origin, countries of destination and migrants and their families.

a) The focus here is on movements that are essentially voluntary, but there are obviously persons who are forced to move and for whom there is an established international protection regime.

ations. However, a human rights perspective is never prominent in the Report. The Introduction sets the discussion parameters more in terms of economic marketability:

> The issues to be addressed extend well beyond the unquestionably important formulation and implementation of minimum standards of protection. In a globalizing labour market, migrant workers seek to move across international borders in part because they have, at the very least, potentially competitive assets in terms of skills, wage expectations, and cultural attributes. The difficult challenge here is to have a policy regime that allows this competitive edge to be put to advantage and enables the realization of these assets, while precluding the 'commodification' of migrant workers (p. 9).

Finally, Points 9 and 10 state that much research and coordination is required for countries to understand and reap the benefits of migration. They match the central purpose of the Report: to make understood the potential benefits of labour migration for all participants in the international economy and the prerequisites for achieving them.

9.4.3 The Migration-Development-Trade Triangle: Reason to Cooperate?

Because of the centrality of Point 6 above, the matching of demand and supply, we lay out more fully the associated argumentative elements provided in the Conclusion (we use a second level index for each element).

6a. "Both countries of origin and destination stand to benefit from securing the involvement and cooperation of the widest range of stakeholders.... Bilateral cooperation offers many possibilities. Bilateral agreements are flexible instruments that can be used to match labour supply and demand in a planned, predictable and rights-based manner, while also contributing to the mitigation of irregular migration" (p. 396).

6b. There are three difficulties in regard to cooperation: nation states' territorial entrance prerogative may limit willingness to cooperate; problems in achieving nationally coordinated policy positions among interested domestic agencies; and differences in priorities among countries (Paraphrase from p. 396).

6c. "Despite these hurdles, however, numerous consultative mechanisms on migration policy have emerged over the last decade or so" like the Abu Dhabi Dialogue of 2008 (p. 396). "Such consultative processes, characterized by their informality and open-endedness, deserve to be further developed as forums for confidence building and information exchange" (p. 396) and as discussion workplaces.

6d. The outcomes of these informal, non-binding consultative exercises "are strikingly convergent. All of them take as their starting point the increasing political visibility and importance of international migration; all of them acknowledge that mobility is an unavoidable economic and social reality; all of them point to benefits that flow from properly managed flows; all of them draw attention to the risks of not managing those flows; all of them assert that it is possible to arrive at common understandings and principles, and propose remarkably consistent lines of action. They also confirm the need for clearer linkages to be established between the domain of human mobility proper and closely adjoining policy fields, especially those of development and trade" (p. 397).

Points 6a to 6d propose a solution for the migration challenges faced. First, the potential of cooperation to match supply and demand, in the form of bilateral agreements of the type that we saw questioned by Geiger (2005), is set forth in point 6a. The terms 'planned' and 'predictable' stand here for business concerns, while 'rights based manner' opens the economic outlook to a broader perspective. However, the absence of analysis in the Report of how these different concerns will coexist smoothly is significant. Second, the three obstacles to cooperation presented in 6b are countered in 6c and 6d by the positive experience shown by recent migration consultation exercises. 6d's last element bridges to the discussion of the migration-trade-development policy triangle and presents the only not entirely clear win-win prospect. It takes us to point 7, which attempts to solve the conflict between migration benefits and brain drain for sending countries, by exploring the potential if cooperation is achieved. For point 7 too, we use a second level index with letters to present the fuller set of arguments given in the Conclusion.

7a. "For all countries, progress in this continuously evolving and complex area is first and foremost subject to a better understanding of the impact of international labour mobility on domestic labour supply; the impact of migration on productivity in the domestic economy; and the impact of remittance flows on development. It will also depend on the establishment of genuine partnerships between countries of origin and destination to attain mutually satisfactory outcomes" (p. 397).

7b. "The migration and trade nexus is at least as complex as the migration and development equation. At the global level, tariffs and other barriers to cross-border investment and trade in goods have been very substantially reduced" and global exchanges expanded. "Facilitation of the movement of people has been identified as a potential avenue to further economic gains through trade liberalization, but the policy intersections between migration and trade need to be more clearly mapped out and fully explored. One specific issue to be addressed is the fundamental tension between trade-oriented policy objectives driven by market dynamics and premised on planning and predictability, and approaches to migration management that favour discretion and the adaptation of policy strategies to changing circumstances" (pp. 397–398).

7c. "At the doctrinal level, trade theories have yet to agree whether trade and migration are substitutes (viz. supporting local economic growth and boosting exports would have the effect of easing migration pressure) or complements (viz. both trade and migration can increase, and can be mutually supportive). Trade theories need to be reviewed from the trade-migration vantage point and relevant supporting evidence gathered", including on the fast-growing "trade in services and knowledge-based trading patterns, both of which rely heavily on the mobility of human resources" (p. 398).

7d. "In the context of international trade negotiations, GATS Mode 4 is seen as a promising means to facilitate the temporary movement of service personnel; however, so far its scope of application has been largely limited to the international movement of highly skilled personnel, and considerable creativity and persistence are still needed to allow these negotiations to move forward". Similarly with regional and bilateral initiatives, but these already incorporate labour mobility and provide relevant experience for work on global approaches. "Finally, policy coherence requires...the integration of worker mobility in national, regional and international employment and migration policies and strategies; and, second, the definition of the particular roles and responsibilities of all key stakeholders" (p. 398).

The macro-structure of the text had already proposed a causal relation between migration and development, which is now backed by a list of economic, social, political and cultural benefits of diasporas (p. 397). In point 7a, various economic relations between migration and development, here meaning national economic development, are proposed. The declaration that these relations hold for all countries makes developed and developing countries appear to be on a 'level playing field', and helps to manoeuvre the argument around developing country objections to brain drain. Point 7b acknowledges that we need more evidence on possible intersections between migration and trade, but it first presents further labour mobility as an identified expected source of benefits; and point 7c conveys impatience by speaking of doctrinal, rather than scientific or theoretical, work on the relations between trade and migration. Given the declared lack of scientific clarity on the relations in the migration-development-trade triangle, point 7d returns to the pragmatic potential of cooperation, on the basis of successful recent negotiation experiences, although these have been queried heavily from other viewpoints, which are not discussed in these chapters.

9.4.4 The Naturalness of Labour Movements and of other Migration

In this policy argument structure, the case for migration is governed by the claim of a need to attain labour market equilibrium in the global economy: supply must equal demand. Several topics in the Introduction and Conclusion reflect this, such as: "Labour Migration, a Key Aspect of Human Mobility and the Global Economy" (p. 4); and the Conclusion's Point 6, about the need for coordinated not unilateral policies in order to match labour demand with supply. The focus within human mobility is on labour that moves as an item of purchase in the global economy.

Neoclassical economics finds it natural to view labour as a factor of production, and as another item of trade, just as goods or currencies. A humanist perspective, such as human rights, holds that labour migrants are human beings and not merely another item of trade. The authors call for future research and planning on migration to include human rights issues (Point 8). But the manner of the move reveals the tension between an unclear stance on human rights and the use of an orthodox economics framework in which the meaning of human development reduces to 'human resource development' from a market perspective: "Nevertheless, there are signs pointing to policy convergence in this area built around the notions of human resource development and migration management" (p. 395). What rights are included is not clear; the Conclusion mentions labour rights, but only twice (pp. 393, 398) and human rights are not reducible to labour rights alone.

Let us return to the aporia on the nature of human migration, presented early in the Introduction as part of explaining the challenges of the Report's task. We saw the following rhetorical figure, brought in as the first of the many questions that the Report sees as underlying the problems to reach a consensus on the "fundamental nature of migration" (p. 2): "Should migration be considered an entirely 'natural' part of human behavior that has occurred throughout history, or rather as 'unnatural', in the sense that it involves painful uprooting of individuals from their place of birth and their equally difficult relocation in other countries?" (p. 2) The authors link the 'nature of migration' with the 'nature of being human'. The second possible answer that they give optimistically presents pain as unnatural. We are steered towards the first interpretation, which naturalizes migration as part of the mobile nature of humans. Historically, geographic movement has indeed been a major feature of human societies. However, the concept of migration defined as movement with respect to borders between communities and between states as a point of reference was only constructed from the middle of the 17th century (Farer 1995: 73).

The Conclusion's text box similarly recalls the pastoralist societies of "time immemorial" and their nomadic way of life, as a "response mechanism to climate stress", and as prelude to mentioning the expected migration response to climate change (p. 399). The text box, while attributed to a different author, supports the Report's central policy proposal for cooperation by the international community to attain further benefits from the triangle migration-trade-development by fulfilling labour market 'needs'. That main theme here is backed up by the threat of future massive mobility as a response to climate change unless there is adequate development in low-income countries.

> A number of analysts, of whom Norman Myers of Oxford University is perhaps the best known, have undertaken to estimate the number of people who will be forced to move over the long term as a direct result of climate change. Myers predicts that, by 2050, 'there could be as many as 200 million people overtaken by disruptions of monsoon systems and other rainfall regimes, by droughts of unprecedented severity and duration, and by sea-level rise and coastal flooding' (Myers 2005: 1)[10] (p. 398).

The next paragraph underlines the intensity of the threat by comparing this figure with the current (international) migrant population of 200 million. Here the naturalization of migration includes environmental threats. The climate change cloud is used to argue for increased cooperation, noting that the resulting forced migration has been ignored by the international community (p. 399). However, in the current context of increasing suspicions that imagined national identities are threatened by persistent immigration, and most governments' reluctance to take a more open response to immigration, this line of discussion is not necessarily effective. Conflict prevention literature warns about appealing to threats (Gardner 2002; Stewart 2002). Adaptation requires that actors not be pushed to purely defensive positions, otherwise it may lead to the stronger imposing the bulk of costs upon the weaker, and can even open the door to violent conflict. Conceivably, this helps us understand why forced migration has no chapter in the *2008 World Migration Report*–in contrast to the inclusion of business, tourist, and student mobility–and indeed hardly any attention: environmentally induced migration is only mentioned in the final pages as a brief supplementary warning. Promoting 'managed migration' might not be helped, some of its sponsors may intuit, by an emphasis on threats. The Report adopts instead a business perspective on mobility.

9.5 Rhetorical Analysis and Local Meanings

Next, following van Dijk's sequence for discourse analysis, we deepen our picture of the Report's main messages by exploring the chapters' rhetorical resources and important local meanings. 'Local meanings' are particular interpretations and propositions that arise in a discourse. They are derived and interpreted within the umbrella of meaning provided by the global topics, the semantic macrostructures; but their concrete particularity gives them a greater vividness and potential lasting impact, so that sometimes readers remember them more clearly. We will consider how the most important rhetorical figures in the text, especially the key metaphors, contribute to the content, coherence, and degree of persuasiveness of the arguments presented.

9.5.1 Genre and Style

In congruence with its genre–the international policy document–and its search for authority, the style of the text is of impersonal narrative, written in passive voice and third-person: "style indirect inevitable" (McCloskey 1994: 325). For example, rather than stating, "We think that avoidance is not an option", the narrators write: "it is already apparent that neither avoidance of the issues nor a passive laissez-faire approach are likely to lead to the policy responses needed to realize the social and economic potential of mobility..."

10 See at: <http://www.osce.org/documents/eea/2005/05/14488_en.pdf> (10 December 2009).

(IOM 2008: 395). In this way, they assign the responsibility for statements to Reality or Everyone or All Those Who See Reality. Similarly, right after the topic of human mobility is presented at the outset of the Conclusion, the second paragraph declares: "Today, a great deal of policy attention tends to fall on highly qualified workers, [whereas] low and semi skilled workers remain a much more challenging and contested category" (p. 393). No agents are specified: whose attention, whose challenges, whose contestation?

In this genre of international report, an authoritative impersonal narrator evaluates the behaviour, preferences and policy choices of binomially categorized protagonists: developed and developing countries. A major implicit reader group are the governments of both country categories. The persuasive strategy of the text is to invite them to broaden the scope of their policy choices, and, to behave in a way consistent with their membership in a single international market and community. The term 'the international community' itself, though, can sometimes mean something else, as we see later: not a comprehensive group, but rather the dominant powers and their allies.

The arguments are given a technical appearance, consistent with the readership at which the text is directed, especially people in intergovernmental organizations, government personnel and other actors participating in international affairs. Thus, the relation between the author and the readers is relatively equal in the sense that technical jargon is often taken for granted. At the same time, there is an implicit claim of high status of the authors, based in the authority of science; for example in a phrase like "the place of migrant labour in the complex equations that are meant to yield the best economic outcomes" (p. 5), a euphemism for a hunt for cheaper labour worldwide. Similarly: "...the movement of human resources at all skills levels is now *factored into the equations intended to yield new economic gains*. In other words, labour market dynamics are increasingly operating across international borders" (p. 394; italics added). This quote reproduces the lack of specification of agents and outcomes ("new economic gains" does not specify gains for whom). It reflects the alienated business style of some management and policy thinking, and an assumed expertise or jargon familiarity in the reader.

9.5.2 Language of Flows

Since the text follows a neoclassical economics framework, many of the tropes (the non-literal uses of language) that are common in such economics discourse occur. Some core metaphors can even be seen to be part of the global meanings that guide the local meanings throughout the chapters, as predicted by van Dijk (2001, 2009) and Lakoff and Johnson (2003).

A master metaphor that pervades the text is that of human and monetary movements as 'flows'. The Report's authors apply this metaphor in two local meanings: remittances, or 'cash flows'; and migrants, or 'human flows'. Table 9.1 gives a concordance for the uses of 'flow' in the Conclusion; it examines each use of the term and identifies the words with which it is partnered in each case.[11] The Conclusion makes as many as eight references to migrant in- and out-flows and one to migrant 'stocks'. The word 'flow' or 'flows' appears three times in reference to remittances (p. 397).

The metaphor of 'flows', taken from movements of water and now used to describe movements of people or money or goods, matches well with the naturalization of the phenomenon concerned. It can convey not just 'natural' status and inevitability, but also danger and the need for management.[12] This flow mood becomes further applied to the process of building acceptance of adaptation to such inevitable flows and management needs. The previously cited quote on the recent major "consultative exercises" (p. 397) on international migration illustrates the flows imagery in, one might say, full flow.

> ... all of them [the Berne Initiative, IOM's International Dialogue on Migration, the UN General Assembly's High-Level Dialogue on International Migration and Development, and the Global Forum on Migration and Development] point to benefits that *flow* from properly managed *flows*; all of them draw attention to the risks of not managing those *flows*; all of them assert that it is

11 See Alexander (2009) on concordance as a method in discourse analysis.

12 Charteris-Black (2006) examines the use of metaphors of receiving countries as containers threatened by incoming tides, waves or flows of immigration. Griffin adds how the metaphors present migrants as an undifferentiated mass, and how the use of abstract nouns such as 'immigration' lead to a de-personalization of those referred to. See at: <http://www.york.ac.uk/res/researchintegration/Integrative_Research_Methods/Griffin%20Discourse%20Analysis%20April%202007.pdf> (6 November 2009). Griffin, Gabriele, 2007: "The Uses of Discourse Analysis in the Study of Gender and Migration".

Table 9.1: Concordances table for use of 'flows' in Conclusion chapter. **Source:** Campillo and Gasper's own analysis.

Preceding text		Subsequent text	Denotation	Page
Large intra-regional	flows	of migrant workers,	Migrants	395
strong South-North migratory	flows	from Latin America and the Caribbean to	Migrants	395
while they are all affected by migratory	flows,	they are not all affected	Migrants	396
all of them point to benefits that	flow	from	Economy	397
properly managed	flows;	all of them draw attention to	Migrants	397
the risks of not managing those	flows;	all of them assert that it is possible	Migrants	397
the recipients of	flows	of remittances that	Economy	397
the impact of remittance	flows	on development.	Economy	397
data on migrant stocks,	flows	and trends are indispensable	Migrants	400
newly affected by migratory	flows;	to formulate policy	Migrants	400
data on migrant	stocks,	flows and trends	Migrants	400

This table presents all the fragments of phrases that use the words 'flow', 'flows' and 'stocks' in the Conclusion chapter of the *World Migration Report 2008*; specific pages are indicated in the last column.

possible to arrive at common understandings and principles, and propose remarkably consistent lines of action (p. 397, emphases added).

9.5.3 Language of Needs as Determined in the Market

Given the sensitivities around immigration, a noun like 'needs' proves invaluable in building arguments for inflows. It requires no specified agent, except the anonymous We of buyers in the market. Their demands become taken as establishing a need. For example, as we saw:

> The focus of Chapter 3 is on the re-emergence of low and semi-skilled migration programmes - a seemingly surprising development considering the economic and socio-political problems that brought large-scale temporary worker programmes in both western Europe and the U.S. to an abrupt halt more than 30 years ago, but one which reflects the recognized *need* for foreign labour as spelled out above... (p. 13; emphasis added).

The past participle 'needed' evolves into an adjective to serve the same roles: "Today, a great deal of policy attention tends to fall on highly qualified workers and their *needed* skills, drive and energy. Developed countries are conscious of the *need* to offer competitive conditions of entry, residence and employment if they are to attract *needed* talent from abroad..." (p. 393, emphases added). The term 'needs' appears 16 times in the Introduction and six times in the Conclusion; 'needed' appears four and eight times respectively. A full concordance exercise would probably yield further insights.

The general implication of the asserted needs is the master need to match the demand for (cheaper) labour with a supply, as stated in bold on the Introduction's page 11 and repeated in point 5 of its summary (p. 17): "...the *need* remains for a broad and coherent global strategy to better match demand **for migrant workers with supply in a safe, humane and orderly way.** *World Migration 2008* has been designed to gauge the nature and magnitude of that *need*..." (p.11; bold in the original, italics added).

An assumed priority for demands as expressed in the market compels agents to respond and arrange supplies. Developing countries in particular can try to upgrade their workers to higher skill levels by pursuing human resource development policies and can then try to place workers in identified external labour niches. At best, they can hope that negotiations will provide for non-abuse and bring better conditions of work, but subject to the principle of economic gains and the proviso that they are willing to accept the return of their workers:

> For countries of origin, this means taking on the challenge of formulating policies and setting priorities able to both satisfy local labour market and economic needs, and nurture talent to compete for work placements abroad. This is best achieved within a comprehensive *human resource development* (HRD) framework.... Foremost among these are measures to uphold the integrity of recruitment processes and, more generally, protect migrant workers from exploitation and abuse. Access to authoritative, accurate and up-to-date information is of great importance, but so are welfare and support services for the workers while abroad and, when

> needed, appropriate arrangements to facilitate their return and reintegration in the home country (pp. 395-396).

In the last sentence, the workers' return and the associated facilitation arrangements will come 'when needed' - needed by the market? by the destination countries? by the workers?

For countries of destination, the picture given is more complex. Their interests appear more inclusive: "Countries of destination, for their part, wish to admit various categories of foreign workers to fill certain domestic labour shortages, while also ensuring the integrity of their sovereign territory and frontiers, and respect for national cultural and social core values" (p. 395). Their "cultural and social core values" deserve respect, and there is an unstated assumption about a possible threat of migrant workers to some essential qualities of destination countries: their identity and territorial integrity. Thus, the Conclusion adopts a priority of the interests of destination countries; after all, they are the destinations that workers from developing countries wish to reach.

9.5.4 Rising or Sinking of Boats Amidst the Flows: Holes in the Boats and in the Arguments

Possible omissions in the flows-related arguments become evident when we compare with another common trope for globalization of the labour economy: the metaphor of 'a rising tide lifts all boats'. It presents a win-win situation from participation in international labour markets (Kornprobst 2008).[13] The Report claims that the cooperation of the international community in matching labour demand and supply will provide benefits for all. It lists many benefits of diasporas (p. 397), such as: "extensive social and cultural networks", promotion and conduct of trade, provision of "investment funding and business know-how", "humanitarian assistance in times of crisis" and even a "meaningful contribution to democratic processes in countries of origin" (p. 397).

Danaher suggests a counter argument that considers inequality more profoundly: a rising tide will not raise leaky boats or sinking countries. The Report explores a similar consequence as a "downside of the picture" (p. 397). The negative partner of positive remittances is known by another familiar metaphor, the 'brain drain', leakage of talent and high skilled labour out of developing countries. Under present world economic arrangements, many African countries now have more of their highly trained personnel resident outside their borders than inside.

This 'downside' aspect is mentioned twice in the Conclusion. The second time is as one of the pulls in the dilemmas posed by the threat of climate change (pp. 399-400).

> There is a dilemma here. Relaxing immigration rules as part of a concerted policy to 'release the population pressure' in areas affected by climate change could accelerate the brain drain of talented individuals from the developing world to the developed - and thereby worsen the 'hollowing out' of affected economies, which is itself a driver of migration. On the other hand, closing borders in both source and destination countries undermines remittance economies and denies developing countries the benefits of access to the international labour market (p. 400).

The emerging situation can start to be seen not as win-win but as win-lose, in which many developing countries are threatened by climate change and also are subject to a high degree of brain drain. Mention of redistributive justice, and of "some analysts who are beginning to argue" (p. 399) that historical greenhouse gas emissions should be considered when allocating climate change responsibilities, suggests possible counterbalancing measures. Indeed, in the absence of such measures, much in futures studies and human security research indicates how climate change and its likely impacts in terms of migration and many other respects are capable of generating lose-lose scenarios worldwide (e.g. Stockholm Environment Institute 2002; UNDP 2008)..

9.5.5 Necessary Implications of Globalization?

Why should all countries follow the logic of needs identified by markets? One line of argument is to refer to the implications of previous commitments: the economic liberalization policies already chosen by the international community are responsible for the phenomenon of labour migration (pp. 5, 394). This seeks to ensure that both developed and developing countries accept some costs in terms of migration policies. A second line of persuasion is to propose possible win-win scenarios, to be achieved via judicious choices. A third line of argument is to rule out the viability of any alternatives, by evoking two imperious giants, "the global economy" (pp. 4, 5, 7, 12, 15) and

13 See at: <http://www.globalexchange.org/campaigns/econ101/sevenArguments.html> (13 May 2010). Danaher, K., 2007: "Seven Arguments for Reforming the World Economy", in: Global Economy 101; Global Exchange.

'globalization'. The latter term is used 12 times in the Introduction: half of the uses come during the stage-setting in pages 2–4, and as many as four uses come on page 12 when beginning the descriptive survey. 'Globalization' also occurs three times in the much shorter Conclusion chapter.

The first substantive reference to 'globalization' is modest, a reference to "the processes of economic and social integration that are collectively known as globalization" (p. 2). However, by the time of the Conclusion's summary, the concept has been reified into "the phenomenon of globalization" (p. 17). The umbrella term evolves into something more unified, which sets imperatives: "the forces of globalization are changing the way enterprises do business, giving rise to more integrated labour markets and, consequently, creating demand for increased labour mobility" (p. 12). Richer countries want more relatively cheap labour; the role and/or opportunity for poorer countries is to provide it.

The idea of 'human resource development' in the Report suggests that developing countries can prepare labour resources for external markets – without reference always to the amounts involved in such investment – in the hope that they generate returns in the form of remittances: "Central to such a [HRD] framework is a properly resourced education system capable of providing the necessary formal learning opportunities and complemented, where necessary, by practical work experience and training, to be formally assessed and certified by recognized educational and professional authorities" (p. 395). Migrant and remittance flows are treated as if there are no other international economy flows. This type of restricted analysis can be characterized as 'synecdochal'; the rhetorical device of synecdoche means taking a part as representing the whole, or vice versa.

The authors adopt neutrality regarding the processes now "collectively referred to as globalization" (p. 394). They mention wage disparities as a cause of migration, but make no effort to explore their causes, which represent the missing part of the synecdoche around migration flows and labour markets. There is no investigation of how rich countries are the ones to benefit most out of the market needs that *must* be met. Such recognition would widen the framing beyond the remittance benefits and would entail recognizing cases of win-lose. We sense thus a pro-developed countries stance in the analysis, especially when this omission is compared with the earlier mentioned listing of benefits deriving from diasporas, which could appear hyperbolic if the 'painful uprooting' of individuals mentioned in the Introduction, as an argument for not regarding migration as natural, had real relevance for the authors.

9.5.6 Flowing Towards Policy Consensus: Manoeuvring (via) the International Community

Product of an intergovernmental organization operating in an extremely sensitive policy area, a report like the *World Migration Report* is not merely a research document. Our assessment of it cannot be limited to identifying the marks of its location within a global power system. We need to ask also how it functions as an attempted instrument of influence for evolution within the system.

First, an organization such as IOM will not jeopardize its activities by antagonizing its major funders, but will plead "for the identification and development of clear linkages between the domains of migration proper and those of development, employment and trade within the broader framework of established global economic interests" (p. 17); and will typically repeatedly call for ongoing major research (p. 17: points 7–10). Even so, such a massive centre of multinational expertise feels it has other important things to say and contribute.

Second, and similarly, the discourses of policy and management, especially in international organizations, often proceed in terms that leave objectives and criteria conveniently vague. Terms like "optimal outcomes" (pp. 17, 395) should make us ask: optimal for whom, for what purposes and according to what values. Similar questions arise for terms like 'management' itself (used 19 times in the Introduction and eight times in the Conclusion), 'effective' (eight times and once respectively), and 'appropriate' (12 and five times respectively); for example in formulae such as "appropriate management strategies" (p. 1) and "appropriate management of contemporary labour mobility" (p. 15). The phrase "to realize the social and economic potential of international labour mobility" (p. 16; also pp. 17, 395) plays a similar role.

Third, implicitly the unit of discussion for evaluation and recommendation is the nation-state. Consider a statement like the following:

> Given the importance of cross-border movements for the purpose of employment, the development of appropriate policies in countries of destination is widely acknowledged as a key component in a comprehensive framework for the management of international labour mobility. However, there is no 'one-size-fits-all' formula.

> The challenge for each country of destination is to develop a planned and predictable labour migration policy (p. 15).

In contrast, the unit of discussion for analysis and explanation is the globe. The nationalism is in continual tension with the globalism (cf. Gore 1996). Intergovernmental international organizations like IOM, especially those not centrally committed to a human rights agenda, constantly walk a tightrope of accepting an evaluative nationalism while drawing out the implications of explanatory globalism.

Fourth, when the Report advocates specific policies, countries are referred to in broad categories: 'developed' and 'developing', or 'countries of destination' and 'countries of origin'. In contrast, for some purposes of general persuasion for reorientation of attitudes, actors and benefits are referred to in collective, communitarian terms, sometimes using the trump term 'the international community': "the international community stands to gain very significant economic benefits from the lifting of constraints on worker mobility" (p. 3). Sometimes the term invokes instead a smaller group of lead countries (as in "the international community was called upon to act primarily on issues of protection and humanitarian assistance", p. 4), but it always contains a bid for authority. It occurs frequently early in the Introduction (five of the ten uses occur during pp. 1–5), and again towards its end (three times more on pp. 17–18). The Conclusion proceeds in terms of evaluative nationalism until almost the end; then three of its four uses of 'the international community' appear in the final two pages of main text (pp. 399–400). The term appears thus at beginnings and endings: when seeking to set the stage for a discussion and when trying to wrap up a broad action conclusion.

9.6 Conclusion

The analysis of the macro-structures of the Report's two overview chapters shows us the central argument that steers the details of text content. The policy claim is a 'need' for cooperation of the international community in the area of labour migration, because of a proposed relation between migration and development worldwide, and an implied relation between migration and trade, which is in turn held to be naturally associated, again, with development. The policy option to match demand and supply and thus to manage labour migration is elaborated and advocated in detail. The objective of the authors, to make countries see the virtues for all parties of migration-for-development, is supported by a range of warrants, including the assertion that international migration is the logical result of the preceding international liberalization of economic policies, and in the background, the possibility of future massive migration impacts of climate change unless there is more development in low-income countries now.

This IOM report provides an example of discourses constructed in an international bureaucracy, which present a simplified vision of a globe divided into developed and developing worlds, but which at the same time aim to create an international policy unity. The text is oriented to persuade countries to cooperate in working within the international economic system framed by the mental models of neoclassical or neoliberal economics. This purpose exists in tension with a subordinated human rights stance, represented by the occasional choice of the term 'human mobility'. The contradiction is present throughout the two chapters, with the neoliberal framing dominant in the Introduction and a human rights and human security framing attaining slightly increased voice in the Conclusion but still subordinate.

Intergovernmental organizations, such as the IOM, purport to pursue impartially the interest of some imagined international (or regional) community. Their reports such as the WMR each bid for global authority in a particular policy arena. However, the selectivity of the arguments in the *World Migration Report* 2008 shows the authors' alignment, with respect to the balance of different national interests and especially with respect to migrants, whose agency is subject to an overwhelming domination of economic priorities that reflect market power. Migrants' opinions lack weight in the text. The positions attributed to their governments are also framed by an assumed primacy of markets. The positions on labour rights or human rights, vaguely treated, fade away before strong convictions on the compelling nature of 'market needs', which are treated as exogenous realities to which individuals and social groups must adapt. The role of governments appears secondary, and there is no effort to counter the partiality of the assumptions involved in an international system dominated by elites in rich countries. The authors do not conceive patterns of life not dominated by market rationality. Although issues of inequality are marginally included in the text, the assumptions entailed in a system that legitimates unlimited self-interest as an acceptable dominant value are never questioned, even when promoting cooperation and arguing about international shared interests.

That international agencies, which are overwhelmingly funded and directed by rich countries, do not confront elite interests in rich countries will come as no surprise. That they recommend arrangements, which imply continuation and augmentation of their own funding and importance, is also no surprise. However, we saw more than this. The *World Migration Report* 2008 represents a statement of a major shift from a more restrictive to a more open form of global economic order, even though it is constructed and expressed in a fashion–frequently veiled about issues of agency, criteria and direction–that reflects its institutional location.

In its final pages, the Report adopts a somewhat more internationalist tone. It provides the emphatic list that we cited of shared conclusions from the series of recent major international consultative exercises. In addition, it raises, belatedly but in a substantial text box, the enormous future migration implications of climate change due to the carbon-guzzling record of rich countries (pp. 398–400). This is not enough to outweigh the overall orientation of the study, which helps us understand why a group of labour exporting developing countries were so insistent on locating one of those international consultative fora well away from the IOM: the new "Global Forum for Migration and Development".

The *World Migration Report* 2008 is an enormous document, and getting to grips in a systematic way with even its two overview chapters is not a small exercise. In doing so we have not been able to introduce comparisons with other documents, which would be a relevant target of further research. It is possible to compare quickly a whole set of documents, each examined in an impressionistic way. We have instead explored the key sections of a single but large document more systematically, using a specific discourse analysis methodology and various conscious methods, notably including identification and analysis of the structures of argumentation, the central terms and their concordances and ambiguities, and the key metaphors which guide the discussion. To undertake the same exercise on earlier WMRs, and on documents produced by other important international organizations working on migration–including organizations representing migrants or otherwise directly defending migrants - would be very interesting. It would allow grounded comparison of perspectives and identification of changes over time, and could help in finding ways forward, to bridge between perspectives and/or create modified ones. That would be a large but worthwhile project. We hope that the present more limited study is useful in illustrating potential fruitfulness of this type of investigation, and for those seeking to construct intellectual alternatives to the positions IOM represents and who wish to relate more effectively to it and similar organizations.

Part III Migrant Experiences: Agency in the Grey Zone

10 Mission Impossible? Voluntary and Dignified Repatriation of Nigerian Victims of Trafficking

May-Len Skilbrei and Marianne Tveit

10.1 Introduction

In the wake of increased internationalization of prostitution markets, European authorities are facing new challenges regarding policy choices between the need to protect the rights of persons trafficked for the purpose of sexual exploitation on the one hand, and to control illegal entry on the other. The Norwegian case is no exception: the largest cities have seen a dramatic change in the composition of both street and indoor prostitution arenas in the last ten years. The number of migrant women in this sector has increased dramatically. The last few years saw a new development: prostitution arenas of larger Norwegian cities have seen an influx of Nigerian women, from only two spotted in street prostitution in the capital Oslo in 2003 to 638 in 2008, out of a total 1,230 women in street prostitution.[1] One of the most important questions posed by the deliberations in Norway on this emerging phenomenon is whether the Nigerian women are victims of trafficking, and if so, how can Norwegian authorities meet their needs?

This chapter attempts to answer the above question by drawing from the knowledge gained from field research on the situation of Nigerian women who have been identified as possible victims of trafficking in Norway. The focus is on the issue of repatriation given that it is one of the rights of victims of trafficking. We first describe the Norwegian authorities' obligations towards victims of trafficking, and then we present a background on women's migration from Nigeria and their current situation in prostitution in Norway. Our central argument is that knowledge about the similarity, complexity *and* diversity of women's migration out of Nigeria and their recruitment into prostitution in Europe is essential to understand the dilemmas they face with regard to repatriation. We conclude with some reservations about the return programme being able to meet the terms stated in international conventions, which the Norwegian government has ratified. The causes, process and consequences of trafficking and how its practices crosscut smuggling arrangements should be examined more carefully.

10.2 State Obligations and the Right of Return

Having ratified the 2000 UN Convention on Transnational Crime, both Norway and Nigeria are obliged to take the responsibility for the physical, psychological, social, practical, legal and security needs, and ensure the safety, of victims of trafficking.[2] The Convention has two supplements: "Protocol to Prevent, Suppress and Punish Trafficking in Persons, Especially Women and Children" (henceforth the Trafficking Protocol) and "The Protocol against the Smuggling of Migrants by Land, Air, and Sea" (henceforth the Smuggling Protocol). The Trafficking Protocol contains 20 articles outlining the obligations of ratifying parties to prevent trafficking, prosecute traffickers, protect and rehabilitate victims of trafficking. Article 8 states that "State Party shall facilitate and accept, with due regard for the safety of that person, the return of that person without undue or unreasonable delay" and that return will mean going back to a state "of which that person is a national or in which he or she had, at the time of entry into the territory of the receiving State Party, the right of permanent residence". Article 8 also mentions that such return shall be voluntary.[3] Return involves

1 The Pro Centre (2009); Året 2008 (Oslo: Oslo Municipality, 2008).

2 Before ratifying the Palermo Protocol the Norwegian authorities introduced a trafficking Act to meet its standards.

3 See at: <http://www.unodc.org/documents/human-trafficking/Toolkit-files/08-58296_tool_7-4.pdf> (1 April 2010).

T.-D. Truong and D. Gasper (eds.), *Transnational Migration and Human Security*, Hexagon Series on Human and Environmental Security and Peace 6, DOI 10.1007/978-3-642-12757-1_10, © Springer-Verlag Berlin Heidelberg 2011

the transfer of victims from the responsibility of one state to another plus the cooperation between State Parties to ensure their safety.

The Trafficking Protocol is an important document that frames the activities of the Norwegian authorities in this domain. In addition to this, the Norwegian authority has also ratified the European Convention on Action Against Trafficking in Human Beings (hereafter Council of Europe Convention) in 2008.[4] Several articles in this Convention apply to the question of the treatment of victims of trafficking after identification. Article 12, on assistance to victims, requires that signing states must implement measures to "assist victims in their physical, psychological and social recovery" while in the country. The Convention is thus sensitive to the needs of the victims following the period of identification and to the needs of governments to obtain information with the victims' cooperation.[5] The Convention regulates many of the same issues related to the treatment of victims as the Trafficking Protocol but goes further on some points.

Article 16 of the Council of Europe Convention is particularly relevant for our purposes since it deals with repatriation and return of victims. It states that the country of origin has to accept the return of victims of trafficking "with due regard for his or her rights, safety and dignity". Moreover, the country to which the victim returns has to ensure treatment "with due regard for the rights, safety and dignity of that person and for the status of any legal proceedings related to the fact that the person is a victim", and return "shall preferably be voluntary".[6] The same article states that the signing parties have to cooperate in ensuring that repatriation is possible and establishing repatriation programmes involving relevant national or international institutions and non-governmental organizations. Hindering exploitation and victimization must be a goal in this cooperation, with the aim of eventual reintegration into his or her home society. Both the Trafficking Protocol and the Council of Europe Convention influence Norway's domestic debates on efforts to prevent and combat trafficking as well as protect and assist victims.

Norway has put in place several instruments to assist victims of trafficking. One is the Re-establishment, Organizing safe places to stay, Security, Assistance (ROSA) through which victims can have access to a safe place, a certain level of security and different forms of assistance.[7] The second instrument is a reflection period for six months for persons who have been identified as a victim. This period can be prolonged for another six months if cooperation with the police and prosecution is established in building a trafficking case. An identified victim has also the right to apply for a temporary residence permit, or asylum. The third instrument to assist victims is the possibility to participate in a return programme.

An additional dimension has entered debates on trafficking policy brought about by the realities endured by Nigerian women in prostitution in Norway. These women rarely arrived in Norway directly. In nearly all cases, their first country of entry is a member state of the Schengen Agreement.[8] Some have acquired a residence permit from a Schengen member-state, for example Italy or Spain, before coming to Norway. Under the Dublin Convention the country of their first entry into Europe (Italy or Spain) must be responsible for them; for Norway they are 'third-country nationals'.[9] Some have received a resident permit in Italy under Section 18 of "The Comprehensive 'Immigration' Enactment" Law of 6 March 1998 (40/98)[10] and would risk having it withdrawn if they are known to engage in prostitution. Those who entered,

4 St.prp.nr. 2 2007–2008: "Om samtykke til ratifikasjon av Europarådets konvensjon 3. mai 2005 om tiltak mot menneskehandel" [The consent to ratification of the Council of Europe Convention 3 May 2005 on action against trafficking] (Oslo: Ministry of Justice).

5 However, article 12 states explicitly that the help offered cannot be dependent on victims' willingness to stand witness against their traffickers.

6 See at: <http://conventions.coe.int/Treaty/EN/treaties/Html/197.htm>, (1 April 2010): 43–46.

7 See at: <http://www.rosa-help.no/> (13 April 2010).

8 The Schengen Agreement is a European treaty that effectively removes border control between 25 countries in what is known as the Schengen Area. While loosening border controls between member countries, the agreement also tightens borders with non-member nations.

9 This convention came into force in 1997. It regulates the relationship between asylum seekers and States that signed the convention. The first country of entry has the responsibility to examine the asylum application. The full name of the convention is "Convention determining the State responsible for examining applications for asylum lodged in one of the Member States of the European Communities".

10 Section 18 of this Law provides for the issue of a temporary permit to stay for social protection for trafficking victims who decide to quit the streets and enrol in programmes designed to enable them to find employment and a proper place in society. See at: <http://www.unicri.it/wwd/trafficking/nigeria/docs/dr_italy_eng.pdf> (1 April 2010).

without a visa or legal residence permit from a Schengen member-state, would come under the responsibility of Norway as their first country of entry.

The reflection period was initially offered to victims who entered Norway as the first country of entry, but it was later extended to those with a visa or residence permit from another Schengen member state since they face similar problems despite differences in legal status. As the reflection period is only temporary, the question of what happens next quickly arises. Many of the victims, who stay in Norway for the duration of the reflection period, make use of the assistance programme and apply for asylum. There are several cases pending, but it is doubtful that asylum will be attainable for many victims of trafficking. The few individuals who have been granted asylum to date have been special cases and have had to prove direct threats to their family in their homeland.

The repatriation programme appears relevant not only for victims who are classified as 'irregular migrants' (having no legitimate travel document), but also to those with a residence permit from a Schengen member state who may have their permit withdrawn because of their engagement in prostitution. A key question concerns whether the Norwegian government can fully adhere to the terms stated in the Trafficking Protocol and Council of Europe Convention and ensure 'rights, safety and dignity' of victims of trafficking when implementing the return programme, to their first country of entry or to Nigeria.

The Nigerian government, having signed and ratified the Palermo Protocol, has subsequently introduced a law against trafficking: Trafficking in Persons Prohibition and Administration. This law facilitates the establishment of a Nigerian federal organ in 2003 – the National Agency for Prohibition of Traffic in Persons and Other Related Matters (NAPTIP)[11] – endowed with the responsibility for prevention schemes, legal investigation, prosecution, and the rehabilitation and protection of victims. NAPTIP is also the party that negotiates with government representatives of other countries in order to prepare bilateral agreements. These bilateral agreements concern different issues surrounding trafficking, mainly aimed at strengthening cooperation between the signing countries on issues such as repatriation and rehabilitation of victims and prosecution of traffickers. Nigeria has various agreements in place with some European countries, such as Italy, Spain and United Kingdom. In 2007, Norwegian authorities funded a return programme managed by the International Organization for Migration (IOM) office in Nigeria, which would cover the costs of voluntary return for up to 20 Nigerian victims of trafficking. In the first year, no victims made use of the programme. In the following sections we draw on the voices of Nigerian women in prostitution in Norway to illustrate the challenges faced by both the Norwegian and Nigerian states in implementing the return programme.

10.3 Methodology

The foundation for the argument in this chapter comes from two research projects on the migration and prostitution of Nigerian women in Norway. The first project intended to create knowledge of a group new to the Norwegian prostitution market. In this study, we focused on the women's situation before, during and after migrating to Norway and with the question of whether what had happened to them can be termed trafficking (Skilbrei/Tveit/Brunovskis 2006; Skilbrei/Tveit 2008). We found that the women had been and were in a difficult situation and that their reasons for leaving Nigeria and their migration histories were complex. The women were very vulnerable in different ways while in Norway, both because of prostitution and different forms of debts and obligations. These findings generated a need for further knowledge in order to find solutions to the problems they faced. Therefore, we undertook a second project to seek new understanding about the circumstances influencing women's wish, or resistance, to return to Nigeria (Skilbrei/Tveit 2007: 1). The Norwegian Ministry of Justice funded both projects and they were part of Norwegian authorities' efforts to improve assistance to victims of trafficking. The second study was commissioned as a part of the preparation for establishing the return programme.

Following the observation made by Skrobanek/Boonpakdi/Janthakeero (1997) with regard to the fact that victims of trafficking are rarely asked what they want and need in the process of devising policy, both projects were qualitative studies primarily aimed at bringing the victims' voices into the ongoing debate on what can and should be done about the situation

11 Several organizations are cooperating with NAPTIP in different ways. UNICEF took part in establishing NAPTIP, which has since cooperated with international organizations such as IOM and Programme Against Forced Labour and Trafficking in West Africa (ILO-PATWA). Its trafficking prevention and rehabilitation facilities are co-funded by many different bodies, including foreign states.

of Nigerian victims of trafficking in Norway. The underlying assumption is that an understanding of victims' situations and views is central to the development of strategies to help them, whether through repatriation and rehabilitation schemes or through alternative means.

We interviewed Nigerian women operating in prostitution arenas, and we accompanied social workers working with women in prostitution settings in Oslo and Stavanger.[12] In the course of the two projects, we conducted individual open-ended in-depth interviews with 25 women, of whom half were interviewed at least twice.[13] Additionally we had discussions at various lengths on the issues at hand with approximately 125 more Nigerian women, both individual discussions and in smaller groups of two-to-three women. In total we interviewed and discussed with 150 different women. This number is about one-third of the total number of Nigerian women in prostitution in Norway during 2006. The data collection took place in two periods of three months each from January to March and August to October 2006. We aimed at interviewing women who are in different situations and might have different needs as regards possible repatriation and rehabilitation schemes. All of the women interviewed were still active in prostitution but identified as victims of trafficking by social workers.

Despite a proportionately great number of Nigerian women in prostitution we have reached, we cannot be certain that all concerns are included. The women least willing to talk to us, or women frequenting neither the social service centres nor the traditional prostitution arenas, may be in different and possibly more vulnerable situations than the women we interviewed. However, our extensive fieldwork has enabled us to establish contact with women who were reluctant to speak with us initially, especially in the presence of other women. They, as well as those who initially expressed a negative and reserved attitude, sometimes opened up on occasions that were more private. A wide range of women representing differences in age, length of stay in Europe, migration history, and personal needs and worries had cooperated in providing us with new understandings about the problem of return from the victim's perspective. There is good reason to think that these women constitute a representative selection of Nigerian women working in prostitution in Norway.

10.4 Leaving Home

Our research disclosed different pathways through which Nigerian women enter prostitution in Norway. A common area concerns their reasons for leaving Nigeria. The women spoke of individual poverty and family responsibilities. Many carry a great deal of responsibility for their younger siblings and/or their own children, and become the family's provider in Europe when they migrate. Molly said:

> When we stand on the streets, we are suffering... but, like me, I sacrificed my life for my family. Being here in Europe I have to work to feed my family. If not, my family will die of hunger or they will die of pain.

Several of our informants refer to the deterioration of their family's life situation (caused by, for example, the loss of a parent or provider) as a key element for them to take responsibility. Their migration process often started as a family decision: sending a family member to Europe was seen as an investment for the whole family, in addition to the hope of improving the life of the migrant herself. The claims made by our informants vary as to whether they and their families knew that they would sell sex in Europe. In spite of information circulated in the home country about Nigerian migrant women working in prostitution in Europe, some interviewees said either that they did not really believe it, or that they thought they could find better options for themselves. Others said that it was common knowledge when they left Nigeria, but this still did not prevent them from migrating.

To get from Nigeria to a European country through legal channels was impossible for the women. Getting a residence permit, or a tourist visa, from a Schengen member-state is very difficult for Nigerians since Nigeria is listed as a country of high risk (Carling 2006). Many migrated illegally, becoming dependent on human smugglers or criminal networks using unofficial channels. How women came in touch with the people that arranged their travel to Europe varied. Some had actively sought information and assistance. Others said total strangers contacted them

12 We met and interviewed women in prostitution areas in Oslo and Stavanger with the help of several organizations: the Pro Centre, a social service centre and national competence centre on prostitution; the Church City Mission Nadheim in Oslo; the Church City Mission Albertine in Stavanger; ROSA and various women's shelters that house identified victims of trafficking.

13 The interviews lasted from one-to-three hours. Of those women we interviewed more than twice, the third and in some cases up to tenth interview tended to be no more than one hour each.

on the street, while a large group met the 'travel agent' through family, friends and personal networks. According to those we interviewed, the final cost of illegal travel to Europe varied between US$ 13,000 and 80,000, often closer to the latter sum. Some knew the whole amount from the time they made the deal, but may not have had an accurate idea about how much this amount actually involved, or the hardship they must go through to repay. They agreed to the deal partly because they believed it would be easy to do so once they got to Europe. Moreover, if they wanted to migrate, this is the only choice. Camilla said: "I knew it was too much money, but there was no other way that I could leave Nigeria except this."

The kind of service the women bought from the agents in Nigeria differs. Some of the women's agents only sold information about how to migrate, but did not offer transport or any other kind of practical assistance. Other agents arranged the whole trip, including airplane tickets, false passports and visas for the destination country. The women who only bought information in Nigeria typically left without further assistance. They usually travelled by bus through West Africa, then further over land to North Africa by different transportation and by foot, then finally by boat from North Africa to Spain. To travel from North Africa to Europe, most migrants were dependent on assistance in getting both documents and transport, which creates a market for human smugglers that demand exorbitant amounts in advance or when the customer arrives in Europe. Given that these practices do not involve the direct exploitation of women's labour, they are legally defined as human smuggling - considered as a 'victimless crime'.[14] Yet a danger prevails to the extent that smugglers can use their power to control the life and destiny of the migrants they smuggled. Many migrants who use smugglers on their own accord have become victims of trafficking.

14 The United Nations "Protocol Against the Smuggling of Migrants by Land, Sea and Air" defines human smuggling in the following terms: "Smuggling of migrants' shall mean the procurement, in order to obtain, directly or indirectly, a financial or other material benefit, of the illegal entry of a person into a State Party of which the person is not a national or a permanent resident." See at: <http://www.unodc.org/unodc/en/treaties/CTOC/index.html> (13 April 2010).

10.5 Being in Norway

Many Nigerian women who came to Norway had stayed in the Schengen Area for several years already, having entered Italy or Spain initially through illegal means mostly. Some had a resident permit in Spain through a legalization programme for irregular migrants, which allows them to apply for legal residence and work permits. Others received resident permits in Italy through Article 18 of the Law of 6 March 1998 (40/98) previously referred to. The women we met primarily commute from the first country of entry to Norway to sell sex, either regularly or on special occasions to solve immediate economic difficulties. Some stayed in Norway for three continuous months, others for only a couple weeks. Most of the women we interviewed came directly to Norway from larger cities in Italy and Spain on low-budget flights within the Schengen Area. The jobs they were able to get in Southern Europe seldom covered both their own living expenses and remittances to family in Nigeria. The women entered prostitution in different ways, some through traffickers who set them up in street prostitution in Italy, Spain or Norway to repay their debts, others through women they knew who sold them information on how to get started. Most of the women lived with several other Nigerian women, with one 'Madam' functioning as a pimp.

The women often lived in cramped apartments, with three-to-six persons together in one tiny space. They have little to do while in Norway other than prostitution. Many had serious health problems and were in great need of many forms of assistance. They also met with many problems while selling sex. Many described the working environments or ways of selling sex unsafe, and seemed particularly vulnerable to abuse by clients compared to other groups of women we had interviewed in previous studies. The women are also particularly vulnerable because they lack knowledge about their rights and options in Norway. Many assumed Norwegian police were corrupt and therefore not to be trusted. Social workers had found it difficult to assist the women, and have to put in considerable time and effort in order to establish contact, rapport and trust with the women.

The situation of our Nigerian informants (their migration processes, current living conditions, the vulnerabilities they face as female migrants in prostitution) illustrates the fine line between the different types of migration assisted by informal networks and trafficking as a crime. The women generally share similar vulnerabilities regardless of the definition and categorization of their migration process. In the life worlds of the prostitution of Nigerian women in Norway, diverse practices (trafficking, people smuggling, pimping and assistance in the organization of migration and initial entry to prostitution) are intermeshed, making it difficult to differentiate between Nigerian women who are victims of trafficking and those women who are not (Skilbrei/Tveit 2008).

Nevertheless the division between victims and non-victims is still of great importance in many situations. When identified as a victim of trafficking a migrant has access to certain rights and assistance that other migrants do not have. In the current Norwegian situation, the question of whether someone is a 'real' victim of trafficking is not important regarding his or her rights to different forms of assistance. Norwegian authorities decided to set the bar low, and if someone defines him or herself as a victim or if social workers think a person qualifies, he or she can claim the rights of a victim.

10.6 Sources of Fear to Return

Entry with false identity papers, or with a valid identity paper from another member state of the Schengen Area that is conditional on their exit from prostitution, is a primary reason behind the fear of deportation. Deportation as 'illegal migrants' is becoming a reality: lately the Norwegian authority has expelled several Nigerian women as illegal migrants claiming to be victims of trafficking. Several other factors also contribute to their fear of repatriation through formal channels: 1) uncertainty regarding their ability to continue to provide for their family when they return; 2) the stigma attached to prostitution and to a 'failed migrant'; 3) anxiety about their treatment by the Nigerian authorities.

When we first met Hannah in Oslo (a 28-year-old woman from a village outside Benin City) she was quite optimistic and ready to start her new life in Europe, having paid off her debt. After being arrested, she realized that everything was much more complicated and difficult than she had anticipated. The identification papers, for which she had paid a fee of US$ 1,400 to a woman broker, were false. She is now placed in the category of illegal migrants. She applied for assistance through the programme for victims of trafficking in Norway, but was told that she was not entitled to assistance because she paid her debt and was no longer under threat. Slowly she understood that she could not go anywhere else in Europe because she has an illegal status. The only thing she could do is to apply for asylum in Norway, which the Norwegians would almost certainly reject. She might have somewhere between 10-to-12 months left to stay in Norway while her asylum application is processed, and then she will be deported to Nigeria.

In contrast to deportation, repatriation is framed as an appropriate way of meeting the needs of victims of trafficking according to international conventions and Norwegian law. The return programme appears a good alternative for Nigerian women who are staying illegally in Norway, or struggling between countries in the Schengen Area generally. Yet women's responses to the return programme are mixed.

Some women who have a residence permit from a member-state of the Schengen Area, but are struggling between Norway and another member-state of this Area, felt trapped in a very difficult situation. They wished for the possibility to return to Nigeria and leave their 'European' problems behind. Many others held a negative attitude towards return. The demand for money by their families in Nigeria is continuous and makes it difficult for women to consider returning because they then would be unable to meet their family obligations. The ordeals they had endured after having left Nigeria and entered prostitution would not be compensated. Hannah explained that she could not go back to Nigeria without money because she could not bear the thought of having gone through all this for nothing. "I went to Europe and have been forced to pay US$ 47,000 of debt with my own body. How can I ever go back if this is the only thing I got out of it? Two years of selling my body in the streets of Norway and no money?"

Leaving Europe without compensation for the suffering they had endured would also mean, for many women, giving up on the dream of a better future, whereas staying on in Europe would give them an opportunity to wait for a more fortunate moment. Many women claimed that they would voluntarily go back if their efforts in Europe enabled them to invest in a future in Nigeria. Their dream was to save enough money to start a profitable business there. Significantly, all of our informants emphasize the lack of stable employment and income in Nigeria, making entrepreneurship seem the only viable solution. Similar to other women interviewed, Claire said she would need between US$ 13,000 and 27,000 to start a business in Nigeria. The money would go to establishing and renting the business premises. In Nigeria, US$ 27,000 would go a long way, and the sums she and others believe are necessary to start up a business means that they have the ambition of a whole other life than what is common in their places of origin in Nigeria.

Another obstacle that many women cite is the difficulty to return to Nigeria as long as they only have a temporary residence permit in a European country. Without a secure income in Nigeria, they are likely to return to Europe; without a more durable permit they would have to start the migration process anew, again accumulating debt. The ones do who have a legal identity document in a member country of the Schengen Area are afraid that their documents might be stolen. Those women without a valid document know that they risk being found out if they cross a border between the Schengen Area and another state. Some women also say that they cannot return to Nigeria as long as they owe money, because the traffickers may then steal their documents to use for trafficking someone else.

Nigeria seems more distant over time to some women. They are acclimatized to living in Europe, and life at home is less and less tempting. Aisha is an example. Despite missing her parents and siblings, she never thinks about going back, and will do anything in her power to stay in Europe. "After everything you passed through, you like to fight for yourself". After four years in Europe, she is no longer paying her madam and plans to save money to finish her education. She believes her future lies in Europe, not Nigeria.

The women emphasized that Nigeria is a violent society, and one in which the police and other agents of the federal and state governments can actually increase a citizen's insecurity. Overall, the women were critical of Nigerian authorities, demonstrating little faith that the government is concerned with improving living conditions of the poor. Many pointed to the fact that Nigeria, like Norway, is an oil-rich country, but cannot even feed its own citizens.

Alongside poverty, corruption and political and economic disenfranchisement, the women express frustration with the lack of gender equality in Nigerian society. Experiencing exploitation and abuse in Europe to support the family back home can also lead women to change their perceptions of gender and family relations. This makes life in Nigeria appear considerably worse to many of them. Aisha describes the Nigerian society as one in which men have power over women and women are unable to circumvent male domination. Aisha said that men in Nigeria treat women they are in a relationship with poorly, and reflected on how her time in Europe changed her view of gender relations.

> Sometimes I think that had I been in Nigeria, maybe I would not know this. I would be living in our culture; I would support them [the men]. You understand me? I would even support the men that are treating the women bad. Maybe. Because it is within that culture. [Now] I have communicated with people, I have travelled, I have learnt more cultures... and that is my own view. I did not know when I was there. But since I have travelled and seen all that I saw, I like it. Women have to fight.

Even if women wanted to give up on building a better future in Europe, they fear mistreatment at the hands of Nigerian authorities upon return. Many of our informants had heard of women returning to Nigeria only to face arrest and potential prosecution. It is illegal for Nigerians to sell sex abroad (Okojie/Okojie/Eghafona/Vincent-Osaghae/Kalu 2003), and the women repeatedly spoke of this fact. Camilla explained,

> When they came back to Nigeria, first and foremost, they were put in prison. The information went to Nigeria that they were caught in the streets here and they were prostitutes, you know. The parents had to look for money to come and bail them out from the prison.

Camilla's last point is crucial. When the women describe the likelihood of detention upon return it does not necessarily mean they will face a trial and prison sentence for prostitution. Detention most likely relates to corruption; airport and/or police officials can detain women returning from Europe and demand a bribe to release them, potentially a profitable source of income. One of the women we interviewed had previously returned to Nigeria, and describes how she was supposed to bribe the officials at the airport.

> They say if I have something [money] there, I should give it to them, so that they can go and stamp my passport. It is for the deportation. If they leave me for the police to catch me, I will pay big money and I will suffer. I should give them something so they would not give me to the police.

It is worth noting that Nigerian women in Denmark have told similar stories about detention at the Lagos airport when returning to Nigeria (Holm 2005: 15). Furthermore, numerous reports on the situation in Nigeria mention some form of incarceration of women returning from Europe (Holm 2005: 15). Officially, women expelled from Europe were supposed to be met by the federal anti-trafficking organ in Nigeria, NAPTIP, at the airport, where an interview should be conducted to decide whether they are victims of trafficking or not (Skogseth 2006). However, this does not always happen due to lack of communication between the countries deporting the women and NAPTIP, and lack of immediate resources in Nigeria (Skogseth 2006; UNDOC 2006: 108). If the women return as part of a repatriation programme, IOM Nigeria would meet them at the airport. Whether the negative impressions the women have of Nigeria and Nigerian authorities are true or not, the women's lack of faith in the authorities at home constituted a major obstacle to a successful return. In interviews, many added that they would be more positive towards returning if Norwegian authorities or organizations were active in the process, particularly on the Nigerian side.

In addition to facing detention and corruption upon return, the women fear possible social consequences of being associated with prostitution. They describe prostitution as shameful in their home societies, even when they had been trafficked. Several claimed that because of information campaigns to prevent trafficking, and newspaper articles, many people suspect women returning from Europe to have taken part in prostitution. Dina is well aware that people in Nigeria suspect that Nigerian women in Europe make their living from prostitution. This fact worries her family.

> People in Benin City know that prostitution is common work for Nigerian girls in Europe. But when I was in Italy, I said no to my family, I am not doing that job. I never tell my family the truth. They will be so sorry and my mother will not let me send her money. My sisters want to come, but I don't tell them what I do. I tell them that it is very hard to get a job. My family tells me, don't try the street! I say that I have never tried it.

It is important to note that the women fear both the association with prostitution and the more general stigma of being a failed migrant. Vanessa tells us that this is her second time in Europe. She stayed in Italy for some years earlier, but was deported back to Nigeria because she had false identity documents. She describes her return to Nigeria as very traumatic. Although her mother and sisters were happy to see her, other relatives and neighbours had laughed and said "Shame on you! Being in Europe and coming home empty handed"! The situation grew worse during the following months, and she felt she had nothing – no money, no work, no status and no property.

> My situation is very bad. I wanted to hang myself. I was coming home with empty hands, everyday cry, cry, cry. So my mother tried to raise her hand to me, slap me. She said, how many years am I going to cry for? I say, I am still crying for my property but... I am crying, I don't know how to read, I am crying where am I going to start? I am crying for many things.

Vanessa ended up migrating illegally back to Europe, by buying new services from the same woman who provided her with false documents the first time. The second time around she promised Vanessa a resident permit and normal job in Norway, after Vanessa insisted she did not want to work in prostitution. Upon her arrival in Norway, however, Vanessa learned that she did not have any legal papers and had to work in prostitution after all. Vanessa knows that if she contacts the police, she would eventually be sent home to Nigeria again, a destiny she finds unbearable.

Reports on the views towards women returning to Nigeria from prostitution in Europe differ. The Danish Immigration Service (2005) claims that there is little stigmatization of returning women, mostly because they earn people's respect due to the money and prosperity they have or are associated with. This is of course dependent on the women returning with money. Adepoju relates what women returning to Nigeria face.

> When deported, their reintegration is made difficult by the stigma of failure, and the local communities are wary that the repatriated victims may spread diseases they contracted abroad. Many such victims of trafficking end up engulfed in, rather than escape from, the trap of poverty, bringing in its wake personal trauma and dishonour to their families (Adepoju 2003: 83–4).

It is difficult to know whether women's experiences with prostitution in Europe will have serious consequences for their prospects of a new life in Nigeria. Prostitution brings stigma upon women in most countries in the world and in Nigeria the trafficking of women into prostitution stigmatizes the country as a whole, as it tarnishes the image of Nigeria internationally (Bamgbose 2002). Bamgbose (2002: 587) writes that women with prostitution experience in Europe are even more vulnerable to prejudice upon return to Nigeria, due to international attention: "There is no opportunity for the reintegration of prostitutes into the society without the stigma and label of prostitution". A UNODOC report from 2006 concludes, "The government agencies (police and immigration) lack the facilities to provide adequate care for victims while they are still in custody" and that "fighting trauma and stigmatization experienced by victims is a particular challenge" (UNODOC 2006: 108).

Another issue for some of the women is the lack of family or other social networks in Nigeria. This may be exacerbated for women who spent many years in Europe. Christina, who herself plans to return to her family in Nigeria in the near future, claimed that life in Nigeria is very difficult for a single woman. "It is difficult if you don't have a family to stay with. Maybe the family lives in the village, but you can't live in the village if you have lived in Europe for many years."

Aisha's concerns are the same. She has a resident permit in Spain, and therefore does not have to fear involuntary repatriation, but was asked to imagine how it would be to return if she did not have a family back home. "I don't know. Worst imaginable. Imagine, I am a girl, I will just... any man who talks to me on the street, I will agree. Because I need a shelter, I need help; I need somebody to be on my side, somebody to talk to me, somebody to help me".

Felicity is an educated woman in her late twenties lured into prostitution in Europe by a woman in her village. She said that no woman would go back to her parents' house poor and deported, ashamed and disgraced. If she is sent back to Nigeria without money she will not tell her family but instead go to live in another part of Nigeria. She states that the only way she will be able to make a living on her own without a network, family, money or job is to work in prostitution.

We often found ourselves surprised by how impossible the women said it would be to succeed in Nigeria without family help and support. The importance of family makes relocation within Nigeria as a means to protect and reintegrate victims of trafficking difficult. In addition, there is the potential stigma of being without a family. UNHCR writes:

> Leaving their family signifies social and economic exclusion for the large majority of Nigerians and in particular for women. There are NGOs who might take her in for a while, but they will not be able to support her forever. The only option for women in such cases would be prostitution (UNHCR 2006: 45).

Entering local prostitution markets would increase women's marginalization and make them vulnerable to different forms of exploitation, including re-trafficking. Dina does not have a resident permit in Europe, and is highly at-risk of being sent back to Nigeria herself. She says:

> If I were deported to Nigeria, I would of course go back to Europe as soon as possible. I would have to borrow more money. That would be difficult because I still have only paid US$ 20,000 of the other money [owed to trafficker for the first trip], but I would still find a way to go back to Europe. I know girls that are deported; they come back to Europe again.

Alice has two children in Nigeria. She ran away from her madam because she did not want to work in prostitution. Nevertheless, when she could not find any other way to make money in Europe, she found herself forced into selling sex. Now she cannot go back to Nigeria because she has not paid the debt to her madam and, if she does not continue to sell sex, her children will suffer because of lack of remittances. The conditions of her resident permit forbid her from selling sex in Italy because she has received assistance as a victim of trafficking,[15] so she commutes to Norway to make money. She misses her children terribly and relates an incident when her 11-year-old daughter called her crying from Nigeria, demanding to know why her mother had left them. Alice believes she can never go home because of retaliations from her madam. She feels helpless.

> When I see the families - families that are well organized, well loved, I have to... I can't even.... If I killed myself, then my children would still remain you know, their life will remain miserable, so I am not so much... I am not so happy, you know. So I don't know what to do. And I can't, even if I have the money, I can't go to Nigeria because of my problem. So you know my life is just a...I don't know what to do really, I don't know what to do.

Julie, who is in a similar position as Alice, says that the only solution she could imagine to her problem is to marry a European man. That would gain her a permanent resident permit and allow her to apply for family reunification for her children. She prays that God will give her a kind man who understands her situation, but knows it will most likely never happen.

> It is not that hard to get a man, but... as I am working in the street, I can't get a responsible man. As I am working in the street, no man will like to take me. Because I am working in the street.

As with Alice, many women we talked to were afraid of some form of retaliation from their trafficker or pimp if they were to end prostitution or return to Nigeria without having repaid the money they owed. Our informants reported debt up to US$ 80,000 upon arrival in Europe, which is consistent with findings in other reports (Okojie/Okojie/Eghafona/Vincent-Osaghae/Kalu 2003; United Nations Office on Drugs and Crime 2005). While they may be scared of punishment and sanctions, many also emphasize that they have made an agreement, and that it is only fair

15 Victims of trafficking are awarded a set of rights through Article 18 in Law of 6 March 1998 (40/98): the Italian Immigration Law. Identified victims can obtain a temporary stay and work permits that may become permanent over time. Importantly, if a woman drops out of the programme or continues/goes back to work in prostitution, she will immediately lose her permits and be deported back to Nigeria.

that they keep it.[16] Several women also say that they were taken to a local *juju* priest before they left Nigeria, but how the women relate to the function and effects of the *juju* rituals varies.[17] Some women sincerely believe in the power of the *juju* rituals they have gone through, while others consider it a mere contract ritual with no magical powers. A significant number however, express fear of retaliation from agents if they do not repay their debts. Some are not worried about their own safety, but fear that the agents and their contacts may harm their families in Nigeria if the debt is not paid.

We also met women who had chosen not to pay their debt or only pay part of it because they considered the sum too large, the working conditions unbearable, or both. For some of these women, standing up to the traffickers seems to have worked; some threatened to contact the police, others discussed the conditions with their traffickers, argued that the agreement was unreasonable and actually got off by paying only part of the total sum owed. Others find that the risk of refusing to pay is too big. Reports as to the veracity of the threats Nigerian women face vary. In the report from the Danish Immigration Service (2005), most professionals interviewed claimed that revenge upon victims by traffickers is rare, and that the returning victims face intimidation at worst. Furthermore, there is conflicting information about the ability of traffickers or madams to seek reprisals against victims upon their return to Nigeria. While some sources believe that there is a real risk of such reprisals, they have no knowledge of this having happened whereas other sources are aware of rare (one or two) incidents (UK Home Office 2006: 10). Nevertheless most women are not willing to put themselves at potential risk, not to mention risking the safety of their family members.

16 See Testaì (2008a, 2008b) for new research among Nigerian victims of trafficking in Italy on the diversity of victims' situations, how they relate to traffickers and the debt they accumulate.

17 *Juju* can be defined as 'traditional medicine', which is linked to a belief in magical powers induced by rituals or fetishes. These powers are included in belief systems widespread in West Africa, but are configured differently in different ethnic groups and over time (Bastian 2002). In relation to trafficking, juju rituals are used in binding victims to traffickers in agreement, and in breaking that agreement; the victims may fear physical retribution or more misfortunes that are magical.

10.7 Conclusion

Summarizing findings on West African migration systems, Truong notes that "the decision-making process to enter migration networks in order to improve livelihood (or to prevent its erosion) is based on a careful assessment of household resources" (2006: 61). Women's entry into prostitution after being sent from the home community to earn and support their family is also revealed by several studies. Policymakers have to be concerned about a woman's situation before and during a trafficking situation, as well as when they manage to get out. Getting out of a trafficking situation does not mean getting out of prostitution.

Our findings on the case of Nigerian women in Norway left us with questions on whether the women in current circumstances should be repatriated to Nigeria at all. Many do not want to return under any circumstances, others are more positive towards returning when they have achieved their goal of building a small fortune. In forcing women who are still searching for a better life in Europe to return to Nigeria there is great risk that they return to Europe yet again - not necessarily with better hopes of avoiding trafficking and other forms of exploitation. There are even arguments against returning women who volunteer to return. After many years in Europe, many are desperate or depressed, and even if they give up and join the repatriation programme, there is a danger that it will be too difficult to reconcile their lives back in Nigeria and that they will soon be looking for a way out again. The women who had the hardest time in Europe, and therefore may be positive towards returning, may not be aware of the difficulties they will face when they return without money and honour. The majority of these women emphasize that it would be almost impossible to go home empty-handed. Europe represents winning the Golden Ticket for Nigerians; no one will understand that a woman can come back from Europe without having anything to show for it.

The reasons they were motivated to leave Nigeria in the first place have often not changed, neither in terms of the family's financial situation nor in terms of their ability to influence their own destiny. When the women describe that large amounts of money are necessary in order to build a new life in Nigeria, it is evident that they seek a very different life than the one they knew before they left. To understand the women's attitudes towards returning to Nigeria, it is important to consider what they left behind, what they invested along the way, and what it takes to make it all worthwhile.

A key consideration in establishing agreements and routines for repatriating victims of trafficking to Nigeria (voluntarily or involuntarily) is dependent on securing the women's rights, safety and dignity – both in Norway and in Nigeria. In light of the concerns voiced by the women themselves, it is difficult to envisage a repatriation and rehabilitation scheme that could meet the challenges of family obligations, corruption in Nigeria, loss of hope for the future, stigmatization, lack of networks, and threats of retaliation.

There are substantial differences between the women in our study in several domains: 1) their actual and perceived situations, 2) their needs if they return and 3) whether they are in a trafficking situation or only suffering the consequences of having been in one. In this light, taking an undifferentiated approach to assisting victims of trafficking can make the situation worse. "Anthropological and sociological studies exist that document dramatic differences between trafficked women, but often a 'one size fits all' model drives prescriptions to assist the victims" (Demleitner 2001: 276). If these differences are not taken into account, there is a chance that life in Europe and return to Nigeria will accentuate the socio-economic divisions that exist between the women, with the likely effect that the same women who struggle most in Europe will struggle most in Nigeria.

11 Migrant Women and Their Vulnerability in the Trafficking-Migration Continuum: Evidence from Asia

Yu Kojima

11.1 Introduction

A spate of recent studies on women engaged in cross-border migration underscored how such movements have come to form part of the regional and global service economy characterized by gender-based labour market niches (Agustín 2003). Parreñas (2000) and Hochschild (2002) for instance, analysed how global care chains are structured by differences in class and ethno-racial power hierarchy involving female labour (Hochschild 2000). Other studies offer historical and structural accounts of the expansion of sex industry in industrialized countries, materialized through the constant supply of foreign migrant labour that satisfies particular sexualized images (Macklin 2003; Tyner 1996). Limoncelli (2009) emphasizes the gender-based structure in international political economics responsible for gender-based niches of labour markets. To date, the debate on trafficking largely disregards this point by either ignoring women's economic rights or defining the scope of such rights in a limited way. Taking all these views into consideration, there is a need to reorient the debates on women's migration towards the intersecting inequalities that reinforce their vulnerability.

This chapter addresses the complexities in the migration-trafficking continuum in two gender-based employment niches - *private care services* (PCS) and *commercial sexual services* (CSS)[1] in Asia to show how intersecting inequalities can arise from a policy framework that treats trafficking and migration as two fixed and distinct categories. This framework distinguishes undocumented migrant women either as victims of trafficking or criminals of illegal migration and it does not always reflect the reality of migration involving women (Pearson 2002). The 2006 Report of the United Nations Office on Drugs and Crime acknowledges that human trafficking is an ongoing process rather than a single offence, and exploitative relations in this mode of migration are bound to be more complex, while migrant smuggling by definition ends upon arrival at the destination and hence is less exploitative (UNODC 2006: 57). The main attempt here is to bring to the fore how a legal demarcation between the categories of victim and criminal underplays the fact that smuggled migrants and trafficked persons undergo similar duress and equally exploitative conditions during migration.

A major point to register is the fact that since the 1990's, forms of recruitment and modes of cross-border migration have diversified, and the conceptual difference between practices of human trafficking and migrant smuggling has nearly vanished,[2] posing a practical difficulty for sustaining these distinctive legal categories (Aronowitz 2001; Musto 2009). The inability of the victim-criminal framework to curb human trafficking effectively is partly explained by the scope of present legal measures, which do not fully reflect the complex process and context of migration in which women are involved. There is a dire need to reinvigorate the debate on trafficking in women to go

1 Care work involving migrants who are predominantly women could be categorized into two groups, namely, 1) managing care for nursing homes and homes for the elderly operating under state regulations; and 2) private care within individual households mediated through private agents. Care work in this category often involves various types of housework, including care of pets, livestock and shop-keeping jobs.

2 Migrant smuggling features a historically different conceptual background from human trafficking. While trafficking of human beings has been predominantly market driven throughout time, the notion of smuggling people has been associated with action out of compassion or duty, as witnessed during the Holocaust of WWII. Some studies show how migrant smuggling evolved as a business venture in different parts of the world (Koser 2008).

T.-D. Truong and D. Gasper (eds.), *Transnational Migration and Human Security*, Hexagon Series on Human and Environmental Security and Peace 6, DOI 10.1007/978-3-642-12757-1_11, © Springer-Verlag Berlin Heidelberg 2011

beyond the victim-agency dichotomy, which had shaped the policy framework, and to give greater significance to intersecting aspects of inequality and vulnerability.

The structure of this chapter is as follows. First, the main analytical approaches to female migration and trafficking in women under globalization and structural changes in the domain of care and sex services in specific regions are reviewed. A key concern is how this debate conceptualizes structure and agency and how to delimit its contextual relevance. Drawing from the narratives of women and youth[3] who experienced the trafficking-migration continuum, the chapter will reveal the key aspects of intersectional discrimination they undergo. An understanding of structural vulnerability experienced by female migrants requires an inductive approach that begins with their location and its affiliated relations of subordination, which may shift at different stages of their migration process. Such an approach is compatible with intersectionality as a normative and empirical research paradigm (Hancock 2007). This approach seeks to discern forms of vulnerability both at the level of institution and at the level of the subjectivity of individuals who hold particular intersectional traits. This chapter concludes by showing how acknowledging the importance of intersected processes of discrimination against migrant women and youth will have significant implications for policy.

11.2 Female Migration and Trafficking in Women: Analytical Approaches

Studies of migration adopt a variety of disciplinary approaches ranging from demographics, economics, history, law, political science, sociology and anthropology. One way to understand these diverse approaches is to pay attention to the levels/units of analysis. Macro approaches focus on immigration policies or on market forces and socio-economic structure. Micro approaches relate to the migratory experiences of an individual migrant or ethnic group, both in emigration and immigration processes (Brettell/Hollifield 2000: 3). Dominant economic migration paradigms known as neoclassical macro-economic theories and dependency theories have been criticized for their primary focus on economic disparities and their exclusion of different migration experiences across gender and ethnic groups (Urzúa 2002). In addition, they deny the aspect of agency of individual migrants as agents in migration. These weaknesses are particularly apparent in theorizing on international migration processes involving women in care and sex work, where economic factors alone do not mobilize them to move across borders.

Analytical approaches for studying the causes and effects of female migration and trafficking in women evolved in response to changing realities of migration. With the rise of more complex and transient forms of migration involving women in the early 1980's, feminist anthropology began to play a key role in the study of female migration. In her analysis on the historical trajectories of migration study from a gender perspective, Brettell (2000: 111) highlights that the initial focus was concentrated on the women's changing power and status in domestic and public spheres – a perspective inspired by Marxist feminism.[4] Analyses of women's decision-making in migration in developing countries that focussed on the domestic sphere have shed light on diverse experiences of those who migrate as part of household strategies (Chant 1992; Sweetman 1998).

The scope of analytical approaches has further expanded as the anthropological theory of female migration evolved with new insights drawn from post-modern feminism and political economic theory. The post-modernist approach has attempted to explain the complexity of identities that female migrants uphold in connection with intertwined social positions of women as a result of interaction between state policies, class, gender, race and ethnicity (Brettell 2000: 111). Drawing on examples in the United States, Asia, Southern Europe and Latin America, theories on gender and migration offer deep insights on the dynamics involved in changing gender roles in the household and women's agency, and in shaping their identity in relation to the family, kinship relations and social networking in the migration process (Floya/Lazaridis 2000; Curran/Saguy 2001; Houdagneu-Sotelo /Avila 2001; Suzuki 2003).

3 The author acknowledges the legal definition of a child in the context of development is highly disputed. In this respect, the author adopts the UN definition of youth (age between 14–24) (www.unicef.org) so as to reflect the age range of interviewees in this article. The term youth in the discussion henceforth signifies young women between ages 14–24.

4 See Moore (1988) for a fuller discussion of the domestic and public spheres from an anthropological perspective.

Emerging theories of gender in migration depict the way in which gender relations are understood in specific contexts. This is well demonstrated in the victim-agency debates[5] derived from an analysis of vulnerability of migrant women particularly in prostitution. Whereas, abolitionists consider the flow of migrant women into the sex industry from the *Violence Against Women* (VAW) perspective (Barry 1995; Hughes/Roche 1999; Jeffreys 2004) and emphasize that these women are victims of abuse and misuse of power for men's sexual gratification, scholars in favour of a sex-work approach underscore the idea of prostitution as work and that women's autonomous rights in relation to the sale of sex should be recognized at the policy level (Bindman 1997; Kemapadoo 1998; Doezema 2002).

From the labour migration perspective recent work stresses that neither the victim nor agency visions fully represent the reality of migrant women. Agustín (2005) draws on the voices of undocumented migrant women engaged in sex and domestic work to show that women's visions on migration intertwine a 'pragmatic, future-oriented focus' and a sense of self-reproving derived from the stigma attached to prostitution that cannot be simply addressed through an abolitionist or sex workers rights strategy. Instead, she argues that theorizing agency of migrant women in prostitution should go beyond this dichotomous and ethically engineered framework and geared towards effective future policy direction in line with migrant women's interest: migrant women's prime concern is their illegal status, not prostitution.[6] Given the complex power dynamics involved in prostitution, recent works are also critical of simplified use of binary labelling against women in prostitution. They argue for understanding women's status in relation to their material experience, so as to recognize that in striving to fulfil their interests and survival needs of their own and their families women could be both victims and agents (Roces 2009).

In pursuit of a more effective response to changing realities of migration involving women, some feminist scholars began to urge for a feminist political economy approach in the analysis on female migration and associated vulnerability of migrant women in the global service economy. Limoncelli (2009: 262) argues that this approach is useful in analysing the vulnerable position of women's labour in the international sex trade facilitated by intersecting inequalities under global capitalism. This would help to reposition the victim-agency trafficking debates in a more constructive way by focusing on the material dimensions and practices that have evolved around global prostitution. Jeffreys (2009: 317) fundamentally agrees that it is necessary to develop a feminist political economy approach. However, she stresses that critical inquiry into economic processes would not change conditions of women in prostitution in reality unless we dare to identify male domination as the root cause of commodification of women's bodies under neo-liberalism.

Turning to the global organization of care services involving migrant women, the demand for female labour has been analyzed in the context of restructuring of the care domain in both industrialized and developing countries (Razavi 2007; Parreñas 2002). These authors point out how the vulnerable status of migrant women as care workers has been reinforced partly by social policy on care labour. The provision of care has shifted from the family to the state and to the market in response to socio-economic changes. Demographic changes (Bettio/Simonazzi/Villa 2006; Escrivá/Skinner 2008) and lifestyle changes (Enhrenreich/Hochschild 2002; Anderson 2001; Esim/Smith 2004) play an important role. State promotion of paid care work without a real attempt to revalue care labour as part of regulated work categories has repressive consequences on migrant women and women from the lower social strata employed in the care sector.

In sum, existing theories contributed greatly to advance our understanding of the life of female migrants. Yet conventional theoretical explanations of the vulnerability of migrant women in PCS and CSS are limited to analyses that address issues related to working conditions, legal status and occupational stigma independently. Theories that weigh on the

5 Contemporary feminist thought views women in prostitution in conflicting ways–as an outcome of woman's autonomous choice, as a woman's survival strategy and as victimization (Truong 1998). The emergence of a pro-prostitution lobby attempted to de-stigmatize women in prostitution through legal recognition of the industry in order to protect them from abuse and exploitation. The mainstream however, continues to uphold a patronizing moral judgment against women in prostitution, as victims.

6 Outshoorn (2004) for instance urges that feminist solidarity concerned for situations of migrant women in prostitution should reflect the changing political landscape in which trafficking in women for prostitution is framed at the individual state policy level. For instance, migrant women in the sex industry increasingly face punishment based on their illegal status as the result of shifting state policies in European countries to legalize prostitution with some conditions.

structural aspect of causal complexity show weakness in downplaying the dynamics of individuals' vulnerabilities arising from their diverse responses to situations they encounter during migration. Theoretical propositions which intend to counter the simplified understanding of victimhood, by posing migrant women as an autonomous social agent, provide powerful insights. Nevertheless, such explanations are inevitably bound with given institutional contexts in which structural discrimination against migrant women occurs.[7] More recently, scholars began emphasising a need for more pragmatic interpretations of the complexity of women's agency in migration in line with their interests and given the changing political economy of women's labour under globalization (Agustin 2007; Outshoorn 2004).

11.3 Research Sites and Methodology

The data presented in this section are part of a broader research project conducted during the period of April 2003 to November 2005. A multi-site approach was adopted to compare experiences of migration and trafficking among women. The primary site was Thailand (Bangkok, Chiang Mai, Chiang Rai) as a sending as well as receiving country. Secondary sites were Sri Lanka (Colombo), Cambodia (Phnom Penh) and Laos (Vientiane) as primarily sending countries, although Cambodia has also emerged as a receiving country of trafficked persons for prostitution.

To gain a complete picture of current patterns of female migration for PCS and CSS, four categories of migrant women and youth were included: 1) women and youth recorded as trafficked cases and detained in shelters;[8] 2) undocumented migrants in an International Detention Centre (IDC) in Bangkok with trafficking/exploitative migration experiences but not registered themselves as trafficked;[9] 3) undocumented migrants who were not under police custody (still working); 4) returned documented and undocumented migrants.

In total, interviews were conducted with 63 individuals of nine nationalities and two ethnic minority groups[10] from IDC-Bangkok, government offices, NGO shelters, and private homes in the countries visited. A semi-structured interview was used for individual migrants while successive group discussions were conducted to identify concerns and needs of specific groups. The timeline method[11] was adopted to gain insights on their migratory experience as an unfolding process to capture the essential forces shaping a given turning point (entry into, exit from, and re-entry into an occupation). This method recognizes the importance of tracing the migration trajectory of a person because it enables us to obtain insights on the conditions under which certain decisions are made and the consequential actions. It also assists us in identifying the forces behind a turning point and how, at a given point, the migrant may experience an overlap of status, such as having a legal status but doing illegal work, or having a legal status that is conditional on being 'bonded' to the employer.

In addition, exploratory interviews were also carried out with migrant women and youth engaged in other types of work (water factory, drug trafficking, rubber plantation, small vendor clerk, and hairdresser).[12] It is common for undocumented migrant women and youth to move from one job category to another for survival. Exposure to the wider scope of the group was useful to capture a holistic picture of the socio-economic environment in which migrant

7 Recurring challenges against pro-prostitution movements in developing countries reflect this tension given that moral autonomy in the sale of sex is highly contextual. The women's autonomy and freedom of expression considered self-evident for women in western countries are not necessarily guaranteed for women in developing countries. Lack of such autonomy often reinforces the vulnerability of those engaged in the sex industry. See Seshu and Bandhopadhyay (2009).

8 For details on the Thai government's repatriation and reintegration programme, see Jayagupta (2009).

9 IDC-Bangkok detains undocumented migrant women who are classified as criminal for breaching the Thai immigration law, whereas persons who could prove themselves victims of trafficking are qualified to enter shelters. In principle, any person under 18 years old with a foreign nationality should be kept under custody of government-run shelters (Government of Thailand 2003).

10 Women and youth interviewed hold nationality from Burma (including ethnic minority group Taiyai): Cambodia; China (including ethnic minority group Taiyai): Laos; North Korea; Sri Lanka; Thailand (including ethnic minority group Kao tribe); Uzbekistan and Vietnam. In addition, a handful of African nationals (from Liberia and Zaire-Congo) detained in IDC-Bangkok were interviewed.

11 The study by Davies (1996) on women's life course provides inspiring insights on this research method.

12 Some of these interviewees were suspected of being involved in prostitution, but this aspect was not revealed clearly in the interview sessions.

women and youth find themselves. This helps to place the character of their work in PCS and CSS in context.

The concept of intersectional discrimination was used to discern particular forms of discrimination based on more than one status. Discrimination against a person or group can take place in the form of structural exclusion (outcome of a historical process), or single events in individual lives that can be sequential or compounded (Crenshaw 2000). In all forms it is reinforced by institutional norms and social practices targeted at particular marginalized social groups (Makkonen 2002). Both Crenshaw and Makkonen emphasize the benefits of intersectional discrimination as a promising legal paradigm in addressing problems faced by marginalized social members and groups. This is because the present international human rights framework operates on the basis of ground-specific contexts (gender, race, age) and is equipped only to address each particular form of discrimination separately, not in intersected forms. An explanation of vulnerability derived from intersectional discrimination experienced by migrant women would be beneficial to the search for legal and social remedies.

Following this line of thinking data on discrimination against migrant women in PCS and CSS were organized along a combination of two sub-sets of power relations: 1) the historically formed ethno-racial hierarchy in which a particular marginalized group is placed; 2) the exclusion of PCS and CSS from regulated work categories, buttressed by dominant gender norms. A third dimension is the fact that during migration, the social locations occupied by the migrants are both spatially circumscribed as well as shifting. Thus the position of each migrant is constantly redefined as they shift to a different position within the same occupation, or shift to another occupation, or shift from one country to another. A fourth dimension results from the legal ambiguity regarding PCS and CSS: discriminatory practices against the migrants engaged in such activities frequently occur while female migration for PCS and CSS work has become more institutionalized. Discerning the positions of the migrants and interpreting their agency thus requires moving beyond conventional class or gender analyses.

11.4 The Vulnerability of Women and Youth in the Migration-Trafficking Continuum

11.4.1 The Migration Process: a Series of Decisions

In the Asian context of regional labour migration, trafficking is increasingly featured as part of an overall movement rather than an independent process. Those who have migrated through a combination of official and unofficial channels generally shared this account (Kojima 2007). Our research has revealed nine stages as the major components of the migratory trajectory. Information drawn from interviews and existing studies suggest that these stages are evident in both regular migration and trafficking cases. They are: 1) Pre-migratory (life before migration); 2) Recruitment (periods of decision to migrate and risk assessment); 3) Travel (obtainment of travel documents and the travel process itself); 4) Pre-job placement;[13] 5) Job placement; 6) Post-employment (as result of rescue, arrest, escape, termination or completion of contract); 7) Investigation and action for legal remedies;[14] 8) Returning home, or deportation; 9) Post-migration and reintegration.

---

13 According to our research findings, most in the sex industry experience a pre-job placement period, while domestic workers tend to find work right away. Women are kept for an average of a week before they start work. This period is often used to get women and youth prepared by taking them shopping to purchase necessary clothes and cosmetics and in some cases they even undergo cosmetic surgery and health examinations. Women also learn basic communication skills to entertain clients during this period by engaging a waitress (individual interviews 2003–2004).

14 Women's experience of investigation and action for legal redress is conditional. For instance, there is a tendency for both Thai and foreign women and youth in trafficking/exploitative migration not to seek legal remedies unless they obtain financial and technical support of local rights advocates (Field interviews 2003 & 2009). In the case of Sri Lanka sending legal domestic workers to the Middle East, female migrants are likely to have very limited chances for successful investigation or compensation of their losses once they leave the country of destination (Interview with SLBFE 2004). Overall, the prosecution process is time-consuming and often overlaps with the reintegration/post-migration stage (stage 9).

A comparison of the narratives of women and youth shows a common feature: the migration process is composed of a series of decisions. When they plan to work overseas, all have a dream of successful migration. They also are aware that some price will have to be paid, and each has her own individual tolerance level. Some are prepared to settle at any cost, while others are not.

The threshold of tolerance may be understood as a turning point in the individual's decision to leave or remain in a situation. This level of tolerance may differ at each migratory stage, affecting the way they perceive themselves and the migration experience as a whole. Different forces define the threshold of tolerance. Cultural elements related to family and educational background and social exposure before migration are significant. Material factors, such as the presence or absence of options, certainly also determine each person's standards as to what is morally acceptable.

The migrants undergo critical situations that may challenge their threshold of tolerance during migration processes. These points are identified in three stages: 1) recruitment, 2) job placement I, and 3) job placement II (the work after the initial debt is paid off). Women's and youth's decision to stay or leave in a given situation at each stage is not as straightforward as it appears at first. As women and youth enter the job-placement stage, they are exposed to a number of incidents and moments that cause them to reconsider their involvement in the work. A decision to stay or leave the job is not always one's own choice but is also dependent on circumstances, such as the work arrangement, which can involve the reselling and rotating of workers.

Careful attention to the narratives helps to understand how the particular decision women make at each stage defines their vulnerability that may not always be connected with the use of force (considered a significant component of human trafficking in legal terms). The present forms of trafficking are not necessarily characterized by constant physical and psychological coercion.[15] Such characteristics appear and disappear throughout the different stages of the migration process. Depending on the scope of individual tolerance, women and youth develop different types of coping strategies alongside their own unique understanding of their position and status in the migration process.

11.4.2 Intersectional Discrimination: How Structural and Subjective Variables Operate

The following six case studies[16] bring to the fore the main features of vulnerability in the migration-trafficking continuum. Women and youth's vulnerability may be understood as the intersection of three types of discriminatory practices: 1) flaws in the legal system which (a) exclude PCS and CSS as economic activities from regulatory frameworks and (b) legal distinction between trafficking and smuggling which offers protection to the former and penalizes the latter; 2) ability of broker, trafficker and employer to exploit these flaws with impunity; 3) stigmatization of the migrant's ethnic and work identities which prevents her from gaining access to social support. The case studies show the need to understand the contextual significance of intersectional discrimination and corresponding responses by those affected.

Case 1: Mon, a 16-year-old Lao domestic worker

> When her mother asked whether she was interested in going to Thailand, Mon accepted an offer from a Thai female stranger to work as a maid for the period of one year. Mon took the job in the hope of supporting her mother, who was in great debt. She travelled with five other people from her village by car. Along the way, everyone was dropped off at different employers and Mon happened to witness a broker receiving money from one of the employers. That was when she realized that she had been tricked and would be sold to her employer. For the next four years, Mon worked in three different households and had no wages for the first two and one-half years. The initial promise that she could go home after a year was broken. The work intensity and conditions were extremely tough. She was abused and left pregnant with her employer's baby. Eventually, she was kicked out of her employer's house. Looking back, Mon confessed that she never intended to leave her employers. She explained, "In the first two families, I was told that I was in debt so I had

15 Discussions with rights advocacy groups in the field repeatedly suggested that classic cases characterized by constant physical and psychological coercion and exploitation still exist but cases bordering on exploitative migration have become more visible in recent years (Field interviews 2003 & 2009).

16 Cases presented here are reconstructions of narratives gathered in the field. Names are changed to protect identity of interviewees.

no choice but to stay and pay back the money. When I moved to the third family, I was paid Thai Bht 2,000 (US$ 60) every month. I wanted to save some and take the money back home since I was the only one in the family who had left to work in Thailand." With no place to go, Mon was arrested by the police while she was roaming the streets and jailed for more than a week before being brought to the shelter.

Case 2: Rat, 21-year-old, Tai-Yai hill tribe, China; in Thai sex industry and household

Rat was not keen to join the trip to Thailand when a Tai-Yai man from a different village came to her community and asked whether anyone was interested in working as a domestic worker in the country. Rat was aware of the risks involved in such an offer, since she had heard about the cross-border migration experiences of many people in neighbouring villages. However, she was convinced by the recruiter that it was a well paying job. Her friend also wanted Rat to accompany her daughter who was excited at the prospect of going to Thailand. Rat travelled from her village in China to Bangkok through Mae Sai. During her travel, she met five brokers at different places who guided Rat's group and a dozen other men and women of different nationalities along the way. During her stay at a female broker's place in Mae Sai, Rat witnessed a Thai man paying money to this broker. This Thai man eventually took Rat and her group to Bangkok. In Bangkok, Rat spent the next two weeks learning how to read and write Thai from the Thai man. The man then informed her that she had been sold by the female broker in Mae Sai and she had to work for him in prostitution to clear her debt. Rat worked for the next three months until the police raided the brothel. However, she managed to hide and was not caught by the police. Then Rat was resold by the Thai man to another employer as a maid. The second employer forced Rat to carry out domestic chores in his house, including working at a chicken farm and washing for the women who worked in his brothel. Several months later, another police raid took place and Rat managed to escape to Korat (northeastern town of Nakorn Ratchasima province), this time on her own. She worked for a karaoke shop for one week and was later arrested by the police while shopping at the market. Rat refused to share in our interview how she felt about the job and how her clients treated her. She simply answered, "I did whatever they [clients] asked me to do since I was afraid that they might report it to my employer. I was afraid of the police and could not plan to escape. I did not know the language well and had no place to go". When Rat was interrogated at the IDC, she refused to inform the police that she had been trafficked. As the result, Rat was jailed at the IDC.

Case 3: Yuri, a 17-year-old Thai youth in Japanese sex industry

Yuri[17] was attracted to a waitress job offer in Japan, brought by her aunt. She anticipated seeing the country and earning a good sum of money. Since her aunt had worked as a waitress in Japan as well, Yuri trusted the offer. She also wanted to help her aged father who was in great debt, according to her. Yuri did not suspect that she was being tricked into prostitution until she saw the shop on her first day on the job. Yuri wanted to escape but was afraid she would never be able to return home if she left her *mama-san's*[18] place. She decided to stay and work hard to clear her debt, which amounted to almost five million yen (US $53,000).[19] She roughly calculated her debts and found that she could repay them in two to three months if she worked very hard. To her surprise, however, Yuri soon realized that the debts would never disappear. This is because Yuri was charged for accommodation, food and clothing, which were deducted from her wages. Out of disappointment and frustration, Yuri decided to accept her fate. Yuri explained, "It [the work at the brothel] was better than being sold on the black market[20] where Yakuza (members of Japanese organized crime syndicates) told me that suffering is unimaginable and they would sell me if I don't earn enough". She carefully observed the situation around her and realized that she could make her life easier by working hard to earn *mama-san* and Yakuza's trust and becoming popular among clients. "Obedience was the key", Yuri explained.

---

17 Japanese name given by her mama-san. Name was changed to protect the identity of individual.

18 This word originates in Japanese language. It literally means 'mother', a term specifically used in brothel establishments. Mama-san plays a managerial role in the establishment.

19 Exchange rate as of May 2010.

20 A couple of informants confirmed that exchanges taking place on the black market were known as being associated with the worst forms of prostitution business in Japan.

Soon, Yuri found herself being given some privileges, such as being allowed to go out alone shopping and the ability to reject clients who refused to use a condom. Moreover, the trust she earned from *mama-san* eventually enabled her to escape from the brothel with help from one sympathetic client who arranged her safe return with the Thai Embassy and a local NGO.

Case 4: Sert and Jiw, Lao nationals in Thai households and sex industry

Sert, 19 years old, made friends with Jiw, 16 years old, in a house where they worked as maids. Sert had been recruited by a Thai man who told her the job was to work in a noodle shop in Thailand. Jiw took up her aunt's offer for work in the north, which she thought was in Laos. Neither of them had consulted anyone. Sert said, "I was afraid and knew it was risky but I wanted to give it a try so I did not want to talk to anybody about the job. If I had, they [the family] would have stopped me from going". On weekdays, they helped to prepare food and cleaned dishes in the noodle shop. On weekends, they worked as domestic servants. The employers treated them badly, imposing heavy workloads, paying no wages and they were abused. Two months later, a neighbouring couple with another job offer in the restaurant approached Jiw. "It [the work] sounded like better conditions and good money. But I did not want to be cheated again so I decided to go home and discuss the offer with Sert". Following night, Sert and Jiw decided to sneak out of the house and went to see the couple who took them to the restaurant. For several days, they worked as waitresses. They were then forced to engage in prostitution for more than a year. Jiw recalled, "After three days, they put me to work [in prostitution]. I gave in to protect myself. But I still had some reservations about making money this way". At one time, Sert and Jiw managed to sneak out of the brothel with the help of a client. However, the brothel owner found and brought them back to the brothel soon after. After this incident, the owner and his family regularly imposed severe physical punishment on them in front of the other employees. The brothel owner also ordered all his employees to keep their eyes on Jiw and Sert as they may run away from the shop again. Jiw and Sert decided to join with their Cambodian and Lao colleagues who were planning to run away. One night, after the owner went to sleep, one of them managed to sneak out of the brothel and hopped on a motorcycle and rushed to the nearby police station to report the situation. A brothel raid by the police took place soon after. Jailed for illegal entry, it took several weeks for Jiw and Sert to be transferred to a government shelter.

Case 5: Kamala, a 36-year-old documented Sri Lankan housemaid in Kuwait

After two years in Saudi Arabia, Kamala decided to continue to work as a maid in Kuwait since she was told that salaries were better there. Her first employer was tough and abusive. Kamala decided to run away from the family and went to the Sri Lankan Embassy for help. Kamala stayed at a safe house at the embassy for a couple months. Ashamed to return home empty-handed like many others, Kamala chose to stay and sought relocation to another family through an agent. This was against the rules and regulations set by the government. The second house was worse. She was paid no wages, had to work almost 19 hours a day and slept in the kitchen since she was not given a private room. The verbal and physical abuse by her employer was also severe. Kamala said, "They [employers and their families] treated me badly because I think they were in the relocation business".[21] In desperation, she returned home without completing her two-year contract, hoping for some official compensation. Only upon her return home, Kamala learned that she had to have registered an official complaint when she was sheltered at the embassy to qualify for compensation. As a consequence, Kamala realized that her chances of getting compensation for her loss were nil.

Case 6: Mira, a 24-year-old Uzbek sex worker in Thailand

Mira had migrated to Thailand to work in prostitution. She was a college student in Uzbekistan but could not complete her last six months of study because of the economic crisis in the country. Mira shared, "I knew that I had to work in prostitution before I came to Thailand. But I felt tricked because I had to stand on the street and solicit clients. I was told by the agent that clients would find their way to meet me in the establishment". Because of the great demand in Uzbekistan for overseas migration, Mira complained that the

21 Relocation business is carried out through reselling domestic workers to different families repeatedly while incurred profits are shared by agents and employers (Field interviews 2004).

service charge for job procurement rose too high after 2000. The first time Mira migrated, she had a female agent to whom she owed about US $300. It took her a month to settle the debt. Then she was resold to another place and had to work for another six months. The second time Mira migrated, she had an agent in Uzbekistan and had to pay her US $1,500 for the service.[22] She first entered Bangkok on a legitimate visa[23] and then was resold to a Thai female sponsor in Pataya and worked there for four months. "It [the working conditions in the second period] was tougher than I thought. I was under tighter control than the previous time". With the visa fee and all other expenses, Mira was US $5,000 in debt, which she managed to reduce to $1,000 with the help of her former client from Kuwait. Then she moved back to Bangkok and worked there for another two months until she was arrested by the police and jailed for immigration violations.

These six cases illustrate variations of the context in the migration-trafficking continuum women and youth often experience. They demonstrate how different social traits interact to create a specific predicament that left migrant women or youth vulnerable to exploitation in the hands of their employer, client, family and law enforcement authority. The traits include: gender (female identity); a stigmatized sexual identity; nationality and/or ethnicity; immigration status (undocumented/documented); class (income). These traits interact with additional contextual variables (such as family obligations) and may reinforce the vulnerable positions of migrant women and youth.

A striking common feature is high mobility in job placement. The first reason for this mobility relates to business management. To help with business promotion and prevent workers from establishing regular contact with clients who might help them escape, constant workplace rotation is common in the sex industry (Case 3). Shifting jobs also occurs voluntarily as women and youth aim for better wages and conditions (Case 4). Shifting jobs to the extent of drifting between specific countries is common among Uzbek women engaged in CSS (Case 6). Many women overstay their visa in one country to continue to work off the debt, and move on to other countries to freelance. Some Uzbek women reported that they also drifted between popular destinations in Bahrain, Dubai, Japan, Hong Kong and Malaysia before ending up in Thailand.

The lack of legal recognition of PCS and CSS occupational categories is found to have enhanced the vulnerability of migrant women and youth regardless of their legal status.[24] As demonstrated in Cases 3 and 6, for instance, the government's failure to admit that entertainer visas cater to the supply of foreign labour as 'unskilled' sex workers,[25] condoned severe abuse and exploitation of female migrants in Japan for decades.[26] In response to the stricter immigration control policy, other types of visas for marriage, tourism and study are reportedly being used to enter Japan, Thailand and other popular destinations for migrant labour engaged in CSS.

PCS can be a regulated work category with minimal protection when it comes to labour export schemes. Case 5 show that this protection is mere window dressing. The legal protection for migrant workers in PCS in the destination country is strictly tied to the employer who issues the initial contract

22 Recruiting agencies in Uzbekistan have different services for their clients, ranging from travel, job procurement and even financial assistance. For instance, the air ticket between Thailand and Uzbekistan costs about US$ 500 but often the agency overcharges. It was also reported that as much as US $900 was requested from the agency as commission to facilitate women's entry into prostitution. Lastly, most of those who wish to work in Thailand need some financial service from an agency to start off. Consequently, individual debts range from US $ 500–2,000 (Field interviews 2003).

23 At the time research was conducted, Uzbekistan was covered by visa exemption agreements, allowing Uzbek nationals to apply for a tourist visa on arrival. As of September 2003, a two-week tourist visa for Uzbek nationals cost about US $300. Many Uzbek women used this visa to enter the country to work in prostitution. However, in response to the growing visibility of Uzbek women in prostitution, the Thai government decided to exclude Uzbekistan from visa exemption agreements.

24 For a detailed legal analysis, see Ramirez-Machado (2000) for domestic work and Bindman (1997) for prostitution.

25 Similar misuse of entertainment visas has been reported in South Korea (Yea 2004).

26 In response to increased incidents of sex trafficking involving women from the Philippines, the Government of Japan amended in 2005 the Immigration Control and Refugee Recognition Act No. 16. With the new revision, it is no longer possible for sending countries to certify the quality of entertainer skills. This is to reflect the fact that many women who entered Japan with entertainer certificates issued by the Philippines authority do not have such skills.

and provides legitimacy for permission of official entry. Owing to the ordeals PCS workers have to go through, particularly in the Middle East, Sri Lankan female domestic workers who migrate through authorized channels are shifting employers (Field interviews 2003). When they do so they no longer have the eligibility to claim compensation. This raises questions about the claim that migration for domestic service is considered 'safe' and can be promoted.

In Thailand, by convention, domestic work is considered 'an informal work' routinely performed by female members of the family or women from the lower social strata or ethnic groups (Burmese or Laotian). Work conditions and job expectations are shaped by feudalistic relationships, thus forging a link between submission in domestic work and ethnicity. A study conducted in Hong Kong with domestic workers from Thailand, Indonesia, and Philippines suggests that nationality also defines types of abuse to which one is exposed (AMC 2001).

Paitoonpong, Jailin and Weerawan (2002) show how social norms that locate migrant women in a marginalized position in the society along the lines of prevalent ethno-racial and gender orders reinforces the gendered and racialized maltreatment of migrant women and youth. Treatment of female migrant workers based on their ethnicity rather than skills has become the norm in both sectors of PCS and CSS in other countries in the region. This is particularly evident in working conditions. Yeoh and Huang (1998) and Wong (1996) shows that in Singapore, wages and off-days differ for Filipinas ($300-350/2 days off), Sri Lankans ($180-240/1 day off), and Indonesian ($220-250/ no day off). Filipina maids have the best working conditions due to bilateral agreements.

As illustrated in cases 1, 3 and 6, migrant women and youth make certain decisions hoping to satisfy their moral obligations as daughter and mother, which put them in vulnerable situations at the consequent stage in the migration process. The oppressive nature of family virtue is poignant. In this respect, several empirical studies stressed the vital role played throughout history by daughters as economic actors in Thai households (Phongpaichit 1983; Whittaker 1999). Support for their natal families is a critical virtue for daughters, and obedience to parents is another moral obligation. The narrative of a girl who was sex trafficked to Japan with the consent of her parents confirms this aspect. At the time of the interview, her parents were pressuring the girl to drop criminal charges against a trafficker since they already received and spent the compensation money.

> I feel pity for my parents. They are too poor. I will ask them why they sold me if there is a chance to in the future. But I know they really did not mean to hurt me (Field interview at shelter 2003).

> Whatever happened in the past, it is over. I suffered and did not like what happened to me but I want to move on. Why should I make a problem out of it and feel sorry for nothing. (Field interview with a detainee from Mekong sub-region at IDC 2003).

As with case 2, it is common for women detained at the immigration prison to refuse to report their trafficking experiences to authorities, partly because of the limited trust they have in authorities and the justice system. In addition, they are aware that exposing such experiences in public often results in repressive consequences. There is apparently very limited social space available for women and youth who fail in the post-migration phase. In contrast, financial power imparted by savings brought back from overseas migration offers female migrants a sense of reward visible in the form of appreciation from immediate family or recognition as a popular marriage candidate. Women and youth have further impetus to migration in such communities where migration is established as an acceptable livelihood option.

11.5 Agency and Coping Strategies

As evident in the six cases above, economic incentive combined with strong personal aspirations and in some cases family violence, plays a significant role in women's decision to migrate. A closer look at each case shows that the social location of women and youth in migration for PCS and CSS (which defines the relations of subordination) shifts as they proceed through the migration process. This is because the vulnerability of women and youth changes according to the negotiation skills and social space they acquire or lose along the way. Their level of vulnerability also fluctuates depending on their relationship with employers and colleagues, conditions of employment and forms of resistance.

Resistance documented in this chapter can be either covert or overt. Covert resistance is that done in secret or disguised manner on an individual basis and overt resistance takes the form of visible resistance against the 'rules' or negotiations conducted in the open through the system already in place. Escaping or refusing to satisfy the quota imposed by brothel owners are examples of overt resistance. Women's agency can be understood in terms of the shifting positions of vulnerability among women and youth in the migration process and how a particular coping strategy is formed and influences their self-perception of status in the migratory experience.

Patterns of fluctuation of vulnerability are diverse across the six cases. The social and physical locations and entailed vulnerability of Mira (case 6) fluctuated dramatically as she transferred from the position of debt bondage to freelancer in the sex industry. Yuri's story (case 3) is another case regarding how covert coping strategies can enhance one's welfare and security in a constrained environment. Yuri built her bargaining power within the brothel not only by totally complying with the 'house rules', but also by manipulating them to secure a privileged position in the establishment.

While some women are successful in making the most of what little they are given, others are caught in changes that worsen their position, and their vulnerabilities increase as they move along. Cases 4 and 5 describe how other women and youth react when caught in unfavourable conditions. The narratives of both Jiw and Sert (case 4) and Kamala (case 5) illustrate how a small attempt to improve one's working conditions can lead to a worse nightmare, as they ended up in the wrong people's hands. A documented migrant domestic worker such as Kamala (case 5) can suffer a deterioration of her legal position. Despite her choice of the most open form of resistance of all six types described above, Kamala slowly lost her bargaining power when she decided to stay on and work for the second family, thus breaching regulations. Her situation suggests that her conditional legal status confirms other structural disadvantages, enhancing her vulnerability to discrimination rather than protecting her.

These cases exemplify how external factors in combination with an individual's agency shape the various coping strategies. For instance, complete confinement in a private space leaves maids most vulnerable to abuse and exploitation as demonstrated in case 1; there is limited space for resistance apart from escape. Prostitution, on the other hand, allows some social exchange to take place with clients, colleagues and employers, depending on the working environment. It is therefore possible to resort to a coping strategy that does not challenge the entire authority in the house, but manoeuvres internal rules and relations to improve one's position and well-being.

These narratives suggest the mechanism of tolerance, by which the borderline of what is acceptable, is composed of layers. There is variety within the unacceptable frame by which some issues could be negotiable, depending on the conditions and what the women expect from the migration experience. Threshold of tolerance may also change in the migration process and be drawn in a consultative manner. By shifting the borderline of tolerance, women and youth cope with unexpected situations and attempt to make sense of the gap arising between their expectations and the challenging reality. The way Uzbek sex workers understand debt bondage reaffirms this point; they foresaw that unfavourable conditions would be imposed until they cleared their debt. They recognize such conditions as part of the package that comes with the particular work arrangement (Group discussion and personal interview 2003).

11.6 Shifting Self-Image

The previous section maps out the structural and subjective variables that shape shifting social locations of women and youth in migration processes and defines their vulnerability. How do these variables then shape ideas of selfhood of individuals? Evidently, their self-image is reflected in the choices they make in their migration processes. The narratives that we recorded suggest that their perceptions are not as clear-cut as 'victims' or 'illegal migrants', as some authorities and rights advocates conclude. This is partly because their self-image fluctuates along with shifts in their social locations and entailed vulnerabilities.

In this connection, the majority of those who are in the grey zone may admit that they failed in their dream of successful migration but may not necessarily consider themselves 'victims'. For instance, Nok, a woman in her twenties from Laos, expressed her strong determination to return to Thailand despite her experience of debt bondage in three different occupations. "Now I have learned all the steps [I need to know to go to Thailand]. I can travel without being cheated, if there is a second chance" (Field interview 2003).

On a similar note, another Uzbek migrant sex worker refused to be seen as a victim and dared not seek assistance from the Thai women's group to get compensation for her losses. Rather, she expressed a wish to return home as quickly as possible to make a fresh start. Having worked in Dubai and Pakistan as a sex worker, her life in Thailand was a combination of classic sex trafficking and freelance work.

> It was stupid of me to come to Thailand. I curse myself sometimes that I made a bad decision and am stuck in prison wasting my time. My savings and things I col-

> lected at my apartment are all gone! So next time, you know, I will go back to the Middle East to work, no more Thailand. I think that is what I'll do when I return home (Field interview at IDC 2003).

Additionally, understanding of complexity of the migration experience and self-image is well demonstrated through remarks made by Yuri (Case 3) and Mira (Case 6) who articulated the benefit they gained from sex trafficking experience as follows.

> The experience [that I was being trafficked] really made me an adult, and I got to know the real world.... It was negative and bad. But because I was tricked, I was able to go overseas and saw and have done things in Japan, the kind of experiences that my family could not afford for me to have because they are poor and things that my friends at home would not be exposed to (Field interview with Yuri 2003).

> I like the work because I can get to know new interesting people from all over the world.... But I do not want my family to find out what I was doing for a living in Thailand (Field interview with Mira 2003).

From these voices, we can extrapolate a social function of migration as part of women and youth's resistance to the conventional life course, the oppressive nature of which has begun to be revealed. Undeniably networks of trafficking/smuggling of migrants do facilitate opportunities for some individuals to gain a sense of elevated lifestyle; but such 'advancement' tends to be of limited duration and have particular constraints. Moreover, migration through these channels does not equip women and youth to challenge the extant discriminatory systems to the extent of reconfiguring the material and symbolic conditions in order to enhance respect for their human dignity.

11.7 Conclusion

This chapter discusses the complex and dynamic nature of the material and subjective conditions associated with the migration-trafficking continuum and how intersectional discrimination as an approach can be useful in meeting challenges this continuum has posed to policy. Two main aspects should be noted in this regard. First, patterns of intersection between migration and trafficking, involving women and youth are increasingly becoming visible. Migration for PCS and CSS may well have become an integral part of the general female migration process in Asia for reasons related to changes in regional political economies and changing lifestyles. Second, the vulnerability of women and youth in the migration process is an outcome of intersecting forces, which points to the significance of the 'intersectional vulnerability' created by a combination of structural (law and policy) and subjective (identity) social forces. Coping strategies are embedded in the specific context of 'intersectional vulnerability' in which changing self-image and the threshold of tolerance of the individual play an important role.

An assessment of the nature of individual's participation in migration based on information on the mode of recruitment and job description available at a pre-migration stage may be ineffective particularly when high mobility in job placement is a common feature of migration experience for women in PCS and CSS. In addition, policy solutions that rely on the establishment of migrant labour law that does not necessarily question the associated cultural valuing mechanism, are considered only tentative measures. This is because international migration for PCS and CSS involving women and youth has its foundation on the structure and value that is both gendered and racial. Insights into vulnerability of women and youth suggest that policy strategies should recognize the critical role of associated cultural valuing mechanisms that reinforce the institutional practice of disrespect and demeaning treatment of migrant women in PCS and CSS. Future policy strategies for rights protection of female migrant workers for PCS and CSS could thus benefit from an inclusive approach that embraces more rigorous understanding of the process of marginalization and subordination of women and youth in migration.

12 The EU's Ambiguous Position on Migrant Underage Workers

Roy Huijsmans

12.1 Introduction[1]

Independent child migration for purposes of work has received considerable attention over recent years (Camacho 1999; Iversen 2002; Punch 2002; Whitehead/Hashim/Iversen 2007; Yaqub 2009). This body of literature mainly concentrates on internal and international child migration taking place outside the European context. These studies demonstrate that young people under 18 years of age leave their families and communities for a number of reasons. This frequently encompasses work, and often involves a considerable degree of strategic decision-making on the part of parents, children or both (Camacho 1999; Iversen 2002; Punch 2002; Whitehead/Hashim/Iversen 2007). Some argue, therefore, that these migratory dynamics cannot be reduced to human trafficking despite exploitation and abuse taking place (Bastia 2005; Whitehead/Hashim 2005; Huijsmans 2008). Yet, the policy space to address the phenomenon of minors migrating for work autonomously as anything other than human trafficking has been described as "very narrow" (Whitehead/Hashim 2005: 4). This, despite indications that policies stemming from the human trafficking discourses amount to anything but making migration safer for minors (Busza/Castle/Diarra 2004) and do not discourage migrant minors from involvement in work (Dottridge 2006: 11).

This chapter fills a void in studies on child migration for work by focusing on migration by underage workers between member-states of the European Union (EU), given that the literature on child migration has, thus far, concentrated on the South exclusively. The case of the enlarged EU is of particular interest since under its provisions for free movement of workers[2] minors from an EU member-state are legally entitled to work in fellow EU-member states, and are entitled to legal protection equal to that enjoyed by their peers in the host-country (Stalford 2000a; Ackers/Stalford 2004: 90).

EU provisions on free movement of workers were not drawn up with children's rights in mind (Stalford/Drywood 2009: 149). The presence of such a framework can, nonetheless, be far-reaching in that it can provide the legal basis for safe migration approaches for underage migrant workers. Thereby, the issue of underage migrant workers between EU member-states constitutes a fascinating case to critically engage with the emerging notion of 'safe migration' which has been coined as a response to the 'don't migrate message' propagated by anti-trafficking initiatives (Dottridge 2006).

This chapter addresses legal, conceptual and empirical aspects regarding the issue of migrant minors involved in the world of work in an intra-EU context. The EU provisions for free movement of workers will be presented first, with attention to how they may relate to underage migrant workers. Next, we turn from policies to data in order to explore the empirical state of knowledge on minors' involvement in intra-EU migrant work. The third section reveals the tension between the presence of a legal framework endorsing intra-EU migration for work at a minor age and sparse empirical evidence of the phenomenon on the one

1 Earlier versions of this chapter were presented at a Save the Children Sweden sponsored conference entitled "Focus on Children in Migration - from a European research and methods perspective" (Warsaw, Poland, 2007), at the Annual Conference of the Royal Geographical Society with IBG (London, United Kingdom, 2007), and at a conference entitled "International Migration, Multi-Local Livelihoods, and Human Security", at the Institute of Social Studies (The Hague, The Netherlands, 2007). This chapter has benefited greatly from the many constructive comments received at these occasions. Remaining errors are however the full responsibility of the author.

2 Council of European Communities, 1968: *Regulation (EEC) on Freedom of Movement of Workers with the Community*, 15 October 1968 (No. 1612/68/L257): 0002-0012.

T.-D. Truong and D. Gasper (eds.), *Transnational Migration and Human Security*, Hexagon Series on Human and Environmental Security and Peace 6, DOI 10.1007/978-3-642-12757-1_12, © Springer-Verlag Berlin Heidelberg 2011

hand, and a dominant view condemning this practice on the other. This view then is contrasted with an analysis of EU youth programmes, showing how forms of mobility promoted under these programmes come close to promoting the involvement of minors in the world of work. The penultimate section returns to the notion of safe migration and theoretically explores the question of the desirability and potential for an EU-wide framework to safeguard migrant minors from abuse and exploitation when they are involved in the world of work within the EU. The chapter concludes with a call for further research on the issue of underage migrant workers in the EU and recommends a move away from the prevailing ambiguity.

12.2 EU Provisions on Free Movement of Workers and their Applicability to Underage Migrant Workers

Key to the EU as an economic and strategic project is its principle of free movement of workers. This principle dates back to Article 39 of the founding Treaty of the European Economic Community, the ancestor of the current EU, the Treaty of Rome of 1957. This Treaty remains significant, as visible through the campaign on the 'Year of the Mobile Worker' in 2006. The following excerpt illustrates the main motivation behind the prominence attached to the principle of free movement of workers in the EU. "Free movement is a means of creating a European employment market and of establishing a more flexible and more efficient labour market, to the benefit of workers, employers and Member States" (Commission of the European Communities 2002: 3).

Thus, the principle of free movement of workers is first celebrated as an economic instrument for its labour market adjusting effects. However, the quote also illustrates that the merits attributed to the idea of free movement of workers are not limited to the logic of economics alone (Ackers/Stalford 1999; Stalford 2000a). Couched in liberal terms, the principle is presented as enhancing individual well-being in several respects: " ... mobility of labour within the Community must be one of the means by which the worker is guaranteed the possibility of improving his living and working conditions and promoting his social advancement, while helping to satisfy the requirements of the economies of the Member States."[3]

The EU provisions on the free movement of workers do not impose age restrictions on the definition of worker. Instead, the definition employed is limited to qualifying the term work and the employment relation to which the EU provisions apply. Thus, the term worker is defined as follows. A person "who (i) undertakes genuine and effective work (ii) under the direction of someone else (iii) for which he is paid" (Commission of the European Communities 2002: 6).

For details on the extent to which the EU provisions of free movement of workers may apply to minors, one has to turn to the EU Directive on the Protection of Young People at Work 1994 (henceforth 'The Directive'). This Directive defines "young people at work" as, "any person under 18 years of age having an employment contract or an employment relationship defined by the law in force in a Member State and/or governed by the law in force in a Member State" (EU 1994: Article 2.1).[4] Importantly, this Article further stipulates that Member States "may make legislative or regulatory provisions for this Directive not to apply, within the limits and under the conditions which they set by legislative or regulatory provision, to occasional work or short-term work involving: (a) domestic service in a private household, or (b) work regarded as not being harmful, damaging or dangerous to young people in a family undertaking" (EU 1994: Article 2.2.).

In its detailed description of the terms and conditions under which young people may be employed, the Directive distinguishes between: 1) a young person; 2) a child; 3) an adolescent. A 'young person' is defined as any person under 18 years of age. A 'child' is "a young person less than 15 years of age or who is still subject to compulsory full-time schooling under national law". 'Adolescent' is defined as a "young person of at least 15 years of age but less than 18 years of age who is no longer subject to compulsory full-time schooling under national law" (EU 1994 Article 3). The Directive thus uses the age of 15 years, or the end of compulsory education, as the upper limit for childhood.

Based on the terminology set out above, and which is used in this chapter, the Directive sets out a principal prohibition on the employment of children: "...prohibit their employment and ensure that the minimum working or employment age is not lower

3 Regulation (EEC) on The Council of European Communities: P. 0002-0012. 15 October 1968. See at: <http://ec.europa.eu/social/main.jsp?catId=458&langId=en> (23 April 2010).

4 See at: <http://eur-lex.europa.eu/smartapi/cgi/sga_doc?smartapi!celexplus!prod!DocNumber&lg=en&type_doc=Directive&an_doc=1994&nu_doc=33> (23 April 2010).

than the minimum age at which compulsory schooling as imposed by national law ends or 15 in any event" (EU 1994). Despite this principal prohibition, the Directive provides for a series of exceptions in which children may be employed. For example, Section 3 of Article 5 states that "in the case of children of at least 13 years of age, Member States may authorize, by legislative or regulatory provision, in accordance with conditions which they shall determine, the employment of children for the purposes of performance in cultural, artistic, sports or advertising activities" (EU 1994). In practice, children may thus under specific terms and conditions, be employed from the age of 13 provided that such work may under no circumstance be detrimental to regular school attendance or prevent full benefit of education.

Such exceptions to a general prohibition on the employment of children below 15 years of age are in line with the international regulations advocated by the International Labour Organization and developed in national level legislation. For example, the Dutch child labour regulations (Ministerie van Sociale Zaken en Werkgelegenheid, 2004) set out in much detail the precise terms and conditions under which children from the age of 13 may be employed.

Once young persons have become adolescents, according to the Directive, their employment is no longer subject to principal prohibition. In fact, the Directive is facilitative to the employment of adolescents in the sense that it provides for protection from adversities related to employment and does not aim to keep adolescents off the work floor. Across the EU, children may thus be employed subject to national legislation under certain terms and conditions from the age of 13, an age at which they are also still subject to compulsory education. Adolescents however, may be legitimately out of school and in work or may combine non-compulsory education with employment (Melchiorre 2004).

This regulatory framework of the Directive sets the contours for national child labour legislation in the EU, and thereby also the terms and conditions under which migrant children and adolescents from one EU-member state may be employed in another member-state. Drawing from Article 1.1 of Regulation (EEC) No. 1612/68 (1968) which specifies that when employing workers from other member-states, the receiving state needs to ensure that the terms of employment are "in accordance with the provisions laid down by law, regulation or administrative action governing the employment of nationals of that State" (1968). This means in effect that a Dutch employer, for example, may lawfully employ a Polish or French adolescent or child as long as it is in accordance with Dutch laws and regulations concerning the employment of children and adolescents in the Netherlands.

Furthermore, in the Netherlands young persons, aged 16 and above, from other EU member-states are also entitled to register independently[5] for residency with the *Gemeentelijke Basis Administratie*, something that is required for non-Dutch EU-citizens who reside in the Netherlands for longer that four months within a six month period.[6] Adolescents from other EU member-states who are at least 16 years of age can thus become full-fledged migrant workers in the Netherlands, as they are, under certain conditions, entitled to work and to take up residence in the Netherlands independently.[7]

12.3 Intra-EU Underage Migrant Workers: what do the figures have to say?

The few studies that deal with the issue of underage migrant workers in the EU are limited to young people whose national origins are non-EU (Pang/Ghrib/Ghrib/Pollman/Markova/Vicari/Venicz/Mestre 2002; Terrio 2008). The absence of studies on under age people who are of EU origin and who migrate for work between EU member-states may indicate either the fact that the phenomenon does not exist, or that it has not been addressed. This section explores a range of secondary data to find indications of its existence and shows what mechanisms might have contributed to its invisibility, and thereby, its lack of attention.

A first indication of the likelihood that EU children and adolescents may migrate and be involved in the world of work within the EU is provided by employment participation and school attendance rates. Eurostat data (Education and Culture/Eurydice/Eurostat 2005: 142)[8] on school participation across EU member-states show that school participation rates drop considerably once the minimum age for leaving

5 Without adult authorization.

6 Registration in the *Gemeentelijke Basisadministratie* is generally translated as "registration with Municipality".

7 The age of majority in the Netherlands is 18 years. Only under special circumstances, e.g. young mothers, and upon request of the young person concerned, is majority status granted from age 16.

8 See at: <http://eacea.ec.europa.eu/ressources/eurydice/pdf/052EN/004_codes_052EN.pdf> (23 April 2010).

Table 12.1: EU Enlargements. **Source:** Adapted from Table 1.1 in Kvist 2004, cited in Doyle, Hughes, and Wadensjö (2006: 15), and complemented with data from Europa Nu, n.d.: "Lidstaten Europese Unie"; at: <http://www.europa-nu.nl/9353000/1/j9vvh6nf08temv0/vh72mb14wkwh>.

Year	Acceding Countries	Number of EU Countries Prior to Accession	Acceding Populations	
			Absolute (1,000s)	Relative % of EU Population
1973	Denmark, Ireland and United Kingdom	9	64,227.8	30.8%
1981	Greece	10	9,700.8	3.5%
1986	Portugal and Spain	12	48,498.9	16.7%
1995	Austria, Finland and Sweden	15	29,339.3	8.4%
2004	Cyprus, Czech Republic, Estonia, Hungary, Latvia, Lithuania, Malta, Poland, Slovakia and Slovenia	25	74,100.0	19.5%
2007	Bulgaria and Romania	27	29,689.0	6.1%
Official Candidates:		Croatia, Republic of Macedonia, Turkey		
Potential Candidates:		Albania, Bosnia and Herzegovina, Montenegro, and Serbia		

school is reached, which is 15 years in most EU member-states. It is thus a plausible conclusion that from the age of 15, a significant proportion of EU adolescents are likely to be looking for gainful employment. Surveys on work activities of children and adolescents who attend school in EU member-states show further that being in full-time education by no means prevents children and adolescents from active participation in the labour market (Dorman 2001). In fact, regular surveys of the Dutch secondary school population consistently show that the majority of Dutch school-going adolescents work in addition to full-time school attendance (de Zwart/Warnaar 1995; van de Berg/Boer 2000; NIBUD 2005). These national level data sources indicate that work during childhood and adolescence is widely prevalent in EU member-states, yet, these data sources are silent on the question of underage migrant workers.

A qualitative research with young people in rural communities on both sides of the pre-2004 EU border shows, however, that the young participants encountered, amongst other things, the problem of "no work for young people" in proximity of their border communities (Hipfl/Bister/Strohmaier 2003: 846). This suggests that working elsewhere, within or beyond national borders, may for young people in certain parts of the EU be a realistic response to limited work opportunities in their own localities. It is however impossible to estimate the extent to which such observed realities translate into migrant underage workers because EU statistics on foreign workers are generally collected in an age-aggregated format (FRA 2009: 15).

Data on intra-EU migration flows following the 2004 EU round of enlargement, which are perhaps the best-documented intra-EU migration flows, are slightly more insightful on the issue of underage migrant workers. As Table 12.1 illustrates, in 2004 ten new countries joined the EU, raising the number of EU member-states from 15 to 25 countries, which increased the total EU population by approximately 20 per cent.

The right of free movement of workers was only extended with immediate and unrestricted effect to two (Malta and Cyprus) out of the ten acceding countries following the 2004 round of EU-enlargement. With regard to the remaining eight acceding countries (A-8 countries), the 15 established EU member-states were entitled to restrict access to their labour market for a maximum period of seven years. This policy is called the 2-3-2 scheme and stems from fear that immediate and unrestricted implementation of the free movement of workers provision would, in the case of the A-8 countries, lead to an inflow of cheap labour with detrimental effects for national workers and to 'welfare tourism' (Currie 2006; Doyle/Hughes/Wadensjö 2006).

Only Sweden refrained from entering the 2-3-2 scheme and fully opened its labour market and associated social policies without any restrictions or limitations for workers from the A-8 countries immediately after the 2004 round of enlargement. Ireland and the UK also opened their labour market for workers from A-8 countries, yet with restricted access to associated social benefits (Currie 2006). The remaining 12 established EU member-states all entered the 2-3-2 scheme and put transitional measures in place that seem more drastic, ranging from granting no access at all to their domestic labour market for citizens from A-8 countries to various forms of strictly regulated access.

Out of the three established EU member-states that opened their labour markets to the greatest extent following the 2004 enlargement, two (Sweden and Ireland) present figures on migrant workers from A-8 countries only in an age-aggregated format. Furthermore, in Sweden, effective 30 April 2006, registration was no longer required in cases of migrant workers from A-8 countries who stay for a period of less than three months. Swedish migration statistics thus do not capture temporary and seasonal work by migrants from A-8 countries. Long school holidays, combined with a demand for seasonal labour in several sectors of the economy (e.g. agriculture, tourism, service sector), provide opportunities for employment for many national children and adolescents from EU member-states. Short term and seasonal employment is likely to be similarly important when it comes to migrant children and adolescents; yet, in the case of Sweden and Ireland, aggregate data prevent further exploration (Doyle/Hughes/Wadensjö 2006).

The UK case offers greater scope for analysis than the Swedish and Irish data sources. The UK Home Office has made its data on migrant workers from A-8 countries, based on the Worker Registration Scheme, publicly available and presents the data disaggregated by age-cohorts. Data covering the period May 2004 to March 2006 show that the bulk of migrant workers are young people aged 18–24 (43 per cent), and a small proportion, less than 0.5 per cent are younger than 18 years of age. This means that out of 374,555 registered migrant workers from A-8 countries working in the United Kingdom, less than 1,872 were younger than 18 years. Moreover, the report argues that among young migrant workers there is considerable seasonal variation, with significantly more young migrant workers from A-8 countries registered during the summer months June, July and August (UK Home Office 2006: 10).

A final source that sheds some light on the involvement of children and adolescents who migrate for work within the EU is the data obtained from the Dutch Tax and Customs Administration presented in Table 12.2. It shows the incidence of young persons aged 13–17 with non-Dutch, European nationality employed in tax-paying jobs in the Netherlands.[9] Employment was predominantly of a temporary nature with the exception of some adolescent migrant workers employed for the entire year.

Table 12.2 shows that almost one-half of the non-Dutch young persons working in the Netherlands originate from the two neighbouring countries, Belgium and Germany. In addition, an upward trend in total numbers developed over the four years covered particularly from 2002 to 2004. The data furthermore indicate a marginal gender disparity with slightly more boys and young men employed than girls and young women. In terms of age variation, the dataset includes nine (1 per cent of total) 13-year-olds, five per cent (43) are aged 14 years, 14 per cent (111) aged 15, and the bulk (31 per cent or 254 and 49 per cent or 403) for those aged 16 and 17-years-old respectively. The various second-hand data analysed above are valuable insofar that they confirm that children and adolescents from other EU member-states are employed in the Netherlands and other EU member-states. However, the limitations of the data are considerable. First, the numbers of young persons from one EU member-state working in tax-paying jobs in another, or having complied with registration requirements, are in all likelihood only a partial reflection of the actual magnitude and distribution of the phenomenon (see Currie 2006). Second, neither the UK nor the Dutch data indicate whether these young persons reside in the Netherlands, or the UK, with or without parents or adult relatives. Thus, it cannot be determined whether we look at independent migrant workers of minor age, or at young people who have migrated with their families and stay with them or are accompanied by other adults. Finally, one can only guess about what each single number represents; the actual experiences and stories behind them are not revealed. Nevertheless, this latter aspect is crucial in order to gain a more informed opinion about this little known but highly delicate social reality.

12.4 EU's Position on Migrant Minors Involved in Work: Condemned, but Promoted in Disguise

Despite a legal framework that endorses the employment of children and adolescents from one EU member-state in another and some sparse evidence of its

9 Children with a double nationality, of which one is Dutch, are excluded from the sample. Furthermore, no additional information is available about the legal status of employment of child-aged migrant workers from non-EU countries or from the 2004 and 2007 accession-states included in Table 12.2.

Table 12.2: Employment of Non-Dutch Children and Adolescents with European Nationality in the Netherlands, 2002-05 (n=820). **Source:** Dutch Tax and Customs Administration. **Comment:** Sending countries whose total contribution of young persons involved in migrant work in the Netherlands exceeds five per cent are highlighted.

Nationality	2002	2003	2004	2005	Total	per cent
Austrian	1	3	4	4	12	1.5%
Belgium	**25**	**42**	**36**	**41**	**144**	**17.6%**
Bosnië-Herzegovina	3	5	2	3	13	1.6%
British	**23**	**17**	**19**	**18**	**77**	**9.4%**
Bulgarian		2	5	5	12	1.5%
Croatian		1	1		2	0.2%
Danish	2	2	6	3	13	1.6%
Estonian				3	3	0.4%
Finnish	2			1	3	0.4%
French	8	11	11	7	37	4.5%
German	**43**	**43**	**47**	**43**	**176**	**21.5%**
Greek	**8**	**16**	**20**	**17**	**61**	**7.4%**
Hungarian			1	3	4	0.5%
Irish	2	1			3	0.4%
Icelandic		1	2	2	5	0.6%
Italian	3	1	4	10	18	2.2%
Latvian			2	1	3	0.4%
Lithuanian			3	1	4	0.5%
Norwegian		1	1	2	4	0.5%
Polish	**6**	**10**	**19**	**25**	**60**	**7.3%**
Portuguese	**15**	**16**	**16**	**20**	**67**	**8.2%**
Romanian	3	3	5	3	14	1.7%
Russian	1	3	11	14	29	3.5%
Slovenian			3		3	0.4%
Slovakian			1	1	2	0.2%
Spanish	7	8	5	5	25	3.0%
Swedish	1	1	2	2	6	0.7%
Swiss	1	1		1	3	0.4%
Yugoslavian	5	2	5	5	17	2.1%
Total	**159**	**190**	**231**	**240**	**820**	**100%**

empirical existence, this co-exists with a dominant view that condemns the involvement of migrant minors in work. The Dutch argument for enacting age-based criteria for issuing work permits to A-8 workers after the 2004 EU round of enlargement illustrates this well. "...it is not desirable that young people under the age of 18 leave their home country for the Netherlands with the main purpose of obtaining paid employment".[10] A similar view emerges from Dottridge's analysis of anti-trafficking initiatives in countries neighbouring the EU: "Some organizations that target young women have progressed from the 'don't migrate' message to offering information about how to check whether job offers abroad are safe and how to migrate abroad without being trafficked. Relatively few of these initiatives have been aimed at adolescents under the age of 18, apart from general advice to graduating students [on] how to look for and apply for jobs" (Dottridge 2006: 11).

These examples serve to illustrate that discussions on migrant minors involved in work fall far below the level of maturity that has now become the norm in debates on child labour. In child labour studies working children are now increasingly seen as "capable *as well as* vulnerable" [emphasis in original] (Ennew/Myers/Plateau (2005: 52), and work during childhood and adolescence is regarded as potentially "fulfilling and developmental *as well as* harmful and exploitative" [emphasis in original] (Ennew/Myers/Plateau 2005: 52). In various studies on work by children and adolescents in EU member-states this nuanced position is empirically demonstrated (Van Beckhoven 1991; Morrow 1994; Frederiksen 1999; Leonard 2002; Hungerland/Liebel/Liesecke 2007). Moreover, this theoretical position has contributed to a gradual shift in focus of child labour policies. It is thus increasingly recognised that the problem of child labour is not the involvement of children and adolescents in work, but the harm this work may inflict on them (White 2005: 332). Hence, it is argued that harmful or exploitative working conditions ought to be the focus of intervention, rather than efforts to ban all sorts of work before a certain age (Bourdillon/White/Myers 2009). The debate on underage migrants involved in the world of work is not so nuanced, as involvement in any sort of migrant work is generally seen as undesirable in case of minors.

Ironically, the EU constitutes a rare case in which the legal framework reflects greater sensitivity to varied realities, than the all-or-nothing constructs in which issues and positions are pre-fixed. Underlying

10 "Brief SZW inzake Wet arbeid vreemdelingen" (Letter from Social Affairs and Employment regarding Law on Employment of Foreigners) in: *The Netherlands* (27 022, Nr 14), 31 August 2000. Translation by author.

the discursive representation is a dichotomous conceptualization of adulthood and childhood, which hinges on the age of 18 years, the point at which young people cease to be children according to the 1989 *United Nations Convention on the Right of the Child* (UN-CRC).[11] Based on this dichotomy, certain forms of migration involving minors appear benign, as they are generally associated with dominant ideas of what constitutes a proper childhood. This includes migration for purposes of learning or family formation and reunification (Stalford 2000a, 2000b; King 2002; Welbourne 2002; King/Ruiz-Gelices 2003; Baláž/Williams 2004; Bhabha 2006: 1530). Excluded is migration for purposes of work, because work is generally associated with adulthood. In addition, separation from parents is regarded as potentially traumatic for children. Importantly however, an adult-child dichotomy set in the inflexible format of chronological age fails to acknowledge important differences in this regard between, for example, six-year-olds and 16-year-olds.

EU programmes concerning young persons and migration sidestep this adult-child dichotomy by employing the terms *youth* and *mobility*. It is worth noting however, that the EU definition of youth includes all young persons whom the Directive defines as 'adolescents', as well as a proportion of those whom the Directive defines as 'children'. According to the new EU 'Youth in Action Programme' (2007-2013), youth includes young people aged 13–30 years, a departure from the 15–25 age group, which the original EU White Paper on youth defined as youth (EU 2001).

Constructed in terms of youth and mobility, EU policy papers leave no room for doubt about the importance it attaches to exposing its young population to intra-EU cross-border experiences: "...mobility must become an integral part of learning *from a very early age*. Programmes must therefore be accessible to all young people regardless of their socio-economic or geographical origin" (italics added by author, EU 2001: 55). The EU's current stock of youth is its future stock of flexible and mobile EU workers. Moreover, early involvement in intra-EU mobility will, it is assumed, stimulate the formation of a European identity and European consciousness (King/Ruiz-Gelices 2003: 233–234). Hence, stimulating intra-EU mobility at an early age is vital for realizing the economic and strategic objectives underlying the EU as a project.

Programmes designed to facilitate mobility of EU youth include studying abroad, traineeships, working abroad (seasonal work during holidays as well as longer term), au pair arrangements, volunteering and exchanges.[12] In cases of 'working abroad', it is clear that the mobility experience involves working in another EU member-state. However, in other forms of youth mobility this is less obvious. Here, work or elements of work are disguised. For example, au pair arrangements are presented in terms of 'learning' and 'helping' (see for example the definition employed in: Government of the United Kingdom 2007)[13], yet, in practice the ways in which au pair arrangements may differ from work performed by a live-in migrant care worker or child-minder is frequently unclear. Furthermore, while 'volunteering', 'traineeships' and 'exchanges' connote ideas of learning, which is compatible with the idea of a proper childhood, these practices also contain work-like elements.

A further case in point is studying in another EU member-state. Although studying is a type of work generally regarded as the ideal type of occupation during childhood and youth, it is argued above that full time schooling is often combined with involvement in paid employment. This appears little different when it comes to studying abroad. Migrant students frequently combine their studies with part-time work as Table 12.3 illustrates (see also King 2002: 99). The data presented in Table 12.3 are collected through an anonymous online poll (n=24,114) on the European Youth Portal website (European Union), which unfortunately does not allow for any form of disaggregation. Table 12.3 underscores the prevalence of involvement in the world of work amongst young EU citizens in EU member-states of which they are not nationals. It shows that more than half of all respondents worked abroad in some way or another.

Pointing out that EU youth mobility programmes border on migrant work, contain elements of work, or allow for involvement in migrant work, is not to discredit these forms of mobility. Rather, it serves to bridge an artificial gap, which analytically sets EU youth mobility programmes apart from EU migrant minors involved in non-institutionalized forms of work.[14] Making this analytical connection between

11 In some specific articles, the UN-CRC employs an age-based disaggregation, without however connecting this to different terms as with the Directive.

12 It is important to note that each specific form of mobility offered by EU programmes comes with its own eligibility criteria, including age.

13 Government of the United Kingdom, 2007: *The Accession (Immigration and Worker Authorisation) Regulation 2006* (London: Statutory Instrument 2006 No. 3317).

Table 12.3: EU Youth Poll: Have you ever Worked Abroad? **Source:** Adapted from European Youth Portal website; at: <http://europa.eu/youth/index.cfm?l_id=en>.

As an intern / stagier	6.7%
As an au pair	5.3%
While studying abroad	17.2%
During holidays	6.5%
Employed full time	21.8%
Employed part time	2.5%
Never	40.0%

these seemingly different forms of mobility and migration foregrounds the important question of why certain forms of underage mobility and migration are presented as benign and others condemned without any apparent need for testing these assumptions empirically. Overcoming this artificial distinction is particularly important for arriving at an informed position on underage migrants involved in forms of work that are not so easily classified as good or bad. This includes work experiences of migrant minors that do not resonate the human trafficking narratives, but are also not part of EU youth mobility programmes.

12.5 Desirability and Potential of a Legal Framework Endorsing Underage Migrants' Work

Since EU youth mobility programmes already offer scope for migrants at minor age to be involved in the world of work within the EU, albeit in disguised terms, it may be argued that there is no need for an additional wide-ranging framework endorsing non-institutional avenues through which migrant minors may become involved in the world of work. In fact, it may be argued that EU youth mobility programmes (due to their institutional nature) offer far more scope for protection from potential abuse and exploitation for under age migrants involved in different forms of migration for work within the EU, than the unregulated alternatives provided by EU provisions under the principle of free movement of workers. On these grounds a claim could be made that a safe migration approach would constitute promoting EU youth mobility programmes and discouraging, possibly facilitated by prohibiting, employment of underage migrant workers through non-institutionalized channels within the EU.

At this point, studies on intra-EU student mobility are insightful. Intra-EU student mobility is a particularly heavily promoted form of EU youth mobility, which can be traced back to the late 1980's with ambitious, yet unrealized, goals of one in ten EU students studying at a university in an EU member-state of which she/he is not a national (King 2002: 99; King/Ruiz-Gelices 2003: 232–233). King and Ruiz-Gelices (2003: 231–232, 236) observe that students whose parents perform manual work and whose parents do not have an international profile are under-represented in intra-EU student mobility. This illustrates that involvement of EU students in study abroad programmes is characterized by an elitist tendency, despite significant effort on the part of the EU to promote this form of mobility amongst all EU students in an undifferentiated manner.

Research would have to demonstrate whether other components of EU youth mobility programmes, particularly those involving the youngest within the category 'youth', fare any better in this respect. However, if King and Ruiz-Gelices' work (2003) is taken as indicative of participation patterns in EU youth mobility programmes other than study, it follows that these programmes may offer scope for protection for some minors involved in certain forms of intra-EU migration, yet, this is a highly select few. In other words, as an avenue for safe migration, EU youth mobility programmes seem limited and selective in scope and therefore, in terms of potential coverage, by no means supplant the regulations stemming from EU provisions on free movement of workers, which under certain terms and conditions apply to all migrant minors from EU member-states.

The question remains whether it is desirable to sanction minors' involvement in non-institutionalized forms of work as migrants. It may be argued that sanctioning non-institutional forms of work contributes to bringing migrant minors into situations with an inherent risk of exploitation and abuse. The argument that there is an inherent risk of harm to underage migrant workers is based on the claim that these workers lack protection from their parents or adult caregivers while working in an unfamiliar context. Familiarity with the social context in which work is situ-

14 Note that there is no legal gap here. The new definition of youth corresponds at its lower limit (13 years) with the absolute minimum age set out in The Directive at which children may under specific circumstances start doing some light work.

ated and residing with parents or adult caregivers undoubtedly safeguards most young workers from exploitation and abuse better than any legal framework could achieve. Moreover, classical development psychology depicting adolescence as a time of storm and stress would add that it is particularly during this time that young people need the proximity of their parents and local community to mitigate risk-taking behaviour associated with adolescence.

Could a theoretical case be made to distinguish legally between children and adolescents working within national borders and children and adolescents working beyond these borders, and on this basis, pursue an argument in favour of outlawing employment of underage migrants based on their own best interests?[15] After all, the legal framework that endorses intra-EU underage migrant workers follows from the Directive on the Protection of Young People at Work, which is primarily designed to guide national child labour legislation in EU member-states, thus concerning member-states' children and adolescents and not migrant children and adolescents.

Given the limitations of available data on underage migrant workers within the EU, it is not possible to address this question empirically. What remains is therefore a theoretical exploration. Without denying the protective qualities that accompany residing with parents or adult caregivers in most cases and with work situated in a wider social context familiar to the young worker, it does not necessarily follow that in cases where minors work abroad they stay isolated from networks and contexts with such protective qualities, and are therefore by default, victims of exploitation and abuse as the human trafficking discourse suggests. Qualitative and quantitative research on independent child migration in a series of developing countries shows that even if children migrate without their parents or adult caregivers their migrations are usually facilitated by networks of kin, peers or other relations (Iversen 2002; Whitehead/Hashim/Iversen 2007). These networks often, but not necessarily, provide some level of protection, and ease young migrants' integration in the social context at migration destination (e.g. finding a job). Moreover, these studies have shown that underage migrants are active agents in migration processes and do make strategic, yet often constrained, decisions that frequently amount to minimizing risks.

The reference above, to Stanley Hall's development psychology, which depicts adolescence as a period of storm and stress (Arnett 2006), questions the amount of faith one should have in the agency of adolescents. To be precise, this line of thought would not deny that underage migrants exercise agency; yet, it would not attribute the same qualities to this as to adults' agency. In fact, it suggests that adolescents' agency amounts to anything but risk-minimizing behaviour. Based on this view adolescents need the corrective proximity of, ideally, committed parents to mitigate their inclination towards risk-taking behaviour. This constitutes an argument against legislation that endorses adolescent involvement in non-institutionalized work through migration within the EU, based on their best interests.

While compelling, and in line with widespread contemporary discourses about adolescence, this line of thought finds little support in contemporary work on adolescents' risk-taking behaviour:

> ...[t]he best demographic, crime, and health statistics show that adolescents do not take excessive risks compared to adults, adolescent risks are associated much more significantly with conditions of poverty and corresponding adult behaviors than with uniquely adolescent factors, and middle-aged adults exposed to the same high poverty levels as American youth display similar or higher levels of crime, violent death, firearms mortality, traffic fatalities, and other behaviours conventionally associated with adolescents (Males 2009: 3).

In sum, an observable elitist bias in participation in EU youth mobility programmes suggests, that as a potential avenue for safe migration, such institutionalized migrations and mobilities are limited and selective in scope, and therefore not comparable with the potentially wide-reaching framework the EU provisions of free movement of workers present. Furthermore, the idea that harm is inherent to underage migrant work and that the only safe form of work at minor age is *non-migrant* work, which would imply outlawing and discouraging migrant underage work, is found unsubstantiated. This can be justified neither

15 Note here also the contradiction between the Universal Declaration of Human Rights and the UN-CRC. States Parties to the UN-CRC committed to protecting any child working on their soil from, amongst other things, 'economic exploitation' and 'hazardous work', since Article 2 of the UNCRC stipulates that States Parties shall respect and ensure the rights set forth in the UN-CRC to each child within their jurisdiction (1989: Art 2), including migrant minors. However, this awkwardly co-exists with a legal reality in which there is no such thing as a right to migrate. To be precise, the Universal Declaration of Human Rights states in Article 13 that "everyone has the right to leave any country, including his own, and to return to his country" (1948). Importantly, it does not include a right to enter a country other than one's own.

based on theories of 'the adolescent brain', nor on the claim that underage migrants work in social settings in which they lack protective potential of social networks. It remains unclear whether evidence from developing countries will hold for the context of the EU. However, at a theoretical level this section suggests that the EU provisions of free movement of workers provide - by endorsing the right of migrants at minor age to work and making it subject to national level labour law - a framework with the potential of making involvement of migrants at minor age in the world of work safer, by targeting exploitation and abuse and not the phenomenon itself.

12.6 Conclusion

This chapter explained how the EU provisions on free movement of workers relate to children and adolescents. It has shown that underage EU nationals may under specific conditions be lawfully employed in other EU member-states and, when doing so, fall under the protection of the labour laws of their host countries. A review of available data on the involvement of underage migrants in the world of work inside the EU yielded evidence that this is not only a theoretical possibility, but also an empirical reality. The EU-wide legal framework, which endorses migrant minors' involvement in work within its territory, co-exists with a general view that condemns this very practice. The exception is constituted by a series of EU programmes which, using the terms 'youth' and 'mobility', present to EU minors the opportunity to participate in institutionalized forms of mobility that border on work, contain elements of work, or that are often combined with involvement in the world of work as migrants.

Available data on participation in EU youth mobility programmes suggest an elitist tendency. Hence, the idea of "shrinking of a borderless Europe" (King 2002: 101), which these programmes convey, is a reality for only a select few. Furthermore, although EU provisions on free movement of workers are not born out of any children's rights concerns, this framework nonetheless presents a legislative framework that applies to a much wider range of migrant minors involved in a much greater variety of work in the EU than the institutionalized EU youth mobility programmes. The potential this framework offers to a children's rights approach to safe migration is supported by a theoretical argument, which claims that statements suggesting that abuse and exploitation are inherent to involvement of underage migrants in the world of work are unsubstantiated, whether they are based on theories of the adolescent brain, or assumed characteristics of work among underage migrants. Outlawing the practice, to the extent that this would be effective at all, and thereby distinguishing between involvement of underage migrants in the world of work within and between EU member-states, seems to have little to offer if the objective is to avoid harm.

Since the EU is a constantly enlarging entity (see Table 12.1) with an increasingly uneven socio-economic landscape, a wide-reaching framework seems appropriate and timely, and a solid basis on which to found the emerging notion of safe migration. However, it must be stressed that it cannot be assumed that the legal provisions stemming from the EU provisions on free movement of workers alone affect the lived experience of migrant minors involved in the intra-EU world of work in any meaningful way. This remains subject to empirical investigation. Yet, research on minors involved in forms of intra-EU migration for work has focused predominantly on worst-case scenarios (human trafficking research), and institutionalized forms of migration (EU youth mobility programmes). The impact that the EU provisions of free movement of workers has, or may have, on making migration safer is likely to be greatest in the grey area constituting forms of migration for work involving minors, which lie somewhere between those scenarios depicted by the human trafficking narratives and EU youth mobility programmes. We know least about these sorts of activities, both qualitatively and quantitatively. Furthermore, whatever protective potential may lie in this legal framework remains largely dormant until EU children and adolescents are sufficiently aware of it. This of course is a policy question that first requires that the EU itself, and its member-states, take a less ambiguous position on minors' migration within the EU for work. Again, this particularly concerns the forms of migration for work which cannot be easily classified as good or bad.

13 Learning How to Work the Grey Zone: Issues of Legality and Illegality among Indian Students in Australia

Michiel Baas

13.1 Introduction

Australia is currently one of the biggest players in the world offering/selling education on a commercial basis. The export education industry is allegedly Australia's third largest service export industry with an annual turnover close to 7.5 billion Australian dollars.[1] At the end of 2006, there were nearly 350,000 international students enrolled across all educational sectors in Australia.[2] For the past few years the two largest groups of students come from India and China. The majority of Indian students are observed to enrol in full-fee paying courses that either lead to diplomas in particular trades, or masters in particular fields (Birrell 2005; Baas 2006: 7). In total, Indian students spent 585 million Australian dollars on education in Australia in 2005. While studying there, they also spent money on housing, food, clothes and other necessities, making their total contribution to the economy a lot larger. As a result, international students have become crucial sources of income on which not only education providers have come to rely on quite heavily, but also on which quite a number of jobs depend now. Some even go so far as to value the export education industry currently at 15 billion Australian dollars.[3]

Statistical research by Birrell (2005) and anthropological fieldwork conducted by Baas (2005–6) (see Baas 2006, 2007, 2010) show that the propensity for Indian students applying for an Australian Permanent Residency (PR) after graduation is very high; nearly three quarters are expected to do so. In order to be eligible for a PR, a student needs to score 120 points on a points test.[4] Getting these 120 points is a fairly straightforward and easy process as long as one meets the criteria. Generally, this works as follows: a student under 30 years of age receives 30 points for age. Another 20 points can come by successfully passing the International English Language Testing System (IELTS) test at level six. Most Indian students meet both requirements easily. Once they complete their two years of full-time education in Australia, they can collect another five points. The real problem comes with the particular skills category. The skilled migration programme is divided into three different categories, worth 40, 50 and 60 points, respectively. Professions such as IT and engineering were included under the 60 points category at the time of this research (2005–6). A profession such as accounting, however, received an additional 15 points, making a total of 75, because it appears on the Migration Occupation in Demand List (MODL).

In 2009 it was estimated that the population of Indian students was about 100,000. Indian students have clearly become very visible, especially in Melbourne and Sydney. Media attention to their presence has increased considerably in recent years, focussing on the following themes: 1) Indian students' experiences with racist attacks; 2) the often abysmal housing/living/working situation they must cope with; 3)

1 See at: <http://www.aph.gov.au/senate/committee/eet_ctte/international_students/report/c01.htm> (23 April 2010).

2 There are five categories in the Australian education system: higher education, vocational education, school education, ELICOS, and other courses including enabling, foundation and non-award. See at: <http://aei.dest.gov.au/AEI/MIP/Statistics/StudentEnrolmentAndVisaStatistics/Recent_TableE_pdf.pdf> (30 September 2009).

3 See at: <http://www.theaustralian.com.au/news/education-debacle-to-cost-us-badly/story-e6frg6n0-1225755726871> (13 September 2009).

4 Please note that immigration systems/laws change frequently and this article deals with the situation of 2005–6. Although Australian immigration laws change almost on a half-yearly basis, current rules and requirements are comparable and have generated similar issues. It must be noted though that with each change it has become harder for students to obtain a permanent residency after graduation.

T.-D. Truong and D. Gasper (eds.), *Transnational Migration and Human Security*, Hexagon Series on Human and Environmental Security and Peace 6, DOI 10.1007/978-3-642-12757-1_13, © Springer-Verlag Berlin Heidelberg 2011

the appalling quality of education they receive at the low-fee colleges where many of them are enrolled; 4) the entanglement of education and migration at such colleges (sometimes referred to as 'PR factories'); 5) the implications this has for Australia's self-image as a safe, welcoming and non-racist country; and finally 6) the damage the attacks and subsequent media coverage has done (and is doing) to the image of the Australian education industry as one of the largest income earners in trade in services (Baas 2009, 2010).

This chapter situates Indian students in contemporary immigration policy in Australia and analyses the emerging mutually dependent relations between educational institutions, international students and access to permanent residency. A perspective on international studentship as a new form of migration is provided, which questions the key assumptions behind migration theory and offers a number of tools for analysis. By revealing aspects of the life and work situations of Indian nationals in their dual position of student and migrant, the chapter analyses how the thin line separating education and immigration, legality and illegality, affects the way they cope and are represented in media. This will be contrasted with how institutions involved in the business of education and/or migration accommodate this separation, pointing to the formation of a grey zone where 'normalcy' is defended when it comes to activities that could also be understood as quasi-legal, semi-legal and illegal. The everyday life problems faced by students reflect a broader process of institutional changes in which education providers and immigration agents fulfil certain needs of the local/central government(s) - such as jobs for the labour department, skilled migrants for the migration department, and income from full fee paying international students for the education department. The ability of the Australian education industry's institutions to test the flexibility of, and thus bend, the rules in an attempt to regulate international education as well as migration may partly explain its success. The chapter concludes with a proposal to give international studentship a more prominent place in the study of transnational migration, in light of the rise of the knowledge economy, higher education as trade in services and the battle for talents in the global economy.

13.2 Understanding International Studentship as a New Form of Migration

Using international studentship as a route for migration is not new. In the 1960's, this phenomenon was referred to as the 'problem of non-return' resulting in what became commonly known as a 'brain drain'- an unplanned outcome of the process of acquiring an education abroad. What is new about the current situation of Indian students is that, from the start, they plan to acquire an Australian Permanent Residency (PR) after graduation. Many Indian students come to Australia with the idea of migration; some even made an informed decision to enrol in a course that is of no real interest to them, solely to get a PR. The question is why do young, middle class Indians want to leave their country?

'Why migrate' is a central question in migration studies. To date answers are mainly derived from a neo-classical 'push-pull' model. Although most migration scholars will agree that the model assumes too much functionality and rationality in migrants' decisions, it is nevertheless still a popular way of understanding migration; the popularity of the terms 'economic' and 'political' migrants certainly testifies to this. A push-pull model typically underscores that there might be reasons behind the economic and political realms for migrating. More importantly, the model creates the idea of permanency or the belief that people leave home to stay somewhere else rather than returning. Sceptics have remarked that issues related to 'return' are often a 'recurring' feature in migration studies (Bolognani 2007; Walton-Roberts 2004). Nonetheless, conventional approaches to migration revolve around the concept of permanency elsewhere, thus the need for integration or assimilation remains essential, though this can be framed as being problematic for some groups.

Brettell and Hollifield (2000: 15) argue that, within anthropology, one of the dominant paradigms in migration theory is the assimilation model which forged the idea that once migrants crossed a border they would stay in the new place, purportedly to improve the material aspects of their lives.[5] Stephen Castles, for instance, argues that the most obvious cause for migration is wage level disparity, employment opportunities and differences in "social well-being"

5 Annelies Zoomers (2006) refers to it as the Harris-Todaro model.

(2000: 272). Yet, he also acknowledges that causes of migration are more complex. Arango (2000: 285) turns away from the neo-classical model which he summarized as follows: "Migration is [seen as] the result of individual decisions made by rational actors who seek to improve their well-being by moving to places where the reward of their labour will be higher than the one they get at home..." He discerned two main reasons for challenging the neo-classical model: the inability to answer the question of why so few people migrate and the failure to explain differential migration - why some countries experience much higher rates of out-migration than others (Arango 2000: 286).

Appadurai opened a new avenue of analysis with the observation that more people than ever before are able to imagine that they or their children will live and work in places other than where they were born (Appadurai 1996: 6). He later also noted, "[m]ore persons in more parts of the world consider a wider set of possible lives than they ever did" (Appadurai 1996: 53). This remark clearly directs our attention towards the idea that more and more people are able to imagine, and thus consider, a (possible) life in a different place than where they were born. Attention to the 'imaginative' part of transnational migration may help shed new light on the reasons why Indian citizens migrate to Australia by way of international studentship. A focus on students' migration trajectory, their experience and where they end up is helpful to integrate subjective and objective dimensions. In this chapter the focus will be specifically on how ideas on legality and illegality are reworked, renegotiated and ultimately reimagined to cope with the in-between situation Indian students, on their way to a PR, are in.

13.3 Indian Students in Australia's Education Industry

Various actors - Indian students, education and migration agents, education providers and the local/central government - are entangled in the same dynamics, creating zones in which the line between legality and illegality is no longer so clear-cut. Four examples, based on field interviews during 2005–2006, are presented here to show the close relationships between these actors and their operations in an emerging grey zone.

13.3.1 Rajneesh and His Quest for Work and Study

Rajneesh was still sleeping when his friend Anish opened the front door and let me in for an interview. In the living room, a number of mattresses lay on the floor, one of which was occupied by Rajneesh who had partly covered himself with a dark green bedspread. Unshaved and fully dressed in a worn-down pair of jogging pants and a sport jacket, he apologized for the mess. None of the other housemates appeared to be at home; they were all at work. Rajneesh had meanwhile gone into the kitchen to wash his face, asking his roommate, Anish, if there was anything left to eat in the fridge.

Rajneesh had hoped to find a professional job, one in which he could use the qualifications he had gained in India, but in Australia the reality of having to pay the bills and the high cost of studying had quickly led him to accept a job in a petrol station. In fact, he had shifted jobs several times, each time working as a console operator in similar 24-hour petrol stations. The previous semester, he explained, he had usually worked shifts for three consecutive days a week, alongside, of course, studying.

> I did not sleep for three days. The first day I would start uni [university] at 9:00 and finish at 5:30. Then it would take me one and one-half hours to get home and then on to my job. So, I would start that job at 8:00 in the evening, I would finish at 7:00 in the morning and at 9:00, uni [university] would start again. And then again, I would do the nightshift. Often I would work more than 20 hours. It was all cash in hand so that was not a problem.

Rajneesh had recently switched jobs again, and was now working for a different petrol station - one that he claimed was a better paying one. They now paid him 18 dollars an hour and he was no longer only working night shifts. The hours were by no means guaranteed though.

> There is this Hyderabadi guy who works there, also a student. He makes 12 dollars per hour. There is a lot of competition in these jobs. So that guy will work for less and he will get the good shifts. Sometimes they even work for five or six dollars.

According to Rajneesh, such petrol pump owners (who are themselves migrants) know that Indian students like him need the money and, when desperate, will do anything for it. Rather angrily, he commented: "That Hyderabadi guy spoils it for all of us." Rajneesh displayed an interesting way of reasoning. For one, overseas students are not supposed to work more than 20 hours per week. That many of them do so anyway became perfectly clear from the stories of other students as well and, in fact, working more than the permitted maximum was quite common.[6] And like Rajneesh, many students considered it normal; working more than 20 hours a week would usually be done cash-in-hand: no taxes were paid and no paper trail. If one did pay taxes, this would show up on official records as one of the many student-visa violations, entailing cancellation of the visa.

Stories such as the one narrated by Rajneesh were indeed common, although there were also plenty of students who stuck to the 20 hours rule. Usually these students managed to find a steady call-centre job, which paid relatively well. Almost everybody seemed to be aware of the various ways there were "not to go on TFN [Tax File Number]". In Rajneesh's case, he would simply pay taxes based on 15 hours; the rest was cash in hand. But there were other ways; on paper, a student would be paid legal minimum wages for, say, 15 hours, but in reality would have to work 30 hours for the same money. Petrol stations, 7-Eleven supermarkets and Indian or Chinese restaurants regularly appeared to adopt this practice. According to students like Rajneesh, this had a lot to do with the fact that others knew about the financial pressures they were under and exploited that. As some remarked, it was seen as something an Indian migrant simply had to put up with.

Having been in Australia for more than a year now, Rajneesh was well aware that his options were similar to others. Talking about his work and the way he dealt with various rules and regulations he showed a great deal of ease about breaking the law. His student visa clearly came with a set of rules, which he was not supposed to break; doing so could have serious consequences. Yet, this had only played a marginal role in the decision-making process of actually involving himself in such activities. It simply seemed the normal thing to do. It may be illegal, but at the same time, it seemed like there was no other option. While the loan played a central role in this, it was not solely about repaying loans or taking care of living expenses and semester fees. In Rajneesh's and others' narrations, the highly commercial and, in their eyes, often-exploitative education industry, which used 'their' rupees to fund Australian universities, played a part in this. Where they perceived the industry to be profiting from them, and in some cases not particularly delivering what had been promised, they saw this as a way to make (take) some of the money back.

Rajneesh and other Indian students' way of reasoning reminds one of what Ranabir Samaddar (1999) describes on the first pages of his inquiry into transnational migration from Bangladesh to the state of West Bengal in India. Rethinking the very clear physical border between the two territories, he recalls his amazement at how the border was nothing exceptional to the people who lived on both sides of it. Even if it was, people found ways to deal with it; after sunset cartloads of goods and vegetables would start crossing the (legal) border, something that, if it meant ferrying goods without due leave, was clearly illegal. "But there were ways to normalize such a situation. In other words, the illegal no longer remained exceptional if it could be adapted as part of the 'normal'" (Samaddar 1999: 53), but for Samaddar it felt as if he had walked into a twilight zone of legality and illegality, exceptionality and normality.

International students are clearly not illegal migrants. They are in fact not even migrants, at least not on paper. It is surprising, then, that activities and situations often associated with illegal migration can be connected to a group of perfectly legal, although temporary, Australian residents. Working as much as possible, Rajneesh had been well aware that he was risking deportation from Australia. At the same time, it was not something he was afraid of; the risk simply came with the situation he was in, he reasoned. Although he had every intention to stay on in Australia after graduation to start an import business, he was unsure if he would meet the requirements and so wanted to make as much money as possible given the investment he had made. He jokingly argued that Australia was profiting enough from him, as he was a full-fee paying overseas student who wasted one year of education at an expensive university. He was now no longer using family money to pay for his fees but his own, which he had earned working locally. This seemed the most sensible thing to do. That this came with a certain amount of risk, he figured, was only normal.

About half of the students interviewed in Melbourne had come to Australia through IDP Education (International Development Program), the biggest Australian recruiter of overseas students, operating on a non-profit basis worldwide and jointly owned by

6 Overseas students in Australia are allowed to work a maximum of 20 hours per week during semesters. This rule is dropped during semester breaks when they are allowed to work an unlimited number of hours. The rule was put in place to prevent students from coming to Australia only to work.

Australian universities and representatives of all education sectors. The rest had come through private agencies, some very large and others one-person businesses, virtually unknown outside the region in India they operated in. When enquiring about education agencies, whether big or small ones, answers from students suggested they had been initially introduced to what they emphasized as the Australian education 'industry' by these private agencies in India.

While these agencies guided them in finding the right courses and universities, and of course with the necessary paperwork, it was clearly understood that these companies were in the business for the profit. Many agencies actually did not charge anything to the students directly. Often they simply made their money through the commission they received from the respective university for bringing in students. Service without charge often gave students the impression that they were dealing with not-for-profit operations that would not be influenced by commercial interests. Yet besides the larger operators in the field such as Planet Education and IDP, many agents appeared to offer only courses with a limited number of institutes. This was not only a question of less work, but also that certain deals had been closed where such dedication was compensated in a proper way. During interviews with students enrolled at institutes with the lowest fees, it became clear that such students almost never came through organizations like IDP. They would usually have been advised to attend such an institute by an agent who had only a limited number of alternatives. Usually such an agent would also advise them on which course to take in order to 'secure residency'. Thus, it became clear that the entanglement of education and migration extended well across Australia's border and far into the urban/regional centres of India.

13.3.2 The Gupte Agency in the Education Industry

Housed on the first floor of a neat office building in the centre of Melbourne, The Gupte Education Agency meets with Indian students throughout the day. Chandra, the Indian woman in charge, is in her thirties. Two of her sisters are also involved in the business; one helps with office-related matters in Melbourne while the other manages the office in New Delhi where most of the actual student recruitment takes place. The family has been active on the Australian market since September 1991

150 students to Australia per semester. Based on students' background the agency tries to guide them as much as it can, going through what the student in question has studied before and what kind of expectations they have before making some suggestions of universities that might be an option.

Chandra was quick to add: "We never push them into anything. It has to be their own choice". People in the business of student recruitment frequently repeated this statement, emphasizing the terms "their own choice". Most agencies active in the recruitment business specialize in a number of universities, but also act as a representative for all of them.

The money the agency makes comes from the universities. "They pay us for the students we enrol with them." How much they receive differs though. Chandra added vaguely: "the amounts vary between and 1,000 [Australian] dollars...but it really depends". Within the education industry commissions are a closely guarded secret among all parties involved. A safe estimate is probably an average of ten per cent of the first year's fees (Sidhu 2006). Indian media, though, reports that some agents now take as much as 2 to 7,000 Australian dollars as a fee for each student they recruit, or as much as 40 per cent of a year's tuition fees.[7] Chandra made clear that "We don't take it into account when we guide students though...We are an ethical business and we like to keep it that way.... We follow the ESOS act and there is a very fine line between migration and education in it. So we stick to that."

The Education Services for Overseas Students (ESOS) Act is supposed to regulate the education and training sector's involvement with overseas students studying in Australia on student visas. In principle, the Act is meant to protect the interests of overseas students by providing tuition and financial assurance. Closely connected to this Act is the National Code[8], the purpose of which is to provide nationally consistent standards for Commonwealth Register of Institutions and Courses for Overseas Students (CRICOS) registration[9] and for the conduct of CRICOS-registered providers. The Code has proved to be especially relevant when it comes to understanding the thin line walked by education providers, education and immigration agents, and others when dealing with, and making money from, overseas students. Under the bracket of "marketing and student information", the Code states that the CRICOS-registered provider is re-

7 See at: <http://www.fisa.org.au/content/education-agents-take-big-slice-pie> (23 April, 2010)

sponsible for ensuring that marketing of its education and training services is carried out with integrity and accuracy.[10] Important here is that the code also stresses that it must uphold the reputation of Australian international education and training. A little further on, the Code states that: "recruitment of overseas students must be conducted in an ethical and responsible manner". Significantly, when it comes to recruitment agencies the Code stresses that

> The registered provider must not accept or continue to accept overseas students recruited by an agent... if they know, or reasonably suspect the agent to be: engaged in dishonest practices, including suggesting to overseas students that they come to Australia on a student visa with a primary purpose other than full-time study.[11]

In the case of Indian overseas students, it is clear that coming to Australia is not only about studying. This is known in India, as reported recently: "Most Indian students are looking at a return on investment and... outcomes are better in Australia than in the U.S. & U.K.," Racquel Shroff, Manager, Chennai branch of IDP Education Australia was quoted as saying.[12] As was noted earlier, IDP, like other agents recruiting students, is not supposed to 'talk' about migration; but the manager of IDP in Chennai clearly refers to the desire for PR here. This shows how the two (migration and education) are inextricably linked. While interviewing five teachers from the same department at a large university in Melbourne one afternoon, it became clear that the reality of migration was known to all of them. Some of them had been on so-called 'road shows' to India in order to recruit students for the university and had soon realized that the most important question on most students' minds was 'will this course get me PR'? Most admitted that answering such questions was unavoidable, and that you had to find a way to deal with it. The teachers were aware that they were not supposed to recruit migrants but students, yet they also knew that with 'selling education' came something else that students wanted as well and it was not just wanting, some explained. These teachers frequently found themselves faced with questions relating to how to get a student loan and associated payback schemes, as well as students wanting to know what their chances were of getting a job in their field in Australia and what their potential earnings would be. In fact, the course itself was not something potential students wanted to know all that much about, having often already spent time online, comparing course programmes and universities. Other teachers and university staff at the Australian International Education Conference (AIEC) 2005, held at the Gold Coast Exhibition Centre in the state of Queensland, painted a similar picture of these road shows during interviews. Everyone had been overwhelmed by questions related to PR and career opportunities in Australia while touring India. The university and the courses themselves were often of limited interest to students. The conference itself avoided the subject. Most sessions dealt with recruitment related practices, from how to build a successful website to types of information needed while travel-

8 When the National Code was revised in 2006, it elicited considerable protests from education providers and agents: "New Federal Government rules on overseas students are extremely confrontational and will cost universities millions of dollars to set up and administer, vice-chancellors warned. But the greater cost could be the loss of students, as the charges are passed onto them." Changes included checking students' attendance at all lectures and tutorials and making sure they meet with visa requirements. The Australian Vice-Chancellors' Committee (AVCC) calculated that the changes would cost universities up to AUS $ 41 million extra. (*Sydney Morning Herald*, 31 May 2006).

9 The ESOS act requires providers of courses to international students to register their institution and the courses they offer with *Department of Education, Training and Youth Affairs* (DETYA). See at: <http://cricos.deewr.gov.au/> (10 October 2009).

10 It doesn't matter whether this is (actually) conducted by 1) the provider, 2) their agents, or 3) those involved in the provision of a course under an arrangement with the registered provider.

11 See also: *University and their Students: Principles for the Provision of Education by Australian Universities*, published December 2002 by the AVCC. "Universities should ensure that Australian Diplomatic Missions and relevant government education agencies overseas are fully cognisant of their involvement in promoting, marketing and delivery of education to international students and that such involvement meets all official in-country rules and regulations.... Universities should ensure that their promotions and advertisements, including those involving third parties, truthfully and accurately describe the education services, including the nature of courses, facilities and opportunities available to international students. Statements about the merits of courses offered by other universities, or about the universities themselves, should be fair and not misleading or malicious" (p. 29). Similar rules and regulations can also be found in earlier publications such as *A Guide for Providers of Education and Training Services to Overseas Students* (1999), which was based on an earlier version of the ESOS Act (1997).

12 *The Hindu* (9 April 2006).

ling in 'source countries'. Migration almost seemed a non-topic, something that those in the business of education knew they were not supposed to talk about. Some even claimed that, by law, they were not allowed to refer to migration. Some also referred to the ESOS Act and National Code. This also meant that they did not have brochures or sections of their agent's or college/university's websites devoted to answering detailed questions about PR. The biggest recruiter in the field, IDP, co-organized the conference and seemed to have even an official policy of not engaging in answering questions related to PR. This was no surprise to students. Yet, standing in a huge conference centre where hundreds of people had come together to discuss the business of overseas students - of which India is the second biggest source country - it was fascinating to observe how everybody seemed to know that migration was an integral part of the business, and somehow had found ways of dealing with this, chiefly by avoiding the topic in public.

13.3.3 The Marketing People on the Fine Line between Education and Migration

Jake, a well-muscled, suit-clad and smooth talking senior marketing officer for one of the bigger universities in Australia clarified that even higher up the ladder universities are well aware of what the industry is producing. Most of his job consists of looking at markets, figures and predicting for the university how things will develop over time. In addition he was also closely involved with setting up marketing programmes to lure more students to his university and interacting with a team of people who travel to 'source countries' regularly. He was hesitant talking about PR at first. As he initially put it:

> India is a price sensitive market. Many of the students are also interested in PR... Indian students have always been interested in PR, but they are now much more aware of it. We don't push the PR issue however; it is not something we advertise with.

Asked why, he explained that they are not allowed to market PR. "We look for other avenues. We want to offer a distinguishing product. We underline the prestige of the degree". Yet talking about the issue a little more, he also admitted that at times they do try to encourage faculties to change their programmes so they come closer to what the market demands (i.e. providing courses that meet criteria for achieving PR), but that it takes time to change a programme. Referring to Central Queensland University - a large institution with a rather low reputation when it comes to education and research - he added that universities of such standing "are what we call picking the low-hanging fruit; it does not help the industry at all to behave in such a way".

Jake's colleague Jason, who introduced himself as the one responsible for the recruitment team at the university in question, explained that in his previous job, he had regularly headed the India missions. "We would go there on these three-week missions to recruit students." These recruitment teams would talk to the students, their parents and everybody else involved during such missions. "We would organize these educational fairs there. But also do these interview programmes, and we would provide training to agents." In addition information sessions are also organized. Reportedly, Indian students rarely asked questions about Australian education itself; and generally time was limited to answer in detail. PR was certainly a familiar topic but Jason was quick to add universities are basically supposed to provide education: "students are mostly outcome driven so you cannot really ignore the fact that they come here for that reason; they see it as a pathway to something.... and the government is clear that it wants skilled migrants".

But here Jake, who had stayed silent for a while, was quick to reassure me that they were not involved in actually recruiting migrants, posing the almost rhetorical question to Jason, "but we don't promote it, do we?" Jason agreed, "we don't promote it as such but we try to answer questions as best we can". Yet talking about this a little more, Jason also remarked that some say this is a 'migration market'. Jason was well informed about the motives of Indian students coming to Australia. Yet, PR and student recruitment continued to be awkward (if not illegal) bedfellows in the world of overseas education.

The ambivalence between Jake and Jason, sometimes correcting themselves or each other when they felt that they were saying something out of tune, given the rules and regulations in place to regulate the industry, made the interview a particularly interesting one. It showed how complex, and at times confusing, an environment it could be to work in. As Jason made quite clear, "It is a civil offence to give advice on PR." He was of the opinion that his university also did not need to use PR in marketing material, as the Indian students already seemed to know everything about it. Jason seemed to think that not being able to use PR as a marketing tool was actually working in his favour. The marketing department was perfectly aware which courses would be of interest to students. Promoting these courses was daily reality for a student recruiter abroad. These courses were directly linked with migration opportunities. However, also knowing that the conditions for obtaining a PR regularly change, the university did not have to commit itself to anything. They were not in the business of migration; that the industry was actually producing migrants was not their problem (or responsibility) and in fact could not (fortunately) legally be so.

13.3.4 Operators in a Permanent Residency Factory

Most Australians in the business of student recruitment produced similar accounts to those presented above. The general narrative on what those within the industry generally refer to as 'dodgy providers' of PR or 'PR factories' usually concerned much smaller, newly established colleges, often located in city centres, and often catering to students from one particular country (China, India, Malaysia) or region (East Asia, South Asia or South East Asia). A college located in the Central Business District of Melbourne had appeared in articles in a number of local Indian papers, owing to the fact that some of the students who had enrolled there had ended up in detention centres because of visa violations. In 2005, the institute had 65 students enrolled. Recruitment had been down for a while but as they were developing new courses, they expected business to pick up soon.

When asked about the courses the college offered, the director (Gerry) replied that they were mostly accountancy-related, thus fetching the highest points when applying for PR: "We have quite a bit of experience with the MODL list." In the past, the institute used to run courses in marketing and IT but as these are now fifty points occupations there are no students in them anymore. Gerry admitted that most of the students that attended his college came to Australia for migration purposes: "They have borrowed a lot of money. And they have come here with falsified documents. So they know the risk they have taken." He added that in a way they have mortgaged their lives. The college would be starting cookery courses such as Indian cooking, professional cooking and all that. "The trend is now that only MODL courses make it; students want the 75 points and so they choose courses that offer that. [And if that is not an option,] they will go bush," he said, referring to the option of studying in a regional area for which students will be able to claim bonus points. "Or they do NAATI (National Accreditation Authority for Translators and Interpreter)," he remarked, referring to the possibility of claiming extra points by becoming a certified translator. "But with 75 points you don't have to worry about that at all." At the moment of the interview, the director was specifically aiming his products at this group of students, or those who did not (seem to) care much about the type of course they would be taking in Australia as long as it ultimately led them to an Australian PR.

A similar college, located a couple of blocks from Flinders Street train station, appeared to view the business of education in similar terms. Calling itself an institute of technology, it seemed to be suggesting an association with the Royal Melbourne Institute of Technology (RMIT) - a large and well-respected university located nearby. Founded and co-owned by three men (one Australian, two Indian) who all had international education-related backgrounds, the institute was a relative newcomer in the field of international education. The director in charge of daily affairs, previously the international director of a large TAFE college, was quick to point this out. His two Indian colleagues were both education/migration agents with offices in both Australia and India. The institute had grown rapidly: in July 2005 they had 40 students, only half a year later this number had grown to 300, almost all Indian (about 97 per cent). The intention to get a PR seemed to be the main reason for this.

Although the institute referred to itself as an institute of technology, they had stopped offering any technology-related courses soon after the institute had opened its doors. It was now totally dedicated to offering cookery courses and a practice area had even been arranged in a local Indian restaurant.

13.4 Production and Processing of International Student-Migrants

13.4.1 The Permanent Residency Factory in Action

A report by the Centre for Population and Urban Research (Monash University) published early in 2007 found that in recent years, there had been a spike in the number of overseas students enrolling in such courses as cooking and hairdressing (Birrell 2007), because they both provide a cheap and easy path to a permanent visa.[13] Moreover, only a minority worked

13 See in: *Sydney Morning Herald* (22 April 2010); at: <http://www.smh.com.au/news/national/schools-in-for-stayers/2007/07/03/1183351209855.html>.

in those occupations once they graduated. Besides reporting on a failing skilled migration programme and that the need for cooks and hairdressers was far less than the numbers coming into Australia to learn these trades, many newspapers were highlighting that other education/trade categories were not attracting anywhere near the same numbers, although demand was supposedly much greater (trade occupations in for instance metal, electrical and construction industries). Attention also went to situations where smaller colleges were clearly profiting from opportunities created by the immigration law.

When describing how some students were becoming Australian residents by means described above, the media began using such phrases as 'cutting corners', 'exploiting a loophole' and 'rorting' [to take unfair advantage] Australia's skilled migration programme."[14] Bob Birrell, one of the authors of the controversial report, explained it as "the whole system [has] been hijacked by the migration industry...". Such colleges have been coined PR factories, a term often used among Indian students themselves (Baas 2006). Yet the practice of considering migration rules and regulations when offering particular courses to overseas students was surely not limited to these colleges. Although several universities have specifically developed a reputation among Indian students for catering to students interested in obtaining an Australian PR, my fieldwork showed that almost all have to come to terms with this aspect of the 'overseas student market', and have, in fact, already found ways of dealing with it.

Education and migration intertwine to the point that it is nearly impossible to separate them. The financial dependence of Australian universities and colleges on overseas students has become so high that the Australian government has no choice other than to consider the education industry when making changes to its skilled migration programmes. Christopher Ziguras (2005: 99) argues that if governments discouraged international education (with declining overseas student numbers a consequence), "the financial viability of many Australian universities would be threatened". However, it could just as well be argued that discouraging students to stay on in Australia and become permanent residents (by introducing stricter rules) might ultimately result in (vastly) declining student numbers from source countries such as China and India, making it hard for certain universities to survive.

13.4.2 In-between Legality and Illegality

The concept of *in-betweenness* proves particularly useful when trying to come to an understanding of situations where migrants do not exactly seem to fit into (match) particular clearly defined concepts or situations. Specifically, *in-betweenness* seems to intersect, interact and interrupt with fixed ways of interpreting what is legal and illegal. By challenging this very idea of knowing and/or understanding the borders that demarcate zones of legality and illegality, we can free ourselves of the idea that social experience actually reflects the defined lines.

It is clear that the day-to-day understanding of the terms illegal and illegality remains a matter of perception and of flexible interpretation depending on the particular situation. Analysing everyday realities of people living in Naples (Italy), Pardo (1995: 47) explains that most ordinary Napolitans conduct their lives without strictly abiding by the law: "Small transgressions such as those against traffic laws are common, and so are various activities that according to formal definition fall in the gray area between legality and illegality or are unequivocally illegal." This so-called grey area covers anything from evading taxes to purchasing smuggled or stolen goods. What defines something as illegal is a 'legal' as well as 'social' process. The legal and the social might provide different opinions about what can or, should be legal or illegal. In this sense a distinction can also be made between state perspectives, which work largely with the dichotomy of legal-illegal spheres, and how people see this themselves, namely often in terms of licitness (legitimate activities) and illicitness (illegitimate activities). Coutin (2002) frames this division in legitimate and illegitimate social spheres, arguing that individuals located in an illegitimate domain survive, at least in part, through unauthorized means or what she dubs 'quasi-illegal practices'. Such quasi-illegal practices show some serious overlaps with the concept of informal activities, which Kloosterman and Rath (2002: 27) use to describe activities "aimed at producing a positive effect on income (for the person executing the activities and/or for the person receiving the results), for which the terms of legislation and regulations (planning requirements, social security legislation, collective labour agreements, and the like) applicable to the activities are not being met". Although in their understanding, knowing that immi-

14 See at: <http://www.theage.com.au/national/foreign-students-could-be-forced-to-leave-20090609-c28h.html> (22 April 2010).

grants often have difficulty accessing regular jobs, such activities might very well contribute to their social and economic advancement.

On occasion, the public at large also seems to understand it this way. Activities that migrants are involved in might very well be in conflict with the law, yet they are seen as normal when it involves persons with apparently limited options. Once when discussing the difficulties faced by Indian students on the work floor, recounting stories of exploitation, an Australian woman who happened to work in social sciences herself commented that Indian migrants are used to such conditions and they always manage to find a way to deal with it. This belief in Indian immigrants' capacities to cope with difficult circumstances (abuse, exploitation, illegality) went hand in hand with the belief that there was nothing abnormal about them having to face such circumstances; it was something normal. Students would often frame it as follows: "This is what we Indians face abroad." One student commented in an interview: "Everybody else is going through it, so 'you' are not alone in that."

Rarely do such perceptions of what is normal for a(n) (Indian) migrant (and/or student) form in a social vacuum. Thus, the issue is one of morality, at least in part; the way moral ideas shape people's understanding of social information, and the way they respond (personally or collectively) to other people (Heyman 2000: 635). As Heyman and Smart (1999: 3–4) previously concluded in understanding why people engage in particular (illegal) activities, informal processes of influence through subcultures and peer networks often have an influence on this. The perception that the practice is commonplace regularly came up during interviews. Working more than the allowed number of hours was seen as something one was not alone in doing; 'everybody else' was doing it as well. This 'social knowledge' worked in two ways: on the one hand it provided legitimacy to an illegal activity and on the other it created peer pressure, in the sense that students often felt stupid if they were not making 'much more' money, as 'others' always seemed to be doing.

13.4.3 The Question of Liminality and Inbetweenness

In an article on El Salvadoran and Guatemalan immigrants in the United States, Cecilia Menjívar speaks of a 'grey area' of liminal legality. In her work, she deals with the in-between area created by black and white conceptualizations of documented and undocumented migration. Referring to Victor Turner's work, she argues that immigrants' uncertain legality transforms them into transitional beings "neither one thing or another, or maybe both, or neither here nor there, or maybe nowhere... and are at the very least 'betwixt and between' all the recognized fixed points in space-time of structural classification" (Turner 1967: 96). Menjívar's (2006: 1007) concern is mainly with 'uncertain legality', which then further shapes social and cultural aspects of immigrants' lives. For Indian students this is of course slightly different since they enjoy legal status, yet it is their uncertain future status in terms of PR that affects their lives. Menjívar's concept of liminal legality expresses the temporariness of such a situation. Yet it is important to note that for many Central Americans in the US this has extended indefinitely (2006: 1008).

The concept of liminality as conceptualized by Turner (1967, borrowing on the work of Van Gennep 1960) more than 40 years ago is a useful way of further understanding not only how *in-betweenness* characterizes Indian students' lives in Australia, but also how this further connects with the entanglement of education and migration in the Australian case in general. A liminal phase typically involves one or all three kinds of separation: spatial, temporal and social/moral. As Guobin Yang notes, "liminality can be seen as in an inverse relationship with bureaucracy... a liminal situation is characterized by freedom, egalitarianism, communion, and creativity" (2000: 383). In organization studies such as those conducted by Christina Garsten (1999) and Tempest and Starkey (2004), the concept was further used to make better sense of the situation temporary workers are in and the way their temporariness challenges the old boundaries of industrial society.

Liminality or the liminal phase can be understood to be almost the same thing as the concept of *in-betweenness*, save for one major difference. The concept of liminality urges us to think in terms of a free space where 'temporarily' the (old) rules no longer apply. Those in that space form a strong community and revel in that new, temporary, freedom. Yet, exactly those binding rules and regulations that require temporary renegotiation to fit certain situations define the concept of *in-betweenness*. *In-betweenness* does not mean freedom from, in fact, it can mean the opposite: being locked in-between certain narrowly defined realms. Menjívar realized this too when she studied the case of Central American immigrants in the US who are prisoners of narrowly defined rules and regulations.

In the case of Indian students, a further complicating factor in their *in-betweenness* is the entanglement of education and migration. This is in terms of there being both an education industry as well as a skilled migration programme that recruits from the pool of freshly graduated overseas students. Yet this entanglement makes certain *in-betweenness* situations slippery and unclear. In particular, we could argue that, in the Australian case there is a certain grey zone where what can be considered legal and illegal is renegotiated to fit in with the reality of the situation students, agents, educational providers and even the government are faced with or involved in. A grey zone is thus an in-between space where strict interpretation of what is legal and illegal is reworked into categories of licitness and illicitness. Students know about the prohibition against working more than 20 hours per week during school semesters. Yet, the *in-betweenness* that characterizes their situation as student-migrants creates a zone where they can argue that there is a certain normalcy to what they are doing. It is accepted as part of their position in Australian society. At the same time, this is also what the industry and the government do. Universities need international students for the money they bring in. The government needs them for the potential skills they bring to the country. Yet the government has ruled that universities may not recruit students for reasons other than education. This is all done with an understanding of the large number of overseas students who come to Australia for residency and that universities are dependent on the money this brings in. As such, all stakeholders now operate in a grey area where terms of 'legality and illegality' have been reworked to adhere to the reality under slogans like 'not strange', 'simply a consequence', 'acceptable' and so on.

13.5 Conclusion

This chapter has raised the question of how issues of legality and illegality in terms of activities and situations play a part in the lives of Indian students in Australia. This is connected to how such issues also play a part among those who profit from these students - such as education providers, immigration agents, and (the) local/central government(s). Education and immigration are highly entangled in Australia. Students often turn out to be migrants as well, while those providing education also provide migration channels. This has created a particularly difficult situation where rules and regulations do not always have the desired result. Clearly, the option of becoming a PR holder after graduation was not created to stimulate the influx of foreign students. Yet, it had that outcome as a result. Education providers realized that in order to recruit students they had to consider them as potential migrants. The Australian government, however, faced a dilemma. The growth of the education industry was not only necessary because universities and colleges depended on the money the industry generated, but also because of all the other jobs in other industries that were now dependent on this industry. Yet the immigration department is not satisfied with the kind of migrants this system produces. Throughout the years, it continued adapting the system to regulate laws more effectively. Knowing that this could negatively influence the growth of the number of full fee-paying students coming to Australia, they had to acknowledge this in their policy changes and updates. This situation continues to influence politics in Australia and has more recently resulted in intense debates on the state of Australia's education industry. Recent debates on the state of the education industry also link to other recent reports on the lives of Indian students in Australia including newspaper reports on poor housing, exploitation of students by local employers and racist attacks.

This chapter argues that better understanding of the grey area that seems to be both separating and overlapping the realms of legality and illegality can be achieved through the use of the concept of *'in-betweenness'*. Where the lines/borders between categories and definitions have become blurred, grey areas pose tremendous difficulties for regulators to deal with. Regulations can also create situations where it is unclear who is exactly responsible for what, and how the safety (both physical and financial) of foreign students can be protected. It will be a challenge for the Australian government to deal with and for social scientists to investigate how this situation unfolds and what effect it has.

Part IV Transnational Identities and Issues of Citizenship

14 Gender, Technology and Migration in Export-Production of Shrimps: Identity Formation and Labour Practices in Surat Thani Province, Thailand

Bernadette P. Resurreccion and Edsel E. Sajor

14.1 Introduction[1]

Biotechnology applications in the shrimp industry fall in line with Thailand's strategy to become 'Kitchen of the World' which assigns an export-oriented role to the food and agriculture sectors.[2] Surat Thani Province is one of the biggest shrimp producer areas in the south of the country with a labour force comprised mainly of migrants from Northeast Thailand, Laos and Myanmar. The competitiveness of the shrimp industry in Thailand appears to be associated with low wages, facilitated by the use of migrant workers.[3] This chapter analyzes the relationship between gender, technology and migration, particularly focusing on the manner in which the concept of 'place' defines 'work' and how the identities of 'gender', 'migrant' and 'worker' interact to produce specific labour control practices affecting wage levels and migrant workers' social well-being.

Our choice of focus is derived from an awareness of the main shortcomings of gender analyses of migration that draw on political-economic and neoclassical approaches and use the concept of 'gender' as a fixed social construct. Women and men as central subjects in migration are conceptualized as being in static opposition; and, *a priori*, women are regarded as being in a disadvantaged position in comparison to men when they move in search of work. Our research uses a post-structuralist approach to show how, under the competitive conditions of shrimp farming, the legal and social conditions are such that migrant men and women as actors constantly create and re-create gender meanings for adaptation. This creates diverse patterns of subordination which cannot easily be reduced to women being always in a subordinated position. Inter-ethnic differences do exist, and men who are members of a marginalized ethnic group may well find themselves worse off than women belonging to the dominant ethnic group.

We begin with a brief discussion on the theoretical premises of the study, followed by a description of the research site and methodology and analysis of our empirical findings. The conclusion highlights the main cultural and discursive practices that are steered towards profit-making objectives, and how they have created diverse identities on the basis of an interaction between notions of 'gender', 'place' and 'work'. Our findings and reflections are connected with the growing trove of ethnographic and feminist geography studies that dwell on the constitution of work and place through the production of 'gender' (Hanson/Pratt 1995; Nagar/Lawson/McDowell/Hanson 2002; Secor 2003; Boyer 2006; Harris 2006; Nightingale 2006). Beyond this, we also see the necessity to situate gendered micro actions at different scales within a broader chain of production governed by different systems of rights and entitlements.

14.2 Intersecting Subjectivities in the Constitution of Work: A Conceptual Pathway

Gender studies that follow the conventional political economy approach often make linkages between gender and globalization, calling attention to the effects of globalization on women in developing regions.

1 An earlier version of this chapter was published in: *International Migration*, 48,5 (2010).
2 According to Flegel (2006) Thailand has been the world's leading producer of cultivated shrimps since 1992 with its export earnings alone reaching more than 1 billion US dollars per year.
3 See at: <http://www.econ.nida.ac.th/people/faculty/Piriya/publications/Piriya-Migration-Journal-format.pdf> (10 April 2010).

T.-D. Truong and D. Gasper (eds.), *Transnational Migration and Human Security*, Hexagon Series on Human and Environmental Security and Peace 6, DOI 10.1007/978-3-642-12757-1_14, © Springer-Verlag Berlin Heidelberg 2011

This perspective usually adopts a structuralist outlook that views globalization as a process driven by 'global capitalism', propelled by neoliberal logic, which inevitably influences and determines international governments, households and families in ways that disfavour women (Connelly/Li/MacDonald/Parpart 1995; Peterson 1996). Themes such as the effects and impacts of the internationalization of labour markets, global production regimes, and the position of women within the global economy often project a dismal picture, depicting the harsh effects of globalization on women as inevitable due to persisting gender inequality (Sen 1996; Shiva 2000[4]; Ghosh 2001; Chow 2002; Beneria 2003). Scholars and practitioners in the field of gender and development refer to this as "the economistic turn" (Davids/van Driel 2001). Variants of the structuralist perspective also underpin discussions on gender, globalization and migration. For example the debate on the growing 'care deficit' in developed regions of the North emphasizes how attempts to cover this gap through importing migrant female labour from the labour-abundant South have created care chains in global and regional political economies.[5] This perspective views labour demand and supply as principal determinants of the movement patterns of women, from rural areas and less developing countries as unskilled, semi-skilled, or low-skilled workers, and gradually to economically vibrant regions. Many attribute global economic restructuring as the principal driver of the mobility of women into cities and across borders. Adopting a one-dimensional view, that reduces explanations of women's decision-making concerning migration, and its outcomes at the destinations, to economic considerations, can bypass significant interactions between economic, legal and cultural forces that shape their identities and experiences at the work place. These can in turn reinforce hierarchical relations within the local political economy and beyond.

Feminist studies today posit that women's undervalued work has buttressed and given shape to economic globalization. For instance, Nagar/Lawson/McDowell/Hanson (2002) and Harstock (2001) argue that different sets of relationships – those between high-skill and low-skill work, formal and casualized economies, productive and caring work, globalized and marginalized places (in the South and the North) – have allowed global capitalism to assume its contemporary forms. Bonds' work (2006) on call centres in the rural American West has unpacked the ways they are linked to processes of transnational capitalism and rural restructuring, underscoring the role of the 'new information economy' that relies on women in occupations clustered at the bottom of the occupational hierarchy. From Pratt's (1997) work, we learn how three discursive constructions of Filipina[6] have shaped Filipinas' labour market experiences in Vancouver as well as the flows of female migrant aspirants to the nursing profession. Pratt's (1997) analysis demonstrates that theories of subject formation can contribute more textured understandings of labour market dynamics and segmentation. Secor (2003) also shows that in Turkey, the discourse of a deferential femininity, or what makes 'a good woman', is a significant part of restructuring local economies and the growth of low-wage, low-status and often casual jobs, for which women are seen as ideal recruits.

Taking this line of reasoning further, we employ a number of key theoretical steps that countervail the view of gender as a fixed structure of power. First, we recognize the contingent link between (a) the production of 'gender' and 'migrant' identities and (b) the constitution of the notions of 'work' and 'place'. By examining migration processes and practices at work places, we discern the production of place, gender and migrant-differentiated identities through iteration. Being a 'woman worker', 'male employer', or 'male migrant' are products of practices, and concrete cultural and historical circumstances, and thus cannot be treated in a pre-determined way. What it means to be a migrant woman or man is context-dependent; and to discover this, we focus on how identities are created, differentially and fluidly, through daily interactions and discourses on work and in the creation of distinct places where migrants are allocated according to their status and employers' preferences.

Second, premised on current theorizing on gender subjectivity (particularly instructive in understanding the production of identities and positions) we underscore the view that women and men as subjects enter into social relationships that are fluid and most often provisional. Rather than viewing the 'subject' as fixed and stable, it is more insightful to understand 'subject

4 See Vandana Shiva, 2000: "Lecture 5: Poverty and Globalization", Reith Lectures, BBC; at: <http://www.bbc.co.uk/radio4/reith2000/lecture5.shtml> (21 May 2008).

5 A care chain is an arrangement through which care responsibilities (for the young and old) are transferred from one socio-economic class in one country to another (see Enhrenreich/Hochschild 2002).

6 As 'supplicant' pre-immigrant; as inferior 'housekeeper'; and, within the Filipino community, as 'husband stealer'.

formation' as a process of becoming (McDowell 1999). This view cautions against *a priori* and reified perceptions on women's roles and redirects attention to the diverse ways women and men enter into, and engage in, social relationships (Rao 1991) and how identities are formed through interaction. Strathern (1988: 128) emphasizes this point as follows: "It is the interactions of women and men that make men, men." Additionally, Butler's (1990, 1994) treatment of 'gender identity' as instantiated by discourses and practices that contribute to cementing ontological differences between women and men urges attentiveness to the iteration of certain practices that makes sex difference appear as natural and stable, therefore turning gender into "the factness of difference" (Butler 1994: 9). Cornwall's (2007) advice regarding the need to take cognizance of the relations of inequality and uneven power that the iteration of practices maintain and co-produce is crucial to analyse the intersection between gender and differentiated migrant identities. Male and female identities as workers can be self-defined as a result of concrete discursive practices which buttress the actual organization of labour in shrimp farms. Reflecting on the links between different scales of production (local, national and global) and connecting gender practices at local sites, we suggest that the creation and re-creation of identities occupy a significant place in the formation and sustaining of social hierarchies within global capitalism.

14.3 Methodology

This study is part of a wider research project on policymaking processes in biotechnology, where a much earlier random survey of 214 shrimp farms in Surat Thani Province was conducted in 2006. The results of that survey are presented in figures 14.2 and table 14.2 to provide additional information on the context. The research for this chapter employed a mixed-methods approach with three sets of qualitative interviews and a survey conducted between October 2006 and May 2007 in 120 shrimp farms in this province. The first set of interviews involved 11 farm owners and focussed on issues of production and labour employment. The second set of interviews involved 30 Lao and Burmese male and female migrant workers,[7] and focussed on migration processes, brokerage networks and the general working conditions in Surat Thani. The key findings from these two sets of interviews informed the selection of items in a survey designed to test the pervasiveness of these initial findings among a wider population. The survey later used a purposive sample of 147 Thai, Burmese and Lao female migrant workers. Tables 14.3, 14.4, 14.5 and 14.6 present findings from this survey.

The third set of interviews, involving 41 female migrant workers selected from participants in the survey[8] aimed at a deeper investigation of labour and employment conditions in shrimp farms by gender. These 41 female migrants were part of the survey and we now purposively interviewed them since their narratives could shed light on their social positioning as labour migrants and as women in paid work on shrimp farms. Questions in this last set of interviews explored historical shifts in livelihoods, marriage and social status, spatial mobility and gendered conditions of the migrants' present employment. The researchers along with Thai graduate students, who translated the conversations from Thai to English, conducted and recorded all three sets of interviews on-site. Later, researchers clustered all interview notes into different themes to enable accessibility of reference.

14.4 Thai Migration Policy, Surat Thani's Shrimp Farms, and the Production of Gender Identities and Work

The uneven spread of economic opportunities and political conditions in Myanmar and Laos, and in the Mekong region as a whole, have prompted people from disadvantaged countries in this sub-region to seek better employment opportunities elsewhere, especially in neighbouring Thailand. Moreover, uneven stages of economic development in the Mekong region also create a differentiated sub-regional labour market: Thailand faces a labour shortage in certain low-skilled sectors, while Laos, Cambodia and Myanmar face an unskilled labour surplus due to rural poverty, underdeveloped infrastructure and low or poor-quality education. Disparities in income accompany these conditions, accounting for part of the cross-border migration flows between Thailand and these other countries.

Thailand's economic growth in the 1980's led to labour market expansion and an acute shortage of unskilled labour towards the 1990's. Local Thais were no

7 9 Lao men, 6 Laotian women, 12 Burmese men, and 3 Burmese women.

8 12 Northeast Thais, 13 Burmese and 16 Laotians.

longer interested in the unskilled labour market, but showed increasing preference for work in the services sectors, where incomes were relatively higher. As a result, the private sector pressured the government to allow them to employ migrant workers. Then, in 1992, Thailand started to adopt an immigration policy for unskilled foreign workers (Chantavanich 2007). Over time, the Thai government began to develop migration policies that implicitly recognized industries' growing need for low, semi-skilled and cheap labour that will enable them to carve a competitive niche within the export market, while simultaneously keeping migration flows in check through stringent legal monitoring systems.

Figure 14.1: Surat Thani Province, Thailand. **Source:** http://th.wikipedia.org/wiki/ ไฟล์:Thailand_Surat_Thani.png.

The shrimp industry in Surat Thani Province (figure 14.1) is the second biggest producer of shrimp in Thailand largely because of shrimp farming intensification and upgraded technologies. The growth of the infrastructure-driven and technology-intensive shrimp industry in Surat Thani Province created an increasing demand for low- and semi-skilled migrant workers, many from neighbouring Myanmar and Laos.

In 2003, a new 'open door' policy to manage rather than reject migrant workers was proposed. This approach requires registration of employers who employ migrant workers, and for employers to issue public announcements of job vacancies first to the Thai labour force. This is completely new for Thailand given that previous policies aimed at registering workers to monitor their presence in the Kingdom, rather than registering employers. On 2 March 2004, a cabinet resolution directed the Ministry of the Interior to develop a database for aliens from Burma, Laos and Cambodia. All aliens living in Thailand were to report for registration, with fines and imprisonment for those who violated this order, including workers, employers, and those who provided accommodations for aliens.[9] Employers were required to pay government fees to register their migrant employees.

Early assessments of the new approach to migration management revealed various challenges, such as when employers refused to pay the required registration fees because they were too expensive, thus slowing down the registration process (Chantanvanich 2007; Muntarbhorn 2005)[10]. Official records indicate that Burmese migrants form the largest proportion of workers with permits. Interviews with farm operators in Surat Thani revealed that many of them comply with the government requirements for registration. They in turn deduct the required fees from workers' wages. Table 14.1 shows the numbers of Laotian and

9 The new requirements are registration of both migrant workers and their employers; failure to come forward to register subjects the former to deportation and the latter to punishment; a medical test, which migrant workers have to pass, leading to a medical certificate; failure to undertake and pass the test subjects migrant workers to deportation, while passing the test leads to the granting of a work permit as well as medical and social welfare paralleling that of the local population (Muntarbhorn 2005: 5–7).

10 However, it was found that there were more migrant registrants than in the past. Whereas 568,249 alien workers registered in 2001, in 2004, 1,269,074 aliens were reported (702,351 men and 566,723 women). The majority (905,881) were from Burma (497,372 men and 408,509 women). In all, 181,614 of the registrants (80,981 men and 100,633 women) were from Laos (Ministry of Interior 2004, in Thongyou/Ayuwat 2005).

Burmese workers who have work permits, and of Thai employers who have permission to employ migrant workers in the Province.

Table 14.1: Number of Laotian and Burmese with work permits and Thai employers with permits to employ migrant workers, Surat Thani Province. Source: Migrant Labour Administrative Office, Ministry of Labour and Employment, 2006

Thai Employers (with permits to employ)	Burmese migrants (with work permits)	Laotian migrants (with work permits)
5,381	22,345	647

In-migration trends in Thailand indicate that the Thai economy is absorbing migrant labourers for low-skilled work that Thai citizens do not find desirable. Migrants from poorer labour-supplying neighbouring countries, like Laos and Myanmar, continue to seek work in Thailand because of the informal infrastructure made up of networks of brokers who charge relatively modest fees (5,000–7,000 baht) (Martin 2002). Employer dependence on migrant labour is likely to persist as industries in Thailand expand given the need to reduce production costs to become more competitive in the global market. Thai migration registration policy is therefore concessionary, ceding to the need to redress the scarcity of low- and semi-skilled labour for growing industries like technology-intensive shrimp farming on the one hand, and to the perceived need to control the flow of migrant workers through legal means that mete out stiff penalties to violators of existing requirements on the other.

Surat Thani Province is one of 14 provinces of Thailand's Southern Region. According to 2006 estimates, the province has 14 per cent of total registered immigrants in this region, estimated to include about 168,114 persons from Myanmar, Lao PDR and Cambodia. In the same period, estimates show that the Southern Region had about 13 per cent of all registered immigrants in the country (Kingdom of Thailand 2006a).

Surat Thani's shrimp farm operators tap into the mobility flows of Northeast Thais, Laotians and Burmese, to address the demands for rapid, superior quality, high-volume production of shrimp for export, with minimum labour cost and maximum control of labour delivery. This pursues the track of export-oriented economic growth, framed specifically by the market niche Thailand defined for itself: the 'Kitchen of the World'. Surat Thani's shrimp production accounted for ten per cent of Thailand's total shrimp export for 2004 (Kingdom of Thailand 2006). All farm operators – big, medium and small – strive to produce shrimp of standard size and quality suitable for the global market.

Shrimp farms vary according to the degree of capital, the volume of production and earnings, the types of technology, and the nature of labour investments. According to Smith (1999), systems of shrimp production are classified as extensive, semi-intensive and intensive, with reference to their stocking levels and pond size. The largest farms in Surat Thani stock as many as 400,000 broodstock per rai,[11] compared with the traditional practice of 5,000 broodstock per rai.[12] The shrimp harvest may be two or three times a year, depending on the degree of infrastructure and labour monitoring. Successful large farms in the province can generate a net profit of 600,000 baht to 1 million baht per shrimp pond. The research project's earlier random survey of 241 farm operators in 2006 showed that large individual or corporate farm operators usually operate more than 20 ponds, with an average annual operating capital of 32 million baht.

Large individual and corporate shrimp farm operators in Surat Thani are successful in super-intensive farming because of their capability to nurture superior broodstock through updated information and close connection with suppliers who use genetic engineering to improve seed and domestication techniques; good farm management practices; and the use of new shrimp farming technologies. An example of these updated farm technologies is the bio-secure system that uses polyethylene lining on the pond bed and walls, good roofing, water chlorination and intense water quality monitoring by a test kit specifically designed for the purpose. The large individual and corporate farm operators are able to harvest high yields in their ponds due to the good survival rate of the superior broodstock, and their use of upgraded technologies. Thus, large farm operators are able to produce huge quantities of large-sized and highly priced shrimp that are attractive to foreign buyers.

Our earlier random survey of 214 shrimp farm operators in 2006 revealed that small-scale farms usually operate one to five active ponds. They do not have a water storage pond, due to land limitations.

11 1 rai is approximately equivalent to 16,000 square metres; 1 hectare is equivalent to 6 rai.

12 Traditional, land-intensive shrimp farming used to be widely practiced in Surat Thani up to the mid-1980's but is no longer practiced.

Table 14.2: Technologies typically employed, by type of farm operator. **Source:** Based on the authors' random survey of 214 farmer operators in Surat Thani (2006). N=214 farm operators.

Type	Technologies	Specific Use	Annual Mean Capital Investment (Baht)
Small n=159	Boat (100%)	Feeding Check water quality	865,000
	Net (100%)	Animal protection	
	Aerator (100%)	Supply oxygen	
	Test kit (100%)	Check water quality	
Medium n=47	Boat (100%)	Feeding Check water quality	4,210,000
	Net (100%)	Animal protection	
	Aerator (100%)	Supply oxygen	
	Test kit (100%)	Check water quality	
	Water storage pond/Wastewater treatment pond (63.8%)	Water storage/ Water treatment	
	Polyethylene (PE) (58.1%)	Pond lining to prevent soil contamination	
Big n=8	Boat (100%)	Feeding Check water quality	32,000,000
	Net: (100%)	Animal protection	
	Aerator (100%)	Supply oxygen	
	Test kit (100%)	Water quality check	
	Water storage pond/Waste water treatment pond (100 %)	Water storage/ Water treatment	
	Polyethylene (PE 75%)	Pond lining to prevent soil contamination	
	Chlorination (75%)	Disinfection	
	In-house laboratory (50 %)	Water quality and disease check	

Medium-sized farms have 6 to 20 active ponds, and have separate water storage ponds. Large-scale farms have more than 20 active ponds for shrimp cultivation. They have water storage ponds, and each pond is generally 5–7 rai in size. For big farms, it is important to maintain a water storage pond to earn a *Certificate of (Good) Conduct* (CoC) from the government, which certifies good quality control standards required by shrimp export protocols. The 2006 survey also revealed that most shrimp farms in Surat Thani are small (74 per cent) and medium-size farms (22 per cent).

The range of technologies used differs widely between small, medium and large type farms. Large farm operators have their own laboratories that can thoroughly check water quality and diagnose shrimp diseases, according to our 2006 survey. They also have basic equipment such as boats, nets and aerator test kits. In contrast, medium-size farms employ a more limited range of technology; while the small-scale operators use only the most basic equipment (see table 14.2).

The number of active shrimp ponds and the nature of farm technology usually determine the labour force on the farms. Usually, one worker takes care of one shrimp pond. Large farm operators hire many workers to apply chlorine, feed shrimp stock, replace polyethylene, operate aerators, regularly monitor water quality in both shrimp and storage ponds and treat wastewater. High-skilled workers work in in-house laboratories, machinery maintenance and financial management. Farms also hire security guards to prevent thefts of any kind. Small- and medium-sized farms, however, require a smaller work force as shown

Figure 14.2: Average number of hired migrant workers in small and medium farms, by nationality, Ganjanadit and Punpin Districts, Surat Thani Province (N = 154). **Source:** Authors' Survey.

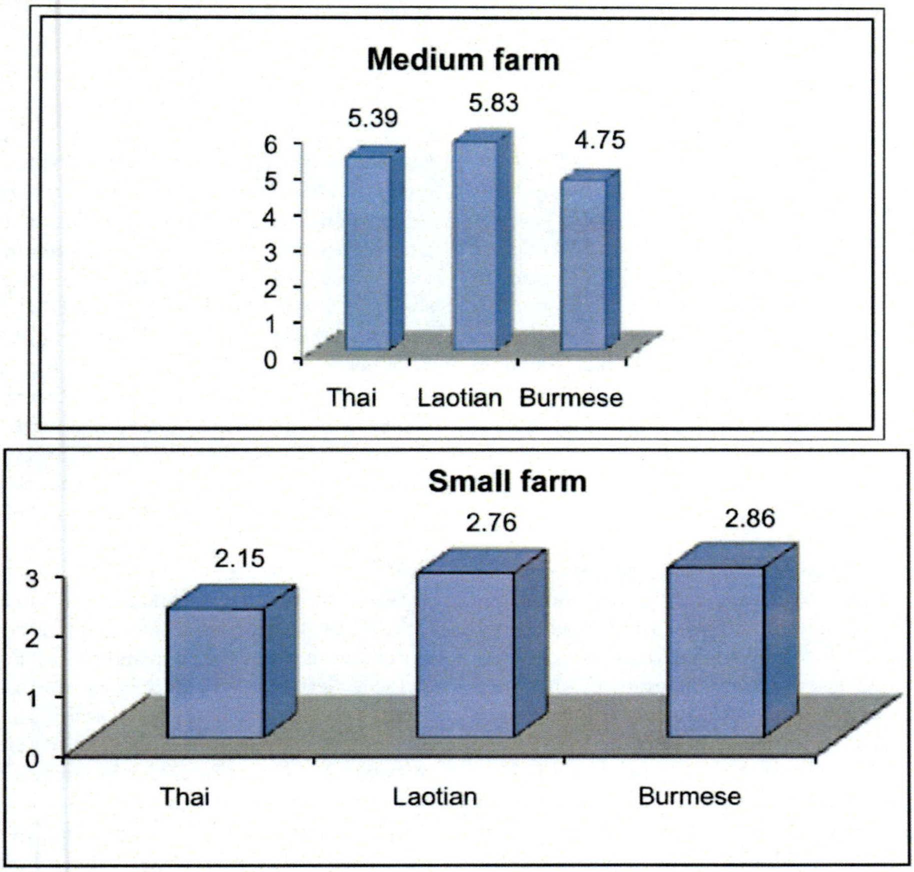

in table 14.2. Due to the lower number of ponds in small-scale farms, family and kin usually undertake hands-on management of the farms, but some migrant workers are also hired.

Interviews revealed that large farm operators hire mainly Thai men from the northeast of Thailand. Medium and small farm operators, on the other hand, hire Burmese and Laotian migrant workers, many of whom are couples. Mr Srisuban, an owner of a large farm, remarked:

> Actually, a Burmese wage is cheaper. But if we hire Burmese workers, they should be legal, not smuggled. However, hiring Thais...hmm...can also be difficult. They return to the northeast during Songkran (Thai New Year) holidays, so we are left without workers. Some farm owners I know don't want to hire Thais, especially from the southern region, since this is the area of shrimp trade outlets. These workers can steal the shrimp from us and bring them there since they know their way around.

In the same interview, another farm owner added, "Some employers prefer to hire the Burmese. They are usually afraid of being arrested, so they don't roam about and this is good for the shrimp farm." A farm owner from Jaidee Farm also expressed his preference for Burmese workers, pointing out that if the employer is fair; the Burmese are generally grateful and diligent. "They do not drink like the Laotians or the Thais since they are a very religious people and pray a lot", he remarked.

From a survey of 154 small and medium type farms[13] in Ganjanadit and Punpin districts, by other researchers in the larger project, the number of migrant workers appears to be actually higher than

13 The total number of surveyed farms was 214 as mentioned in the methodology section. The number of medium and small-sized farms was 154.

the number of Thai workers in aggregate terms. Figure 14.2 show this pattern.

Most workers in these farms are migrant couples, and this is not a coincidence. Cultural and economic processes intersect as shrimp farms in Surat Thani evolve into an emerging migrant niche in South Thailand. Farm employers and migrant workers continue to produce and re-employ meanings around technology-intensive work that serve to sustain shrimp farming as a viable source of profit from global and domestic trade. Unlike others who have studied migrant identities with reference to an ethnic group, place of origin, or nationality that effects or pervades trans-local or trans-national identities, we will view the migrants under study through their worker identities produced by concrete social practices and discourses (Yeoh/Willis/Abdul Khader Fakhri. 2003; Toyota 2003).

14.4.1 The Production of Place

Surat Thani's shrimp farms have become migrant enclaves of a distinct type, exemplifying the notion that "place itself is a *process* that makes and is made by migration" [italics added for emphasis] (Silvey 2006). All Thai, Burmese and Laotian migrants in the Surat Thani farms under study are working couples. Most of these couples are at a stage in their life where there is motivation to 'start up', that is, generate savings for the future and secure a place to live albeit temporarily and away from places of origin. Many of these couples also have small children. Table 14.3 presents differences in civil status according to nationality among the sampled migrant workers.

Table 14.3: Civil status of migrant workers by nationality on small and medium shrimp farms, Surat Thani Province. **Source:** Authors' Survey (2007).

	Thai (%)	Laotians (%)	Burmese (%)	Total
Married	32 (30%)	28 (26%)	47 (44%)	107 (100%)
Living together	10 (25%)	17 (42%)	13 (33%)	40 (100%)
Single	0	0	0	0
Total	42 (29%)	45 (31%)	60 (40%)	147 (100%)

Migrant couples disclosed that many of them met, began to live together and/or married each other elsewhere in Thailand, or in their places of origin. They then travelled south to settle and work on one of Surat Thani's shrimp farms. Almost unanimously, migrants acceded to the fact that living and working on a shrimp farm was comfortable, and allowed them to live together as a couple.

A Laotian couple from Mooring Ta Kag, close to the Thai border, have worked on a shrimp farm for two years. Mod said that she and her partner, Boontawee, arrived at Surat Thani, a month apart. "I came later so that he could first find us a home. He found work here on the shrimp farm, where we could also stay." During the slack season immediately after the harvest, their boss employs Boontawee in his factory. Boontawee prefers this arrangement instead of working for a construction firm like other Laotians he knows. "It is quite good to live and work here. I feel as though I am staying at home. Working for a construction firm is difficult since you need to move from place to place. It may be all right if you only have your wife with you. It will never work since we have a child."

Ta, a shrimp farm worker from Northeast Thailand, recalls that prior to settling in Surat Thani, she worked as a domestic in Bangkok for a year and a half. She left her workplace after she met her boyfriend: "so I moved here to live with him. We met in Cha-am (3 hours south of Bangkok) where he was working on a shrimp farm and we later married in Nakonpanom our hometown, just prior to coming to work in Surat Thani." As a domestic, Ta used to receive a monthly pay of 4,500 baht, a little less than what she is currently receiving as a shrimp farm worker (only 5,000 baht, which she has to share with her husband). She reasons: "If I didn't marry I wouldn't have quit my job in Bangkok. But living on this farm with my husband is not bad at all because the cost of living is low. We are given rice and gas, so I can still send some money home to my parents in Nakonpanom." In Surat Thani, she did not attempt to apply for a job as a domestic since, as she pointedly says, "It's not good because we are a couple."

Sorn is from Ubon Ratchathani, or the Isan region in Northeast Thailand. She also worked as a domestic in Bangkok, married her boyfriend, and moved to Don Suk, where he worked in commercial fishing. They later moved to Surat Thani, working on a shrimp farm for the last two years. She thinks Surat Thani is a better place for her: "Here we have a place to stay and we both earn, at the same time, we have a baby. I only help my husband so I have time to care for the baby. That would not have been possible in

Don Suk, since I was not earning – only my husband [was]."

Tai, a Burmese female worker says, "If a woman is single, she has no choice but to work in a rubber plantation, be a merchant, or work in a store, since she has no husband." Her husband, Seng, adds, "Women cannot work on shrimp farms, only men can. But they can stay with their husbands and help with the housework." His wife, Tai, informed us that she and her husband work on the shrimp farm "for the price of one worker." In the same conversation, another Burmese female worker, Teem, counters that on the shrimp farm, "We are comfortable. We pray a lot, do the laundry and sweep our houses and the owner's as well."

Owners of small and medium type farms prefer to hire couples because they feel assured of a greater sense of responsibility from these worker-couples than from single women or men. In their view, couples work together to stay together. Interviews also revealed that due to the precariousness of shrimp farming – the risks of theft, and needs for regular feeding and close monitoring of shrimp health, water quality and temperature – farm owners are inclined to hire couples who can easily take turns to do the work and can flexibly share these tasks. These farms do not require a huge workforce but can afford to employ couples or small families to live within their farm compounds to keep round-the-clock watch over the ponds. One farm owner remarked, "I prefer to hire a good, reliable male worker who can watch and care for the ponds and have his wife with him to make sure that he is not lonely so that he does not go on drinking bouts with other workers." Owners of large farms, on the other hand, prefer to hire individual male workers to operate and maintain the numerous pieces of equipment and infrastructure on their farms. They are provided individual living quarters on the farm compounds where they are subjected to a more corporate regimen of labour control and management. Women may not live on these premises.

A number of migrant couples on small and medium size farms have young children. This, however, is temporary as when the children reach school age, they are sent back home. Table 14.4 shows that most workers do not have their children living with them on the farm.

Farm owners restrain workers from keeping too many children in the compounds, to avoid crowding, disturbances at work, and accidents in ponds. Female workers are relatively freer to travel to visit their older, left-behind children, since husbands are responsible for the farm work much more than their female partners who are largely considered secondary work hands (to be discussed later). As migrants, women also experience the 'friction of distance' from children differently than do men, thus they take principal responsibility for their children even from a distance (Hanson/Pratt 1995). For instance, they take it upon themselves to remit earnings to caretaker relatives at home for their children.[14]

Table 14.4: Number of children of migrant workers living on shrimp farms, Surat Thani. **Source:** Authors' Survey.

Number of children living in the shrimp farm	Frequency	%
0	66	45
1	59	40
2	22	15
Total	147	100

Migrants and employers have created small and medium type shrimp farms collectively as a place where workers can lead their lives as couples, simultaneously residing and earning a living, yet mostly without their children. The absence of children is a stark reminder that the migrants continue to live in flux, as migrants-in-temporary-settlement, while the overriding concern of employers for acquiescing to the conjugal arrangement is primarily to employ a distinct, work- and-cost-efficient pool of workers who can provide high productivity for the markets. Studies of women workers and labour markets, notably by Hanson and Pratt (1995), demonstrate the spatial terms by which women select their jobs due to childcare obligations. The migrant workers in this study prefer locations where they can earn a living and keep their small children by them. Indeed, employers and migrant workers unwittingly coalesce behind a particular organization of conjugal labour, premised on the need for a couple's intimacy and proximity for economic production, built into the constitution of shrimp farms as a distinct migrant niche and place for working couples.

14 Paying for a broker who can physically bring money to their families left behind is common especially for Burmese and Laotian women.

14.4.2 The Production of Identity: A Worker vs. 'Not a Real Worker'

Feminists in different disciplines have explored the ways gender inflects the meaning, representation, and experience of work (Hanson/Pratt 1995; Mohanty 1997; McDowell 1998; Phillips 1998; Elson 1999; Lawson/Silvey 1999; Pratt 1999). "Women do not do unskilled or low-skilled jobs because they are naturally bearers of inferior labour. Rather, the jobs they do are unskilled because women enter them already determined as inferior labourers compared with male labour" (Elson/Pearson 1981). As early as the 1980's, a consciousness of the socially constructed character of female labour had provided explanations (for cheap female labour, the occupational segregation of women and their slow career mobility) that challenged biologically determined explanations. Butler (1990) adds to the conundrum on women's work, drawing attention to the idea that female work identity does not precondition work, but is an effect of it. Butler's argument is thus substantially at odds with earlier deterministic notions of gender on labour, and the *a priori* gender-typing of jobs. Gendered work in our analysis is formed by particular conditions and practices that materialize 'gender', making it appear fixed, natural and common sense while actually it is iterative, negotiated and contingent (Nightingale 2006; Risseeuw 1989). A number of interviews with farm owners and workers reveal this aspect clearly. Below some of these interviews are presented in full to demonstrate the nature of the discursive and behavioural practices that materialize gender.

> "Working on a shrimp farm is too laborious for a woman. A male worker is more agile. A female worker mostly works in the 'store' – meaning doing administrative work. On our farm, we have about 30 per cent female workers. But on small farms, the proportion of female to male workers is probably one to one," explains Mr Srisuban, owner of a large shrimp farm.

Interview 1: with Deam, a female Burmese worker on Mr Chai's shrimp farm:

Interviewer: For how long have you been working on Mr Chai's farm?
Deam: Three years.
Interviewer: Did you come to Surat Thani directly from Myanmar?
Deam: Yes, but I worked in the city first. I was in a factory that sorted out fish for export.
Interviewer: Why did you leave your work in the city?
Deam: I got married.
Interviewer: How many ponds are you responsible for?
Deam: Only one pond. I help my husband with his work on the pond.
Interviewer: Do you get paid separately by Mr Chai?
Deam: No, only my husband receives a salary. Wives are 'not real workers' (*ah lote tha marr a sit ma hote par*).

Interview 2 with Ae, a female Lao worker from Khun Thong:

Interviewer: How much salary do you receive?
Ae: 7,000 baht. My husband and I receive this amount.
Interviewer: How many ponds are you responsible for?
Ae: Two ponds.
Interviewer: How much will you get if you take care of one pond?
Ae: 4,000 baht. They used to give us 6,700 baht for two ponds.
Interviewer: Are there single people working here?
Ae: No, only people who have families or are married.
Interviewer: If a family quits, will the owner hire a family again?
Ae: Yes.
Interviewer: What is your duty here?
Ae: Feeding the shrimp. Helping my husband with the motor of the aerator. Cleaning the office of our boss.
Interviewer: Does your husband also clean the office of your boss?
Ae: No, only women here do that.

Couples who work on the shrimp farms often receive a 'couple wage', not the sum of two individual wages. Some owners pay the working couples for every pond they care for. For instance, Mu, a Burmese female worker, compares working on a palmsugar farm to working on a shrimp farm:

> A family or a couple can also live on a palm farm together. But the wife is only paid when she does actual work on the palmsugar farm. Here on the shrimp farm, we are paid per pond. So even if I only help my husband, I still get paid. We get paid together.

Table 14.5 presents the responses of 143 female workers when asked whether they receive a separate wage from their husbands.

Table 14.5 indicates that most female Burmese workers do not receive a separate wage from their em-

Table 14.5: Female workers' receipt of a separate wage by nationality. **Source:** Authors' Interviews.

Do you receive a s eparate wage from your husband?	Thai (%)	Laotians (%)	Burmese (%)	Total (%)
Yes	26 (58%)	12 (27%)	7 (15%)	45 (100%)
No	16 (16%)	32 (33%)	50 (51%)	98 (100%)
Total	42 (29%)	44 (31%)	57 (40%)	143 (100%)

ployers, whereas most Thai female workers do. The data invites us to conclude that the nature of work performed on shrimp farms differentiates between women and men, and evidently, nationalities and legal status.[15] Instituting a couple wage and public admissions of gender-specific work and capacities produce and reproduce coherent identities of women as 'not real workers'. These serve as discursive and material means by which differentiated identities and social places of workers come to cohere as fixed and indisputable, thus further cementing differences and inequalities between women and men.

Indeed, conscious of being 'not real workers', the women nonetheless both know and try to rework their social place, in order to negotiate and promote their own purposive goals (Brunt 1992; Villareal 1992; Williams 2005). It is in the interstices between accepting and resisting their identity as 'not real workers' that they are able to create latitude for exploring multiple livelihoods apart from their present one, and to perform social reproductive obligations, especially childcare.

Although paid a separate wage, trans-local female migrants from northeast Thailand are not considered 'real workers' (*mai chai khon ngan*) either. This identity provides them with room to manoeuvre to engage in multi-local livelihoods, as they are generally mobile and are able to juggle shrimp farming with other livelihoods. Twenty-two year-old Sorn, who has been working on a shrimp farm for the last three years, says that after the shrimp harvest, she joins work teams on nearby house construction sites. "They pay us a bit more than 100 baht per day", she said. However, Sorn admits that being a brick layer is not sufficient livelihood and so after the slack period of shrimp farming, she resumes her work on the farm with her husband, who earns a bit more from his work at the farm than she does. Sorn, then, is less dependent on shrimp farm work since she does not place her shrimp farm worker status on equal terms as her husband, making it possible for her to explore multiple jobs.

Unlike Thais from the northeast, who explore supplementary sources of income, some Laotian female migrants prefer to stay with their husbands on the shrimp farms. A number of them bring their children. They capitalize on 'not being a real worker' (*bor man kam ma kone*) to attend to their childcare duties, although this is not the only reason why they have opted for singular jobs. The following conversation details a worker's experiences.

Interview 3 with Mod, Laotian female worker:

Interviewer: You've been working here for two years. Have you ever worked elsewhere in Surat Thani, or taken up other jobs while working here at the shrimp farm?
Mod: Never, only here.
Interviewer: Does the employer pay workers per person or per pond?
Mod: They pay per couple. Each couple receives 5,000 baht.
Interviewer: Is there anything else they provide?
Mod: Rice is free. But I have to pay for the fuel, water and electricity.
Interviewer: Would you be interested in being a domestic while working for the shrimp farm with your husband?
Mod: I cannot do other work since I have a child.
Interviewer: What is your work here?
Mod: Most of the time I do housework for the owner and take care of my child.
Interviewer: While your husband works on the pond?
Mod: Yes.

For Burmese female transnational migrants, "not being a 'real worker'" (*ah lote tha marr a sit ma hote par*) serves to tie them more firmly to their husbands who work as bonded labourers on shrimp farms, due to the mobility limitations posed by their legal statuses in Thailand. Compared with other types of mi-

15 This may be largely due to better platforms for negotiation by Thai workers – an altogether important yet separate issue that deserves discussion elsewhere.

Table 14.6: Supplementary jobs of female workers simultaneous with shrimp farming by nationality. **Source:** Authors' Survey (2007).

	Thai (%)	Laotians (%)	Burmese (%)	Total (%)
Had a second job/livelihood while being a shrimp farm worker	14 (47%)	9 (30%)	7 (23%)	30 (100%)
Never had a second job/livelihood while being a shrimp farm worker	27 (24%)	34 (30%)	53 (46%)	114 (100%)
Total	41 (28%)	43 (30 %)	60 (42%)	144 (100%)

grant workers, Burmese migrants are highly dependent on their individual farm employers for their legal status and livelihood security. The new migration policy in Thailand that requires both employers and workers to jointly register and pay government fees has tied both workers and employers to each other. As Teem's husband says resentfully:

> If we have a working license, it is usually kept by our boss. He is afraid that his employees will leave and go elsewhere. You see if any one of us is questioned or arrested by the police, our boss will be in trouble. Thai people are the headmen here, while the Burmese people are the workers.

When queried on whether they would seek second jobs, a number of Burmese female workers responded:

Dao: The boss will not allow. The boss says that a good employee is hard to find.

Tik: No, I must ask my husband first.

Aye: The boss allows me to take up a job when I don't have work. But I don't go. I don't have a legal ID.

Oma: I worked in a seafood factory when I was single. But now, I do not search for other work since my husband will not allow me. I concentrate on my work here, that is, washing, cooking and sometimes feeding the shrimp.

As shown in table 14.6, among the three groups of migrants, Burmese female migrants do not usually take up supplementary jobs compared with Thais and Laotians.

'Not being a real worker' has translated into diverse practices and strategies by Thai, Laotian and Burmese female migrants. Circumstances have also enabled or constrained these practices. In particular, authorities usually overlook the presence of Lao migrants since they tend to blend well with the local population due to their ability to speak Lao-Thai, whereas the Burmese emerge more visibly as culturally distinct and they have a record of being irregular migrants in Thailand. These practices differentiate them as migrant national subjects based on the extent of their 'bondedness' to their employers, often determined by legal immigration policies. Differentiated employment conditions, legal regulatory structures, and possibly, perceived marital norms circumscribe the latitude that migrant women have to secure their livelihoods and perform their reproductive obligations. Yet, as agents fully aware of their social place, they navigate their lives with dexterity, using their status to attain livelihood and reproductive security, albeit short-term and largely irregular.

14.5 Conclusion

This chapter has analysed the experiences of people who migrate as couples to work in a major export industry in Thailand and illustrates how the diverse relationships with, and meanings within, the workplace have emerged through gender and identity practices. By placing social practices that produce gender subjects and their ontological differences at the centre of our analysis, the chapter has revealed the finer aspects of subject positions available to women through labour practices and migration processes.

For migrant couples from Northeast Thailand, Laos and Burma, the shrimp farms are a conjugal comfort zone – a temporary fix in the flux of their mobile migrant lives, where they can both reside and earn a living. For shrimp farm owners, especially those of small and medium size farms, employing migrant couples is preferable since by paying the lower cost of a couple's wages, they have a flexible work team of two persons attending to the delicate and round-the-clock monitoring of shrimp ponds. The creation of 'place' as niche for temporary migrant workers is layered with different rationalities, the conjugal requirements of couples to stay intimately together while earning a living and employers' labour efficiency target. Creation of the female worker subject, publicly categorized as 'not a real worker' through the couple wage, further differentiates the conjugal workforce. By paying a 'couple wage' to migrants, employers recreate and solidify discourses on the work and labour capacities that differentiate women and men on shrimp farms. This discourse, however, does not face opposition as women workers themselves reproduce it. Female workers employ and invoke their status to achieve certain ends, such as exploring supplementary income sources as well as expanding latitude for the care of young children while still being virtually on the farm's payroll. Women workers' enactments of 'not being a real worker' create, reproduce and differentiate migrant national subjects and relations of inequality.

Düvell's (2004: 205) view on political economy, as being founded on the politics of differences that can be translated into different systems of rights, remains valid. Our case shows how immigration status, labour policies, attitudes of farm owners and migrants' behaviour do interact in ways that have consequences for practices of labour control, affecting wage levels and workers' well being. In addition, the production of place and, concurrently, of subject identities (gender and migrant) that occurs through the labour process plays a significant role in ensuring conformity. Indeed, the purported 'Kitchen of the World' is premised not only on huge investments of capital, science and infrastructure, but equally on cultural and discursive practices steered towards profit maximization to lend support to a coherent organization of largely cheap, bonded and gendered migrant labour.

15 Changing Identities, Multi-local Politics and Citizenship: Reflections on the Agency of Migrants from Indonesia and their Descendants in the Netherlands

Ton van Naerssen

15.1 Introduction[1]

Studies on intergenerational identities of migrant groups - who originate from Indonesia and have been resident in the Netherlands for more than half a century - focus on the issue of their integration in Dutch society while maintaining their own but changing identities over generations. The change in identities is explained by the interplay between migrant policies in the country of settlement and shifts in the socio-economic and family positions of migrant generations, for example intermarriage with native Dutch (de la Croix/Dumpel/van Naerssen/Portier 2006; de Vries 2009; Rinsampessy 2008; van Leeuwen 2008). Some studies have compared the experiences of the two largest migrant groups from Indonesia, the *Indisch Dutch* or *Indo's* from mixed Asian and European descent[2] and the Moluccans, stressing differences in the expectations of the immigrants and the reception in the country of arrival (Bosma 2009; van Amersfoort/van Niekerk 2006).

This chapter elaborates on the same themes as it focuses on the identities of migrants from Indonesia spanning over three generations and explicitly compares the two migrant groups. However, contrary to the previous studies, the themes reside within the context of socio-political changes and events in *both* the country of settlement and the country of origin. The underlying proposition is that the formation of migrants' identities can better be understood by using a transnational perspective (Levitt/Waters 2002; Levitt/Glick/Schiller 2004). It is argued that multi-local politics and the politics of international relations between the country of origin and the receiving country have inter-generational impacts that extend beyond the first generation. In particular, attention is paid to the ability of migrants and their descendants to respond to and to be able to change policies in their country of settlement and of origin. This chapter also differs from earlier studies by including the migration-development nexus and citizenship into the debate. The emergence of the migration-development nexus is acknowledged as a new space for the construction of meanings and practices that add new dimensions to the formation of migrant descendants' identities, including the meaning of their citizenship.

Examining the major activities and associations of the Eurasians and the Moluccans over three generations in the Netherlands shows that the contents and meanings of their identities are continuous, fluid and dynamic (de la Croix/Dumpel/van Naerssen/Portier 2006; de Vries 2009; Rinsampessy 2008; van Leeuwen 2008). The first and largest migrant group, the Eurasians, defines its citizenship as belonging to the Dutch nation-state. The second group, the Moluccans, seem to have a pervasive ambivalence among migrants of third generations towards the notion of citizenship and the nation-state, as well as more pronounced elements of transnational connections with the region of origin, the Moluccas (also called the Moluccan Islands). Understanding the formation of migrants' identities as co-created by migrants and the socio-cultural and political environment may help us to grasp the contextual and nuanced differences between the two groups.

1 The author wants to thank the anonymous reviewers for their comments on the first drafts of this contribution.

2 In other words, they are Eurasians. Most of them bear European family names. Their history can be traced back to the 17th century (Bosma/Raben 2003). Note that the *Indies Dutch* are different from other European repatriates such as the *pied noirs* and the *retornados* in respectively France and Portugal, since in the colonies of these countries less intermarriage between different ethnic groups had taken place (Smith 2003: 14-15, 22-23).

T.-D. Truong and D. Gasper (eds.), *Transnational Migration and Human Security*, Hexagon Series on Human and Environmental Security and Peace 6, DOI 10.1007/978-3-642-12757-1_15, © Springer-Verlag Berlin Heidelberg 2011

15.2 Theorizing Migrants' Identities and Transnational Connections

The main body of literature on intergenerational identity formation among migrant communities addresses issues concerning the second generation. A generally accepted idea is that contrary to the first generation that purportedly brings its identity to the country of destination, the second-generation migrant has to constitute an identity for itself. Portes' studies of 2nd generation *Latinos* in the US are representative of this view (1995, 1996). In an extensive longitudinal research on adaptation patterns, trajectories and social mobility of second-generation migrants, Portes and Rumbaud (1996) concluded that both upward and downward social mobility are part of adaptation patterns. In the latter case, the second generation adapts to the underclass in poor urban areas of the US. However, upward mobility is also significant; hence, they argued that *segmented assimilation* processes take place.

Levitt and Waters (2002) connected assimilation processes to transnationalism and argued that "although it is unlikely that the children of immigrants will be involved in their ancestral homes with the same frequency and intensity as their parents, the extent to which they will engage in transnational practices is still an open question" (2002: 2). An important aspect of these practices are the private (family) and development-oriented remittances (small-scale and locally situated economic and welfare development projects) to the countries and regions of origin. In this vein, the emergence of the migration-development nexus in policy circles (Nyberg-Sørensen/van Haer/Engberg-Pedersen 2002) has led many studies to focus on the positive role of migrants in development processes in countries of origin through remittances, knowledge transfer, investments and initiating trade (van Naerssen/Spaan/Zoomers 2008). An example of an in-depth study on the impact of remittances on a regional economy is a study by de Haas (2003) on the socio-economic impact of out-migration in the Todgha Oasis Valley in Morocco. He concluded that out-migration has led to a substantial improvement in the living conditions and new local economic activities in the region. Kabki (2007) and Smith (2007) each make an explicit link with transnationalism in their studies on the impact of remittances on both the countryside and the urban environment (Accra) in Ghana. In a general overview, Adams and Page (2005) reached the conclusion that a ten per cent increase in per capita official international remittances will (on the average) lead to a 3.5 per cent decline of people living in poverty.

Remittances by individual migrants to their families at home, who use the money for food, consumer goods, education of children, construction and small business enterprises, attract most of the attention. The migration-development nexus as a space for constructing meanings and practices, however, also embraces remittances used for small development projects such as schools and health clinics, the transfer of knowledge, skills and ideas, investments in private businesses and support to political movements. Thus, migrants initiate what Farrant/MacDonald/Sriskandarajah (2006) have called *diasporic flows*, consisting of a triad of knowledge, investment and trade that has a direct and visible impact on the economic development in countries of origin.[3] These flows exist because migrants and, to a greater or lesser degree depending on the specific context and history, their descendants maintain social relations in the regions or countries of origin. In the formal language of the United Nations, it is now commonly accepted that migrants of different types (diasporas, circular and return migrants) transfer knowledge, offer access to capital and information for companies, constitute markets that would otherwise not exist, and are a source of tourism (United Nations 2006; World Bank 2006; UNDP 2009).

While still embedded in transnational networks, migrants also establish their own social networks in the settlement countries. They create formal and informal ethnic, national or regional organizations to 'feel at home away from home' and to accommodate and facilitate the arrival and stay of newcomers in a foreign and largely unknown environment. The organizations usually aim at socializing in the countries of settlement, but members bring their transnational networks with them and these help establish linkages with areas of origin. In time, collectively contributing to development at home becomes an explicit goal of some of the organizations, which then commit themselves to small-scale development projects and programmes in education, health and infrastructure in the communities and regions of origin. Migrants

3 While the mainstream in the current discourse on the migration-development nexus stresses the positive impact of the diasporic flows, one should note that the concept of development remains often undefined and that more empirical evidence about the assumed positive effects is needed especially regarding sustainability aspects (van Naerssen/Spaan/Zoomers 2008: 8, 15-16).

might also collectively contribute through knowledge transfer (Meyer/Brown 1999), among other ways by temporary return of skilled people.

Individual migrants contribute to economic development through family remittances but they can also play an important role in social change by consciously or unconsciously breaking through traditional customs and taboos, for example, by promoting the emancipation of women and minority groups in countries of origin. Collectively, through their *transnational community organizations* (TCOs) migrants also strive to encourage political debates and democracy and to strengthen civil society through sustaining local organizations in the countries of origin.[4] The direct role of TCOs in home politics is more problematic and contentious, as for example analysed by Ellis and Zafar Khan (2002) for the Kashmiri migrant and Oestergaard-Nielsen (2002) in the case of the homeland politics of Kurds in Germany. This role builds on a tradition (Sheffer 1986) and, in the case of TCOs involved in human rights advocacy at home, in Western Europe its roots go back to the Third World movement of the mid-1960's and 1970's.[5] This tradition continues through the current interest in the role of TCOs in conflict interventions and peace initiatives (Nyberg-Sørensen/van Haer/Engberg-Pedersen 2002; University for Peace 2006)[6].

National governments have discovered that they can use the development potential of their migrant (also former) citizens. Increasingly, home governments are capitalizing on migrant initiatives and multilateral organizations that widely propagate 'good practices' support them. As far as the economy is concerned many developing countries now appreciate the role of TCOs. Previously, emigrants and their immediate descendants were looked upon as traitors but they are now considered as compatriots living abroad. There is thus a change in attitude in countries as diverse as Vietnam, the Philippines, India, Cape Verde and Kenya. International migration is regarded as a major instrument of national economic development, in which a combination of migration, remittances, brain-gain, government and organized migrant support might substantially contribute to economic growth in countries of the South. Interestingly, the concepts of nation and territory are increasingly becoming less intertwined, as expressed in the Philippine concept of the 'Global Nation' and the option of double citizenships in such countries as Argentina, Morocco and Turkey.

15.3 Identity Formation among Migrants from Indonesia in the Netherlands

In 2008, the population of the Netherlands was about 16.5 million persons. Of these, some 1.7 million were born abroad and 3.3 million were considered *allochtonen*; a term that comes close to but differs from words such as aliens, immigrants and foreigners. In the Netherlands it indicates that a person or one of his or her parents was born outside the country; there is no difference whether this person is a Dutch passport holder or not. Other Dutch are called *autochtonen*, which translates as indigenous or natives. The introduction of the notion of *allochtones* in the debates on international migration issues in the Netherlands was originally to facilitate affirmative actions on behalf of migrants and to support the creation of a multicultural society. However, around 2000 with rising anti-immigrant and anti-Islamic sentiments within Dutch society, the expression *allochtones* became a derogatory concept to many immigrants and their descendants. In their view, it implies that they are not fully recognized as Dutch citizens, since even if they possess Dutch nationality, as the majority of them do, they are considered different from 'real Dutch'.[7]

Migrants and their descendants from Indonesia constitute the largest group of the Dutch *allochtones*. They entered the Netherlands shortly after the Second World War, during and after the Indonesian struggle for independence.[8] Some 300,000 people with the status of 'European' in colonial Dutch East Indies, about half of whom were Indisch Dutch of

4 The expression '*transnational community organizations*' (TCOs) is preferred to the notions of 'migrant' or 'diaspora' organizations because the organizations concerned do not, in general, encompass migrants only but their descendants and members of the native population such as spouses, friends and sympathizers. A diaspora normally concerns an entire ethnic group living abroad regardless of the length of stay in the country of settlement, which could be for centuries (Jewish and Armenian diasporas for example). TCOs comprise two or three generations and their members live, mentally as well as behaviourally, in two countries and are thus transnational although to varying degrees.

5 As the author can testify, since he was involved in activities of TCOs advocating and lobbying for human rights in various Southeast Asian countries from 1965-1995.

6 University for Peace, 2006: "Capacity Building for Peace and Development: Roles of Migrant", Final Report Expert Forum Migrant Conference 2006, 19-20 October (Toronto: University for Peace): Mimeo.

mixed ethnic origin[9] and soldiers in service of the colonial army, many of them from the Moluccas, left Indonesia. Although for many of the Indisch Dutch it was the first time they had ever been to the Netherlands, in general they are considered as repatriates rather than refugees[10] (Willems 2001: 332), since the latter usually have nationalities that differ from the people in the country of settlement. The Moluccans were soldiers in the Dutch army and came to the Netherlands on army orders.[11] They were opposed to the unitary Indonesian Republic and wanted to return to the Moluccas after the intended establishment of an independent *Republik Maluku Selatan* (RMS; South Moluccan Republic). Like other ethnic groups in the archipelago, interrelations, similarities and differences existed between the Indisch Dutch and the Moluccans, but as we will see, the variation in reception in the Netherlands accentuated and strengthened the differences.

The Indisch Dutch and their descendants currently number around 500,000. They consider themselves Dutch although with (traces of) a mixed, hybrid and transnational culture that came into existence near the end of the 19th century (Bosma 2005). Hence, there was a sense of Indisch Dutch ethnicity. Once they arrived in the Netherlands, they had no wish to return or were not able to do so because of the political and economic circumstances in Indonesia and the tense relations between the two countries up to the mid-1960's.[12] On the other hand, the Moluccan group initially considered themselves as temporary guests in the Netherlands, as they expected to return to the Moluccas after the establishment of the South Moluccan Republic. However, this Republic never came about in an independent Indonesia and they had to stay in the Netherlands, where their current number is estimated at some 50,000 (Rinsampessy 2008: 16, 323).[13] Including young children, both groups now consist of four or five generations. They have their own associations that substantially differ in activities and character. Immigrants do not constitute homogenous groups and, particularly among the Indisch Dutch, many will not consider ethnicity as important to their identity in Dutch society. However, for the third generation of Moluccans, their ethnicity and the region of origin are still important.

15.3.1 The Indisch Dutch

Policymakers consider the integration of the Indisch Dutch in the Netherlands a successful case of assimilation and smooth absorption into the larger society. A quarter of a century after their arrival and contrary to the initial expectations, they were relatively easily absorbed in the Dutch labour market. On average, the Indisch Dutch were less skilled and educated than *autochthones* and the majority of them became lower skilled workers and employees in government services, the same positions they occupied in the former Dutch East Indies. The migrants' belief that there was 'no way back' facilitated assimilation. Vice versa, once the Dutch government realized that the deteriorating political relations between the Netherlands and Indonesia prevented return migration, "....politically as well as ideologically, tolerance and acceptance were stressed" (Willems 2001: 332). Knowledge of the Dutch language and the Christian background of most of the migrants were also favourable to the assimilation process.

The relatively quiet path followed by the integration process is the major reason why, in a report on ethnic minorities of the Ministry of Home Affairs in 1981, no mention was made of the Indisch Dutch (Ministerie van Binnenlandse Zaken 1981). In other words, the report assumed that they had lost their specific *mestizo* culture and ethnic identity. However, there were efforts to preserve ethnic identity as demonstrated by the existence of Indisch Dutch organiza-

7 Based on personal communication. The author is member of the Global Society Foundation (SMS), a meeting point for refugee and migrant associations. SMS prefers the term New Dutch (www.sms-vluchtelingen.nl/english), which recently was adopted by the Minister for Integration in his "Integration Letter" to the Dutch Parliament (www.vrom.nl/). *NRC Handelsblad*, 7 November 2009: 1, headlined "Minister: *Integratie is voor een groot deel geslaagd*" ("Minister: Integration for a large part has succeeded"). Also see at: <www.buitenlandsepartner.nl/forum> for a discussion on the term.

8 In the 1960's, smaller groups consisted of Papuans, refugees from West Papua (*Irian Barat*) that became part of Indonesia, and Indonesian political refugees after the *coup d'état* of 1965.

9 The Indisch Dutch belongs to a larger group of immigrants, comprising also ethnic Dutch and Indonesians.

10 For an exception, see Ex (1966).

11 According to Smeets/Steijlen (2006: 64-68), the matter is more complex but here I follow the opinion of most of the Moluccans in the Netherlands.

12 But some 50,000 re-migrated to the United States; specifically to California and 7,000 went to Australia (Willems 2001: chap. 10 and 11).

13 Although Beets/Walhout/Koesoebjono (2002) estimated their number at 40,000 at the beginning of the 21st century.

tions, the popularity of the widely read periodical *Tong Tong* (in the Dutch East Indies this was a hanging wooden block beaten for announcements)[14] and the activities of its vocal chief editor Jan Boon (1911–1974).[15] In fact, many members of this model-assimilated group maintained major characteristics of their cultural background.

In the mid-1960's, Ex asked his Indisch Dutch respondents for their opinion of the native Dutch:

> They're freer than we are in their relations with others. They are often tactless in what they say and sometimes downright rude. They lack courtesy, especially towards women, and their lack of respect for superiors is very noticeable. Whatever they are thinking and feeling, they are speaking it out loud, while we conceal it all; it's part of our Eastern mentality, I suppose (Ex 1966: 42).

This quote represented general opinion among the Indisch Dutch fairly. Moreover, as Dumasy, second-generation Indisch Dutch, born in 1948, recalled, "I learned from childhood to think in terms of 'us' and 'them'. Our Indo-European group was different from the Dutch group and again different from the Indonesian group" (2007: 58). This feeling was not only culturally related but was also an inheritance of the socio-economic position of Eurasians in the former Dutch East Indies, where they were considered inferior to the thoroughbred Dutch and superior to the native Indonesians. In the Netherlands, much of what was preserved of the Indisch Dutch culture remained inside the homes and concerned matters such as food, the importance of the grandparents and parents in family life, the way of receiving guests, and the belief in the supernatural. In due time these were mixed with typically Dutch customs, for example the celebration of St. Nicolas birthday (5 December) and the placing of a decorated conifer tree in the living room during the Christmas period. One can indeed say that the concept of a hybrid migrant or postcolonial culture also applied to the Indisch Dutch.

However, there were few public signs of the Indo culture. The most visible one was the yearly event *Pasar Malam Besar* (the Great Night Market) in The Hague that currently continues under the name *Tong Tong Fair*. The *Pasar Malam Besar* started in 1959 and developed from a rather restricted ethnic event coloured by homesickness into a 10-day event with cultural shows of invited guests from Indonesia and other Southeast Asian countries and tens of thousands of visitors. Today many *autochthones* visit the market too, if only because of the food. It is a transnational and culturally hybrid phenomenon. The Indisch Dutch also claim to have introduced rock-and-roll to the Netherlands in the early 1960's by way of so-called 'Indo Rock' bands and they were or may still be overrepresented in badminton clubs, an extremely popular sport among the Indisch Dutch.

In the 1960's, a shift in the geopolitical context occurred. After a bloody coup d'état in 1965, Sukarno, the first president of independent Indonesia, was removed and replaced by General Suharto in 1967, who established a military dictatorship with a friendly attitude towards Western countries - especially the United States. The first-generation Indisch Dutch applauded these developments, in particular because they regarded Sukarno as having been the major actor in driving their forced migration from Indonesia. The political relations between Indonesia and the Netherlands improved, strengthening economic as well as cultural links between the two countries. Because of these developments, many Indisch Dutch started to visit the country of their birth and found similarities as well as differences with the pre-war social and cultural situation. It is not a coincidence that at the same time, the hybrid Indisch Dutch culture gained a certain nostalgia to *Tempo Doeloe* (The Good Old Times) as expressed in songs, movies and TV series. The notion of *Tempo Doeloe* refers to the colonial period around 1870–1914 in the Dutch East Indies, when Dutch private capital entered the country to establish plantations (sugar, tea, coffee) and mines (tin, bauxite, petroleum), the Dutch established their colonial rule in the whole of the Dutch East Indies and everything looked so adventurous, exotic, peaceful and relaxed.[16] However, sometimes the nostalgia embraced the entire pre-Second World War colonial period, which could be characterized as a post-colonial phenomenon, since its popularity also included many native Dutch with indirect or weak colonial ties. Thus,

14 In later years, the journal was re-named *Moesson* (Monsoon).

15 Jan Boon wrote essays and short stories under the pseudonyms of Vincent Mahieu and Tjalie Robinson. A translation of short stories has been published under the title *Hunt to Heart* (Mahieu 1995). The Dutch scholar Wim Willems published an extensive biography of Jan Boon, titled *Tjalie Robinson: Biografie van een Indo-schrijver* (Biography of an Indo-Writer) (2008).

16 For Europeans of course. It should be noted that in 1908, at the end of the *Tempo Doeloe* period, the first native political society in the Dutch East Indies, *Budi Utomo* ('Pure Endeavour') was founded. Today, Indonesia commemorates 1908 as the birth year of nationalist awakening.

it is claimed as part of the colonial heritage of the entire Dutch society (van Leeuwen 2008: 125-137).

Another new development with an impact on identity formation concerned changes within Dutch society, which impacted the demands raised and the revival of Indo self-consciousness in the 1980's, after a quarter of a century of public silence. During these 25 years, substantial numbers of new migrants entered the Netherlands, in particular Surinamese from the former colony of Dutch Guyana (South America) and Moroccan and Turkish 'guest workers'. The latter groups came to the Netherlands as low-skilled migrant labour for factory work (textile, shipbuilding) during 1964-1974 and the intention was that they would stay temporarily. However, when the factory work shifted to low-income countries and many of the labour migrants became unemployed, they preferred to stay in the Netherlands. Return migration was low and this was precisely the reason why the Ministry of Home Affairs published the minorities report in 1981. The slogan was "integration with retention of culture" and the ethnic minorities as defined by the Ministry received special provisions to realize this aim (Obdeijn/Schrover 2008: 288-293; Sleegers 2007: 9-16).

Many Indisch Dutch compared this policy with the one when they came to the Netherlands, which they perceived as forced assimilation. Thanks to the 'open society' that had developed in the Netherlands, grievances could now be voiced in public. Partly based on feelings of resentment, the first generation in particular demanded the payment of salary arrears of government employees and military due to Japanese occupation in Indonesia during the Second World War, and recognition of and compensation for suffering during the war. Among others, the intended visit of the Queen of the Netherlands to the Emperor of Japan led to an unexpected and strong reaction from the Indisch Dutch community, who recalled the traumatic events of the Japanese occupation. Since then, the Dutch state has changed its policy and supported various initiatives that made the Indisch Dutch more visible by proclaiming 15 August as Liberation Day (the day Japan surrendered) and the unveiling of an *Indisch Monument* in The Hague, commemorating the suffering in Indonesia under Japanese rule during the Second World War.

Nevertheless, this was not sufficient. A visit of the Japanese Prime Minister in July 1991 and a statement by the Dutch Prime Minister Ruud Lubbers that "it is all over" triggered new protests. The Dutch government then started discussions with a number of Indisch Dutch organizations, which were encouraged to start a common platform for negotiations. It also started to fund historical studies and granted substantial financial support to the so-called *Indisch House*, which according to the stereotype of Indisch Dutch, went bankrupt within four years due to lack of management and financial skills. In 2001, the Dutch government initiated a foundation called *Het Gebaar* ('The Gesture') to grant financial compensations of some 175 million Euros to the first generation Indisch Dutch because of the "poor reception by the Dutch government in the 1950s". The foundation also manages some 125 projects and programmes[17] (such as historical studies and a movie) initiated by members of the Indisch Dutch community.[18]

In the 1980's, a second generation of Indisch Dutch made itself visible. Alejandro Portes (1995), who studied 2nd generation *Latinos* in the USA, stated that, contrary to the first generation that has already found its identity, second-generation migrants have to create an identity for themselves. This is precisely what happened with the Indisch Dutch. The earlier quoted Dumasy (2007) expressed this as follows:

> When I was about twelve years old, I felt I was confronted with an unavoidable dilemma and had to make a choice. I had to opt either for the Indo-European culture with the promise of better relations with my family or for the Dutch culture although it could mean estrangement and loss of identity (Dumasy 2007: 66).

Dumasy opted for Dutch culture but at a later age changed his mind and in an effort to confirm his Indisch Dutch identity, studied the history of the Dutch, the Indisch Dutch and Indonesia. Like many other second generation Indisch Dutch people, he visited Indonesia several times, staying with family members and travelling through the country.

In 1984, a group of second-generation Indisch Dutch held a large demonstration in Paradiso, the centre of youth culture in Amsterdam, to assert themselves as a group with its own culture. A year earlier, the then 30-year-old artist and novelist Marion Bloem, had published her *Not an Ordinary Indisch Girl* (1983) that became a bestseller. New Indisch Dutch organizations came into existence and along with supporting the claims of the first generation[19] formulated their own political demands. In Paradiso, these were defined "in solidarity with other ethnic minority groups" (van Leeuwen 2008: 142).

---

17 The total budget was 17.5 million Euro.

18 See at: <www.gebaar.nl> for more information.

Another aspect of the second generation, stressed by de Vries (2009), concerns what she calls 'mental decolonization'. In her view, the inferiority feelings of the first generation Indisch Dutch towards the 'real Dutch', a heritage of the colonial context wherein they had lived, transferred in part to the second generation. They had to liberate themselves from feelings of subordination and to develop a more assertive attitude in the country of settlement. According to her, this mental decolonization contributed to an increased self-awareness.

Today, the Indisch Dutch does not constitute a clear-cut community within Dutch society. Measured by indicators such as levels of education, employment and intermarriage, the Indisch Dutch are well integrated in Dutch society.[20] Nevertheless, it is striking how individual members of the third generation still cherishes an Indisch identity, denoted by certain qualities such as politeness, hospitality, conflict-avoiding behaviour, taking things easily and lack of initiative. Not all of these are perceived as positive, since functioning in Dutch society requires a more assertive attitude (de la Croix/Dumpel/van Naerssen/ Portier 2006; de Vries 2009; Young/de Vries 2009).

The following quotes are from de la Croix/ Dumpel/van Naerssen/Portier 2006 who interviewed 41 second- and third- generation Indisch Dutch.[21] Robert, a third-generation male, answered the questions: "Does an *Indisch* identity exist and what is it based on" as follows.

> Yes, if you mean with identity an 'own' culture, I am convinced that an Indisch identity exists. I notice that when Indisch Dutch are sitting together they unerringly recognize each other because of a certain behaviour, appearance, and words. If such a feeling of solidarity exists then there is certainly a specific culture (de la Croix/Dumpel/van Naerssen/Portier 2006: 153).

Explaining a "typical Indisch lifestyle", Ron says:

> There exists, so to say, relaxed blood in Indisch Dutch, 'lazy blood' some people say.... Indisch Dutch don't place themselves that easily in the forefront. They are quiet, calm, think twice before they decide to be involved into certain activities (de la Croix/Dumpel/van Naerssen/Portier 2006).

Due to widespread intermarriage of their parents, many third-generation Indisch Dutch do not distinguish themselves physically from native Dutch. For example, Elisa, born in 1985, says:

> I don't consider myself as very Indisch; I have no clear Indisch appearance such as my mother. I have a good relationship with my grandfather and grandmother who live in the house below ours. It is because of them that I feel Indisch.... I am fairly proud of this feeling, it is a part of me. Some people say that I possess a number of typical Indo characteristics (de la Croix/Dumpel/van Naerssen/Portier 2006: 159).

Significantly, de Vries titled her book on second-and third-generation Indisch Dutch *Indisch is een gevoel,* which translates as "Indisch is a Feeling" (de Vries 2009).

Some third-generation Indisch Dutch like to present themselves as Asian and organize Asian and 'I love Indos' parties together with new Asian migrant groups such as second-generation Filipinos. A third-generation organization, called *Darah Ketiga* (Third Blood) started in 2001, was blaming the second generation for not asserting their Indonesian roots (Molemans 2004: 120–136). There appears one important difference with the earlier, more demanding and politically involved, Indisch Dutch organizations. Indisch identity is limited to Indo culture or as *Darah Ketiga* states on its website, "We are an independent organization meant for the preservation of Indo culture and cultural development."[22] Another youth organization, called *Nasi Idjo* ('Green Rice', in other words young, not full-grown rice) established in 2003, aims at keeping the Indisch Dutch identity alive among the younger generation. It proclaims:

> We, of the Indisch Dutch youth organization *Nasi Idjo,* are of the opinion that being Indisch Dutch has nothing to do with appearance. It doesn't matter whether you are brown, white or black, or whether you wear jeans or

19 A typical example was the unveiling of a stone to commemorate the Second World War in the Dutch East Indies, in the hometown of the author of this chapter, Nijmegen, on 14 August 2007, more than 50 years after the war. It was an initiative of second-generation Indisch Dutch people involved in the Platform of Indisch Dutch Associations in Nijmegen.

20 This does not say that the differences in these fields are completely levelled out. Until now, systematic studies do not exist but it is the author's clear impression that in higher education and political participation, the Indisch Dutch are still underrepresented.

21 The interviews were part of the book project initiated by the *Stichting Arisan Indonesia* (SARI; at: <www.stichtingsari.nl>). The Foundation is based in Gelderland province, where the interviews were carried out during the year 2004. The interviews were in-depth and with a few exceptions took place in the houses of the respondents. The authors of the book themselves are Indisch Dutch and the project received scientific backing from members of the Radboud University Nijmegen.

22 See at: <www.darahketiga.nl>.

a *sarong*.[23] No, being Indisch Dutch is about a feeling, a connection. Being Indisch Dutch is in your heart.[24]

Although some will argue that only a small minority of the Indisch Dutch occupy themselves actively with this 'optional ethnicity' (de Vries 1999: 43),[25] it is striking that, up to now, the flow of publications and initiatives to keep the Indisch Dutch identity alive continues.[26] It is also surprising how many Indisch Dutch associations still exist at the national and local level. The database Postcolonial Migrant Organisations of the International Institute of Social History (IISG) comprises more than 300 Indisch Dutch organizations, with various aims (cultural, welfare, virtual meeting place), of which 58 started in the period 2000-2009.[27]

With the normalization of relations between the Netherlands and Indonesia, remittances to Indonesia gradually surpassed the stage of family remittances and ethnic support to Indisch Dutch who had opted for Indonesian citizenship and lived in poverty in the country of origin. Transnationalism, in the sense of "...multiple ties and interactions linking people and institutions across the borders of the nation-states" (Vertovec 1999: 447), is not strong among the Indisch Dutch but many of their organizations initiate and support small-scale projects in Indonesia such as schools and clinics. The majority of these projects concern private initiatives. Some have the explicit aim of support to the country of origin; many more combine social or cultural activities in the Netherlands, with support to local projects in Indonesia. Disasters lead to social responses too. The tsunami in the beginning of 2004, showed an unexpected generous amount of donations for relief activities. More recently, an earthquake in the Javanese city and cultural centre of Yogyakarta in May 2006 resulted in spontaneous collections at the *Pasar Malam*, at locally organized dance parties and in (Indisch Dutch) homes for the elderly. These and other forms of altruistic collective behaviour have a welfare and symbolic value and keep the memory of the country of origin alive.[28] As Bosma remarks, "The postcolonial history of the Indisch Dutch is a fine example of the more it becomes clear that settlement in the Netherlands is for good, the more transnational ties are tightened" (Bosma 2009: 279).

15.3.2 The Moluccans

The case of the Moluccans in the Netherlands shows much stronger transnational ties. The ideal of a Moluccan republic, the *adat* (traditional law) and *pela* (kinship) connections have a strong impact in constituting the Moluccans as a social group with a specific ethnic identity. However, the cultural identity was reinforced by policies of the Dutch government, as spatially expressed by their housing. Upon arrival in the Netherlands, they were accommodated in special barracks or camps[29] all over the Netherlands and in later years in special designated neighbourhoods or streets. This policy is explained by the expectations of both the Moluccans and the Dutch government who, as we have seen earlier, during the first decades after arrival expected their stay in the Netherlands to be temporary. Nowadays most of the Moluccans live outside the special areas and among native Dutch, but the Moluccan neighbourhood still has a strong symbolic meaning (see for example Rinsampessy 2008).

The relation between the Dutch state and the Moluccans is substantially more contentious and complex than in the case of the Indisch Dutch. The major point of contention relates to the demands of the first-generation Moluccans that the Dutch government should support the claim of a free *South Moluccan Republic* (RMS). A government in exile, based in the Netherlands, cherishes the establishment of a free state, independent of the Republic of Indonesia, as an ideal. Politics are clearly decisive in the identity formation of the Moluccans in the Netherlands, although for successive generations, this ideal increasingly became and has become problematic. Among others,

23 Indonesian dress
24 See <www.nasi-idjo.nl>.
25 De Vries referred to a study of M.C. Waters (1990). Optional ethnicity is self-chosen it is not inescapable.
26 The extensive biography of Jan Boon, who played an important role for the 1st generation Indisch Dutch in the 1950's-60's, was published in 2008. In the same year, Hans van Wessel edited a book meant for secondary school teachers on Indisch Dutch history called 'Indisch tracks'. In 2009, Dutch cinemas showed the first Indisch Dutch movie "Far from the Family", a DVD titled "Indo Nu" (Indo Now) entered circulation, and Young and de Vries published a book on experiences of Indisch Dutch outside the Japanese camps. The Dutch government via the foundation, *Het Gebaar* (The Gesture) sponsored the movie, DVD and book.
27 See at: <www.iisg.nl/research/migrantorganisations>.
28 Guarnizo (2003) reminds us that along with contributing to development processes and keeping the homelands alive, motives such as obtaining status and recognition in the places of origin might also play a role.
29 Life in a barracks or camp is well pictured by Frans Lopulalan in his short novel, *The Barrack*.

Voutz and Rinsampessy (2008: 22–30) mention the increasing interaction with Dutch people, including intermarriage, the move from the barracks to urban neighbourhoods and the difficult position of second-generation Moluccans in the labour market.

Activist practices of the second generation were also of importance. In the 1970's, the feelings about a free South Moluccan Republic were still strong and dominant. Contrary to the Indisch Dutch, the coming to power of General Suharto was not perceived as a positive change because in April 1966, when he was already de facto leader of Indonesia, he ordered the execution of Chris Soumokil, the RMS leader of a guerrilla group on the island of Ceram. The Moluccans blamed the Dutch government for establishing good relations with Indonesia and not being supportive to their cause. The dramatic dilemmas facing the second generation were demonstrated when young radical Moluccans hijacked a train in 1975; two years later, they again hijacked a train and a school as well. The killing of the train driver and two passengers in 1975 and the military intervention in 1977 with eight deaths (two of them hostages) sent shock waves through both the Moluccan community and Dutch society. In 1978, a fourth armed action in the offices of the Province of Drenthe did not obtain the support of the Moluccan community and its leaders and by consequence, failed (Smeets/Steijlen 2006: 237–241).

The hijackings marked a turning point in the relationship between the Moluccans and the Dutch government. Sylvia, a second-generation Moluccan woman comments:

> The government became conscious of the fact that the presence of Moluccans in the Netherlands was no more a temporary affair, for the Moluccans it meant that they could never count on the support of the Dutch government to realise the RMS ideal. For both parties it was a turning point, a turnover.... I personally decided to build my life in the Netherlands. It implies that I will fruitfully contribute to this society (Molemans 2004: 59–60).

The Dutch government took measures to encourage dialogue with the Moluccan groups in the Netherlands and in the Moluccas as well. The *Inspraakorgaan Welzijn Molukkers*, an official body to promote welfare among the Moluccans, started its activities after the first train hijacking (Smeets/Steijlen 2006: 242–243). There was an urgent need to devise a social policy for the Moluccans because the levels of unemployment and incomes were substantially worse compared with the Dutch, including the Indisch Dutch. Two years later, the government published a report on the problems among the Moluccans. Among other measures, the Dutch government put efforts into training Moluccan social workers and funding 'orientation trips' to the Moluccas (Pollmann 1982). In fact, at the end of the 1970's, a process of integration into Dutch society, at that time defined by many as a multicultural society, was started (Voutz/Rinsampessy 2008; Smeets/Steijlen 2006: 281–329).

What does the integration process mean for third-generation Moluccans? A 31-year-old Moluccan woman with higher degrees in economy and communication management who works in Brussels says in her own words how she feels both Dutch and Moluccan:

> I have long looked for my identity: the comparison with being Moluccan here in the Netherlands but also the feeling of being Moluccan with the family in the Moluccas. I have always had that bond but more when Moluccan family members visited us. Till 2006 I was never in the Moluccas.... In 2006 I went for the first time to the Moluccas, together with my grandparents and other family members.... Yes, in the Moluccas I had the feeling: 'Here I am really a Moluccan', while I am also Moluccan in the Netherlands. But here you have, so to say, to divide yourself in a Dutch and Moluccan part (Rinsampessy 2008: 315).

Although Moluccans are Dutch citizens in the formal sense of Dutch passport holders, the recognition that they are Moluccan Dutch is still not generally accepted. However, mixed marriages with native Dutch are increasingly common and the children feel more Dutch than the earlier generation. Verkuyten (1999) asked 20 young mixed origin Moluccans whether they felt Moluccan, Dutch or bicultural. Fourteen respondents defined themselves as both Moluccan and Dutch, and five answered that they considered themselves primarily Moluccan.

> I don't think about whether I am Moluccan or not, I am, this is simply what I know. Am I Moluccan or Dutch? No, I am Moluccan. My friends usually call me a light half-breed. They consider me as Moluccan and not as Dutch (Verkuyten 1999: 99).

According to Verkuyten, the context determines which identity prevails but in general, these Dutch-Moluccans indicate that they do not belong to the Moluccans nor to the Dutch but that they are in-between (Verkuyten 1999: 100).

A powerful symbol of identification is the ideal of an independent Moluccan Republic that still exists, albeit less widespread among the third generation (Voutz/Rinsampessy 2008: 29; Smeets/Steijlen 2006: 340; van der Foort 2008). In September 2009, the new president of the Moluccan government in exile declared that the population of the Moluccas has to decide in freedom about its future political structure and that both the government in exile and the Indonesian government have to commit themselves to the outcome of this referendum. In other words, the government in exile no longer has the creation of an independent South Moluccan Republic as its sole option.[30]

The Moluccans in the Netherlands tend to organize according to villages of origin. Today, there are about 80 *kumpulans* in the Netherlands, meaning Moluccan groups from specific villages. Kinship relations are important in keeping up the links with Moluccan islands in East Indonesia and are often considered more important than religious bonds (most of the Moluccans are Christian but there is a Muslim minority). *Pela* refers to the relationship between two or more villages and traditional law forbids marriages between members of the villages. The *pela* is still important for understanding the Moluccans in the Netherlands, although the prohibition of marriages within the *pela* is less strict than before. The relation usually consists of mutual help. For the aim of this contribution, it is relevant to know that over the years, the Moluccans have supported their villages of origin as well as the villages by which they are linked through the *pela*.[31] On a larger scale, an interesting, recent effort is the so-called 'Hundred Villages Plan' of the TCO TitanE that works together with the Moluccan TCO Women for Peace, the Moluccan History Museum and various other Moluccan organizations. The aim is to contribute to poverty alleviation and to the *Millennium Development Goals* (MDG) of the United Nations. The provision of clean water and good governance with 40 per cent participation by women are tools to reach the aims.[32]

The Postcolonial Migrant Organisations' database mentions some 450 Moluccan organizations. Of these 76 are classified as organizations with (primarily) "an orientation to the country of origin", of which 22 were set up from 2000-2009.[33] Again, as in the case of the Indisch Dutch, but in the case of the Moluccans much stronger, transnational ties are alive and continue to be developed. Earlier in this chapter, we met second-generation Sylvia, who after the hijackings of the 1970's, decided to build a future in the Netherlands. She saw no prospect of an independent Moluccan Republic and decided to choose a 'new route':

> Many of my family members live in the Moluccas. While I live in the Netherlands and lead a comfortable life, my family there has no easy life. If an independent RMS is not feasible, how can I support them? By looking around and observing that I live in a country of overabundance, in a country where you can obtain much knowledge. Money and knowledge are the best ways to help the people of the Moluccas (Molemans 2004: 60).

By consequence, via a *kumpulan*, she supports a potable water project in the village where her father was born.

In 1999-2001 (shortly after the Asian crisis and the fall of Suharto's dictatorship), violent ethnic and religious conflicts occurred in the region of origin, during which at least 5,000 people died and 500,000 were displaced. Islamic groups attacked Christian villages and *vice versa*. Rumours blamed the Indonesian army for deliberately creating unrest and trying to abort the newly established Indonesian democracy of 1998.[34] The *kerusuhan*, as the riots in the Moluccas are called, led to the founding of a Union of *Kumpulans* (*Vereniging van Kumpulans*, VKN), since it was clear that the village-based organizations had to work together. The Moluccans in the Netherlands undertook various initiatives and demonstrations to express their solidarity, thereby stressing joint efforts by Christian and Muslim Moluccans. They pressured for peace, called for an end to the violence and approached politicians in the Netherlands and in Indonesia as well. A delegation of prominent members of the Moluccan Dutch community met political leaders in Indonesia twice.

The Moluccan TCOs also became involved in relief efforts. They held campaigns to collect money, at the national level by way of a national aid campaign supported by two Dutch mayors and the Dutch Red Cross, as well as through numerous local activities. The national campaign raised around 2.75 million Euros. Over time, the emergency assistance developed into development-oriented small-scale projects. The interethnic conflict of 1999-2002 in Indonesia has reinforced the ethnic identity of the Moluccan com-

30 *Eigen Molukse Republiek niet langer heilig* (Independent Moluccan Republic no longer sacred), in: *Nederlands Dagblad*, 17 October 2009: 1, 3.

31 See for example: <www.tuhaha.nl> and <www.tulehu. nl>.

32 See for example: <www.titane.org> and personal communication.

33 See for example: <www.iisg.nl/research/migrantorganisaties>.

34 General Suharto was president of Indonesia from 1967 to 1998. The so-called 'New Order' was a military dictatorship that ended after the Asian crisis of 1997 and domestic unrest in 1997-98. Since then, a delicate balance exists between political parties, the elected president and the army.

munity in the Netherlands and strengthened transnational ties with an impact on the identity formation of the third generation (Steijlen 2004; Smeets/Steijlen 2006: 340–356). Many members of this generation seem preoccupied with their Moluccan identity and emphasize Moluccan values and use of the Malay language (Voutz/Rinsampessy 2008: 28, 31; Verkuyten/van de Calseijde/de Leur 1999).

15.4 Conclusion

The two migrant groups cited and their descendants from Indonesia show remarkable differences in their patterns of integration in the Netherlands, their agencies, their shift in identities over the generations, and their transnational relations. The cases demonstrate how relations between migrant groups and their regions and countries of origin could be controversial, maintained for decades and intergenerational. They show the mutual impact of the agencies of migrants and their descendants and multi-local policies, the latter in the sense of socio-political changes, events and trends in both the country of settlement and the country of origin and bilateral international policies as well. This interaction shapes and transforms identities over the three generations. The involvement in diasporic flows between the country of settlement and the country of origin, in particular in the sphere of social remittances, and, in the case of the Moluccans, ambivalent feelings of belonging towards the country of settlement all belong to this identity. Our contribution shows how state interventions can reconcile contentions between ethnic identities and Dutch citizenship. In particular, this occurs by mobilizing Dutch state institutions and funding agencies to support TCOs, among others for development in the region of origin.

In the old model of international migration, over the years the ties and interactions between people and institutions across the nation states fade away. However, globalization and new means of communication imply the start of new forms and meanings of transnationalism among the next generations. Significantly, among both the Indisch Dutch and the Moluccans, an increase is discerned in the number of organizations with a transnational orientation. For the period 1945–1989, the database of the International Institute of Social History classifies 1.5 per cent of the Indisch Dutch organizations and 9.3 per cent of the Moluccan ones as transnational, while for the period 1990–2007, the percentages are respectively 4.1 and 29.1.[35] It is difficult to predict the direction of the new forms of transnationalism. Much depends on the further development of means of transportation and communication techniques. Moreover, as argued, it depends on socio-political developments in both the country of origin and the country of settlement. In the contemporary Dutch context of strong resistance to both immigration and the idea of a multicultural society, it could well be that, as a response, second- and subsequent-generation descendants of immigrants will preserve more of their ethnic identity and cultural heritage than one would currently expect.

Would this affect their citizenship? This question is more relevant to the Moluccans than to the Indisch Dutch. The latter already possessed formal Dutch citizenship or easily obtained a Dutch passport upon arrival in the Netherlands. Transnational practices definitely still exist but compared to the Moluccans they are much weaker. The Moluccans were stateless until they could obtain Dutch passports in 1976 (Act relating to the Position of the Moluccans). As demonstrated, for decades, the relationship with the Dutch government was contentious. Transnational relations are still strong and cover a diversity of practices: family and social remittances, knowledge transfer, tourism and political activism. This relates to the specific identity of the Moluccan Dutch, who feel Moluccan and Dutch but for whom explicitly expressing the latter side of their identity is still a taboo. According to Voutz and Rinsampessy (2008: 16), the Dutch side of their identity will *preferably*, not be mentioned in public. Young Moluccans do not consider themselves foreigners in the Netherlands but they do not feel Dutch either (Smeets/Steijlen 2006: 353–358; Verkuyten 1999). In this sense, their citizenship continues to be ambivalent.

35 See: <www.iisg.nl/research/migrantorganisations>.

16 Pro-asylum Advocacy in the EU: Challenging the State of Exception

Helen Hintjens, Richa Kumar and Ahmed Pouri

In a landscape where the principle of deterrence is deliberately punitive, offering assistance becomes ever more problematic for an organization and for the individuals working within it, as the fight is not only for refugee rights but for resources and legitimacy (Cambridge/Williams 2004: 103).

History teaches us how practices first reserved for foreigners find themselves applied later to the rest of the citizenry.[1]

16.1 Introduction[2]

This chapter explores examples of how pro-asylum advocates challenge the harsh measures used to punish those who try to enter or reside in the EU illegally, taking examples from The Netherlands and the UK. We explore organized resistance to the '3-Ds', which are so typical of EU-wide migration policies: destitution, detention and deportation. Together these are the backbone of policies of deterrence. Sections 2 and 3 explore how 'global apartheid' and the 'state of exception' within the EU connect. Giorgio Agamben (2005) first theorized the "state of exception" and Kohler, "global apartheid" (1978). The state of exception is the regional context for pro-asylum advocacy work, and global apartheid is the global context within which the EU-wide state of exception can be understood (Webber 2000; Migreurop 2009)[3]. In section 4, the 'shared injustice frames', or common worldviews, of pro-asylum advocacy networks in the EU, are briefly explored.

Section 5 presents examples of pro-asylum advocacy work from the UK and the Netherlands. These examples draw on our own background experience and research. We explore how two pro-asylum advocacy organizations, one a loose network, the other a small NGO, have tried to organize to protect those seeking sanctuary against the 3-Ds.[4] The right not to be deliberately made homeless, not to be imprisoned at will, and not to be forcibly expelled to dangerous countries, are thus the main focus of these organizations, and of section 5. In section 6, we briefly explore some positive recent developments, such as the 'sanctuary campaign' in the UK, but also how resistance to deterrence policies has had to go 'underground' in the face of criminalization in both the EU and elsewhere, such as Canada (Fekete 2009; Nyers 2003). The first example we explore is the National Coalition for Anti-Deportation Campaigns (NCADC), a UK-wide loose coalition of members and asylum support groups. We consider in particular NCADC's 2007 anti-deportation campaign around a charter flight to

1 Giorgio Agamben: "No to Political Tattooing", in: *Le Monde*, 10 January 2004; at: <http://www.ratical.org/ratville/CAH/totalControl.pdf> (24 June 2007).

2 This chapter draws on an earlier paper by Helen Hintjens, International Institute of Social Studies, The Hague and Ahmed Pouri, *Participating Refugees in Multicultural Europe* (PRIME), The Hague, entitled "Advocates in Fortress Europe: Working for Refugee Rights, which was presented at the International Conference on Migration at the Institute of Social Studies, on 30-31 August 2007.

3 See at: <http://www.poptel.org.uk/statewatch/news/2005/aug/crimes-of-arrival.pdf> (20 August 2009); <http://www.migreurop.org/article1574.html> (6 January 2010).

4 The UK Independent Asylum Commission (2008) proposes the term 'sanctuary' instead of asylum; at: <http://www.independentasylumcommission.org.uk/> (3 May 2010).

T.-D. Truong and D. Gasper (eds.), *Transnational Migration and Human Security*, Hexagon Series on Human and Environmental Security and Peace 6, DOI 10.1007/978-3-642-12757-1_16, © Springer-Verlag Berlin Heidelberg 2011

the Democratic Republic of Congo. In the Netherlands, our example is Participating Refugees in Multicultural Europe (PRIME), a Hague-based affiliate of Landelijke Ongedocumenteerde Stichting (LOS) [the National Organization for the Undocumented], an umbrella organization.[5] We consider how PRIME worked with those who sought to benefit from the general pardon, or amnesty, announced for some failed asylum seekers in 2008. At the end of section 5, we also present two individual profiles, two women - one in PRIME, the other in the NCADC network in the UK - who reflect on the state of exception and how pro-asylum advocacy has impacted on their lives. These global, EU-wide, national, local and individual aspects of pro-asylum advocacy are all connected in this chapter, just as they are for many advocates and those seeking sanctuary.

Our research is based on pro-asylum research conducted in both the UK and the Netherlands over several years.[6] The rise of racism in particular, explains our decision to connect global apartheid with the state of exception inside the EU. During our research, we became interested in how and why ordinary people, including refugees and asylum seekers, engage in pro-asylum advocacy. They encountered the harsh realities of deterrence policies, through experience and close contacts rather than by design or conviction alone. Section 6 reflects on how growing harmonization of deterrence policies in the EU poses a danger to legitimate, organized resistance to the 3-Ds. The conclusion shows that it is becoming more urgent, and more difficult to do this work in the EU today (Fekete 2009). Some of the many contradictory forces besetting pro-asylum rights advocates in the EU should become clearer by the end of this chapter.

5 Stichting *Landelijke Ongedocumenteerden Steunpunt* (LOS), or the National Advice Centre for Undocumented. Information about LOS from an interview with Rian Ederveen, Coordinator of LOS, The Hague, 2 April 2007.

6 By being involved in PRIME, in NCADC and other refugee organizations, including UNHCR, the three authors of this chapter have been involved in campaigns, challenges to new laws, faith-based organizations, schools, voluntary groups and trade unions that have resisted the rise of racism and indifference to the suffering of asylum seekers and the undocumented.

16.2 Why 'Global Apartheid'?

Popularly referred to by Thabo Mbeki and Fidel Castro, among others, the term 'global apartheid' has also been used analytically by scholars like Anthony Richmond, Titus Alexander and Patrick Bond (Richmond 1994; Alexander 1996; Bond 2000). For Ali Mazrui, global apartheid resembles a global caste system (Mazrui 2007), and interestingly, during the formal apartheid era in South Africa the concept had already been theorized (Kohler 1978). In his classic *Immigration Law and Practice*, Ian MacDonald compared UK nationality and immigration laws with apartheid laws, since both created different categories of 'nationals', with unequal resources and unequal access to the national territory (MacDonald 1983). The concept of global apartheid usefully conveys not only the scale of global inequalities, but also laws and policies aimed at their legitimization, and processes of coercive state enforcement. Dominant and protective self-determination underlies global apartheid, as it did South African apartheid, with mainly white heartland populations claiming to be in danger (Kohler 1978; Richmond 1994). On the other hand, both global and South African forms of apartheid claim to protect the culture of the excluded peoples.

State-designed, racially encoded, religiously loaded and (mostly) legally sanctioned internal controls to prevent cross-border movement and exclude those defined as 'undesirable' have been intensifying internationally for some years (Bond 2000; Bauman 2004). "[F]orcible isolation of people who are different" was already part of colonial segregation and expulsion, and in this sense is nothing new (Richmond 1994: 206). Like colonial surveillance, today's strategy is to screen entire groups of people out of entitlements and benefits, enforcing unequal life chances, this time in the hope of deterring future cross-border movements (Zureik 2001; Albrecht 2002). Surveillance and control, neglect and violent exclusion are affected through a global grid of changing laws, as well as walls, barriers, sanctions and surveillance techniques. Many state policing functions are contracted out to transnational security corporations, making the role of corporate capital in global apartheid analogous to the part it played in South African apartheid (Falk 2005; Bacon 2005).

The border controls, detention centres, deportations and internal controls and surveillance, are deliberate deterrence policies, as are the 3-Ds domestically (Webber 2000). Their success is limited, however, and it seems governments compete between each other with ever-more draconian sanctions against undocumented people, seen as the source of insecurity (Bhagwati 2003; Bigo 2001). An estimated half million undocumented people reside in the UK, and around 150,000 in the Netherlands. Yet from 2002 until 2008, progressively fewer people were able to reach the UK or the Netherlands to claim asylum (Jandl 2004: 6).[7] Fleeing one's 'homeland' does not imply reaching one's destination and gaining sanctuary.[8] "Scooped up like so many fishes, expelled by new security and policing systems, migrants are redefined as smugglers or smuggled, traffickers or trafficked, and asylum seekers have a hard time reaching safety, whatever they pay for the journey" (Loescher 1993).

Almost by definition, "...the asylum seeker's flight...is tortuous...[and] is likely to be indirect, facilitated by commercial intermediaries and false documents" (Bhabha 2002: 156). This makes criminalization relatively easy for EU governments. Ever-wider circles of border controls have made the EU almost impenetrable (e.g. FRONTEX polices the seas off the Canaries; EU funding helps pay for detention centres in Libya and Morocco). Neighbouring countries thus detain people for the EU, as 'Fortress Europe' seeks to close Mediterranean and North Africa routes (Migreurop 2007; Maas 2007; van Houtum 2007; Bigo 2001, JRS 2010[9]). Even the principle of *non-refoulement* (not being sent back across a border before an asylum case is properly heard), is routinely violated, not by disobedient officials, but by obedient ones. There lies the heart of the problem of global apartheid and the state of exception for pro-asylum advocacy (Fekete 2001: 26; Helton 2002: 123; Maas 2007).

In the UK, Heaven Crawley talks of the emergence of a marked 'culture of disbelief' among Border Agency staff, including in relation to minors (Crawley 2006). Similar attitudes have been reported in the Netherlands (HRW 2003).[10] Violent assaults during detention and deportation have been documented across Europe (Fekete 2005). Rejected asylum seekers, especially those without children, tend to go underground rather than wait to be detained and forcibly deported. Unable to work, they cannot claim benefits, shelter or health care, and are subject to detention and deportation without notice if caught. Torture and rape victims experience re-traumatization, and families become separated, all in the name of effective border controls. As one lawyer explains:

> ...when people are subjected to routine fingerprinting, when they are locked up, when they are restrained by body belts and leg shackles and thirteen feet of tape, or forcibly injected with sedatives to keep them quiet as they are bundled on to an aircraft, it seems reasonable to ask: what have they done? The answer is that they have tried to come to Western Europe, to seek asylum, or to live here with their families, or to work here. And the whole panoply of modern policing, with its associated rhetoric, is applied against them (Webber 2000: 1).

Between Europe's heartlands and the impoverished homelands, are in-between places that grow in number and variety; refugee camps, confined lands, militarized border zones; deserts criss-crossed by barbed wire, gun posts and walls (Bhagwati 2003; Collyer 2007; Migreurop 2009). Meanwhile, governments and pliant media whip up collective insecurity, exaggerating the threats migrants pose, to justify new and more draconian exclusions imposed on undocumented migrants (Bhabha 2002: 160–161; Bauman 2004). Among many pro-asylum advocates in the EU today, a sense of urgency is tangible, in the face of organized human rights violations resulting from the 'state of exception' within the EU.

16.3 An EU-wide State of Exception

Along with the barbed wire, armed guards and walls, sophisticated biometric and satellite-tracking techniques combine to produce multiple zones of simultaneous entrapment and exclusion. 'Apartheid walls' slice through space, while high-tech monitoring techniques assist with random checks of civilian populations, for example at airports and checkpoints (at the US border with Mexico, across Palestine). Within the EU, detention camps mushroomed after the Cold War, as the state of exception grew and moved beyond the effective reach of international human rights norms and mechanisms. Free movement for goods and capital has meant more confinement for the world's poor and desperate (Andreas 2000; Richmond 1994; Alexander 1995; Cohen 1987). The philosopher Giorgio Agamben first developed the concept, 'state of exception', which refers to the combined might of state and

---

7 Jo Woodbridge, 2005: *Sizing the Unauthorized (illegal) Migrant Population in the United Kingdom in 2001*, Online Home Office Report No. 29.05; at: <http://www.homeoffice.gov.uk/rds/pdfs05 rdsolr2905.pdf>: 5.

8 For this kind of analysis applied to Uganda, see Himbara/Sultan (1995), and for a more critical view on the use of "bantustan" in this way, see the comment by Doornbos (1996).

9 See at: <http://www.with.jrs.net/files/DoTheyKnow.pdf> (4 January 2010).

10 See at: <http://www.hrw.org/en/reports/2003/04/08/fleeting refuge-0> (4 January 2010).

corporate power to suspend normal rules of governance and legality, and to do so *wherever and whenever they so choose* (Agamben 2005; Migreurop, 2009).

Even prisoners have more rights than those held in this state in detention centres and camps across the EU.[11] Detention is supposed to be used only as a last resort, or immediately prior to deportation, but instead is routinely used as a form of deterrence, both in the UK and the Netherlands (Bacon 2005: 4). Even the sick, disabled and small children, can disappear through forced deportation. Those who struggle, fearful of deportation, are sometimes restrained and drugged during the removal process. Thus, every day on chartered and civilian long-haul flights international law is violated (Migreurop 2007; Fekete 2005, 2009). Pro-asylum advocates try to bring such stories of resistance to media attention, but often the media feels that these stories are not news. Only when the unusual and sensational occurs (a suicide or hunger strike among detainees or, a fire in a detention centre) do the media report on the detention centres (Hintjens/Jarman 2003; Athwal 2006).[12]

Under the state of exception, living conditions are made as harsh as possible for undocumented people, to encourage them to leave Europe voluntarily. But this strategy seems not to be working (Albrecht 2002; Bacon 2008). Governments can force people onto the streets, lock them away in detention centres, take their children into foster care, but conditions in their country of origin remain life threatening, and very few people will voluntarily return to Democratic Republic of Congo (DRC), Iraq or other dangerous places. In a world where increasing pressures push people to move, and where the displaced are denied "rights and equality as they do what they have to do to survive", there is no obvious, politically acceptable solution (Bacon 2008: vi). Under such global conditions, the most likely response to deterrence is evasion and illegal flight (Bacon 2008; Athwal 2006).

A cat-and-mouse game ensues between private 'fixers', ships' captains, border police and lifeguards, in which rescue at sea is reclassified as smuggling, and people can be locked up for helping those drowning off-shore. Private security firms are heavily involved in detention and deportation, and run most of the UK's immigration centres (Bacon 2005). Their profits depend on government failure, since the detention centres would be redundant if nobody could enter the UK. This is not likely to happen, as violent conflicts, human rights violations and growing global inequalities fuel these movements (Bhagwati 2003).

Overt physical and mental abuses are widely reported across EU detention centres (Migreurop 2009). In 2009, riot police attacked peaceful hunger strikers in Schiphol detention centre in the Netherlands without warning, causing serious injuries, not long after they began to refuse food.[13] In a separate incident, families with children on hunger strike in Yarlswood in the UK, experienced almost exactly identical attacks (Fekete 2009: 89).[14] Physical use of force is symptomatic of the state of exception, and of the deterrence logic underpinning migration policies across the EU (Agamben 2005; Migreurop 2009).

Agamben has compared torture in detention today with torture in Nazi concentration camps, and insists that, "...situation is legally speaking actually comparable [since]...the detainees of Guantanamo do not have the status of Prisoners of War, they have absolutely no legal status.... They are subject only to raw power; they have no legal existence."[15] Those in asylum detention are similarly forgotten, although less completely removed from the rule of law, and can find their basic rights arbitrarily suspended. There are some parallels between the 'terror estate' and the 'detention estate' (Bacon 2005). Images of 'scrounging' and 'criminal' detainees are reinforced by media and

11 A map, regularly updated by the French migrants' rights organization, MIGREUROP, shows the number and types of open and closed detention centres and migration and refugee camps across Europe, and makes for horrifying comparisons with similar maps of concentration and forced labour camps during World War 2. See at: <http://www.migreurop.org/IMG/pdf/carte-en. pdf> (20 December 2009).

12 Helen Hintjens, 2007: "The War for Illegals", in: Bad Subjects website special issue on 'Hope'; at: <http://bad.eserver.org/issues/2007/78/> (29 November 2008).

13 Ahmed Pouri; Helen Hintjens: "Hunger Strikers attacked inside Schiphol's Detention Centre", in: PRIME Press Release, 9 March 2009; at: <http://indymedia.nl/nl/2009/03/58112.shtml> (2 June 2009).

14 Helen Hintjens: "Unveiling the Truth in The Netherlands: Attack on Hunger Strikers Inside Amsterdam's Schiphol Airport Detention Center", PRIME Press Release; at: <http://theporcupine.org/?p=135> (2009); *National Coalition of Anti-Deportation Campaigns* (NCADC), at: <http://www.ncadc.org/> includes a list of successful cases defended, 141 in all, totalling more than 300 people.

15 Giorgio Agamben: "No to political tattooing", in: *Le Monde*, 10 January 2004; at: <http://www.ratical.org/ratville/CAH/totalControl.pdf> (24 June 2007).

public bias, creating an increased sense of insecurity and resentment against asylum seekers (Bigo 2001).

The state of exception explains how spaces created by governments, with corporate partners, can be placed outside normal 'rules of the democratic game' and beyond due process (Agamben 2005). In this state, a person can be moved about at will, mistreated and ignored. In Agamben's terms, this is the human being in the condition of 'naked life' (*homo sacer*) (Agamben 1998). What the public sees is usually another side of the story, as when: "our television cameras [are] focused on the gallant policemen rounding up the 'illegals' and *sans papiers* and transporting them to the nearest refugee camp" (Bauman 2007: 22). Inside the camp, the cameras usually stop rolling, and there is "not much to report".

Within the EU, the state of exception means enforced detention, forced destitution and implementation of annual deportation quotas and targets. Pro-asylum workers, including teachers, social workers, lawyers, doctors and family members, friends, church or mosque members, know about the state of exception, through experience, and through seeing the experience of others, and most recently through a range of 'crimes of solidarity' (Fekete 2009). Starting with a 2002 EU Directive and Framework Decision, which requires "member states to create offences of directly or indirectly aiding the unauthorized entry, movement or residence of non-EU nationals", governments have been arresting and convicting those who support undocumented people, including in the UK (Fekete 2009).

Humanitarian NGOs and human rights advocates, and those living with anyone classified as illegal or liable to deportation, are themselves criminalized for helping undocumented migrants. Prosecutions have already begun in a number of EU countries (Fekete 2009: 84), and pro-asylum advocacy has become a riskier business (Black 2003; Nyers 2003; Fekete 2009; Webber 2000; Athwal 2006). Some common level of understanding of what confronts them has forged a kind of identity among pro-asylum advocates, in the form of a shared worldview.

16.4 Shared Injustice Frames and Pro-asylum Stories

The notion of a 'shared injustice frame', as elaborated by Olesen (2003), is a useful way to reflect on shared worldviews that arise among those involved in pro-asylum advocacy networks in the EU. A common view is widely shared of how the world works, and what people confront in asserting their rights. These frames derive their power from their ability to bridge divisions of class, identity, refugee status, gender, professional training and political and religious ideas. As resistance to deterrence policies and laws has grown across the EU, shared understandings have risen that such policies and laws are both unjust and unworkable. For pro-asylum advocates, the state of exception is illegitimate, and involves impunity for state and corporate crimes against vulnerable people. A shared identity has thus started to emerge among pro-asylum advocates (Olesen 2005). How such shared injustice frames or transnational grievance perceptions, as Olesen calls them, produce shared forms of identification is interesting, since: "...in contrast to a legitimating frame, [a shared injustice frame provides]...an interpretation of what is happening that supports the conclusion that an authority system is violating the shared moral principles of the participants. An alternative to the legitimating frame, it provides a reason for non-compliance" (Olesen 2005: 31).

For pro-asylum advocates whether they support free movement or not, everyone seeking sanctuary in the EU has the right to claim protection and to fair and humane treatment in doing so. International law provides strong support for this premise (Loescher 1993; Helton 2002). For pro-asylum advocates, deterrence-based approaches to migration are clearly incompatible with human rights principles and practices, and with any sense of justice or fairness. Through a wide range of responses, such as media pressure, diplomatic dialogue, legal challenge, street demonstrations and public citizen campaigns, pro-asylum advocacy networks resist the official view that such policies can be justified. Cases are taken to court, debates organized in Parliaments, media and civil society training programmes conducted, and information communicated through radio, press, film and internet. While strategies may vary, the challenge of delegitimizing official claims that cruel policies are unavoidable to deter future inflows is a shared challenge. Inside knowledge of detention and deportation regimes helps to discount such official claims. Most advocates have first-hand evidence of the state of exception and the way it violates all basic human rights principles. The localized practices of contestation they use also have in-built connections to perceptions of global injustices. As Sassen puts it:

> (these) types of political practice(s)...are not the cosmopolitan route to the global. They are global through the knowing multiplication of local practices. These are

> types of sociability and struggle deeply embedded in people's actions and activities. They are also forms of institution-building work with global scope that can come from localities and networks of localities with limited resources and from informal social actors (Sassen 2004: 662).

Advocates thus inform the wider public about what they can do, and tell harrowing, but also hopeful, stories of individuals, families and minority groups daring to challenge the deterrence logic and the state of exception. Advocates thus strategically make public what should otherwise remain private experiential or professional knowledge (Carpenter 2007; Athwal 2006). Through stories of what refugees can do in the face of official indifference and abuse, advocates can show how the deterrence regime dehumanizes both those subject to the state of exception, and those who enforce it. Senior policymakers, and others distanced from the harsh realities of the 3-Ds, can thus be confronted with firsthand stories, making advocates interlocutors of the undocumented, enabling them to speak directly in most cases by straddling several spheres through internet or other forms of media (Cambridge/Williams 2004). Charles Tilly explains that stories are a powerful instrument, since, "...like the plow [stories]...use a simple application of force to dig deep... they frustrate purists: they condense complex life into simple plots" (Tilly 2006: 95). If it suits their purposes, governments may be exposed as failing to meet their international legal obligations, and in extreme cases it may be easy to find public sympathy, especially where stories concern the most vulnerable, especially children (Crawley 2006).

By sharing a common view of what is wrong with the world, and by telling stories to highlight what is wrong, political identities of pro-asylum advocates are constructed upwards, as it were, from shared experiences and insights. Shared injustice frames thus work to produce broader, overlapping alliances and relationships, among pro-asylum advocacy networks within, and also beyond, the EU. As a "transnational advocacy network", those involved in pro-asylum advocacy are "bound together by shared values [and] a common discourse" (Keck/Sikkink 1998: 2). Our starting point is this shared analysis by pro-asylum advocates of the problems they confront both under global apartheid and under the EU state of exception. As they do their work, such advocacy networks seek also to persuade others that official policies are illegitimate, and to extend their shared injustice frames through the media and greater public involvement.

16.5 Pro-Asylum Advocacy: Examples from the UK and the Netherlands

Advocacy can be defined as, "the process of identifying with and representing a person's views and concerns, in order to secure enhanced rights and entitlements..." (Cambridge/Williams 2004: 98). Locality, gender, class, profession, refugee status, training and politics will all influence the experience and practice of advocacy. Awareness is the product of lived experience and professional training, and since most pro-asylum advocacy networks operate informally and on a small scale, there are generally few material incentives to do such work; on the contrary. Offices of migrant and refugee organizations are generally small, cluttered and open long hours; almost nobody is on a permanent salary, many people work on goodwill alone. A few core people generally do most of the work.

Even small organizations like NCADC and PRIME can have significant impacts on how national and more global immigration policies are imagined and resisted, and perhaps redefined (Sassen 2004). Translocal pro-asylum networks include a range of actors, from priests to politicians, lawyers to actors, office workers to poets, trade unionists, teachers, intellectuals, postal workers, unemployed and retired people, as well as lawyers and domestic workers. Many or most are themselves refugees, or asylum seekers. Others are locals who may consider themselves 'citizens of the world', but who work mainly in a highly localized way within their own city, region or neighbourhood. They often see themselves as engaged in a defensive war to protect basic human rights for some of the most vulnerable people in their society (Migreurop 2007).[16]

In one of the opening quotations to this chapter, Agamben suggests why people might get involved in pro-asylum advocacy networks, including for self-interested reasons. Enlightened self-interest and solidarity with those at the bottom of the social hierarchy are not necessarily opposed to one another. 'There but for the grace of God go I', is a common sentiment expressed whatever the original reason for getting involved. The question of how people get involved in pro-asylum advocacy networks is difficult to answer, and there may be an element of pre-disposition through identification, as the two individual profiles presented in this chapter illustrate. We will not repli-

16 Helen Hintjens, 2007: "The War for Illegals", in Bad Subjects website special issue on "Hope"; at: <http://bad.eserver.org/issues/2007/78/> (29 November 2008).

cate earlier survey work on social movement members in the European context (Della Porta/Tarrow 2005). Instead we focus on some limited cases, where our shared experience has made it possible to observe longer-term processes of engagement from within.

Campaigning involves the shared goal of making visible those whose experiences are denied in official migration deterrence policies (Cohen 2001; Sereny 2003). A common response is outrage at the cruelties of official policies among pro-asylum advocacy groups. However, a sense of horror can turn people off, as well as engaging them. Refugees and asylum seekers may both engage and withdraw, at different times, depending on the nature of their responses to the horror and disgust they feel on learning of some new injustice perpetrated. Some are paralysed as they are re-traumatized in the asylum process; others avoid depression by becoming even more actively engaged (Cohen 2001; MacDonald 2006). Those involved in pro-asylum advocacy networks tend to share not only a sense of being 'in the know', but also of having shared projects based on defending principles of human rights and solidarity. Individual and group deportations, hunger strikes and similar actions can help produce forms of resistance-based identities. These identities enable people involved in pro-asylum advocacy to remain engaged, even in the face of growing risks to themselves. Some pro-asylum advocates view "...autonomous migration [as]...a form of resistance to global apartheid enforced at nation-state [level]" (Spener 2008: 115), but this is not true of everyone. As with all 'weapons of the weak', resistance against the state of exclusion and global apartheid can take covert and sublimated forms. For PRIME in The Hague and NCADC across the UK, the focus is on protecting individuals, families, and groups of mostly undocumented, non-nationals from the triple threat of destitution, detention and deportation.

16.5.1 The UK case: NCADC

By 2007, the UK government claimed to have 'mastered' immigration flows, and was *Tipping the Balance*. As, "the number of failed asylum applicants removed each year exceeds the number predicted to have unfounded claims", deportations exceeded applications from asylum seekers that were refused in 2006. A Home Office press release reported, "...in 2006 asylum applications reached their lowest level since 1993, while the number of removals and deportations by the Immigration and Nationality Directorate hit an all-time high".[17] A year later, Meg Hilliard, speaking for the Border Agency that had replaced the Immigration and Nationality Department of the Home Office, stated, "We will be pressing on, not going backward...there is no need for an amnesty."[18] "A lot of hard work from a lot of people", the Minister claimed, had gone into Tipping the Balance. Removals rose to 71 per cent of rejected and withdrawn asylum claims ('unfounded' in Home Office terms) in 2005, compared with just 49 per cent in 2004. In December 2006, deportations were 109 per cent of the target, averaging 103 per cent for 2006 as a whole. This meant that 18,235 forced or voluntary deportations took place from the UK, compared with the 17,780 people whose claims for asylum were denied or dropped.

In the press, Alibhai-Brown described this achievement as "policies and practices of institutionalised savagery, rebranded as efficiency".[19] Efficiency criteria like these, commonly used across Europe, are not peculiar to the UK and can be seen as part of the underpinning of global apartheid (Fekete 2005: 5–9). Pro-asylum advocates in the UK are becoming aware that refusal quotas and targets are part of inter-EU harmonization, and of agreements like the Dublin Convention, which have made matters worse for those seeking asylum. EU support for tighter controls may backfire, however, with questions starting to emerge - including in the European Parliament - about whether detention, expulsions and high refusal rates are inflicting too high a price.

The NCADC has been able to secure longer-term funding, but has come under pressure to change its campaigning style. For many years, NCADC had only one full-time, permanent campaigner, John O., who reluctantly retired in May 2010. The consistent emphasis of NCADC mailings has in the past been on connecting global, national, regional and individual

17 See at: <http://www.ind.homeoffice.gov.uk/6353/aboutus/tippingpointsresults4amend.pdf> (May 2009). UK Home Office, 2007: *Public performance target: removing more failed asylum seekers than new anticipated unfounded applications* (London: The Stationery Office)

18 The quotations in this paragraph derive from a letter sent in reply to Alan Williams (Swansea West) MP, 17 July 2007, in response to a letter on behalf of two constituents taken into detention.

19 Yasmin Alibhai-Brown: "The Brutal Reality of our Asylum Policy", in: *The Independent*. 27 February 2007; at: <http://www.independent.co.uk/opinion/commentators/yasmin-alibhai-brown/yasmin-alibhaibrown-the-brutal-reality-of-our-asylum-policy-437980.html> (12 July 2009).

injustice issues. Weekly e-mails reported on media reports, on court rulings, official government reports, international NGO research on countries of origin, academic studies and cases from all over the world. John O. also circulates individual cases and group campaigns related to charter flights, which ask for support in the form of faxes, e-mails and letters to MPs, airlines and government ministers. Individual and group cases mainly relate to the UK context, although news on campaigns in other EU countries also circulates periodically, and are posted on the website. To safeguard its future, in 2008, NCADC secured National Lottery funding for three years, and became a registered charity. One condition of charitable status, however, is not to engage in political campaigning, and NCADC must therefore appear independent if it is to remain financially secure in the future. Most NCADC members feel uneasy with the forced political neutrality of the shared injustice frames because they blame the government for detentions and deportations as well as sharing a sense of moral outrage at the, unavoidably political, act of human rights violations. Three paid staff positions now depend on meeting charitable status conditions that tend to undermine the appeal of NCADC, which is precisely its interconnected, holistic and very political worldview.

Created in 1995, NCADC has engaged with the rise of forcible deportation policies, through a growing engagement with government ministers, but also with private security companies, regular and charter airlines. Since 1996, NCADC takes credit for preventing 165 deportations, as well as other (uncountable) cases where their intervention may have helped prevent deportation. Although this figure is tiny in relation to the numbers of deportations, NCADC claims that running a campaign using the NCADC website and e-mail list, writing letters, signing petitions, and sending faxes, involving MPs, neighbours and the media, can work. In recent years, national campaigns have also been mounted by NCADC affiliates against group deportations and charter flights, for example to Iraq, Afghanistan, Zimbabwe and the Democratic Republic of Congo (DRC). An outstanding example of such an NCADC campaign was the 2007 DRC (Congo-Kinshasa) anti-deportation charter flight campaign.

16.5.2 The DRC Charter Campaign: A Qualified Failure

Even after more than ten years of continuous warfare and violence, with millions of documented deaths and hundreds of thousands of cases of rape, forced deportations to the DRC continue from most West European countries. Estimates suggest that up to 10 million Congolese have died due to chronic hunger, displacement, sexual violence and killings resulting from the war that started in 1998. Forced labour affects the population in mineral-rich areas, few public services operate at all, and hunger, disease, child labour and sexual violence are all rife. The regime in power views returned asylum seekers as political enemies who can be detained, tortured and even killed (Hintjens 2006; Fekete 2006). In 2007 Rudi Vis, MP, tabled an early day motion in the UK House of Commons (EDM 926, 21.22007) demanding an end to deportations to DRC, because of human rights violations by the Kinshasa government. EDM 926 called for cancellation of a charter flight due to deport 30 Congolese on 26 February 2007, since their removal would constitute "a grave violation of their Article 3 human rights as provided for in the Geneva Convention". Before 26 February, five MPs had signed EDM 926.[20] Forty-five more signed after the charter flight had left.

The NCADC campaign was significant for several reasons. As John O. reported, this campaign mobilized "the biggest and best response to an appeal to stop a deportation in the 12 years of [NCADC's] existence".[21] A loose network of affiliated campaign groups shared the view that whatever could be done to prevent deportation, even at the last minute, should be done, in this case, and however slim the chances of success. Outrage at human rights violations involved was the basis for counter-politics of hope, since, as the NCADC website put it:

> Unjust and inhumane deportations are tearing families apart, forcing asylum seekers back to countries where

20 The text is as follows: EDM 926 DEMOCRATIC REPUBLIC OF CONGO 21.02.2007, Vis, Rudi "That this House believes that further deportations to the Democratic Republic of Congo should be suspended with immediate effect based on evidence that failed asylum seekers risk being subjected to serious mistreatment and imprisonment on return and that this amounts to a grave violation of their Article 3 human rights as provided for in the Geneva Convention; and that, in particular, the mass removal of Democratic Republic of Congo asylum seekers on 26th February 2007 on a specially chartered XL Airways flight should not be allowed to proceed". See at: <http://edmi.parliament.uk/ EDMi/EDMDetails.aspx?EDMID=32646&SESSION=885>.

21 Personal E-mail from John O. in response to a question by the researcher, 27 February 2007.

> they face persecution, denying gay and lesbian couples the right to a relationship. These are the reasons that motivated campaigners and supporters to get together with those facing deportation and do something about it.... Never doubt that a small group of dedicated people can defeat an attempt to deport someone. An Anti-Deportation Campaign involves organizing resistance to restrictive immigration legislation, and simply means making the government change their minds regarding an individual case.[22]

The central method of all NCADC advocacy is to write, send faxes and e-mail airline companies, government Ministers, private companies, and to contact MPs and media to support campaigns for people not to be deported, but to be allowed to remain in the UK. Court cases are also undertaken, concerning country-based deportation policies, for example in relation to the DRC. What was new about the DRC campaign was how it managed to mobilize existing, global and UK-wide networks of anti-corporate campaigners. A company called XL.com, an on-line global travel company, operated the DRC Charter. Mass faxing and letter writing was accompanied by both physical picketing of XL.com's headquarters, and heavy use of the customer complaints facility on the XL.com website.[23] The campaign letter appealed to XL.com's commercial self-interest as follows: "I would therefore urge you to reconsider your involvement, present and future, in such schemes, until your company has fully appraised itself of the available evidence. There seems a great risk that negative media attention to the outcomes of such 'deportation charters' to war zones could be commercially damaging for XL airlines."[24]

On 26 February 2007, in spite of the largest campaign in NCADC history to-date, the UK government forcibly deported "more than 40 people" back to DRC. They, "were loaded onto the plane that day, handcuffed and distressed, the children crying, and ... accompanied by around 150 police and escorts". Showing its more political side, the NCADC e-mail also commented that "the whole exercise smacked of conspiracy between the British and DRC authorities".[25] For example, a party held at the deportees' arrival in Kinshasa was reportedly filmed, footage that could have been used to show that those deported to DRC were not in any danger. Congolese in UK were meanwhile taking the government to court, disputing continued deportations to DRC. The UK government eventually won this case, after a hearing in 2008, and documented video evidence from the BBC of torture risks facing returned asylum seekers did not convince the judge that the UK government should stop deportations to DRC. The suggestion made by NCADC is of collusion between sending and receiving countries in denying basic rights to former asylum seekers (Fekete 2005). In Europe, as also "[i]n many African countries...refugees are accused of being the cause of economic hardship and social ills" (Kibreab 1999: 400), and refugee militarization can lead to former asylum seekers being accused of criminal activities (Muggah 2006).

Despite mounting evidence of serious human rights abuses, torture and killings on return, the UK Home Office (and other EU governments) continue to deport people by force to war zones in the DRC, Iraq and Afghanistan. The DRC anti-deportation campaign failed to achieve its goal, as expressed in EDM 962. Even so, the campaign can be considered successful. Considerable pressure was brought to bear on

22 National Coalition of Anti-Deportation Campaigns (NCADC) at: <http://www.ncadc.org/> includes a list of successful cases defended, 141 in all, totalling more than 300 people. See at: <http://www.ncadc.org.uk/about/profile.htm>.

23 XL.com's website was flooded with customer comments in the form of "polite complaints" from members of NCADC, NoBorders and anti-corporate networks used to challenging private corporations on their own commercial turf, as it were. Just 18 months later, XL.com filed for bankruptcy. See at: <http://www.flyertalk.com/forum/british-airways-executive-club/865321-xl-com-now-collapses-3rd-biggest-uk-tour-operator.html> (2 December 2008). A company with the same name continues to operate from a French-registered website in France. The controversy with XL Airlines and NCADC was later reported. See at: <http://www.indymedia.org.uk/en/2007/08/379320.html> (21 August 2007).

24 Dear XL Airlines letter, from NCADC website. The decision to stop charter flights was reported in an article in the independent. See Verkaik: "Major airline refuses to help with forcible removal of immigrants", in: *The Independent, Monday, 8 October* 2007; *at:* <http://www.independent.co.uk/news/uk/crime/major-airline-refuses-to-help-with-forcible-removal-of-immigrants-394451.html> *(18 December 2009)*. The article reports that "In an email to a campaign group which supports failed asylum seekers, XL said its chief executive had told the Government it had not 'fully understood' the political dimensions of these flights. In February, one of its aircraft was used to deport 40 failed asylum-seekers to the Democratic Republic of Congo as part of the Government's 'operation castor'".

25 NCADC e-mail, 5 March 2007, sent to NCADC list by Liz Atherton.

XL.com, because it had contracted to carry deportees, portrayed as innocent women and children. This threatened to damage the company's reputation, and XL.com soon announced that the company would no longer charter planes for deportation purposes. The company even declared its "sympathy for all dispossessed people in the world".[26] Here is a case where NCADC anti-deportation advocacy benefited from involvement of the Congolese themselves, mobilized and organized around the pending court case against the UK government, and involvement of mainstream anti-corporate protest movements, with their on-line and direct action tactics and strategies tried and tested. When airline (and other) companies accept contracts to deport and detain, they can expect to face public scrutiny, and as in this case, organized objections and direct protests. The nexus of rights advocacy formed during the DRC campaign enabled the NCADC campaign to reach the soft commercial underbelly of XL.com, using public interest and human rights arguments effectively.

Through John O., NCADC consistently reports human rights violations by private companies in the detention estate, companies such as Group 4 and GSL (Global Solutions Ltd). Official reports of Her Majesty's Prison Inspector, Anne Owens, find repeatedly that there is inadequate medical care, poor legal support and poor facilities, including for children's education. During the deportation process, the use of force has become evident across the EU (Fekete 2005). In mid-2008, Medical Justice, a UK charity connected with NCADC, released: *Outsourcing Abuse*, a report that documentted dozens of cases of beatings and brutality against detainees, by private security company staff.[27] Home Secretary Jacqui Smith soon appointed Nuala O'Loan, former Police Ombudsman for Northern Ireland, and now in the House of Lords, to conduct an independent enquiry. Results were still awaited at the time of finalizing this chapter. However, new legal and financial sanctions for those who refuse voluntary removal indicate the direction of government thinking on the rights of deportees. A person who refuses to leave with the The International Organization for Migration (IOM) can be denied re-entry to the UK for 5 to 10 years, and may even be charged the full cost of their deportation.

16.5.3 Netherlands: Generaal Pardon and Criminalization of PRIME

Meanwhile, in early 2007, the Netherlands announced a general pardon. After years of campaigning and petitioning the Queen, 26,000 undocumented people were to benefit from the regularization process. However, when viewed from within an organization like PRIME that works mainly with undocumented migrants themselves, most of them former asylum seekers, what followed the announcement was quite different. Just as success lay behind the failed DRC anti-deportation campaign, here there were mainly failings that prevented many who had hoped to be eligible from qualifying for amnesty. The way that the Generaal Pardon linked explicitly to speeding up deportation measures against those who were not eligible for legalization, belied the façade of generosity. The campaign backfired in a way, for it led to some gain at the expense of others who were more easily singled out and deported; the amnesty offer acted like a lure.

PRIME's tiny offices have moved several times in recent years, weakening an organization that has worked with the undocumented since the mid-1990's. PRIME suffers from chronic under-resourcing, and there are few full-time volunteers left. The organization has depended on only two or three people for many years for its core activities, which include visiting and phoning people in detention centres, liaison with the destitute, campaigns, publishing news and responding to urgent requests from those confronting destitution, detention and deportation. Some years ago, PRIME was quite a large organization, with a sizeable budget, including from the local municipality, and ran several 'safe houses' for people forced into destitution. By 2005, the organization focused entirely on anti-detention and anti-deportation work, mostly with people who spoke Farsi or a related language. Research on this chapter started around 2006, right before amnesty. PRIME staff and volunteers were intensively involved in assisting individuals hoping to benefit from this new policy at this time.[28]

PRIME estimates that less than half of the original figure of 26,000 were in fact regularized after 2007.[29]

26 Robert Verkaik: "Major airline refuses to help with forcible removal of immigrants", *The Independent*, 9 October 2007; at: <http://news.independent.co.uk/uk/legal/article3038391.ece> (30 November 2009).

27 Robert Verkaik, "Investigations into claims of abuse on asylum-seekers", *The Independent*, Tuesday 30 September 2008; at: <http://www.independent.co.uk/news/uk/home-news/investigation-into-claims-of-abuse-on-asylum-seekers-946106.html> (16 November 2009).

28 Helen Hintjens, 2007: "The War for Illegals", in Bad Subjects website special issue on "Hope"; at: <http://bad.eserver.org/issues/2007/78/> (29 November 2008).

One Afghani man's experience highlights his vulnerability. PRIME supported his case, but in 2009, he received a refusal from the Dutch Immigration and Nationality Department (IND). Fearing deportation to Afghanistan, he decided to move to the UK, where he had discovered his brother had full refugee status. The Afghani was detained on arrival in UK, without papers, and placed in a private correctional facility. Here he was held for four months, unable to contact his brother. Yet by being in detention, he had fallen foul of a rule attached to the General Pardon, that anyone detained for more than three months (for any reason) was not eligible to be regularized. Detention for immigration purposes in the EU, however, does not imply any criminal activity (Bacon 2006). This man decided to continue living underground, but was now more vulnerable to deportation.

Using an amnesty to expose illegal migrants from their hiding places was a cynical ploy, but is understandable in the context of heightened surveillance and harassment of the undocumented across Europe. Rian Ederveen of Stichting LOS confirms that charities working with the undocumented were subjected to close police controls after Generaal Pardon was announced. Lia Matheu works on migrant's rights in The Hague, an advocate for Portuguese-speaking Africans. She explains starkly that "(t)hey are chasing people out; and deportations have been explicitly linked to the Generaal Pardon ruling" (interview, 11 June 2007). When central government, seeking to speed up deportations, tried to oblige local governments to hand over lists of undocumented people, however, almost all refused to comply.[30] As PRIME has tried to explain to policymakers, distrust is reinforced by such underhanded ways of operating.[31]

Even PRIME has received unwelcome police attention since 2007. One day in 2008, staff and volunteers who left the PRIME offices were picked up, one by one, and taken to the local police station. They were not allowed to phone anyone, and were told they were being held under anti-terrorism legislation. This started at 4 p.m. and continued until 9 p.m., when Ahmed Pouri was the last to leave the building. The police released everyone, and later explained that under new anti-terrorism laws, they were obliged to follow up on all accusations. A man had gone to the police station, someone known to have mental health problems, and had alleged that PRIME were making bombs in their offices. Anti-terrorism procedures then required police to take everyone to the police station for questioning, before releasing them. The next day, flowers were sent to PRIME by way of an apology, but for some volunteers the whole experience proved too distressing and they stopped coming to PRIME. Some volunteers had no papers, and so felt especially terrified to be detained by police. While seasoned campaigners laughed the incident off, volunteers were intimidated in a perfectly legal way, thus undermining PRIME.

With fragility and under-funding of many pro-asylum advocacy organizations across the EU, it is hard to come across serious, legitimate leadership. Pro-asylum advocacy networks attract few resources, and working against the democratic government's policies is not an attractive option for society's most prominent, as well as most marginalized, people. Asylum advocates may be settled refugees who combine pro-asylum advocacy with a paid job, or may simply volunteer. They may be Europeans who find the inhumanity of the asylum regime disturbing enough to be galvanized to get involved. Lawyers, social workers and religious leaders may all get involved because they deplore the secrecy and lack of accountability they see in the immigration regime and in detention and deportation policies. In Australia, media people are prominent in pro-asylum advocacy, as are artists and intellectuals (Hintjens/Jarman 2003). Within the 'spaces outside the law', as Agamben calls them, it is very possible however to be forgotten by the rest of society (Agamben 2005).

29 Ahmed Pouri; Helen Hintjens: "Hunger Strikers attacked inside Schiphol's Detention Centre", PRIME Press Release, 9 March 2009; at: <http://indymedia.nl/nl/2009/03/58112.shtml> (2 June 2009).

30 Edestad, "Geen medewerking aan uitzetting vreemdelingen die buiten pardon vallen", 19 July 2007; at: <http://www.edestad.nl/index.php/module\615> (4 August 2008).

31 Interview with Lia Matheu, pro-asylum advocate, The Hague, 20 June 2009; Ahmed Pouri; Helen Hintjens: "Hunger Strikers attacked inside Schiphol's Detention Centre", PRIME Press Release, 9 March 2009; at: <http://indymedia.nl/nl/2009/03/58112.shtml> (2 June 2009).

16.5.4 Two Individual Advocates[32]

The two women we will call Susan (UK) and Femke (the Netherlands) were each involved voluntarily in pro-asylum advocacy work for many years. Susan worked with Asylum Justice, a local organization in South Wales, loosely affiliated with NCADC. Femke has worked with PRIME in The Hague for many years and in pro-asylum advocacy for almost 30 years. Neither woman, however, had any formal legal training. Both Susan and Femke suffer from serious clinical depression, and must take medication. They have their depression in common with many failed asylum seekers. Although Susan has a full-time day job, Femke does not, and for both women, the work on asylum rights has become a way of life, something pivotal to their worldview. They both see asylum as a metaphor for the injustice in the world, but also for a politics of hope, which they share. Each identifies herself closely with the broader refugee experience of displacement and isolation. Each can make sense of the world and identify her own small, inter-connected, contribution to promoting the rights of those even worse off than herself. Susan's involvement with asylum issues started in 2005 following the forced dispersal of asylum seekers to her town in the UK. Femke began to help in a local detention centre during the 1970's. Each has been involved in all aspects of pro-asylum work, from the mundane, involving social events, to the most technical, assisting in legal cases and training in asylum law and human rights. They have translated documents, visited detained people, campaigned against deportations and helped destitute people and families.

Each woman now has a wealth of experience of the asylum regime, and as intermediaries between the system and the individual claimants. Femke makes this clear when she explains how she helped interpret between asylum seekers and officials in the detention centre, translating the asylum seekers' stated needs into terms understood by the officials, lawyers, bureaucrats, doctors and other professionals working in the centre. Susan also sees her work with Asylum Justice in terms of interpreting the law for asylum seekers who wish to lodge appeals, for example. Femke visits many individual detainees who phone her to tell her of their experiences in the prison or detention centre. Her work has mainly involved facilitating access where possible to a lawyer, a doctor, somewhere to live. In South Wales and in The Hague, most charities hand out food donations, but rarely get involved in legal, housing, health or employment rights.

Susan became involved a few years after Asylum Justice was first set up to resist the claim of the official legal aid system that it "...sifts out worthy from unworthy forced migrants" (Bhabha 2002: 160). Susan and Femke each talked at length about how destructive the asylum process can be of individual applicants' personal potential and talents. Both women remarked on the chronic failure of the system to provide adequate legal aid. Each expressed frustration that without legal aid, asylum seekers could not convince the courts (or get bail in the UK). Few would win their appeals and many would be deported, or living in destitution once more. This depressed both women, but they were also determined to do something positive to influence the situation they found around them, together with others.

Susan and Femke share disgust at the mainstream media attitudes towards asylum seekers and undocumented people, and both admit to a deepening sense of outrage at public and political attitudes, which have worsened since a few years ago. Each expressed fear that the stress and anger their awareness of the asylum system brought had not only taken over their lives, but was also damaging their health. Campaigning against the 3-Ds, Susan and Femke knew many individuals and families who daily inhabited a state of exception, and were alternately destitute, detained and subject to deportation. Each woman described how this altered her previous sense of normality. The cruelty inflicted on people they knew, or had met and spoken to, shocked these women, and Susan helped—together with a refugee friend—to set up a group for refugee and asylum seeker women, caring for children while mothers met for shared activities. Volunteer work by women like Susan and Femke keeps most pro-asylum advocacy organizations going, and makes their networks operate in a way that is open and receptive to people in crisis. Both women consider it a waste of human potential, that destitute and detained people, women and children, and isolated and rootless young men remain trapped in the 3-Ds, or in fear of them, despite many already having experienced torture, rape and political persecution at home.

The two women report that their lives have changed completely through their growing involvement with pro-asylum advocacy in the UK and the

32 Interviews and discussions were conducted with Susan (not real name) and Femke (not real name) in Swansea and The Hague, respectively, in December 2008 and September 2009. We are grateful to both women for their insights, and for being so open with us. We hope to publish these interviews in full elsewhere, along with others gathered during this research.

Netherlands. Global and national injustices manifested in individuals, motivated them to become involved, and to become pro-asylum advocates. They both opposed what they saw as a globally designed, locally manifested system of separations, unjust laws and physical controls (global apartheid). It is interesting that both women, through their pro-asylum advocacy work, have re-evaluated their own depression, and have radically reorganized their worldviews, as well as their private lives, to hold a broad set of 'shared injustice frames'.

16.6 Harmonizing Exclusion

Across the EU, and beyond, serious rights violations are being justified in the name of the priority of secure borders (Huysmans 2006), even to the point of compromising the right to seek asylum. Non-discrimination principles are flouted, the right to a fair trial and a fair hearing of one's case are ignored, and the right not to be arbitrarily detained is disappearing. Citizenship and the right to family life are being eroded, and most undocumented people have little or no access to education, health, work or legalization. Those seeking sanctuary can fall outside of the protection of international, regional and national human rights provisions, if they are refused. Under 'fast-track' asylum procedures in the UK, as in the Netherlands, deportations happen almost on arrival (Dummett 2001; Bhabha 2009, Webber 2000). Although Article 31 of the Geneva Convention specifically ensures that a person can seek asylum, and lodge their claim, whatever their documented status, legislation across the EU is making it a crime to enter a country with false papers. There are few signs that this 'migration deterrence regime' is weakening; on the contrary (Fekete 2001). EU harmonization has simply speeded up the process. As Helton reminds us, "Cooperation...is not necessarily synonymous with generosity. In Western Europe it has been directed mainly at enforcement measures designed to frustrate the arrival of asylum seekers and to encourage them either to remain in their home country or locate in a nearby country of asylum" (Helton 2002: 272).

And setting numerical quotas and rejection targets arguably violates the legal basis of refugee law, by promoting the speedy return of people to countries where they may face danger and further risk of persecution (Helton 2002: 123). The Congolese charter flight campaign is an example of where security concerns receive priority over human rights or even legal procedures; the DRC court case was pending at the time of the 2007 deportation.

Ministers, and some policymakers, claim that all this harsh treatment is unavoidable to make life unpleasant for those who abuse the system. Bogus asylum seekers, criminal networks, smugglers, traffickers and all manner of scroungers and spongers are to be warned off by ever greater cruelty. They must be stopped from exploiting loopholes in border controls; they must be deterred from misusing the asylum system. The claim is that in this way, asylum will be safe for 'genuine' asylum seekers. However, the question remains how the latter are to get through the minefield laid down for everyone else. By blaming supposedly 'bogus' claimants for their own policies of victimization, the government get off the hook, blaming the victim for using deterrence (Ryan 1971; Nyers 2003; Webber 2000). Victim blaming tends to "normalize or naturalize unjust and violent social and political conditions" (Leatherman 2005: 12). At the same time, welfare and employment guarantees for citizens have all but dried up, and states feel "[n]o longer in full charge of the economy, security or culture", unable to provide, "...the whole-life protection from the cradle to the grave which [they] not so long ago strove to provide" (Bauman 2007: 45). Victim-blaming occurs when "...refugees...[are] accused of being the cause of economic hardship and social ills" (quotation Kibreab 1999: 400; Muggah 2006). In the heart of 'Fortress Europe', growing "[i]gnorance, incredulity and indifference...may be as significant hurdles...as disagreement or hostility" (Bhabha 2002: 158). Media reports on illegal immigrants reinforce a climate of denial equated with, "...criminal organizations, terrorists and drug traffickers [that] threaten the citadels of civilization" (quotation Nederveen Pieterse 2004: 110; Bauman 2007: 128; Bhabha 2002: 161–2).

16.7 Conclusion

This chapter has tried to contextualize the shared perspectives and frames of pro-asylum advocates within the EU, using examples familiar to us. We proposed that both global apartheid and the EU-wide state of exception are underpinning deterrence policies of individual governments towards asylum seekers and other migrants. The 3-D strategy, based on destitution, detention and deportation, is a particular focus of pro-asylum advocacy and resistance to the existing legislation and policies. The state of exception, for example in asylum detention camps, makes sense as a way of reinforcing global inequalities. We see crude physical barriers combine with increasingly sophisticated forms of internal surveillance of the population, to screen people out as well as in. In short, under global apartheid and the EU state of exception, "the institution of asylum has become a key pressure point, complicating the filtering process...designed to separate eligible from ineligible travelers" (Bhabha 2002: 161). At the same time, basic social and economic rights have been severely eroded across Europe, for everyone. As the quotation from Agamben at the start of this chapter made clear, ever more ingenious forms of exclusion and surveillance of non-nationals can end up being used against all EU citizens and those living in the EU, as wider processes of rights-erosion are facilitated and obscured (Fekete 2001, 2009, Webber 2000). Engaged in an unseemly 'scramble to make themselves unattractive', EU member states pay little attention to the European Convention on Human Rights (Harvey 2000: 368). Cross-EU harmonization snares innocents, as genuine refugees are caught in traps set for traffickers, smugglers and all manner of 'illegal' persons as if they were game animals (Harvey 2000; Collyer 2007). Across the globe, camps are "made permanent by a blocking of their exits" (Bauman 2007: 45), which works to "reinforce...the mouldy and decaying walls meant to guard the hallowed distinction between the 'inside' and the 'outside' [in a]...world that pays little if any respect" to this distinction (Bauman 2004: 58). Blatant contradictions result, with myths of inclusiveness and daily strategies of victim-blaming coexisting in, "a borderless economy and a barricaded border" (Andreas 2000: p. x).

Just as South African apartheid and colonial segregation were enshrined in law, so the 'state of exception' that underpins today's deterrence regime across the EU is legally encoded and based on EU-wide provisions. The key starting point was a 2002 EU Directive and Framework Decision on, "Strengthening the penal framework to prevent the facilitation of unauthorised entry, transit and residence." This has created more and more difficulties and obstacles for pro-asylum advocacy work as "the authorities have widened the net of those suspected of unacceptable solidarity" (Fekete 2009: 84). However, Fekete sees in this an "intention ... not so much to prosecute more people but to warn those in civil society and public office that the threat of prosecution is real and imminent" (Fekete 2009: 84). Moreover,

> ...threat of prosecution now hangs over those who take part in direct action in support of the refugee sanctuary movement or hunger strikers, those who provide housing for the undocumented or refuse to provide information to the authorities on their residence status, those who expose conditions within detention centres or simply defend the rights of detainees (Fekete 2009: 84).

It is becoming illegal in more and more countries of the EU to help undocumented migrants, or to support struggles for their basic rights, including the right to legalization. In France, an underground movement has emerged. In the UK, grassroots support for the idea of sanctuary is growing. Already there are 11 or so 'Cities of Sanctuary' in the UK, including Sheffield, London, and Swansea in South Wales. As government threatens to convict those that campaign for undocumented people, whole cities are declaring themselves supportive.[33] Small pro-asylum advocacy organizations across the EU, like NCADC and PRIME, are struggling during the present financial crisis, besieged by an atmosphere of fire-fighting and stretched resources. Strategic and tactical alliances with progressive lawyers, well-meaning policymakers and various communities have become more urgent than ever. Working against the 3-Ds in the UK or the Netherlands has become more difficult as the deterrence regime is stepped up and the legacy of the 'war on terror' appears to merge with the 'war on insecurity'. This painful and contradictory situation attracts new supporters, because of the mounting evidence of official abuses, of even children and the disabled (Crawley/Lester 2005; Bauman 2004). This also frightens off otherwise well-meaning people from getting involved. When members of the UK Royal Society for the Protection of Birds, for example, are threatened with legal action, to prevent them demonstrating against environmental damage, it is high time everyone sat up and acted to protect our civil liberties.[34]

Eventually, any system of segregation that excludes increasing numbers of people from its protective surveillance starts to lose legitimacy and finds itself confronted with widespread resistance (Richmond 1994; Cohen 1987). Failed asylum seekers, 'illegals', undocumented migrants and people *sans papiers* are *helots*, or as Bauman puts it "...the dregs, the waste and rejects of...global free trade and economic progress" (Bauman 2007: 22; Cohen 1987). Caught between the "unheard-of-affluence" of the few and the "unspeaka-

33 See at: <http://www.cityofsanctuary.com/> (13 January 2010).

34 Martin Hickman "Heathrow puts up legal barricades to keep away protesters", *The Independent*, 27 July 2007. See at: <http://www.independent.co.uk/news/uk/this-britain/heathrow-puts-up-legal-barricades-to-keep-away-protesters-459177.html> (12 November 2009).

ble poverty and humiliation" of the many, pro-asylum advocates also are subjected to "fears and gruesome premonitions" of a world divided against itself (Bauman 2007: 22). In this context, pro-asylum advocacy is an increasingly uphill struggle, and increasingly indispensable.

Tentatively, then our conclusions are that, arising from global apartheid as reinforced by the state of exception at EU level, pro-asylum advocacy networks share common perceptions of the global system as fundamentally unjustifiable. They operate to resist the dominant logic of deterrence in the EU, and it is this, rather than shared tactics or strategies of resistance per se, that creates solidarities among such advocates. Today, within the EU, direct citizen action against the 3-Ds continues, within a context that requires close coordination. Even in a hostile legal and political climate, pro-asylum advocacy make sense to those involved, given the shared worldviews that have emerged to connect people across barriers of class, belief, legal status and local context to defend the right to sanctuary.

17 Human or Public: The Referents of Security in Discourses on Migrants in Japan

Tatsuo Harada with Kenji Kimura

17.1 Introduction[1]

This chapter offers a critical perspective on 'human security' in Japan by contrasting the meaning of the term as written in the country's Official Development Assistance (ODA) reports with that applied in discourses on, and practices towards, migrant workers. The aim is to show how the 'human being' as a referent of security – promoted under concern for 'distant others' reachable through ODA policy – has been displaced when 'distant Others' arrive on Japan's soil as migrant workers. The human dimension of security is indeed overwritten by 'public security' concerns.

First an overview is provided of the key features of Japan's restrictive immigration policy and its relationship with national identity. Next, it is shown how the combination of the demographic crisis (aging population and low fertility rate) and economic downturn has shaped the adoption of measures to import labour without allowing the visible presence of migrant labour to jeopardize the link between national identity and 'ethnic purity' (see chap. 22 by Mushakoji). New patterns of migration and new migrants that have emerged in Japan in the last two decades have politicized debates on migration, and since the events of 9/11 migration has acquired the meaning of 'public security' fuelled by the politics of fear of 'Otherness'. A paradox of security[2] prevails and operates between society's majority groups and its plural minorities.

Using data from Aichi in the Chubu Region (2005–2007) we highlight the experiences of human insecurity and their contextual differences. This region is known for its economic recovery from the burst of the economic bubble (1991–2003), which lasted until the global economic crisis began to unfold in 2008. The region also has one of the highest percentages of migrant workers compared to other regions.[3] Our analysis seeks to extend the scope of migration studies in Japan[4] by drawing attention to the complex interaction between different aspects of security (human and societal) which produce the fear of migrants and legitimize both their criminalization and exclusionary practices of an overt and/or subtle nature. The situation calls desperately for a rapprochement between these different meanings of 'security'.

17.2 Japan's Immigration Policy: Protecting National Identity and Coping with a Demographic Crisis

17.2.1 Immigration Trends in Japan in the Post-war Period

During the post-war era the Japanese government had only a fragmented immigration *control* policy and no integrated immigration approach. Until the 1970's Japan's domestic labour pool operated reasonably well, without having to consider the alternative of labour immigration as in other industrialized countries undergoing post-war economic growth. The massive inflow of a young male Japanese labour force from rural to urban areas, followed by female labour (as espe-

1 The authors are deeply grateful to Thanh-Dam Truong, Des Gasper and the essay's anonymous reviewers for their insightful comments on this chapter. All errors in the text are those of the authors.

2 Mushakoji (2003) inspires and emphasizes this perspective of human insecurity and migrants in terms of the security dilemma

3 See at: <http://www.moj.go.jp/PRESS/080601-1.pdf> (10 April 2010)

4 This field of study has have grown rapidly in Japan, especially after the bubble economy, though much attention has been devoted to the economic and social conditions of specific ethnic groups.

T.-D. Truong and D. Gasper (eds.), *Transnational Migration and Human Security*, Hexagon Series on Human and Environmental Security and Peace 6, DOI 10.1007/978-3-642-12757-1_17, © Springer-Verlag Berlin Heidelberg 2011

cially housewives) and young part-time workers had kept the domestic labour force in balance. The control of entry of foreigners into the country was primarily conducted at the national border for public security purposes.

Beneath this seemingly unproblematic domestic labour pool is the dominant myth that Japan is an ethnically homogeneous nation, which is partly accountable for the neglect of its multi-ethnic reality and has led to the marginalization of its minorities. The presence of the Koreans as a minority ethnic group has long contested official policy discourses on homogeneity. The number of Koreans in Japan was half a million at the end of the Second World War, after about 600,000 Koreans who had been conscripted into the workforce and military during the war had returned home.[5] After 1952, with the help of the U.S. government and the Japanese Red Cross, the Japanese government devised a scheme for the repatriation of Koreans to North Korea. Because Koreans were the largest minority group debates on the migration-security nexus and the social construction of 'Otherness' had most focussed on them, until recently.

Morris-Suzuki (2007: 204) notes the following report by one U.S. officer:

> The Koreans...have been an underprivileged, economically poor group living in isolated communities within major urban areas. As a result, they have been a major crime problem and a drain on the national and local social services. The Japanese, beset by their own employment problems, have not welcomed this additional burden.

The above perspective, which established a connection between being a migrant, economic hardship, and crime, was applied to the Koreans and now becomes the archetype for Japan's policy towards foreign workers, including those of Japanese descent.[6]

The 1965 Treaty on Basic Relations between Japan and the Republic of Korea marked a turning point in Japan's external relations. Japanese capital supported by the government re-entered Korea, and eventually its ex-colonies in Asia, through ODA. The period of Japan's peak economic growth (between the end of the 1960's and the beginning of the oil shocks in 1970's and through to the 1980's) saw political leaders and business officially weighing the costs and benefits of a comprehensive import of Asian migrant workers. Ochiai (1974) pointed out that practices of bringing in workers under the guise of 'trainees' began in the late 1960s to help alleviate labour shortages, particularly unskilled and semi-skilled labour in small and medium enterprises; pressure from business followed and insisted that employers be able to import workers from other Asian countries independently of the trainee system (Kuptsch/Oishi 1995).

Japan's political system has been slow in appreciating the far-reaching implications of a globalized economy, especially when it comes to migration. Having ratified the International Covenants on Human Rights in 1979 and the Refugees Convention in 1981, Japan had made amendments in social security laws to guarantee social rights to refugees and non-Japanese persons who settled in the country. Accepting new migrant workers in addition to long-term residents would mean facing the obligation to address their social rights as well. Although the domestic labour pool was showing problematic signs - fertility has declined sharply and has been below replacement level for decades and industries were pressured to hire foreigners - the government refused their demands and instituted instead policies that restructured domestic work forces for longer-term competitiveness (Meissner/Hormats/Walker/Garrigues/Ogata (1993: 68-69).[7]

The first official breakthrough was the establishment of the Japanese International Training Cooperation Organization (JITCO) in 1991. In the following two years, the government launched its Technical Internship Training Program (TITP) initially designed to be part of a larger effort to facilitate the transfer of technical skills to neighbouring developing countries through trainee programmes while also allowing Japanese employers to avail themselves of rotating pools of workers. A key element of this programme was the establishment of training centres in particular sending countries, which would select applicants wishing to migrate for work and give them brief instructions on elementary industrial production techniques and Japanese language and customs. A two-year contract period with medical care and other benefits was envisaged, after which these workers would be rotated back to their home countries. Upon their return these training centres were supposed to perform a labour-placement and exchange role (Meissner/Hormats/Walker/Garrigues/Ogata 1993: 67-68). The

5 See at: <http://www.han.org/a/fukuoka96a.html> (10 April 2010).

6 For a global history of "the emergence of migration as a security issue" see: Kleinschmidt (2006: 78-87).

7 For example: greater promotion of the participation of women and senior citizens in the labour market, introducing flexible work schemes.

trainee system with its rotating mechanism may be seen as a device to respond to both domestic labour demands and the government avoidance of the commitment to ensure social rights to migrant workers. Preventing their long-term settlement appeared to be a solution.[8]

17.2.2 Internationalization of Japan and the New Immigrants

Population Statistics of Japan 2008 show the projected population by age group with the proportion of people over 65 years old at 20.2 per cent in 2005, 26.9 per cent in 2015, 30.5 per cent in 2025 and, finally, 40.5 per cent in 2050.[9] According to *UN Population Prospects: the 2008 Revision Highlights* in 1990, the aggregate per woman birth rate for the previous year was 1.57, the lowest recorded birth rate since the end of the war; and it was estimated to be 1.27 during the period of both 2005–2010 and 2010–2015.[10] Japan experienced its first population decline in 2005; the last low point according to official records available was 1899.

Japanese immigration statistics show that the largest number of registered foreign nationals in Japan has changed from the Koreans (645,373 in 1997 to 593,489 in 2007) to the Chinese (252,164 in 1997 to 606,889 in 2007). In a controversial paper, a former immigration officer Sakanaka (1989) once summarized and predicted "the disappearance of Koreans in Japan" due to decades-long assimilation.[11] Changes in the composition of the population of immigrants stemmed from Japan's amendments of its immigration law in the 1990s to accept new migrants to join the domestic workforce in response to the acuteness of the demographic problem. A major amendment in Immigration Law was the use of *Jus sanguinis* to encourage the return migration of *Nikkeijin*,[12] and groups responded at an increasing annual rate from Brazil (233,254 in 1997 to 316,967 in 2007) and Peru (40,394 in 1997 to 59,696 in 2007).[13] In addition, three tenets underpinned the foreign trainee system: 1) admitting foreign workers, on whatever basis, should be a last resort; 2) unskilled workers should not be admitted; 3) all foreigners should be admitted on a temporary basis only (Cornelius 1994: 386–387).

The neoliberal policy package implemented by successive cabinets of the Liberal Democratic Party (LDP)[14] included financial deregulation and flexible labour market policies, and stimulated spatial and industrial urban restructuring through the construction of more business facilities in metropolitan areas, particularly during the bubble economy. This created an enormous demand for new types of labour – especially for construction and cheap services supporting sophisticated consumer and specialized corporate/producer services (Sassen 1991).[15] Deregulation allowed many companies to replace full-time employees with part-time and temporary workers and to circumvent the foreign trainees system, thus creating a social space in which migrant workers function, formally or informally.

Despite the principle for introducing the trainee system being the transfer of technical skills to neighbouring developing countries plus meeting domestic labour shortage, there are institutional 'security holes' that have caused foreign trainees and interns to suffer, some of which are: 1) their passports have been taken away; 2) off-the-job training for foreign trainees is incomplete or not undertaken; 3) trainees must work overtime during working days or on their days off; 4) trainees do not receive training allowances; 5) trainees are not paid their wages, nor do they receive compensation for overtime work; 6) restrictions on everyday life, including the prohibition of mobile phone use, staying up overnight, and taking extended trips. The number of the trainees supported by JITCO is increasing (28,011 in 1997 to 51,012 in 2004), whereas the av-

8 Little is known about past efforts in receiving foreign trainees, especially on a private basis, but today many researchers and practitioners have become very interested in the arrangements being made under Economic Partnership Agreement/Free Trade Agreement (EPA/FTA) with the Philippines and Indonesia to accept caregivers officially.

9 See at: <http://www.ipss.go.jp/p-info/e/psj2008/PSJ2008-02. pdf > (10 April 2010).

10 See at: <http://www.un.org/esa/population/publications/wpp2008/wpp2008_highlights.pdf>, (10 April 2010).

11 Sakanaka (1989: 159–160) summarized the immigrant policy for Koreans in Japan (*Zainichi Chosenjin*) as follows: "Koreans in Japan today are legally 'foreigners,' but in fact 'quasi-Japanese'. We can suppose that they are going to be Japanese in the future and should be called 'Korean-Japanese (nationals).'"

12 *Nikkeijin* are Japanese descendants living outside Japan. Those who return were mainly living in Latin America at the time. They are entitled to permanent residence but are segregated from mainstream society due to 'cultural difference', especially the younger generation.

13 See at: <http://www.moj.go.jp/content/000007316.pdf> (10 April 2010).

14 From Nakasone (1982–87) to Koizumi (2001–2006).

15 Indeed, Tokyo and other urban areas have been transformed from national to global cities during this period.

Table 17.1: Comparison between industrial training and technical internship. **Source:** Compiled by the authors

	Industrial training	**Technical internship**
1. Scope of eligible duties and occupations	Activities that are not purely repetitive of the same task, complying with the Immigration Control Act and ordinances.	The 63 occupations and 116 selective works covered by the National Trade Skills tests and other similar tests.
2. Target skill levels	Basic Grade 2 of the National Trade Skill tests (by the end of one-year training).	Grade 3 of the National Trade Skill tests (by the end of the second year of internship).
3. Measures for ensuring skill acquisition	Formulation of and adherence to training plans	Formulation of and adherence to internship plans
4. Required residence status	"Trainee"	"Designated Activities"
5. Worker status	Trainees have no worker status and are not permitted to work.	Interns are treated as workers.
6. Overtime work and work on regular days off	Not allowed	Allowed
7. Protective measures	Protection implemented under the Immigration Control Act and ordinances. A training contract is between the sending/ accepting organizations.	Protection implemented under the Labour laws and regulations. A Technical Internship contract is between the technical intern and the accepting company.
8. Clarifications of terms and conditions	Trainees are provided with a "Notification of Conditions to Trainees" stipulating the training hours, allowances and other terms and conditions.	Interns are provided with a contract of employment or a "Notice of Employment Conditions," stipulating the working terms and conditions
9. Welfare guarantee provided by the accepting organization	Trainees are paid a training allowance to cover their living expenses. Allowances are decided based on the agreement between the sending organization and the accepting organization	Interns are paid wages for their labour. Wages are described in each employment contract between the technical intern and the accepting company. The Minimum Wages Law applies as in the case of Japanese employees.
10. Insurance against accidents and illness	Comprehensive Insurance for Foreign Trainees is arranged on a compulsory basis.	The Workers' Accident Compensation Insurance Law applies during the technical intern period; the Comprehensive Insurance for Foreign Technical Intern also applies.

Note: The Industrial Training Programme is designed for young and middle-aged people from developing countries to acquire technologies, skills and knowledge in specified industries ad occupations in companies in Japan. The Technical Internship Programme is a scheme that enables trainees to master the technologies, skills and knowledge they acquired through training in practical and professional ways while being employed for a period up to three years, including the training period.

Source: JITCO (2009) *Industrial Training and Internship Programmes: Operative Manual for Sending Organizations*, (Tokyo: Japan International Training Cooperation Organization).

See at: <http://www.jitco.or.jp/download/data/sendorg_manual_English.pdf>; <http://www.jitco.or.jp/english/overview/pattern.html> (23 May 2010).

erage monthly allowance is decreasing (Hatate 2006: 87–88).[16]

Business in Japan has always been cautious of absorbing the social costs of migrant labour. Even during the bubble economy period, the so-called *Kaikoku-Sakoku Ronsou* (debates on closed- or open-door policy for immigrants), this attitude prevailed. Today business owners seem to be confident about their experiences in making use of various types of immigrant labour, formally or informally.[17] Importing unskilled labour is becoming less and less of a taboo subject, politically and/or economically.[18] The category of 'technical intern' has now been added to the foreign trainee system. This new category allows trainees who passed a skills examination after the training period to change their visa status to one permitting them to engage many types of paid jobs (up from 17 in 1993 to 64 in 2009) and remain in Japan for a period of three years. Since the trainee system has been functioning as an informal measure recruiting cheap unskilled workers, adding this new category means the possibility to extend the legal time frame, job coverage, and perhaps receive better protection.

"Entertainer" as a visa category has also been subject to much criticism. Data shows that in the 1970s the Republic of Korea was the largest supplier of this category of migrant workers, followed by the Philippines in the 1980s (David 1991). Today 'entertainers' come from many countries in Asia, Latin America and Eastern Europe. This category has been widely used to bring women into the country to work in the sex industry. Pressure to address human rights abuse in sex trafficking has increased since Japan's ratification of the Transnational Convention against Organized Crime (2000).[19] Being placed in Tier 2 and thus on the watch list in the U.S. Trafficking in Persons Report 2004, Japan has sought to improve this status. Crackdown measures have led to a notable decline of the number of entertainers since 2005.

Figures for foreigners' status of residence show "an increasing trend until the end of 2004, but decreased at the end of 2005 and 2006 due to decrease in the number of foreign nationals entering Japan with the status of residence of 'entertainer'".[20] This sharp drop (from 32,297 in 1999, 64,742 in 2004 to 15,728 in 2007) stemmed from the introduction of stricter control of entertainer status granted to Filipinos and Thais.[21]

Crime control led to the expansion of the activities of the immigration bureau on public security, focussing mainly on Taiwanese, Chinese, Colombian, Romanian and Nigerian networks who have been active in the last twenty years in informal global networks of drugs, human trafficking and small arms. Given that the Japanese authority considers overstaying to be the first step that makes a person vulnerable to, and a potential target for, criminal activities, *overstayers* have become an important focal point for scrutiny and public security. *Overstayers* are those who remain in the country beyond the period authorized by their visas, not only because they have slipped through the government's strict control but because of its tacit tolerance in view of the need to satisfy labour demands by small and medium-size companies.

Recently, *Immigration Control 2007* proudly announced that the reason why the number of *overstayers* has been steadily decreasing was attributable partly to:

> ...the conducting of strict immigration examinations, concentrated efforts for close cooperation with other related agencies to detect violation of the Immigration Control Act and active performing of publicity activities to prevent illegal employment, as well as the fact that the year 2006 was the third year of the five-year plan to

16 For further information, refer to the Advocacy Network for Foreign Trainees, see at: <http://k-kenri.net/>, (5 May 2009). Interestingly enough, in their Trafficking in Persons report (2007, 2008, 2009), the US State Department has criticized the Japanese foreign trainee and intern system as a type of trafficking in persons. See at: <http://www.state.gov/g/tip/rls/tiprpt/index.htm>. The Japanese government thus announced revisions to the system on their website, only available in Japanese, See at: <http://www.jitco.or.jp/cgi-bin/press/detail.cgi?n=260&ca=2>, 20 Oct 2009.

17 For another brief explanation of unskilled labour migration to Japan in a regional context, see Shuto (2006: 206–210).

18 For instance, on 14 November 2004, *Nippon Keidanren* (Japan Business Federation) issued a report entitled *Gaikokujin Ukeire Mondai ni kansuru Chukan Iken Torimatome (Interim report on receiving foreigners)*, in which it called for preparing and promoting the acceptance of a wide range of foreigners, including specialists, care workers and manual labourers. This can be said to be the very first official announcement by business associations regarding immigration.

19 The Japanese government obtained the approval of the Diet for it, but has not, to date, concluded the convention because it has not yet provided for the necessary domestic legislation to implement it. Further, three protocols have not yet been concluded: 1) Protocol to prevent, suppress and punish trafficking in persons, especially women and children, supplementing the United Nations Convention against Transnational Organized Crime, 2) Protocol Against the Smuggling of Migrants by Land, Sea and Air, Supplementing the United Nations Convention Against Transnational Organized Crime, and 3) Protocol Against the Illicit Manufacturing of and Trafficking in Firearms, their Parts and Components and Ammunition, Supplementing the United Nations Convention Against Transnational Organized Crime.

20 Immigration Bureau of Japan, 2008: "Immigration Control 2008". See at: <http://www.moj.go.jp/NYUKAN/nyukan80-3.pdf>, 21 (10 May 2008).

21 As Japan Times online reported, Japan is trying to limit the number of foreigners entering the country on entertainer visas - most of whom are Filipino women - to tighten controls on human-trafficking. Many of the women, who often land in hostess jobs, end up in the sex industry. See at: <http://search.japantimes.co.jp/cgi-bin/nn20050218a4.html>, (14 June 2008). Also see at: <http://search.japantimes.co.jp/cgi-bin/nn20060602f2.html>, (14 June 2008).

halve the number of illegal foreign residents implemented by the Immigration Bureau.[22]

The number of foreign detainees has subsequently risen sharply nationwide. Thirty per cent of the total prisoner population in Tokyo was foreign (2005) with foreign females outnumbering Japanese female prisoners by 55 per cent (Iwai 2007: 8). The rapid increase in the number of foreign detainees is far beyond the administrative capacity of the prison system for domestic criminals. Part of the foreign detainee population is classified as belonging to the 'F class' who do not understand Japanese or are not accustomed to Japanese customs. There is no special treatment for this group: they are put in the same prison as the Japanese (male foreigners in Fuchu or Osaka Prison; females in Tochigi), or temporarily at the East and West Japan Immigration Centres.

Public access to information on foreign detainees at the East and West Japan Immigration Centres is highly limited. Takahashi (2007) points to the following problematic practices: 1) forced imprisonment in every case, including people undergoing treatment for work-related accidents, pregnant women, elderly persons, and those who are unfit; 2) indefinite or long-term imprisonment; 3) family members separated by juvenile imprisonment; and 4) prisoners abused by immigration officers. It has been reported that police officers readily subject foreign detainees to violence and inhumane treatment.[23]

Coutin's analysis of 'the space of nonexistence' in the U.S. holds true with the case of Japan:

> The undocumented have been referred to as 'shadow' people who slip in and out of sight and who live in an 'underground' or a 'netherworld.' Official U.S. policy is to detain and eventually deport these troubling, ambiguous, shadowy people, and thus to remove the trace of their physical presence. Even if they are not deported, the undocumented are set apart from the juridically authorized by laws that dispense rights and services on the basis of legal identity. The undocumented therefore exist in a non-domain, a space of illegality (Coutin 2003: 174–175).

To recapitulate, the neoliberal framework of governance of migration in Japan seems to be navigating between two objectives: 1) to preserve the myth of ethnic purity, and 2) to avoid absorbing the social costs of migrant labour. The archetype of policy inherited since the end of the Second World War premised on a view that links migrants with poverty, economic burden and crime has veiled their positive contributions. Circumventions of the legal framework had been possible given this widespread belief – even in the case of the *Nikkejin* who can enter Japan, work legally and enjoy access to social security services, but who are segregated from mainstream society due to 'cultural difference' which makes them vulnerable to being treated as disposable labour in a way similar to other migrant workers. Deregulation has permitted the creation of new ill-defined zones outside the formal boundaries of legality. The underlying logic of relation between ethnic purity and social space for migrant workers is hierarchical, and status (defined on the basis of ethnicity, mode of entry, skill-level) thus serves to differentiate both the place and position occupied by these workers as well as the relations between them and mainstream society. Recent measures to crack down on crime have turned immigration detention centres into what has been termed as a new place of 'bare life' and a 'zone of arbitrary treatment' (Buck-Moss 2000; Agamben 1998) for those removed from the system.

17.3 Discursive Practices on Human Security: The 'Distant Human' in ODA versus the 'Proximate Other' in Migration

17.3.1 Human Security as Framed in Japanese ODA

Since the turn of this millennium Japan ODA policy has concentrated on the areas of international peace and economic development as one of the limited ways to show its diplomatic presence – the constraints of Article 9 of the country's Constitution limits Japan's military role to that of self-defence. Its philosophy on human security has not necessarily been clear to the international community. At the end of the Cold War Japan became a leading ODA donor

22 Immigration Bureau of Japan, 2007: "Immigration Control 2007", See at: <http://www.moj.go.jp/NYUKAN/nyukan68-3.pdf>, (10 May 2008).

23 According to Johnston, Eric; Matsubara, Hiroshi, 2004: "Detainees stage hunger strike: Ex-Vietnamese boat people protest indefinite detention", in *The Japan Times Online,* 25 Vietnamese (later 23) being held at the West Japan Immigration Centre were on a hunger strike to protest their prolonged incarceration. Some had been held for nearly two years, partly because the Vietnamese government had refused to take them back due to their status as former boat people, and they had therefore lost their public presence for two years. See at: <http://search.japantimes.co.jp/cgi-bin/nn20040611a3.html> (4 June 2008).

prompting the government to initiate its own development assistance strategy which does not necessarily follow the developmental prescriptions of the West. The Cabinet approved Japan's Official Development Assistance (ODA) Charter in 1992, and Japan co-hosted the Tokyo International Conference on African Development (TICAD) in 1993. The co-organizers of TICAD were UN agencies – OSSA (Office of the Special Advisor on Africa) and UNDP. The key concept guiding TICAD has clearly become human security especially since TICAD's Tenth Anniversary Declaration at TICAD III (2003).

Since the introduction of the ODA Charter of Japan in 1992 successive leadership in the Japanese government has made reference to the human security agenda. According to the chronology of activities related to human security by the Japanese Government, in December 1998, Prime Minister Keizo Obuchi expressed his views on human security in "Intellectual Dialogue on Building Asia's Tomorrow"; in March 1999 the United Nations established the Trust Fund for Human Security. Prime Minister Obuchi stated in his keynote speech that the concept of 'Human Security' would be reflected in Japan's concrete foreign policies. In February 2003 the co-chairs of the Commission on Human Security, Sadako Ogata and Amartya Sen, submitted a summary of the final report of the Commission to Prime Minister Koizumi. In October 2000 Japan also chaired the first FHS (Friends of Human Security) meeting – an unofficial and open-ended forum based in New York. The purpose of FHS is to provide an informal forum for United Nations Member States, as well as relevant international organizations, to discuss the concept of human security from different angles in order to seek a common understanding and explore collaborative efforts for mainstreaming it in United Nations activities.[24]

Most recently, in the pamphlet of the Trust Fund for Human Security (UNTFHS) for a 'human centred' 21st century, Japan explains its diplomatic position as follows. To overcome the global issues, including ethnic and racial conflicts, the smuggling of people, arms and drugs as well as infectious diseases, "...[t]he traditional concept of 'state security' alone, whose objective is to protect the boundaries and the people, is no longer sufficient. Indeed, the importance of state security will not and should not shrink at all, but additional responses are necessary to address diverse threats comprehensively".

Against this background, the notion of human security, an important pillar of Japan's foreign policy, has increasingly gained relevance. Human security aims to protect people from critical and pervasive threats to human lives, livelihoods and dignity, and to enhance human fulfilment. For these objectives human security tries to integrate and strengthen initiatives that emphasize 'human-centred perspectives'. Japan presented four basic policies in its revised ODA Charter: supporting the self-help efforts of developing countries; the perspective of 'Human Security'; the assurance of fairness; and the utilization of Japan's experience and expertise. It is important to note that from the Japanese perspective, human security is understood in practice as follows:

> In order to address direct threats to individuals such as conflicts, disasters, and infectious diseases, it is important not only to consider the global, regional, and national perspectives, but also to consider the perspective of human security, which focuses on *individuals* [italic added]. Accordingly, Japan will implement ODA to strengthen the capacity of local communities through human resource development. To ensure that human dignity is maintained at all stages, from the conflict stage to the reconstruction and development stages, Japan will extend assistance for the protection and empowerment of individuals (Ministry Foreign Affairs 2003: 2).

In line with the ODA Charter and in view of its commitment to reduce vulnerabilities faced by people, communities and countries by employing the concept of 'human security', the Medium-Term Policy on ODA describes Japan's position on four priority issues: poverty reduction; sustainable growth; global issues; 'peace-building'. Global interdependence is also included.[25]

Japanese development assistance policy lies in sharp contrast to its domestic migration policy. Ironically, addressing 'vulnerabilities' faced by individuals located in foreign countries is not a policy focus when dealing with the challenges faced by foreign people (and migrant workers) on Japanese soil. It appears as though there are two types of people: those who deserve to be protected, strengthened, empowered and respected; and those to be placed under control regardless of their being exploited, voiceless and ex-

24 Ministry of Foreign Affairs, 2008: "Friends of Human Security" see at: <http://www.mofa.go.jp/policy/human_secu/friends/index.html> (1 Oct 2009).

25 Ministry of Foreign Affairs, 2009: "The Trust Fund Human Security for the 'Human Centred' 21st Century", See at: <http://www.mofa.go.jp/policy/human_secu/t_fund21.pdf> (1 Oct 2009).

Table 17.2: Some indicators of economic activities by Prefecture of the Chubu Region in 2005.

Prefecture	Foreign Residents	Foreign Workers	Nominal GDP by Prefecture	Nominal GDP by Industrial Sector		
				Primary	Secondary	Tertiary
Aichi	150,115	83,354	35,819,911	208,639	13,907,916	22,814,718
Shizuoka	70,721	44,203	16,415,050	192,667	7,068,315	9,910,591
Gifu	36,793	25,020	7,247,705	77,728	2,490,547	5,008,871
Mie	34,249	20,778	7,699,787	116,776	3,206,302	4,688,957
Sub Total (Chubu Region)	291,878	173,355	67,182,453	595,810	26,673,080	42,423,137
Tokyo	248,363	93,501	92,269,424	47,177	13,324,590	84,428,097
Osaka	175,766	73,688	38,529,386	30,232	8,431,234	31,546,718

Notes:

1. Data of Economic Activities in 2005 from the Cabinet Office, Government of Japan; see at: <http://www.esri.cao.go.jp/jp/sna/kenmin/h17/main.html> (10 April 2009)
2. Data of Foreign Residents and Workers in 2005 from the Statistics Bureau and the Director-General for Policy Planning (Statistical Standards); see at: <http://www.stat.go.jp/data/kokusei/2005/gaikoku/zuhyou/syuyou.xls> (10 April 2009)
3. Unit of GDP: one million yen.
4. GDP by Industrial sector includes import tax, consumption tax on total capital formation, and imputed interest; GDP by prefecture does not.

cluded from official assistance. We call this contrast the Distant Human versus the Proximate Other.[26]

This bifurcated vision of human security is reflected in academic work. Since 2000 there have been many publications in Japan under the label of 'human security'. They fall into two broad categories. One focuses mainly on development policy, ODA and poverty reduction (Taya 2000; Yoshida 2004; JICA 2007); the other is mainly based on peace studies (Katsumata 2001; Matsukuma 2008). Most of them follow the definition of the Sen-Ogata Report on human security and shed light on the topics and cases of human security and insecurity in developing countries from their specialized perspective. This perspective is tightly connected to the definition of human security as 'freedom from fear and want', thus orienting policy towards humanitarian intervention and 'human-centred' development assistance. The basic assumption is that human (in)security is a problem 'over there' (or abroad) rather than one arising from global interdependence. No attention has been given to the interrelationship between the forms of insecurity faced by people 'over there' and those experienced by the foreign nationals who have moved 'here' to Japan. Japanese research on human security that follows the notion of global interdependence displays more sensitivity to human (in)security 'here' and 'there' and provides an interconnected perspective on 'people on the move' inclusive of the migrant population (including migrant workers) from developed countries. In the following section the interconnected aspects of human insecurity are spotlighted in a major manufacturing region in Japan where a high number of migrants are concentrated.

17.3.2 Human Faces of Migration and Security in the Chubu Region: A Focus on the Aichi Prefecture

As pointed out earlier, Chubu is a manufacturing centre for Japan. The region is also a major point of attraction for migrant workers. Manufacturing exports (especially automobiles) to the US and BRIC countries (Brazil, Russia, India, and China) have recently led the Japanese economic recovery after the burst of the bubble economy. The head office of Toyota is located in Chubu. This contributed to the expansion of

26 The contradictory attitude of Japanese government becomes most apparent when reading the part on 'target peopleí and situations in the UNTFHS documents. See Item b) in Ministry of Foreign Affairs (2009: 9): b) Supporting and empowering refugees, internally displaced persons (IDPs), economic migrants and others on the move. Particular attention should be given to the socioeconomic impact on the displaced and their host communities.

Table 17.3: Number of registered foreign residents in the Aichi Prefecture by selected cities (2007). **Source:** Department of Regional Development and International Affairs, Aichi Prefectural Government See at: <http://www.pref.aichi.jp/0000012581.html> (10 April 2009)

Nationality/Rank	Aichi						
Brazilian	79,899	Toyohashi	12,840	Toyota	7,813	Nagoya	6,213
Chinese	41,755	Nagoya	19,552	Toyota	2,646	Ichinomiya	1,712
Korean	41,456	Nagoya	21,217	Kasugai	2,473	Toyohashi	1,900
Filipino	23,701	Nagoya	6,842	Toyohashi	1,715	Ichinomiya	1,275
Peruvian	8,277	Toyohashi	1,015	Nagoya	891	Komaki	882
Prefectural Total	221,389						

the export base of the region, which has been most recently hit hard by the current economic turmoil.[27]

Within Aichi prefecture there is a concentration of 'oldcomers' (Koreans and Chinese) in the capital city (Nagoya) where there are various job opportunities for those well integrated into Japanese society, and a concentration of mainly 'newcomers' (migrant groups who arrived in Japan in increasing numbers after 1980's) in other industrial cities (Toyohashi, Toyota, Okazaki and Komaki).

Occupational distribution by nationality may also be noted. Almost all migrants from developing countries are highly concentrated in factory work as labourers, which is a part of the reason they are *invisible* to the public eye. Thais and Filipinos are concentrated in the service sector in close interaction with the Japanese people in daily life. They work in the commercial zones of Aichi, as well as Nagoya (Harada 2005: 40). In addition to these patterns of employment of formal migrants are those concerning informal residents and workers, or *overstayers*. How specific groups of migrants experience human insecurity may differ according to their legal status but it is noteworthy that they all rely on self-help organizations to achieve daily needs, sometimes with the involvement of the local government and actors in the Japanese civil society.

Rather than providing an in-depth ethnographic analysis of the variations of human insecurity experience in this region, the intention here is to highlight those aspects which help direct attention to the web of relationships shaping these experiences. Data obtained of two groups of immigrants – the Japanese-Brazilian and South Asian workers – help to illustrate how, under a specific legal and economic environment, social and cultural factors can propel and influence interactions in ways that affect insecurity in daily life for particular groups.

The situation of Japanese-Brazilian children in education was studied from October 2006 to June 2007 in Komaki City, an industrial city located in the suburbs of Nagoya in Aichi, using several methods (participatory observation, group and individual interviews and analysis of secondary materials).[28] The main findings suggest that Japanese-Brazilians with formal visa status who stay for a long period – even when they enjoy relatively stable economic positions – face problems regarding the education of their children, including learning languages (Japanese or Portuguese), school dropout and juvenile delinquency. Circular migration and job-hopping nationwide by the parents has brought about serious insecurity for the young generation.[29]

An important factor to be noted is that the principle of mandatory education applies only to Japanese nationals, and therefore the education of foreign children has not been regarded as an obligation of the state but as a favour (*onkei*) – despite Japan's ratification of the Convention on the Rights of the Child in 1994 (Sakuma 2006). Foreign children have no guaranteed right to education.[30] Children of Japanese-Bra-

27 For more information on the Japanese automobile industry and the Chubu region during the post-war period, see Jacobs (2003). See also the Japan Times online article: "Over the past few months, layoffs among foreigners nationwide, especially those who are temp workers. employed by auto parts manufacturing plants in the Kanto and Chubu regions, continue to grow as Toyota and other leading automobile firms struggle with declining demand. Many now out of work would return home if they could, but the rising cost of airplane tickets due to increased fuel surcharges makes it difficult.î See at: <http://search.japantimes.co.jp/cgi-bin/nn20081224f1.html> (24 Dec 2008).

28 Kenji Kimura conducted the field research in this section.

zilian parents who drop out of primary school have limited educational choices, and those who cannot gain substantial help from their parents often become isolated from Japanese society. Consequently, some have begun to commit crimes and eventually separate themselves from local society. With active support from the local government and NGOs (non-governmental organizations) some dropouts can now work in the Homi apartment complex,[31] also known as 'Little Brazil'.

Since many Japanese-Brazilians do not really rely on municipalities for support, self-help organizations have played an essential role in the education of their children. Volunteers have begun to offer Japanese and Portuguese language classes privately, not just for learning but also as a means for communicating and making friends. This is considered to be an effective way to curb child dropouts and juvenile delinquency. Currently only a few public schools accept these volunteer groups in Komaki but substantial progress has been made. In 2009 this city has become an official member of the *Council for Cities of Non-Japanese Residents,* which networks its member cities.[32] Until now, long-staying formal immigrants like the Japanese-Brazilians have not received a full-range of social support other than from self-help groups. Under the current system and policies they will have to continue living as secondary citizens or aliens, unless Japan makes a concerted effort to extend and ensure them equal rights. Paradoxically, problems of school dropout and juvenile delinquency have led to better communication between young people of both Japanese-Brazilian and Japanese origin.

Turning to the South Asian *overstayers* similar reliance on self-help groups is found plus a nebulous distinction between the legal and illegal. Those who participated in our interviews in 2006[33] invited us to their homes - old Japanese-style one-storey houses located near the firms where they worked. They prepared their stories before being interviewed because the moderator had told them our purpose in advance. While they read the stories we interjected with several questions. One of the informants, over 50 years old, was formerly a political leader back in his home country.[34] He had been working in Japan for 13 years in different places: factories for chemicals, printing, fertilizer and meat processing. At the time of the interview he was working at a factory producing car plastic parts in Aichi. His bad working conditions and struggles for just treatment were clearly a challenge to him. Here he notes:

> My worst experience was at a fertilizer factory. Our employer usually ordered us to work for 12 hours (8am-8pm) and once for 36 hours without any break! He criticized me for breaking bags when I carried them, so they reduced my wages (from $100 to $50 for a few weeks). I consulted a local labour union and brought my case to the local police station, which didn't arrest me for overstaying. We won the case. The brokers were not worth trusting; they acted in collusion with the employer.

29 The economic recession in 2008–2009 is changing their life plan drastically. The government support policy provides $300 per person for foreign workers of Japanese descent to return to their home country, plus $200 per dependent. "The policy was enacted in response to the waves of layoffs that have hit foreign-born workers as the economic situation worsens, and while it forbids re-entry to Japan there are many workers of Japanese descent who say they would like to come back once the economy gets back on track." And "According to the Ministry of Health, Labour and Welfare (MHLW), the prohibition on a return to Japan 'for the time being' is 'to prevent people of Japanese descent from using the support for short trips to their home countries'". This policy was introduced in April 2009, and many policy-makers and the Brazilians themselves are divided on this issue. See at: <http://mdn.mainichi.jp/mdnnews/national/archive/news/2009/04/30/20090430p2a00m0na0020 00c.html> (5 May 2009).

30 Historically, this stems from the implementation of the Alien Registration Law when the San Francisco Peace Treaty took effect in 1952. Under this law, Korean and Taiwanese residents became disenfranchised of the Japanese nationality they had held during colonial rule, and were recognized as foreigners regardless of how long or how many generations they had lived in Japan (Douglass/Roberts 2000: 6). See also Yamanaka, Keiko, 2002: "Ana Bortz's Law Suit and Minority Rights in Japan", JPRI Working Paper No. 88, The University of San Francisco Centre for Pacific Rim, See at: <http://www.jpri.org/publications/workingpapers/wp88.html> (18 Aug 2007).

31 The Homi public apartment complex is located in Toyota City where the headquarters of the carmaker is located. The Homi is a place where Japanese-Brazilians go when they leave the factory, where their children return after school, a surrogate home away from home. See: Linger (2001).

32 Its member cities number 27, of which cities in Chubu account for 20: three in Gifu, seven in Shizuoka; six in Aichi; and three in Mie. See also the *Council* website at: <http://homepage2.nifty.com/shujutoshi/> (10 April 2010).

33 Professors Youngku Koh and Tatsuo Harada from Chubu University conducted these interviews.

34 For security reasons, the identities of informants are kept anonymous.

South Asian *overstayers* suggested that they often received as much in wage as their Japanese counterparts, but they felt more insecure and unjustly treated due to the lack of access to medical care and other pertinent social benefits. Some assert that the Japanese government knows of their expired residency permit. One respondent asked:

> Why don't Japanese employers officially request the authorities to allow them to hire foreign workers? They know about our presence. It is easy for them [employers] to report to the authorities after we worked for a few months without any official assistance. We easily fall sick because of bad working conditions. We are exploited.

Despite the lack of public medical services these *overstayers* have solicited contributions from their fellow nationals to donate medical machines to a hospital in their own country, for which they seemed very proud. Meetings of a self-help organization held in Aichi were attended by those with a formal status and *overstayers* - young and old, both male and female - suggesting that this group is organized, has no particular fear of the local police, is apparently familiar with the insufficient cooperation between immigration authorities and the local authority, and is aware that their presence, while considered 'illegal', is tolerated owing to the contributions they make to the local economy.

This nebulous distinction between legality and illegality also finds its expression in the ways firms employ *overstayers,* some of which encounter curious tactics of criminal networks or anti-migrant groups. According to one respondent who is director[35] of a firm that assembles interior part of automobiles, Toyota had long known that many undocumented foreign workers were employed in subcontracted factories. Despite this, Toyota continues to limit the prohibition of illegal employment of foreigners to only a few of its subcontractors. Our employer-respondent has devoted himself to evolving better working conditions for foreign workers (informal or formal). He has encountered curious manoeuvres of extortion.

> "I have heard of this one strange case about some factories being blackmailed by members of the Yakuza or rightwing organizations. They said, "We will inform the police or the immigration office that you're committing the illegal employment of foreign workers unless you pay an amount of money [meaning a few hundred thousand yen] as hush money." How could they learn about this secret? They waited outside the factory, met the foreign trainees after these had finished working overtime and asked them: "Hey guys, are you working very hard overtime?" The trainees, who aren't allowed legally to work overtime in their first year, trusting them, answered, "Yes, we are tired!", or something along this line. This is proof of violating the law, which those groups use to blackmail factory directors."

According to him, cases of foreign trainees running away from companies are not uncommon. The decision to extend the contract terms is generally based on a company's interests, and not those of foreign trainees. An extension period without breaks can be too long for some trainees; those who have 'escaped' from the company had relied on a friend or someone whom they knew they can contact. Escaping these dire working/training conditions only meant one thing - that they have ventured into the illegal zone of categorically being labelled as *overstayers.*

In sum, the variations of human insecurity discerned show multi-causes and intersecting aspects that have produced distinctive experiences, although these are mainly related to the absence of a social policy (education and medical care) for the migrants and a work environment favouring the interests of producers. In this respect it is important to point out that to achieve human security goals would first require a social policy that is not restricted to national membership. Mutual support self-help groups formed among those having the same ethnicity, sometimes with enabling action by the local government, are the main avenues through which the immigrants receive help. New dynamics in personal and collective interactions emerging at a local level seems to aim for these goals, even if they currently are very weak. Local communities have shown a more open attitude to multi-ethnic realities; yet local restructuring and shrinking public support do place limits on the possibility of extending social policy to the new immigrants. Despite a more open attitude to multi-ethnic realities among some people at the local level, the absence of a wider public support places limits on the possibility of and opportunities for extending social policy to the new immigrants. The dialectic of inclusion and exclusion, or association and dissociation, experienced by different ethnic groups should be considered in the broader context of the transformation of local society in Japan.

---

35 It had been very difficult to have contact with employers of foreign workers, especially undocumented. We interviewed an employer at several meetings held in 2005 and 2006 who has long hired many Asian workers: informally at first and now formally. This case is special in that the respondent is married to someone who had been a foreign intern at his factory. He thus seems to have a deep compassion regarding the working conditions of foreign interns.

17.3.3 Transformation of the Local Public Sphere

In Japan, those accepting the neoliberal world of fragmented labour have accused foreigners of being potential opponents to the social order, branding them as criminals. Neighbourhood-watch groups and security cameras have increasingly become common due to this fear of 'otherness'.[36] Japanese discourses and policy on immigrant control presuppose a 'preventive public security' in which foreigners are viewed as potential criminals and terrorists – just as human security discourses in Japanese ODA proclaim preventive diplomacy and development.

A missing element in this perspective is how neoliberal deregulation has reshaped many local communities and generated different forms of insecurity for the local population. One example of the destructive impact on local life space is the Large Scale Retail Stores Law in 2000, which permitted large chain stores and shopping malls to open on every corner of local cities. This suburbanization led to the closing down of local shopping streets due to competition. Homogeneous suburban spaces for consumers became dominant nationwide. With local businesses being hollowed out, communities have become more competitive as well as security-oriented.

Spatial homogenization has made every local life space unappealing for young and old generations. The elderly, in particular, lost their community – as they knew it. For them, neighbourly and family relations have become more inaccessible. For young people who have been disassociated from mainstream society (as well as gangster groups formed for other reasons) this context provides a sense of legitimacy for their hostile reaction against the presence of the 'Others' in what they perceived to be 'their' space (or the life spaces on the edge of mainstream society shared also by the unemployed and homeless). The presence of foreign trainees, *Nikkeijin* and undocumented migrants, employed by many manufacturers and agricultural producers in suburban areas, has in many ways intensified this antagonism. The 'unease' suffered by some Japanese citizens who feel discarded (because they cannot cope with the uncertainty of everyday life) has been fuelled by the " securitization" of immigration policy (Bigo 2002: 65). This unease is not only psychological, but also reflects the structural unease in a 'risk society' – framed by neoliberal discourse which always associates 'freedom' at its limits with danger and in/security (Bigo 2002).

Furthermore, local provision of social services has been deteriorating due to the financial burdens placed on local governments, thus further intensifying the 'felt' insecurities among local citizens. In the name of autonomy and decentralization, local governments are required to become independent from the central government's budget allocation. Many local governments suffer from financial collapse, and must raise taxes and social insurance contributions, including care insurance. The elderly take such a major hit that some are forced to leave their hometowns to escape the increasing financial burden. More and more local public hospitals are being closed or consolidated for financial reasons.

The Act on Assurance of Sound Financial Status of Local Governments (2007) defines the organization for early correction as a 1st step; and fiscal reconstruction as the 2nd step in accordance with one of four indicators: 1) real deficit ratio; 2) consolidated loss ratio; 3) real debt expenditure ratio; and 4) fiscal burden in future. The second indicator is of special importance. This act consolidates general with special accounts of local finance for correction and reconstruction – the latter account includes public expenses, some of which are related to the domain of social policy and tend to build up deficits. When the indicator falls below the mark, the local government has to show budget austerity to the central government. This stimulates the financial and organizational restructuring of local care systems such as hospitals.

The much discussed option to import foreign care workers under the *economic partnership agreements* (EPA) between the Philippines and Indonesia may serve to illustrate the messy impact of this Act on local society. Formally, these agreements were based on the reason that there is an insufficient supply of Japanese medical workers nationwide. Yet in 2008 and 2009 the numbers of actually accepted nurses and care workers were far below initially planned targets, mainly because of the lack of systematic acceptance mechanisms; this in addition to the collapse of local medical care systems and worsening working conditions of care workers generally.[37] The national perspective does not seem sensitive to the fact that financial tightening policy developed by the central government does limit the room for local govern-

36 One of Japan's nationwide surveillance systems is called the 'N-system' in the name of crime control (first introduced in 1987). It has been set up at more than 400 points of arterial roadways and automatically records information regarding the car registration number, the driver and other passengers.

ments to accommodate foreign workers who come to Japan under terms of bilateral agreements. The postwar social welfare system in Japan is based on local community organizations (such as the Japan National Council of Social Welfare) thus once foreign care workers arrive the local organizations must be responsible for them, as has been the case for foreign trainees (Harada 2007: 68). Financial tightening means a reduction of local capacity to comply with established standards, creating a situation in which invited guest workers are not properly protected; and their presence has come to be seen by citizens as an impingement on the local life spaces over which they have a sense of 'ownership'. This domestic security tension is yet to be taken up in Japanese ODA discourses on human security.

17.4 Reformulating the Referent of Human Security

What are the key elements of human security conception and practice, following the discussion above? The first element is that the notion of human insecurity is a less contestable normative concept than human security as formally defined; thus we can more easily go beyond the formal definition and identify forms of human insecurity experienced by individuals and groups within a specific context of transnational connections and multi-local livelihoods (Truong/Gasper 2008). In other words human insecurity allows a more embedded understanding and a theorizing enriched by on-site experiences and life stories. Beyond the international migration management perspective the existential sufferings of some specific immigrant groups in Japan should be researched in ways that reveal the new local dialectical interactions on 'security'. This helps illuminate the rift between official discourses on human security under ODA and those on public security under domestic immigrant control.

The second element is that 'people on the move' represent one of the most significant individual and collective living proofs of transnational networks, through which forms of human insecurity arise and spread in a mode that connects different regions, localities and nations. If this interconnectivity is ignored, the policy orientation of universalistic human security (presented in UNDP's 1994 report) remains within the expedient policy talk of the distant 'Human' versus the proximate 'Other'.

The third element is that the dichotomy between the definition of human security (as "freedom from fear and want") and the policy orientation of "protection and empowerment" (first chapter of the Human Security Commission Report) should be overcome. The former is embedded in the traditional framework of national security and development policy, and the latter is directed at the improvement of the living conditions of vulnerable people in developing countries.[38] Instead of clinging to these respective definitions one should comprehend the historical development of three interrelated security concepts - national, social and human security – and their historical constructions. The problem is how these seemingly different concepts of security can be bridged in a positive way. That is the core theoretical question. In Japan, social security has developed with national security and national integration since the Second World War. Human security, however, belongs to an age of "post-national membership" (Soysal 1994: 3), and is often not based upon the universalistic human rights as formally proposed (Castles and Davidson 2000: 17–19) but upon more contextual realities. The concept of human security should be made more sensitive to contextual social interactions.

The fourth element is to reconsider the questions of 'who is human?' and 'what is humanity?' within the concept of human security. Arnold Gehlen views the nature of humanity as fragile and vulnerable, due to neoteny[39] (born to be powerless) and the lack of a set of instincts to adapt itself to the natural environment - unlike other animals. Thus he called man and woman 'deficient beings'. Instead of a natural and strong action-programme based upon instincts, humanity is equipped with learning abilities and has built institutions like language, technology and culture (Gehlen 1988). Recognizing this fundamental powerlessness of human existence is vital to acknowledge the capability and human need to care for, and to ac-

37 See at: <http://mdn.mainichi.jp/perspectives/news/20090516p2a00m0na013000c.html>, (20 May 2009): *The Mainichi Daily News*; see also: Harada (2007); Onuki (2009).

38 For a narrow conception of human security, see MacFarlane and Khong (2006: 251). They claim, "it is also the case that the 'security' in social security has little analytical function. The more widely used descriptors of the programme are 'social insurance' and 'social welfare'". In their conception the main target of human security is direct violence. As a result, structural and cultural violence (Galtung 1990) are missing from their depiction.

39 Neoteny is a kind of *pedomorphosis* in development biology.

cept care from 'others' as a vital core of 'being human'.[40] Societal institutions built on the recognition of such caring interaction can be more open and help make life more secure. Extending feminist knowledge to human security, Truong sheds fresh light on an ontology of relational self, care and human security. "Built on a 'relational ontology' care offers an alternate understanding of social reality. ...the constitution of each and every entity in the human-scale reality is made up of a nexus of relationships...and mutual constitution. Caring for the self in this regard also means an openness to 'otherness'" (Truong 2009b: 19). Clarifying the relationship between the ethics of care and human security, she writes:

> Concerns about the narrow understanding of group rights and about a singular understanding of identity require security to be more epistemologically grounded and rooted in particular geo-political contexts. The demand for such 'situated' understanding and action does not imply a whole rejection of universal norms, rather, a more reflexive approach to: (a) the existing institutions; (b) their contextual performance; and (c) their capacity to pursue (or dislocate) human security goals.... In this vein, the ethics of care can strengthen a vision on human security, as it accords significance to diversity, particularity and context (Truong 2009b: 21–22).

Thus, though we may find the agency of migrants in Japan very weak, their resiliency through caring for each other remains the key to their survival.

17.5 Conclusion

The long-standing fragmented and dual labour markets in Japan have been deepened by a neoliberal deregulative capitalist regime. This has affected Japanese nationals and immigrants simultaneously, bringing them into competition and antagonistic interactions. In addition *selective and exclusive* immigrant control policies, and the deepening of concerns for public security, have placed the onus on migrants, resulting in practices that place them in a zone of nonexistence and consequently enhancing their insecurities outside the boundaries of the law and the public sphere. This is in sharp contrast to the Japanese ODA discourse on human security which promotes the *inclusion* of all vulnerable people in developed countries or conflict areas.

The security dilemma between the majority and minority communities in Japan is worsening with the economic recession. Multi-ethnic Japan is of a local nature; so are its problems. In this respect the human insecurity of migrant workers within Japan can be overcome by making human security thinking more socially sensitive to embrace all people living and working in Japan, moving beyond national membership and paying particular attention to the specific realities at the local level. The challenge now is to build a new form of solidarity based upon a new contextual post-national platform, working with local membership groups in the name of human security to overcome social and economic turmoil in realistic ways and promote a shift in the national position from below.

---

40 According to Roach, "caring is the mode of human being" and it is "the most common, authentic criterion of humanness" (Roach 1987: 2). As Gaylin mentioned, "powerlessness, care and survival are interconnected" (Gaylin 1976: 20).

18 The Global Forum on Migration and Development: 'All Talk and No Action' or 'A Chance to Frame the Issues in a Way that Allows You to Move Forward Together'?

Bernice Roldan and Des Gasper

18.1 Introduction

In 2006, the United Nations, for the first time in its history, held a high-level multilateral dialogue on international migration and development. With migration trends and issues increasingly common in international discussions - including on remittances, brain drain, feminization of migration, irregular migration, and violations of migrants' human rights - sustained pressure had been exerted on the UN to convene a major forum. To some, the Dialogue was a way to address the lack of support by labour-receiving countries for the UN International Convention on the Rights of All Migrant Workers and Members of their Families.[1] In Dauvergne's words, for those countries, national migration law has been "transformed into the new last bastion of sovereignty" (Dauvergne 2004: 588). Various governments, of major labour-sending countries in particular, lobbied the UN for years to convene a keynote meeting. There were delays as the organization gave priority to other issues and conferences (MFA 2007), but eventually a 2003 agreement of the General Assembly led to the Dialogue on 14–15 September 2006 at the UN headquarters in New York City. The objective was to address how to increase development benefits of international migration and reduce negative impacts.

Given adamant opposition by major immigration countries to any machinery for binding global regulation of migration, the preparations for the Dialogue led to design of a purely consultative and purely intergovernmental Global Forum on Migration and Development (GFMD). The Forum now exists outside of, although in cooperation with, the UN system, and has become a standing inter-governmental forum on international migration, how it relates to development, and the status of migrants' rights. It aims to build international cooperation on migration, in thinking, policy and practice, and "to foster practical and action-oriented outcomes at the national, regional and global levels".[2]

For some civil society groups this outcome was a bitter disappointment. One issue surrounding the GFMD concerns its non-binding character, given the background history of non-ratification of the Convention on migrant workers. Another is that by taking the forum out of the auspices of the UN and making it a meeting of governments, many voices are excluded, including those of migrants, their families and communities, and civil society in general. Many in international civil society hold that issues of human rights and sustainable development are thereby downplayed. A different perspective comes from others such as the

1 See at: <http://www.mfasia.org/mfaActivities/MWC-RatifyMonitor.html> (4 January 2010). Opened for ratification in 1990, the Convention only achieved sufficient ratification to come into force in 2003. Only 40 State Parties have ratified it to date. Thus far, no major labour-receiving country has ratified the Convention. In contrast, the Convention against transnational organized crime achieved sufficient ratification within two years. That the two most common objections to the migrant rights Convention–concerning limits to state sovereignty and the provision for family reunification to regular migrant workers already residing in the labour-receiving country–do not hold upon a close look at the Convention's text, shows labour-receiving countries' degree of suspicion and domestic political dispute in this area. MacDonald and Cholewinski (2007: 12) argue that the relevant Articles (44 and 79) have extremely qualified language, "leaving such a wide discretion open to states, it is difficult to see any obligation of any sort, let alone one that could present a serious obstacle to ratification".

2 See at: <http://government.gfmd2008.org/forum_info/objectives.html> (30 March 2009).

T.-D. Truong and D. Gasper (eds.), *Transnational Migration and Human Security*, Hexagon Series on Human and Environmental Security and Peace 6, DOI 10.1007/978-3-642-12757-1_18, © Springer-Verlag Berlin Heidelberg 2011

Washington-based think tank Migration Policy Institute, which wrote that while many circles had written off the 2006 UN Dialogue as "all talk and no action, it may yet be the beginning of a new era. Nearly all participating countries said they would like to continue a dialogue on migration and development but that such a forum should be state-led and should only promote cooperation, not produce binding agreements".[3]

Since 2006, while power relations between labour-sending and receiving countries inevitably remain in play, the Forum has evolved into a significant space for bilateral negotiations on international migration and how it relates to development, in particular concerning migrant labour (MFA 2009), as seen in its subsequent annual conferences in Brussels (2007), Manila (2008) and Athens (2009). Plans for subsequent annual meetings (in Mexico, Spain and Morocco, successively) are underway, before the Forum returns to the UN in 2013.

This chapter looks in detail at two speeches - the opening address to the 2006 High-Level Dialogue by then UN Secretary-General Kofi Annan, and the closing address of the 2008 Manila conference by the conference chair - each in its entirety, using selected tools of discourse analysis. We aim to cast light on the intended rationale of the Forum, whose proponents see its non-binding, restricted character as a strength and not a weakness, given the starting points of fear and confusion in labour-receiving countries and profound international mistrust. We further aim to cast preliminary light on how the Forum's approach fares in practice, including whether and how it starts to build trust and reduce fear.

We especially aim to illustrate the usefulness of discourse analysis tools, in helping to reveal and test influential assumptions and frames and contrast them with other perspectives. Discourse analysis is particularly relevant in the field of international migration, given that the field abounds in fears and stereotypes, paradoxes and inconsistencies. The choices of categories and the creation or loss of trust are of central importance for the direction of discussion (cf. Griffin 2007).[4] To reach a wide and relevant audience, we need tools of discourse analysis that are relatively accessible and yet take us beyond the level of insight of ordinary reading. In this chapter, we employ basic elements of rhetorical analysis, giving attention to each of logos, pathos and ethos (roughly speaking: appeals to logic and evidence, to feelings, and to the credibility of the author), and to the choices made in framing, especially through the choices of metaphor.

18.2 Visionary Pragmatism? Address by Secretary-General Kofi Annan to the 2006 High-Level Dialogue

In just over 1,000 words, Kofi Annan's opening address[5] to the New York 2006 Dialogue presented a major message. It rewards careful attention. The core audience was from UN member states at the ministerial and highest civil servant levels. UN agencies and other inter-governmental bodies and organizations, such as the International Organization for Migration (IOM), were present as observers. While civil society and the private sector involved in issues of international migration were not present, everyone was aware that these actors were intensively monitoring the UN process. There had already been an interactive UN consultation with international civil society two months earlier.

In the analysis table below, we divide Annan's text into sections and comment on the choices of focus, language and structure. In doing so, we gain more insight into the layers of tacit meaning. To take us beyond the level of intuitive appreciation, such an analysis table forces the reader to examine a key text in a different way. It slows us down, ensures that we give attention to all elements and provides a more reliable route in looking for themes. We can then subsequently reconstruct the patterns of argumentation-cum-suggestion conveyed by the speech, more revealingly than through ordinary reading.

We identify five parts in the speech. First, an unusually bold and unapologetic opening, that describes international migration in language that brings legitimacy in dominant countries, not least the country where the speech was given: individual striving, opportunity and creative identification of possibilities for mutual benefit. Second, given the shared recognition now of the great potential for joint advantage between countries, the speech offers an emphatic endorsement of the timeliness of the initiative. The third and central aspect is a perspective for the ongoing

3 See at: <http://www.migrationinformation.org/Feature/display.cfm?id=544> (25 February 2009).

4 See at: <http://www.york.ac.uk/res/researchintegration/Integrative_Research_Methods/Griffin%20Discourse %20Analysis%20April%202007.pdf> (6 November 2009).

5 See at: <http://www.un.org/migration/sg-speech.html> (16 February 2009).

Table 18.1: Analysis table for Kofi Annan's New York speech, 14 September 2006

U.N. Secretary-General Kofi Annan's Address to the High-Level Dialogue of The General Assembly on International Migration and Development New York, 14 September 2006	**Commentary** We have inserted in brackets five implied section headings. Italics in this column indicate a paraphrase or implication of a part of the speech.
Madam President, Excellencies, Ladies and Gentlemen:	[**Governments start to see migration as an opportunity**]
Migration is a courageous expression of an individual's will to overcome adversity and live a better life. Over the past decade, globalization has increased the number of people with the desire and capacity to move to other places.	After the conventional formal greetings, a bold opening captures attention and legitimacy, by direct reference to individual humans and their aspirations and choices, and unapologetically praises migrants. In addition, he links migration to globalisation.
This new era of mobility has created opportunities for societies throughout the world, as well as new challenges. It has also underscored the strong linkages between international migration and development.	Opportunities are highlighted before challenges; opportunities for all.
Just a few years ago, many people did not think it possible to discuss migration at the United Nations. Governments, they said, would not dare to bring into the international arena a topic on which their citizens are so sensitive.	
Yet here you are, and I sense that the mood is changing.	*You [the assembled governments] have been daring.* Annan establishes a tone of confidence, openness; he also makes the audience individually self-reflective by saying "you" are here, not here "we" are. "Mood" - emotions are involved;
More and more people are excited about the ways in which migrants can help transform their adopted and their native countries. More and more people understand that governments can cooperate to create triple wins—for migrants, for their countries of origin, and for the societies that receive them.	"excited" - the alternative mood. "More and more" repeated, to build a sense of a new majority. "Understand", not merely "feel" or "hope", acknowledges cognition as well as emotion involved. "Triple wins" - confidence-raising business jargon. "Their countries of origin", not "their countries" as if they did not belong also in the country of arrival.
No one can deny that international migration has negative aspects—trafficking, smuggling, social discontent—or that it often arises from poverty or political strife. But by being here today you show yourselves willing to tackle migration's challenges through dialogue and cooperation, rather than antagonism and isolation.	Again "you", not "we"; thus putting each of the audience in the spotlight rather than hidden in a crowd.
Your presence is also a tribute to the infectious energy and visionary pragmatism of my Special Representative, Peter Sutherland. His efforts have reassured and inspired everyone. I am deeply grateful to him.	Sutherland: the Irish former head of WTO – a Northern advocate of free trade, thus able to reassure rich nations "reassured": nervous worries have been overcome. Praise for one of the key organisers of the event implies praise too for those who participate in it.

As you begin your Dialogue, let me suggest three reasons why this is the right moment for it.	**[You have made the right choice, to participate in this event and process]**
First, to put it simply, we are all in this together. More countries are now significantly involved in, and affected by, international migration than at any time in history. And they are no longer so easily divided into "countries of origin" and "countries of destination". Many are now both. Countries that are very different in other respects face surprisingly similar migration challenges.	The first use of "we". Until this point the Secretary-General stressed the Dialogue as the product of the choices of individual governments (e.g., "your Dialogue"). Now, as the speech moves from the chosen entry of each government to the Dialogue, on to the substantive issues for the Dialogue, he stresses what all countries share.
Second, the evidence on migration's potential benefits is mounting. With their remittances reaching an estimated 167 billion dollars last year, the amount of money migrants from the developing world send back to their families exceeds the total of all international aid combined. And money is far from being the whole story. Migrants also use their skills and know-how to transfer technology, capital, and institutional knowledge. They inspire new ways of thinking about social and political issues. They form a dynamic human link between cultures, economies, and societies. As a result, we are better positioned than ever to confront the challenges of migration, and seize its opportunities.	*International migration is now central to economic, social and political development of poor countries, and in many vital global interlinkages.* Again, use of the unifying "we", though for the last time (apart from one use of "us"). In the rest of the speech, the Secretary-General returns to using "you", to strengthen the feeling of Forum ownership by individual states.
Third, Governments are now beginning to see international migration through the prism of opportunity, rather than of fear. You are focused on magnifying the positive, mutually beneficial aspects of migration: on sharing your experiences, developing practical ideas, building partnerships.	Third use of "opportunity". Having unified the audience by the terms adopted in his presentation, he reinforces this by praising their bold and constructive stance. The sentence 'You are focused...' is a garland of praise-terms: "positive", "mutual", "sharing", "practical", "building partnerships".
For all these reasons—and also because people migrate not only between neighbouring countries or within regions, but from almost every corner of the world to every other—international migration today cries out for a global discussion.	Again, implicitly: *we are all in this together.*
	[The way forward: dialogue and voluntary cooperation, controlled by you]
Of course, it also stirs passionate debate. It can deprive countries of their best and brightest. It can divide families. It can generate social tensions. Sometimes criminals and terrorists exploit it. But the answers to many of these problems can be found through constructive engagement and debate.	"Of course" makes an appeal to shared knowledge, shared experience, shared understanding and shared challenge. "Best and brightest" – implies that the term does not apply only in rich Northern countries. The three-fold repetition of "It can" gives emphasis. "Constructive" figures as favourable counterpoint to the earlier "passionate".
That's why I think the dialogue you are starting today should not end tomorrow. I am especially delighted that so many of you have embraced my proposal for a Global Forum on Migration and Development, and asked me to help set it up. And I am particularly grateful to the Government of Belgium for offering to host the first meeting next year.	He takes upon himself responsibility for the initiative on this issue "so sensitive"' that others said Governments would not dare to discuss it together. Hence, no one can say it is only an initiative from Government X or Group Y.
I believe such a Forum can foster practical, evidence-based cooperation among governments. It can give you a chance to frame the issues in a way that allows you to move forward together, to discover areas where you agree, and to find ways of improving cooperation.	From here onwards, he conveys how the Forum he proposed is now owned by the governments, not by the UN: "you" frame, consult, and choose. The speech supplies a nourishing diet of praise-language: from "practical" and "evidence-based", through "move forward", to "cooperation".

Clearly, there is no consensus on making international migration the subject of formal, norm-setting negotiations. There is little appetite for any norm-setting intergovernmental commission on migration. But, as I understand the thinking of the countries that back it, the Forum would be the opposite of that. It would be informal, voluntary, consultative. Above all, it would not make binding decisions.	"Clearly" is added to help avoid spending time on a non-productive issue, and to instead sweep on towards more "visionary pragmatism". "Little appetite": a gentler phrase than "intense opposition", it eases the way towards cooperation. He now presents the thinking as that of the Forum's backers, not his; ownership has been transferred. The Secretary General presents himself as a modest global facilitator, working with the grain.
The Forum would allow us to build relationships of trust, and to bring together the best ideas that different countries have developed: facilitating remittances; engaging diasporas; exploring new ways to reduce poverty; building educational partnerships; and so on.	Another treasure-house of praise language: "build", "trust", "bring together", "facilitating", "engaging", "exploring", "building".
Finally, it would show that Governments are now willing to address this complicated, volatile issue in a thoughtful, constructive fashion.	The praise accompanies an elegant implied criticism—*that governments were previously unwilling to deal thoughtfully and constructively*—in order to again promote self-reflection.
	[The UN will help you along this path]
The Forum must be led and overseen by States. But the United Nations System, and I personally, stand ready to support it. I have decided to extend the mandate of my Special Representative on Migration beyond this Dialogue. I trust that the Special Representative will form an essential link between the proposed Forum and the entire United Nations system. Also, I stand ready to create a voluntary Trust Fund to help support the Forum's work, should you find this useful.	Having calmed fears of an international process that would pressurise unwilling governments, Annan calms fears that the government-led process will lack technical and financial support or coordination with related work. He outlines a series of facilities, to reassure and encourage participants and to reinforce his own and the UN's standing.
The United Nations is rising to the challenges of international migration in other ways as well. Last spring, I established the Global Migration Group, which brings together UN offices, Funds, Programmes, and Agencies engaged in various aspects of international migration and development, as well as the International Organization for Migration. You are no doubt familiar with the important work done by the constituent members of the Group – from supporting labour migration to helping developing countries connect better with migrant communities abroad, from outstanding demographic analysis to research on remittances, from efforts to secure the rights of migrants to combating trafficking in human beings. The Global Migration Group is working to ensure stronger coordination and greater coherence among its members.	He relies heavily on his personal stature as a globally trusted global leader—using the authority and the freedom conveyed by being near the end of his ten years in post. The repeated "I" language conveys confidence and strength, to help energise the new Forum. By subsequently stressing the myriad relevant and coordinated activities of the UN system, he then transfers this personal authority to their work that will continue after him.
Ladies and gentlemen,	**[*Envoi:* It is time for serious work; let us put childish things behind us]**
This High-level Dialogue will succeed to the extent that it ushers in an era of sustained, thoughtful consideration of international migration and development issues. For far too long, migration policy has been based on hunches, anecdotes, and political expediency. It is now time to turn to the evidence, and use it to build a common understanding of how international migration can bring benefits to all.	Implicitly: *In the past, we have not acted in migration policy like thoughtful, well-informed and mature judges.* If we do so, then success—benefits to all—awaits us.
Thank you very much.	

management of this arena through a continuing forum for voluntary inter-state sharing of ideas. Fourth, reassurance that the Forum would not be an international mechanism to exert pressure on states to move in directions they do not wish, but could rely on support from the established UN system to make progress. Finally, as the send-off to his audience: Annan gives a gentle call for maturity by governments and a pointer to the benefits for all that it can bring. Later we will investigate the central, third, section of the speech in more detail.

Overall, from our initial reading, Kofi Annan's speech is well suited to its audience composed of senior government figures and representatives of intergovernmental and international agencies. The language is diplomatic, with judicious use of metaphor ("little appetite for", "prism of opportunity rather than fear", "move forward together"), juxtaposition (maximizing opportunities, minimizing risks; volatile problems, constructive solutions), a cast of characters suitable for motivating the audience (courageous individuals, visionary pragmatists, dangerous criminals and terrorists), and hints of pathos. Praise and criticism terms provide familiar signposts, and are often used in partnership. Having praised governments for their boldness in joining this new process - "you have been daring" - Annan underlines that the process represents their intelligent self-interest - for "we are all in this [intensively interconnected world] together" - and gently criticizes the previous lack of intelligent, well-informed and constructive attention.

Our commentary in the right-hand column of Table 18.1 adheres to the three central categories of classical rhetoric: *logos*, the direct arguments provided, examined in detail below; *pathos*, the emotions appealed to, as in the opening and concluding sections where Annan extols the courage and enterprise of migrants, and then quietly calls for courage, enterprise and intelligence from governments; and *ethos*, the role adopted and authority acquired by the author in relation to the audience. Some key aspects in this construction of ethos are as follows. Annan shows that he understands the worries and concerns in rich countries, as well as those of migrants; he calls for evidence; he buttresses the credentials of the UN as a wise and helpful support of governments, not infringing their sovereignty but strengthening their rationality. He presents the United Nations system as deserving the standing that he individually had gained: as sufficiently broadly accepted and trusted, endowed with a global perspective and substantial relevant expertise.

We now look in more detail at the central section of the speech. Having already encouraged, praised and unified the audience, the Secretary-General here moves to identify the required work that lies ahead and how it should be structured and conducted. As is usual in political speeches and in much other communication, many of the assumptions and suggestions remain tacit, only hinted at, for it could be clumsy, unnecessary or counterproductive to make them explicit. Table 18.2 employs a more refined, three-column, analysis format, that includes dedicated space for identifying his assumptions and conclusions, both stated and unstated, the definite and the only hinted at. This will give us a basis for specifying the logical structure of the core of the speech, as the system of propositions in Table 18.3. The main value-added from the more detailed analysis provided in Table 18.2 will be seen then in the synthesis of Annan's arguments that we arrive at in Table 18.3. (For exposition and fuller illustration of this linked pair of formats, and their rationale as introductory tools in argumentation analysis and discourse analysis more generally, see Gasper 2000, 2002, 2004b.)

Our closer study of this core passage confirms that the UN was well aware that in its first official meeting on international migration and development it was under scrutiny from various sides. The language is vivid when touching on the social costs of migration (families divided; countries deprived) and muted on causalities and broader societal problems. It made clear that the outcome after New York City would be a GFMD process where governments would take the lead and the UN would play a supporting role. The central passage ends with a subtle criticism of and warning to governments, while offering them the prize of better outcomes and a better image if they follow the path of constructive dialogue.

Table 18.3 organizes the Secretary-General's points in this central passage into a logical system. The first row below the column headings shows how the overall proposal, that governments should proceed to cooperate within the new Global Forum, stems from a set of more factual claims (Data) and a series of posited principles or judgments (Warrants), largely those which we identified in the final column of Table 18.2. Each of those supporting elements rests in turn on some other background posited Data and Warrants, as we show in the other rows for most of the elements. The procedure helps us to draw out further the unstated assumptions and conclusions that we sought in the final column of Table 18.2, to show the interconnections, and to better assess what Annan

Table 18.2: More detailed analysis table for the key central passage of Annan's 2006 speech
Stated assumption = SA Stated conclusion = SC
Unstated assumption = UA Unstated conclusion = UC Unstated suggestion = US.

Components of the text	Further comments/Clarification of meanings Italics in this column indicate a paraphrase or implication of a part of the speech.	Identified assumptions/ conclusions/ suggestions
	1. Challenges of migration	
Of course, it [international migration] also stirs passionate debate.	Acknowledges the strong sentiments on migration in international debate	US: "I understand your worries".
It can deprive countries of their best and brightest. It can divide families. It can generate social tensions. Sometimes criminals and terrorists exploit it.	Pathos of labour-sending countries. "Generate social tensions": a vague description (and without clear causality) in contrast to "deprive" and "divide". Migration seems like an omnipresent force that can deprive and divide. But what are its underlying causes?	US: Labour-sending countries have a difficult situation. The UN understands that too. US: Unless we manage migration, criminal groups will manage it.
	2. Proposed solution: the Forum	
But the answers to many of these problems can be found through constructive engagement and debate.	"But": *pessimism is unjustified.* "Constructive engagement and debate" – neutral, diplomatic solutions to emotive problems.	UA: Controversial emotive problems require calm structured communication.
That's why I think the dialogue you are starting today should not end tomorrow.	"dialogue *you* are starting today"; having provided an optimistic perspective, he associates it with the work of those who have assembled	US: Member states have ownership of the dialogue, not the UN.
I am especially delighted that so many of you have embraced my proposal for a Global Forum on Migration and Development, and asked me to help set it up. And I am particularly grateful to the Government of Belgium for offering to host the first meeting next year.	"delighted", "so many", "embraced", "particularly grateful" – *things are going great* "Asked me to help set it up" – *I am your agent.* A rich country takes the lead.	US: Governments are in control, while the UN will provide support. US: Other rich countries can feel secure.
	3. Conditions for cooperation among member states	
I believe such a Forum can foster practical, evidence-based cooperation among governments.	Soothing, encouraging words.	UA: Member states start with different views, but
It can give you a chance to frame the issues in a way that allows you to move forward together, to discover areas where you agree, and to find ways of improving cooperation.	Uses panoply of praise terms, associated with: *You, you, you.* *The Forum offers so much that governments would wish for.*	SC: cooperative work will increase the areas of agreement, which will reinforce the cooperation.

	4. Dialogue as voluntary, non-binding, consultative process	
Clearly, there is no consensus on making international migration the subject of formal, norm-setting negotiations. There is little appetite for any norm-setting intergovernmental commission on migration.	"No consensus" – understatement, neutral term.	UC: It is not feasible to implement binding resolutions and sanctions at present, as there is insufficient acceptance of an intergovernmental migration commission to lead this. SA: There is little demand to set up such a commission
But, as I understand the thinking of the countries that back it, the Forum would be the opposite of that.	Highlights role of the UN as outsider and supporter, and the countries as owners and leaders of the process.	UC: An informal, voluntary, consultative and non-binding dialogue is more desired and feasible than a norm-setting intergovernmental commission on migration.
It would be informal, voluntary, consultative.	"Informal" might be vague, particularly for a high-level meeting, but "voluntary" and "consultative" are praise terms.	
Above all, it would not make binding decisions.	Emphasis via "above all", to reassure the fearful.	UA: Non-binding character of the Forum is seen positively by most member states, and UC: is thus an accepted priority.
	5. Fostering trust and sharing good ideas	
The Forum would allow us to build relationships of trust, and to bring together the best ideas that different countries have developed: facilitating remittances; engaging diasporas; exploring new ways to reduce poverty; building educational partnerships; and so on.	Uses a series of praise terms, to encourage, persuade, reassure	SA: Trust is built when member states share good practices to minimise the risks and maximise the opportunities from migration. UC: it will reduce the need to create a formal, binding process.
	6. Addressing a sensitive issue fruitfully	
Finally, it would show that Governments are now willing to address this complicated, volatile issue in a thoughtful, constructive fashion.	Juxtaposition of problem/criticism terms –"complicated", "volatile"–with solution/praise terms: "thoughtful", "constructive".	US: Governments were previously not thoughtful and constructive.

said. Assessment is the task of Table 18.3's last column, where we present possible qualifiers and objections. It could be interesting, for example, to explore further Annan's judgment that it is not feasible to have binding resolutions and sanctions in the absence of a responsible and accepted intergovernmental migration commission.

Overall, the Secretary General argued that in the global system of nation states, a Global Forum for inter-state mutual familiarization and cooperation is the best available option. The United Nations, itself an inter-state organization, offers no route for fast-tracking migrants' rights. An attempt to take such a route raises fears and will be obstructed by labour-receiving countries. If Annan's problem analysis indicates fear and mutual ignorance as central constraints, including fear that global-wide principles are too standardized and unconditional, then his solution analysis points toward countering the fears and ignorance and promoting 'sustained, thoughtful consideration'. Let us move to look at the character of the Forum in practice.

Table 18.3: Synthesis table to show logical structure of key passage of Annan 2006 speech.

I propose that (Claim)	Given that (Data)	And the principle that (Warrant)	Unless (Rebuttal / Qualifications/Queries)
Overall Claim: You should go ahead to work in the Global Forum for Migration and Development	D1. Disagreements exist; and a heritage of casual, non-thoughtful, non-constructive behaviour. D2. Alternatives are not feasible. D3. GFMD is feasible.	W1. We must manage migration. W2. Controversial emotive problems require calm, structured communication. W3. GFMD will be fruitful.	[See below, for possible objections and queries concerning the inputs to the proposition.]
W1. We must manage migration	There are many associated problems and strong sentiments.	Migration yet offers great opportunities (see elsewhere in speech). US: Unless we manage migration, then criminal groups will.	We = who?
D2. Alternatives to GFMD are not feasible	SA: There is little demand to set up such an Intergovernmental norm-setting commission on migration	UC: It is not feasible to implement binding resolutions and sanctions at present, as there is insufficient acceptance.	Do binding general rules depend on having a norm-setting commission?
D3. GFMD is feasible	US: Member States have ownership of the dialogue, not the UN. US: Governments are in control, while UN will provide support. US: Rich countries will feel secure.		Various other stakeholders want an intergovernmental commission: migrant organisations, some labour-sending countries, some human rights groups.
W3. GFMD will be fruitful	UA: Non-binding character of the Forum is seen positively by most member states, and UC: is thus an accepted priority.	SC: Cooperative work will increase the areas of agreement, which will reinforce the cooperation. SA: Trust is built when states share good practices to minimise the risks and maximise the opportunities from migration. An informal process is more effective and can be sufficient, for it tackles the root problem of lack of trust.	Provided that civil society consultations take place and feed into the inter-governmental process. Annan assumes that all governments will have strong participation at the Forum. Labour-sending and labour-receiving countries will in fact have different degrees of interest. In addition, the non-binding character could produce non-participation, lack of commitment and distrust among member states.

18.3 Frame and Metaphor Analysis of the Report of the 2008 Manila Global Forum on Migration and Development: 'Continuing the Journey' and 'Harvesting the Fruits'?

Our second text for analysis is the concluding report by Esteban Conejos, Jr., the Philippines Undersecretary for Migrant Workers Affairs, at the GFMD conference in Manila in October 2008. The speech appears as an appendix to this chapter (Box 18.1). The Undersecretary was the focal person from the Philippine government in the GFMD process and the Chair of GFMD Manila. He presented the report at the closing of the inter-governmental meeting, to more than 600 delegates (government leaders and representatives) from 164 countries.[6] More than 1,100 delegates participated in the meeting as a whole.

Migrant associations were kept out of the intergovernmental meeting but this provided a focus and inducement for an enormous wider forum. The event organizers provided for:

> a section dedicated to civil society participation: the Civil Society Day(s) held before the government meeting. While there had been only one day provided for migrants' representatives to meet in Brussels, this part was expanded to two days in Manila, including an 'interface' session with the representatives of government. Here, the topics of the Roundtable sessions mirrored the ones from the government meeting, thus Roundtable 2.2. dealt in both cases with 'Managing Migration and Minimizing the Negative Impacts of Irregular Migration' and so forth. Apart from the 'interface', a delegation of civil society representatives was given [30 minutes] during the government meeting to present its recommendations.... [In addition the] 2nd GFMD would see an especially wide scope of parallel events; in fact, the impressive level of activities taking place over nine days from October 22 until October 30 amounted to a more comprehensive, more inclusive and one might even say: more relevant event than the GFMD proper (Rother 2009a: 101).

In an interview with the Philippines' leading news network, when asked what would be discussed at GFMD Manila, Mr. Conejos had replied, "We are going to shine the spotlight on the human face of migration. In the first meeting in Brussels, they were [very much] concerned with the economic side: what the economic benefits of remittances are, the transfer of skills, the diaspora contributions to the communities. But in Manila, we will not focus on the money. We will focus on the person itself" (sic).[7] Despite this, when compared to Kofi Annan's speech in terms of 'visionary pragmatism', his closing report leans far towards the pragmatism side. As we will see, the 'focus on the person' seems to concern as much the 'migro-crats', those involved in inter-governmental and inter-organizational processes of mutual education and negotiation on migration, and their trust-building direct interaction.

18.3.1 Frames and Framing

The Conejos report is three times as long as Annan's speech. We will not employ the same micro-textual analysis and argumentation analysis formats, for that would be arduous and would still require use of additional complementary tools to seek out general themes and principles guiding this larger text's construction. To illustrate this latter type of investigation, we will use frame analysis methodology to comment on aspects of inclusion, exclusion, prioritization and patterning of choices in the speech. Following Rein and Schön's "frame-reflective policy analysis" approach (Rein/Schön 1977; Schön/Rein 1979), we trace how the report uses a series of framing devices to transform worries over a complex policy issue into an orderly problem formulation.

In policy development, problem setting is the stage of inquiry undertaken to arrive at a problem definition and diagnosis, as a stage in moving towards a prescription for action. It starts with a problematic situation, where our existing knowledge is not sufficient to cope with the problem, so that worries ensue, which we attempt to overcome through ordered formulation of the problem (John Dewey, in Rein/Schön 1977: 238). Conceptual frames guide us towards a problem definition and diagnosis. They focus our thoughts by highlighting and including certain things, while omitting and ignoring others. They link together certain features to create a pattern, thus suggesting relationships, creating order out of complexity and making sense for us out of problematic issues. Policy frames build a particular orientation towards action.

To make tacit frames implicit, we can look for what is the remedial action proposed, for that typically implies a perceived flaw that needs correcting, and the perception of flaw typically reflects a whole system of perceptions. In this case, some of the remedial actions to correct perceived flaws were mentioned in the themes of the Manila roundtable discussions (RTDs) – RTD 1: Migration, development and human rights (paragraph 14); RTD 2: Secure, regular migration can achieve stronger development impacts (paragraph 24); RTD 3: Policy and institutional coherence and partnerships (paragraph 31). The third title is of particular importance, for the master theme of the report appears to be communication: that a consultative process can gradually improve everything and bring advantages to everyone. Supporting this master theme are sub-themes, on particular aspects of

6 See at: <http://government.gfmd2008.org/news/press-releases/second-global-forum-on-migration-and-development-formally-opens.html> (30 March 2009).

7 See at: <http://www.abs-cbnnews.com/features/10/14/08/esteban-conejos-we-will-shine-spotlight-human-face-migration> (30 March 2009).

the process, on necessary supportive structures, and on the expected fruits.

18.3.2 Master Frame: Collegial Consultative Process Will Bring Benefits For All

Staying close to the GFMD's character as a high-level forum that is "informal, voluntary, consultative", the report's overall style remains relatively informal and easy to grasp. Paragraph 3 sets the tone. It invokes "an ongoing process that is changing our thinking and actions on migration and development, but *more importantly*, that is changing the way we deal with each other on these two complex, but interrelated, issues", migration and development (emphasis added). Paragraph 9 elaborates, as follows: "The informal nature of the Forum has allowed new *friendships and partnerships* to blossom between migrant-sending and -receiving countries" (emphasis in the original). Paragraphs 10, 13 and 40 continue the mood. Interaction unpressured by fear of imminent worldwide legal instruments provides the space for sharing information and for growth of mutual and joint understanding, leading to identification of mutually beneficial options, case-by-case. The final paragraph (47) restates the theme of a flexible discussion process, providing ongoing opportunity-oriented dialogue rather than attempting to specify a standard worldwide regime of rules.

18.3.3 Secondary Theme 1: Win-win Solutions, Doing Well by Doing Good

The theme of benefits for all is elaborated in paragraphs 14, 16 and 29. By a harmonizing hand, the protection and empowerment of migrants will benefit not only them but also their countries of origin and destination (paragraph 14); the right thing to do is also the smart thing to do (paragraph 16); and new smarter policies such as planned circular migration and "market-based migration policies" (paragraph 29) will benefit all these groups, by precluding the activity of smugglers and traffickers, who constitute the real alternative if instead of orderly managed migration the governments of labour-receiving countries attempt to limit migration drastically.

18.3.4 Secondary Themes 2, 3: Changing the Perceptions of Possibilities and of 'We'

Finding benefits for all relies on patient joint work, which rests on and in turn promotes a mutual acceptance, the formation and strengthening of a feeling of 'we', at least for these purposes. The theme recurs again and again, from paragraph 1 on "harvest[ing] the fruits of our labour together" and paragraph 3 on "changing our thinking and actions" by "changing the way we deal with each other", through paragraph 9 on "new friendships and partnerships" and paragraph 30 on "the theme of partnership and cooperation", to paragraph 38 on handing on "the GFMD torch" from low-income Philippines to high-income Greece. The cooperative 'we' is described as engaged in a process that changes and generates ideas (paragraphs 2, 3, 13, 22) and moves towards much more shared understanding and concrete agreements.

18.3.5 Secondary Theme 4: Jointly Approved Research and Dissemination

The speech repeatedly states a need for research related to migration and development (paragraphs 21–23, 28, 32, 33 and 37), to provide evidence to guide policymakers; for instance in paragraph 21 on "disseminating information and the results of research on migration and development [to] inform governments about how to provide an enabling environment to empower migrants". Paragraph 32 echoes Kofi Annan on the previous fear-based reliance on 'intuition and anecdote', the reason why the GFMD is needed.

Paragraph 21 is silent on whose research results and information will be disseminated and used. Will it be that of a labour-sending or labour-receiving country? Policy-oriented research is typically the subject of many criticisms, including that it is used merely to legitimate government action and discredit other courses of action, to support limited reforms that have already been formulated along preconceived lines, and to mobilize belief to back up such action (Rein/Schön 1977: 236–237). The GFMD appears in contrast to aspire to be a source or channel for more broadly acceptable research, including through commissioning or assembling studies on matters of widely shared interest, notably on 'good practices'.

Paragraph 28 says that both regular and irregular migration will be studied, to analyse their costs and benefits. However, a preconceived line of action is already embedded in RTD 2, whose title asserts that "secure, regular migration can achieve stronger development impacts". Although irregular migration also needs some 'overdue research', paragraph 24 declares, that "the best frameworks to protect and empower migrants for development are likely to be regular migration programs that are accessible, transparent, and non-discriminatory".

18.3.6 Secondary Theme 5: A Flexible Approach to Policy; 'Good Practices' not 'Best Practices'

Undersecretary Conejos twice uses the stereotypical jargon term 'best practices' (paragraphs 12, 20), a notion that can transfer authority to global centres of research and research funding like the World Bank that claim to synthesize global experience and, on that basis, declare what are best practices. However, his report largely shifts instead to a far more flexible, case-specific concept of "good practice" (paragraphs 20, 23, 26, 27), and explicitly opposes a "one size fits all" approach (paragraphs 26, 36).

18.3.7 Secondary Theme 6: A Light Supportive Structure

The report combines a predominant language of flow that stresses informal process, with a secondary language of solidity ("building on the substantive achievements...and consolidating the structures", paragraph 4). The open ongoing process requires some supportive structures (paragraphs 4, 38-39, 40–42), including ad hoc working groups and good working links with the UN system, but not a new, large and costly bureaucracy. Implicitly such an organization can become financially beholden to rich countries, and would be largely staffed by rich country professionals and/or cut off from the urgency of action, lost in "the usual talk-fests of international conferences" (paragraph 40). The International Organization for Migration, with almost 7,000 staff, headquartered in Geneva, receives no mention in the report.

18.3.8 Generative Metaphors

A metaphor is a device of seeing something abstract or unfamiliar in terms of something else that is familiar, creating in the process new insights. Metaphors are used not only to simplify and analyse complex issues, but also to construct social realities. The metaphors we use day after day function as various sorts of 'mirrors' (that may reflect the plain truth, lie, or take us beneath the surface), 'magicians' (that transform realities), or 'mutinies' (that expose and mobilize against forces considered to be oppressive) (Kornprobst 2008).

Metaphors typically play a central role in the frames and stories used in public policy for problem setting and for pointing towards solutions (Schön/Rein 1979). Frames usually "contain generative metaphors that enable us to reason from the familiar to the unfamiliar. Familiar concepts are brought to unfamiliar situations and in the process transform the unfamiliar, providing a way of organizing and understanding it, while they are themselves transformed" (Rein/Schön 1977: 240–241).

Some metaphors in the GFMD text are perhaps only decorative, like paragraph 9's "blossoming of friendships and partnerships". However, some are generative, in the sense described: notably, "harvesting the fruits of our labour" (paragraphs 1 and 11), "passing the torch" (paragraphs 38 and 45), and most pervasive and basic: "moving ahead". Each indicates a system of ideas and a course of action.

"Harvesting the fruits of our labour" likens the GFMD process to painstaking, productive work that is for the eventual benefit of all, building mutual understanding and trust (paragraph 3). Compared to Kofi Annan's address, the report is relatively silent on the labour of the migrants themselves. The focus is on governments, portrayed to be working with as much effort as the migrant workers, towards a goal that will benefit the migrants too.

The metaphor of 'passing the torch', from Brussels to Manila and from Manila to Athens, conveys perseverance, victory and legacy. It mobilizes the imagery of the Olympic Games: heroic endeavour within a community of international cooperation. The broader metaphor of a journey is central to the whole speech, from paragraph 1's "endings and beginnings", through to "the road ahead" (paragraph 41) and the very final paragraph (47). Whereas the penultimate paragraph (46) resorts to a hackneyed military metaphor ("We have gained much ground") to convey pride in GFMD effort and achievements, the final paragraph reverts to the primary theme, ongoing process: "The GFMD remains a 'work in progress' – to be completed... to be continued".

While 'change' is repeatedly emphasized (paragraphs 2, 3 [twice], 29 and 40), we are secured along the journey by the partner emphasis on 'continuity' in the process (paragraphs 2, 4, 11, 29). The terms provide more than decorative relief and reassuring conventional juxtapositions. A journey suggests exploration and advance, and hence praise. In paragraph 2, for example, we find a great cache of praise terms: achievements, continuing, advancing, consultation, collaboration, changing. Some of the praise may be intended for the Philippines host, for the Brussels meeting in 2007 had concentrated on other things and did not bring the process as far as Manila claims to have done: "changing the way the world looks at migration and development" and, "more importantly...changing the way we deal with each other on [migration and development]" (paragraph 3).

18.3.9 Silences

Identifying which topics are excluded or downgraded, and assessing this, is part of a frame analysis. Especially given the 3,000-word length and considerable repetitions in the GFMD Chair's report, we are entitled to remark that several major issues and actors received little attention.

First, while traffickers and smugglers are in the frame, other villains or challenges receive little or no mention: human rights violations against migrants; poverty, unemployment and underemployment in the home country that push migrants to resort to irregular migration; the global systems that contribute to these pressures; and the inability of national police forces, as well as lack of political will, to prosecute transnational human trafficking and smuggling.

Second, paragraph 25 presents "growing crimes of smuggling and trafficking" as a threat to the migrant worker's capacity to "earn and support families back home". Left out are other villains such as the extremely high charges that money transfer companies impose on clients who send remittances home. Another villain could be the lack of training for migrants and their families in financial literacy, management and sustainable entrepreneurship, to help them to manage their remittances to uplift their quality of life (Villalba 2002).

Third, the role of civil society including non-governmental organizations is only touched on. Paragraph 18 states that civil society and NGOs have an important role to play in the 'shared responsibility' of protecting the rights of migrant workers, but no detail is given. Paragraph 42 adds that as governments, "We need to continue working on our relations with...Civil Society. We are still feeling our way in this process...".

Fourth, the importance of institutionalizing human rights treaties for the protection of migrant workers is mentioned once, in paragraph 19, but only in the form of referring to 'some recommendations', calls and 'suggestions' from some of the delegates, without any explanation, emphasis or endorsement.

18.3.10 Development

We could extend the analysis in many ways, for example through exact examination of how the key terms are used and in what contexts. Let us illustrate with one central term: 'development'. It appears 34 times (besides the uses implied in the name GFMD). Half of these uses are in conjunction with 'migration', as in "migration and development" (paragraphs 2, 3, 13, 21, 30, 31, 32, 33, 35, 36, 42), "empower[ing] migrants for development" (paragraphs 7, 23, 24), "impacts of migration on development" (paragraph 28), and "development friendly migration" (paragraph 29). The other uses confirm the treatment of migration as instrumental to development (e.g., "development benefits they can bring" - paragraph 7; "contribution to [economic] development" - paragraphs 16, 21, 23 [twice]; "development impacts" - paragraph 24; "development needs" - paragraph 26). In particular the implied definition of development is that human development is only a "facet of development" (paragraph 7); human development is not the encompassing UNDP concept, but the narrower concept used in development banks: "human beings who are healthy, educated, employed, and able to care for their families" (paragraph 16), which is contrasted to "economic development", towards which it is instrumental (paragraph 16). Thus, overall, migration is discussed in terms of instrumentality towards economic development.

18.4 Is the Mood Changing?

The Manila Forum Chair's report maintains the perspective presented in the Secretary-General's New York speech, without much erosion or accretion. It lacks Annan's initiating flair and authority, and reflects a subsequent stage of routinization. Amongst its intended audiences, the report may achieve its desired effect. 'Development' is a potent idea; few would oppose the benefits of 'development'. The needs that are then articulated (for particular policies, better research, partnerships and so forth) are plausible, but limited and thus potentially misleading.

How much will be generated by the GFMD process in the longer-term remains to be seen. This would be no surprise to Kofi Annan and his advisers. His 2006 speech concluded: "This High-level Dialogue will succeed to the extent that it ushers in an era of sustained, thoughtful consideration of international migration and development issues". It did not guarantee such an era. However, as we have seen, the proposed logic of his position was to start from where we are, from conceptions of 'development' that remain dominated by economic measures and from a system of nation-states that guard their sovereignty, and to establish improved channels of regular and constructive communication that have some potential to bring evolution. The GFMD is part of this. As Rother suggests (2009a: 95): "...it provides a perspective, albeit a vague one, for a possible way out of the gridlock between the sending and receiving states of migrants".

At one level, the new track of meetings between government delegates is expected to gradually create its own chemistry, generate expectations, proposals and alliances and, establish a more constructive dynamic. "...as Peter Sutherland phrased it, it can be seen as an advancement when sending, receiving and transit countries of migration sit around the same table 'instead of yelling at each other'. Indeed, the fact that e.g. the Saudi Arabian government showed willingness to speak about migrants' rights at all should be seen as an, albeit small, progress" (Rother 2009a: 104).

At a second level, the GFMD meetings become a catalyst and focal point for much more. Non-governmental organizations target the meetings, commission research, initiate campaigns and grab some of the attention. That different NGOs pull in different directions on this stage can be seen not as a problem but as part of "the cunning of history": it creates pressure for information and innovation, change and creativity; it ensures that positions are tested hard. At the Manila Forum,

> [S]ome associations were pursuing an 'inside-outside' strategy: while taking part in the GFMD process, they also founded the Peoples' Global Action on Migration, Development and Human Rights (PGA), which then organized workshops - as well as public rallies for migrants' rights. Migrant associations are active in many countries. However, the movement is split. The International Migrants' Alliance (IMA), which was founded in Hong Kong in 2008, opposes the PGA because it considers the GFMD unacceptable. The IMA argues that the GFMD treats people as commodities and promotes neoliberal policies. (Rother 2009b: 333)

Rother concludes: "It will be worth observing and researching which of the approaches -'inside-outside' or 'outsiders by choice' - will turn out to be the more effective strategy in the long term" (2009a: 106). Perhaps the real point is that these approaches are both necessary and are complementary, and that the presence of the Forum catalyses them.

18.5 Conclusion

This chapter had two sets of objectives: at the immediate level, to explore the proposed rationale of the Global Forum on Migration and Development, and, at a deeper level, to show the relevance of some accessible tools of discourse analysis for better understanding of and better participation in migration policy. Discourse analysis may be particularly germane for migration policy, for as Griffin (2007) noted, stereotypes, inconsistencies and mistrust are so prevalent there.

We took first Kofi Annan's speech in which he launched the Global Forum. Through use of analysis tables for comprehensive precise attention (Tables 18.1 and 18.2), we identified the speech's resources and themes, both stated and unstated. We saw Annan's skilful use of appeals to governments' self-image as intelligent and constructive, his confidence- and responsibility-building allocation of Forum ownership to the governments, and his reassuring lending of his own authority and commitment of support from the UN system. We then organized the elements from the central part of the speech as an explicit logical system, in a synthesis table (Table 18.3). Annan's advocacy of the Forum was seen to rest on a series of claims: that migration must be managed; that the present position is one of entrenched disagreements and mistrust; that to proceed will require constructive structured communication; that the Global Forum can provide this and is a feasible way forward; that alternatives to the Forum are at present less feasible; and that the Forum will be not merely feasible but fruitful, through processes of increased mutual education and mutual acceptance. Expression in this synthetic form helps us to clarify content, assess cogency and compare criticisms and alternatives. While not always feasible for longer texts, the approach is helpful for key passages; and such use strengthens one's awareness and skills when tackling longer texts in ways that are more selective.

While Annan's position could be expressed as a logical system, some of the component meanings are not openly or emphatically stated in the speech and we draw them out fully only through the unusual form of reading done for the analysis table. Further, much of the work of persuasion is seen to be done not through bald logic but through a combination of suggested causal linkages with effective use of *pathos*—mobilization of relevant values (including here: respect for migrants, respect for nations, respect for open communication, and self-respect)—and *ethos*, concerning the reasons for giving trust and credence to the speaker (including respect for not just his experience, post, and organizational resources but his range of sympathies and understanding, his combination of boldness and finesse). Central was Annan's subtle alternation between 'you' and 'we' in addressing the assembled government representatives.

How does Annan's case for the Forum fare in practice? Does it outlast Annan's presence in an important facilitating role? We looked for evidence from the second GFMD conference. While it is too early to identify success, it might be early enough to sense failure. There were no signs of that yet in the Manila concluding report, which gave an upbeat restatement and emphatic elaboration of the proposed rationale of the Forum: that from a starting position of major divergence and mistrust between national governments in a world polity of nation states, a non-coercive forum of open communication can help to identify mutually beneficial good practices and in the process strengthen mutual trust and solidarity. Discourse analysis helped us clarify both the imaginative and emotional content of the claims for the Forum, with their talk of moving forward, passing on torches, and reaping harvests, the central hypothesis of gradual growth of collegiality, and the silences, the issues neglected.

Evidently, in the world of the GFMD, governments of labour-sending and receiving countries are mandated to be the managers in migration and development, and are not necessarily attuned to perspectives promoting the human rights and well-being of migrants. The GFMD is a Forum for 'migro-crats', representing nations who meet not in a Habermasian ideal discourse situation but with very unequal powers. Migrants and civil society are involved at best in consultations and lobbying, but the Forum provides a valuable focal point for their mobilization and for wider public attention. No one format or line of action will suffice, but the GFMD adds a space for 'migro-crats' too to 'see the world' and enrich their understanding, as well as be subject to public pressures.

Much more can be done in trying to understand, monitor and assess the Global Forum. We can examine its other meetings, relate it to the preceding and parallel other fora and events in the international migration policy scene, and compare their respective impacts (cf. MacDonald/Cholewinski 2007). We can employ also much more complex forms of discourse analysis. In this chapter we hope though at least to have illuminated central aspects of the speeches and, especially, to have illustrated some widely accessible and yet helpful ways to probe key texts in migration policymaking. In doing so, we aim to facilitate involvement from all actors in a more informed and creative fashion in these realms of meaning-making and world-making.

Box 18.1: Final Conclusions and Recommendations of the Chair, Esteban B. Conejos, Jr., Undersecretary of Foreign Affairs for Migrant Workers' Affairs and Special Envoy to GFMD, Republic of the Philippines , Manila, 30 October 2008.

1. We have reached that exciting point in our Global Forum meeting, where we can harvest the fruits of our labour together over the past 18 months, and share some thoughts about the future of the Forum. This may well be the end of the Manila meeting, but it is also the beginning of the next phase of the GFMD.
2. I see the two overriding achievements of our meeting this year as being *Continuity* and *Change*. Continuing and advancing the process of consultation and collaboration begun in Brussels last year, and changing the way the world looks at migration and development.
3. What we have achieved in the past two days is to move forward by a few more decisive steps an ongoing process that is changing our thinking and actions on migration and development, but more importantly, that is changing the way we deal with each other on these two complex, but interrelated, issues.
4. We have done this by building on the substantive achievements of the first meeting in Brussels and consolidating the structures that will assure continuity in this process.

Turning to the substance or the themes of the Forum

5. The Brussels meeting focused on the first two priorities identified by governments in a survey undertaken at the outset of the GFMD process - labor mobility, and remittances and other diaspora resources. The Manila meeting took up the next two priorities, namely, rights and security.
6. These formed the basis of the RT 1 discussions on protecting and empowering migrants, and the RT 2 discussions about the policy frameworks that could foster such protection and empowerment by better balancing facilitation and control of migration. The third thematic area, policy and institutional coherence, has been continued from one meeting to the

next as it provides the underpinnings of roundtables 1 and 2.

7. What is different about the Manila meeting is the spotlight on the human face of migration, and the human development facet of development. The Philippine Government chose the theme 'Protecting and Empowering Migrants for Development' to shift the debate away from the usual rational arguments about economic benefits of migration, and back to the migrants and their families. The greatest wealth of any country is its people, and the development benefits they can bring to their communities and countries are only possible when they are properly protected and supported.
8. As a major country of origin, managing huge outflows and diasporas for some 30 years now, the Philippines was well positioned to take up this cause, on behalf of our own migrants and their families, but also to share with other governments our hard-won good practices and lessons learned over this time.
9. The informal nature of the Forum has allowed new *friendships and partnerships* to blossom between migrant sending and receiving countries, which can lead to better deals for migrants in the future. It also helps the messages of the Manila Forum to reverberate more widely among countries around the world.
10. The informality of the process - the fact that we are not aiming for Declarations or binding agreements, but rather at efficiencies and effectiveness on the ground that serve everyone's interests, particularly the migrants - has also helped us achieve more than may be possible in formal international debates about principles, norms and doctrine.

Outcomes of the Roundtables

11. But, having assured the continuity of the GFMD process, what exactly have we achieved with the Roundtable discussions? What are the real fruits of the Manila Forum? And where do we take them from here?
12. Our GFMD rapporteurs have shared with us a number of concrete outcomes resulting from the Roundtable sessions - studies, pilot programs, compendia of best practices, working groups - and these projects are important for connecting this meeting with last year's in Brussels and with next year's in Athens. They should bring fresh evidence and information to the Athens roundtable discussions.
13. But these outcomes tell us something more about the GFMD process. They tell us that we are beginning to achieve a certain *consensus of understanding* about the important connections between migration and development, where the gaps of knowledge are and how to fill those gaps. They take us one step closer toward common solutions to our common challenges. They bring us closer to a *consensus on action.*
14. In Roundtable 1 on 'Migration, Development and Human Rights' we sought to highlight the condition of migrants and their families, and show how their protection and empowerment could result in development not only of their person, but also of their countries of origin and destination.
15. We wanted to see how principles and doctrines of protection and empowerment were working on the ground - a 'bottom up' approach to policies that protect migrants' rights. We also identified elements of an enabling environment for empowering migrants and diaspora to mobilize their resources more effectively for development.
16. There was consensus in RT 1 that migrants' rights must be protected, not only because they contribute to economic development, but because it is their basic human right. *Protecting the rights of migrants is not only the right thing to do, but also the smart thing to do.* People are our biggest national asset. Economic development cannot occur without human development, that is, without human beings who are healthy, educated, employed, and able to care for their families.
17. In this regard, the need to protect the rights of women migrant workers, child migrants, and migrants in irregular situations was emphasized.
18. Protecting the rights of migrants is a shared responsibility of governments of origin and host countries. There is a need for political will at both origin and destination to translate the concept of 'shared responsibility' into tangible policies and programs on protecting migrants' rights. Non-government actors like the civil society and private sector also play an important role in this.
19. Many delegates called for ratification of the 1990 International Convention, ILO Conventions and other core international human rights treaties. There were some recommendations to review the provisions of the 1990 Convention or devise mechanisms that would improve rates of ratification and implementation. There were also suggestions to look at complementary approaches in applying the principles of international treaties in practical and concrete ways.
20. The GFMD plays an important role in facilitating an exchange of good programs and policies in this regard. These best practices include the Philippines' comprehensive lifecycle approach to migration management, and the Abu Dhabi pilot project in deepening dialogue and cooperation, which may be replicated with possible assistance from other agencies and countries.
21. The GFMD could also be useful in disseminating information and the results of research on migration and development, which can inform governments about how to provide an enabling environment to empower migrants. It could help governments and other relevant stakeholders identify effective elements that encourage migrants to better contribute to development, such as strong reliable domestic institutions in countries of origin, secure legal status for migrants, and incentives and tools in both countries of origin

and destination. The GFMD could likewise promote partnership between source and destination countries in facilitating diaspora's financial, technological, and social contributions in both countries.

22. The GFMD could consider other suggestions made to empower migrants, such as ensuring greater exercise of political rights by migrants, establishing a common lexicon or dictionary of terms to promote commonality of understanding, and the feasibility of issuing diaspora bonds in order to harness diaspora assets beyond merely their income flows.

23. In view of the foregoing, I propose that the GFMD considers setting up an ad hoc *Working Group on Protecting and Empowering Migrants for Development,* which could conduct a study on the actual links between protections for migrants and their capacity to contribute to development. It could also catalogue good practices in joint arrangements to protect and support migrants and the diaspora for their contribution to development. I invite you to join the governments of the Philippines, the UAE, Belgium, and El Salvador - Co-Chairs of RT Sessions 1.1 and 1.2 - in forming this small and informal consultative mechanism.

24. In Roundtable 2 on 'Secure, Regular Migration Can Achieve Stronger Development Impacts', we discussed how the best frameworks to protect and empower migrants for development are likely to be regular migration programs that are accessible, transparent and non-discriminatory. This is particularly so when legality is enforced through strong, effective measures to reduce exploitative and abusive practices such as migrant smuggling and trafficking in persons.

25. Migration programs that better match skills with real jobs, and are affordable and accessible to migrants, offer the best incentives to migrate by choice rather than by necessity. Enforcement alone has not prevented or solved the growing crimes of smuggling or trafficking, which can disempower migrants and reduce their capacity to earn and support families back home. We looked at more comprehensive approaches that combine enforcement with facilitation in a more balanced way.

26. While we all agreed there is no 'one size fits all' approach to migration, there are some emerging 'good practices' such as circular migration and bilateral labor migration arrangements that take account of the labor market and development needs of both the country of origin and host country. We saw that where labor mobility is managed flexibly between countries it can also help workers increase their skills abroad and contribute to sectoral development back home.

27. Governments are already able to benefit from the *Compendium of good practices in labor migration* established by the Moroccan and Spanish Governments as a follow-up to the GFMD meeting in Brussels last year. And we hope to expand and elaborate on that further before the next meeting in Athens.

28. Some *pilot circular migration programmes* that have also resulted from the Brussels meeting will also be followed up and evaluated for the lessons they may yield in the coming year or so. We hope to continue the work begun last year on how to engage the private sector better in *lowering the costs of migration for migrants;* and to undertake some overdue *research on the costs and benefits,* and impacts, of regular and irregular migration on development.

29. Coming back to my observations about 'continuity and change', all of these outcomes are connected to the labour mobility theme of the Brussels Forum and the protection an empowerment theme of Roundtable 1 this year. They point to new and smarter policy approaches that could foster more development-friendly migration, such as circular migration and market-based migration policies that could compete with smuggling and trafficking businesses.

30. They also link with the theme of partnership and cooperation in Roundtable 3. Thailand's suggestion that a meeting be held next year for heads of regional consultative processes to share information on migration and development-related activities and achievements is a welcome effort to link the aims of Roundtables 2 and 3, and to reinforce coherence within the GFMD substantive frame.

31. In Roundtable 3 on 'Policy and Institutional Coherence and Partnerships' we looked at the institutional and policy elements that need to be in place to achieve the aims of Roundtables 1 and 2 - the red thread of coherence runs through all other Migration and Development themes.

32. *First,* without a clear sense of those priority areas where strengthened data and research are required to assess the impacts of migration on development, and of development on migration, our arguments for policy and institutional coherence, joint approaches or partnerships are weak and will remain based on intuition and anecdote. We need more comparable data and must work towards common definitions and methodologies across countries. We need to improve our way of working, and promote new approaches to produce evidence-based information that can be of immediate use to policy makers in all regions.

33. The proposal arising from Roundtable 3.1 to set up an ad hoc *Working Group on Data and Research on Migration and Development* should thus be taken forward as part of our common effort to furnish this information. This working group can help us work towards more coherence and cooperation among key actors in these areas.

34. *Second,* the issue of policy, program and institutional coherence needs to be addressed both in terms of the concrete institutional and organizational arrangements governments are putting in place to achieve coherent policy making, and in the way these arrange-

ments and resulting policies can subsequently be assessed and evaluated.

35. The second GFMD survey on policy coherence undertaken by Sweden, following the one undertaken for Brussels, has clearly demonstrated the political will and commitment by many governments to work towards such a coherent approach in addressing the migration and development nexus. The proposal of Roundtable session 3.2 to create an ad hoc *Working Group on Policy and Institutional Coherence* is well taken and should be pursued actively, including for the purpose of relying on the GFMD website to ensure on-going exchange among interested GFMD participating governments. This working group will also ensure that the critical issue of policy and institutional coherence remains on future GFMD agendas.

36. *Third,* we had a highly interesting debate on international cooperation, both within and across regions, including new initiatives for dialogue and cooperation at the inter-regional level. The effectiveness of regional and inter-regional consultations for development will be strengthened through an assessment of the impacts of such processes on country policies, and a pilot programme will study the implementation of policy-relevant recommendations on migration and development. Governments also agreed to further strengthen the link between regional and inter-regional fora and our Global Forum in order to assure greater consistency and coherence of the positions they take in all these processes.

37. Our discussions in all Roundtables have confirmed again that coherence must stay on the agenda of the GFMD. The Global Forum can provide the framework for periodic reviews of data, research, methodologies, evaluation techniques, pilot programs, how governments integrate migration into their national development strategies and so on.

Finally, to the structures and modalities of the GFMD

52. Our work of the past 18 months, and your conclusions during the Future of the Forum meeting, have ensured that the right structures and modalities will be in place to take the GFMD process forward to the next meeting and beyond. As you know, we are honored to hand the GFMD torch onto Greece for 2009, and after that at least three other countries have indicated their interest in hosting the meeting.

How has Manila strengthened the structural foundations of the GFMD?

53. We have continued to use the structural framework and the working methods set up in 2007 - the network of country focal points, the Roundtable teams of governments, the Chair's Taskforce, comprising national and international experts, the Friends of the Forum, a Steering Group; and to help 'govern' the process, the Troika of past, present and future Chairs.

54. We have retained the practical and results-oriented roundtable approach, which in itself is a change from the usual talk-fests of international conferences on these issues. Countries at every point on the migration continuum - at origin, transit and destination - have cooperated in teams to prepare the roundtable discussions *together,* explore ideas and good and bad practices *together,* and agree on some new policy approaches and partnerships that can benefit everyone, not just one side of the emigration/immigration equation.

The road ahead

55. Out of our Future of the Forum deliberations, most governments have agreed to add to the existing structural framework a light Support Unit to assist future Chairs-in-Office with the daily administrative management of this fast-growing process.

56. We have also considered other governance and strategic questions deemed important for the future of our Forum, such as its linkages with the UN, its relationship with the Global Migration Group (or GMG) and with Civil Society generally, future funding sources and responsibility for follow-up activities. Most of us agree that the GFMD is now firmly established as an ongoing government-led, non donor-driven process with links to the UN, particularly through the Secretary General's Special Representative for Migration and Development. We need to continue working on our relations with the GMG and Civil Society. We are still feeling our way in this process, and new questions arise as the process grows, but also as global circumstances change.

57. The current global financial crisis, for example, is a sober reminder to us of the importance of good planning and coordination within and between governments at any time. But sound policies and institutional coherence are also the best buffers against the shocks of such a global crisis for the migrants, their families and home economies.

58. How we find the right answers to all the lingering and newly emerging questions in the future will determine the continuing relevance and usefulness of the process. It will be incumbent upon my successors to carry the suggestions you have made in respect of these crucial issues to a fruitful conclusion.

59. I can assure you that the Philippine government is prepared to fully play its future role as Troika member and to assist the in-coming Greek Chair whenever possible, notably in the follow-up to the conclusions reached here in Manila. The Government of the Philippines will hand the GFMD torch over to the Greek Government on 15 December 2008.

60. We have gained much ground in Manila, but there is still more to be done.

61. The GFMD remains a 'work in progress' - to be completed ... to be continued....

Part V Ethics of Modern Day Transnational Migration: A Human Security Perspective

19 International Migration, Well-being and Transnational Ethics

Des Gasper

19.1 Introduction[1]

Migration involves a search for well-being and security, but is not guaranteed to bring either. In the short run, it quite often reduces both. What are the hoped for benefits for which the risks are undertaken? Insecurity can generate migration, and in the case of refugees fleeing conflict areas, migration is primarily insecurity driven. Apart from people fleeing the most extreme physical insecurity, however, the reasons behind migration (and the subjective definitions of security) are diverse. Migration can itself put people's security in jeopardy: migrants are often unavoidably risk-takers and sometimes decide on the basis of bad information, miscalculation or duress. It would be self-contradictory to risk everything for the hope of security alone. Some people even flee a security they view as stifling or dull. Overall, migration involves considerable uncertainty and vulnerability. Some migrants achieve an acceptable or even admirable outcome while others end up in situations of great insecurity and distress. Some lose their lives. The risks are greatest for illegal migrants.[2]

This chapter looks, first, at migrant lives, including at ill-being, well-being and plain 'be-ing', and at degrees of security.[3] Security concerns the security of holding goods, and the associated risks. Starting by looking at 'be-ing', the contents of migrant life, we can move to consider its evaluation, as well- and ill-being and the justice and injustice of their generation and distribution. One aspect of well- and ill-being that demands reflection is the frequent divergence between 'subjective' (personal intuitive self-assessments) and 'objective' judgments (assessments in terms of explicit socially validated criteria of advantage or disadvantage) by or for migrants. Justice concerns the interpersonal distribution of goods and of risks, as well as the nature of processes of distribution. The themes of justice and security overlap strongly, with reference to distribution of risks.

From this examination of aspects of being, well-being and distributive justice, the chapter will address themes of transnational ethics. My interest is as much in the significance of migration for global ethics as in commenting on the global ethics of migration. Migration jumbles up the contents of the national 'societies' that are treated by 'realist' international relations and nationalist ethics theorists as separate and discrete units in the global order. As David Harvey declared: "[We require] a more unified critical geographical understanding of the world to parallel the contemporary striving for a cosmopolitan ethic.... The geographical point is not to reject cosmopolitanism but to ground it in a dynamics of historical-geographical transformation" (Harvey 2000: 557, 560). The topic of migration helps us to consider the content and possible bases and barriers for the value changes required in evolution towards more humane global ethics.

The chapter aims to raise considerations relevant for ethical analyses of migration, with special reference to issues of well-being, not to build a normative model or methodology. It provides a background to such work. In reaction to much philosophical literature on international relations, which lacks adequate empirical basis and reflection on its own categories – such as well-being, identity, community, peoples, and societies – it seeks to encourage empirical attention and better grounded conceptual reflection as a basis for philosophical argument, let alone philosophical system building.

---

1 Acknowledgement: My thanks to two referees for valuable guidance, and to Thanh-Dam Truong for involving me in this work and for continued stimulation and support.

2 Illegal migrant' refers, except perhaps in China, to international rather than intra-national movements. This chapter concentrates on international not intra-national movement and relocation, whether permanent, temporary, indefinite or recurrent.

3 The philosophical term 'be-ing' helps to promote our attentiveness to and reflection on the contents and character of daily life, both in routines and in crises.

T.-D. Truong and D. Gasper (eds.), *Transnational Migration and Human Security*, Hexagon Series on Human and Environmental Security and Peace 6, DOI 10.1007/978-3-642-12757-1_19, © Springer-Verlag Berlin Heidelberg 2011

19.2 Being, Well-Being and Distributive Equity in Migration

In the first half of the chapter, we try to identify some of the relevant dimensions in human lives that involve or are otherwise affected by international migration. We also use them to guide evaluative discussion of the well-being and ill-being effects and their interpersonal (including intergenerational) distribution.[4]

19.2.1 Be-ing

'Home' connotes security. Migration means leaving home, changing location. There are various types of home and of migration. Migration in space is central to economic development. It may be circular or permanent. Birds and nomads are circular migrants; and so, increasingly, are some other humans. It was the standard pattern in Southern Africa in the 20th century. Migration in time constitutes life's story, from birth through to death. It includes both gradual evolutions and major life turning points, such as marriage and incapacitating illness. Economic development and modernization, political conflict and cultural evolution frequently bring existential (not merely physical) migrations, including major shifts in people's life-worlds, social contexts, values and identities. In Marshall Berman's words, modern urban environments promise us "adventure, power, joy, growth, transformation of ourselves and the world - and at the same time, [threaten] to destroy everything we have, everything we know, everything we are" (Berman 1983: 15). Migration in space thus typically involves existential migration too, and thereby represents a life-turning point.

Migration in one sense or other is normal. So is a craving for security. In most cases, migrants in space achieve security, an existential home, through bonding into a new or old identity grouping, for example a religious group.

Migration builds liminal identities, whether conscious or unconscious.[5] A person's identity is inherently plural, a vector, as discussed for example by Sen (2006). Migration creates new liminal zones. It increases the plurality within identity. In most cases, a core loyalty group remains paramount at the level of conscious identification. Today, international migration is less decisive and irreversible, less of an indisputable shifting of one's allegiance than in 19th and early 20th century moves to another continent.[6] Movement back and forth is easier now. Even without movement back, migrants are retaining homeland identities and notions of the land of origin as 'home' on a greater scale. These generate calls for overseas voting rights and dual citizenship. More important than physical movement is the magic carpet of cheap, unlimited electronic communication, especially satellite- and cable-television. The residents of what Buruma (2006) calls (satellite) 'dish-cities' are mentally transported back 'home', or to an idealized version thereof, in the same way that American military personnel on foreign bases have long stayed secure in havens of taped Hollywood entertainment.

Liminal identities, created by migration, communications, trade and travel, could contribute to "The global spread of plural loyalties [which] is essential to the creation of a new world order: it is the psychic infrastructure without which the emergence of such an order remains impossible" (Goulet 1982: 127). The contribution is possible rather than inevitable. The Indian who has moved to the USA and gradually acquired dual loyalty is certainly not necessarily a cosmopolitan with global loyalties. Goulet himself observed that people acquire additional identities in part because they find that it is the best way to maintain their original identities, through coping and succeeding in their new location. Dish-city society has taken us further in this direction. Even so, while a plural identity is not a global identity, communication and co-mingling and the sharing of universalist languages of development and human rights contribute to weakening the traditional domestic-versus-international dichotomy. Toni Erskine (2000), David Held (2004) and others discern a world system of a myriad of overlapping communities, not self-contained nation-states. Through the overlaps, individuals are simultaneously members of many communities, and this may promote a broadening of perspectives and sympathies.

'Other-ing' is the great counterforce. Creation of stereotyped simplified visions of perceived other groups is a standard feature in the processes of iden-

4 For elaboration of the framework, see Gasper and Truong (2010b) .

5 Liminal means at or on both sides of a margin, transition, boundary or threshold.

6 South Asian migrants to East Africa provide an interesting test case. Because return to India was considerably easier physically and financially than for their compatriots in South Africa, Fiji and the Caribbean, the East African 'Asians' kept far less diluted South Asian identities than those other groups did.

tity formation and maintenance of any group. The 'other' is typically perceived as having a connected, incorrigible set of characteristics that are inferior, one by one and especially collectively, to the matching set of characteristics of the self-describer group (Connolly 2002; Hansen 2006; Kuus 2002). Such representation is central to the mutual antagonisms assumed in 'realist' theories of international relations (Odysseos 2002). Mushakoji (2007b and chapter 22 in this volume) notes the 'outsider' situation of minorities in strongly nationalistic countries like Japan. Othering of migrants by 'host' country groups reinforces any tendencies the migrants may have towards introspective and/or 'home' country-oriented identity formation.[7]

The weakest migrant groups suffer loss of rights as well as loss of status. Their main identity in the recipient country can become one of identity-less-ness as well as other-ness (Ehrenreich/Hochschild 2003). A twilight, liminal zone of illegal migrants serves employers' and governments' interests: employers pay less and are restricted less; governments play innocent of the sin of admitting the 'other' and acquire no obligations to them; the voters who select governments have access to low-cost goods and services from groups without effective rights who can often be summarily evicted when no longer wanted. Sex workers are invariably one major such group (see Mushakoji 2004; Mushakoji/Kamal Pasha 2008). Single migrants, especially single men, provide a demand for sex-work, to add to the clienteles already living in host countries that are generated by urbanism, liberalism, capitalism and affluence. Desperate, naïve or overly hopeful and risk-taking migrant women provide the supply: persons seeking alternatives and exits from their conditions in the home country, those who believed unwisely in the promises of their recruiters, and those who hoped for better things but now must take whatever unskilled work they can get.[8]

Most of the above could have been written two or more decades ago (Phizacklea 1983; Lycklama 1989; Truong 1990, 1996; Skrobanek/Boonpakdi/Janthakeero 1994). However, globalization has recently taken major steps, advises Thomas Friedman in *The World is Flat*, which was reportedly the bestselling nonfiction book worldwide in 2006–2007. 'Flattening' comes from the Internet, the ease now of electronic uploading rather than only downloading, the seamless integration of computer technologies, and so on. Michael Sandel points out that the metaphor of flatness alludes to this elimination of barriers and not to the medieval notion of a flat world that ends somewhere, contrary to the cover picture for the American hardback edition (Friedman 2006: 236–7). A sphere is a better image for comprehensive interconnection than is a bounded plane.

One side effect of the recent global unification is that some highly skilled labour has less need and wish to emigrate. The Indian or Chinese computer engineer can and generally now does choose to stay in Bangalore or Shanghai. The question arises whether this will become true for other regions. Rwanda's attempt to leapfrog electronically into the 21st century economy is perhaps one test case. And will the 'stay home' transition ever occur for less skilled labour too? Perhaps not for a very long time. The sex trade, the care sectors and the other labour intensive service industries in rich countries appear unlikely to be substantially replaced by electronic services or displaced by other gadgetry. In addition, at present we see the continuing operation of huge push and pull factors domestically, from west to east in China, or to Delhi, Mumbai, Bangalore and other major cities in India; including the pure push forces of compulsory displacement, enforced by the State and/or private muscle. Internationally we see sustained high flows, from sub-Saharan Africa to South Africa, from Central America and Mexico to the US, and from Eastern to Western Europe; and still from most of the South to the North, which is deliberately targeting higher-level knowledge workers and all levels of care workers (IOM 2008; UNDP 2009).

A trend more relevant for less skilled labour migrants than telecommuting from home is 'transnational' multiple involvement and circulation. Transnationalism involves the intensive routine integration of what were previously largely separate national spaces. People, commodities, ideas and money now move much more readily, to and fro. Indian engineers come and go between India and the US, and Ghanaian traders and professionals move between Ghana and the

---

7 Surveys show, for example, how extraordinarily little most native white/*autochtoon* Dutch residents know of the great diversity of ethnic and cultural backgrounds amongst immigrants to the Netherlands from Turkey and Morocco.

8 Truong and Barajas (2006: 16): '"You know, most of the women that are working here have experience as prostitutes in their countries of origin. But other women come looking for another kind of job possibilities, cleaning houses or as nannies, but when they find difficulties to survive because of unemployment, for example, their circumstances force them to switch to the sexual work. Once they begin, it is very difficult to leave that activity... " [interview C47]'.

Netherlands. Often they maintain bases, operations and even companies in both. So too now, even if to lesser degree, do individuals of many other types.

19.2.2 Well-being: Risking everything for the sake of security?

> "Look, I always want something better"
> Latin American migrant to The Hague (quoted by Truong/Barajas 2006: 23).

Filipino and Nigerian migrants have a reputation for public cheerfulness. However, cheerfulness cannot be taken as the primary measure of well-being or advantage. Some of the cheerful Filipinos and Nigerians may rank their lives far less favourably when asked a question like "How satisfactory are your life circumstances?" and not, "How happy are you as an individual?" There are differences between individuals, and differences on average between culture groups, in responding to the same circumstances. In all groups, one is likely to find a number of mental coping strategies for living with stresses and difficulties. Religion is one great source of solace and strength, not least amongst Filipino and Nigerian emigrants. Depression and unhappiness can hinder rather than spur response to problems, so when one is objectively disadvantaged why should one let oneself suffer subjectively too? Nevertheless, successful subjective coping does not mean absence of objective disadvantage. As capability theory has insisted, this shows the inadequacy (not irrelevance) of happiness measures of well-being or advantage. We must look at criteria of well-being that offer a more objective view, including capabilities (attainable valued functionings) and achieved functionings. People should be involved in specification of these 'objective' measures of their well-being – involved thus in prioritizing particular functionings – since the measures are certainly not value-free. When used for public purposes they should reflect careful and public valuation. Reference to functioning, rather than capability, has priority for children and the mentally infirm, and, ironically, for the dead. The capability to have a decent funeral is no longer sufficient when a person is dead; the actual functioning of a decent event is what is required.

Emigration contains innumerable different pathways and stories. No attempt is made here to estimate an overall balance since the balance varies with time and place, sector and person. A favourable overall balance in some time-place-sector cases does not absolve us from understanding problem cases at sub-group and individual levels. It would not justify inequitable distribution or inattention to areas of major stress and suffering. We need, first, to refine the system of accounting; second, to reflect on the common pattern of apparent rises in objective well-being accompanied by declines in subjective well-being; and third, to look at the distribution and the justice of distribution of these costs and benefits.

Cortez (2007: 25) illustrates several types of effect on well-being in the case of Filipino temporary migrants, and reports an attempt to draw an overall balance.

> The negative long-term effects of temporary migration on the country and to the migrants' families include disintegration of the family, disruption of family relationship, health issues of children as a result of the absence of migrant working parents, juvenile delinquency (early pregnancies, drug addiction, malnutrition) and school dropout. A four-country (Indonesia, Philippines, Thailand and Yunnan-China) study by the ESCAP proved that despite problems encountered by migrant workers, the positive outcomes outweigh the negative consequences (ESCAP 2002). The economic benefits that accrue to the migrant worker and his/her family according to Go (2002), is the single most tangible positive effect of migration. The effects are visible in the assets accumulated, small businesses acquired and the social status achieved (Go 2002). Go sees the Filipino family as stable because they have continued to be resilient and have been adaptive to changing situations. Caretakers and other relatives have been playing key roles in taking care of the children left behind.

The gains mentioned are direct economic benefits to the worker and family. The possible losses are diverse serious forms of social damage (including euphemistically labelled 'health issues'), especially affecting children who remain in the land of origin. The costs very possibly bring long-term repercussions, including far outside the family, but those are not mentioned nor is the category of community. Reportedly, coping strategies in which other family members typically compensate for absent parents mitigate these dangers. Other family members are described like shock absorbers: 'stable', 'resilient' and 'adaptive'. The extra burdens on them are not mentioned as costs.

We must look too at the non-economic effects on the migrants themselves. Some can be favourable: perhaps access to better education and healthcare, especially for children who accompany their parents; access to many more ideas and opportunities, including options for adult migrants. Some effects can be unfavourable: loss of friends and family life, especially separation from one's children (although such losses do not apply in all cases), sometimes loss of respect, identity, meaningfulness and peace of mind, in a hostile or anomic 'host' country. "This society has lost it", comments one Latin American immigrant in the Netherlands (Truong/Barajas 2006: 28). Sex-work in many cases offers significant economic gains but severe non-economic costs to the migrant and her children. There may be few or no economic gains if they chose to enter the trade out of desperation or as a fallback, or if it was not chosen voluntarily, or if it was chosen on the basis of bad information or poor reasoning (see Baas/Kojima and Skilbrei/Tveit in this vol.; also Ehrenreich/Hochschild 2003).

In some cases, reports indicate rise in migrant objective well-being indicators but not subjective ones. This might reflect transfer of many of the recorded benefits to other people. Even in cases where the reports are more informative about the content of a person's own life, mental states can adapt; for example, new advantages may become taken for granted, while some disadvantages may perhaps wisely become overlooked. In addition, the criteria used for 'objective' well-being could sometimes be misleading: overweighted and incomplete. People seek not only material comfort but also security, stimulation and respect. "Every person and society wants to be treated by others as a being of worth, for its own sake and on its own terms, regardless of its utility or attractiveness to others" (Goulet 1975: 232). For many persons this involves 'well-dying' (Gasper 2007a) as a major concern, including even a wish to be buried in their land of origin. Many Ghanaian migrants to the Netherlands are able to fulfil this wish, although not necessarily through their own savings; rather through the contributions of family, friends and co-community members after the migrant's death.

In reverse cases, we find rises in the migrant's subjective well-being indicators but not in the conventional objective ones. This could reflect cheerful self-sacrifice for the benefit of others at home, adaptation of mental states to make the best of a bad job, or the absence of conventional well-being measures of some aspects important to the migrant, such as felt stimulation and freedom from social restraint (see Thieme 2008's Kirghiz case studies). Stability in subjective indicators, despite decline in objective indicators for the migrant (but perhaps not his or her dependants) can reflect adaptation. Some argue that migrants' resilience here sustains injustice (Truong/Barajas 2006: 32) yet the alternative, lack of resilience, would be worse.

One may feel certain misgivings in some of the cases where both subjective and conventional objective well-being indicators rise. Much of the flattened global market's unification is around trivia, of which Friedman's *The World is Flat* provides breathless case studies, as of world-class Indian professionals working to their limit to produce escapist computer games for the US market. Money power commands talent. As money power accumulates in the South, the direction of allocation of talent will change somewhat, but it will take something more fundamental for people to become influenced by ethically weightier forces. Indeed organized wealth readily funds support for the claim that it is ethically weighty, as expressed in certain forms of libertarian political theory. Let us move to consider the issues of distributive justice.

19.2.3 Distributive Justice

> "...they have nothing here or there" (priest) ... "We did it for the children" [woman] (Truong/Barajas (2006: 23–24)

Migration raises many questions of justice: are migrants coerced by traffickers, are they mishandled by state officials, and/or are they misinformed of their rights by employers and officials? Besides those dimensions of culpable wrongdoing, how just are the outcomes of processes where there is no specific wrongdoer? Thinkers such as Hayek (1976) and Nozick (1974) and their politician disciples asserted that in such cases the concept of justice was inapplicable.

19.2.3.1 Parties

Let us first simply list the main groups of affected people, before looking at the redistributions that can arise.

1. The relocated: men, women; some drop contact with their place of origin, but most maintain it and remit funds.
2. Their accompanying children. It is important to distinguish this group since their experiences may be quite different from the adults. Potentially they are a major beneficiary group, but they experience exposure to significant risks.[9]
3. Those whom the migrants leave behind: family; government and taxpayers who in various ways paid for their education and upbringing; and labour market competitors who now find it marginally easier to get jobs. These groups' costs and

9 See for example studies on the lack of guaranteed and adequate education for children of Japanese Brazilian migrants to Japan, including studies in this volume, by Harada and Kimura as well as Mushakoji.

benefits depend on whether contact is retained and funds remitted, whether tasks must be taken over, and many other factors.

4. The intake country's employers, consumers and government, all of whom may gain.
5. Intake country workers and cultural conservatives, who may feel threatened.[10]

19.2.3.2 Redistributions

Migrant workers often show enormous altruism for the benefit of their children and family back home. In cases of Latin American migrants in The Hague, studied by Truong and Barajas (2006), the sacrifices by some of the migrants were extreme. They had become 'other-ed' from all sides: 'other-ed' in the land of immigration; distanced by those whom they support back home - because seen as privileged, absent from their duties, and/or dirty or corrupted, for example as sex workers - and reduced to a 'wallet' function; and liable to be still mistrusted and distanced if they return.[11]

Migrant workers enrich the receiver country in various ways, including often culturally and emotionally. In the 'heart trade', skilled and sympathetic carers from poor countries leave behind their own children, parents and other intimates and dependants, to care for the elderly, the infirm, and the children of the well-to-do in rich countries. They invest not only time and labour, but also affection (Ehrenreich/Hochschild 2003).[12] Highly attractive to rich countries, the arrangement brings financial benefits to poor countries but at great emotional and social cost. As in the case of the trade in human organs, neoclassical economics declares that the trade must be considered *beneficial* since entered into by willing sellers who know their own needs and preferences better than anyone else does. The argument rests on numerous assumptions, including that choosers are capable, well informed and not coerced. Further, the *justice* of the arrangement is conditional, in part, on the justice of the starting point. A kidney sale from a poor parent desperate to fund an operation for a child is unjust, when we view it in a broader perspective, even if entered into voluntarily and in full cognisance of the risks. Similarly, a life separated from one's own children, due to absence of opportunities to fulfil social expectations and requirements by staying at home, is unjust, even if entered into voluntarily and in full cognisance of the implications, which is certainly not always the case.

19.2.3.3 Criteria

In the case of universally 'other-ed' migrant workers, we used a desert criterion of equity: the migrant workers deserve more than they receive; given how much they have worked, sacrificed and given (Gasper 1986, section 6.1).[13] Consistent with an emphasis on desert criteria, Bagchi (2007) notes critically the self-satisfaction of the privileged, such as in the historically immigrant nation of the US where present day citizens may enjoy the fruits of past dispossession of others, in addition to the legacy from the effort, ingenuity and good fortune of preceding generations, and thus enjoy benefits not due to their own work or sac-

10 The Netherlands journal *The Broker* (issue 1, April 2007, p.13) reports that "Harvard economist George Borjas has calculated that in the United States immigration has resulted in a redistribution of wealth of some 2 % of GDP from the poor to the rich", since it keeps low-skill wages down. World Bank estimates of such impact are far lower; for they include indirect impacts, which include benefits for poorer groups too, via lower product prices, more investment and more readily available services.

11 Truong and Barajas (2006: 23–24), A priest from a Latin American parish reported, "... these women [sex workers] work very hard here in order to support their families in their countries of origin, to save for their old age, and get company when they will go back. But the money disappears very easy and finally they have nothing. The remittances they sent are used for their relatives in other things and are not spent as they wanted.... I know a lot of cases of women who returned to the country of origin and are rejected even by their relatives, because they suspect about their activity here.... There is a distrust factor about how they got the money. Generally they don't find the investments they expected of the money they sent.... The rest of the family ask help for each thing they need in such a way that easily expects the woman who works here to solve all kinds of needs of a wide network of relatives there. It's very sad indeed. It's the same case as the former Spanish labour migrants: they have nothing here or there". For a survey of all types of Latin American migrants to the Netherlands, including many who are more successful and fortunate, especially the large group who are recognized partners of Dutch nationals, see: Barajas (2008).

12 Ehrenreich and Hochschild (2003) write of 'exporting love'. I adopt the term 'heart trade' in analogy to terms like 'organs trade' and 'sex trade'.

13 'Desert' is the term used in philosophical ethics to describe merit-worthiness based on past contributions that establish a claim to a share of benefits (Stanford Encyclopaedia of Philosophy, 2008: 'Desert', at: <http://plato.stanford.edu/entries/desert/>).

rifice. Rich countries in general also continue to reap benefits from attracting skills of professionals to whose education they did not contribute, while the poorer countries that did contribute may barely gain from the resulting services. This leads us to Jagdish Bhagwati's notion of a tax on the earnings of 'brain drain' personnel, to be sent to the government of their country of origin.[14]

In the case of enforced separation from loved ones, we used a fair opportunity criterion of equity. People who inherited too few entitlements to maintain and stay with their closest family cannot be said to have fair opportunity in relation to others with lavish inherited entitlements. Extreme market-based ethics assert that whatever results from voluntary market processes must be seen as a fair outcome, and consequently as providing a fair starting point for subsequent activity. This assertion requires supplementation by a very particular and peculiar morality of inheritance or theory of identity to convert it into a claim that, at this starting point for subsequent activity, those who inherit nothing from their parents are in a fair relation to those who inherited enormously. Inheritance has nothing to do with desert.

These claims about process equity would not excuse past forced dispossession. Typically they are combined with a claim that market operation in the long-term benefits all, as judged in comparison to the real alternatives to markets. The two aspects of defence - the claim of mutual benefit and the way that past historical processes are conceptualized - interconnect. It is nearly always possible to posit a baseline for comparison that is so low that it makes a present day outcome appear to be an improvement even for less advantaged groups. Thus, if one places a 'veil of ignorance' (Rawls 1971) over the historical record of dispossession, domination and discrimination, holding that past events and their impacts are too obscure and disputable to have clear implications for distributive justice - as for example does the prominent American philosopher Thomas Nagel when writing on global justice (Nagel 2005; Gasper 2005a; Bagchi 2008) - and if one has no criterion of desert, then desperation behaviour in the organs trade, the 'heart trade' and the sex trade becomes morally unexceptionable.

14 See e.g. Subramanian (2005). Cortez (2007) reports the explosive unpopularity amongst migrant workers and their families of a 'Bhagwati tax' proposal in the Philippines.

19.3 Ideas for a Grounded Transnational Ethics

The second half of this chapter presents and uses selected ideas from transnational ethics and political ethics in general, rather than attempting to create a separate and distinctive transnational ethic of migration, well-being or migrant well-being. It outlines Nussbaum's critique of the tradition of social contract theory, in order to generate a central commitment to basic human rights instead. Next comes the observation that the trend in much of practice and some of theory has gone in another direction: towards unification of the globe as a moral arena, unlike in Rawls's version of social contract theory, but unified as a moral arena dominated by market principles rather than principles of humanity. Last, in contrast to that, I draw attention to and support the call for a cosmopolitan egalitarianism, in the particular direction indicated by Mushakoji: that of universal human rights but framed within the humanly richer and more conflict-aware perspectives of human security theory and pluralist cosmopolitanism. As a prelude to those three stages in the argument, the following subsection highlights underlying dimensions of debate in these sorts of discourse, including arguments about what truly furthers one's self-interest, and, more profoundly, arguments about the character of the 'self' and the 'we', the content of one's 'interests', and the span of one's identifications as well as one's responsibilities.

19.3.1 Finding Alternatives to Injustice via Reinterpretations of Self and of Interests

A first theme, or focus for debate, in global ethics and human security studies is that life contains considerable injustice and misfortune. People often do not reap according to what they have sown. Therefore, there is a role for ethically driven reconsideration and rectification. The theme is basic in ethics in general and, certainly in development ethics and global ethics in particular. Similarly to Mushakoji in this volume, we take development ethics as the field that asks, in Nigel Dower's terms, "How ought a society to exist and move into the future?", as partner to the traditional field of personal ethics that asks, "How ought one to live as an individual?" The emergent field of global ethics asks the former question in terms of world society (Dower 1988).

A second theme in development and global ethics is that responses to opportunities created by scientific, technical and economic change are not pre-fixed:

a range of alternative possible responses exists. This space for alternatives gives the opportunity, not only desirability, for reconsiderations and rectifications. Societal trajectories will depend upon ethical perspectives, feelings of identity and security, concepts of humanity and rights. Mushakoji's work (2004, 2007, and in this vol.) illustrates this with reference to migration to Japan and the debates over Japanese national identity.

Using the space for ethical consideration of alternatives involves, among other aspects, building arguments in terms of enlightened self-interest, and eventual reconsideration of 'self' and 'interest'. In the former area, Mushakoji stresses how mainstream Japanese need to feel that they contribute to their own security by having secure and respected minority groups within Japan who will also help to link them to the rest of the world. Enlightened self-interest arguments connect to the theme in globalization and human security studies of 'common security', namely that not respecting others' security will undermine your own security. In an interconnected world, where one deals with intelligent others who have agency, at least sometimes one does indeed reap according to how one sows. Others' coping behaviour, moral outrage and reactions can mean that injustice eventually brings a cost to the perpetrators, and sometimes will be overthrown. This is a third theme in global ethics. It is potentially encouraging, since any rethinking of the contents of 'self' and 'interest' cannot be rushed, and may be dependent on a prior phase of respectful coexistence motivated by enlightened self-interest.

A fourth key theme in global ethics and human security studies goes beyond appeals to enlightened self-interest based on understanding of complex interconnection. It is that international relocation gradually changes the cast of actors – the 'selves' – and makes it other than presumed in the conventional stories about justice. Thomas Nagel (2005) and many Northern philosophers and politicians propose that the notion of justice does not apply to contexts that lack a sovereign power, and thus not to relations with members of 'other societies'. In contrast, they presume that their own national societies are well defined, cohesive and distinct. The rise of transnational society and the large-scale presence of members of 'other societies' within one's own society destabilize this vision (which was already grossly idealized). Mushakoji in this volume explores how the emergence under economic globalization of large immigrant communities in Japan in the past generation, for example, brings a confrontation with the Japanese state's ideal of a culturally homogeneous nation striving as one for national development. While the developmentalist Japanese state insists on multi-culturalism in the international arena, it rejects it internally. Mushakoji discusses possibilities for how this impasse might evolve.

19.3.2 From Social Contract to Human Rights

John Rawls revived attention to the theory of justice in modern academic normative political philosophy. He returned to the notion of a fair social contract that all can accept, indeed that all do accept in a notional fair bargaining position in which none know what will be their eventual social identity. He explicitly limited his model to within nation-states of a certain type. *A Theory of Justice* considers closed societies: "...persons enter only by birth, and exit only by death" (Rawls 1999: 26). Consider however a central feature of America's historical and contemporary experience: international migration; and suppose, as is reasonable, that one does not know whether one will eventually become a cross-border migrant. Yet Rawls excluded migrants from his model; they overstrain it. The model does not fit in our real, globalized, social world.

We need to distinguish social contract theory in its original territory, of the essentially isolated nation-state; the attempts by other authors than Rawls to extend his principle of fairness to the world arena; and Rawls's own very different response. Even for social contract theory's original isolated national territory, Nussbaum shows how problematic its assumptions are. The contractors are assumed to make arrangements only for themselves, not others, or are taken to represent the interests of those dependants adequately; otherwise they are assumed to value only their own concerns, and to be indifferent to each other's wishes, gains or losses. In reality, many people (such as those involved in or affected by domestic and international migration) make arrangements for others who are not part of the contract discussion, sometimes with great altruism, sometimes with indifference or hostility. Nussbaum (2006: 377) argues persuasively that we should not exclude the typical human motivation for fellowship with others from the set of basic principles that will guide a theory of justice. The point applies for the international arena too, she argues, and it undermines authors who seek to retain Rawls's social contract perspective and to envisage a self-interested bargain between all persons in a world community. Regarding such a position, Bagchi warns that, "Since

Rawls's theory is based on the notion of a contract implicitly or explicitly entered into by citizens of a democratic state, it is virtually impossible, without altering the structure of the basic axioms, to extend it into the international arena" (Bagchi 2008: 199).

Rawls himself tried to handle the international arena by using instead the assumption that the sole relevant moral agents are self-sufficient states or, in his later work, emotionally united 'peoples' (Rawls 1999). Peoples are in reality not so strongly internally united and externally indifferent. Instead we see a spectrum and, as in the 'heart transplants' described by Ehrenreich and Hochschild in parts of the care sector, quite a lot of affective trade.

Preserving analytic convenience, Rawls dealt with international migration in an extraordinarily cavalier fashion. *The Law of Peoples* lists the following causes of migration: persecution of religious and ethnic minorities; political oppression; and flight from starvation or population pressure, both of which he declared typically related to profound political failures (Rawls 1999: 8–9). None of these causes are present in 'well-ordered states', he declared, those states among whom a global social contract can be arranged. Therefore, he ignored migration explicitly in his elaboration of such a contract (Rawls 1999: 8). In the case of population pressure, his notion, as articulated by Seglow, was that "Pressure to emigrate can only mean that a people has not sufficiently taken care of its territorial asset" (Seglow 2005: 323). And that, "...[peoples have] to recognize that they cannot make up for their irresponsibility in caring for their land and its natural resources by conquest in war or by migrating into other people's territory without their consent" (Rawls 1999: 39). Such a conclusion delegitimizes the colonization by Europeans of the present-day United States. Further, the inadequacy of its framework of explanation becomes apparent as Northern-led global warming drives increasing numbers of people in other countries out of their coastal or otherwise environmentally marginal homes.

Nussbaum concludes that "Rawls's theory of international justice neglects the inviolability of each person that is a key to Rawls's domestic theory" and to its intuitive appeal (Nussbaum 2006: 253). His discussion in *The Law of Peoples* contains no reference to literature on migration in the social sciences, arts and humanities or journalism, despite the centrality of migration in American history and contemporary life. Whereas his own life experience and exposure could serve him to some substantial degree in providing raw materials for essaying *A Theory of Justice,* he had far less grounding for his essay in global ethics. Active respect for each person worldwide, based in some informed awareness of the contents of their lives, is needed. It is what the sort of existential survey illustrated in the first half of this chapter points towards. Much fuller examples are found in studies such as Ehrenreich/Hochschild (2003), Jordan/Düvell (2002), Mushakoji/Kamal Pasha (2008), and Truong/Gasper (2008), and in novels such as Tremain's *The Road Home.*[15]

The way to capture the intuitive appeal of offering respect for each person while dropping Rawls's misleading contractualist infrastructure is, Nussbaum argues, a human rights approach, reformulated and justified in the language of capabilities theory. She offers a conception of basic human rights, specified in the form of basic capabilities, and grounded in identification of basic needs, those needs prerequisite for human dignity. Her own brand of philosophy relies on intense existential immersion, drawing from life testimonies, literature, biography and legal cases.

Nussbaum applies her theory of basic rights/capabilities in some detail in several arenas, but not yet that of international migration. One could envisage such an application, and could then compare it with for example Benhabib's (2004) or Piper's (2008) work on the rights of migrants. As part of his cosmopolitan egalitarianism, Bagchi (chapter 20 in this volume), proposes that the right to migrate voluntarily is a human right. He hints at the hypocrisy of any historically immigrant nations, nations indeed of immigration against the wishes of the original inhabitants, which would then control immigration with an iron rod. He contrasts too, as does Thomas Pogge (2005), the prevention of legal immigration of people from poor countries with, on the other hand, the emigration of capital from those countries often without even basic checks on propriety and legality, and on a scale that dwarfs international assistance and in some cases indirectly forces the migration of people.

15 Jordan and Düvell's book deserves special mention. It records a rich investigation into the lives of Brazilian, Polish and Turkish/Kurdish 'irregular migrants' (people working without a work permit) in London, and the work of the UK agencies and officials that deal with them. This is then used to ground a detailed proposal for a long-term goal of open borders combined with a system of unconditional 'basic income' in each country. Mushakoji's work similarly builds an ethical perspective around careful ethnography and historical study in addition to broad philosophical reading. For a comparable study see also Truong and Barajas (2006).

19.3.3 From National Social Contract to Global Market Contract

As Bagchi observes, not merely have rights declared within national boundaries not been extended to a global context, basic rights within national boundaries are often flouted, even in cases of sustained and strong international attention like the forced displacement of population in India's Sardar Sarovar Project (2007: 6–7). Pushing against the international human rights movement are a worldwide system of property rights and the influence that property can buy. While the international human rights movement is a form of egalitarian cosmopolitanism, more powerful so far are forms of non-egalitarian cosmopolitanism. These treat the world as a single moral arena but one in which mutual obligations extend at best to contract observance, and then only for actual contracts, including contracts agreed in conditions of great inequality and not from an ideal Rawlsian starting point (Gasper 2005a). Generalized tax evasion and organized opposition to redistributive expenditure are two symptoms of rejection of more extensive public obligations, especially to the poor, let alone to immigrants. "The affluent [in India] seem to have become semi-detached in their own country, inhabitants of a quasi-apartheid system moving further in the direction of Brazil or South Africa. In effect they declare that if the elites and middle classes of other parts of the globe are entitled to live in a certain way, then so are they – by the principle of equal real income (post-taxation) for equal work.... The principle espoused by many has become, 'If we are obligated to the poor here in India [no longer "our poor"], then so are you. Since you are not, then nor are we'" (Gasper 2005a: 7; see also Gasper 1986, sect. 7). In addition, in the global market vision, nobody is responsible for emigrants except themselves.

Various factors act counter to the construction and maintenance of national-level social contracts. Large-scale migration could itself be one, but it is a response not only a cause. Forms of redistribution outside the nation-state framework exist within many communities, certainly not solely through networks that involve emigrants. Emigrants who do not return, and immigrants who do not integrate, are both often presented as weakening national social contracts or the prospects for them. More significant though than the physical migration of some is the mental and financial emigration of many, notably the better off, as is eminently possible and perhaps increasingly common in our flattened globe of unlimited communications.

We see diverse competing global projects: the system of a world of separate national homes, in which international migrants are a complication, considered useful but also a threat; the project of the global market, in which migrants are a mobile factor of production, with few rights; and the vision of a world of international human rights, in which migrants are considered to share and belong rightfully.

19.3.4 Furthering Ethics of Compassion, Plural Identity and Human Security

Bagchi's starting point is a global framework for undertaking explanatory analyses, part of what is elsewhere called 'joined-up thinking' (Gasper 2007b). It is impossible, for example, to understand the levels of migration from developing and transition economies without reference to enormously increased income gaps between many pairs of countries (Bagchi 2008: 202ff). One can also refer to the collapse of basic social provision in some countries and the global spread of aspirations. Only within an acceptance of a shared moral universe does the enormously increased inequality have a moral significance. How is such an acceptance to be argued for and promoted, in a project of cosmopolitan egalitarianism? Most of Bagchi's concrete proposals to sustain such a project – notably, regulation of the export and import of capital in all countries – can be argued for on other grounds too, as for example in Stiglitz's *Making Globalization Work* (2007). Underlying such arguments, however, and evident in Stiglitz's final pages, is acceptance of a shared moral universe, albeit perhaps a gender-blind one. "[The American] Declaration of Independence does not say 'all Americans are created equal', but 'all men are created equal'" (Stiglitz 2007: 292).

Mushakoji warns that it would be futile simply to tell Japanese school children that persecuting their ethnic minority schoolmates violates universal human rights. It could even become counterproductive. How to motivate concern for others, and specifically for migrants, depends on changing people's imaginations and touching their feelings.[16] The growth of acceptance of ideas of universal human rights owes less to philosophers and academics than to the horrors of the 20th century and the increasing spread of vivid re-

16 For a related discussion, see a set of papers in *Development and Change* 37(6), 2006, especially those by Giri and Truong.

portage in newspapers, television, biography and other forms of life narrative, suggest Schaffer and Smith (2004). Like Mushakoji (2004 and in this volume), I see helpful potential here in a 'human security' framework of ideas, to complement, motivate and focus the notions of human rights. His version of the framework goes deeper than that present in most international development agencies, and interconnects reflections on being, well-being, justice and security.

In other work, I have articulated the human security framework as containing far more than simply the concept from which it takes its name (Gasper 2005b, 2007b).[17] The set of ideas forms a discourse, which has a variety of roles and effects.[18] Like its partner discourse of human rights, it gives moral weight to all humans, as persons, not in proportion to nationality, religion or bank balance; we may call this 'joined-up feeling'. Like its second partner discourse, that of human development, it essays 'joined-up thinking' that transgresses national boundaries, disciplinary conventions and organizational mandates. It goes further than discourses of human development in some areas. In particular, it brings a concern for stability not only for expansion, and a prioritizing focus on basic needs, including physical security, giving them a status of basic rights. It essays this same necessary prioritizing role within the human rights discourse, which is otherwise liable to unhelpful proliferation of rights claims. The focus on basic requisites for human dignity is vivid, clearly imaginable and more compelling than more abstracted or generalized languages. It helps to deepen and mobilize awareness and sympathy for concrete other human persons and their life-projects.

Mushakoji argues that a multicultural perspective is vital here to avoid the counterproductive "imposition through external pressures of an essentialist universalism [as in some types of human rights doctrine,] which only adds to the reactionary virulence of essentialist State nationalism" in countries which feel themselves pressured by what they consider Western doctrines manipulated by dominant powers (Mushakoji 2007). Those same countries should likewise recognize the collective right of their internal minorities to physical and social reproduction. Otherwise, they too risk generating a virulent reaction.

Here, human security discourse can valuably complement human rights language, which can be too individualistic in isolation, necessary but not sufficient. Human security thinking links feelings of compassion to an awareness of realities of vulnerability as a universal condition, to be exacerbated or reduced through co-action. It stresses relatedness, and thus helps us to conceptualize afresh who are the relevant actors and groups; and it supports the notion of common security, that one cannot be secure unless one's neighbours are. Mushakoji in this volume notes that the Japanese developmentalist state's quest for identity security through use of an exclusivist notion of Japanese identity undermines the identity security of migrant groups and, ironically, ultimately weakens Japanese security. "...the Japanese system of identity reproduction represented by its educational system, so carefully dedicated to guaranteeing the social reproduction of human security among the Japanese [is] causing different kinds of insecurity to the migrant communities" (p. 305). If the security of the Japanese majority society continues to be based on the insecurity of the diaspora communities, this will give a reproduction of the informal sector in education and in later employment and social organization, which he argues will benefit neither the informal migrant communities nor the majority society.

Like Truong in various papers (e.g., Truong 2009; Gasper/Truong 2010a), Mushakoji proposes a Buddhist epistemology as potentially helpful,

> where the 'self' and the 'others' are not separated by the law of excluded middle, and where they can develop a relationship of 'contradictory identification' ... [including for example] hybridization among different identities ... [and also the possibility] for both the 'self' and the 'others' to be negated and transcended by a higher level identity.... A 'global identity' can thus be built not [of] identical human individuals, but by diverse identity communities preserving while negating their respective differences inside a global identity community (Mushakoji 2007).

He presents the potential of human security discourse to contribute to a feasible path of advance starting from where we are; promoting acceptance of plurality of identity and the perception that one's identity can be enriched rather than threatened by that of others; and with an endorsement of gentle evolution of identity, towards a human identity, unified but not homogeneous.

---

17 Gasper, Des, 2008: "The Idea of Human Security", Garnet Working Paper 28/08, at: <http://www.garnet-eu.org/fileadmin/documents/working_papers/2808.pdf>.

18 See also parallel work by scholars at the Universities of Duisburg and Marburg in Germany, e.g. Debiel and Werthes (eds. 2006).

19.4 Synthesizing Discussion

Issues of international relocation deserve a key role in discussions of global ethics because, to adapt Goulet's phrase, relocation potentially helps to provide the psychic infrastructure for a more cosmopolitan world order. It fundamentally increases mutual exposure and creates liminal identities that are more complex; and, potentially, can counter the 'other-ing' processes that render identities crude and mutually antagonistic.

Both for understanding migration's impact on ethics and for better ethical understanding of migration, we need to immerse ourselves in its experience. The chapter has emphasized not philosophical system building but the essential prior stage of exposure to the range of key considerations, with reference to diverse types of evidence, testimony and reflection. As basis for discussion of migrants' well-being and of the justice of the generation and distribution of well-being, earlier parts of the chapter looked at characteristic elements in migrants' lives, including facing risks, existential migration and migration in identity. The existential migration that spatial migration brings affects not only the spatial migrants, but also the people they leave behind and those where they arrive; in that sense all are migrants.

Such immersion and reflection does not give a universal storyline, or a single balance sheet like that of an evaluation done in terms of GNP. Emigration contains innumerable different pathways and stories. The balance of advantage or disadvantage varies according to time, place, sector and group. Rather than estimate some overall balance sheet, I attempted to refine the system of accounting; reflect on the common pattern of apparent rises in objective well-being accompanied by declines in subjective well-being; and raise considerations on the distribution and the justice of distribution of these costs and benefits.

The 'system of accounting' is also a system of re-counting, of telling the stories, to retrieve the excluded or downplayed elements. We must see well-being as more than a quest for security. I suggested we should use a formulation of well-being that looks specifically at authoritatively valued functionings, and especially at fulfilment of basic human rights (interpreted with reference both to capabilities and actual functionings); in other words, to look primarily at 'objective well-being'. It remains essential for both evaluation and understanding to look also at subjective states and issues of identity. We must attend too to themes of justice not only aggregate well-being, and observe the workings of the virtues of care, compassion and solidarity (Gasper/Truong 2010a).

To judge the fairness of different distributive patterns requires criteria, such as those of appropriate desert and fair opportunity, whether the latter is seen as equal opportunity, equal basic opportunities or some other interpretation. Judgment often requires a comparison case, of what is assumed the relevant alternative for the parties involved. Here it is too easy to specify the comparison case so minimally that whatever happened is thereby vindicated: the heart trade, the organs trade, the sex trade, even the slave trade. Dr. Pangloss's Law declares that these are all not merely Pareto improvements but win-win arrangements for human betterment.

Using more relevant comparison cases in evaluation, we see that unfairness exists: often people do not reap in proportion to what they have sown. Awareness of relevant alternatives can affect action, not only evaluation; injustice can bring resistance, not only resignation, and unfairness is not immutable. Amongst the mechanisms of progress towards justice are the threat of resistance to injustices, and the recognition of other threats too in an interconnected world, including the spread effects from health catastrophes, economic stresses and environmental decline in distant corners of the globe. Public-ills cannot be confined indefinitely to within the worlds of the deprived but will spread and affect the worlds of the privileged. Therefore, sometimes, systems of injustice reap as they sow, eventually. A mutually agreed social contract can arise from a perception that a system of mutual benefit would be more advantageous to each contractor. However, social contract theory based only on self-interest, even enlightened self-interest, is too narrow for several reasons, and unnecessarily so. As Nussbaum suggests, it arbitrarily excludes the typical human motivation or potential for fellowship with others, or arbitrarily restricts it to only within national boundaries.

In the move beyond the confined national boxes of Rawlsian and most other social contract theories, in which international migrants are considered a destabilizing complication, two types of cosmopolitanism compete. First and now predominant is the global market, in which migrants are a mobile factor of production with few rights. Second is the vision of a world of international human rights in which migrants share and belong. Which vision will predominate in the end depends, in part, on which of the potentials from international migration is most fulfilled. Ideally, relocation would enrich the range of identities, connections and loyalties away from that presumed in the traditional international relations picture of separate national boxes.

19.5 Conclusion

This chapter has sketched a case for a transnational ethics in terms of objective wellbeing that includes major elements of human rights thinking complemented by care ethics and sensitivity to subjectivities.[19] The human security framework has promise here. It combines a number of needed features, by its use of both 'joined-up thinking' and 'joined-up feeling'. A critique of predominant European perspectives made some years back by Kishore Mahbubani, then permanent secretary in Singapore's Foreign Ministry, illustrates the centrality of these two dimensions.[20] Mahbubani diagnosed as Europe's fundamental weakness "an inability to accept the simple proposition that other cultures or social forms may have equal validity". This, in part, can be viewed as stemming from a failure of empathy and 'joined-up feeling'.[21] The judgment remains largely relevant, notwithstanding some signs of gradually increasing European humility. Failures in 'joined-up thinking' – lack of a global frame for conceptualization and causal analysis – appear in rich Northern countries' fantasies of disconnection from their global environment. Mahbubani, now Dean of the Lee Kuan Yew School of Public Policy at the National University of Singapore, pointed to the ideas and practices of 'Fortress Europe', including the unwillingness to engage seriously with Turkey and to foresee the dynamics that could be encouraged thereby. He stressed the failure to envisage that in the absence of economic arrangements that are widely perceived by Africa and other low-income countries as just – including allowing them to utilize their potential comparative advantage in agriculture and in low-skill manufacturing – migration into Europe could be unstoppable (Mahbubani 2001, 2008).

Joined-up thinking, a perspective of pervasive interconnection and interdependence, is vital for identifying and inspiring required social change. Arguably, there is more chance of getting people to accept joined-up thinking than joined-up feeling, but the two can be mutually reinforcing. Integrated analyses can conduce to joined-up feeling, including through effects on the perception of 'we'. Joined-up feeling in turn increases the likelihood and wholeheartedness of immersion in the explanatory perspective of interconnectedness.

The human security approach complements human rights thinking, by being less individualistic and giving emphasis and space for the significance of community and identity, including complex and liminal identities. Its concern with distinct and substantive areas of being, well-being and security – including physical security, identity security, uniting children and parents, or repatriating bodies – takes us in the direction of a transnational ethics of well-being and migration that has substance and insight beyond what will be found in an abstract general international or global ethic.

---

19 'Care ethics' stresses the centrality in ethical behaviour of "empathic association with others and a sense of being responsible and caring.... The ethics of care therefore promotes traits...such as sympathy, compassion, fidelity, discernment, love, and trustworthiness" (Honderich 1995: 121).

20 Mahbubani, Kishore, 1994: "You May Not Like It, Europe, but This Asian Medicine Could Help", in: *International Herald Tribune* (1-2 October 1994). He has made similar points regarding the US in his other writings.

21 See Code (2008: 198) for a similar discussion on identities and reductive stereotyping. It draws from her book (Code 2006), which presents an ecology-inspired philosophy that highlights interdependence, mutual constitution and local specificity.

20 Migration, Morality and Finance

Amiya Kumar Bagchi

20.1 Introduction: Migration in the Second Age of Globalization[1]

Human beings are migratory animals and by migrating across seas and land, they have established their settlements around the globe (Diamond 1992). However, like most other animals, they have also had a sense of territoriality. Yet, rights of territoriality were flexibly exercised until the rise of modern, so-called rational-bureaucratic states.[2]

How then should migrants be treated? The simplest answer is that migrants are human beings and should enjoy the same rights as any other human being. However, this answer runs up against the modern state system, under which states treat their own citizens and citizens of other states differently. This differential treatment becomes glaring in the case of so-called illegal, but also many legal, immigrants. In criminal jurisprudence, the cardinal principle is that a person is to be innocent until he is proved otherwise. It is generally the responsibility of the prosecuting authorities to prove the guilt of the person charged with a crime. With immigrants, an opposite principle is generally followed: they are considered guilty until they can prove that they are legal residents in the host country. The problem becomes even more complicated when people become refugees and\or stateless. Not all refugees are stateless, but many of them refuse to return to the jurisdiction of states of which they are citizens and many states refuse to take back persons who claim to be citizens of those states.

Morality concerns a human being's behaviour with regard to other beings and to things outside him/herself as far as they impinge on the fortunes of other beings, especially human beings. Hence, morality necessarily has to assume certain basic propositions about how the lives of human beings are affected by socio-economic and political institutions and changes in them.

The liberal theory of justice takes inequality to be a fact. It seeks to design policies without trying to alter a given social and political arrangement that reproduces and often aggravates structures of inequality worldwide. Applied to migrants, policies arising out of that minimalist view of morality only address how illegal immigrants can be treated more humanely, or how the grosser forms of discrimination against minority communities constituted by immigrants can be ended.

This chapter challenges the minimalist perspective on morality, as applied to migrants. It also challenges the view that dramatic socio-economic inequality will always be with us and that the goal of sensible policy can only be the provision of primary goods and alleviation of poverty in micro contexts. Such a frame of policymaking neglects the macro-structures and policies that reproduce and exacerbate inequality and poverty. Gross international inequality and poverty are the root causes of streams of illegal migrants and refusal to treat those causes can only yield ad hoc solutions, which leave the migrants in a disadvantaged position. In most ethical, legal and economic literature related to migrants, there is also an inadequate appreciation of the asymmetries of resources, information and power that prevail as between the migrants and the authorities who sit in judgment over them. Most of those designated as illegal immigrants do not possess enough information relating to their own economic or legal situation. On the other side, the authorities of the country to which they have migrated

1 I thank Jasodhara Bagchi, Barnita Bagchi, Tista Bagchi, Marie-Claire Calosz-Schopp, Achin Chakraborty, Pierre Dasen and Shubhoranjan Dasgupta for insightful comments on one or other previous versions. I also thank Des Gasper and Thanh-Dam Truong for carefully editing the final version. However, none of them should be blamed for any remaining errors.

2 See, for example, the description of exchanges between agriculturists and pastoralists, and of transhumant migrations in pre-colonial Senegambia, in Curtin (1975: chap. 1).

T.-D. Truong and D. Gasper (eds.), *Transnational Migration and Human Security*, Hexagon Series on Human and Environmental Security and Peace 6, DOI 10.1007/978-3-642-12757-1_20, © Springer-Verlag Berlin Heidelberg 2011

are often woefully ignorant of the home background of the migrants, and demand documentation unavailable to inhabitants of many developing countries.

Three changes in the international politico-economic order appear to underlie the aggravation of inequality internationally and within countries. These are: 1) the turn against the state as a provider of social services and insurer of a long-term strategy for improving the technological and economic capability of developing countries, from the late 1970's; 2) the placing of finance as the sovereign governor of the fates of most market economies; and, 3) the collapse of the Soviet bloc. The signing of the World Trade Organization agreement sealed the first change and connected with the financial liberalization that swept over more and more countries from the early 1980's. The effects of these changes have been the disabling of the state as the regulator of economic institutions and as the provider of social security for the disadvantaged section of population. They have also meant an endemic deficiency of effective demand in practically all developing countries, and the rise of levels of unemployment worldwide.

Before they gave up their model of socialism, the Eastern European states took complete responsibility for education, health and access to work for the population. The total abdication by the state of that responsibility has created an enormous movement of population within and out of those states. The movement often takes the form of trafficking of women.[3] The social democratic Western European states have also reduced the social protection of the sick, the elderly and the unemployed. On the other side, divergent movements in the growth of the working age population (themselves partly the product of unequal access to health care and education in the rich and the poor countries) have produced new tensions in the policies related to labour and immigrants, especially in the richer countries. While international capital movements are not only permitted but, falsely glamorized as the harbinger of innovation and greater efficiency, richer states are introducing increasingly draconian regulations to control immigration and deny basic human rights to so-called illegal immigrants. A proper ethical framework for informing policymaking at the national and international levels needs to address these contradictions and tensions if it is to be a step towards ensuring fuller freedom for all human beings.

In the wake of increased global terrorist attacks, the security approach to migration has found greater favour with policymakers. There are three basic objections to this approach. First, it is likely to have only temporary impact, while increasing the cost of surveillance and protection of the borders. Secondly, the measures taken by the authorities in some countries, such as the US and UK, have violated the constitution and laws of those countries and abridged the freedom of their own citizens: the courts in these nations have often thrown the cases out on these grounds. Finally, they usurp and deny many of these migrants' basic human rights, with little redress from any higher authority. These states effectively practice terrorism against immigrants, especially against those who are stigmatized as 'illegal immigrants', although they might have lived in the host country for many years, often doing menial jobs that the natives, very often descendants of earlier immigrants, refuse to perform.

The search for an alternative paradigm must start with the recognition that the increased inequality between incomes of different countries contributes to a surge of migration from developing and transitional economies. A more decent international order, with the promise of what the ILO calls 'decent work' for most people in most countries, would minimize the need for migration and the eruption of irrational anger expressing itself as terrorism. The restoration of the IMF to its original function of minimizing turbulence in the balance of payments between countries, removing most WTO provisions that damage both agriculture and industry in developing countries, scrutiny of all money transfers at both the point of origin and the point of deposit to prevent haemorrhage similar to what Russia suffered throughout the 1990's, and what sub-Saharan Africa and Latin America have suffered for the last 30 years or more, and restoring the necessary public provisioning by the state, are some necessary items to create an adequate policy to guide the global polity of the future.

20.2 Internal Migration: The Roles of the State and the Market

We will deal briefly with internal migration before moving on to the treatment of international migrants. Migration within the borders of a given state is probably a larger stream than migration across international borders. In the People's Republic of China alone, estimates of actual and potential numbers of migrants range from 150 million to 500 million per-

3 For an analysis of the reasons for the growth of trafficking of women in different parts of the world, see Banerjee 2003; Facio 2003; and Poulin 2003.

sons, whereas the currently accepted estimate of international migrants is around 200 million.[4] The treatment of internal migrants raises many of the same issues of morality and justice as international migration.

The common cause behind internal migration on the part of free agents is the search for better incomes, better environments, better education and other facilities. As noted, human beings have always been migratory. However, many settled states in the past tried to restrict the mobility of their subjects or citizens by penalizing emigration to ensure a tax-base or a base for recruitment of soldiers, and to restrict immigration to protect guild privileges. One of the principal demands of publicists, philosophers and political economists was the removal of restrictions on mobility between places and occupations. The right to migrate voluntarily is a human right. However, especially in the international arena, this right is routinely violated. Domestically too there have been and still are many coerced into migration, such as women forced into sex work, bonded labourers in the sugarcane or cotton fields or brick kilns of South Asia, and other 'unfree' workers in many other developing regions.

Under capitalism, the working of cumulative causation that feeds on economies of spatial agglomeration and increasing returns within firms and among networks of firms is a major factor behind voluntary migration, displacement and coerced migration.

1. When, for some reason, a particular city or region attracts customers and firms, and economic agents in general cluster in that locality, division of labour becomes more complex both within and between firms. The greater specialization through division of labour itself generates economies of scale. In addition, learning by doing and by experimenting makes individuals and organizations more efficient... (Bagchi 2005a: 20).
2. The profits generated through the first set of factors enable the capitalists operating there to accumulate more capital, and to increase their advantage in comparison with those who operate in less-favoured locations. The experience of successful operation of dynamic firms induces the managers and capitalists to venture on further innovations. Moreover, the dynamic cluster acts as a beacon to capitalists and entrepreneurs from other regions (Bagchi 2005a: 20).
3. Workers leave a declining location and migrate to the dynamic clusters. A predominant fraction of such migrants tend to consist of young adults, and in many situations, adult males. The expanding cluster gets the benefit of adult workers whom it had not fed from childhood or educated (when the workers have skills and/or formal education), and the capitalists can offer lower wages than would have ruled if the migration had not taken place (Bagchi 2005a: 20–21).

Under conditions of modern economic growth, internal migration has generally meant moving out of rural to urban areas, out of agriculture into industry or services as the main occupation, or moving from areas of slow growth or stagnation to fast-growing areas. In the developed countries, the major movements out of agriculture into industry or services had been largely completed by the third quarter of the 20th century. Such movements took place rapidly and posed major problems of urban congestion, shortages of housing, clean water and infrastructural facilities, renewal of decaying habitations and so on; and such problems, while less acute than a century ago, remain today.

Developing countries today face similar problems but the scale is much greater because the populations involved are about three to four times those of developed countries. They are also more acute because various ideological and structural reasons have rendered resources for meeting the challenges more scarce. However, the challenges will ultimately have to be tackled at the local level by the people of the developing countries themselves, even as they struggle against an international socioeconomic order that drains resources from the Third World and often undermines the concerned states' capacity to plan for a humane process of structural change.

Several major changes in developing countries have intensified internal migration. The first is the construction of dams, factories or mines in regions mainly populated by economically and politically underprivileged communities. The state carried out many of the projects and was complicit in the work of local capitalists with others. But with the rise of neoliberalism, the private sector assumed a leading role and the protective regulation earlier installed by the state has been stripped away, leaving the affected people even more vulnerable to the pressures of the market, often backed by the force of the police or of security apparatus of the corporate sector. Secondly, in many cases in which the state has faced resistance

4 GCIM, 2005: Migration in an Interconnected World, New Directions for Action: Report of the Global Commission on International Migration, October; see at: <http://www.gcim.org/en/finalreport.html>, 1, 18 Feb 2010.

against such acts of displacement, it has resorted to forcible resettlement and ethnic influx of the national majority community to dilute the strength of the popular resistance. Recently, especially after the advent of the WTO regime, agriculture, which still supports about half the work force of the developing world, is facing a severe crisis. Unemployment and imminent starvation are forcing hundreds of millions of peasants off the land. At the same time, the rate of growth of employment in services and industry is far lower than that of the labour force in most developing countries (ILO 2004).

Stories of the pushing back of indigenous peoples into inhospitable land and their further displacement leading to their forced migration have been repeated all over the developing world and the now affluent North America and Australia, and continue today (Bagchi 2005c: Part III). Tragically, many of the so-called nomadic communities, who are some of the worst victims of state-and market-directed coerced migration, were originally rendered so by earlier changes that damaged their livelihood and uprooted them from their habitats (see Bagchi 1981). The threat of such forced migrations has increased under the neoliberal regime that aims to privatize many goods and resources earlier considered inviolably public goods. The struggle for saving the livelihoods and protecting the fundamental rights of 'oustees' is not simply about compensation for displaced people or the quality of rehabilitation offered to them. It is also about the quality of the democratic process itself. The 150,000 persons displaced in India's Narmada valley by the *Sardar Sarovar Project* (SSP), for example, learned the imminent threat to their homes, their livelihood and their way of living only when survey teams arrived to measure their land. When people resisted this usurpation of their homes, they were met not with consultation and negotiation by the agents of a democratic state but by extreme repression by police authorities. If the benefits of farmers elsewhere outweighed the costs imposed on the oustees, then the state had the obligation to get the two sides together and offer a compensation package that would outweigh the loss of their homes. State authorities decided that these people, who were generally held in contempt by the members of the upper classes and upper castes, would be treated as disposable material to be herded into ghettoes and trampled on as the lowest of the low.

The requirements of a democratic process under a constitution that guarantees the right to livelihood in case of possible displacement of a group of people include 1) the transmission of adequate information to potential victims, 2) a process of consultation with the potential oustees, 3) the preparation of a package of compensation or reparation for the oustees, 4) a judicial review in case of disputes that takes adequate account of the fundamental rights of the oustees, and 5) counselling and training of the oustees in new occupations in cases in which the state cannot provide alternative locations in which the oustees can carry on their earlier patterns of livelihood. In the SSP, practically all these requirements were violated at every step. The same indictment applies for many other dam projects in India, and a fortiori, in the case of the mega projects in China (Aiyar 2006).

When internal displacement occurs through the working of state-sponsored or market-driven development, the moral issues are clear. Any concept of public morality that places both the substantive and formal freedom of persons at the centre of its discourse would want society to provide for people forced into destitution through no fault of their own. Without such a provision, human lives will be lost or rendered intolerable and the freedom of choice that upholders of negative liberty revere will become meaningless. Substantive freedom will be badly curtailed or lost altogether if people who are displaced and coerced into migration because of state action or the depredations of an unregulated market cannot express their discontent about the changes they are victims of. When, for example, women and children are trafficked within a state and especially across state borders, they are often rendered voiceless through the complicity of the employers and authorities.

20.3 Theories of Justice and Morality and their Bearing on the Ethics of Treatment of International Migrants

The scale of international migration as computed by the international bodies monitoring them is impressive. A recent estimate puts the figure of international migrants at about 200 million persons in the beginning of the 21st century.[5] It must be recalled that, 1) 200 million is still a small fraction of the total world

5 GCIM, 2005: *Migration in an Interconnected World, New Directions for Action: Report of the Global Commission on International Migration*, October, See at: <http://www.gcim.org/en/finalreport.html> (18 February 2010).

population; 2) most migrants are in developing countries; and 3) a single country, China, may be handling as many as 120–150 million, mostly rural to urban migrants without any international aid. While we do not know the full scale of injustice perpetrated on the displaced people, China is trying to build infrastructure and housing on an unprecedented scale to provide better living conditions both for permanent urban residents and for migrants from rural areas. It systematically ploughs about 40 per cent of its income into investment. It is able to do so because so far it has not allowed 'diseases of financialization' to enter into its body politic, and because it had effected a transformation of its economy by eliminating the power of property owners and speculative capital.

At the eye of the storm are migrants to developed countries, who are categorized in progressively more pejorative terms as 'undocumented', 'irregular', 'unauthorized' or 'illegal' migrants. Immigrants from the South to both the US and the EU move mainly into agriculture, which the native-born are giving up, into the hotel and restaurant sector, construction, and low-skilled services.[6] Europe needs these immigrants even more than the US, since the European population is aging much faster, but that does not prevent most European nations from violating human rights treaties they have signed, in their treatment of immigrants.[7]

It follows that a discourse on the morality of migration, internal or international, has to address three overarching structures governing the fate of all human beings. These are the prerogatives of the modern state, the regime of property rights as mediated through markets in a property-owning society, and the governance of the family and the power of adult males over women and children.

In the usual systems of morality or justice, the reference persons are subjects or citizens of particular states. These owe their origin to the context of the modern mercantile-absolutist states in Europe in the 16th to 18th centuries and the continual wars in which they were embroiled to acquire hegemonic position (Bagchi 2005c: chapter 4; Blanning 2007). Hugo Grotius[8] put forward the basic system of laws governing relations between states, which dealt with relations between states in peace or war, and did not throw much light on how states should treat people whose status as citizens or residents straddled several territorial jurisdictions.

Conventional political philosophy, including the dominant version of political liberalism, offers little insight into the ethical or political problems surrounding international migration. Such philosophy takes the existing system of states to be a given and says little beyond what had been accepted as the norm between 'civilized' states from the time of Grotius.

The dominant strands of political liberalism, in its social or democratic variants (to borrow a classification made by Plant, 2004), in fact contradict their own consequentialist approach to questions of public morality and justice, the meta-principle that principles for human behaviour must be judged by their consequences. They treat the market as an unanalysed, absolute and given fact rather than as a human institution interacting with other human institutions such as the family and the state. Thereby they not only produce false answers about the way markets perform, but also yield the high ground to neoliberalism that has then made short work of the social or democratic variants of political liberalism.

John Rawls has been perhaps the most influential philosopher of political liberalism since the 1960's, as far at least as academic discourse is concerned. Rawls's theory of justice as fairness demands that everybody enjoys certain inalienable liberties, that 'fair' opportunities for advancing themselves should be available to all citizens, and that only those differences in economic and social arrangements should be tolerated that would be accessible to everybody and maximally benefit the most disadvantaged sections of the population (Rawls 1971, 1999; van Parijs 2003). Compared with many other versions of liberalism, Rawls' work possesses at least two virtues. First, it is an explicitly 'political' theory of justice. There is no pretence that the principles of justice apply to some ideal society, without a state endowed with a monopoly of coercive power. Secondly, the principles of justice are primarily macro-social in nature and are not principles that should guide individual behaviour, as Rawls insisted in the numerous restatements he provided (Rawls 1974, 1999). It is a consequentialist theory and, therefore, judgments about enforcing certain rules necessarily involve analysis of the processes followed, to judge how far they lead to the approved results encoded in the principles of justice.

6 KW 2006: *The Immigration Debate: Its Impact on Workers, Wages and Employers*; see at: <http://knowledge.wharton.upenn.edu/article/1482.cfm> (3 May 2006).

7 KW2006: 2, 54-55, Annex III.

8 Grotius, Hugo, 1625/1901: *De jure belli ac pacis*, translated by A. C. Campbell as *The Rights of War and Peace*, online Library of Liberty; see at: <http://files.libertyfund.org/files/553/0138_Bk_Sm.pdf> (18 February 2010).

Since Rawls's theory is based on the notion of a contract implicitly or explicitly entered into by citizens of a democratic state, it is virtually impossible, without altering the structure of the basic axioms, to extend it into the international arena. Rawls explicitly recognized this in his essay on the "Law of Peoples" (Rawls 1999). Not only is it difficult to extend the Rawlsian contractual approach to problems of citizens who are not members of the state to which the principles of justice apply, it is also exclusionary since as Rawls made clear in his numerous writings, including *Political Liberalism* (Rawls 1993), it cannot apply to nations that do not have the background institutions of his conception of "the reasonably just societies of well-ordered peoples" (Rawls 1999: 17).

As Sen (2002: 458) pointed out:

> The Rawlsian exercise involves institutional reasoning among people 'who are born into that society in which they lead their lives' (Rawls 1993: 23). What is a matter of concern here is the absence of some procedural insistence on forceful scrutiny of local values that may, on further scrutiny, turn out to be preconceptions and biases that are common to a focal group.

Thus, Rawlsian democracy may end up by encoding racism, gender discrimination, not to speak of class biases, directed against strangers or even citizens who do not belong to the focal group.

Rawls also insisted that his principles of justice would embed in production relations that, following James Meade (1964), he dubbed a "property-owning democracy" (Rawls 1987, 1999: 419). He sharply distinguished his concept of a property-owning democracy from that of a welfare state (Rawls 1987, 1999: 419).

> One major difference is that the background institutions of property-owning democracy, with the system of (workably) competitive markets, try to disperse the wealth and capital, and thus to prevent a small part of society from controlling the economy and indirectly political life itself. Property-owning democracy avoids this, not by redistributing income to those with less at the end of each period, so to speak, but rather by ensuring the widespread ownership of productive assets and human capital (educated abilities and trained skills) at the beginning of each period, all this against a background of the equal basic liberties and fair equality of opportunity. The idea is not simply to assist those who lose out through accident or misfortune (although this must be done), but instead to put all citizens in a position to manage their own affairs and take part in social cooperation on a footing of mutual respect under appropriately equal conditions.

However, the outcome of the working of a property-owning democracy may violate some of the basic principles of justice laid down by Rawls. First, in competitive markets some persons may starve because of the working of the market, if the state does not intervene (Coles/Hammond 1995). Second, if workable competition includes monopolistic markets, then some people may be unable to access goods and services because the monopolists find it profitable to raise prices and change the quality of those goods and services out of reach of low-income persons (Atkinson 1995). Even in situations where everyone begins with equal assets, the outcome of monopolistic competition leads to some being denied Rawls' 'primary goods'.

In countries that had a property-owner class using market and non-market coercion, the deprivation of the peasants and the emergence of a landless class of workers were built into the institutional framework (Habib 1965/1995, 1983/1995). Even under legal systems that gave rights to land initially only to actual cultivators, the market produced a class of landless workers. This was true as much of the northern states of the US as of, say, Denmark by the end of the 19th century. In the industrial sphere, the market led to ever-greater concentrations, and when mergers and takeovers were permitted, to greater centralization of economic power. The protection of the actual cultivators or small producers in industry against dispossession could come only through the continuous intervention by the state, as through the operation of the Sherman Act in the US, or the continuous monitoring of land transfers as once exercised in South Korea.

Rawls's programme would involve a periodic redistribution of all assets in society, something that no welfare state has attempted. There are two reasons why in a market economy, with chance associated with external factors such as harvest fluctuations or changes in trade patterns or with endogenous factors such as competition or innovations – themselves spurred by competition – a skewed distribution of assets and income will be generated. Some members of the population subjected to these external shocks would acquire larger values of assets and incomes, and others would get lesser shares of the assets and incomes and an unequal distribution would be inevitable if no purposive action is taken to counter this process (Aitchison/Brown 1957: chapter 3). In addition, a connected set of factors works through the processes of increasing returns to scale and spatial agglomeration noted earlier. Karl Marx's theory of the tendency for concentration of capital in a few firms and the associated tendency of smaller firms consumed by larger ones leading to centralization of capital fits into this schema. Similarly, Schumpeter (1942) stressed the creative destruction wrought by innovations facilitating the growth of oligopolistic firms and further fomenting the growth of such firms; and Kaldor and Myrdal put forward theories of cumulative causation that would lead to growing inequality of distribution of wealth, incomes and regional fortunes and finally, of fortunes of different countries.[9] There are also other theories seeking to explain the rise of inequality to a historic high in most countries of the world (Milanovic 2005).

The point is not to believe that inequality must rise in every country in every period, measured by every criterion; even less do we have to believe in a particular strand of explanation for the tendency of inequality to increase, as measured by many criteria. Moral theorists simply cannot treat the existing market as a competitive mechanism under which everybody is engaged in an equal exchange. John Rawls and many other moral theorists of welfare capitalism have never analysed the nature of the market and its continual transformation under advanced capitalism. They have assumed that capitalists will handle the market while states guided by moral theorists will tackle the undesirable consequences of market operation. This has played into the hands of neoliberals. If markets are taken to be 'naturally' given, then any interference with that market in the form of state or trade union regulation is considered unnatural. A fiscal crisis of the welfare state results when typical measures of social insurance associated with the welfare state support that regulation, but at the same time a low tax regime for the rich is instituted in the belief that it will encourage thrift and enterprise or will check capital flight. The crisis then provides a strong argument for neoliberals to do away with most state regulation, as allegedly against capitalist enterprise.

20.4 Second Era of Finance-led Globalization: Contradiction between Unregulated Movements of Capital and Restrictions on Labour Migration

To grasp the enormity of dislocation that has fuelled migration, especially migration across borders, we have to analyse the political economy of neoliberalism. The problems of international and internal migration acquired new dimensions as neoliberalism moved to strip the state of most functions other than providing security to the property of the rich and transnational firms. It will be helpful to compare the current phase of finance-led globalization, starting around 1971, with an earlier phase, between the mid-19th century and 1914.

The earlier phase of finance-led globalization was likewise associated with a huge swell of migration. Between 1846 and 1924, an estimated 48 million people moved out of Europe into other continents (Massey 1988: table 1). Most of that movement took place from the 1870s to 1914. A much smaller number of people from China, India and other colonial and semi-colonial lands were taken as indentured labourers, mostly to serve in the plantations and mines of the tropical regions. The intercontinental European migration was supported by a massive flow of European – chiefly British – investment to the lands where Europeans settled. That foreign investment was in its turn sustained by large flows of tribute and European profits in the non-white dependencies of the British and other European powers with substantial possessions in Asia, Africa and Latin America (Pollard 1985; Bagchi 2005c: chap. 13 and 16).

The structural transformation attendant on industrialization and the quickening of population growth in several regions, brought about by declining infant and adult mortality, drove European migration in the late 19th century. Germany became a net immigration country from the 1890s; and overseas, the US became the principal destination for European migrants. The total proportions of population as of 1900 who migrated overseas in this period ranged from 1.3 per cent for France, 8.0 per cent for Germany, 29.2 per cent for Italy, 30.1 per cent for Portugal, 35.9 per cent for Norway and 40.9 per cent for the British Isles (Massey 1988: Table 1). The extra-European destination countries were able to absorb these immigrants not only because of the flows of foreign investment received by them, but also because of the immense degree of support given by domestic policies in those countries to both public and private investment. The governments of Germany, US, Australia and Canada all instituted stiff tariff protection against foreign manufacturers, and they built up the infrastructure through generous grants. The concerned governments were also involved in extending education and public health care in various forms. Moreover, in the European heartland, workers' bargaining power improved through their own struggles as well as the tightening of the labour market; government policies

9 For a summary of the processes of cumulative causation see Ricoy (1998).

looked after the young and the old when so many working adults were migrating abroad. The European settlers also grabbed the land and resources of native populations in the US, Canada, Australia, South Africa and Rhodesia (today's Zambia and Zimbabwe). Such acts of usurpation would not be open to today's impoverished migrants, but multinational corporations (MNCs) continue to usurp common property resources all over the world.

The global situation under the second phase of finance-led globalization since the 1970s is, in many respects, different from what prevailed in the first phase of finance-led globalization. From the beginning, policies aimed at curbing worker power, making the state retreat from any activities judged not to be in the interest of capital and to push back the bargaining ability of primary producers, especially producers of oil. The transnational banks domiciled in the US, UK, Switzerland, France and Germany successfully corralled the petrodollars arising out of the quadrupling of the oil price in 1973. In a connected development, the major countries of Latin America were pushed into a debt trap that closed on them in 1982. In the so-called rescheduling of the debt of the heavily indebted countries, the trapdoor was lifted only as far as it allowed the countries to work a treadmill for generating a stream of service payments, without ever getting out of the trap. The domestic investment capacity of practically all the developing counties, except those of East Asia, was battered exactly when they needed to invest more not only in physical capital and economic infrastructure, but also in health, education and technology appropriate for providing employment to a burgeoning labour force.

20.5 Theories of Justice Confronted by Facts of Globalization

We argue above that the social or democratic versions of liberalism have failed to analyse the markets in capital and labour power as they really work. Moreover, they have not taken into account the transformation of these markets since financial engineering wreaked havoc on government support for social sectors or productive investment in all countries that they could cajole or bully, and on the coordination functions of the IMF or World Bank. The latter became international gendarmes at the behest of capital. This failure of the ethical philosophers left the field wide open for neoliberal policymakers all around the world.

Discourses on morality that place responsibility for particular lapses on the actions of particular persons are inadequate to address the issues raised by the way financialization and finance-led globalization has shaped the international economy. These issues relate to what some call 'structural injustice' (Fortman 2006). No single person decides that because of the Asian financial crisis of 1997, for example, hundreds of thousands of Indonesians should find themselves on the verge of starvation. However, the structures that make such hazards impinge on the lives of innocent people demand serious scrutiny; such scrutiny is lacking in most ethical discourses. The Rawlsian discourse displays a gap regarding critical examination of the financial or trade structures that make injustice endemic in most societies.

For examination of how moral theorists should address the ethical treatment of peoples separated by barriers of state structures, Rawls's analysis does not advance beyond Grotius. The 'law of peoples' can apply, properly speaking, in the Rawlsian canon only to properly ordered societies with institutions that are clones of the US system of governance. It would also apply to peoples with non-liberal but 'decent' governments. Rawls does not define what he means by a decent, non-liberal government. Leaving that aside, can people be held responsible for indecent governments ruling over them? Moreover, Rawls imposes on the people the responsibility of taking control of their numbers, a responsibility that Grotius did not know of. This sits badly with his ethical individualism, and is reminiscent of the Social Darwinism that blamed the poor for their 'polyphiloprogenism', to borrow from T.S. Eliot.[10] Rawls's requirement seems influenced by the neo-Malthusian policymakers who think that governments can control fertility and the growth of population, if necessary, by direct or indirect coercion (politely called incentives). In fact, such policies have generally failed, and many such policies violate the freedom of choice beloved of liberals.

In his law of peoples, Rawls would give citizens the right to emigrate. Would this right make sense if people also did not have the right to immigrate into some other country? Thus, unfortunately, the Rawlsian corpus has little to offer by way of guidance to seekers after justice and morality in international relations. In fact, the general trend of his argument might support the action of a so-called democratic society in imposing its rule over another country if the govern-

10 For a critique of Social Darwinism, see Bagchi 2005c: Appendix A.

ment of the latter is judged indecent and is accused of systematically violating human rights.

Financial innovations effected by the major financial powers led by the US and UK and ideological constructs by economists both played a role in the debt-entrapment of the developing countries. In the early 1970s, stock exchanges in both Chicago and New York introduced derivatives futures on commodities, which included options on increasingly sophisticated delivery systems in terms of dates and instruments. Concurrently Black, Merton and Scholes constructed the fallacious formula of option pricing.[11] They assumed that it is always possible to find out the fundamental values of profit from the ownership of a share in a firm or in a stock of goods, and to anchor the formula for option pricing on those fundamental values. But it is well known that prices in the stock market are governed largely by sentiment and operators' guesses about how other operators in the market will behave (for a classic demonstration, see Keynes 1936: chapter 12). Despite that, in 1997, the Nobel Prize for economics was awarded to Merton and Scholes (Black had died by then). The unreliability of the Black-Merton-Scholes formula was proved soon afterwards. In 1998, Long Term Capital Management, a hedge fund founded by Merton and Scholes among others, almost went bankrupt, with a huge exposure to banks in Europe and the US. It was rescued by a bailout operation orchestrated by the Federal Reserve Bank of New York but was finally liquidated in early 2000.[12]

Similarly, in 1973 Ronald McKinnon (1973) and Edward Shaw (1973) published books which alleged that developing countries suffered from what they called 'financial repression'. According to the McKinnon-Shaw doctrine, the regulation of interest rates by the government rather than their determination in a free market, and the direction of funds into designated uses, damage economic growth by discouraging saving and by misallocating resources. This doctrine lacks adequate theoretical and empirical foundation. First, a credit market does not work like a market for apples. Intending borrowers cannot get more credit simply by offering to pay higher rates. Credit markets are always characterized by rationing. Most students of monetary economics knew this and a number of economists have rigorously shown the logic of credit rationing (see Stiglitz/Weiss 1981). Second, in capitalist economies, investment drives saving. Individual saving intentions, stimulated though they may be for some savers by higher rates of interest earned on their savings, cannot lead to a nationally higher rate of investment and growth unless investors act in a venturesome manner. In many cases, a low interest regime can stimulate higher rates of investment. After World War II, most governments of Western Europe and Japan followed low-interest policies and achieved high rates of growth. In more recent times, the high-growth economies of East Asia, including China, South Korea and Taiwan, have followed policies that would be castigated by believers in the McKinnon-Shaw theory as financial repression, with great benefit to their economies (Amsden/Chu 2003; Bagchi 2005b).

More generally, the advocates of neoliberal reforms have argued that the developing countries had done worse under some degree of state direction and protection of home industries in the 1960s and 70s than they did thereafter. Investigations by international bodies such as the United Nations Conference on Trade and Development (UNCTAD) and individual researchers have shown that most developing countries had higher rates both of economic growth and of advances in various human development indices between 1960 and 1980 than they have attained since (Bagchi 2005c: chap. 22 and 23; IOM 2005: chap. 9).[13]

Some reasons why the economic structural adjustment programmes (SAPs) of the 1980's and 90's set back these economies have been well demonstrated. It is useful still to mention them here, because many discussions of new waves of migration from Latin America, the Caribbean and Africa remain silent on the subject. By squeezing domestic expenditure severely, the SAPs damaged incentives to invest. The raising of interest rates under the SAPs both curtailed investment by firms and led to the bankruptcy of many businesses that could not meet their obligations. This in turn often led to a banking crisis, as witnessed in the cases of Indonesia in 1997–98 and Ar-

11 For a short account of the theory, see at: <http://nobelprize.org/economics/laureates/1997/press.html> (16 February 2010).

12 See at: <http://www2.sjsu.edu/faculty/watkins/ltcm.htm> (16 February 2010).

13 See also Weisbrot, Mark; Baker, Dean; Kraev, Egor; Chen, Judy, 2001: *The Scorecard on Globalization 1980-2000: Twenty Years of Diminished Progress* (Centre for Economic and Policy Research), See at: <http://www.cepr.net/index.php/publications/reports/the-scorecard-on-globalization-1980-2000-20-years-of-diminished-progress/> (19 February 2010).

gentina during 2001–02. With vastly diminished incomes and yet the overriding obligation to pay foreign debtors, even apart from the pressure of the new minimalist state orientation, the governments of the highly indebted countries were forced to sell off many productive enterprises. These sales generally went to foreign enterprises at fire sale prices since the currency of the country concerned had drastically devalued and only firms from hard currency areas had the resources to bid for them.

Although many of the problems of both developed and developing countries in Globalization Phase II arise from this footloose behaviour of capital, in the literature there has been little discussion of the justice or even the legality of full capital mobility across international borders. It is taken as axiomatic in some branches of the contemporary Anglo-Saxon literature, centred on the interests of shareholders, that the latter are the only risk-bearers in a firm. But the employees also bear risk, as do subcontractors and suppliers to the firm, and in some cases, even consumers (if, for example, the firm is the only easily accessible seller of an essential drug in a poor country). In the current phase of globalization, firms have been allowed to shift their operations from one country to another without consulting the interests of workers. That kind of relocation or the employment of low-wage workers at the cost of locally employed higher-wage workers has fuelled populist politics of restricting immigration (Crisp 2003; Spencer 2003) and even some leftist economists have supported such moves. Borjas[14] and Rowthorn (2008) have argued that immigration of any workers will have a depressing effect on the wages of the locals, especially in pockets of high unemployment. Such views are contested (Kleinman 2003; IOM 2005: chapter 9).

In assessing the proposed immigration controls, note that for many years the rest of the world has kept the US afloat by sending more than $2 billion dollars a day to that country to meet its balance of payments deficit. A large part of the foreign funds comes from controllers of client states or from businesspersons who are directly or indirectly responsible for creating deprivation and unemployment in their home countries. Another large part of the legitimate US earnings accrues from arms sales to states, in conflict situations or rendered insecure through the activities of NATO member countries, led by the US.

Some, such as Borjas, do not question the capitalist rules of the game, which shore up the growth of the US economy in other ways. The wave of illegal immigrants from Mexico and Latin America helps keep up the profits of private firms in the US. For example, in the reconstruction of the city of New Orleans, devastated by Hurricane Katrina in 2005, about a quarter of the construction workers were reported to be:

> ...illegal immigrants, who are getting lower pay, less medical care and less safety equipment than legal workers, according to a new study by professors at Tulane University and the University of California, Berkeley. These workers reported making an average of $6.50 less than legal workers and had more trouble collecting their wages, the study said. While few workers reported run-ins with the police,...their employers sometimes threatened to have them deported if they complained about missing pay or dangerous working conditions (Eaton 2006).[15]

Thus, the illegality of most immigrants in labour-importing countries acts as a double-edged sword; it makes them work under worse conditions than legal workers do. Simultaneously, the stigma of illegality can be used to beat down worker resistance. The use of illegal workers is not confined to the private sector. For instance, in fire-fighting operations, which are essential especially in the Western states of the US, immigrant workers form half of the contracted workers and an untold number of them work illegally.[16] In 2005, the US issued only two visas to unskilled Mexican labourers, whereas the number of undocumented immigrants from that country was 500,000. According to State Department rosters, it takes 12 years for a naturalized US citizen, born in Mexico, to bring an adult son or daughter to live in the United States (Eaton 2006).

Yet the history of the United States is, in great part, the history of immigrants (Handlin 1973: 3, cited in Hirschman 2005: 595). Throughout history, immigrants have been responsible for its economic, scientific and technological development. Even the evidence of the impact of current immigrants with low skills on the wages of the lower rungs of native-born workers remains inconclusive (Hirschman 2005: 606–

14 Borjas, George J., 2004: *Increasing the Supply of Labour through Immigration: Measuring the Impact of Native-born Workers*, Centre for Immigration Studies, See at: <http://www.cis.org/articles/back504.html>, (14 October 2005).

15 Leslie Eaton: "Study Sees Increases in Illegal Hispanic Workers in New Orleans", in *New York Times*, 8 June 2006; see at: <www.nytimes.com> (9 June 2006).

16 Kirk Johnson: "With Illegal Immigrants Fighting Wildfires, West Faces a Dilemma", in: *New York Times*, 28 May 2006; see at: <www.nytimes.com> (29 May 2006).

608). On the other hand, the demands for the civil, economic and political rights raised by immigrants are freshly energizing native-born workers' struggles for better living conditions.

Neither Borjas nor Rowthorn or other opponents of legal immigration into rich countries from the poorer regions take account of the fact that the financialization that benefited those on Wall Street or Threadneedle Street has led to a decline in rates of investment in most G7 countries (Stockhammer 2004). Rowthorn (1995) blamed this decline on rise in unemployment rates in Europe. To analyse the effects of immigration in developed countries without taking into account these overarching factors seems akin to the proverbial attempt to measure the effect of the weight of a fly on a boat when the fly is sitting on an elephant, without measuring the elephant's weight.

With a rampaging market for mergers and acquisitions reaching new records in terms of the value of assets and the number of workers affected, none of the ordinary stakeholders can be sure where their jobs, their supply contracts or their skills will end up and whether they will have anything left at the end of the deal. Most economists or political science commentators have not questioned the justice of allowing the licentious capital mobility that has caused the problem in the first place.

When it comes to developing countries, the injustice of allowing unrestricted capital mobility is even more glaring. Much of the Third World debt originated in the corruption within and around dictatorial regimes. When businesspersons and politicians in the know thought that the currency of the country concerned was likely to suffer devaluation because of unsustainable balance of payment deficits, they exported capital to hard currency areas. It was well known that before the Mexican debt crisis of 1982, as soon as the government borrowed money abroad, almost half of it was deposited in US banks. On top of that, dictators knew that they might have to flee at some stage from the wrath of the people, as happened with the Shah of Iran, Ferdinand Marcos, Mobutu and others. What is the justice of refusing to hand over the ill-gotten assets of the former Shah of Iran to the Iranian people? Why did it take so long for Swiss banks to hand over only a fraction of the billions that Sani Abacha stole from the people of Nigeria? Abacha died in 1998, but only a part of the money lodged in Swiss banks was returned to Nigeria and under the condition that the World Bank would monitor Nigeria's use of the funds.[17] It was also known that Abacha's ill-gotten wealth was stashed in the UK, Luxemburg, Liechtenstein and Austria as well. Did those banks ever ask how Abacha had obtained his money? If that money (altogether several billion US dollars) had been invested in Nigeria, it would have generated income and employment for several thousand Nigerians, and, at least, part of the incentive to migrate would have vanished.

So long as there are countries and institutions that will accept funds without asking any questions, the structure exists for continuous capital flight from all poor, vulnerable economies. As the research of Boyce and Ndikumana (2002) and other scholars have shown, much of Third World debt is due to capital flight, to which the international agencies, the G7 countries and traditional safe havens such as Switzerland turn a blind eye. Boyce and Ndikumana (2002) estimated that even for sub-Saharan Africa, the poorest of the major regions of the world, total capital flight exceeded the debt owed by them. Baker and Nordin (2005) have usefully distinguished three kinds of dirty money sluicing around the international economy - from official and political corruption; from drugs and arms running, human trafficking, racketeering etc., and commercial. The last receives the least official attention and may be more important than transfers of funds from official corruption.

> Businesses try to hide revenue from their country's tax inspectors by, say, directing buyers to deposit the money in Western bank accounts. Private studies have estimated such practices in developing countries at 5 per cent to 7 per cent of their total trade, or more than $ 200 billion per year illicitly transferred abroad.... Annual foreign aid totals $50 billion or so [pre-2003], while dirty money is upwards of $1 trillion per year, half of which passes from developing and transitional economies to the West.[18]

20.6 Troublesome Issues: Brain Drain, Brain Waste, Stateless and Irregular Migrants and Trafficking

Many of the usual normative discourses in the portals of respectable academia and the more powerful international bodies, with respect to international (and na-

---

17 *BBC News*, 9 September 2005; see at: <http://news.bbc.co.uk/2/hi/business/4230884.stm> (16 February 2010).

18 Raymond Baker, Jennifer Nordin: "While Dirty Money Flows, the Poor Stay Poor, in: *International Herald Tribune*, 13 April 2005.

tional) migration, turn out to be justifications for repressive measures under which troublemakers (read asylum-seekers) and unwelcome migrants may be shot with impunity, and/or subjected to stop-gap humanitarian measures as palliatives. In the same portals, selective, skill-specific immigration is approved of and the ill-effects on the developing countries of opening such side doors and the culpability of developed country governments and employers is often overlooked (except for Özden and Schiff (2006) and a report submitted to the *Global Commission on International Migration* (GCIM) set up by the United Nations). [19] While the agony continues, palliative humanitarian measures will be necessary. However, a long-term, morally appealing solution to the problem of migration will require the dismantling of the structure that continues to promote finance and the interests of capital at the cost of all other human values.

There are several troublesome areas pertaining to the treatment of international migrants, which cause controversies, or about which the mainstream literature is profoundly silent. In some ways, the treatment of skilled migrants has received most attention from researchers and policymakers. However, the treatment of stateless persons, of trafficking of persons, especially women, and finally, of so-called irregular or illegal migrants pose many painful issues.

Consider the migration of skilled or educated persons from poor countries. According to Özden and Schiff (2006: 10):

> Among the positive externalities that are lost with the emigration of educated workers are (a) the positive effect on the productivity of colleagues, employees, and other workers; (b) the provision of key public services with positive externalities, such as education and health, particularly for transmissible diseases; (c) the fiscal externalities associated with the fact that [their payments] are larger than the public services they consume and the public funds expended in their education; and (d) their contribution to the debate on important social issues and their impact on policy and institutions.

We can only mention the grievous effect of inducing the selective migration of highly skilled professionals such as doctors or nurses from developing countries to affluent lands. In some of the poorest nations, such as the countries of Central America and the Caribbean Islands, in 2000 CE, more than 50 per cent of their university-trained graduates were living abroad (Docquier/Marfouk 2006). There were reportedly more Ethiopian doctors practicing in Chicago than in the whole of Ethiopia. The number of Jamaican tertiary education graduates who migrate is 3.7 times the number of such people who stay home. Since 2000, "nearly 16000 African nurses have registered to work in the UK alone. Only 50 out of 600 doctors trained since independence are still practicing in Zambia. And it is estimated that there are currently more Malawian doctors practising in the northern English city of Manchester than in the whole of Malawi".[20] Thus, doctors and nurses trained at great cost by desperately poor countries are being lost to rich nations while sub-Saharan Africa continues to be a region of health disaster, plagued by HIV/AIDS, tuberculosis, endemic malaria and poverty-related diseases such as diarrhoea and other gastro-enteric disorders.

Not only health care, scientific and economic progress are threatened by this brain drain, but the ability of poor countries to protect the biological and genetic resources on which they have depended for survival for millennia is also gravely damaged. Under the Biodiversity Convention and the Trade-Related Aspects of Intellectual Property Rights (TRIPs) clauses of the WTO agreement, the poorer countries may protect their plant genetic resources (Correa 2000: chapter VI). Yet, how can they protect them if they do not retain scientists who can describe and classify them?

Conversely, there is brain waste which benefits nobody except some migrants who may seek to escape unemployment or abysmally low wages at any cost (Özden/Schiff 2006). Ordinary graduates, doctors, scientists from developing countries and Eastern Europe migrate to the EU, Australia and the US and perform menial jobs, either because their home country certification is not recognized in the host countries or because they cannot find jobs that fit their skills.

The case of stateless persons is the most difficult. Persons may be effectively stateless because they have been driven out of their usual homes and neither their home country nor the country to which they have been forced to migrate is willing to bear the cost of their rehabilitation. The cases of Palestinian refugees in West Asia and Rwandan refugees in Africa are noto-

19 GCIM, 2005: *Migration in an Interconnected World, New Directions for Action: Report of the Global Commission on International Migration*, October, See at: <http://www.gcim.org/en/finalreport.html>: (18 February 2010).

20 GCIM, 2005: *Migration in an Interconnected World, New Directions for Action: Report of the Global Commission on International Migration*, October, See at: <http://www.gcim.org/en/finalreport.html>: 24 (18 February 2010).

rious examples of such victims of ethnic cleansing or genocide, but such victims are there in many other regions of the world. The UN High Commission for Refugees (UNHCR) may take care of a fraction of these victims and whole generations of people spend their lives in refugee camps.

Stateless people are not necessarily refugees; in several countries of West Asia such as Kuwait and the United Arab Emirates, there are several hundred thousand inhabitants called *bidun jinsiya* in Arabic, meaning 'without nationality'. Most of them are supposed to have originated in Iran or South Asia. They have no security while they have lived all their lives in some of these countries and may be expelled any time, as happened to half of the population of *bidun* in Kuwait after the 1991 Gulf War (IOM 2005: 53–54).

Cases of so-called irregular immigrants have attracted attention because of atrocities committed against them by developed country governments in the name of law enforcement. One of the worst incidents occurred on 26 August 2001. The Norwegian steamer MV Tampa responded to an Australian Coastal Surveillance alert that an Indonesian boat was sinking and rescued 460 people on the boat. The Australian Prime Minister refused permission - for those boat people who were Afghan natives who had arrived in Indonesia earlier - to land. Ultimately, 150 of them were taken by New Zealand and the rest were landed in the tiny island state of Nauru (Crisp 2003: 85)[21]. Australia's action was against international law and human rights. The Australian government of John Howard was notorious for its treatment of asylum seekers and illegal immigrants, keeping them isolated in detention camps, and some detainees sewed their lips closed in protest (Jordan/Düvell 2003). The International Centre on Migration Policy Development estimates that some 2000 migrants die each year trying to cross the Mediterranean from Africa to Europe. According to Mexican consulates, about 400 Mexicans die trying to cross the border into the US each year.[22] Many Asian immigrants also die when the traffickers deliberately scuttle them in the Mediterranean when a naval patrol chases a boat carrying such immigrants. Others die trying to cross other seas and the Sahara desert.

Trafficking of women raises particularly delicate issues (Poulin 2003; Trépanier 2003). When women are employed as domestic servants or for so-called home care, they may be subjected to various kinds of exploitation beyond what they are supposed to do. All irregular or illegal immigrants suffer from the severe handicap that they cannot have any legal redress against their employers. When such immigrant women are sex workers, their handicap becomes particularly great, if in the host country sex work is itself an illegal activity. In such cases, the traffickers often get away under the usual police procedures but the women face severe penalties. While many feminists and other activists consider sex work a demeaning activity, legalization of sex work at least would free sex workers from harassment by pimps and by the police. On the other hand, some claim that legalizing the sex trade has led to a larger flow of trafficked women from most countries of Latin America and the Caribbean (Facio 2003).

20.7 Towards Cosmopolitan Egalitarianism

Given the contradictions caused by the state system and the widespread deliberate violation of both human rights and international law, the only morally defensible stance is what one might call cosmopolitan egalitarianism. Beitz (1979/1999) argued that neither moral realism or rather, moral cynicism in international affairs, nor an international 'communitarianism' that privileges all domestic institutions equally because they are supposed to reflect a consensual agreement, are morally defensible stances if we value every human being equally (Sen 2002). Under the current regime of national and international migration, the cosmopolitan liberalism that Beitz advocates will not work to protect the persons at risk since it privileges non-interference with the operation of footloose finance and monopolistic firms that concentrate economic power in their grasp. Thomas Nagel (2005) refuses claims of cosmopolitan morality such as from Beitz and instead engages in the delineation of a politically oriented international morality. His argument concerns whether richer states have any responsibility to aid poorer states. He not only takes the international property rights arrangements of a liberal state as his assumed background structure, but also refuses to scrutinize the origins and justice of the current in-

21 See also Suter, Keith, 2001: "Australia's International Humiliation over Boat People"; see at: <http://www.onlineopinion.com.au/view.asp?article=1947> (21 February 2010).

22 GCIM, 2005: *Migration in an Interconnected World, New Directions for Action: Report of the Global Commission on International Migration*, October; see at: <http://www.gcim.org/en/finalreport.html>: 24 (18 February 2010).

ternational economic and political order characterized by deep inequality.

The only defensible moral stance, to protect the human rights of everybody, including migrants, is to ignore the barriers erected by institutions of states and exclusionary communities, as Amartya Sen (2004) argued. The intending immigrants must also respect the human, including cultural, rights of the people in whose territory the migrants are seeking to build new homes. This applies to the rights of those forcibly uprooted by the powerful oligarchs of the market and the state. Global capitalism has been responsible for the displacement, sometimes amounting to genocide, of millions of people around the world (Bagchi 2005c: chap. 14–15, 18; Davis 2001).

To begin to work towards an international order that can address some of the basic issues, certain fundamental changes in the current arrangements governing movements of capital and labour must occur.

1. There should be regulation of the export and import of capital in all countries. Unregulated capital movements hurt the interests of workers, and not only workers, of all countries. Transparent and internationally monitored movements of capital can benefit all countries and can stem the migration of labour from poor countries.
2. Prohibit the export and import of capital by derivatives trading. Derivatives are primarily instruments of speculation and not instruments for minimizing risk. This is certainly true when they involve movements of funds across borders. Banning most derivatives will dampen the enterprise of financial engineers. However, the world has been awash with currency, banking and economic crises since the financial engineers were allowed to shape the money and credit markets.
3. The state should be fiscally empowered to spend on social sectors to enable constant improvement in areas of education, health care and conditions of work. If capital flight and tax evasion by the rich can be minimized, there will be an enormous gain of revenue by the citizens and the state, particularly in developing countries, which can then spend money on several projects. This is especially relevant for developing countries which can then spend more on education, sanitation and health care and expand the urban infrastructure in countries that are undergoing rapid structural transformation. In all countries, governments can spend more on relocation of families and workers adversely affected by investments and technological change and restore the basic features of the welfare states in affluent nations damaged by neoliberalism.
4. If preference is given to immigrants with skills, then part of the taxes originating from their earnings should be remitted to their homes regularly, at least until the costs of providing the extra education to the immigrants are recovered. Such steps will not interfere with the freedom of individuals and families to migrate but will partly address the glaring misdirection of skilled persons.
5. Citizenship should be granted to willing immigrants after a brief period. The current practices of the developed and developing countries in controlling immigration violate basic human rights. As Kymlicka (2003) argued, the acceptance of immigrants is closely associated with the way citizenship is defined. Canada has been one of the few countries which has welcomed immigrants and has tried to integrate them into Canadian society, while recognizing that many of them had different ways of relating, with different kinds of religious bonds and so on. However, as the disasters of the 1990s propelled ever-larger numbers of people to migrate, the attitudes of the developed countries hardened. In the wake of 9/11 and the attack that the US, UK, Australia and their allies mounted on Iraq in 2003, the actions of those countries towards asylum-seekers who were automatically treated as 'terrorists' until proved otherwise, have been more inhumane than ever before (see Chang 2002). The proper thing to do would be to restore traditional habeas corpus rights for everybody, including asylum-seekers and suspected terrorists, and punish only people found guilty of some offence besides having the wrong skin pigmentation or wrong religion.

This chapter sits well with various other proposals for rendering the global financial system more stable, proposals for uniform labour standards (Palley 2004), and for defining members of a global community (Jordan/Düvell 2003). Given that the so-called international community of policymakers has mismanaged the world economy so badly, as far as the lives and security of the majority of humanity are concerned, it is high time we seriously discuss schemes for radical structural change rather than palliatives that have failed so blatantly.

21 Migration Regimes and the Politics of Insiders/Outsiders: Japan and South Africa as Distant Mirrors

Yoichi Mine

21.1 Introduction

This chapter compares the patterns of migration as well as the trends of immigration policies in Japan and South Africa in the recent past. These two countries are regional powers in East Asia and sub-Saharan Africa respectively with economic might disproportionate to their population sizes. The two countries also must reconcile with their 20th century past in order to play a constructive role as legitimate members of the regional communities. Many Asian nations well remember the wartime atrocities committed by the Japanese, while the oppressive domination of Apartheid South Africa inflicted many wounds upon society both within and beyond the country, some of which are still raw.

Beyond such resemblance in regional contexts, at first glance these countries appear to share little. Japan is supposed to be an ethnically homogeneous nation, in spite of the fact that the long process of inward and outward migration has shaped Japanese society. It is known that the prototypical Japanese were formed through the encounters in ancient times between the indigenous population and the immigrants from today's Korea, China and southern islands. After the Meiji Reform period, a substantial number of Japanese emigrated permanently to the Americas and then temporarily to the Japanese colonies in East Asia, while millions of Koreans were brought to Japan before and during the Second World War. However, these historical experiences seldom come to the surface of the mind of the majority of Japanese people immersed within the myth of a monolithic nation. This homogeneity hypothesis of Japan is widely shared in popular opinion in the West, reinforcing the perception that the nature of Japanese society is fundamentally different from those of North America and Western Europe.[1]

In a stark contrast, South Africa is incontestably a country of migration with absolute visibility. White, Coloured and Indian South Africans have diverse ethnic origins outside the continent, notably Western Europe and coastal regions of tropical Afrasia. Moreover, the majority of Bantu-speaking Africans whose ancestors gradually moved south from central Africa in ancient times have been the target of coercive, circular migration between home villages and industrial cities since the late 19th century.[2] South Africa's exploitative labour control and rigid segmentation of society along racial lines is thought to be a unique case in world history.

This chapter argues, however, that Apartheid-style rigid labour control has not become obsolete but forms the keystone of contemporary immigration practices in major host countries around the world, including Japan. The chapter traces the rise and fall of racial segregation in South Africa, examining the political and economic functions of segmentation of the labour market and rural-urban migration. The iron hand of social engineering during the Apartheid era maintained and reinforced the exploitative nature of the workforce division, the end of which is now bringing about uncontrolled migration on a continental scale. The chapter then examines a contemporary Japanese case of selective immigration policy, which consolidates the division of foreign workers along ethnic lines in its specific historical context. Combining the insights gained from a comparison of the two country

---

1 For criticism of the homogeneity assumptions of Japanese society, see Denoon/Hudson/McCormack/Morris-Suzuki (1996), Douglass and Roberts (2000), and Lie (2001). Morris-Suzuki (1998) provides a superb historical contextualization. Sugimoto (2003) contains a good overview of conflicting perspectives of post-war Japanology.

2 The cultural diversity in the early history of South Africa has been emphasized by pioneer liberal historians. See Wilson and Thompson (1969) and Thompson (1990), for examples. As for a comprehensive mapping of the country's diversity, see Frankental and Sichone (2005).

T.-D. Truong and D. Gasper (eds.), *Transnational Migration and Human Security*, Hexagon Series on Human and Environmental Security and Peace 6, DOI 10.1007/978-3-642-12757-1_21, © Springer-Verlag Berlin Heidelberg 2011

cases, the conclusion highlights the significance of forging a unity which transcends divisions between insiders and outsiders imposed by top-down policy practices, to realize truly multicultural societies where all groups can live in dignity.

21.2 South African Experience: Exceptionalism and Unnoticed Commonality

For various reasons, many regard South Africa as an exception, or rather, an anomaly in global history. No other African nation has had such deep penetration of colonial domination and widespread settlement of white immigrants. No other Western colony has had such a lingering continuation of institutional racism and racial segregation into the latter half of the 20th century. Liberal historians attribute the tenacity of Apartheid to the racist, irrational mindset of Afrikaners forged through the history of master-slave relationship in the Cape Colony as well as the perception of their being victimized by the British (Walker 1930; Thompson 1985).

However, there has been another influential thread of interpretation regarding the structural tenaciousness of the Apartheid regime. Besides works giving weight to the involvement of global capitalism (Seidman/Makgetla 1980; Seidman 1985; Hanlon 1986),[3] several scholars have elucidated the internal logic of the reproduction of the segregationist regime in the southern tip of Africa. As a prime example, Mahmood Mamdani has pointed out that South Africa's Apartheid shared the generic form of the African state with decentralized despotism, both Anglophone and Francophone, which inherited the bifurcation of political power engendered during the period of late colonialism: the urban world of civil society and the rural world of customary law. In this divisive framework, universalist civil discourse on human rights tends to be interpreted in rural settings as an alien assault on traditional values, while the rhetoric of customary law, often enforced by the authoritarian chiefs supported by colonial powers, tends to be dismissed by permanent city dwellers as intrinsically backward. Given this dichotomy, what is essential for the politics of emancipation is to unite democratic struggles beyond the urban/rural dichotomy and ethnic fragmentation (Mamdani 1996).

Mamdani illustrates this point through careful case studies of rural Uganda and urban South Africa, and his discussion on political violence in South African urban townships is particularly relevant to the present discussion (Mamdani 1996: chap. 7). The violent conflicts that intensified in the urban spaces of South Africa in the early 1990's were often between permanent city dwellers and temporary migrant workers, 'the rural in the urban', who were uprooted from impoverished rural homelands to work in cities by contract. It has frequently been pointed out that this 'black-on-black' feud was orchestrated by the 'third force': the complex of police, army and mainstream faction of Zulu militant traditionalists.[4] Mamdani's account is quite original in his illumination of structural, historical settings of the manifest political violence. With malicious instigators, the community of urban citizens and the community of rural migrants in the urban space could easily start to distrust each other, trapped as they both were in a security dilemma.

The theory of bifurcation and decentralized despotism presented by Mamdani has breathed new scholarly life into the conventional understanding of the colonial legacy of British indirect rule, which proved to be instrumental in serving the political interests of ruling elites even in late 20th century Africa, including white South Africa.[5] However, our explanation should go beyond the logic of the instrumental expediency of divide and rule for the perpetuation of political status quo. It is crucial to note that the material interests embedded in the dominant economic system of African colonies underpinned the political framework of urban/rural bifurcation. Benefits and subsidies were inadequate to sustain the power base of colonial tribal leaders, which was, in reality, reproduced through the function of the rural economy itself. Colonial powers in Africa have not always served

3 This tradition was revived in a series of recent criticisms of neoliberalism in the South African context by, for example, Bond (2001).

4 The magnitude of the conspiracy has been disclosed through the investigation of a committee chaired by Richard Goldstone. As for the factual records, see *Race Relations Surveys* of the South African Institute of Race Relations in Johannesburg, especially the 1992/3, 1993/4 and 1994/5 editions.

5 The indirect-rule technique of the British colonial authorities in tropical Africa was elaborated in the classic work of Governor-General of Nigeria, Frederick Lugard (1922). Theophilus Shepstone, an influential administrator of the British Natal Colony in South Africa, developed a parallel system in the middle of the 19th century (Welsh 1971).

as modernizing agents, but often tried to *preserve* the economic as well as political systems in non-capitalist rural societies, performing the role of the friend of native traditionalists.[6]

Neo-Marxist scholars like Harold Wolpe (1972) and Claude Meillassoux (1975) elaborated this reasoning. Through a series of laws after the Native Land Act in 1913, the white South African government designated about 13 per cent of the total land area as native reserves, or black homelands, halting the merciless process of land encroachment at the final stage of the colonial conquest and demarcating those homelands as a principal source of temporary migrant workers. In order to obtain access to cash income, male workers moved to mines and cities, harbours and plantations, leaving family members behind, and were forcibly repatriated to their homelands at the end of their labour contracts. As long as the members of the rural subsistence economy - especially women - provided necessary care for the young and old, the sick and the workers in need of recuperation, without compensation from the capitalist sector, the reproduction of the migrant work force remained sustainable even though the provision of capitalist wages stayed below the value of labour power.

In other words, this left the capitalist sector exempt from a substantial part of the social security burden of reproducing a labour force, and collusion between settlers and collaborative chiefs must have controlled the outflow of families from rural to urban spaces.[7] This late colonial super-exploitation based on gender-based division of labour can be construed as a prolonged process of primitive accumulation, the transfer of value from the pre-capitalist to capitalist mode of production.

According to the theory of imperialism set forth by Rosa Luxemburg (1913), the process of primitive accumulation is not just a one-time-only prelude to capital accumulation, but continues throughout the process of expanded reproduction of capital, which always requires predation of a non-capitalist, natural economy as the very basis of its function. Luxemburg's conception is echoed in Mies (1986: 34–35) in a radical feminist perspective as well as in Harvey (2003: chap. 4) in his critique of contemporary imperialism. The thesis of super-exploitation, or of exploitative articulation of modes of production, illuminates that this process of destruction of non-capitalist economy is far from straightforward, and can be concomitant with temporary conservation of diverse non-formal systems of economy and society. In a similar vein, the perspective of 'invention of tradition' (Hobsbawm/Ranger: 1983) elucidates that there was much room for the manipulative consolidation of local ways of life and livelihoods, which was conducive to the rise of modern African decentralized despotism.

21.3 Separation, Integration and Orderly Disorder

In the actual path of South African history, however, predation of the non-capitalist rural economy did not last very long; the lack of productive investment and the population increase, largely due to the forced removal of African households from white areas, have gradually eroded the caring capacity of the subsistence economy in homelands. Nevertheless, under the official scheme of Apartheid social engineering, the process of separation of homelands from the rest of the country continued to the extent that several homelands were granted the status of quasi-independence in the 1970's.

The logical mainstay of Apartheid policy was 'separate development', which means that each segment of the South African population should develop along its own lines in its own space. In the vast area designated for the white population, African urban citizens were robbed of basic rights, being treated as second-class citizens in their birthplace. At the same time, it was becoming increasingly difficult for migrants from ethnic homelands to find good jobs in the urban space, and the mining sector started to rely heavily on the cheaper and more obedient migrant workers from other African countries (Crush/Jeeves/Yudelman 1991). Contrary to the lingering assumption that migrant workers were still taken care of in their homelands, those rural villages were, in reality, transformed to mere dumping grounds of surplus labour with much less reproductive function by the 1950's (Simkins 1981; Wilson/Ramphele 1980: 206–226, 285–

6 It is noteworthy that the exploitative function of imperialist *preservation* practices was emphasized not only by neo-Marxists but also by W. Arthur Lewis, the founder of classical development economics (Lewis 1954; Mine 2006).

7 Thus, the African migrant workers had to live lives as "Men of Two Worlds" (Houghton 1964). As a corollary of the dual system, agricultural production of the rural economy should be kept at a subsistence level through the full involvement of women in farming activities. This explains at least partly, why the status of women is relatively high in sub-Saharan Africa compared to South Asia (Boserup 1970).

292). A logical consequence of separate development would have been that the white government in power should make an effort towards making homeland economy viable, but the recommendations of the Tomlinson Commission Report in 1955 to that effect were rejected in favour of the continuation of unfettered access to African labour (Lipton 1986: 29–37). As the material substance to sustain the super-exploitation hollowed out, the whole system was taking on a more coercive and authoritarian nature and the poverty-stricken rural homelands were taken over by African despots who colluded with the white government.

There was, through, a minor branch of policy framework which placed more emphasis upon gradual integration of urban workforce into the formal economy. Given the numerical preponderance of Africans, industry favoured the existence of permanent African city dwellers as a consumer market as well as semi-skilled workforce. A series of pre-Apartheid government reports advocated partial labour market liberalization, especially the Fagan Commission Report of 1948, which a National Party victory that same year put aside. In the terminal phase of the Apartheid regime, however, the National Party government took up this liberal option. The gradual implementation of the recommendations of the Riekert Commission Report in 1978 guaranteed free movement of permanent city dwellers, yet kept migrant workers under strict control. The repressive pass laws that controlled the movement of Africans were repealed in 1986.

The proportion of Africans estimated to live in urban areas grew from 10 per cent in 1904 to 32 per cent in 1960, but remained nearly stagnant between 1960 and 1980 (Statistics South Africa 2006: 22; Wilson/Ramphele 1989: 26). During the Apartheid era, the authorities tried to stem the influx of rural population into cities. With the result that the African urban workforce, whose numerical expansion the government kept in check, received *relative* protection *vis-à-vis* migrant workers. The pass laws and rigid labour bureau system were the major devices to differentiate the permanent urban workforce from the temporary migrants rooted in the homelands. Throughout the 20th century, Apartheid regimes intensified this structural bifurcation continuously and fostered relatively different identities and aspirations among urban residents and migrants, with a gap in material conditions of their living spaces (Hindson 1987; Posel 1991). This situation constitutes the background of political tension in the early 1990's as depicted by Mamdani.[8]

However, in 1994, with the first democratic general election and the subsequent inauguration of Nelson Mandela as the president of the inclusive South African nation, the Apartheid regime ended decisively. By then, the fragmented labour market with repressive state controls had already begun to phase out in favour of a unified, nationwide labour market. As for the emergent structure of labour in post-Apartheid South Africa, the following three features seem to be discernible.

First, in spite of the abolishment of tight influx control, a massive exodus of impoverished population from former homelands to urban areas, as was anticipated in the 1980's, did not take place. While the urbanization rate of the black South African population reached 47.5 per cent (90 per cent for the white population) by 2001 (Statistics South Africa 2006: 19), the labour absorption capacity of the new economic regime is quite limited, largely due to the neoliberal design of economic policy adopted by the government of Thabo Mbeki, Mandela's successor (Bond 2004). South Africa's Gini coefficient had been aggravated from the already high 0.65 in 1995 to one of the worst in the world, nearly 0.70, in 2000 (Seekings/Nattrass 2005: 303–304, 319). Further polarization of living standards and disintegration of communal order, coupled with a high unemployment rate, 50.2 per cent for the African population in 2001 (Statistics South Africa 2004: 59), exacerbated the crime situation. Young jobless city dwellers were becoming an angry, frustrated mass that apparently refused to become a positive, constituent multitude. The violent nature of city life and limited job opportunities appeared to function as disincentive for internal migration.

Second, the megacities in South Africa (such as Johannesburg) as well as labour-hungry large farms have started to attract a large number of illegal migrants from other neighbouring African countries (estimates vary from 2 to 4 million), notably Zimbabwe, which is in political and economic havoc. By 2008, the office of the Ministry of Home Affairs in Pretoria became an open-air slum full of Zimbabwean asylum-seekers waiting for residential permits. The Ministry eventually decided to allow Zimbabweans to live and work in South Africa without papers for 90 days, granting

8 The economic and political stratification developed not only among urban and rural Africans but also between Africans and Asians in Kwazulu/Natal (and between Africans and Coloureds in Western Cape) along the racial lines (Freund 1995). This is the principal reason why Steve Biko and his comrades strategically tried to expand the definition of 'Blacks' to include those traditionally 'non-African' peoples to counter the Apartheid domination (Biko 1988).

them basic economic and social rights.[9] In Apartheid South Africa, the Riekert Commission Report proposed fines for business firms hiring illegal (mainly South African black) migrants, but as long as such workforce was needed there was lax implementation of such regulations (Lipton 1986: 73–74). The new, post-Apartheid government has employed an even softer immigration policy due to its constitutionally enshrined Bill of Rights, also to the bureaucratic inefficiency partly inherited from the past regime, and, *inter alia,* to the growing demand for cheaper and more compliant labour for South African industry, now exposed to the global competition. The preference of local employers for illegal migrants indicates structural mismatches in the South African labour market.

It is noteworthy that, in the absence of strict immigration control, non-South African migrants fall victim to assaults by groups of xenophobic, desperate jobless people. In May 2008, in townships in Gauteng and other provinces, bands of roving, immigrant-hunting thugs looted immigrants' shops, set fire to their shacks, tortured and killed them claiming the immigrants were criminals stealing jobs from native South Africans. A series of violent events lead to the death of 62 and the injury of nearly 700, with about 100,000 foreigners displaced.[10] Although the normative discourse of citizenship is largely associated with Western cosmopolitanism in Mamdani (1996), the actual practices of citizenship in Southern Africa are extremely hierarchical in terms of boundaries and belonging (Nyamnjoh 2006). In a sense, the function of the rigid top-down influx control of the Apartheid regime has partially been replaced by the informal, 'voluntary' aggression of the citizenry.[11]

Third, as a matter of cultural hegemony, the African city dwellers seem to be held under pressure to become 'good African citizens' as the precondition for assimilation into the order of urban economy. The discourse targets the so-called black middle class, unionized workers, and the newly emerging wealthy classes called 'Black Diamonds'. While the authoritarian measures of 'consultation with Natives' (Fagan 1960), as proposed by liberal Afrikaners during segregation are clearly out of date, the Victorian-style notion of diligence, self-help and family values has resurfaced in cultural interpretations of township life. Sowetans are undergoing 'a punishing apprenticeship' (Holland 1994: 202), to get accustomed to modern urban life, something very Western in connotation. The normative discourse of the post-Apartheid urban space in South Africa is sometimes plainly value-oriented, where a set of fundamental social values that people might eventually opt for is presented as something pre-existing, prescribed for them to choose.

21.4 Japan as a Distant Mirror

The case of South Africa serves as the reference frame to analyse and compare the experience of migrant communities in Japan in light of global trends of labour migration policy. The original pattern of immigration into Japan developed before and during the Second World War. After Japan's annexation of the Korean Peninsula in 1910, the Japanese colonial rule intensified the 'landlord' system in Korea, and the impoverished rural Koreans started to migrate into Japan. Although those who crossed the Korea Strait were mostly single male workers, they gradually settled in Japan and formed permanent family bases there, and by 1930, they reached an estimated population of at least 300,000.

From the end of the 1930's onward with the intensification of the war in East Asia and the Pacific, the Japanese militarist regime mobilized Koreans and Chinese directly into factories, mines and overseas battlefronts, with the mobilization of sex slaves a part of the entire process. At the end of World War 2, in August 1945, more than two million Koreans were in the Japanese mainland, and one-third of them eventually remained for complex reasons including the North-South divide of the Korean Peninsula.[12] The decades-

9 Although the present South African authorities treat immigrants sometimes with cruelty, their immigration policy is rather chaotic, and the pursuit of maniac total strategy concomitant with the erstwhile Apartheid regime is completely missing. Human Rights Watch (2008): "SA Permit Will Improve Zimbabweans' Plight", *The Sunday Independent* (26 April 2009): 6; "SA Opens Zimbabwe Border", *Cape Times* (5 May 2009): 1.

10 "Bloody Injustice: Xenophobic Violence Shattered Thousands of Lives ... A Year Later, What Has Changed?", special supplementary issue, in: *The Star* (19 May 2009). As for a vivid description of the feeling of black South Africans toward *Makwerekwere* (non-South African black migrants), see Mpe (2001). Factual details of recent trends of regional migration are in Kok/O'Donovan/Bouare/Van Zyl (2003).

11 "Xenophobia Emerges As a 'New Apartheid'", in: *Business Day* (1 April 2008): 1, 2. In the context of comparison between 'necklacing' in South Africa in the 1980's and contemporary suicide bombings in Israel, Mamdani argues that we should go beyond the dichotomy between 'settler' and 'native' in favour of "equal citizenship of all those who live in it" (Mamdani 2005: 228).

long gradual immigration of Koreans and Chinese into Japan and their wartime coercive mobilization are both consequences of Japan's colonial expansion, although these two forms of migration are different in terms of the degrees of violence and the directness of control.

After its defeat in the Second World War, Japan underwent a miracle process of economic recovery, this time with no major militaristic aggression. In contrast with Europe, Japan achieved post-war economic growth as a self-contained process, relying principally upon the labour supply from the domestic pool, the agricultural sector in the rural countryside. Combined with relatively high fertility rates in the post-war period, Japan's post-war economic reconstruction started with a labour abundant condition, and it was even a net sender of emigrants until the 1950's. This nature of post-war Japanese society seems to have laid the groundwork for the homogeneity thesis.

However, the continuous growth of the Japanese economy, the declining fertility rates, the spread of higher education and the resultant upward-mobility of a young labour force led to a serious shortage of domestic labour by the late 1980's. In the wake of the 1985 Plaza Accord, in which a drastic depreciation of the US dollar against the Japanese Yen and the Deutsche Mark was agreed, the Japanese economy experienced an unprecedented speculative expansion, often referred to as 'bubble economy'. Labour shortage was seriously felt in economic sectors dominated by 3k (3d) jobs: ***kitsui*** (demanding), ***kitanai*** (dirty) and ***kiken*** (dangerous), or undesired bottom-wage jobs, which local young people had come to avoid (Mori 1997: 32–68).

In order to accommodate the increased demand for un-skilled and semi-skilled labour, the Japanese government initiated a major reform of its immigration regime through amendments to the Immigration Control Act in 1990, the cornerstone of Japan's new immigration policy into the 21st century.[13] Although the Japanese economy entered a prolonged recession in the 1990's after the bubble burst, the demand for cheap labour intensified in manufacturing, service and agricultural sectors, as the Japanese industry now had to compete with Chinese and other Asian counterparts in the world market.

The 1990 Immigration Act and related legislation were to reinforce the hierarchical nature of the Japanese labour market by embedding foreign workers into lower positions designated in the industrial division of labour, by opening up the 'side door' of the immigration regime. The Act first provided for the formal admission of *Nikkeijin,* the descendants of Japanese emigrants to Latin American countries such as Brazil and Peru, with no restriction on employment. Tens of thousands of Latinos often accompanied by their spouses and children entered Japan every year and started to work in factories in Aichi, Shizuoka, Tokyo and other areas of concentrated export industry like automakers including the giant Toyota (Komai 1995; Mori 1997: 106–114). As a result, by 2006, the number of registered foreigners with Brazilian nationality swelled to 313,000 and those with Peruvian nationality to 59,000, even through their numbers had been relatively negligible until the late 1980's (Immigration Bureau 2008: 19[14]). The choice of the Japanese overseas descendants as the subject of the first experimental admission of semi-skilled and unskilled workers was based not only on Japan's juristic principle of *jus sanguinis,* but also on a faint hope that these newcomers would get accustomed to Japanese ways of life relatively easily due to kinship and cultural affinity[15]. However, in reality, many *Nikkeijin* have eventually come to feel treated as outsiders in the country of their ethnic origin. There are frequent reports that Japanese Brazilians have reconsolidated their identity as Brazilians in consequence of their everyday contact with the native Japanese.[16]

---

12 Lee/Murphy-Shigematsu/Befu (2006) outline broad citizenship issues surrounding the Korean minority in Japan. Morris-Suzuki (2007a) provides a vivid historical account of the massive exodus of some 90,000 patriotic Koreans from Japan to North Korea in the late 1950's and early 1960's. At that time, the Japanese high officials wanted to get rid of redundant and 'dangerous' Koreans, who were cheated to work eventually for the Kim Il-sung regime as cheap labour in miserable conditions, due to an implicit collusion between the top elites of the two hostile countries. As for the 'comfort women' issue, see the historical evidence in Tanaka (2002).

13 The English text of the Immigration Control and Refugee Recognition Act (Cabinet Order No. 319 of 1951) reflecting the latest 2009 amendment that can be found at: <http://www.cas.go.jp/jp/seisaku/hourei/data/icrra.pdf > (31 January 2010).

14 See at: <http://www.moj.go.jp/NYUKAN/nyukan80.html>.

15 For a comparison between the return of *Aussiedler,* ethnic Germans, in unified Germany and the acceptance of *Nikkeijin,* ethnic Japanese Latinos, in Japan, see Brody (2002: 87–100).

16 A good amount of detailed ethnography of *Nikkeijin* is now available. See Linger (2001); Roth (2002); Hirabayashi/et al. (2002); Tsuda (2003); Lesser (2003).

In the same year as the Immigration Act of 1990, the government introduced a labour quota system in which un-skilled foreign workers could be recruited and assigned as 'trainees' to labour-hungry small factories and construction firms, as well as farms that are sometimes located in remote villages. The majority of the trainees are Chinese, with 68,000 new entries recorded in 2007, followed by Vietnamese, Indonesians, Filipinos and Thais. Categorized as a form of bilateral development cooperation and 'technology transfer', the 'trainees' often find themselves excluded from formal protection under the Japanese labour legislation in terms of minimum wage and overtime payment (Komai 1995: 37–54; Mori 1997: 114–133; Immigration Bureau 2008: 10–11).[17]

Finally, the 1990 Immigration Act introduced for the first time a penalty system for companies and agents involved in the employment of clandestine foreign workers (Mori 1997: 98–100). The penalty system has been occasionally invoked, making the worst kind of agents operate deep underground. More than ever, this policy creates a clear division among foreign workers based on a dichotomous categorization between the legal and illegal. According to the official estimation, the number of migrants who overstay had been shrinking by 50 per cent since the peak year of 1993, but still some 150,000 foreigners were supposed to be staying in Japan as 'illegal residents' in January 2008 (Immigration Bureau 2008: 31)[18].

At present, Japan's migration regime seems to be in a thorough overhaul. A noticeable direction is that the government tried to elaborate on an institution of controlled temporary migration for specific job categories and for specific duration. Because of public criticism of the huge discrepancy between the stated aims and the actual practice of the trainee system, in mid-2007, three Japanese government ministries in charge of labour/health, industry and justice made respective reform plans public. Contrary to the habits of Japanese bureaucracy, those incongruous proposals have been tabled without prior consensus. At any rate, the future system will turn to admit that Japan purposely recruits un-skilled foreign workers and allocates them to labour-hungry small firms through definite labour contracts.[19] The government is also planning to introduce a more centralized IT registration system for all foreigners in Japan. Based on the 2009 Immigration Act, the central government now takes charge of foreign registration cards, formerly issued by municipal offices.

In the meantime, a new experimental quota system has commenced in the field of recruitment of relatively skilled workers. Since mid-1980's, a number of Filipinas visited Japan as 'entertainers' through the agency of brokers, exposing themselves to the risks of grave sexual exploitation (Ballescas 1992; Komai 1995: 71–80; Mushakoji 2003a). In response to criticism that this is a disguised form of human trafficking the immigration authorities ceased granting this category of visa to Filipinas by 2006. The Japanese government then launched a programme in 2008 to accept Filipino and Indonesian professional nurses and caregivers under bilateral *Economic Partnership Agreements* (EPAs) to meet the pressing demand of the aging society. Two thousand are expected to come to Japan in two years, and only those who pass the qualification exams in Japanese will be allowed to continue to work and stay in Japan after the termination of contracts.[20]

Japanese immigration policy is becoming more selective and hierarchical. Setting aside the international elite in the IT and financial industries, lower-skilled migrant workers are to be accommodated on a bilateral basis as long as there are strong demands in particular job categories, and their permanent settlement can be permitted only on condition that they are well accustomed to the everyday order of Japanese society. The persistence of the trainee system in the face of mounting criticism indicates the strong demand for cheap labour on the part of labour-intensive industries and commercial agriculture in the country. In any case, migrant groups of different origins have little opportunity to interact; the new entrants are placed under strict policy control and segregated from local Japanese communities and most of them are supposed to be repatriated after the end of their contracts. Nevertheless, a considerable number of workers and their family are expected eventually to stay permanently in Japan, as was the case with the postwar German *Gastarbeiter*.

17 See at: <http://www.moj.go.jp/NYUKAN/nyukan80.html>.

18 See at: <http://www.moj.go.jp/NYUKAN/nyukan80.html>.

19 "Competing Foreign-worker Plans Face Off", in: *Japan Times* (7 June 2007): 3; "Immigrant Workers in Japan Caught in a Real Racket", in: *Japan Times* (1 July 2007): 17. The latest 2009 Immigration Act stipulates that the legal protection of trainees in terms of wages and labour conditions should be granted after a short period of on-the-job training, recognizing that trainees are workers.

20 "Filipino Caregivers Face Hurdles", in: *Japan Times* (20 December 2008): 3; see also Mine (2003).

Japan's gradual open-door policy in the early 21st century is likely to be accompanied by strict state regulations. The new policy trend has been supplemented by the eruption of xenophobia in the wake of the global transmission of the September 11 panic. The recidivist, sensational agitation against 'foreign criminals' by Tokyo governor Shintaro Ishihara, the manipulative interpretation of statistics by the police authority to exaggerate the crime of foreigners, and the campaign by the Justice Ministry to call upon citizens to provide anonymous information through the internet about any 'overstayer' they come across, are only a few. Thus, the majority Japanese are induced in everyday life to discriminate between bad foreigners and good foreigners. Under the 2004 Immigration Act, the period of ban on re-entry for unauthorized, 'malicious' immigrants who are arrested is now extended from five years to ten years, while the period for those who appear voluntarily at the immigration authorities is shortened to one year.[21]

Compared with its European and North American counterparts, Japan as a late developer has encountered only recently the question of accommodating massive influx of foreigners in peacetime. While the authoritarian and regulationist reactions to foreigners are widely shared among industrialized nations, the Japanese attitude can also be interpreted as the expression of bewilderment in the face of new challenges.[22] The way to address the long-term situation of more permanent and vocal foreign residents, typically Koreans, may turn out to be a touchstone for future immigration policy in Japan. Although their residential status is much more stable than other foreign residents are, Koreans appear disinclined towards assimilation into Japanese society due to lingering discrimination. Given the historical sequence of immigration, Korean residents are dubbed 'Oldcomers', the recent immigrants from other countries, 'Newcomers' and they have developed specific identities and aspirations.

The argument of Hidenori Sakanaka, the former Director of Tokyo Immigration Bureau (while not well known outside Japan) is relevant to this question. Since 1975, Sakanaka has consistently advocated that Korean permanent residents should consider the option to live as 'Korean Japanese citizens', by acquiring Japanese nationality, yet maintaining their Korean ethnic identity (Sakanaka 2005). Setting aside the merit of this option to attain full Japanese citizenship through naturalization, the anomaly is that the exhortation of spontaneous integration comes from the very person who leads merciless crackdown operations on unauthorized foreigners in Tokyo and Nagoya. Having a wider range of choices on the part of ethnic minorities would be a real advantage in itself, but his case illuminates the benign, authoritarian nature of a possible assimilation policy. Here again, an option that people might eventually choose is presented as something prescribed for them to choose.

21.5 Conclusions

During the age of Apartheid, both antagonists and protagonists of the white supremacy tended to narrate the black population as a monolithic mass. Yet, the history of segregation in South Africa was the history of segmentation of working classes, dissociating the permanent residents in the industrial space from the circular migrants, regularly sent back to their 'homelands'. The ruling classes discriminated against and exploited those insiders and outsiders, but in different ways. The 'Black Unity' against Apartheid was forged through the sedulous efforts of activists to bridge the divides imposed by top-down social engineering, the divides among ethnic groups, the divides between the urban and the rural. Mamdani's bifurcation thesis, its persuasive anatomy of conflicting aspirations of Africans, as well as its warning against the danger of political exploitation of such divides illuminates the nature of such challenges. The popular struggle against Apartheid aimed to dismantle the iron hand of migration control and this dream materialized after the release of Nelson Mandela.

Today, we witness migration regimes in industrialized nations bearing a strong resemblance to the erst-

---

21 "For Visa Violators, It Pays to Come Clean", in: *Japan Times* (1 December 2004): 3. The government ministries contemplate making a Japanese language proficiency test compulsory for foreign residents ("Long-term Residents May Face Language Test", in: *Japan Times,* 16 January 2008: 1, 2), though its feasibility seems to be low.

22 As the economic recession lingers on, a considerable part of Japanese labour of all ages has started to seek jobs in the 3k (3d) sector. "Kanikosen (The Cannery Boat)", an almost forgotten work of the communist novelist who was tortured to death by the police in 1933, has suddenly become a best seller among young Japanese 'precariat' workers in 2008. "1920s Proletarian Novel Strikes Chord with Young Underemployed", in: *Japan Times* (18 July 2008: 3). Although conflicts between Japanese and non-Japanese workers over job opportunities seldom take place, there is little indication of organized solidarity between them either, at least for the moment.

while Apartheid regime in some critical respects. The migration regimes with parallel segmentation appear in many places of the contemporary world, as discussed in the case of Japan, although this country is far from an isolated case. Selective migration policies show up in other industrialized nations, including Japan's neighbours in East Asia such as South Korea and Taiwan, where different foreigners started to receive different treatment. In South Korea, for example, a large number of foreign brides from China (mainly ethnic Koreans), Vietnam and other Asian countries have begun establishing roots in rural villages, provided with support to help them adjust to the local way of life, as they are expected to provide much needed care services for aging communities as well as agricultural labour. By contrast, temporary foreign workers in cities are being rigorously repatriated to their birthplaces after their labour contracts expire.[23]

Temporary labour migration presupposes that migrant workers, whether a trainee, a contract worker or a clandestine worker, who were born, raised and educated in their home countries, will receive gratuitous care after they go back home. Extant inequalities in wage standards between countries make the system attractive for migrant workers, even though agents operating in the home country may misappropriate a significant part of their earnings as kickbacks. The economic sectors of the host country that absorb them still receive substantial benefit, derived from super-exploitation and from avoiding the need to disburse the indirect wage, which is essential to reproduce the labour force over generations.

At the same time, the new patterns of international migration affect the conditions of social reproduction in the host countries as well. The core functions of social reproduction such as caring and nursing in industrialized countries are increasingly performed by foreign workers, mainly women, who leave behind their own family in their own home, like African domestic workers in the white suburbs of South Africa.

One key issue in labour migration is that a real human being is not a simple commodity, and in a place where the principle of equal pay for equal work is not observed, social morality will be lost. Another key issue is that an understanding of the commonality of the political-economic logic of migration should merge with a proper cognisance of historical specificity and the moral frame that supports it. To conclude the discussion, let me suggest possible areas of further reflection regarding the recent experiences in two subject countries of this chapter, South Africa and Japan.

While the contemporary regulatory practices of segmentation of the labour market in industrialized nations mirrors the Apartheid model of divide and rule, today's post-Apartheid South Africa is becoming an experimental field that shows a possible shape of a future society *without* the top-down social engineering aimed at controlling border-crossing migration. Contrary to Mamdani's prediction that in the post-Apartheid regime 'decentralized despotism' might consolidate, what we witness is an anarchical order in which African people move around to make livelihoods with much less authoritarian control, modern or traditional. Despite the frequent outbreaks of xenophobic incidents, in the violently bustling streets of Johannesburg such as Hillbrow, local South Africans and people from former Zaire, Nigeria, Zimbabwe, Mozambique and Somalia live together, doing business, battling with each other, chatting with each other, raising children and praying for whatever they value. The contemporary continental-scale movement of people toward South Africa can be a reverse process of *Mfecane,* the massive, dynamic population movement in the first half of the 19th century driven by the emergence of the Zulu military kingdom.[24] In the long-term, dynamic exchange of experiences among Africans may lead to the formation of a new border-crossing group identity, given the 5,000 years of history of migration of Bantu-speaking Africans (Iliffe 2007).

Turning to the prospect of a multicultural Japan, education is becoming a focal point for potential changes. Despite the fact that the national education system of Japan has been geared to bring up 'good Japanese' rather than 'good citizens', it is undeniable that the lasting quest for education over generations

23 A series of articles on 'Multiculturalism in Korea' appeared in: *The Korea Herald,* from 25 July to 15 August 2006. For the background, see Lim (2006).

24 Conventional wisdom is that the xenophobic attitude is stronger in less-educated, lower-income people, whose worldview could be limited and who are exposed to the competition with illegal migrants in labour market. According to a questionnaire survey conducted in the late 1990's, however, better-educated white people showed unanimous hostility towards illegal migrants, while less-educated, black African population were less so. Besides, contrary to the common perception, Zulu speakers tended to be less xenophobic than the politically mainstream ethnic Xhosa are (Solomon 2003: 92-97).

has made an enormous contribution to the betterment of the material conditions of ordinary people's lives in Japan and other Asian countries. In recent years a sense of solidarity has been forged in this country among children of foreign parents (Koreans, Brazilians, Chinese, Peruvians and Filipinos through the establishment in 2005 of a lively national forum of 'ethnic schools'. In its annual meetings, while people listen to the narratives on contemporary challenges faced by new schools for Japanese Brazilian children, Korean educators muse about the enormous hardships encountered by their parents and grandparents, and all parties feel that they are not alone.[25]

The essence of emancipatory politics is always to unite. Although this chapter has offered only two country cases, a fortuitous combination of analytical insights from countries in Asia and Africa, it is hoped that the lessons of their experiences will be shared by people who face divisive, exploitative and top-down migration control, in any part of the world, premised on the artificial dichotomy of insiders and outsiders.

25 Annual national meetings have been held in Hyogo (2005), Aichi (2006), Tokyo (2007) and Osaka (2008). "Korean School Strives to Keep Its Homeland Culture Alive", in: *Japan Times* (11 December 2005): 15, 16; "Teaching with the 'Enemy'" *Japan Times* (22 May 2007): 16; "Schools for Kids of 'Newcomer' Foreigners Reach 100", in: *Japan Times* (3 November 2007): 2; "Flexible and Diverse: International Schools Thrive", in: *Japan Times* (3 January 2008): 1, 2.

22 State and Immigrant Diaspora Identity in Contemporary Japan: From a Developmentalist National Ethic towards a Multicultural Development Ethic of Common Human Security

Kinhide Mushakoji

22.1 Introduction

Since the turn of the millennium, the defence of human rights in the political/intellectual environment of contemporary Japanese civil society has been facing the challenge of a nationalist backlash to globalization. The press today uses a new expression, 'human rights metabolic syndrome', which is becoming an accepted concept to explain the growing juvenile criminality and the social insecurity caused by an increase in the number of 'illegal' foreigners. Just as the metabolic syndrome is caused by an excessive consumption of nutrients, the threat to 'human security' (as a secure way of life for nationals) is seen as being caused by 'too much human rights' especially when combined with the growing demand by foreigners for their rights.

While it is easy to condemn this trend as a right-wing reaction to the growing importance of human rights introduced in Japan during the American occupation after the 1945 defeat, the matter lies at a much deeper level. In Japan, as in most 'developmentalist' states[1], a tension has always existed between the affirmation of a unique national identity and the acceptance of the 'Others' with their own national identity.[2] The tendency to reproduce an identity community ethically dedicated to its own development is, however, not limited to Japan. China, Singapore, Malaysia, Myanmar and many other Asian states share the Japanese scepticism towards the universal application of human rights that opens the space for the subjugated 'Others' to claim their presence and respect for their identity. States that follow a 'developmentalist' course find this application of human rights limiting to their national development and that it provides dubious pretexts for Western states to intervene in their domestic markets and internal affairs. They all emphasize 'national identity' as a key value on which to base the education of the next generation in order to create a process of social reproduction beneficial to the development of their respective states and nations.

In Japan, the demand by old and newly arrived immigrants for the right to affirm their own identity is now challenging this hegemonic way of defining the 'Self', the 'Other' and the 'nation'. All these identity communities are composed of members who share a specific culture, values and beliefs, and who want to maintain these to affirm their common collective identity – this, seen as crucial for their social and cultural reproduction. Meeting these demands requires an ethical framework that can place their identity development in a concrete collective societal context.

This chapter tries to identify the possibilities of forming such a framework based on a value system that does not reject the rights of any identity community to social reproduction. In doing so, it calls for the acceptance of the reproduction of identity as an important domain, not only for the national majority,

1 The term 'developmentalist state' is used here in line with the Latin American usage of the term 'desarrollismo'. A 'developmentalist state' considers its development as the ultimate goal of all its citizens, and develops a state ethics, which inculcates this belief in all its nationals through education. Discussed elsewhere is the consequence of this state ideology, which I call 'development racism'. Japan is one example of a non-Western state that emerged as a modern state by becoming a developmentalist state, but many non-Western post colonial states tend to fit more or less to this ideal type (Mushakoji 1993: 15-18).

2 Examples of the struggle for recognition of a minority identity, and the importance of collective autonomy as a pre-condition for the survival of a distinctive social group, include for example the Inuit in Alaska, Ainu in Hokkaido, Japan, Tibetan in China, and Shan in Myanmar.

T.-D. Truong and D. Gasper (eds.), *Transnational Migration and Human Security*, Hexagon Series on Human and Environmental Security and Peace 6, DOI 10.1007/978-3-642-12757-1_22, © Springer-Verlag Berlin Heidelberg 2011

but also for all minority and diaspora communities. Accepting the need for reproduction of identity must respect the universal principles of human rights, individual and collective, without distinction of nationality, gender or class.

The chapter is organized as follows. The first three sections bring into focus the realities and challenges faced by Diaspora communities in the field of education in Japan. We map out the evolution of legislation on education built on a perspective of the state being 'developmentalist' and discern the underpinning ethical values that serve as its raison d'être as expressed in the Basic Laws on Education. We then present the responses of four different Diaspora communities to the 2006 reform of the Basic Law on Education. Reflecting on findings drawn from the *Chubu Region Multiculturalism and Gender Equality Research* (CRMGER) study, we show how an educational system framed along the lines of the 'developmentalist ethics' of the Japanese state carries exclusionary aspects that cause insecurity to both Japanese nationals and Diaspora communities. Last, drawing from the lessons learned we argue for the need to revisit development ethics as a field and offer some insights geared towards its reconstruction to counter the negative effects of the ethic of a developmentalist state. The ongoing and growing trends in cultural interactions and the hybridization of society require that development ethics extend its perspective to the right to social reproduction of identities and give significance to inter-group dynamics.

22.2 Human Rights and the Social Reproduction of Identity in Japan

Through the concept of universal human rights, the Enlightenment made the individual human the core unit of assessing the good and bad in a society. Hegel and Fichte, two German thinkers, interpreted the implementation of this ethic as belonging to the state.[3] Both emphasized the role of the state in the realization of civil ethics. The former considered the state as the embodiment of universal and individualistic civil ethics, and the latter saw it as an institution uniting the nation to oppose any aggression from abroad, including a foreign state that claims that its values system is universal.

Japan as a non-Western and 'developmentalist' state has generated a framework of civil ethics of its own, by adjusting its traditional ethics to the requirements of national development within the Hegel-Fichte tradition of the Prussian state. It replaced the universalist dialectics of the former with a historically-based patriarchal ethics particular to the Japanese state, and turned the latter's emphasis on national identity into a state religion (Takii 2003).

The *Kyoiku Chokugo* of 1890 (Imperial Edict on Education) combines Fichte's way of approaching civil ethics with both 'developmentalist' ideas and with the basic concepts of Confucian ethics: filial piety, faithfulness of wives to their husbands, and service to the Emperor as subjects. The Edict stressed the familial ties uniting the nation with the Emperor at its head, and proclaimed the ethical duty of all Japanese subjects to be prepared for eventual mobilization in times of national peril. The Meiji state developmentalist ethics skilfully combined the introduction of Western legal institutions with Japanese ethics. In this regard developmentalist ethics, in the case of Japan is, from the beginning, a *hybrid*.

The ethics of the Meiji modern imperial state chose the phrase 'Japanese spirit with Western skill' (*wakon-yousai*) to build the Japanese nation. It used the family as a core unit for the social reproduction of the Japanese nation. This communitarian ethics defined the Japanese state in an entirely different way from the Western Enlightenment in that it did not pose the individual whose rights are universal as the ultimate unit. It was a developmentalist state ethics *par excellence* in the sense that it had as its focus the reproduction of a homogeneous nation dedicated to the defence and the prosperous development of the state. This ethics of social reproduction of the imperial state attempted to recreate a homogeneous people sharing a common familial tradition under the Emperor, the *pater familias* of the Japanese nation (Eisenstadt 1995: 8–12).

After the defeat in World War II, the Meiji state reformed its educational system under the pressure of the US Occupation Authorities to democratize Japan. Building a democratic society could not be reached without building an educational system geared to the promotion of human individuals conscious of their rights, rather than to the reproduction of faithful subjects. In 1947, the Japanese government enacted a Basic Law on Education (Sakata 2007), which stated the

3 It is well known that Fichte wrote his *Rede an die Deutsche Nation* in order to educate the Germans to appreciate their culture and resist the Napoleonic imposition of French universalism. The revised Basic Law on Education of contemporary Japan shares with Fichte his concern to preserve and develop the *Volksgeist* in the face of the global affirmation of universal values.

basic principles indispensable for the democratization of Japanese education. This Law stipulates, for example, such virtues as 'love for truth and justice', 'respect for individual values', 'work and responsibility' and 'autonomous mind' as the objectives of education. These are all individual qualities stemming from the Enlightenment tradition.

Nearly half a century later, the Abe Government[4] proposed the revision of this Law, seeking to minimize individualism in national education and revive the collectivistic orientation of the Japanese developmentalist state. The new Basic Law of Education enacted in 2006 specifies the main role of the Japanese education to be the raising of citizens dedicated to national aspirations, the creation of a dignified nation and society, and the cultivation of human beings who cherish family, region, nation and life. The law nurtures the Japanese youth, emphasizing 'life and environment', 'appreciation for tradition and culture', and 'love for nation and homeland' while respecting foreign nations and contributing to the 'peace and development of the international society' (Yoshifumi 2006)[5].

At one level the reassertion of the significance of the social reproduction of the Japanese nation, and the subsequent obliteration of individual human rights previously enshrined, can be seen as an ideological reaction of the Japanese government and of the Japanese elite in the face of globalization, which some perceive to threaten the homogeneity of the Japanese nation. At another level the emphasis on national traditions, culture and patriotism indicates a shift from a Hegelian appreciation of the state to an emphasis on national identity typical of Fichte.

This new turn of ethics in the Japanese developmentalist state is not quite a return to the patriarchal Confucian Meiji state ethics. It tries to reproduce a nation that accepts Enlightenment values and is open to engaging with the globalizing forces of the neoliberal international society, while still maintaining a national pride framed by Japanese traditions, culture and a patriotic collective awareness.[6] The Meiji Imperial Edict on Education and the two Basic Laws on Education of 1947 and 2006 have in common the principle that the state is responsible for the education of Japanese nationals. Alien children do not feature in the three documents that define education as a means of social reproduction of the Japanese nation. The legal interpretation of the 2006 Basic Law on Education mentions, in a rather easy-going way, that the education of foreign children who are not included in the Basic Law should be conducted in the same way as for Japanese children. The ethical base of the Japanese educational system is not derived from the principle of universal human rights but from the interest of a 'developmentalist' state in its own social reproduction. Domestic law maintains the gap in education between Japanese children and children belonging to migrant communities.

Under the Westphalian system governing the international community as a community of States, Japan can invoke the principle of non-interference and self-determination applicable to all States to continue to ignore both the rights of migrant children to education and the need for migrant communities to reproduce their own identity. Making the right to social reproduction exclusively applicable to the Japanese state can be based on the following rationale: in order to determine its own affairs and eliminate any danger of external interference, the state has to be sure that its subjects or citizens share a common identity that is reproduced and transmitted to the next generations.

Two different frameworks of understanding of what constitutes 'development' in 'ethics' seem to prevail. The ethics of the 'developmentalist' state emphasizes its own social reproduction in the course of 'development' as modernization. Development ethics is a body of thought on the nature of ethically desirable development, ethical means for achieving such development, and ethical dilemmas arising from practice (Gasper 2004a; Crocker 2008). Beyond the question related to personal ethics, how a person ought to live, development ethics asks how a society ought to exist and move into the future. Extended to the global realm, development ethics inevitably touches upon relations between nation-states and peoples.

As a member of a community of nation-states, Japan emphasizes respect for foreign nations and obligation to contribute to the peace and development of

4 Prime Minister Shinzo Abe took office in September 2006 and resigned abruptly on 12 September 2007 after months of mounting political pressure.

5 Tawara Yoshifumi (2006): *Abe Shinzo no honsho* [The True Nature of Abe Shinzo], Kin'yobi (chap. 4), translated by Nicholas Albertson, See at: <http://ceas.uchicago.edu/celebratingprotest/TawaraDoc.pdf> (9 February 2010).

6 It is interesting to note here that the revised Law on Education stresses the importance of international awareness. The Japanese children should be educated to participate actively in global economic competition. Education on universal norms like human rights is not excluded; however it is only legitimised by the need to participate in the global market, not from any universal ethical principles.

the international society. In foreign policy, Japan follows the basic principle of development ethics to include 'Others' in the consideration of its own actions, and in domestic policy, it follows an exclusionary principle towards 'Others' by virtue of its own need for national development. What is missing is the ability to see the right to self-reproduction as a corollary of the claim to legitimacy of an identity, since identity cannot maintain its legitimacy without self-reproduction. Therefore, this right exists for all states, but cannot be limited to them. It must be broadened to include not only potential nations, but also any community whose identity is legitimate. In this regard, it is important to mention the work of Amartya Sen (2006) - one of the founders of development ethics as a field - who challenges the communitarian philosophy that treats identity as something fixed, to be bolstered by the purported 'singular identity' of cultures and civilizations. To him, pluralities of identity are not only descriptively more accurate than the notion of singular identity, but are also normatively desirable. Identity is fluid and evolving; being related not just to religion but also to language, occupation and business, politics, class and many other aspects; therefore, taking cognisance of this aspect is extremely important to challenge singular polarization.

22.3 The Difficulty of Social Reproduction of Diaspora Identity in Japan

In the last decades, the influx of migrants and growth of Diaspora communities has triggered, in general, a xenophobic reaction denying foreign migrants security and rights, for example in the domain of education and identity reproduction. Discrimination in Japan against people from developing countries often borders on racism[7] and is often exploitative of non-nationals and minorities. Unification and development of the nation is often used as a justification for discrimination.

Parallel to this, Japan is also witnessing a healthy counter-current, which exists in the communities where Japanese citizens live with Diaspora communities. In such multi-ethnic and multicultural local communities, many Japanese citizens try to satisfy the identity needs of the non-Japanese migrants, especially by reducing the insecurity they face in daily life due to the lack of educational facilities for their children.[8] It is possible that these initiatives use the lens of development ethics (which calls for education for all) to interpret the text of the 2006 Basic Law on Education and to redress the gap between the right to education for the Japanese nationals and that of migrant communities. Many Japanese intellectuals who believe in human rights reject as collectivistic and nationalistic any ethical position affirming the right to social reproduction of nationalities and ethnic communities. They focus mainly on the principle of the individual right to education.

We argue here that the search for a development ethics respecting the identity reproduction of all social groups, majority and minorities, is not only indispensable to contemporary Japan, a successful developmentalist state, but also to all other non-Western states whose development process involves the co-existence of a national majority and of multiple ethnic minorities. The problem of discrimination against minorities is common to all of them, and the creation of a development ethics recognizing the necessity of the social reproduction of minority identities is vital to permit societies the ability to overcome development racism and evolve into multi-ethnic democracies.

The cases of national minorities in contemporary Japan indicate the complexity of this evolution. While it is easy to say that majority and minorities must all have equal recognition of their rights to identity reproduction, it is important to recognize a xenophobic ethical conviction that follows the firm belief held by a developmentalist state about its own right to identity reproduction, considered to be the basis of its progress and development in a world that often treats it as retarded and uncivilised.[9] A state interested in distinguishing itself from 'Others' distances itself not only from the 'others' as external powers and their nationals, but also 'others' within its own society.

Japan today proclaims multiculturalism to the outside 'Others', but the 'Others' within are acceptable only as far as they play a positive role in the development of the nation, and they do not interfere in the

7 The term 'developmental racism' is also used to refer to this phenomenon (Mushakoji 2003), which is common to all developmentalist states, which discriminates any human group that does not contribute to the development of the state.

8 *Chubu Region Multiculturalism and Gender Equality Research Group* (CRMGERG), n.d.: "Open Letter to United Nations Special Rapporteur Doudou Diene: Report on Education Issues for Foreign Children in the Chubu Region"; see at: <online at http://www.hurights.or.jp>: 4.1.

nation's identity reproduction.[10] This double requirement was affirmed at the turn of the century by then Prime Minister Mori who voiced support for increased immigration and emphasized the need to invite Indian information technology (IT) specialists to Japan. Simultaneously he insisted on the necessity to teach the younger Japanese generation who have forgotten that Japan was a 'divine country', and to keep the homogeneity of this divine Japanese people intact in the face of globalization. Returning to the principle of the Meiji developmentalist state - 'Japanese spirit and western skills' - the state was to allow foreigners to come and support its technological progress while keeping Japanese national unity and homogeneity. Within this framework, foreign workers were welcomed on the condition that they return to their home countries once the services needed by Japanese society are completed. The only exception is the case of migrants who can be assimilated culturally and become completely 'Japanese', through marriage with a Japanese citizen (which opens the possibility for naturalization), or through permanent residency. Complete assimilation is easier for Korean and Chinese migrants who resemble the Japanese more than many of the 'new-comer' migrants.

Japan's identity reproduction differentiates between the national majority - whose social reproduction serves the developmentalist state - and the migrant minorities - who serve Japan's economic development but whose social reproduction many perceive as an obstacle to national unity and homogeneity. The two Basic Laws on Education assume that formal education aims at forming a new generation of Japanese citizens as the majority, and disregards the education of non-citizen and minority children whose identity is different from the majority. The educational materials, methods and curricula are standardized to meet the daily lives of the majority children and do not permit adjusting lectures, class discussions or homework to the needs of different minorities, even where the teachers are devoted to the ideals of multicultural education.

In 2006, the Chubu Region Multiculturalism and Gender Equality Research Group conducted field research on the situation of children of minority and migrant communities (Korean, Indonesian, Philippine, and Japanese-origin Brazilian). Based on the findings collected through individual interviews and focus-group discussions techniques, the Group wrote an Open Letter to the United Nations Special Rapporteur, Doudou Diene, reporting on the education issues for foreign children in this central region of Japan.[11] Here we will select the key findings to illustrate the concrete problems faced by some of the Diaspora communities in educating their young generation and guaranteeing the identity reproduction of their community.[12]

The Report begins with the Korean minority, commonly called the 'old-comers' (together with the Chinese) because their migration to Japan began at the time of the Japanese annexation of Korea in 1910. The others (called 'new-comers') arrived in Japan in the 1970's and 1980's. For the Korean Diaspora, the major problems they face are defined by the historically tense relationship between Japan and Korea linked to Japanese colonial rule of Korea between 1910 and 1945. The Korean Diaspora in this period were forced migrant labourers who filled in the production gap created by the Japanese serving in the army during the war.

The subsequent division of Korea created two different types of Diaspora communities, one related to the South, the other to the North. Both however share similar issues of discriminatory treatment of their national schools, in the sense that they are neither recognized as formal public education institutions nor eligible to receive any state subsidy. Such subsidy is provided only to legally recognized private schools where the teaching is conducted according to the nationally recognized curricula. In addition to the

9 The Japanese developmentalist state ideology is strongly dominated by this country's historical experience of entering into the international community only after having proven that it was 'civilised' by developing its industrial and military capacity to the extent of winning the Sino-Japanese and the Russo-Japanese wars around 1905. The post-colonial states who met at Bandung in 1955 were not conditioned to the same extent by this obsession to develop and surpass the Western powers, while imitating them and becoming a faithful ally to the strongest among them.

10 In Japanese publications about multi-culturalism, this term has been used more to insist on the need in the international community not to accept the dominance of Western or American cultures. Japan has promoted multiculturalism in UNESCO in this international sense, not necessarily in promoting domestic multicultural education involving minority diaspora communities.

11 *Chubu Region Multiculturalism and Gender Equality Research Group* (CRMGERG), n.d.: "Open Letter to United Nations Special Rapporteur Doudou Diene: Report on Education Issues for Foreign Children in the Chubu Region"; see at: <http://www.hurights.or.jp>.

12 Ibid, 3–5.

exclusion of Korean schools from the legal school system,[13] children belonging to the North Korean Diaspora are additionally the targets of racist harassment by right wing factions of the majority civil society. For example, the North Korean schoolchildren who go to school in their *chimachogori*[14] often experience the piercing of their gown by a razor in crowded trains. Public discrimination such as the restrictive treatment of Korean schoolchildren and graduates by public authorities complement such private acts of racism.

State authorities consider the identity education provided in Korean textbooks incompatible with education standards established by the Ministry of Education and Science. In the case of North Korean schools, their textbooks were, until recently, geared towards awareness-building amongst Korean children about their past subjugation by Japanese colonial rule. This is based on the North Korean *juche* ideology (self-management) where autonomous thinking is promoted, and conformity to the Japanese educational system discouraged.

Despite volatility in Japan-North Korea relations, the situation is improving. The Korean educators in the Chubu Region reported that North Korean schools in Japan have adopted the Japanese educational system and are teaching according to official instructions on educational standards and curriculum. Furthermore, the Japanese Ministry of Education and Science now gives state universities the freedom to admit graduates from Korean high schools. Yet, it is unrealistic to assume that the Japanese state will accept the identity reproduction of the Korean Diaspora to the extent of including narratives of the colonial past in history textbooks. Nevertheless, beyond the universalistic principle of freedom of thought, it appears that developing an ethic that enables the majority and minority to each reproduce their community identity is indispensable, for this would facilitate the acceptance of different interpretations of their common past, while making a shared effort to rectify the same through critical dialogues to clarify memories and interpretations of the past. A development ethics that accepts all identity communities, disallows the publication of Japanese textbooks that gloss over or ignore the colonization and exploitation of Korea by Imperial Japan and the atrocities committed by the Imperial Army, is important for healing painful memories of the past. The case of the Korean Diaspora, thus, provides a precious example of the necessity of a development ethic that promotes efforts to overcome colonialism and other asymmetrical historical experiences between the majority and the minority communities.

The Indonesian Diaspora (a so-called 'new-comer' group) discerns the apparent lack of understanding and respect for Muslim religious practices and Indonesian culture from Japanese authorities and civil society as the major problem. The Japanese state endorsed the separation between religion and politics under pressure from the American occupation authorities. This was crucial in building a secular democracy denying the divinity of the Emperor and of the Japanese people. In recent years State Shintoism has regained some public authority, expressed through the official visits by Japanese Prime Ministers to the Yasukuni Shrine where war criminals are venerated as national heroes despite the strong objections of China and Korea. The Japanese identity reproduction continues to be connected with traditional religious and cultural beliefs that provide the foundation for patriotism.

It is nevertheless important to realize that Japanese culture has been tolerant towards the mixture of different religious traditions. It is common for people to marry according to Shinto rites and have funerals according to Buddhist rites. Today, Christian wedding ceremonies are common for couples who do not belong to any Christian churches. This religious pluralism, however, does not seem to facilitate the free performance of religious obligations for the rapidly growing number of Muslim migrants at schools, at their work places, and more broadly in civil society.

The Japanese developmentalist state ethics was developed in an historic cultural context where Christianity was the only monotheist religion with which the state had to interact. Roman Catholicism was first introduced in the 16th century and then rejected during the Edo Period (17th and 18th centuries) when Japan closed its doors to colonialist pressures from the West (Abdel-Malek 1972: 63–74), which paved the way for the fear of foreigners. The exposure of Japan to Islam was limited to the Muslim presence in China, which made this religion an object of study in the course of Japanese expansion into China in the 1930's. It was

13 The Japanese educational system makes a clear distinction between schools, public and private, which constitute the official educational system under the Ministry of Education and Science, and other schools that are called miscellaneous schools (*kakushu-gakkou*), such as driving, typing and other schools. The Korean schools are treated as miscellaneous schools.

14 Korean national gown adopted as the uniform of North Korean schools

only in the 1970's, after the 1973 Oil Crisis that Islam, once again, became a subject of interest.

Against this historical backdrop, the Japanese educational system poses great difficulties for Indonesian children in receiving an education that allows them to practice the basic requirements of their faith. The current educational system does not permit the observance required for Muslims - such as prayer time and *halal* meals. The absence of an option for *halal* meals implies that Muslim children must bring their own lunches to school. This practice differentiates them from ordinary schoolchildren and turns them into potential targets of racist bullying. The Muslim children in Japan face an educational system that is benevolent according to Japanese standards, but insensitive to the needs of non-Japanese children. It provides lunch rigorously planned to satisfy the nutritional requirements, but according to the preference of the standard Japanese family meals. It is not designed to meet different lifestyles and food habits.[15] The social reproduction of the Japanese lifestyle, being part of the Japanese educational project, completely (and deliberately) ignores the reproduction of non-Japanese lifestyles. The system supports multiculturalism in theory, but makes no effort to permit reproduction of non-Japanese lifestyles in schools and other social environments, where the social reproduction of different identity communities nevertheless takes place *de facto*.

For the Philippine Diaspora communities - many of its members are undocumented - the absence of a legally recognized status is at the crux of the struggle to ensure an education for their children. In contemporary Japan, undocumented migrants are treated as criminals: the Japanese developmentalist state ethic has always considered something to be ethical in terms of what the state authorises, endorses or permits, and something to be unethical in terms of what it forbids. Undocumented migration is unethical and forbidden, hence a crime. A double standard is revealed through the cases of Philippine entertainers whose contracts are violated by their Japanese contractors/employers, but who are not treated as victims of an unlawfully broken contract, rather, as 'illegal' and 'criminal' migrants. Only if married to a Japanese citizen can Filipina entertainers acquire permanent residency. Furthermore unless officially recognized by their Japanese fathers, the children of mothers with an illegal status are also considered illegal.

15 The difficulties met by the Indonesian children in practising their beliefs is quite different from the discrimination based on secularism in France where the veil is forbidden as a practice unacceptable from the point of view of secularism.

Japanese immigration law stipulates that any foreigner has the right to stay in Japan only if authorized by the Minister of Justice who determines when the migrants are performing activities useful to the Japanese state. The criminalization of the undocumented aliens is a manifestation of the more generalized xenophobic attitude of the Japanese state and civil society. Hidden feelings of suspicion against foreigners are historically rooted and remain strong today and have been reactivated by the massive influx of migrants from the 1980s onwards.

The post-9/11 development of the American War on Terror has strongly intensified these xenophobic trends. Surveillance mechanisms now cover not only migrants from Muslim countries, but also undocumented foreigners (including non-Muslim Filipinos and their families) who are seen as potential criminals and terrorists. The insecurity felt by undocumented Filipino families is manifested by parents forbidding their children to play outdoors, and organizing their own clandestine school.

The Japanese developmentalist state ethics, aimed at the reproduction of Japanese patriotism, ignores Diaspora communities in the informal zone where legal or administrative measures do not guarantee the protection of their security and disregard in particular their need to raise their children and educate them properly (Mushakoji 1988: 146-159). This xenophobic ethic does not help the security of the Japanese state and people, given that it traps the unprotected 'illegal' communities in an informal sector where they live in a state of powerlessness and human insecurity (Mushakoji 2003b). So long as the security of Japanese majority society is based on the insecurity of the diaspora communities, there will be a social reproduction of the informal sector, benefiting neither the minority of undocumented migrant communities nor the majority civil society. A new development ethics should consider how to define a common security between civil society and informal communities. This common security is, however, difficult to realize in a situation of asymmetrical relationships, which make minorities in informal sectors of civil society invisible.

The Peruvian and Brazilian Japanese-descent Diaspora are composed of members from the Japanese Diaspora communities in Peru and Brazil. Their communities represent a special case for social reproduction of identity because they form a group of exceptionally non-xenophobic Japanese. Called *Kimin* (rejected people), they are descendents of Japanese people who migrated to Latin America during the Meiji rule as contract labourers, and faced rejection by the Meiji state who renounced its responsibility for them. With almost no means to guarantee their security and well-being in a foreign land, except their own personal ethic, many were able to build more secure and prosperous lives and after several generations, they have successfully climbed the social ladder and now enjoy full middle class citizenship, particularly in Peru and Brazil.

In 1990 the Japanese government used the *jus sanguinis* principle, making a special exception to its tight immigration policy, to encourage descendants of Japanese nationals living in Peru, Brazil and other Latin American countries to return to Japan and work with legal protection and the possibility for eventual naturalization. While authorizing their stay without restriction, this policy, however, did not take into account the necessity to guarantee the social reproduction of these Japanese-descent migrant communities. The Japanese government does not provide enough support to the education of their children who need, for example, bilingual education. In 2006, a statement by the then Foreign Minister Taro Aso created an acute state of insecurity among this group of migrants, by asserting that the policy to admit Latin Americans of Japanese descent based on their Japanese heritage was a mistake. This statement came about in response to the emerging conflicts between the local Japanese and the Japanese 'Latin Americans', which were generated by what popular discourse pinpoints as the latter group's lack of understanding of Japanese customs and language. Therefore, he suggested that Japan should impose a language test for anybody aspiring to migrate to Japan. This may mean that the Japanese-descent Latin American migrants who speak poor Japanese may lose their legal prerogative to stay in Japan. Furthermore this statement contradicts the basic idea of multiculturalism given that the Minister did not mention the need for Japanese citizens to become more open to other cultures. Rather he insisted on keeping the homogeneity of Japanese civil society by integrating selectively only those migrants able to blend into the country's ways of life.

This is an example of a general problem caused by the Japanese cult of homogeneity reproduced by the ethics of a developmentalist state. Sakata (2007: 64–74) explains how the Japanese civil society has been under the influence of this xenophobic belief in the homogeneity of the Japanese people, with one nationality, one language and one culture. The myth of homogeneous society guaranteeing all Japanese people a common security logically accompanies a suspicion of all foreigners who come to break this homogeneity. Many Japanese people consider Japanese-descent Latin Americans as foreign because, despite their identical facial features, they continue to behave according to their Peruvian or Brazilian cultures and national identities. Many of them do not speak Japanese, and had brought with them from their home countries what are considered un-Japanese customs and practices.[16] The most serious problem faced by Brazilian children articulated to the Chubu Regional Research Group is their inability to cope with the 'stiffness of the Japanese educational system'; to them this is a major source of insecurity.

The Brazilian participants of the Chubu Region Research Group all stressed that they faced a convergence of different causes that makes their effort to educate their children ineffective. Beside language problems, which sometimes divide the parents and their children, the work circumstances of the parents did not give them enough time to interact with the children. In addition, a shared uncertainty prevails when it comes to the consideration whether to stay and settle down in Japan, or return home. Job insecurity and unclear future opportunities makes the choice between giving their children a Brazilian or Japanese education difficult. Reproducing the Brazilian identity in Japan among those who have close ties with their home community in Brazil is, however, no easy task. Although the mobility between the two countries is in itself a precious gift to the Japanese Brazilian community, since it permits their members to serve as a bridge between Japan and Brazil, the Japanese education system continues to focus on the social reproduction of Japanese citizens and, thus, does not give the Brazilian Diaspora in Japan the space necessary for their identity reproduction. The emerging generations of both the Brazilian Diaspora in Japan and Japanese citizens must go beyond the present developmentalist ethic and create a new development ethic which per-

16 There have been cases of friction between them and their neighbouring Japanese citizens, because the latter found them too noisy with their habit of singing and dancing during their home parties. More generally the more relaxed way of life of the Japanese-descent Latin Americans should open the less expressive Confucian Japanese civic culture to a more expressive and happy multi-cultural lifestyle. Hopefully, these cultural conflicts will only be transitory phases that Japan has to experience in the present process of multiculturalization.

mits the social reproduction of identities, allowing freedom to travel between the two countries without forcing the Diaspora to choose between their native homeland (Brazil) and their ancestral nation (Japan).

All the problems faced by the four Diaspora communities outlined above indicate that the Japanese system of identity reproduction represented by its educational system, so carefully dedicated to guaranteeing the social reproduction of human security of the Japanese, causes different kinds of insecurity to the migrant communities. All the Diaspora communities seem to face three major common issues – racism, especially racist bullying; uncertainty about staying in Japan or returning home; and the rigid insensitivity and intolerance of the Japanese educational system to cultural pluralism.[17] All the Diaspora communities agree on the legal and administrative difficulties they face, but also report with gratitude that many dedicated educators, administrators and local citizens responded to their problems.[18] This hopeful sign has to be encouraged, to support good deeds performed by public and private social agents in the local communities, and to help produce a bottom-up revision of the now predominantly xenophobic attitude towards people from the 'less developed' countries and the racism of the Japanese educational system based on its developmentalist ethics. A bottom-up process seeking to transform the present state of opposition between the identity reproduction of the majority Japanese and of the migrant minority communities must be the major concern of a new development ethic.

22.4 Towards a Multicultural Development Ethics

The above cases point to the aspects of the human insecurity that the Japanese developmentalist ethic generates. National education represented by the Imperial Edict and the two Basic Laws of Education provides an appropriate field to check the contradictions of this ethic, since education is the state institution that seeks to guarantee a specific type of socialization of the young generation reproducing the national identity of the Japanese people within the state of Japan. Different foreign diasporas, Korean, Philippine, Indonesian and Brazilian, all sought to guarantee the social reproduction of their respective communities through education, which enabled them to raise a next generation that reproduces their national identity.

The Chubu Region Research Group discussions indicate that both the Japanese government and the Diaspora communities share the same educational objectives. They all aimed to guarantee a smooth integration of the next generation into their identity community be it Japanese, Korean, Indonesian, Philippine or Brazilian, with an emphasis on the reproduction of identity perception for the coming generations.[19] There was, however, a difference in defining the conditions necessary to building identity, not only between the Japanese majority education and the education of the different national minorities, but also among the latter.

Evidence shows that the Japanese education system was not designed to fulfil the needs of the Diaspora communities for the social reproduction of their identities because this system is planned carefully for the reproduction of the Japanese national identity (CAPP 2004). The educational reforms that took place under the American occupation included some human rights standards, which could have helped expand the social space for non-Japanese minorities in their search for identity education. Regrettably, despite its incompatibility to today's globalized realities, the present trend in Japan is to revise the Basic Law of Education and return to the pre-1945 principles of identity education, stressing national identity and pride to the detriment of individual identity and rights.

The application of laws and ethics based on universal human rights cannot solve the amount of problems faced by foreign communities in Japan. Although the right to education is universal and should be applied to all children, national education should not limit itself to socializing citizens for the good of the nation. It is vital to find a development ethic that rec-

17 Chubu Region Multiculturalism and Gender Equality Research Group (CRMGERG), n.d.: "Open Letter to United Nations Special Rapporteur Doudou Diene: Report on Education Issues for Foreign Children in the Chubu Region"; see at: <http://www.hurights.or.jp>, 4.6.

18 Ibid, 5.1 and 5.2.

19 The above remarks about identity reproduction of national identity communities is from the perspective of the community itself and not of each individual member of the community who may belong to more than one community as with married migrants. Even in such cases, married migrants belong to the diaspora community of their homeland, the survival of which depends on the reproduction of their home identity even when they also belong to the majority community of the target country of their migration.

ognizes not only individual but also collective rights to identity development. This principle should not be limited only to the states but must apply also to the different identity communities within states (minorities including migrants, indigenous peoples, religious communities, cities, villages and other local communities). Applied to individuals, this principle can ensure the right to choose between, and combine and innovate, aspects of different identities. This makes the system composed by different identity communities very complex, and this complexity increases with the contemporary global process of hybridization, which omits none of the identity communities, be they national, transnational or local. The process of hybridization can develop in positive ways and allow marginal individuals to combine their different identities, avoiding the dangerous path towards an anomic multiculturalism where individuals lose their identity by integration with the cosmopolitan faceless masses. The more hybridization, the more these identity communities have to support the emergence of individuals who belong to many identity communities with a richer set of values and beliefs originating in the different epistemic environments they inhabit simultaneously. In order to enable the development of creative cosmopolitan individuals, the different identity communities have to see their social reproduction guaranteed, materially and also in terms of their lifestyles, traditions, cultures and other features of their identities as specific epistemic communities.[20] This collective guarantee of community identity reproduction should not work as an obstacle to the emergence of creative people, reproducing themselves and their combined identities. Rather, it is expected to contribute to an enrichment of the multicultural complexities of the global societies they constitute with their neighbouring communities in today's hybridized world.

Education is the main formal and official means at the service of the state for this purpose, and the social reproduction of identities takes place through a complex nexus of formal and informal means of socialization. The above examples indicate how asymmetry between the state and national minorities hampers such reproduction, especially for new migrant communities. Furthermore, it is insufficient to define the rights of the concerned identity communities to guarantee their identity reproduction. Legal norms are only a minimal guarantee of sanctions for violations of ethical norms. The likelihood of punishment cannot be sufficient to guarantee the social reproduction of an identity community. Ethical motivations that encourage good practices because of a sense of solidarity with the community are necessary as well.

While development ethics must consider the social reproduction of the communities seeking their development, it is necessary for this ethic to cover realities that are beyond human rights issues concerning individuals. Bullying caused by racist discrimination is but an application to minority children of practices that are already taking place among the Japanese majority children in schools, where a collective discrimination and victimization of some children different from the majority strengthens a sense of belonging to this majority group. A key issue for children of Latin American parents of Japanese descent is that discrimination at school also obstructs the social reproduction of identity in this Diaspora community. It is meaningless though to try to convince Japanese children that racist bullying is against universal human rights law. Their unconscious socialization, emulating the xenophobic homogenizing culture that dominates the Japanese state and civil society, guides their discriminatory behaviour. Therefore, development ethics must include the respect for human rights but cannot be limited to it. This ethic must simultaneously address inter-personal and inter-group relations as part of the existential surroundings where people develop their identity communities.

It is necessary to emphasize here that human rights, in their original individualist definition by the Western Enlightenment, do not necessarily provide a legitimate context for identity education, since rights are considered as belonging to individuals. The basis for social reproduction of collective identities does not necessarily rely on individual rights and therefore requires another source of ethical legitimacy. This is especially important in developmentalist states where assimilation has become the ideal. The government exploits individual rights to become part of majority civil society with a policy of convincing all minorities not to reproduce their collective identity, so that the community disappears and assimilation occurs. To attribute to individuals the right to leave any minority community, without giving to the community the collective right to its social reproduction, leads to the assimilation of minorities into the majority society that is fully cooperative to the developmental state. The dilemma between individual rights versus collective rights in this context becomes a choice between as-

20 As pointed out at the beginning of this chapter, all identity communities are composed of members who share a specific culture, values and beliefs, and therefore constitute one 'epistemic community'.

similating resident aliens or the multicultural development of a pluralist democratic society.

Identity education becomes justified when the concept of collective rights is fully recognized, and when the collectivity (which wants to reproduce itself through identity education) is also recognized as a legitimate identity community. According to the Westphalian tradition, only nation states have this privilege. Developmentalist state ethics benefit from this idea, which gives the state the right to ignore non-state agents who are considered to have no rights to reproduce their identities on the territory of states alien to them. This is where the introduction of the concept of 'human security' becomes essential, because it replaces the focus of security on the state to the focus on human individuals and collectives as units sharing a common 'security'. For all 'identity communities' the major concern for security is their sustainability as a community in a context of social reproduction in a state of flux.

This new concept of 'human security' has come to supplement 'human rights'. The new concept detaches security from the state as its traditional unit. So long as the state was the only agent responsible for security, externally through its military forces and internally through its police forces, security was associated with the monopolization of legitimate force by the states. Now that the Westphalian system is in decay, and many non-state agents hold brute force, the concept of 'national security' is insufficient in keeping international peace. The concept of 'human security' has arisen as a new discourse, which stresses the need to develop endogenous capacity to guarantee one's own security, among different kinds of 'security communities' (Mushakoji 2003b: 103–116). This is especially important in the case of undocumented migrant communities, extremely vulnerable by the fact that they do not benefit from the protection of the state.

As far as 'human security' is concerned, the ultimate goal of an identity community is the elimination of any insecurity affecting the survival of the community. In other words, the *sine qua non* precondition for 'human security' is the social reproduction of the identity community. Consequently, development ethics can cover the issues regarding the social reproduction of identity communities by combining 'human security' with human rights. The new 'human security' approach recognizes the need to empower not only states but also non-state identity communities (or 'security communities') (Mushakoji 2007a: 137–146) experiencing insecurity – such as in conflict and post-conflict situations and among people on the move (migrants, refugees, and victims of trafficking and smuggling). The 'human security' concept also permits us to address the ethical issues involved in coping with 'security dilemmas', broadening application of this concept beyond states. 'Human security' considers such dilemmas between asymmetrical security communities, including the state and the migrant communities, and stresses that the security of the citizens should not derive from or rely upon the insecurity of migrant communities. For a sustainable future, the majority civil society will have to develop a state of 'mutual security' where reduction in the migrants' insecurity contributes to increased security for citizens and vice versa (Mushakoji 2003b: 163–165).

Generally, the principle of common security, articulated in the 1980's, shows that efforts to increase security within one community by strengthening its power and competitive capacities against other communities, entails increased insecurity due to the comparable efforts generated by neighbouring communities. Development ethics must therefore be built on affirming one's own identity, while recognizing the significance of building a 'common security' respectful of each other's identity (Mushakoji 2003b: 161–181). Furthermore, for peaceful co-existence to take place, a newly constructed development ethics will also have to take into consideration the differences in political-economic, socio-cultural and psychological conditions and opportunities of identity communities.

Examples of the encounter between the state of Japan and the Diaspora communities show that finding this 'common security' (peaceful co-existence between the state and the non-state security communities) is not an easy task. The case of the Korean Diaspora[21] reveals the importance of the historical context within which this encounter takes place. In the present global age, historical developments since the 16th century play a crucial role in determining the interrelations both between Western 'industrial democracies' and the non-Western developmentalist states, as well as among the latter group. The Durban Declaration of 2001[22] asserts the significance of inter-state historical context, more specifically, how the his-

21 Chubu Region Multiculturalism and Gender Equality Research Group (CRMGERG), n.d.: Open Letter to United Nations Special Rapporteur Doudou Diene: Report on Education Issues for Foreign Children in the Chubu Region"; see at: <http://www.hurights.or.jp>, 3.2.

22 For more information, see at: <*www.un.org/WCAR/durban.pdf*>.

tory of colonialism and slavery affects the security of non-state security communities in very concrete ways.

A new development ethics must therefore consider the historical context and the power imbalance within which the state and non-state communities interact. Colonialism and post-colonial relationships of dependence (including those between states and communities, as well as those bearing gender and class features and cultural traditions) will have to be taken into account, to find an ethical ground to co-exist and transform one another (Mushakoji 2003b: 239–240). The social reproduction of identities must move from the present state of 'security dilemma' competition into a situation of co-transformation and development.

According to CRMGERG (ses footnote 21) the Indonesian Diaspora in Japan indicates the necessity to develop, between the state and the minority security communities, the possibility to reproduce their respective identity communities without intolerance, in mutual respect of their respective religious beliefs, lifestyle and ethos. This is where it is important to broaden the Bandung Principle of 'peaceful coexistence'[23] and apply it to all identity communities, both state-based and non-state-based. Western modern 'secularism' should also recognize the necessity for the secular state to accept religious minority communities on an equal footing. The non-Western States should also secularize in terms of recognizing the right of different religions, as is the case in Indonesia under the *Panchasila* ethic.[24] The Filipino community in Japan, with a substantial component of undocumented members, indicates the need to overcome the divide between civil societies and the informal sector through the criminalization of undocumented identities. Neoliberal globalization is accompanied by widening gaps, both in the South and the North, and has resulted in a downward spiral of solidarity between peoples on both ends. Any new development ethics must create spaces for the mainstream civil society to realize fully that their own identity reproduction is unsustainable without guaranteeing the identity reproduction of the different migrant communities in the informal sector. It is crucial to develop an ethical principle guaranteeing 'common security' between the citizens of a given state and the dwellers of the informal sector of the society, including the undocumented migrants. Where 'illegal' migrants are treated as potential 'terrorists', it is difficult but essential that the citizens regard 'illegal' migrants as their partners in eliminating their common insecurity, including 'terrorism' and organized crime, through an increased mutual trust, and a recognition of their equal mutual benefit in their socioeconomic and cultural exchanges. Here, the Bandung Principle of 'equal mutual benefit' has to be applied beyond its original limitation to inter-state relations (Mushakoji 2003b: 254–257).

The CRMGERG noted how the cases of the Japanese-descent Latin-American communities indicate among other things, the need to overcome prejudices built by the strict observance of state boundaries. In this global age when territorial states have their borders crossed by capital, information and people, migrants should not be treated as 'guest workers', but rather as mobile people moving across national borders.

Different identity communities must have the freedom to stay in a specific place or to move about, to remain apart or inter-mingle with members of other identity communities. They should receive permission and encouragement to reproduce themselves, with the rich intellectual and cultural creativity of hybridization and fusion. In renouncing assimilation-oriented laws and policies, the state must also guarantee the 'human security' of the migrant communities, otherwise a variety of tensions between the migrant communities and the majority of civil society will accompany this process, leading to a state of mutual insecurity. The reproduction of identity communities now occurs in this global context, and it is vital to understand that the co-development of different states and non-state communities emerges from this creative chaos where identities are no longer mutually exclusive entities divided by state borders.

A new development ethic will have to transcend the exclusive image of identity reproduction. It will have to respect the autonomy of the different identity communities, while recognizing the rights of individuals who leave their communities and those who live on the fringe between their community and the ma-

23 The Bandung Conference held in 1955 was a Conference of the newly emerging States of Asia and Africa who were the only agents of change that decided to form a counter-hegemonic alliance in face of the Cold War bi-hegemony. The realities of the post-Cold-War globalization and the post-9/11 War on Terror require the peoples to form a larger counter-hegemonic alliance beyond nation-states.

24 *Panchasila* is a combination of '*pancha*' in Sanskrit, which means five, and '*sila*' in Pali, which means principle or moral precept. The concept was introduced at the independence of Indonesia in 1945 to promote the cohabitation of different cultures and religious traditions sharing the same country.

jority national community. Married migrants belong to this marginal group, and may develop a special role in mixing the cultural traditions of their communities with the culture of their spouse.[25] Development ethics in this global age has to provide unambiguous principles of legitimacy, inclusive of the identity of all the 'mixed-blood' peoples generated by the predominant process of identity hybridization.[26]

Development ethics is built on an individualistic normative system that ignores the burning needs of identity reproduction of different identity communities, states or Diaspora communities. As a field it faces major problems as globalization advances and creates more complex formations of identity communities. Universalist and individualist ethics following the great tradition of the Western Enlightenment cannot provide an adequate theoretical framework for development ethics unless it is validated in an existential context where different identity communities can satisfy their collective rights to development.

So far non-Western states have adopted and integrated human rights principles into their national identities (Kristeva 1988: 109–115). However, to be addressed still are issues of individual rights within a collectively validated ethical system of an identity community. This requires the acceptance of Western ethical principles as a complement and vice-versa. The universality of human rights and Enlightenment values will remain felt as exogenous, and subject to criticism as ethical impositions of cultural colonialism by the Western 'industrial democracies', unless states can allow Western and non-Western principles to interact and create a 'third' space.

22.5 Concluding Remarks

If new development ethics must guarantee common security between different identity communities, this ethics will have to develop in an epistemological space, which includes, but is not limited to, the doctrine of universal human rights. This space must however become much broader than the universalistic epistemological space of human rights in order to respond to the questions of inequities and imbalances brought about by the colonial history; by the dichotomization of Western and non-Western religious traditions; formal and informal sectors; and the sidelining of realities stemming from mobility, hybridization and fusion. Left unrecognized and unaddressed, this epistemological space will remain a power struggle and will create policies that, more often than not, introduce double standards that benefit the 'industrial democracies' leading the global development process.

With a focus on the human being, the new development ethic must respect the individual as a human person, the basic unit of human rights. It will have, in addition, to recognize that ethics must be based on inter-human relations and collective interactions, involving 'care' as attentiveness, responsiveness and responsibility. This aspect of the social realities covered by 'human security' requires complete integration into the epistemological space of development ethics because all identity communities are epistemic communities sharing also a sense of common security and insecurity.[27] Non-Western concepts like the Gandhian concepts of *swadesh*, *swaraj*, *sarvodaya* and *antyodaya*[28] and their underlying ethical principles to join collective efforts and to care for the most disadvantaged in the community, are examples of non-individualistic and interactive ethical concepts that must be written into the new development ethical discourses without losing the person-centred ethical principles of the Western Enlightenment. This discourse must enable the combination of individual values with a social relational ontology that supports the above-mentioned interactive ethical values (Berman 2004).

The epistemological space of human rights, which is defined by the Aristotelian logic ruled by the laws

25 The author of this report participated in a research project on Married Migrants in Asia organized by ARENA (The Asian Research Exchange of New Alternatives) since 2007, and still ongoing in 2010, comparing married migrants from Vietnam and the Philippines to Korea and Japan. The project aimed to organize the married migrants and start a process of empowerment based on their full citizenship linking their countries of origin and destination.

26 Hybridization develops a complex tree of identities, with imbricated identity communities whose plurality becomes in itself a guarantee that the different identity communities try always to find some grounds for common security, and find some mediating agents among the mixed blood peoples who share the different identities.

27 We already saw that 'identity communities' were 'epistemic communities'. They are also 'security communities' and this triple identity must be granted by development ethics to the non-state identity communities including migrants.

28 The term *antyodaya* in Sanskrit means 'the advancement of the most disadvantaged'.

of identity, contradiction and excluded-middle, must be embedded in the Nagarjuna epistemological space of 'tetra-lemma'[29] (Mushakoji 1988: 20–21) where two other epistemological 'lemmas' play an important role.[30] Aristotelian logic posits that Identity 'A' cannot be Identity 'non-A'. However, what takes place in reality is in stark contrast to this logic: one can belong to more than one identity community. The exclusive construction of identity and the assertion of 'one identity' will therefore need to be challenged to open up the grounds for tolerance. This makes it possible for Identity A to turn itself into a non-A identity, without fearing intolerance and discrimination. Further, at the level of states, a colonialist past identity can turn itself into an anti-colonialist identity. This is the only way for the Japanese state and civil society to overcome the dilemma between maintaining its colonialist identity and becoming a non-aggressive nation. The same problem exists in all former-colonial states now defining themselves as 'industrial democracies'. We often need to achieve states of mind that transcend both A and non-A. Transcending the opposition between one's own identity and another will have to become the ultimate objective of the new development ethics. It is what the social movements in search of 'another world', which is 'sustainable', want to achieve.[31] This would create, for example, a situation where the Japanese forget about their Japanese identity and accept living as equal partners with the Diaspora communities in Japan. Although this is a dream for the moment, we believe that this is the only way for the Japanese people to guarantee themselves a secure and sustainable future.

Examples of such an epistemic meta-community, a kind of 'cosmopolis', transcending exclusionary national identity, and working closely to put together different identities, in society as well as in the mind of individuals, are beginning to form in local communities even in developmentalist Japan. This is why we suggest that the new development ethics should propose the transcendence of existing security dilemmas between asymmetric communities by relativizing the state, which will no longer feel the need to claim monopoly over the right to self-determination and self-reproduction among the different identity communities, competing with each other even on a global scale. The state is important but should not claim the same exclusionary allegiance developmentalist states demand. In order to surmount the state-centred Westphalian epistemology, the new development ethic must adopt the principle of subsidiarity between different security communities, and initiate a bottom-up process of transcending those self-centred identity definitions which currently prevail among both the state and the non-state identity communities. In the case of the migrants and their Diaspora communities, reduction of their human insecurity must take precedence, since the basis for the new ethics will logically rest in caring for the most vulnerable, as a precondition of the sustainable development of the state.[32]

The transcendence of all exclusionary identities is not only the long range objective of 'human security', it is also the epistemological and ethical ideal of 'compassion' and other principles of conviviality, which we suggest – in concluding this chapter – as the cornerstone of a new development ethic, meeting the ethical needs of the present globalizing world.

---

29 The tetralemma is a figure that features prominently in the classical logic of the Greeks. It states that with reference to any logical proposition, there are four possibilities.

30 'Common human security' is possible only when the different security communities, which are themselves epistemic communities, recognize the fact that their identity must always be coupled through an A/non-A formula. They are all epistemic communities, which can and must be coupled with other communities.

31 *Education for sustainable development* (ESD) is promoted by the UN with UNESCO as its lead agency. Sustainability is defined to combine three aspects, ecological, social and economic sustainability. Biodiversity and multiculturalism are inseparable pre-conditions of this sustainability, which gives resilience to the whole ecocultural complex. A new development ethic should provide the groundwork for ESD.

32 An ESD citizen group in Japan working in the Chubu (Central) Region stresses the need to reverse the globalist top-down approach, which ethical chain starts with the Global hegemony (United States>Japan>Central Japan>prefecture>village community>household>individual). The sustainability of development should give precedence to the smaller unit and form a bottom-up chain empowering the larger unit when the smaller one is unable to function alone (individual>household>village community>prefecture>region>nation>global community). This is in line with the idea of 'subsidiarity' developed in Medieval Europe by the Counciliar movement in the Roman Catholic Church, which stressed the priority of local churches over Rome in the governance of the Church.

Abbreviations

A-8 Countries	Eight countries that acceded to the European Union in 2004 on a transitional basis, the so-called 2-3-2 scheme (Czech Republic, Estonia, Hungary, Latvia, Lithuania, Poland, Slovakia and Slovenia)
ACSUR-Las Segovias	Asociación para la Cooperación con el Sur-Las Segovias [The Association for Cooperation with the South]
ACVZ	Adviescommissie voor Vreemdelingenzaken [Advisory Committee on Aliens' Affairs]
AECID	Agencia Española para la Cooperación Internacional y el Desarrollo [Agency for International Development Cooperation]
AIEC	Australian International Education Conference
AMC	Asian Migration Centre
AMSED	Association Marocaine de Solidarité et Développement [Moroccan Association for Cooperation and Development]
ARENA	Asian Research Exchange of New Alternatives
ASEAN	Association of Southeast Asian Nations
ASCIB	Association Ibn Battuta
ATIME	Asociación Trabajadores Inmigrantes Marroquíes en España [Association of Moroccan Immigrant Workers in Spain]
AVAR	Valencian Refugee Aid Association
AVCC	Australian Vice-Chancellor's Committee
BRIC	Brazil, Russia, India, and China
BoP	Balance of Payments
CAD	Development Aid Committee
CAPP	Centre for Asia Pacific Partnership
CBP	Customs and Border Protection [US]
CDHMAP	Centro de Derechos Humanos Miguel Agustín Pro-Juárez [Miguel Agustin Pro-Juarez Centre for Human Rights]
CEAR	Comisión Española de Ayuda al Refugiado [Spanish Commission for Aid to Refugees]
CEAS	Common European Asylum System
CEDAW	Conventions on Elimination of All Forms of Discrimination against Women
CEEC	Central and Eastern European Countries
CEN-SAD	Community of Sahel-Saharan States
CFA	Colonies Françaises d'Afrique [French colonies of Africa]
CFO	Commission on Filipinos Overseas
CISEN	Centro de Investigación para la Seguridad Nacional [Research Centre for National Security]
CMEA	Council for Mutual Economic Assistance
CNDH	Comisión Nacional de los Derechos Humanos [[National Human Rights Commission of Mexico]
CoC	Certificate of (Good) Conduct
CODENAF	Cooperación al Desarrollo en el Norte de África [Development Cooperation in Northern Africa]
COMAR	Comisión Mexicana de Ayuda a Refugiados [Mexican Commission for Aid to Refugees]
COLEF	El Colegio de la Frontera [del Norte/del Sur] [College of the Northern and Southern Border, Mexico]
CPA	Comprehensive Plan of Action for Indo-Chinese Refugees
CPSS	Committee on Payment and Settlement Systems
CQU	Central Queensland University
CRMGERG	Chubu Region Multiculturalism and Gender Equality Research Group
CRICOS	Commonwealth Register of Institutions and Courses for Overseas Students
CRLAF	California Rural Legal Assistance Foundation
CSAO [SWAC]	Club du Sahel et de l'Afrique de l'Ouest Sahel and West Africa Club
CSS	Commercial Sexual Services
CTR	Currency Transaction Report
DETYA	Department of Education, Training and Youth Affairs [Australia]
DFID	Department for International Development [UK]
DHS	Department of Homeland Security [US]
DIF	Desarrollo Integral de la Familia [National Agency for Family Development, Mexico]
EADI	European Association of Development Research and Training Institutes
EC	European Commission
ECOWAS	Economic Community of West African States
ECPR	European Consortium for Political Research
ECRE	European Council on Refugees and Exiles
EEA	European Economic Area
EDM	Early Day Motion [Westminster System]
EMCMO	Euro-Mediterranean Centrum Migratie & Ontwikkeling [Euro-Mediterranean Centre for Migration and Development]
EMIF	Encuesta sobre Migración de la Frontera Norte [Survey on Migration on the Northern Border]

T.-D. Truong and D. Gasper (eds.), *Transnational Migration and Human Security*, Hexagon Series on Human and Environmental Security and Peace 6, DOI 10.1007/978-3-642-12757-1, © Springer-Verlag Berlin Heidelberg 2011

EMIF-GUAMEX Encuesta de Migración Fronteriza Guatemala-México [Survey on Border Migration Guatemala-México]
EPAS Economic Partnership Agreements [Japan]
ESCAP Economic and Social Commission for Asia and the Pacific
ESD Education for Sustainable Development
ESOS Education Services for Overseas Students Act [Australia]
EU European Union

FCNR Foreign Currency Non-Resident [India]
FDI Foreign Direct Investment
FHS Friends of Human Security
FI Financial Institutions
FRA European Agency for Fundamental Rights
FRONTEX European Agency for the Management of Operational Cooperation at the External Borders of the Member States of the European Union
FTA Free Trade Agreement

GA General Assembly [United Nations]
GASEF Grupo de Apoyo para la Seguridad Fronteriza [High Level Group for Border Security]
GATS General Agreement on Trade in Services [WTO]
GDP Gross Domestic Product
GATT General Agreement on Tariffs and Trade
GFMD Global Forum on Migration and Development
GMG Global Migration Group
GRECO Programa Global de Regulación y Coordinación de la Extranjería e Inmegración [Global Programme to Regulate and Coordinate Foreign Residents' Affairs and Immigration, Spain]
GSL Global Solutions Ltd
G-24 The Intergovernmental Group of Twenty-Four on International Monetary Affairs and Development

HRD Human Resource Development

IASC Inter-Agency Standing Committee [United Nations]
ICEM Intergovernmental Committee for European Migration
ICHR Inter-American Court of Human Rights
ICM Intergovernmental Committee for Migration
ICRMW International Convention on the Protection of the Rights of All Migrant Workers and Members of their Families
IDC International Detention Centre
IDP International Development Programme – Education [Australia]
IDP Internally Displaced Person
IELTS International English Language Testing System
IFHR International Federation of Human Rights
IISG International Institute of Social History
ILO International Labour Organization
ILO-PATWA International Labour Organization - Programme Against Forced Labour and Trafficking in West Africa
ILPA Immigration Law Practitioners' Association
IMA International Migrants' Alliance
IMADR International Movement Against All Forms of Discrimination and Racism
IMF International Monetary Fund
IND Immigratie en Naturalisatie Dienst [Immigration and Naturalization Department]
INEF Institut für Entwicklung und Frieden [Institute for Development and Peace]
INM Instituto Nacional de Migración [National Institute for Migration of Mexico]
INS Immigration and Naturalization Service
IOM International Organization for Migration
IVTS Informal Value Transfer Systems

JHA Justice and Home Affairs
JICA Japan International Cooperation Agency
JITCO Japanese International Training Cooperation Organization
JRS Jesuit Refugee Service

LAC Latin American Countries
LDP Liberal Democratic Party
LDW Legal Domestic Worker
LOS Landelijke Ongedocumenteerde Stichting [National Organization for the Undocumented]
LSW Legal Sex Worker

MDG Millennium Development Goals
MFA Migrant Forum in Asia
MFI Micro Finance Institution
MNC Multinational Corporation
MODL Migration Occupation in Demand List
MPDL Movement for Peace, Disarmament and Freedom
MS13 Mara Salvatrucha
MTIN Ministry of Labour and Immigration [Spain]
MTO Money Transfer Operator

NAATI National Accreditation Authority for Translators and Interpreters [Australia]
NAFTA North American Free Trade Agreement
NAPTIP National Agency for Prohibition of Traffic in Persons and Other Related Matters [Nigeria]
NCADC National Coalition of Anti-Deportation Campaigns [UK]
NCSL National Conference of State Legislatures {UK]
NDA National Democratic Alliance [UK]

NR(E)RA	Non-resident External Rupee Account [India]
NGO	Non-Governmental Organization
NIBUD	Nationaal Instituut voor Budgetvoorlichting [National Institute of Budget Information]
NIE	New Institutional Economics
NLDW	Non-Legal Domestic Worker
NLSW	Non-Legal Sex Worker
NRI	Non-Resident Indian
ODA	Official Development Assistance
ODA	Overseas Development Assistance [UK]
OECD	Organisation for Economic Co-operation and Development
OHE	Office of Higher Education [Australia]
OISCA	Organization for Industrial, Spiritual and Cultural Advancement [International]
OSCE	Organization for Security and Co-operation in Europe
OSSA	Office of the Special Advisor on Africa
OWWA	Overseas Workers Welfare Association [Philippines]
PCS	Private Care Services
PE	Polyethylene
PFP	Federal Preventive Police [Mexico]
PGA	Peoples' Global Action on Migration, Development and Human Rights
POEA	Philippine Overseas Employment Administration
PR	Permanent Residency [Australia]
PRD	Partido de la Revolución Democrática [Party of the Democratic Revolution]
PRIME	Participating Refugees in Multicultural Europe
QMV	Qualified Majority Voting [EU]
RABIT	Rapid Border Intervention Teams [FRONTEX]
RCI	Rational Choice Institutionalism
RedCo	Red Codesarrollo [Codesarrollo Network, Spain]
REMCODE	Red Euromediterránea de Cooperación al Desarrollo [Euro-Mediterranean Network of Cooperation and Development, Spain]
RMIT	Royal Melbourne Institute of Technology
ROSA	Re-establishment, Organizing safe places to stay, Security, Assistance [Norway]
RSP	Remittance Service Provider
RTD	Roundtable Discussion
SAR	Suspicious Activity Report
SIOD	Sociale Inlichtingen - en Opsporingsdienst [Social Intelligence and Investigation Service]
SIS	Schengen Information System
SLBFE	Sri Lanka Bureau of Foreign Employment
SMR	South Moluccan Republic
SNE	Servicio Nacional de Empleo [National Employment Service]
SOPEMI	Systeme d'Observation Permanente des Migrations [Continuous Reporting System on Migration]
SPPNA	Security and Prosperity Partnership of North America
SPV	Special Purpose Vehicle
SRE	Secretaría de Relaciones Exteriores [Ministry of Foreign Affairs, Mexico]
SSP	Sardar Sarovar Project
STPS	Secretaría del Trabajo y Previsión Social [Ministry of Labour of Mexico]
TAFE	Technical and Further Education [Australia]
TCO	Transnational Community Organizations
TFN	Tax File Number [Australia]
TICAD	Tokyo International Conference on African Development
TITP	Technical Internship Training Programme
TMB	Treaty Monitoring Bodies
TRIPs	Trade-Related Aspects of Intellectual Property Rights [WTO]
UA	African Union
UN	United Nations
UN-CRC	United Nations Convention on the Rights of the Child
UNCTAD	United Nations Conference on Trade and Development
UNDP	United Nations Development Programme
UNHCR	United Nations High Commissioner for Refugees
UNICEF	United Nations Children's Fund
UNICRI	United Nations Interregional Crime and Justice Research Institute
UNODC	United Nations Office on Drugs and Crime
UNTFHS	United Nations Trust Fund for Human Security
USITC	United States International Trade Commission
VIS	Visa Information System
VKN	Vereniging van Kumpulans [Union of Kumpulans]
WAV	Wet Arbeid Vreemdelingen [Aliens Employment Act]
WCAR	World Conference Against Racism
WMR	World Migration Report
WRR	Wetenschappelijke Raad voor het Regeringsbeleid [Scientific Council for Government Policy]
WTO	World Trade Organization
YMCA	Young Men's Christian Association
YWCA	Young Women's Christian Association

Bibliography

Abdel-Malek, Anouar, 1972: *La dialectique sociale* (Paris: Seuil).

Acebillo, Miriam; Boni, Alejandra; McGee, Rosemary; Peris, Jordi; Calabuig, Carola; Hueso, Andrés, 2009: "Los Discursos de la Accountability en el Sistema de Cooperación Español", A Research Report (Mimeo) (Valencia: Universidad Politecnica de Valencia).

Abrahamsen, Rita, 2005: "Blair's Africa: The Politics of Securitization and Fear", in: *Alternatives: Global, Local, Political*, 30, 1: 55-80.

Acemoglu, Daron; Johnson, Simon, 2005: "Unbundling Institutions", in: *Journal of Political Economy*, 113, 5: 949-995.

Ackers, Louise; Stalford, Helen, 1999: "Children, Migration and Citizenship in the European Union: Intra-community Mobility and the Status of Children in EC Law", in: *Children and Youth Services Review*, 21, 11-12: 987-1010.

Ackers, Louise; Stalford, Helen, 2004: *A Community for Children? Children, Citizenship and Internal Migration in the EU* (Aldershot/Burlington: Ashgate Publishing).

Adams, Richard; Page, John, 2005: "Do International Migration and Remittances Reduce Poverty in Developing Countries?", in: *World Development*, 33,10: 1645-1669.

Adepoju, Aderanti, 2002: "Fostering Free Movement of Persons in West Africa: Achievements, Constraints, and Prospects for Intraregional Migration", in: *International Migration*, 40, 2: 3-28.

Adepoju, Aderanti, 2005: "Review of Research and Data on Human Trafficking in sub-Saharan Africa", in: Laczko, Frank; Gozdziak, Elzbieta (Eds.): *Data and Research on Human Trafficking: A Global Survey Offprint of the Special Issue of International Migration*, 43,1-2 (Geneva: IOM).

Adnan, Shapan, 2004: *Migration, Land Alienation and Ethnic Conflict: Causes of Poverty in the Chittagong Hill Tracts of Bangladesh* (Dhaka: Research and Advisory Services).

Adviescommissie voor Vreemdelingenzaken (ACVZ), 2003: *Immigration and the Fight Against Terrorism* (The Hague: Ministry of Justice).

Agamben, Giorgio, 1998: *Homo Sacer: Sovereign Power and Bare Life* (trans. Daniel Heller-Roazen) (Stanford, CA: Stanford University Press).

Agamben, Giorgio, 2005: *The State of Exception* (Chicago/London: University of Chicago Press).

Aggarwal, Reena; Demirgüç-Kunt, Asli; Martinez Peria, Maria Soleda, 2006: "Do Workers' Remittances Promote Financial Development?", Policy Research Working Paper Series No. 3957 (Washington, DC: The World Bank)

Agustin, Laura, 2003: "A Migrant World of Services", in: *Social Politics-International Studies in Gender, State & Society*, 10, 3: 377-396.

Agustin, Laura, 2005: "The Migrants in the Mistress's House: Other Voices in the 'Trafficking' Debate", in: *Social Politics-International Studies in Gender, State & Society*, 12, 1: 96-117.

Agustin, Laura, 2007: *Sex at the Margins: Migration, Labour Markets and the Rescue Industry* (London/New York: Zed Books).

Aitchison, John; Brown, James Alexander Campell, 1957: *The Lognormal Distribution: With Special Reference to its Uses in Economics* (Cambridge: Cambridge University Press).

Aiyar, Pallavi, 2006: "Damming Spree", in: *Frontline*, 23,11 (16 June): 62-70.

Akram, Susan, 2006: "Are they Human Children or just Border Rats" in: *Boston University Public Interest Law Journal*, 15: 187-96.

Alberola, Enrique; Salvado, Rodrigo César, 2006: "Banks, Remittances and Financial Deepening in Receiving Countries: A Model", Banco de Espana Research Paper No. WP-0621 (Madrid: Banco de España).

Albrecht, Hans-Jorg, 2002: "Fortress Europe: Controlling Illegal Immigration", in: *European Journal of Criminal Law and Criminal Justice*, 10: 1-22.

Alexander, Richard J., 2009: *Framing Discourse on the Environment: A Critical Discourse Approach* (London: Routledge).

Alexander, Titus, 1996: *Unravelling Global Apartheid: an Overview of World Politics* (Cambridge: Polity Press).

Alt, Jörg, 2003: *Leben in der Schattenwelt: Problemkomplex Illegale Migration* (Karlsruhe: von Loeper).

Amsden, Alice H.; Chu, Wan-wen, 2003: *Beyond Late Development: Taiwan's Upgrading Policies* (Cambridge MA: Massachusetts Institute of Technology Press).

Andall, Jacqueline, 2000: "Organizing Domestic Work in Italy: The Challenge of Gender, Class and Ethnicity", in: Floya, Anthias; Gabriella, Lazaridis (Eds): *Gender and Migration in Southern Europe Women on the Move* (Oxford/New York: Berg): 145-172.

Anderson, Bridget, 2001: "Why Madam has so Many Bathrobes: Demand for Migrant Domestic Workers in the EU", in: *Journal of Economic and Social Geography*, 92, 1 (February): 18-26.

Anderson, Philip, 2005: 'Ein spannungsgeladenes Feld: Die Wahrung der sozialen Rechte von Menschen in der Illegalität als Aufgabe der Kommune. Das Beispiel München', in: Jünschke, Klaus; Paul, Bettina (Eds.): *Wer bestimmt denn unser Leben? Beiträge zur Entkriminaliserung von Menschen ohne Aufenthaltstatus* (Karksruhe: von Loeper Literaturverlag): 184-199.

Andreas, Peter; Snyder, Timothy, 2000: *The Wall around the West: State Borders and Immigration Controls in North America and Europe* (Lanham/Boulder/New York/Oxford: Rowman & Littlefield Publishers).

Andreas, Peter, 2000: *Border Games: Policing the US: Mexico Divide* (Ithaca/London: Cornell University Press).

Anguiano, María Eugenia; Trejo, Alma Paola, 2007: "Políticas de seguridad fronteriza y nuevas rutas de movilidad de migrantes Mexicanos y Guatemaltecos", El Colegio de la Frontera Norte, Tijuana.

Appadurai, Arjun, 1996: *Modernity at Large: Cultural Dimensions of Globalization* (Minneapolis: University of Minnesota Press).

Appadurai, Arjun, 2002: "Globalization and the research imagination", *International Social Science Journal*: 51, Issue 160: 229-238.

Apostolopoulos, Yorghos; Sonmez, Sevil; Kronenfeld, Jennie; Castillo, Ellis; McLendon, Lucia; Smith, Donna, 2008: "STI/HIV Risks for Mexican Migrant Laborers: Exploratory Ethnographies", in: *Journal of Immigrant and Minority Health*, 8, 3: 292.

Arámbula, Alma; Gabriel, Santos, 2007: *El flujo migratorio centroamericano hacia México* (México DF: Centro de Documentación, Información y Análisis de la Cámara de Diputados).

Aranda, María Teresa, 2004: "El Programa Interinstitucional de Atención a Menores Fronterizos del DIF", in: Comisión Nacional de Derechos Humanos (CNDH) (Ed.): *Transición democrática y protección de los derechos humanos* (México DF: CNDH).

Arango, Joaquin, 2000: "Global Trends and Issues - Explaining Migration: A Critical View", in: *International Social Science Journal*, 52, 3: 283 -296.

Arbeidsinspectie, 2006: *Jaarverslag* 2005 (Den Haag: Ministerie van Sociale Zaken en Werkgelegenheid).

Arnett, Jeffrey Jensen, 2006: "G. Stanley Hall's Adolescence: Brilliance and Nonsense", in: *History of Psychology*, 9, 3: 186-197.

Aronowitz, Alexis, 2001: "Smuggling and Trafficking in Human Beings: The Phenomenon, The Markets that Drive It, and The Organizations That Promote It", in: *European Journal on Criminal Policy and Research*, 9, 2: 163-195.

Artola, Juan, 2005: *Tráfico de personas: Cruce de fronteras, documentos de identidad y principales rutas* (México: Instituto Nacional de Migración).

Artola, Juan, 2005: *Tráfico de personas: Cruce de fronteras, documentos de identidad y principales rutas* (México: Instituto Nacional de Migración).

Asian Migration Centre (AMC), 2001: *Baseline Research on Racial and Gender Discrimination towards Filipino, Indonesian and Thai Domestic Helpers in Hong Kong* (Hong Kong: Asian Migration Centre).

Athwal, Harmit, 2006: *Driven to desperate measures* (London: Institute of Race Relations).

Atkinson, Anthony B., 1995: "Capabilities, Exclusion, and the Supply of Goods: a Festschrift in honour of Amartya K. Sen", in: Sen, Amartya Kumar; Basu Kaushik; Pattanaik, Prasanta K., Suzumura, Kôtarô (Eds.): *Choice, Welfare, and Development: A Festschrift in Honour of Amartya K. Sen* (Oxford: Oxford University Press): 17-31.

Aubarell, Gemma; Aragall, Xavier, 2005: *Informe Migraciones y Desarrollo. Parte III: Estudio del caso de Marruecos* (Madrid: Centro de Estudios de Cooperación al Desarrollo).

Avila, Fernando Rios; Schlarb, Eva, 2008: "Bank Accounts and Savings - The Impact of Remittances and Migration: A Case Study of Moldova", Working Paper No. 448 (Kiel: Kiel Institute for the World Economy).

Baas, Michiel, 2006: "Students of Migration: Indian Overseas Students and the Question of Permanent Residency", in: *People and Place*, 14, 1: 8-24.

Baas, Michiel, 2007: "The Language of Migration: The Education versus the Migration Industry", in: *People and Place*, 15, 2: 49-61.

Baas, Michiel, 2009: "Curry Bashing Indian Students: Racism, Violence and Alien Space Invaders", in: *Economic and Political Weekly*, XLIV, 34, 22 (August): 37-42.

Baas, Michiel, 2010: *Imagined Mobility: Migration and Transnationalism among Indian Students in Australia* (London: Anthem Press, i.p.).

Bacon, Caroline, 2005: "The Evolution of Immigration Detention in the UK: The Involvement of Private Prison Companies", Working Paper No. 27 (Oxford: Refugee Studies Centre, Universtity of Oxford).

Bacon, David, 2008: *Illegal People: How Globalization Creates Migration and Criminalizes Immigrants* (Boston: Beacon Press).

Bader, Veit, 2005: "The Ethics of Immigration", in: *Constellations*, 12, 3: 331-361.

Bagchi, Amiya Kumar, 1981: *Merchants and Colonialism*, Occasional Paper No. 38 (Calcutta: Centre for Studies in Social Sciences), Reprinted in Bagchi, 2002: 17-70.

Bagchi, Amiya Kumar, 2002: *Capital and Labour Redefined: India and the Third World* (London: Anthem Press).

Bagchi, Amiya Kumar, 2005a: "Inequality, Deprivation and Displacement", in: Banerjee, Nirmala; Marjit, Sugata (Eds.): *Development, Displacement and Disparity* (Hyderabad: Orient Longman): 17-28.

Bagchi, Amiya Kumar, 2005b: *The Developmental State in History and in the Twentieth Century* (New Delhi: Regency Publications).

Bagchi, Amiya Kumar, 2005c: *Perilous Passage: Mankind and the Global Ascendancy of Capital* (Lanham, MD: Rowman & Littlefield).

Bagchi, Amiya Kumar, 2006: "Workers and Migrants: India and China Circa 2005 CE", in: Nielsen, Ingrid; Smyth, Russell; Vicziany, Marika (Eds.): *Globalisation and Labour Mobility in China* (Melbourne: Monash Asia Institute, an imprint of Monash University Press).

Bagchi, Amiya Kumar, 2007: "Migration, Morality and Finance", Paper for the Conference on International Migration, Livelihoods and Human Security, 30-31 August 2007 (The Hague: International Institute of Social Studies of Erasmus University Rotterdam).

Bagchi, Amiya Kumar, 2008: "Immigrants, Morality and Neoliberalism", in: *Development and Change*, 39, 2: 197-218.

Baláž, Vladimír; Williams, Allan M., 2004: "'Been There, Done That': International Student Migration and Human Capital Transfers from the UK to Slovakia", in: *Population, Space and Place*, 10, 3: 217-237.

Baldwin-Edwards, Martin, 2006: "'Between a Rock and a Hard Place', North Africa as a Region of Emigration, Immigration and Transit Migration", in: *Review of African Political Economy*, 33, 108: 311-324.

Ballescas, Rosario P., 1992: *Filipino Entertainers in Japan: An Introduction* (Quezon City: Foundation for Nationalist Studies).

Balmaceda, Gema Santamaría, 2007: "Maras y pandillas: límites de su transnacionalidad", in: *Revista Mexicana de Política Exterior*, No. 81 (Mexico: Secretaría de Relaciones Exteriores).

Balzacq, Thierry (Ed.), 2007: "Editorial - Construire le Voisin: Pratiques Européennes", in: *Cultures & Conflicts*, 66: 202.

Bamgbose, Olyuemisi, 2002: "Teenage Prostitution and the Future of the Female Adolescent in Nigeria", in: *International Journal of Offender Therapy and Comparative Criminology*, 46, 5: 569-585.

Banerjee, Upala Devi, 2003: "Globalization and its Links to Migration and Trafficking: The Crisis in India, Nepal and Bangladesh", in: *Canadian Woman Studies (Le Cahiers de la Femme)*, 22, 3-4: 124-130.

Barajas, Cristina Sandoval Luz, 2008: "Integration and Development Trajectories: Latin American Populations in the Netherlands", Working Paper No. 461 (The Hague: International Institute of Social Studies of Erasmus University Rotterdam).

Barry, Katherine, 1995: *The Prostitution of Sexuality: The Global Exploitation of Women* (New York: New York University Press).

Basch, Linda; Glick-Schiller, Nina; Szanton-Blanc, Critina (Eds.), 1994: *Nations Unbound: Transnational Projects, Postcolonial Predicaments, and Deterritorialized Nation-States* (New York: Gordon and Breach Science Publishers).

Bastia, Tanja, 2005: "Child Trafficking or Teenage Migration? Bolivian Migrants in Argentina", in: *International Migration*, 43, 4: 57-87.

Bastian, Misty L., 2002: '"The Daughter She Will Eat: Agousie in the World of the Spirits' Witchcraft Confessions in Missionised Onitsha", in: *Africa: Journal of the International African Institute*, 72, 1: 84-111.

Basu, Kaushik; Pattanaik, Prasanta K.; Suzumura, Kotaro (Eds.), 1995: *Choice, Welfare, and Measurement: A Festschrift in Honour of Amartya Sen* (New Delhi: Oxford University Press).

Bauman, Zygmunt, 2000: *Liquid Modernity* (Cambridge: Polity Press).

Bauman, Zygmunt, 2004: *Wasted Lives: Modernity and its Outcasts* (Cambridge/Malden MA: Polity Press).

Bauman, Zygmunt, 2007: *Liquid Times: Living in an Age of Uncertainty* (Cambridge/ Malden MA: Polity Press).

Baviskar, Amita, 1995/2004: *In the Belly of the River: Tribal Conflicts over Development in the Narmada Valley* (New Delhi: Oxford University Press).

Bayangos, Veronica; Jansen, Karel, 2009: "The Macroeconomics of Remittances in the Philippines", Working Paper No. 470 (The Hague: International Institute of Social Studies of Erasmus University Rotterdam).

Bayart, Jean-François, 2007: "En Finir avec le Co-développement", in: *Alternatives Economiques*, 257: 26.

Bear, Margaret E., 1999: "Illegal Migration: Personal Tragedies, Social Problems, or National Security Threats?", in: Williams, Phil (Ed.): *Illegal Immigration and Commercial Sex: The New Slave Trade* (London: Frank Cass).

Beck, Ulrich, 2000: "The Cosmopolitan Perspective: Sociology of the Second Age of Modernity", in: *The British Journal of Sociology*, 51, 1: 79-105.

Beets, Gijs; Walhout, Evelien; Koesoebjono, Santo, 2002: "Demografische ontwikkeling van de Molukse bevolkingsgroep in Nederland" [Demographic Development of the Moluccan Population in the Netherlands], in: *Maandstatistiek van de Bevolking*, 6: 13-17.

Behrendt, Stephen, 1999: "Transatlantic Slave Trade", in: Appiah, Kwame Anthony; Gates, Henry Louis (Eds.): *Africana: The Encyclopedia of the African and African American Experience* (New York: Basic Civitas Books): 1865-1877.

Beitz, Charles R., 1999: *Political Theory and International Relations: With a New Afterword by the Author* (Princeton, NJ: Princeton University Press).

Beneria, Lourdes, 2003: *Gender, Development and Globalization* (New York/London: Routledge).

Benhabib, Seyla, 2004: *The Rights of Others: Aliens, Residents and Citizens* (Cambridge: Cambridge University Press).

Berman, Marshall, 1983: *All That Is Solid Melts Into Air: The Experience of Modernity* (London: Verso).

Berman, Michael, 2004: "Merleau-Ponty and Nagarjuna: Relational Social Ontology and the Ground of Ethics", in: *Asian Philosophy*, 4, 2 (July): 131-145.

Bernazzoli, Richelle M.; Flint, Colin, 2009: "Power, Place, and Militarism: Toward a Comparative Geographic Analysis of Militarization", in: *Geography Compass*, 3,1: 393-411.

Bettio, Francesca; Simonazzi, Annamaria; Villa, Paola, 2006: "Change in Care Regimes and Female Migration: The 'Care Drain' in the Mediterranean", in: *Journal of European Social Policy*, 16, 3: 271-285.

Bhabha, Jacqueline, 2002: "Internationalist Gatekeepers? The Tension between Asylum Advocacy and Human Rights", in: *Harvard Human Rights Journal*, 15: 155-182.

Bhabha, Jacqueline, 2006: "The Child - What Sort of Human?", in: *PMLA - the Journal of the Modern Language Association of America*, 121, 5: 1526-1535.

Bhabha, Jacqueline, 2009: "Arendt's Children: Do Today's Migrant Children have a Right to have Rights?", in: *Human Rights Quarterly*, 31, 2 (May): 410-451.

Bhagwati, Jagdish, 2003: "Borders Beyond Control", in: *Foreign Affairs*, 82, 1: 98-104.

Bigo, Didier, 2001: "Migration and Security" in: Guiraudon, V.; Joppke, C. (Eds.): *Controlling and New Migration World* (London/New York: Routledge): 121-149.

Biko, Steve, 1988: *I Write What I Like* (London: Penguin).

Bindman, Jo, 1997: *Redefining Prostitution as Sex Work on the International Agenda* (London: Anti-Slavery International).

Birrell, Bob, 2001: "Chapter 3: 1972-2000", in: Markus, Andrew (Ed.): *Building a New Community: Immigration and the Victorian Economy* (Crows Nest, NSW: Allen & Unwin).

Birrell, Bob, 2005: *Immigration Rules and the Overseas Student Market in Australia* (Melbourne: Centre for Population and Urban Research, Monash University).

Birrell, Bob, 2007: "Cooks Galore and Hairdressers Aplenty", in: *People and Place*, 15,1: 30-44.

Black, Richard, 2003: "Breaking the Convention: Researching the 'Illegal' Migration of Refugees to Europe", in: *Antipode*, 35, 1: 34-54.

Blanka, Garcés-Mascarénas, 2008: "Old and New Labour Migration to Malaysia: From Colonial Times to the Present", in: Schrover, Marlou; van der Leun, Joanne; Lucassen, Leo; Quispel, Chris (Eds.): *Illegal Migration and Gender in a Global and Historical Perspective* (Amsterdam: Amsterdam University Press).

Blanning, Tim, 2007: *The Pursuit of Glory: Europe 1648-1815* (London: Penguin).

Bleahu, Ana, 2007: "With Calluses on Your Palms They Don't Bother You: Illegal Romanian Migrants in Italy", in: *Focal. Journal of Global and Historical Anthropology*, 49: 101-109.

Bloed, Arie, 1988: *The External Relations of the Council for Mutual Economic Assistance* (Leiden: Brill).

Bloem, Marion, 1983: *Geen Gewoon Indisch Meisje* [Not an ordinary Indisch girl] (Haarlem: Uitgeverij In De Knipscheer).

Boekhoorn, Paul; Speller, Trees; Kruijssen, Froukje, 2004: *Operationeel toezicht vreemdelingen; evaluatie van de bevoegdheden in de Vreemdelingenwet 2000 voor het vreemdelingentoezicht door de politie* (Den Haag: Boom Juridische Uitgevers).

Bolognani, Marta, 2007: "The Myth of Return: Dismissal, Survival or Revival? A Bradford Example of Transnationalism as a Political Instrument", in: *Journal of Ethnic and Migration Studies*, 33,1: 59-76.

Bond, Patrick, 2001: *Against Global Apartheid: South Africa Meets the World Bank, IMF and International Finance* (London: Zed Books).

Bond, Patrick, 2004: *Talk Left, Walk Right: South Africa's Frustrated Global Reforms* (Scottsville: University of KwaZulu-Natal Press).

Bonds, Anne, 2006: "Calling on Femininity? Gender, Call Centers, and Restructuring in the Rural American West", in: *ACME - E-Journal of Critical Geographies*, 5, 1: 28-34.

Boserup, Ester, 1970: *Woman's Role in Economic Development* (London: Allen & Unwin).

Bosma, Ulbe, 2005: "The Indo: Class, Citizenship and Politics in Late Colonial Society", in: Coté, Joost; Westerbeeks, Loes (Eds.): *Recalling the Indies. Colonial Culture and Postcolonial Identities* (Amsterdam: Aksant).

Bosma, Ulbe, 2009: *Terug uit de koloniën. Zestig jaar postkoloniale migranten en hun organisaties* [Return from the Colonies. Sixty Years of Post Colonial Migrants and their Organisations] (Amsterdam: Bert Bakker).

Bosma, Ulbe; Raben, Remco, 2003: *De oude Indische wereld* 1500-1920 (The Old Indisch World 1500-1920) (Amsterdam: Bert Bakker).

Bosniak, Linda, 2006: *The Citizen and the Alien. Dilemma's of Contemporary Membership* (Princeton: Princeton University Press).

Bosold, David; Werthes, Sascha, 2005: "Human Security in Practice: Canadian and Japanese Experiences", in: *Internationale Politik und Gesellschaft/International Politics and Society*, 1: 84-101.

Boswell, Cristina, 2007: "Migration Control in Europe after 9/11: Explaining the Absence of Securitization", in: *Journal of Common Market Studies*, 45, 3: 589-610.

Boswell, Cristina; Straubhaar, Thomas, 2004: "The Illegal Employment of Foreign Workers", in: *Intereconomics*, 39: 4-7.

Bourdieu, Pierre, 1990: *The Logic of Practice* (Cambridge: Polity Press).

Bourdieu, Pierre, 1994: "Rethinking the State. Genesis and Structure of the Bureaucratic Field", in: *Sociological Theory*, 12, 1: 1-18.

Bourdillon, Michael F.C.; White, Ben; Myers, William E., 2009: "Re-assessing Minimum Age Standards for Children's Work", in: *International Journal of Sociology and Social Policy*, 29, 3/4: 106-117.

Boutin, Susan B., 2003: "Illegality, Borderlands, and the Space of the Nonexistence", in: Perry, Richard W.; Mauer, Bill (Eds.): *Globalization under Construction: Gov-*

ernmentality, Law, and Identity (Minneapolis MN: The University of Minnesota Press): 171-202.

Boyce, James K.; Ndikumana, Léonce, 2002a: *Africa's Debt: Who Owes Whom?* Working Paper No. 48 (Amherst, MA: University of Massachusetts at Amherst, Political Economy Research Institute).

Boyce, James K.; Ndikumana, Léonce, 2002b: "Public Debts and Private Assets: Explaining Capital Flights from Sub-Saharan African Countries", Working Paper No. 32 (Amherst, MA: University of Massachusetts at Amherst, Political Economy Research Institute).

Boyer, Kate, 2006: "Introduction: Gender, Space and Technology", in: *ACME - E-Journal of Critical Geographies*, 5, 1: 1-8.

Brachet, Julien, 2005: "Migrants, transporteurs et agents de l'État: Rencontre sur l'axe Agadez-Sebha", in: *Autrepart*, 36: 43-62.

Brachet, Julien, 2009a: *Migrations transsahariennes. Vers un désert cosmopolite et morcelé (Niger)* (Paris: Le Croquant).

Brachet, Julien, 2009b: "Migration Towards and Transiting Through the Central Sahara: From International to Local Patterns and Practices", in: Trémolières, Marie (Ed.): *Regional Challenges of West African Migration. African and European Perspectives* (Paris: Club du Sahel et de l'Afrique de l'Ouest/Organisation for Economic Co-operation and Development): 209-218.

Breckenridge, Carol A.; Vogler, Candace, 2001: "The Critical Limits of Embodiment: Disability's Criticism", in: *Public Culture*, 13, 3: 349-357.

Bredeloup, Sylvie; Pliez, Olivier (Eds.), 2005, "Migrations entre les deux rives du Sahara", *Autrepart*, 36: 200.

Brettell, Caroline, 2000: "Theorizing Migration in Anthropology: The Social Construction of Networks, Identities, Communities and Globalscapes", in: Brettell, Caroline; Hollifield, James Frank (Eds.): *Migration Theory: Talking Across Disciplines* (London: Routledge): 97-136.

Brettell, Caroline; Hollifield, James Frank (Eds.), 2000: *Migration Theory: Talking Across Disciplines* (New York: Routledge).

Brody, Betsy, 2002: *Opening the Door: Immigration, Ethnicity, and Globalization in Japan* (New York: Routledge).

Broeders, Dennis, 2007: "The New Digital Borders of Europe: EU Databases and the Surveillance of Irregular Migrants", in: *International Sociology*, 22, 1: 71-92.

Broeders, Dennis, 2009a: *Breaking Down Anonymity: Digital Surveillance of Irregular Migrants in Germany and the Netherlands* (Amsterdam: Amsterdam University Press).

Broeders, Dennis, 2009b: "Tracing, Identifying and Sorting: The Role of EU Migration Databases in the Internal Control on Irregular Migrants", in: Fassmann, Heinz; Haller, Max; Lane, David (Eds.): *Migration and Mobility in Europe: Trends, Patterns and Control* (Cheltenham: Edward Elgar).

Broeders, Dennis; Engbersen, Godfried, 2007: "The Fight against Illegal Migration: Identification Policies and Immigrants' Counter Strategies", in: *American Behavioral Scientist*, 50, 12: 1592-1609.

Brooks, Trevor W; Redlin, Meredith, 2008: "Occupational Aspirations, Rural to Urban Migration, and Intersectionality: A Comparison of White, Black and Hispanic Male and Female Group Chances for Leaving Rural Counties", in: *Southern Rural Sociology*, 23, 2: 130-152.

Brunt, Doreen, 1992: "Mastering the Struggle: Gender, Actors and Agrarian Change in a Mexican Ejido" (PhD Disssertation, Wageningen Agricultural University, Department of Gender Studies in Agriculture).

Bryson, Bill, 2004: *A Short History of Nearly Everything* (London: Black Swan Books).

Buck-Moss, Susan, 2000: *Dreamland and Catastrophe: The Passing of Mass Utopias in East and West* (Cambridge MA: Massachusetts Institute of Technology Press).

Bunyan, Tony, 2010: "Just Over the Horizon – The Surveillance Society and the State in the EU", in: *Race & Class*, 51, 3: 1-12.

Burawoy, Michael, 2005: "For Public Sociology", in: *American Sociological Review*, 70: 4-28.

Burell, Simon; Maxwell, Simon; Menocal, Alina Rocha, 2006: "Reforming the International Aid Architecture: Options and Ways Forward", Working Paper No. 278 (London: Overseas Development Institute).

Buruma, Ian, 2006: *Murder in Amsterdam* (London: Atlantic Books).

Bustamante, Jorge A., 2002: *Migración internacional y derechos humanos* (México: Universidad Nacional Autónoma de México, Instituto de Investigaciones Jurídicas).

Busza, Joanna; Castle, Sarah; Diarra, Aisse, 2004: "Trafficking and Health", in: *British Medical Journal*, 328: 1369-1371.

Butler, Judith, 1990: *Gender Trouble: Feminism and the Subversion of Identity* (New York/ London: Routledge).

Butler, Judith, 1994: "Gender as Performance: An Interview with Judith Butler", in: *Radical Philosophy*, 67: 32-39.

Buzan, Barry; Wæver, Ole; de Wilde, Jaap, 1998: *Security: A New Framework for Analysis* (Boulder CO: Lynne Rienner).

Camacho, Agnes Zenaida V., 1999: "Family, Child Labour and Migration: Child Domestic Workers in Metro Manila", in: *Childhood*, 6, 1: 57-73.

Cambridge, Paul; Williams, Lucy, 2004: "Approaches to Advocacy for Refugees and Asylum Seekers: a Development Case Study for a Local Support and Advice Service", in: *Journal of Refugee Studies*, 17, 1: 97-113.

Carling, Jørgen, 2005: "Gender Dimensions of International Migration", Global Migration Perspectives Paper No. 5 (Geneva: The Global Commission on International Migration)

Carling, Jørgen, 2006: "Migration, Human Smuggling and Trafficking from Nigeria to Europe" (Geneva: International Organization for Migration).

Carling, Jørgen, 2007: "Migration Control and Migrant Fatalities at the Spanish-African Borders", in: *International Migration Review*, 41, 2: 316-343.

Caron, Cathleen, 2007: *Portable Justice, Global Workers and the United States* (New York: Global Workers Justice Alliance).

Carpenter, Charlie R., 2007: "Setting the Advocacy Agenda: Theorizing Issue Emergence and Nonemergence in Transnational Advocacy Networks", in: *International Studies Quarterly*, 51, 1: 99-120.

Carrera, Sergio, 2007: "The EU Border Management Strategy: Frontex and the Challenges of Irregular Immigration in the Canary Islands", Working Document No. 261 (Brussels: Centre for European Policies Studies).

Carter, Donald; Merrill, Heather, 2007: "Bordering Humanism: Life and Death on the Margins of Europe", in: *Geopolitics*, 12, 2: 248-264.

Casillas, Rodolfo, 2005: "De las prácticas visibles e invisibles en la trata en Tapachula" (México DF: El Collegio de Mexico, Latin American Faculty of Social Sciences).

Casillas, Rodolfo, 2006: "La Trata de Mujeres, Adolescentes, Niñas y Niños en México: Un Estudio Exploratorio en Tapachula, Chiapas" (México DF: Instituto Nacional de Migración Centro de Estudios Migratorios).

Casillas, Rodolfo, 2005: "De las prácticas visibles e invisibles en la trata en Tapachula" (México DF: El Collegio de Mexico, Latin American Faculty of Social Sciences).

Casillas, Rodolfo, 2006: *La Trata de Mujeres, Adolescentes, Niñas y Niños en México: Un Estudio Exploratorio en Tapachula, Chiapas* (México DF: Instituto Nacional de Migración Centro de Estudios Migratorios).

Casillas, Rodolfo, 2007: *Una vida discreta, fugaz y anónima: Los centroamericanos transmigrantes en México* (México DF: El Collegio de Mexico, Latin American Faculty of Social Sciences).

Castillo, Manuel Angel, 2000: "Las políticas hacia la migración centroamericana en los países de origen, de destino y de tránsito", in: *Papeles de Población*, 24 (April-June): 133-157.

Castillo, Manuel Angel, 2001: "Los flujos migratorios en la frontera sur de México", in: *Amérique Latine: Histoire et Mémoire*, 2 (Paris: Université Paris VIII).

Castles, Stephen, 2000: *Ethnicity and Globalization: from Migrant Worker to Transnational Citizen* (London: Sage).

Castles, Stephen, 2007: "Comparing the Experience of Five Major Emigration Countries", Working Paper No. 7, International Migration Institute (Oxford: University of Oxford).

Castles, Stephen; Davidson, Alastair, 2000: *Citizenship and Migration: globalisation and the politics of belonging* (London: Macmillan).

Centre for Asia Pacific Partnership (CAPP), 2004: *Peace and Human Rights in the Asia Pacific. Report of the Inaugural Symposium of Centre for Asia Pacific Partnership* (Osaka: Osaka University of Economics and Law)

Chami, Ralph; Jahjah, Samir; Fullenkamp, Connel, 2003: "Are Immigrant Remittance Flows a Source of Capital for Development?" Working Paper No. 03/89 (Washington, DC: International Monetary Fund).

Chang, Nancy, 2002: *Silencing Political Dissent* (New York: Seven Stories Press).

Chant, Sylvia (Ed.), 1992: Gender and Migration in Developing Countries (London: Belhaven Press).

Chantavanich, Supang, 2007: *Thailand's Policies towards Migrant Workers from Myanmar* (Bangkok: Asian Migration Research Center, Chulalongkorn University).

Charteris-Black, Jonathan, 2006: "Britain as Container: Immigration Metaphors in the 2005 Election Campaign", in: *Discourse and Society*, 17, 5: 563-581.

Cheah, Wui Ling, 2009: "Migrant Workers as Citizens within the ASEAN Landscape: International Law and the Singapore Experiment", in: *Chinese Journal of International Law*, 8, 1: 205-231.

Chimni, B. S., 2004: "From Resettlement to Involuntary Repatriation: Towards a Critical History of Durable Solutions to Refugee Problems", in: *Refugee Survey Quarterly*, 23,3: 55-73.

Cholewinski, Ryszard, 1994: "The Protection of the Right of Economic Migrants to Family Reunion in Europe", in: *The International and Comparative Law Quarterly*, 43, 3: 568-598.

Chow, Esther Ngan-ling, 2002: "Globalization, East Asian Development, and Gender: A Historical Overview", in: Chow, Esther Ngan-ling (Ed.): *Transforming Gender and Development in East Asia* (London/New York: Routledge): 9-24.

Code, Lorraine, 2006: *Ecological Thinking* (New York: Oxford University Press).

Code, Lorraine, 2008: "Thinking about Ecological Thinking", in: *Hypatia*, 23, 1: 189-203.

Cohen, Robin, 1987: *The New Helots: Migrants in the International Division of Labour* (Aldershot: Ashgate Publishing Limited).

Cohen, Stanley, 2003: *States of Denial: Knowing about Atrocities and Suffering* (Cambridge/ Oxford/Malden MA: Polity Press).

Coles, Jeffrey L.; Hammond, Peter J., 1995: "Walrasian Equilibrium without Survival: Existence, Efficiency, and Remedial Policy", in: Amartya Kumar; Basu Kaushik; Pattanaik, Prasanta K., Suzumura, Kôtarô (Eds.): *Choice, Welfare, and Measurement: A Festschrift in Honour of Amartya Sen* (Oxford: Oxford University Press): 32-64.

Collins, Patricia Hill, 2000: *Black Feminist Thought: Knowledge, Consciousness, and the Politics of Empowerment* (New York: Routledge).

Collinson, Sarah, 1993: *Beyond Borders: West European Migration Policy Towards the 21st Century* (London: Royal Institute of International Affairs).

Collyer, Michael, 2007: "In-Between Places: Trans-Saharan Transit Migrants in Morocco and the Fragmented Journey to Europe", in: *Antipode*, 39, 4: 668-90.

Commission of the European Communities, 2002: "Free Movement of Workers - Achieving the Full Benefits and Potential" (Brussels: Commission of the European Communities).

Commission on Human Security, 2003: *Human Security Now* (New York: United Nations).

Connelly, M. Patricia; Li, Tania Murray; MacDonald, Martha; Parpart, Jane M., 1995: "Restructured Worlds/Restructured Debates: Globalization, Development and Gender", in: *Canadian Journal of Development Studies*, 16: 17-39.

Connolly, William, 2002: *Identity/Difference* (Ithaca NY: Cornell University Press).

Cornelius, Wayne A., 2001: "Death at the Border: Efficacy and Unintended Consequences of US Immigration Control Policy", in: *Population and Development Review*, 27, 4: 661-686.

Cornelius, Wayne A., 2006: *Impacts of Border Enforcement on Unauthorized Mexican Migration to the United States* (San Diego: Center for Comparative Immigration Studies).

Cornelius, Wayne A., 1994: 'Japan: The Illusion of Immigration Control' in: Cornelius, Wayne A.; Martin, Philip; Hollifield, James (Eds.), 1994: *Controlling Immigration: A Global Perspective* (Stanford CA: Stanford University Press)

Cornelius, Wayne A.; Tsuda, Takeyuki; Martin, Philip; Hollifield, James (Eds.), 2004: *Controlling Immigration: A Global Perspective* (Stanford CA: Stanford University Press).

Cornwall, Andrea, 2007: "Revisiting the Gender Agenda", in: *Institute of Development Studies Bulletin*, 3, 2: 69-78.

Correa, Carlos M., 2000: *Intellectual Property Rights, the WTO and Developing Countries: The TRIPs Agreement and Policy Options* (London: Zed Books).

Cortez, Michael Angelo, 2007: "The Human Development Implications of Temporary Labour Migration: The Case of the Philippines", Paper for the conference on International Migration, Multi-local Livelihoods and Human Security: Perspectives from Europe, Asia and Africa, 30-31 August 2007 (The Hague: International Institute of Social Studies of Erasmus University Rotterdam).

Coutin, Susan Bibler, 2002:"Questionable Transactions as Grounds for Legalization: Immigration, Illegality, and Law", in: *Crime, Law and Social Change*, 37: 19-36.

Coutin, Susan Bibler, 2003: "Borderlands, Illegality and the Spaces of Non-existence," in: Perry, Richard; Maurer, Bill (Eds.), *Globalization under Construction: Governmentality, Law, and Identity* (Minneapolis, MN: University of Minnesota Press): 171-202.

Craig, Edward, 1990: *Knowledge and the State of Nature* (Oxford: Clarendon Press).

Crawley, Heaven, 2006: *Child First, Migrant Second: Ensuring that Every Child Matters*, ILPA Policy Paper (London: Immigration Law Practitioners' Association).

Crawley, Heaven; Lester, Trine, 2005: *No Place for a Child: Children in UK Immigration Detention: Impacts, Alternatives and Safeguards* (London: Save the Children Fund).

Crenshaw, Kimberle, 2000: *Background Paper for the Expert Meeting on the Gender-Related Aspects of Race Discrimination*. A paper prepared for UNIFEM for an Experts' Meeting in Zagreb, Croatia, 21-24 November (New York: United Nations Development Fund for Women).

Crisp, Jeff, 2003: "Refugees and the Global Politics of Asylum", in: *The Political Quarterly*, 74, 1, Supplement: 75-87.

Crocker, David A., 2008: *Ethics of Global Development Agency, Capability, and Deliberative Democracy* (Cambridge: Cambridge University Press).

Crozier, Michel J.; Huntington, Samuel P.; Watanuki, Joji, 1975: *The Crisis of Democracy: Report on the Governability of Democracies to the Trilateral Commission* (New York: New York University Press).

Crush, Jonathan; Jeeves, Alan; Yudelman, David (Eds.), 1991: *South Africa's Labor Empire: A History of Black Migrancy to the Gold Mines* (Cape Town: David Philip).

Curley, Melissa; Wong, Siu-lun, 2008: *Security and Migration in Asia: The Dynamics of Securitisation* (Milton Park/New York: Routledge).

Curran, Sara R.; Saguy, Abigail C., 2001: "Migration and Cultural Change: A Role for Gender and Social Networks?", in: *Journal of International Women's Studies*, 2, 3: 54-77.

Currie, Samantha, 2006: '"Free' Movers? The Post-accession Experience of Accession-8 Migrant Workers in the UK", in: *European Law Review*, 31, 2: 207-229.

Curtin, Philip D., 1975: *Economic Change in Precolonial Africa: Senegambia in the Era of the Slave Trade* (Madison WI: University of Wisconsin Press).

Cypher, James M.; Dietz, James, 1997: *The Process of Economic Development* (London/New York: Routledge).

Da Lomba, Sylvie, 2004: *The Right to Seek Refugee Status in the European Union* (Antwerp/Oxford/New York: Intersentia).

Danaher, Kevin, 1994: 50 *years is enough: the case against the World Bank and the International Monetary Fund*, (Boston MA: South End Press).

Danish Immigration Service, 2005: "Report on human rights issues in Nigeria: Joint British-Danish fact-finding mission to Abuja and Lagos, Nigeria" (Copenhagen: Danish Immigration Service).

Daum, Cristophe, 2000: *Typologie des Organisations de solidarité internationale issues de l'immigration* (Paris: Institut Panos).

Daum, Cristophe, 2008: "Le Codéveloppement, Grandeur et Décadence d'une Aspiration Généreuse", in: *La revue internationale et stratégique*, 68: 48-59.

Dauvergne, Catherine, 2004: "Sovereignty, Migration and the Rule of Law in Global Times", in: *The Modern Law Review*, 67, 4: 588-615.

Dauvergne, Catherine, 2008: *Making People Illegal: What Globalization Means for Migration and Law* (Cambridge: Cambridge University Press).

David, Randolf S., 1991: "Filipino Workers In Japan: Vulnerability and Survival", Paper for the Workshop on International Labour Migration between Japan and the Rest of Asia, March 16 (Kyoto: The Research Institute for Scocial Sciences, Ryukoku University).

Davids, Tine; Van Driel, Francien Th. M., 2001: "Globalization and Gender: Beyond Dichotomies", in: Schuurman, Frans J. (Ed.): *Globalization and Development Studies: Challenges for the 21st Century* (London/New York: Routledge): 153-176.

Davidson, Robert, 2003: "Introduction: Spaces of Immigration 'Prevention' Interdiction and the Non-Place", in: *Diacritics*, 33, 3-4: 3-18.

Davies, Karen, 1996: "Capturing women's lives: A discussion of time and methodological issues", in: *Women's Studies International Forum*, 19, 6: 579-588.

Davis, Mike, 2001: *Late Victorian Holocausts: El Niño Famines and the Making of the Third World* (London: Verso).

Davis, Mike, 1992: *City of Quartz* (New York: Vintage Books).

De Boom, Jan; Engbersen, Godfried; Leerkes, Arjen, 2006: *Asielmigranten en criminaliteit* (Apeldoorn: Elsevier-Overheid).

De Genova, Nicholas, 2007: *Working the Boundaries: Race, Space and 'Illegality' in Mexican Chicago* (Durham NC/London: Duke University Press).

De Goede, Marieke, 2006: "Financial Regulation in the War on Terror", in Libby Assassi; Duncan Wigan; Anastasia Nesvetailova (Eds.) *After Deregulation: Global Finance in the New Century* (London: Palgrave).

De Haan, Arjan, 2002: "Migration and Livelihoods in a Historical Perspective: A Case Study of Bihar, India", in: *The Journal of Development Studies*, 38, 5: 115-142.

De Haas, Hein, 2003: "Migration and Development in Southern Morocco: The Disparate Socio-Economic Impacts of Out-Migration on the Todgha Valley" (PhD Dissertation, Radboud University Nijmegen, Faculty of Social Sciences).

De Haas, Hein, 2005: "International Migration, Remittances and Development: Myths and Facts", in: *Third World Quarterly*, 26, 8: 1269-84.

De Haas, Hein, 2007: "The Myth of Invasion: Irregular Migration from West Africa to the Maghreb and the European Union", Research Report, International Migration Institute (Oxford: University of Oxford).

De La Croix, Humphrey; Inge Dumpel, Inge; Van Naerssen, Ton; Portier, Karen, 2006: *Gelders Blauw. Indische Nederlanders in de provincie* [Gelders Blue. Indisch Dutch in the Province of Gelderland] (Nijmegen: BnM).

De Vries, Marlene, 1999: "Why Ethnicity? The Ethnicity of Dutch Eurasians Raised in the Netherlands", in: Crul, Maurice; Lindo, Flip; Pang, Ching Lin (Eds.): *Culture, Structure and Beyond: Changing Identities and Social Positions of Immigrants and their Children* (Amsterdam: Het Spinhuis): 28-48.

De Vries, Marlene, 2009: *Indisch is een gevoel De tweede en derde generatie Indische Nederlanders* [Indisch is a feeling. The Second and Third Generation Indisch Dutch] (Amsterdam: Amsterdam University Press).

De Zwart, Ronald; Warnaar, Marcel. F., 1995: *Nationaal Scholierenonderzoek* 1994 [Dutch National Student Survey 1994] (Den Haag: Nationaal Instituut voor Budgetvoorlichting (NIBUD))

Debiel, Tobias; Werthes, Sascha (Eds.), 2006: "Human Security on Foreign Policy Agendas: Changes, Concepts, Cases", INEF Report 80/2006 (Duisburg: Institut für Entwicklung und Frieden, University of Duisburg-Essen): 21-38.

Della Porta, Donatella; Tarrow, Sidney G. (Eds.), 2005: "Transnational Processes and Social Activism: an Introduction", in: Della Porta, Donatella; Tarrow, Sidney G. (Eds.): *Transnational Protest and Global Activism: People, Passions and Power* (Lanham MA: Rowman & Littlefield): 1-21.

Demleiter, Nora V., 2001: "The Law at a Crossroads: The Construction of Migrant Women Trafficked into Prostitution", in: Kyle, David; Koslowski, Rey (Eds.): *Global Human Smuggling: Comparative Perspectives* (Baltimore MD: The Johns Hopkins University Press): 257-293.

Denoon, Donald; Hudson, Mark; McCormack, Gavan; Morris-Suzuki, Tessa (Eds.), 1996: *Multicultural Japan: Palaeolithic to Postmodern* (Cambridge: Cambridge University Press).

Denzau, Arthur; North, Douglass C., 1994: "Shared Mental Models: Ideologies and Institutions", in: *Kyklos*, 47, 1: 3-31.

Department of Homeland Security (DHS) 2006: *Yearbook of Immigration Statistics* (Washington, DC: Office of Immigration Statistics).

Department of Homeland Security (DHS), 2008: *Appropriations Act*, 2008 (Washington, DC: The Library of Congress).

Desarrollo Integral de la Familia (DIF), 2005, 2006, 2007: *Programa Interinstitucional de Atención a Menores Fronterizos, Anuarios Estadísticos* (México DF: Ministry of Health).

Department for International Development (DFID) and UK Remittance Working Group, 2005: "UK Remittance Market" (London: Overseas Development Administration).

Diamond, Jared, 1992: *The Rise and Fall of the Third Chimpanzee* (New York: Harper Collins).

Diario Oficial de la Federación, 1999: *Ley General de Población* (México DF: Secretaría de Gobernación).

Diario Oficial de la Federación, 2005: *Acuerdo por el que se reconoce al Instituto Nacional de Migración como In-*

stancia de Seguridad Nacional (México DF: Secretaría de Gobernación).

Díaz, Gabriela; Kuhner, Gretchen, 2007: "Women Migrants in Transit and Detention in Mexico," in: *Migration Information Source* (Washington, DC: Migration Policy Institute).

Docquier, Frédéric; Marfouk, Abdeslam, 2006: "International Migration by Education Attainment", in: Özden, Çaglar; Schiff, Maurice (Eds.): *International Migration, Remittances and the Brain Drain* (Washington, DC: World Bank/Palgrave Macmillan): 151-199.

Doezema, Jo, 2002: "Who Gets to Choose? Coercion, Consent, and the UN Trafficking Protocol", in: *Gender and Development*, 10, 1: 20-27.

Doornbos, Martin, 1996: "Uganda: a Bantustan?", in: *Review of African Political Economy*, 23, 69: 425-427.

Dorman, Peter, 2001: *Child Labour in the Developed Economies* (Geneva: International Labour Office, International Programme on the Elimination of Child Labour).

Dottridge, Mike, 2006: *Action to Prevent Child Trafficking in South Eastern Europe: A Preliminary Assessment* (Lausanne/Geneva: Terre des Hommes/UNICEF).

Douglass, Mike; Roberts, Glenda S. (Eds.), 2000: *Japan and Global Migration: Foreign Workers and the Advent of a Multicultural Society* (London/New York: Routledge).

Dover, Robert, 2008: "Towards a Common EU Immigration Policy: a Securitization Too Far", in: *Journal of European Integration*, 30, 1: 113-130.

Dower, Nigel, 1988: *What is Development? A Philosopher's Answer* (Glasgow: Centre for Development Studies, University of Glasgow).

Doyle, Nicola; Hughes, Gerard; Wadensjö, Eskil, 2006: *Freedom of Movement for Workers from Central and Eastern Europe: Experiences in Ireland and Sweden* (Stockholm: Swedish Institute for European Policy Studies).

Drozdz, Martine; Pliez, Olivier, 2005: "Entre Libye et Soudan: la fermeture d'une piste transsaharienne", in: *Autrepart*, 36: 63-80.

Duffield, Mark, 2002: "Governing the Borderlands: Decoding the Power of Aid", in: *Disasters*, 25, 4: 308-320.

Duffy, Mignon, 2005: "Reproducing Labour Inequalities: Challenges for Feminists Conceptualizing Care at the Intersections of Gender, Race, and Class", in: *Gender & Society*, 19, 1: 66-82.

Dumasy, Edu, 2007: "Multicultural Educational Experiences in Brabant", in: Corner, Trevor; Van de Bunt-Kokhuis, Sylvia (Eds.): *The Space between Words: Cross-Cultural Essays in Education* (Tilburg: Tilburg University Press): 56-71.

Dummett, Michael, 2001: *On Immigration and Refugees* (London/New York: Routledge).

Düvell, Franck, 2003: "Some Reasons and Conditions for a World Without Immigration Restrictions", in: *ACME: An International E-journal for Critical Geographies*, 2, 2: 201-209.

Düvell, Franck (Ed.), 2006: *Illegal Migration in Europe: Beyond Control?* (London/New York: Palgrave Macmillan).

Ehrenreich, Barbara; Hochschild, Arlie R. (Eds.), 2003: *Global Woman: Nannies, Maids, and Sex Workers in the New Economy* (New York: Metropolitan Books).

Eisenstadt, Shmuel Noah, 1995: *Japanese Civilization: A Comparative View* (Chicago: University of Chicago Press).

Eisenstadt, Shmuel Noah, 1995: Japanese Civilization: A Comparative View (Chicago: University of Chicago Press).

El Colegio de la Frontera Norte (COLEF), 2002: *Encuesta sobre migración en la frontera norte de México* (Tijuana: El Colegio de la Frontera Norte).

El Colegio de la Frontera Sur (COLEF), 2004: *Encuesta sobre migración en la frontera Guatemala-México* (Tapachula: El Colegio de la Frontera Sur).

El Colegio de la Frontera Norte (COLEF), 2006: *Encuesta sobre migración en la frontera norte de México* (Tijuana: El Colegio de la Frontera Norte).

Ellermann, Antje, 2008: "The Limits of Unilateral Migration Control: Deportation and Interstate Cooperation", in: *Government and Opposition*, 32, 2: 168-189.

Ellis, Patricia; Khan, Zafar, 2002: "The Kashmiri Migrant: Influences in Kashmir", in: Al-Ali, Nadje; Koser, Khalid (Eds.): *New Approaches to Migration? Transnational Communities and the Transformation of Home* (London: Routledge): 169-201.

Elson, Diane, 1999: "Labor Markets as Gendered Institutions: Equality, Efficiency and Empowerment Issues", in: *World Development*, 27, 3: 611-627.

Elson, Diane; Pearson, Ruth, 1981: "'Nimble Fingers Make Cheap Workers'. An Analysis of Women's Employment in Third World Export Manufacturing", in: *Feminist Review*, 7: 87-107.

Engbersen, Godfried, 2001: "The Unanticipated Consequences of Panopticon Europe: Residence Strategies of Illegal Immigrants", in: Guiraudon, Virginie; Joppke, Christian (Eds.): *Controlling a New Migration World* (London: Routledge): 222-246.

Engbersen, Godfried, 2003: "The Wall around the Welfare State in Europe: International Migration and Social Exclusion", in: *The Indian Journal of Labour Economics*, 46, 3: 479-495.

Engbersen, Godfried. 1996: "The Unknown City", in: *Berkeley Journal of Sociology*, 40: 87-112.

Engbersen, Godfried; Staring, Richard; Van der Leun, Joanne P., 2002: "Illegal Immigrants in the Netherlands", in: Engbersen, Godfried; Snel, Erik; De Boom, Jan; Heyl, Erwin (Eds.): *Migration, Immigrants and Policy in the Netherlands: Report for the Continuous Reporting System on Migration (SOPEMI) of the Organisation of Economic Co-operation and Development (OECD)* (Rotterdam: Risbo, Erasmus University): 76-84.

Engbersen, Godfried; van der Leun, Joanne P., 2001: "The Social Construction of Illegality and Criminality", in: *Eu-*

ropean Journal of Criminal Policy and Research, 9, 1: 51-70.

Engbersen, Godfried; Van San Marion; Leerkes, Arjen, 2006: "A Room with a View Irregular Immigrants in the Legal Capital of the World", in: *Ethnography*, 7, 2: 209-242.

Engster, Daniel, 2007: *The Heart of Justice: Care Ethics and Political Theory* (Oxford: Oxford University Press).

Enhrenreich, Barbara; Hochschild, Arlie Russell, 2002: *Global Woman - Nannies, Maids and Sex Workers in the New Economy* (London: Granta Books).

Enloe, Cynthia H., 1989: *Bananas, Beaches & Bases: Making Feminist Sense of Interna-tional Politics* (London: Pandora).

Ennew, Judith; Myers, William E.; Plateau, Dominique Pierre, 2005: "Defining Child Labor as if Human Rights Really Matter", in: Weston, Burns H. (Ed.): *Child Labor and Human Rights: Making Children Matter* (Boulder, CO: Lynne Rienner Publishers): 27-54.

Erskine, Toni, 2000: "Embedded Cosmopolitanism and the Case of War: Restraint, Discrimination and Overlapping Communities", in: *Global Society*, 14, 4: 369-390.

Economic and Social Commission for Asia and the Pacific (ESCAP), 2002: "International Migration: An Emerging Opportunity for the Socio-Economic Development of the ESCAP Region", Social Policy Paper No. 6 (Bangkok: Economic and Social Commission for Asia and the Pacific).

Escrivá, Angeles; Skinner, Emmeline, 2008: "Domestic Work and Transnational Care Chains in Spain", in: Lutz, Helma (Ed.): *Migration and Domestic Work: A European Perspective on A Global Theme* (Adelshot, Hampshire: Ashgate Publishing Limited): 113-126.

European Commission (EC), 2001: *A new impetus for European youth* (Brussels: European Commission).

European Council on Refugees and Exiles (ECRE) and Refugee Council, 2007: "Refugee Council and the European Council on Refugees and Exiles' Joint Response to Select Committee on the European Union Sub-Committee F (Home Affairs): Frontex Inquiry" (Brussels: European Council on Refugees and Exiles and Refugee Council).

European Union Agency for Fundamental Rights (FRA), 2009: *Developing Indicators for the Protection, Respect and Promotion of the Rights of the Child in the European Union: Summary Report* (Vienna: European Agency for Fundamental Rights).

Esim, Simel; Smith, Monica, 2004: *Gender and Migration in Arab States: The Case of Domestic Workers* (Beirut: Regional Office for Arab States, International Labour Organization).

Espiritu, Rose Ann, 2004: "The Evolving Filipino Perceptions of Citizenship" (MA Thesis, International Institute of Social Studies of Erasmus University of Rotterdam in The Hague, Public Policy and Management).

Ewing, Walter A., 2006: "Sabotaging National Security: The Paradox of U.S. Border-Enforcement and Immigration Policies", Lineae Terrarum International Borders Conference (El Paso TX: University of Texas).

Ex, J. 1967: *Adjustment after Migration* [with a foreword by Prof. F. J. Th. Rutten] (The Hague: Martinus Nijhoff).

Facio, Alda, 2003: "Trafficking in Women and Children for the Sex Trade: Reflections from a Latin American Human Rights Feminist", in: *Canadian Woman Studies (Le Cahiers de Femme)*, 22, 3-4: 136-142.

Fagan, Honour A., 1960: *Our Responsibility: A Discussion of South Africa's Racial Problems* (Stellenbosch: Die Universiteits-Uitgewers en -Boekhandelaars).

Fagan, Honor A.; Munck, Ronaldo, 2009: *Globalization and Security: An Encyclopedia, Volumes 1/2* (Santa Barbara: Praeger Security International).

Faist, Thomas, 2000: *The Volume and Dynamics of International Migration and Transnational Social Spaces* (Oxford: Oxford University Press).

Faist, Thomas, 2006: "Espacio Social Transnacional y Desarrollo: una Exploración de la Relación entre Comunidad, Estado y Mercado", in: *Migración y Desarrollo*, 5: 2-34.

Faist, Thomas; Ette, Andreas (Eds.), 2007: *The Europeanization of National Policies and Politics of Immigration: Between Autonomy and the European Union* (Basingstoke: Palgrave Macmillan).

Fajnzylber, Pablo; López, Humberto J. (Eds): *Remittances and development: Lessons from Latin America Door* (Washinton DC: World Bank).

Falk, Richard, 2005: "Towards Authoritativeness: the ICJ Ruling on Israel's Security Wall", in: *The American Journal of International Law*, 99, 1: 42-52.

Farer, Torn, 1995: "How the International System Copes with Involuntary Migration: Norms, Institutions and State Practice", in: *Human Rights Quarterly*, 17, 1: 72-100.

Fargues, Philippe (Ed.), 2005: *Migrations méditerranéennes: Rapport* 2005 (Florence: Institut Universitaire Européen).

Farrant, Macha; MacDonald, Anna; Sriskandarajah, Dhananjayan, 2006: *Migration and Development: Opportunities and Challenges for Policymakers*, IOM Migration Research Series 22 (Geneva: International Organisation for Migration).

Featherstone, Kevin, 2003: "Introduction: In the Name of 'Europe'", in: Featherstone, Kevin; Radaelli, Claudio M. (Eds.): *The Politics of Europeanization* (Oxford: Oxford University Press): 3-26.

Fekete, Liz, 2001: "The Emergence of Xeno-Racism", in: *Race and Class*, 43, 2: 23-40.

Fekete, Liz, 2005: *The Deportation Machine: Europe, Asylum and Human Rights* (London: Institute of Race Relations).

Fekete, Liz, 2009: "Europe: Crimes of Solidarity", in: *Race and Class*, 50, 4: 83-97.

Ferguson Sidorenko, Olga, 2007: *The Common European Asylum System* (The Hague: T.M.C Asser Press).

Fernández, Mercedes; Giménez, Carlos; Puerto, Luis Miguel, 2008: *La Construcción del Codesarrollo* (Madrid: La Catarata).

Fischer-Lescano, Andreas; Löhr, Tillmann; Tohidipur, Timo, 2009: "Border Controls at Sea: Requirements under International Human Rights and Refugee Law", in: *International Journal of Refugee Law*, 21: 256-296.

Flegel, Timothy William, 2006: "Detection of major penaeid shrimp viruses in Asia, a historical perspective with emphasis on Thailand", in: *Aquaculture*, 258: 1-33.

Floya, Anthias; Lazaridis, Gabriella (Eds.), 2000: *Gender and Migration in Southern Europe Women on the Move* (Oxford/New York: Berg).

Flynn, Michael; Cannon, Cecilia, 2009: "The Privatization of Immigration Detention: Towards a Global View A Global Detention Project", A Working Paper, Graduate Institute of International Relations and Development (Geneva: University of Geneva).

Flyvbjerg, Bent, 1998: "Habermas and Foucault: Thinkers for Civil Society?", in: *British Journal of Sociology*, 49, 2: 210-233.

Fog, Karen Olwig; Sorensen, Ninna Nyberg, 2002:"Mobile Livelihoods: Making a Living in the World", in: Fog, Karen Olwig; Sorensen, Ninna Nyberg (Eds.): *Work and Migration. Life and Livelihoods in a Globalizing World* (New York: Routledge): 1-19.

Fortman, Bas de Gaay, 2006: "Human Rights", in: Clark, David A. (Ed.): *The Elgar Companion to Development Studies* (Cheltenham: Elgar).

Fortuny, Karina; Capps, Randy; Simms, Margaret; Chaudry, Ajay, 2009: *Children of Immigrants: National and State Characteristics* (Washington, DC: The Urban Institute).

Foucault, Michel, 1975: *Surveillance et Punir: Naissance de la Prison* (Paris: Editions Gallimard).

Foucault, Michel, 1984a: "What is Enlightenment?", in: Rabinow, Paul (Ed.): *The Foucault Reader* (New York: Pantheon Books).

Foucault, Michel, 1984b: "Foucault" (under the pseudonym Maurice Florence, with F. Ewald), in: *Dictionnaire des Philosophes*, I (Paris: Presses Universitaires de France): 941-944.

Foucault, Michel, 1984c: "Des Espaces Autres" (conférence au cercle d'études architecturales, 14 mars 1967), in: *Architecture, Mouvement, Continuité*, Octobre, No. 5: 46-49.

Foucault, Michel, 1991a: "Questions of Method", in: Miller, Peter; Gordon, Colin; Burchell, Graham (Eds.): *The Foucault Effect: Studies in Governmentality* (Chicago: University of Chicago Press).

Foucault, Michel, 1991b: "Governmentality", in: Miller, Peter; Gordon, Colin; Burchell, Graham (Eds.): *The Foucault Effect: Studies in Governmentality* (Chicago: University of Chicago Press).

Foucault, Michel, 2001: *Fearless Speech* [Pearson, J. (Ed.)] (Los Angeles, CA: Semiotext(e)).

Foucault, Michel, 2007: *Security, Territory, Population: Lectures at the Collège de France* 1977-1978 [Senellart, Michel (Ed.), Burchell, Graham (Trans.)] (London: Palgrave Macmillan).

Frankental, Sally; Sichone, Owen B., 2005: *South Africa's Diverse Peoples: A Reference Sourcebook* (Santa Barbara CA: ABC-CLIO Inc.).

Fraser, Arvonne, 2001: "Becoming Human: Women's Human Rights in the Private and Public Sphere", in: Agosín, Marjorie (Ed.): *Women, Gender, and Human Rights* (New Brunswick NJ: Rutgers University Press).

Frederiksen, Lisa, 1999: "Child and Youth Employment in Denmark: Comments on Children's Work from their own Perspective", in: *Childhood*, 6, 1: 101-112.

Freeman, Gary P., 1995: "Modes of Immigration Politics in Liberal Democratic States", in: *International Migration Review*, 29, 4: 881-902.

Freeman, Samuel (Ed.), 2003: *The Cambridge Companion to Rawls* (Cambridge: Cambridge University Press).

Freund, Bill, 1995: *Insiders and Outsiders: The Indian Working Class of Durban*, 1910-1990 (London: James Currey).

Frieden, Jeffry A., 1995: "Capital Politics: Creditors and the International Political Economy", in: Frieden, Jeffry A.; Lake, David A. (Eds.): *International Political Economy: Perspectives on Global Power and Wealth* (New York: St. Martin's Press): 282-298.

Friedman, Thomas, 2006: *The World is Flat: The Globalized World in the 21st Century* (London: Penguin).

Fritz, Barbara; Ambrosius, Christian; Stiegler, Ursula, 2008: *Financial Development and Macroeconomic Stabilisation through Remittances? Potential Contribution and Modes of Governance*. Paper presented at 12th EADI conference, Geneva, 24-28 June 2008 (Bonn: European Association of Development Research and Training Institutes).

Gabriella, Lazaridis, 2000: "Filipino and Albanian Female Migrant in Greece: Multiple Layers of Oppression", in: Floya, Anthias; Gabriella, Lazaridis (Eds.): *Gender and Migration in Southern Europe Women on the Move* (Oxford/New York: Berg): 49-80.

Gallagher, Ann, 2008: "Human Rights and Human Trafficking: Quagmire or Firm Ground? A Response to James Hathaway", *Virginia Journal of International Law*, 49, 4: 789-848.

Galtung, Johan, 1990: "Cultural Violence", in: *Journal of Peace Research*, 27, 3: 291-305.

Garcés-Mascareñas, Blanca, 2008: "Old and new labour migration to Malaysia: From colonial times to the present", in: Schrover, Marlou; van der Leun, Joanne; Lucassen, Leo; Quispel, Chris (Eds.): *Illegal Migration and Gender in a Global and Historical Perspective* (Amsterdam: Amsterdam University Press): 105-122.

Gardner, Anne-Marie, 2002: "Diagnosing Conflict: What Do We Know?", in: Osler, Fen Hampson; Malone, David (Eds.): *From Conflict Reaction to Conflict Prevention:*

Opportunities for the UN System (Boulder, CO: Lynne Rienner): 15-40.

Garsten, Christina, 1999: "Betwixt and Between: Temporary Employees as Liminal Subjects in Flexible Organizations", in: *Organization Studies*, 20, 4: 601-618.

Gasper, Des, 1986: "Distribution and Development Ethics", in: Apthorpe, Raymond; Krahl, Andras, (Eds.): *Development Studies - Critique and Renewal* (Leiden: Brill): 136-203.

Gasper, Des, 2000: "Structures and Meanings - A Way to Introduce Argumentation Analysis in Policy Studies Education", in: *Africanus*, 30, 1: 49-72.

Gasper, Des, 2002: "Fashion, Learning and Values in Public Management: Reflections on South African and International Experience", in: *Africa Development*, 27, 3: 17-47.

Gasper, Des, 2004a: *The Ethics of Development* (Edinburgh: Edinburgh University Press).

Gasper, Des, 2004b: "Studying Aid: Some Methods", in: Gould, Jeremy; Marcussen, Henrik Secher (Eds.): *Ethnographies of Aid - Exploring Development Texts and Encounters* (Roskilde University, Denmark: International Development Studies): 45-92.

Gasper, Des, 2005a: "Beyond the Inter-National Relations Framework - An Essay in Descriptive Ethics", in: *Journal of Global Ethics*, 1, 1: 5-29.

Gasper, Des, 2005b: "Securing Humanity - Situating 'Human Security' as Concept and Discourse", in: *Journal of Human Development*, 6, 2: 221-245.

Gasper, Des, 2007a: "Human Well-Being: Concepts and Conceptualizations", in: McGillivray, M. (Ed.): *Human Well-Being: Concept and Measurement* (Basingstoke: Palgrave): 23-64.

Gasper, Des, 2007b: "Human Rights, Human Needs, Human Development, Human Security - Relationships between Four International 'Human' Discourses", in: *Forum for Development Studies*, 1: 9-43 (Norwegian Institute of International Affairs).

Gasper, Des, 2010: "The Idea of Human Security", in: O'Brien, Karen; St. Clair, A. L.; Kristoffersen, B. (Eds.): *Climate Change, Ethics and as Human Security* (Cambridge: Cambridge University Press): 23-46

Gasper, Des; Truong, Thanh-Dam, 2010a: "Development Ethics through the Lens of Caring, Gender and Human Security", in: Esquith, Stephen; Gifford, Fred, (Eds.): *Capabilities, Power and Institutions: Towards a More Critical Development Ethics* (University Park, PA: Penn State University Press): 58-95.

Gasper, Des; Truong, Thanh-Dam, 2010b: "Movements of the 'We': International and Transnational Migration and the Capabilities Approach", in: *Journal of Human Development and Capabilities*, 11, 2: 339-357.

Gavrielatos, Angelo; Hopgood, Susan, 2009: *Submission to the Senate Inquiry into the Welfare of International Students* (Southbank VIC: Australian Education Union)

Gaylin, Willard, 1976: *Caring* (New York: Alfred A. Knopf).

Geddes, Andrew, 2005: "Europe's Border Relationships and International Migration Relations", *Journal of Common Market Studies*, 43, 4: 787-806.

Gehlen, Arnold, 1988: *Man: His Nature and Place in the World* (New York: Columbia University Press).

Geiger, Martin, 2005: "Managing Migration for an Enlarging Europe: Intergovernmental Organizations and the Governance of Migration Flows", in: *The Romanian Journal of European Studies*, 4: 19-30.

Ghosh, Bimal, 1998: *Huddled Masses and Uncertain Shores: Insights into Irregular Migration* (The Hague: Martinus Nijhoff).

Giddens, Anthony, 1984: *The Constitution of Society* (Cambridge: Polity).

Giddes, Andrew, 2005: "Europe's Border Relationships and International Migration Relations", in: *Journal of Common Market Studies*, 43, 4, 787-806.

Giménez, Carlos; Martinez, Julio; Fernandez, Mercedes; Cortes, Almudena, 2006: *El Codesarrollo en España. Protagonistas, Discursos y Experiencias* (Madrid: La Catarata).

Giri, Ananta K., 2006: "Cosmopolitanism and Beyond", in: *Development and Change*, 37, 6: 1277-1292.

Gnisci, Donata (Ed.), 2008: *West African Mobility and OECD Migration Policies* (Paris: Club du Sahel et de l'Afrique de l'Ouest/Organisation de Coopération et de Développement Economiques).

Go, Stella P., 2002: "Migration, Poverty and Inequality: The Case of the Philippines", Paper presented for the 5th International Conference of the Asia Pacific International Migration Network, Coral Coast, Fiji, 24-26 September 2002 (De La Salle University: Philippine Migration Research Network).

Goldstein, Bruce, 2006: "Merchants of Labour in Three Centuries: Lessons from History for Reforming 21st Century Exploitation of Migrant Labour", in: Kuptsch, Christiane (Ed.): *Merchants of Labour* (Geneva: International Institute for Labour Studies, International Labour Office).

Gómez Gil, Carlos, 2005: "Nuevas Vías para el Codesarrollo en la Cooperación Descentralizada", in: *Cuadernos Bakeaz*, 72: 1-16.

Gómez Gil, Carlos; González Parada, José Ramón; 2006: *El Camino hacia el Codesarrollo: Un Acercamiento al Debate desde la Perspectiva de la Cooperación al Desarrollo* (Córdoba: Ayuntamiento de Córdoba).

Goodwin-Gill, Guy S., 1985: *The Refugee in International Law* (Oxford: Clarendon Press).

Gore, Charles, 1996: "Methodological Nationalism and the Misunderstanding of East Asian Industrialization", in: *European Journal of Development Research*, 8, 1: 77-122.

Goulet, Denis, 1975: "The High Price of Social Change - on Peter Berger's Pyramids of Sacrifice", in: *Christianity and Crisis*, 35, 16: 231-237.

Goulet, Denis, 1982: "Development Policy and Social Stratification", in: Goulet, Dennis (Ed.), 2006: *Development Ethics at Work: Explorations* 1960-2002 (New York/London: Routledge): 120-134.

Gozdziak, Elzbieta M, 2008: "On Challenges, Dilemmas, and Opportunities in Studying Trafficked Children", in: *Anthropological Quarterly*, 81, 4: 903-923.

Graham, David T.; Poku, Nana, 2000: *Migration, Globalisation, and Human Security* (Routledge: New York).

Grant, Kevin, 2005: *A Civilised Savagery: Britain and the New Slaveries in Africa*, 1884-1926 (New York: Routledge).

Grillo, Ralph; Riccio, Bruno, 2004: "Translocal Development: Italy-Senegal", in: *Population, Space and Place*, 10: 99-111.

Groenendijk, Kees, 2002: "New Borders Behind Old Ones: Post-Schengen Controls Behind the Internal Borders and Inside the Netherlands and Germany", in: Groenendijk, Kees; Guild, Elspeth; Minderhoud, Paul E. (Eds.): *In Search of Europe's Borders* (The Hague: Kluwer Law International): 113-146.

Gryzmala-Kazlowska, Aleksandra, 2005: "From Ethnic Cooperation to In-Group Competition: Undocumented Polish Workers in Brussels", in: *Journal of Ethnic and Migration Studies*, 31, 4: 675-697.

Gubert, Flore, 2008: "(In)cohérence des politiques migratoires et de codéveloppement françaises. Illustrations maliennes", in: *Politique africaine*, 109: 42-55.

Guild, Elspeth, 2006: "The Europeanization of Europe's Asylum Policy", in: *International Journal of Refugee Law*, 18, 3-4: 630-651.

Guild, Elspeth, 2009: *Security and Migration in the 21st Century* (Cambridge: Polity Press).

Guimont, Aude; Silvestri, Martina; Proli, Paolo, 2008: *The UN Treaty Monitoring Bodies and Migrant Workers: a Samizdat* (Brussels: December 18 VZW).

Gutting, Gary, 1994: *The Cambridge Companion to Foucault* (Cambridge: Cambridge University Press).

Habermas, Jürgen, 1984: *The Theory of Communicative Action. Volume 1. Reason and the Rationalization of Society* (Boston: Beacon Press).

Habib, Irfan, 1965, 1995: "The Social Distribution of Landed Property in Pre-British India: A Historical Survey", in: *Enquiry* (New Delhi), New Series, II, 3 [reprinted in Habib, 1995: 59-108].

Habib, Irfan, 1983, 1995: "The Peasant in Indian History", in: *Social Scientist* (New Delhi), 11,3 [reprinted in Habib, 1995: 109-160].

Habib, Irfan, 1995: *Essays in Indian History: Towards a Marxist Perspective* (New Delhi: Tulika).

Hampshire, James, 2005: "The Politics of Immigration and Public Health", in: *The Political Quarterly*, 76, 2: 190-198.

Hancock, Ange-Marie, 2007a: "Intersectionality as a Normative and Empirical Paradigm", in: *Politics and Gender*, 3, 2: 248-254.

Hanlon, Joseph, 1986: *Beggar Your Neighbours: Apartheid Power in Southern Africa* (London: Catholic Institute for International Relations).

Hansen, Lene, 2006: *Security as Practice – Discourse Analysis and the Bosnian War* (London: Routledge).

Hansen, Randall, 2003: "Migration to Europe since 1945: Its History and its Lessons", in: *The Political Quarterly*, 74, 1, Supplement: 25-38.

Hanson, Susan; Pratt, Geraldine, 1995: *Gender, Work and Space* (London/New York: Routledge).

Harada, Tatsuo, 2005: "Objective and Methods for the Study on the Cities of the Chubu Region: A Preliminary Rough Sketch", in: *Journal of Human Security in the Networks of Global Cities*, 1: 36-50.

Harada, Tatsuo, 2007: "A Brief Overview over Local Care Workers in Japanese Context: the Intersection of Human and Social Security Approach", in: *Journal of Human Security in the Networks of Global Cities*, 3: 66-68.

Harada, Tatsuo; Mushakoji, Kinhide, 2009: "Human (in)Security of Migrants in Japan", in: Mushakoji, Kinhide; Pasha, Mustapha Kamal (Eds.): *Human (In)Security in the Networks of Global Cities: the Final Report* (Kasugai: Center for Human Security Studies of Chubu University): 122-144.

Hardy-Fanta, Carol, 2007: *Intersectionality and Politics: Recent Research on Gender, Race, and Political Representation in the United States* (London: Taylor and Francis).

Harris, Leila M., 2006: "Irrigation, Gender, and Social Geographies of the Changing Waterscapes of Southeastern Anatolia", in: *Environment and Planning D: Society and Space*, 24: 187-213.

Hartstock, Nancy, 2001: "*Domination, Globalization: Towards a Feminist Analytic*" Paper presented at the InkriT Conference on Domination and Ideology in High Tech Capitalism, 24-27 May 2001 (Berlin: Institute for Critical Theory).

Harvey, Colin, 2000: "Dissident Voices: Refugees, Human Rights and Asylum in Europe", in: *Social and Legal Studies*, 9, 3: 367-96.

Harvey, David, 2000: "Cosmopolitanism and the Banality of Geographical Evils", in: *Public Culture*, 12, 2: 529-564.

Harvey, David, 2003: *The New Imperialism* (Oxford/New York: Oxford University Press).

Hashiya, Hiroshi, 2004: *Teikoku Nihon to Shokuminchi Toshi* [Imperial Japan and Colonial Cities] (Tokyo: Yohikawa Kobunkan Publishers).

Hatate, Akira, 2006: "Gaikokujin Kenshu/Ginou Jisshu Seido wo Dousuruka" [How to Change the Foreign Trainee and Intern System], in: Gikokujin Kenshusei Mondai Nettowaku [Advocacy Network for Foreign Trainees] (Ed.): *Gikokujin Kenshusei: Working with an Hourly Labor Rate of 300 JPY* (Tokyo: Akashi Shoten): 83-97.

Hatton, Timothy J.; Williamson, Jeffrey G., 2005: *Global Migration and the World Economy: Two Centuries of Policy and Performance* (Cambridge: The Massachusetts Institute of Technology Press).

Hayek, Friedrich A., 1976: *The Mirage of Social Justice* (London: Routledge).

Hayter, Teresa, 2004: *Open Borders: the Case against Immigration Controls* (2nd edition) (London: Pluto Press).

Held, David, 1983: "Introduction: Central Perspectives on the Modern State", in: Held, David; Anderson, James; Gieben, Bram; Hall, Stuart; Lewis, Paul; Parker, Noel; Turok, Ben (Eds.): *States and Societies* (New York/London: New York University Press).

Held, David, 2004: *Global Covenant* (Cambridge: Polity Press).

Helton, Arthur C., 2002: *The Price of Indifference: Refugees and Humanitarian Action in the New Century* (Oxford/New York: Oxford University Press).

Hernandez-Coss, Raul; Brown, Gillian.; Buchori, Chitrawati.; Endo, Isaku.; Todoroki, Emiko.; Naovalitha, Tita; Noor, Wameek; Mar, Cynthia, 2008: "The Malaysia-Indonesia Remittance Corridor: Making Formal Transfers the Best Option for Women and Undocumented Migrants", World Bank Working Paper No. 149 (Washington, DC: World Bank).

Hew, Cheng Sim, 2003: *Women Workers, Migration and Family in Sarawak* (London: Routledge).

Heyman, Josiah M., 1999: "Respect for Outsiders? Respect for the Law? The Moral Evaluation of High-Scale Issues by US Immigration Officers", in: *Journal of the Royal Anthropological Institute*, 6: 635-652.

Heyman, Josiah M.; Smart, Alan, 1999: "States and Illegal Practices", in: Heyman, Josiah M. (Ed.): *States and Illegal Practices* (Oxford/New York: Berg).

Higuchi, Naoto; Tanno, Kiyoto, 2003: "What's Driving Brazil-Japan Migration? The Making and Remaking of the Brazilian Niche in Japan", in: *International Journal of Japanese Sociology*, 12, 1: 33-47.

Himabara, David; Sultan, Dawood, 1995: "Reconstructing the Ugandan State and Economy: The Challenge of an International Bantustan", in: *Review of African Political Economy*, 63: 85-93.

Hindson, Doug, 1987: *Pass Controls and the Urban African Proletariat in South Africa* (Johannesburg: Ravan Press).

Hintjens, Helen, 2006: "'Like Leaves in the Wind': Desperately Seeking Asylum in the UK", in: *Race and Class*, 48: 79-85.

Hintjens, Helen; Jarman, Alison, 2003: "Acting for Asylum: the Nexus of Pro-Refugee Activism in Melbourne", in: Leach, Michael; Mansouri, Fethi (Eds.): *Critical Perspectives on Refugee Policy in Australia* (Burwood Victoria: Deakin University): 59-87.

Hipfl, Brigitte; Bister, Anita; Strohmaier, Petra, 2003: "Youth Identities Along the Eastern Border of the European Union", in: *Journal of Ethnic and Migration Studies*, 29, 5: 835-848.

Hirabayashi, Lane Ryo; Kikumura-Yano, Akemi; Hirabayashi, James A. (Eds.), 2002: *New Worlds, New Lives: Globalization and People of Japanese Descent in the Americas and from Latin America in Japan* (Stanford CA: Stanford University Press).

Hirschman, Charles, 2005: "Immigration and the American Century", in: *Demography*, 42, 4 (November): 595-620.

Hobsbawm, Eric; Ranger, Terence (Eds.), 1983: *The Invention of Tradition* (Cambridge: Cambridge University Press).

Hoddinott, John, 1994: "A Model of Migration and Remittances Applied to Western Kenya", in: *Oxford Economic Papers*, 46, 3: 450-475.

Hoerder, Dirk, 2002: *Cultures in Contact: World Migrations in the Second Millennium* (Durham NC: Duke University Press).

Holland, Heidi, 1994: *Born in Soweto: Inside the Heart of South Africa* (Harmondsworth: Penguin).

Holm, Maibrit Gamborg, 2005: *Nigerianske kvinner i prostitusjon i Danmark* (Copenhagen: Reden-STOP Kvindehandel).

Honderich, Ted (Ed.), 1995: *The Oxford Companion to Philosophy* (Oxford: Oxford University Press).

Houdagneu-Sotelo, Pierrette; Avila, Ernestine, 2001: "I'm Here, But I'm There: The Meanings of Latina Transnational Motherhood", in: *Gender and Society*, 11, 5: 548-571.

Houghton, D. Hobart, 1964: *The South African Economy* (Cape Town/New York: Oxford University Press).

Hout, Wil; Robison, Richard, 2009: "Development and the Politics of Governance: Framework for Analysis', in: Hout, Wil; Robison, Richard (Eds.): *Governance and the Depoliticisation of Development*, (London: Routledge): 1-11.

Hout, Wil, 2009: "Development and Governance: An Uneasy Relationship", in: Hout, Wil; Robison, Richard (Eds.): *Governance and the Depoliticisation of Development* (London: Routledge): 29-43.

Hudson, David, 2008: "Developing Geographies of Financialisation: Banking the Poor and Remittance Securitisation", in: *Contemporary Politics*, 14, 3: 315-333.

Hughes, Donna M., Roche, Claire (Eds.), 1999: *Making the Harm Visible: Global Sexual Exploitation of Women and Girl: Speaking Out and Providing Services.* (Kingston: Coalition Against the Trafficking of Women).

Huijsmans, Roy, 2008: "Children Working Beyond their Localities: Lao Children Working in Thailand", in: *Childhood*, 15, 3: 331-353.

Human Rights Watch, 2008: *Neighbors In Need: Zimbabweans Seeking Refuge in South Africa* (New York: Human Rights Watch).

Human Security Centre, 2005: *Human Security Report 2005: War and Peace in the 21st Century* (New York: Oxford University Press).

Hungerland, Beatrice; Liebel, Manfred; Liesecke, Anja, 2007: "Paths to Participatory Autonomy: The Meanings of Work for Children in Germany", in: *Childhood*, 14, 2: 257-277.

Huysmans, Jef, 2000: "The European Union and the Securitization of Migration", in: *Journal of Common Market Studies*, 38, 5: 751-777.

Huysmans, Jef, 2006: *The Politics of Insecurity: Fear, Migration and Asylum in the EU* (London/New York: Routledge).

Iliffe, John, 2007: *Africans: The History of a Continent*, 2nd ed. (Cambridge: Cambridge University Press).

Immigration Law Practitioners' Association (ILPA), 2007: *Ilpa submission to the select Committee on the European Union Sub Committee F- Frontex Inquiry September* 2007 (London: Immigration Law Practitioners' Association).

Immigration Bureau, 2008: 2008 *Immigration Control* (Tokyo: Immigration Bureau, Ministry of Justice).

In?iguez Ramos, J, MartiÌn, 2005: *Los maras: ø Problema de seguridad puÌblica o nacional? (México DF: Instituto Nacional de Migración).*

Instituto Nacional de Migración (INM), 2005a: *Flujo de entrada de extranjeros por la frontera sur terrestre de México registradas por el Instituto Nacional de Migración* (México DF: Centro de Estudios Migratorios, Instituto Nacional de Migración).

Instituto Nacional de Migración (INM), 2005b: *Diagnóstico general de los flujos de trabajadores temporales de la frontera sur de México: Resumen de principales hallazgos y tendencias a futuro* (México DF: Centro de Estudios Migratorios, Instituto Nacional de Migración).

Instituto Nacional de Migración (INM), 2005c: *Propuesta de política migratoria en la frontera sur de México* (México DF: Centro de Estudios Migratorios, Instituto Nacional de Migración).

Instituto Nacional de Migración (INM), 2007: *Statistics* 2004-2007 (México DF: Centro de Estudios Migratorios, Instituto Nacional de Migración).

Instituto Nacional de Migración (INM), 2009: *Statistics* 2008-9 (México DF: Centro de Estudios Migratorios, Instituto Nacional de Migración).

Interamerican Court of Human Rights (ICHR), 2003: *Report of the Visit to Mexico of the Rapporteur for Migrant Workers and Members of their Families* (Washington, DC: Interamerican Court of Human Rights).

International Federation of Human Rights (IFHR), 2008: *United States-Mexico: Walls, Abuses, and Deaths at the Borders* (USA: International Federation of Human Rights).

International Labour Office (ILO), 2004: *Global Employment Trends for Youth* (Geneva: International Labour Office).

International Organization for Migration (IOM), 1997: *Combatiendo la migración irregular y el tráfico de migrantes: Elementos de una respuesta*. Document prepared for the Second Regional Conference on Migration Panama, 13-14 March, (Geneva: International Organization for Migration).

International Organization for Migration (IOM), 2005: *World Migration 2005: Costs and Benefits of International Migration* (Geneva: International Organization for Migration).

International Organization for Migration (IOM), 2008: *World Migration Report 2008: Managing Labor Mobility in the Evolving Global Economy*, vol. 4 (Geneva: International Organization for Migration)

Iversen, Vegard, 2002: "Autonomy in Child Labor Migrants", in: *World Development*, 30, 5: 817-834.

Iwai, Shunji, 2007: *Gaikokujinn Hanzisha: Kareraha Naniwo Kangaeteirunoka* [Foreign Criminals: What Do They Think About?] (Tokyo: Chuoukoron).

Jackson, Cecile; Palmer-Jones, Richard, 1997: "Work Intensity, Gender and Sustainable Development", in: *Food Policy*, 22, 1: 39-62.

Jacobs, Andrew James (2003): "Embedded Autonomy and Uneven Metropolitan Development: A Comparison of the Detroit and Nagoya Auto Regions, 1969-2000," in: *Urban Studies*, 40, 2: 335-360.

Jandl, Michael, 2004: "The Estimation of Illegal Migration in Europe", in: *Studi Emigrazione/Migration Studies*, XLI, 153: 141-55.

Japan International Cooperation Agency (JICA), 2007: *Ningen no Anzenhoshou: Hinkon sakugen no Atarasii Shiten* [Human Security: A New Approach to Poverty Reduction] (Tokyo: Kokusai Kyoryoku Shuppankai).

Jayagupta, Ratchada, 2009: "The Thai Government's Repatriation and Reintegration Programmes: Responding to Trafficked Female Commercial Sex Workers from the Greater Mekong Subregion", in: *International Migration*, 47, 2: 227 - 253

Jeffreys, Sheila, 2004: "Prostitution As a Harmful Cultural Practice", in: Stark, Christine; Whisnant, Rebecca (Eds.): *Not For Sale. Feminists Resisting Prostitution and Pornography* (Melbourne: Spinifex): 386-399.

Jeffreys, Sheila, 2009: "Prostitution, Trafficking and Feminism: An Update on the Debate", in: *Women's Studies International Forum*, 32, 4: 316-320.

Jencks, Christopher, 2007: "The Immigration Charade", in: *New York Review of Books*, LIV: 49-52.

Jesuit Refugee Service, 2005: *Detention in Europe: Administrative Detention of Asylum-seekers and Irregular Migrants* (Brussels: Jesuit Refugee Service).

Joppke, Christian, 1999: *Immigration and the Nation-state: The United Sates, Germany and Great Britain* (Oxford: Oxford University Press).

Jordan, Bill; Düvell, Franck, 2002: *Irregular Migration: The Dilemmas of Transnational Mobility* (Cheltenham/ Northampton MA: Edward Elgar).

Jordan, Bill; Düvell, Franck, 2003: *Migration: The Boundaries of Equality and Justice* (Cambridge: Polity Press).

Jorry, Hélène, 2007: "Construction of a European Institutional Model for Managing Operational Cooperation at the EU's External Borders: Is the FRONTEX Agency a Decisive Step Forward?", Challenge Paper No. 6 (Brussels: Centre for European Policy Studies).

Kabeer, Naila, 2000: *The Power to Choose – Bangladeshi Women and Labour Market Decisions in London and Dhaka* (London: Verso).

Kabki, Mirjam, 2007: *Transnationalism, Local Development and Social Security: The Functioning of Support Networks in Rural Ghana* (Leiden: African Studies Centre).

Kannan, Kappadath P. M.; Hari, K.S., 2002: "Kerala's Gulf Connection: Remittances and their Macroeconomic Impact", in: Zachariah, K.C.; Kannan, Kappadath P.; Rajan, Irudaya S. (Eds.): *Kerala's Gulf Connection: CDS Studies on International Labour Migration from Kerala State in India* (Trivandrum, Kerala: Centre for Development Studies): 119-227.

Karafolas, Simeon; Sariannidis Nikolaos, 2008: "The Banking Network as a Transmission Channel of Migrant Remittances: The Case of Greek and Italian Banks in Albania", in: *Transition Studies Review*, 15, 4: 674-684.

Kategekwa, Joy, 2006: "Extension of Mode 4 Commitments to Include Unskilled Workers in the WTO. A Win-win Situation, especially for LDCs", Paper for the OECD Development Centre Panel on Migration and Development in the WTO Public Forum, titled "What WTO for the 21st Century?", 25-26 September 2006 (Geneva: World Trade Organization).

Katsumata, Makoto (Ed.), 2001: *Gurobaruka to Ningen no Anzenhoshou* [Globalization and Human Security] (Tokyo: Nihon Keizai Hyoronsha).

Kaur, Amarjit; Metcalfe, Ian, 2007: "Migration Matters in the Asia-Pacific Region: Immigration Frameworks, Knowledge Workers and National Policies", in: *International Journal on Multicultural Studies*, 9, 2: 135-157.

Keck, Margaret E.; Sikkink, Kathryn, 1998: "Transnational Advocacy Networks in International Politics: Introduction", in: *Activists Beyond Borders: Advocacy Networks in International Politics* (Ithaca NY: Cornell University Press): 1-37.

Keenan, Jeremy, 2008: "Demystifying Africa's Security", in: *Review of African Political Economy*, 118: 634-644.

Kempadoo, Kamalam; Doezema, Jo (Eds.), 1998: *Global Sex Workers: Rights, Resistance, and Redefinition* (New York: Routledge).

Ketkar, Suhas; Ratha, Dlip, 2001: Securitisation of Future Receivables: a Useful Tool for Developing Countries, in: *Finance and Development*, 38, 1.

Keynes, John Maynard, 1936: *The General Theory of Employment, Interest and Money* (London: Macmillan).

Kibreab, Gaim, 1999: "Revisiting the Debate on People, Place, Identity and Displacement", in: *Journal of Refugee Studies*, 12, 4: 384-410.

Kimball, Ann, 2007: *The Transit State: A Comparative Analysis of Mexican and Moroccan Immigration Policies* (San Diego CA: The Center for Comparative Immigration Studies, University of California San Diego).

King, Russell, 2002: "Towards a New Map of European Migration", in: *International Journal of Population Geography*, 8, 2: 89-106.

King, Russell; Ruiz-Gelices, Enric, 2003: "International Student Migration and the European 'Year Abroad': Effects on European Identity and Subsequent Migration Behaviour", in: *International Journal of Population Geography*, 9: 229-252.

Kingdom of Thailand, 2006: *Results of Employment Needs, Quota and Extension of Work Permit for Immigrant Workers, Myanmar, Laos and Cambodian Nationality between 1-30 June* 2006 (Bangkok: Ministry of Employment, Department of Labour, Office of Foreign Workers Administration).

Kingdom of Thailand, 2006: *Fisheries Statistics of Thailand* 2004 (Bangkok: Ministry of Agriculture & Cooperatives, Department of Fisheries).

Kjaer, Anne Mette, 2004: "Introduction: The Meaning of Governance", in: Kjaer, Anne Mette (Ed.): *Governance* (Cambridge: Polity): 1-18.

Kleinman, Mark, 2003: "The Economic Impact of Labour Immigration" in: *The Political Quarterly*, 74, 1, Supplement: 59-74.

Kleinschmidt, Harald, 2006: "Migration, Regional Integration, and Human Security: An Overview of Research Developments", in: Kleinschmidt, Harald (Ed.): *Migration, Regional Integration and Human Security: the Formation and Maintenance of Transnational Spaces* (Aldershot: Ashgate): 61-102.

Kloosterman, Robert; Rath, Jan, 2002: *Working on the Fringes: Immigrant Businesses, Economic Integration and Informal Practices* (Amsterdam: Universiteit van Amsterdam, Institute for Migration and Ethnic Studies).

Kohl, Ines, 2007: "Going 'Off Road': With Toyota, Chech and E-Guitar through a Saharian Borderland", in: Hahn, Hans Peter; Klute, Georg (Eds.): *Cultures of Migration. African Perspectives* (Berlin: LIT Verlag): 89-106.

Koh, Pieter; O'Donovan, Michael; Bouare, Oumar; Van Zyl Johan, 2003: *Post-Apartheid Patterns of Internal Migration in South Africa* (Cape Town: Human Sciences Research Council).

Kohler, Gernot, 1978: *The Meaning of Global Apartheid* (New York: Transaction Publishers).

Kojima, Yu, 2007: *Women in Trafficking-Migration Continuum: From Perspective of Human Rights and Social Justice* (Maastricht: Shaker).

Komai, Hiroshi, 1995: *Migrant Workers in Japan* [Wilkinson, Jens (translation)] (London - New York: Kegan Paul International).

Komai, Hiroshi, 2001: *Foreign Migrants in Contemporary Japan* [Wilkinson, Jens (translation)] (Melbourne: Trans Pacific Press).

Kornprobst, Markus (Ed.), 2008: *Metaphors of Globalization: Mirrors, Magicians and Mutinies* (Basingstoke: Palgrave).

Koser, Khalid, 2008: "Why Migrant Smuggling Pays", in: *International Migration*, 46, 2: 3- 26.

Koulish, Robert, 2009: *Immigration and American Democracy: Subverting the Rule of Law* (Milton Park/New York: Routledge).

Kristeva, Julia, 1988: *Étrangers à nous-mêmes* (Paris: Fayard).

Kuptsch, Christiane; Oishi, Nana, 1995: *German and Japanese Schemes for Workers from Transition Economies or Developing Countries* (Geneva: International Institute for Labour Studies, International Labour Office).

Kuptsch, Christiane (Ed.), 2006: *Merchants of Labour* (Geneva: International Institute for Labour Studies, International Labour Office).

Kuus, Merje, 2002: "European Integration in Identity Narratives in Estonia: A Quest for Security", in: *Journal of Peace Research*, 39, 1: 91-108.

Kyle, David; Koslowski, Rey (Eds.), 2001: *Global Human Smuggling. Comparative Perspectives* (Baltimore MD/ London: The John Hopkins University Press).

Kymlicka, Will, 2003: "Immigration, Citizenship, Multiculturalism: Exploring the Links", in: *The Political Quarterly*, 74, 1, Supplement: 195-208.

Lacomba, Joan, 2004a: *Migraciones y Desarrollo en Marruecos* (Madrid: La Catarata).

Lacomba, Joan, 2004b: "Migración y Desarrollo Rural en Marruecos. El Papel de los Emigrantes y sus Asociaciones", in: Escrivá, Ángeles; Ribas, Mateos Natalilia (Eds.): *Migración y Desarrollo* (Madrid: Centro de Investigación y Cooperación para el Desarrollo): 185-212.

Lacomba, Joan, 2005: "Marruecos: Realidades de las Migraciones y Posibilidades del Codesarrollo", in: Abad, Luis V.; Aragall, Xavier; Aubarell, Gemma; Gómez Galán, Manuel; Lacomba, Joan; Moré, Iñigo; Moreno, Luisa; Ramón, Consuelo (Eds.): *Codesarrollo: Migraciones y Desarrollo Mundial* (Madrid: Centro de Investigación y Cooperación para el Desarrollo): 147-170.

Lacomba, Joan; Boni, Alejandra, 2008: "The Role of Emigration in Foreign Aid Policies: the Case of Spain and Morocco", in: *International Migration*, 46, 1: 123-150.

Lacroix, Thomas, 2005: *Les Réseaux Marocains du Développement. Géographie du Transnational et Politiques du Territorial* (París: Les Presses de Sciences Po).

Lahav Gallya; Guiraudon, Virginie, 2006: "Actors and Venues in Immigration Control: Closing the Gap between Political Demand and Policy Outcomes", in: *West European Politics*, 29, 2: 201-223.

Lakoff, George; Johnson, Mark, 2003: *Metaphors We Live By* [updated ed.] (Chicago, IL: University of Chicago Press).

Lavenex, Sandra, 2001: "The Europeanization of Refugee Policies: Normative Challenges and Institutional Legacies", in: *Journal of Common Market Studies*, 39, 5: 851-874.

Lavenex, Sandra, 2006: "Shifting Up and Out: The Foreign Policy of European Immigration Control", in: *West European Politics*, 29, 2: 329-350.

Lavenex, Sandra; Uçarer, Emek M., 2004: "The External Dimension of Europeanization -The Case of Immigration Policies", in: *Cooperation and Conflict* 39, 4: 417-443.

Lawson, Victoria; Silvey, Rachel, 1999: "Placing the Migrant", in: *Annals of the Association of American Geographers*, 89, 1: 121-132.

Leatherman, Janie, 2005: "Global Arrogance and the Crisis of Hegemony", in: Leatherman, Janie; Webber, Julie A. (Eds): *Charting Transnational Democracy: Beyond Global Arrogance* (New York/Basingstoke: Palgrave Macmillan): 3-27.

Lecocq, Baz; Schrijver, Paul, 2007: "The War on Terror in a Haze of Dust: Potholes and Pitfalls on the Saharan Front", in: *Journal of Contemporary African Studies*, 25, 1: 141-166.

Lee, Soo im; Murphy-Shigematsu, Stephen; Befu, Harumi (Eds.), 2006: *Japan's Diversity Dilemmas: Ethnicity, Citizenship, and Education* (Lincoln NE: iUniverse).

Leerkes, Arjen, 2009: *Illegal Residence and Public Safety in the Netherlands* (Amsterdam: Amsterdam University Press).

Lemke, Thomas, 2007: "An Indigestible Meal? Foucault, Governmentality and State Theory", in: *Distinktion: Scandinavian Journal of Social Theory*, No.15: 1-25.

Leonard, Madeleine, 2002: "Working on Your Doorstep: Child Newspaper Deliverers in Belfast", in: *Childhood*, 9, 2: 190-204.

Lesser, Jeffrey (Ed.), 2003: *Searching for Home Abroad: Japanese Brazilians and Transnationalism* (Durham NC: Duke University Press).

Levinson, Amanda, 2005: "The Regularization of Unauthorized Migrants: Literature Survey and Country Case Studies", Centre on Migration, Policy and Society (Oxford: University of Oxford).

Levitt, Peggy; Glick-Schiller, Nina, 2004: "Conceptualizing Simultaneity, A Transnational Social Field Perspective on Society", in: *International Migration Review*, 38, 3: 1002-1039.

Levitt, Peggy; Waters, Mary (Eds.), 2002: *The Changing Face of Home: The Transnational Lives of the Second Generation* (New York: Russell Sage Foundation).

Leyshon, Andrew; Thrift, Nigel, 2008: "The Capitalization of Almost Everything: the Future of Finance and Capitalism", in: *Theory, Culture and Society*, 24, 7-8: 97-115.

Lie, John, 2001: *Multi-Ethnic Japan* (Cambridge MA: Harvard University Press).

Lietaer, Bernard, 1997: "Beyond Greed and Scarcity: a Dialogue with Sarah van Gelder", in: *Yes! A Journal of Positive Futures*, Spring 1997: 34-39.

Lim, Timothy C., 2006: "NGOs, Transnational Migrants, and the Promotion of Rights in South Korea", in: Tsuda, Takeyuki (Ed.): *Local Citizenship in Recent Countries of Immigration: Japan in Comparative Perspective* (Lanham MD: Lexington Books): 235-269.

Limoncelli, Stephanie A., 2009: "The Trouble with Trafficking: Conceptualizing Women's Sexual Labour and Economic Human Rights", in: *Women's Studies International Forum*, 32, 4: 261-269.

Linger, Daniel Touro, 2001: *No One Home: Brazilian Selves Remade in Japan* (Stanford, CA: Stanford University Press).

Lipsky, Micheal, 1980: *Street-level Bureaucracy* (New York: Russel Sage Foundation).

Lipton, Merle, 1986: *Capitalism and Apartheid: South Africa*, 1910-1986 (Totowa N.J: Rowman & Allanheld).

Lisborg, Anders, 1998: *Købte kroppe - Om Prostitutionsrelatert Migration fra Thailand til Danmark*, Working Paper No. 139 (Roskilde: Roskilde Universitetscenter)

Loescher, Gil, 1993: *Beyond Charity: International Cooperation and the Global Refugee Crisis* (Oxford/New York: Oxford University Press).

Lopulalan, Frans, 1985: *Onder de sneeuw een Indisch graf* [Below the Snow an Indies Grave] (Amsterdam: Uitgeverij De Geus).

Loser, Claudio; Lockwood Caitlin; Minson Adam; Balcazar, Lucia, 2006: "The Macro-Economic Impact of Remittances in Latin America: Dutch Disease or Latin Cure?", Paper for presented at Presented at the G-24 Technical Group meeting in Singapore on September 13-14 (Washington, DC: Inter-American Development Bank).

Lucas, Robert E.B., 2005: *International Migration and Economic Development: Lessons from Low-income* (Cheltenham: Edward Elgar).

Lugard, Frederick J.D., 1922: *The Dual Mandate in British Tropical Africa* (Edinburgh: William Blackwood) [a reprint, 1965 (London: Frank Cass)].

Luxemburg, Rosa, 1913/2003: *The Accumulation of Capital* [Schwarzschild, Agnes (Translation)] (London: Routledge).

Lycklama à Nijeholt, Geertje, 1989: "Trade in Maids: Asian Domestic Helpers in Migration Theory and Practice", in: Heyzer, Noleen; Lycklama à Nijeholt, Geertje; Weerakoon, Nedra (Eds): *The Trade in Domestic Helpers: Causes, Mechanisms and Consequences* (Kuala Lumpur: Asian and Pacific Development Centre): 21-59.

Lyons, Lenore; Ford, Michelle, 2007: "Where Internal and International Migration Intersect: Mobility and the Formation of Multi-Ethnic Communities in the Riau Islands Transit Zone", in: *International Journal on Multicultural Studies*, 9, 2: 236-263.

Maas, Maria Wies, 2007: "Fleeing to Europe: Europeanization and the Right to Seek Refugee Status" (MA Thesis, International Institute of Social Studies of Erasmus University Rotterdam in The Hague, Governance and Development Programme).

MacDonald, Euan; Cholewinski, Ryszard, 2007: *The Migrant Workers Convention in Europe - Obstacles to the Ratification of the International Convention on the Rights of All Migrant Workers and Members of their Families: EU/EEA Perspectives* (Paris: United Nations Educational, Scientific and Cultural Organization).

MacDonald, Ian, 1983: *Immigration Law and Practice* (London: Butterworths Law).

MacDonald, Kevin, 2006: *Global Movements: Action and Culture* (Malden MA/Oxford: Blackwell).

MacFarlane, Neil Stephen; Yuen Foong Khong, 2006: *Human Security and the United Nations* (Bloomington IN: Indiana University Press).

Macklin, Audrey, 2003: "Dancing Across Borders: Exotic Dancers, Trafficking and Canadian Immigration Policy", in: *International Migration Review*, 37, 2: 464-500.

Mahbubani, Kishore, 2001: *Can Asians Think? Understanding the Divide Between East and West* (Hanover NH: Steerforth).

Mahbubani, Kishore, 2008: *The New Asian Hemisphere: The Irresistible Shift of Global Power to the East* (New York: Public Affairs).

Mahieu, Vincent, 1995: *The Hunt for the Heart. Selected Tales from the Dutch East Indies* (Kuala Lumpur/Oxford: Oxford University Press).

Makaremi, Chowra; Kobelinsky, Carolina (Ed.), 2008: "Confinement des étrangers: entre circulation et enfermement", in: *Cultures & Conflicts*, 71: 192.

Makkonen, Timo, 2002: *Multiple, Compound and Intersectional Discrimination: Bringing the Experiences of the Most Marginalized to the Fore* (Turku: Institute for Human Rights, bo Akademi University).

Males, Michael, 2009: "Does the Adolescent Brain make Risk Taking Inevitable? A Skeptical Appraisal", in: *Journal of Adolescent Research*, 24,1: 3-20.

Malgesini, Graciela; Ochoa, Javier; Lacomba, Joan; Cloquell, Alexis, 2007: *Guía Básica del Codesarrollo: Qué es y cómo Participar en El* (Madrid: Centro de Investigación y Cooperación para el Desarrollo).

Mamdani, Mahmood, 1996: *Citizen and Subject: Contemporary Africa and the Legacy of Late Colonialism* (Princeton NJ: Princeton University Press).

Mamdani, Mahmood, 2004: *Good Muslim, Bad Muslim: America, the Cold War, and the Roots of Terror* (New York: Pantheon).

Marglin, Stephan A.; Schor, Juliet (Eds.), 1990: *The Golden Age of Capitalism: Reinterpreting the Postwar Experience* (Oxford: Clarendon Press).

Markose, Sheri M., 2003: "Computability and Evolutionary Complexity: Markets as Complex Adaptive Systems (CAS)", in: *The Economic Journal*, 115, 208: 159-192.

Marquina, Antonia; Selim, Mohammed, 2003: *Security Concepts, Institutions and Strategies for Cooperation Partnership and Conflict Prevention in the Mediterranean*. A Discussion Paper, Unidad de Investigación sobre Seguridad y Cooperación (Madrid: University of Madrid).

Martin, Philip, 2002: *Thailand: Improving the Management of Foreign Workers*, Second Edition (Bangkok: International Labour Organisation and International Organisation for Migration).

Martin, Philip, 2004: "Policy Responses to Unauthorized or Irregular Workers", in: *Intereconomics*, 31, 1: 18-20.

Martin, Philip; Miller, Mark, 2000: "Employer Sanctions: French, German and US Experiences", International Migration Papers No. 36 (Geneva: International Labour Organization).

Massey, Douglas S., 1988: "Economic Development and International Migration in Comparative Perspective", in: *Population and Development Review*, 14, 3: 383-413.

Massey, Douglas S.; Arango, Joaquin; Hugo, Graeme; Kouaouci, Ali; Pellegrino, Adela; Taylor, J. Edward, 1998: *Worlds in Motion: Understanding International Migration at the End of the Millennium* (Oxford: Oxford University Press).

Matsukuma, Jun, 2008: *Ningen no Anzenhosho to Kokusaikikou* [Human Security and International Organizations] (Tokyo: Kokusai Shoin).

Mattoo, Aaditya; Carzaniga, Antonia, 2003: *Moving People to Deliver Services* (Washington, DC: Oxford University Press/The World Bank).

Mazrui, Ali, Al'amnin 2007: "Global Apartheid? Race and Religion in the New World Order", in: Das Gupta, Tania; James, Carl E; Maaka, Roger C.A.; Galabuzi Grace-Edward; Andersen, Chris, (Eds): *Race and Racialisation: Essential Readings* (Toronto: Canadian Scholars Press): 95-100.

McCloskey, Donald N., 1994: "How to Do a Rhetorical Analysis and Why", in: Backhouse, R.E. (Ed.): *New Directions in Economic Methodology* (London: Routledge): 319-342.

McDowell, Linda, 1998: "Capital Culture: Gender at Work in the City", in: *American Journal of Sociology*, 104, 3: 960-962.

McDowell, Linda, 1999: *Gender, Identity and Place. Understanding Feminist Geographies* (Cambridge: Polity Press).

McKeown, Adam, 2004: "Global Migration, 1846-1940", in: *Journal of World History*, 15, 2: 155-190.

McKinnon, Ronald Ian, 1973: *Money and Capital in Economic Development* (Washington, DC: Brookings Institution).

McKleever, David; Schultz, Jessica; Swithern, Sofia, 2005: *Foreign Territory: the Internationalization of EU Asylum Policy* (Oxford: Oxfam UK)

McRae, Robert Grant; Hubert, Don (Eds.), 2001: *Human Security and the New Diplomacy: Protecting People, Promoting Peace* (Montreal: McGill-Queens University Press).

Meade, James Edward, 1964: *Efficiency, Equality and the Ownership of Property* (London: Allen & Unwin).

Meillassoux, Claude, 1975: *Femmes, greniers et capitaux* (Paris: François Maspero).

Meissner, Doris M.; Hormats, Robert D.; Walker, Antonio Garrigues; Ogata, S., 1993: *International Migration Challenges in a New Era: Policy Perspectives and Priorities for Europe, Japan, North America and the International Community*, Report No. 44 (New York/Paris/Tokyo: Trilateral Commission).

Melchiorre, Angela, 2004: "At What Age are School-Children Employed, Married and taken to Court?" (London: Right to Education Project).

Mendola, Mariapia, 2006: *Rural Out-migration and Economic Development at Origin: What do We Know?* Working Paper No. 40, Migration Research Programme (Brighton: University of Sussex)

Menjívar, Cecilia, 2006: "Liminal Legality: Salvadoran and Guatemalan Immigrants' Lives in the United States", in: *American Journal of Sociology*, 111, 4: 999-1037.

Merchant, Carolyn, 1980: *The Death of Nature: Women, Ecology, and the Scientific Revolution* (San Francisco CA: Harper).

Merchant, Carolyn, 2003: *Reinventing Eden: The Fate of Nature in Western Culture* (New York: Routledge).

Mernissi, Fátima, 2004: *Les Sindbads Marocains: Voyage dans le Maroc Civique* (Rabat: Editions Marsam).

Meyer, Jean-Batiste; Brown, Mercy, 1999: *Scientific Migrants: A New Approach to the Brain Drain*. Paper for the World Conference on Science, 26 June - 1 July (Budapest: International Council for Science, United Nations Educational, Scientific and Cultural Organization).

Mies, Maria, 1986: *Patriarchy and Accumulation on a World Scale: Women in the International Division of Labour* (London: Zed Books).

Migrant Forum in Asia (MFA), 2007: UN High-Level Dialogue on International Migration and Development: A Report Prepared by Migrant Forum in Asia (Quezon City, Philippines: Migrant Forum in Asia).

Migreurop, 2007: *Guerre aux Migrants: le livre noir de Ceuta et Melilla* (Paris: Editions Syllepse).

Migreurop, 2009: *Europe's murderous borders* (Paris: Editions Syllepse).

Milanovic, Branko, 2005: *Worlds Apart: Measuring International and Global Inequality* (Princeton: Princeton University Press).

Miller, Mark J., 2001: "The Sanctioning of Unauthorized Migration and Alien Employment", in: Kyle, David; Koslowski, Rey (Eds.): *Global Human Smuggling: Comparative Perspectives* (Baltimore MD: The John Hopkins University Press): 318-336.

Mine, Yoichi, 2003: "The Political Economy of Population Change in Japan: Implications for South Africa", in: Alden, Chris; Hirano, Katsumi (Eds.): Japan *and South Africa in a Globalising World: A Distant Mirror* (Aldershot: Ashgate): 239-262.

Ministerie van Binnenlandse Zaken, 1981: *Ontwerp Minderhedennota* [Memorandum on Minorities] (The Hague: Ministry of Internal Affairs).

Ministerie van Sociale Zaken en Werkgelegenheid, 2004: *Werk: Kinder en Jeugdarbeid aan Strenge Regels Gebonden [Work: Child and Youth Labour Strictly Regulated]* (The Hague: Ministry of Social Affairs and Employment).

Mohan, Rakesh, 2008: "Capital Flows to India", *Reserve Bank of India Monthly Bulletin*, No. 2048.

Mohanty, Chandra Talpade, 1997: "Women Workers and Capitalist Scripts: Ideologies of Domination, Common Interests and the Politics of Solidarity", in: Mohanty, Chandra Talpade; Alexander, Jacqui (Eds.): *Feminist Genealogies, Colonial Legacies, Democratic Futures* (London/New York: Routledge): 3-29.

Molemans, Griselda, 2004: *Met vlag en wimpel. Erfgenamen van Indië* [With Flying Colours. Heirs of the Indies] (Utrecht/Antwerpen: Kosmos-Z/K Uitgevers).

Montiel, Antonio, 2007: "Globalización, Subdesarrollo y Responsabilidad Internacional", El Papel de la Cooperación Descentralizada en el Desarrollo Humano Global, La Cooperación Técnica para el Desarrollo (Valencia: Fundación Centro de Estudios Políticos y Sociales).

Moore, Henrietta L., 1988: *Feminism and Anthropology* (Minneapolis MN: University of Minnesota Press).

Moravcsik, Andrew; Nicolaïdis, Kalypso, 1999: "Explaining the Treaty of Amsterdam: Interests, Influence, Institutions", in: *Journal of Common Market Studies*, 37, 1: 59-85.

Mori, Hiromi, 1997: *Immigration Policy and Foreign Workers in Japan* (Basingstoke: Macmillan).

Morris-Suzuki, Tessa, 1998: *Re-Inventing Japan: Time, Space, Nation* (New York: M.E. Sharpe).

Morris-Suzuki, Tessa, 2007a: *Exodus to North Korea: Shadows from Japan's Cold War* (Lanham, MD: Rowman & Littlefield).

Morris-Suzuki, Tessas, 2007b: "Cross-Border Migration and East Asian Regional Integration", in: *International Journal on Multicultural Studies*, 9, 2: 158-173.

Morrow, Raymond, 2008: "Re-thinking Buroway's Public Sociology: A Post-Empiricist Construction", in: Jeffries, Vincent (Ed.): *Handbook of Public Sociology* (Lanham MD: Rowman & Littlefield Publishers, Inc.).

Morrow, Virginia, 1994: "Responsible Children? Aspects of Children's Work and Employment Outside School in Contemporary UK", in: Mayall, Berry (Ed.): *Children's Childhoods: Observed and Experienced* (London/Washington, DC: The Falmer Press): 128-143.

Mpe, Phaswane, 2001: *Welcome to Our Hillbrow* (Pietermaritzburg: University of Natal Press).

Muggah, Robert (Ed.), 2006: *No Refuge: the Crisis of Refugee Militarization in Africa* (London/New York: Zed Books).

Muntarbhorn, Vitit, 2005: *The Mekong Challenge: Employment and Protection of Migrant Workers in Thailand: National Laws/Practices versus International Labour Standards?* (Bangkok: International Labour Organisation).

Mushakoji, Kinhide, 1988: *Global Issues and Interparadigmatic Dialogue: Essays on Multipolar Politics* (Torina: Albert Meynier).

Mushakoji, Kinhide, 1992: "Development and Racism in Asia and the Pacific", in: *IMADR Yearbook*, 4: 15-30.

Mushakoji, Kinhide, 1993: "Post-Modern Cultural Development in East Asia: Beyond the Japanese Version of Confucianism", in: Massini, Eleonora; Atal, Yogesh (Eds.): *The Future of Asian Cultures* (Bangkok: United Nations Educational, Scientific and Cultural Organization, Principal Office for Asia and the Pacific): 57-80.

Mushakoji, Kinhide, 2001: "Engendering the Japanese 'Double Standard' Patriarchal Democracy: The Case of the 'Comfort Women' and Military Sexual Slavery", in: Kelly, Rita Mae; Bayes, Jane H; Hawkesworth Mary E.; Brigitte Young (Eds.): *Gender, Globalization, and Democratization* (Lanham, MD: Rowland and Littlefield): 205-222.

Mushakoji, Kinhide, 2003a: "Social Reproduction of Exclusion: Exploitative Migration and Human Insecurity", in: Bakker, Isabella; Gill, Stephen (Eds.): *Power, Production and Social Reproduction* (Basingstoke: Palgrave): 146-161.

Mushakoji, Kinhide, 2003b: *Ningen Anzenshou Ron Josetsu: Grobaru Fashizumu ni Kouite* [Introduction to Human Security: Facing Global Fascism] (Tokyo: Kokusai Shoin).

Mushakoji, Kinhide, 2004: *Gender Dialectics and the Quest for Ontological Democracy – Social Reproduction and Human (In)security*. Paper for the Fifth Pan-European Conference, ECPR Standing Group on International Relations, 9-11 September, The Hague (Essex: European Consortium for Political Research).

Mushakoji, Kinhide, 2007a: "'Wa' no Sai-kochiku to jinken no Saiki-teki Naihatsu-ka" [The Reconstruction of 'Wa' and the Reflexive Endogenization of Human Rights], in: Miyanaga, Kuniko (Ed.): *Global-Ka to Paradox* [Globalization and Paradox] (Sekai-Shiso-Sha): 107-147.

Mushakoji, Kinhide 2007b: "*Common Human Security and Development Ethics: State and Diaspora Identity in Contemporary Japan*", Paper for the conference on International Migration, Multi-local Livelihoods and Human Security: Perspectives from Europe, Asia and Africa, 30-31 August 2007 (The Hague: International Institute of Social Studies of Erasmus University Rotterdam).

Mushakoji, Kinhide, 2007c: "Note on Migration and Human Security", Project on Human Security and Global Cities (Chubu University, Japan).

Mushakoji, Kinhide; Kamal Pasha, Mustapha (Eds.), 2008: *Human (In)Security in the Networks of Global Cities* (Chubu: Center for Human Security Studies, Chubu University).

Musto, Jennifer Lynne, 2009: "What's in a Name?: Conflations and Contradictions in Contemporary U.S. Discourses of Human Trafficking", in: *Women's Studies International Forum*, 32, 4: 281-287.

Myers, Norman, 2005: "Environmental Refugees: An Emergent Security Issue", 13th Economic Forum, 23-27 May, Session III – Environment and Migration, Organization for Security and Co-operation in Europe (OSCE), Prague, Doc. EF.NGO/4/05.

Nadi, Dalila, 2007: "Installations dans une ville de transit migratoire. Le cas de la ville de Tamanrasset en Algérie", in: Boesen, Elisabeth; Marfaing, Laurence (Eds.): *Les nouveaux urbains dans l'espace Sahara-Sahel. Un cosmo-*

politisme par le bas (Paris: Karthala/Centre of Modern Oriental Studies [Zentrum Moderner Orient]): 279-294.

Nagar, Richa; Lawson, Victoria; McDowell Linda; Hanson, Susan, 2002, in: "Locating Globalization: Feminist (Re)Readings of the Subjects and Spaces of Globalization", 78, 3: 257-84.

Nagel, Thomas, 2005: "The Problem of Global Justice", in: *Philosophy and Public Affairs*, 33, 2: 113-147.

National Conference of State Legislatures (NCLS), 2009: *State Laws Related to Immigrants and Immigration in* 2008 (Revised 27 January 2009) (Washington, DC: Government Printing Office).

Nationaal Instituut voor Budgetvoorlichting (NIBUD), 2005: "Nationaal Scholierenonderzoek 2004/2005" [Dutch National Pupil Survey 2004/2005] (Utrecht: Nationaal Instituut voor Budgetvoorlichting)

Neal, Andrew William, 2009: "Securitization and Risk at the EU Border: The Origins of FRONTEX", in: *Journal of Common Market Studies*, 47, 2: 333-356.

Nederveen Pieterse, Jan, 2004: *Globalization or Empire?* (New York/London: Routledge).

Newman, Edward; Van Selm, Joanne (Eds.), 2003: *Refugees and Forced Displacement: International Security, Human Vulnerability and the State* (New York: United Nations University Press).

Nightingale, Andrea J., 2006: "The Nature of Gender: Work, Gender, and Environment", in: *Environment and Planning D: Society and Space*, 24: 165-185.

Noll, Gregor, 1999: "Rejected Asylum Seekers: The Problem of Return", in: *International Migration*, 37, 1: 267-288.

North, Douglass Cecil, 1990: *Institutions, Institutional Change and Economic Performance* (Cambridge: Cambridge University Press).

North, Douglass Cecil, 1994: "Economic Performance Through Time", in: *American Economic Review*, 84, 3: 359-395.

Nozick, Robert, 1974: *Anarchy, State and Utopia* (New York: Basic Books).

Núñez, Jesús (Ed.), 2004: *Redes Sociales en Marruecos. La Emergencia de la Sociedad Marroquí* (Barcelona: Icaria).

Núñez-Neto, Blas, 2005: *Border Security: The Role of the U.S. Border Patrol*, Report for Congress, 10 May (Washington, DC: Congressional Research Service)

Nussbaum, Martha, 2006: *Frontiers of Justice* (Cambridge MA: Harvard University Press).

Nyamnjoh, Francis B., 2006: *Insiders and Outsiders: Citizenship and Xenophobia in Contemporary Southern Africa* (London: Zed Books).

Nyberg-Sørensen, Ninna; Van Haer, Nicolas; Engberg-Pedersen, Poul, 2002: "The Migration-Development Nexus Evidence and Policy Options State-of-the-Art Overview", in: *International Migration*, 40, 5: 3-47.

Nyers, Peter, 2003: "Abject Cosmopolitanism: The Politics of Protection in the Anti-Deportation Movement", in: *Third World Quarterly*, 24, 6: 1069-1093.

O'Brien, Gerald V., 2003: "Indigestible Food, Conquering Hordes, and Waste Materials: Metaphors of Immigrants and the Early Immigration Restriction Debate in the United States", in: *Metaphor and Symbols*, 18, 1: 33-47.

Obdeijn, Herman; Schrover, Marlou, 2008: *Komen en gaan. Immigratie en emigratie in Nederland vanaf* 1550 [Arriving and Leaving. Immigration and Emigration in the Netherlands since 1550] (Amsterdam: Bert Bakker).

Ochiai, Eiji, 1974: *Ajiajin Rodosha Yunyu* [Import of Asian Labor in Japan] (Tokyo: Gendaihyoronsha Publishers).

O'Connell Davidson, Julia, 2005: *Children in the Global Sex Trade* (Cambridge/Malden, MA: Polity Press).

Odysseos, Louiza, 2002: "Dangerous Ontologies: The Ethos of Survival and Ethical Theorizing in International Relations", in: *Review of International Studies*, 28: 403-418.

Oestergaard-Nielsen, Eva, 2002: "Working for a Solution through Europe: Kurdish Political Lobbying in Germany", in: Al-Ali, Nadje; Koser, Khalid (Eds.): *New Approaches to Migration? Transnational Communities and the Transformation of Home* (London: Routledge): 186-201.

Oishi, Nana, 2005: *Women in Motion: Globalization, State Policies, and Labor Migration in Asia* (Stanford CA: Stanford University Press).

Okojie, Christiana E. E.; Okojie, Obehi; Eghafona, Kokunre; Vincent-Osaghae, Gloria; Kalu, Victoria, 2003: *Trafficking of Nigerian Girls to Italy: Report of Field Survey in Edo State, Nigeria* (Torino: United Nations Interregional Crime and Justice Research Institute).

Olesen, Thomas, 2005: *International Zapatismo: The Construction of Solidarity in the Age of Globalization* (London/New York: Zed Books).

Olsen, Johan, 2002: "The Many Faces of Europeanization", in: *Journal of Common Market Studies*, 40, 5: 921-952.

Onuki, Hironori, 2009: "Care, Social (Re)production and Global Labour Migration: Japan's 'Special Gift' toward 'Innately Gifted' Filipino Workers", in: *New Political Economy*, 14, 4: 489-516.

Ostrom, Ellinor, 1990: *Governing the Commons: The Evolution of Institutions of Collective Action* (Cambridge: Cambridge University Press).

Oumarou, Hamani, 2008: "Le rôle des ressortissants et des migrants à Bambey face à la crise", in: *Afrique contemporaine*, 225: 199-216.

Outshoorn, Joyce (Ed.), 2004: *The Politics of Prostitution: Women's Movements, Democratic States and the Globalisation of Sex Commerce* (Cambridge: Cambridge University Press).

Özden, Çaglar, 2006: "Educated Migrants: Is There Brain Waste?", in: Özden, Çaglar; Schiff, Maurice (Eds.): *International Migration, Remittances and the Brain Drain* (Washington, DC: World Bank/Palgrave Macmillan): 227-244.

Özden, Çaglar; Schiff, Maurice (Eds.), 2006a: "Overview", in: Özden, Çaglar; Schiff, Maurice (Eds.): *International*

Migration, Remittances and the Brain Drain (Washington, DC: World Bank/Palgrave Macmillan): 1-17.

Özden, Çaglar; Schiff, Maurice (Eds.), 2006b: *International Migration, Remittances and the Brain Drain* (Washington, DC: World Bank/Palgrave Macmillan).

Paitoonpong, Srawooth; Plywej, Jailin; Sirikul, Weerawan, 2002: "Migrant Housemaids in Thailand: A Case Study" in: *Thailand Development Research Institute Quarterly Review* (Spring): 21-28.

Palley, Thomas I., 2004: "The Economic Case for International Labour Standards", in: *Cambridge Journal of Economics*, 28: 21-36.

Palriwala, Rani; Uberoi, Patricia (Eds.), 2008: *Marriage, Migration and Gender* (New Delhi/ Thousand Oaks/ London/Singapore: Sage Publications Pvt. Ltd).

Pang, Ching Lin; Ghrib, Assia; Pollmann, Uwe; Markova, Evgenia; Vicari, Annalisa; Venicz, Elizabeth; Mestre, Ruth Maria, 2002: *Trafficking in Unaccompanied Minors in the European Union: Belgium, France, Greece, Italy, The Netherlands, Spain* (Geneva: International Organization for Migration).

Paranjape, Suhas; Joy, K. J., 2006: "Alternative Restructuring of the Sardar Sarovar: Breaking the Deadlock", in: *Economic and Political Weekly*, 41,7 (18 February): 601-602.

Pardo, Italo, 1995: "Morals of Legitimacy in Naples: Streetwise about Legality, Semi-legality and Crime", in: *Archives Européennes de Sociologie*, 36: 44-71.

Parreñas, Rhacel Salazar, 2000: "Migrant Filipina Domestic Workers and the International Division of Reproductive Labour", in: *Gender and Society*, 14, 4: 560-581.

Parreñas, Rhacel Salazar, 2001: *Servants of Globalization: Women, Migration, and Domestic Work* (Stanford CA: Stanford University Press).

Parreñas, Rhacel Salazar, 2002: "The Care Crisis in the Philippines: Children and Transnational Families in the New Global Economy", in: Enhrenreich, Barbara; Hochschild, Arlie Russell (Eds.): *Global Woman- Nannies, Maids and Sex Workers in the New Economy* (London: Granta Books): 39-54.

Passas, Nikos, 2003: "Hawala and Other Informal Value Transfer Systems: How to Regulate Them?", in: *Risk Management*, 5, 2 (Special Issue: *Regulation, Risk and Corporate Crime in a Globalised Era*): 49-59.

Passas, Nikos, 2004: "*Informal Value Transfer Systems [IVTS] and their Mechanics*", Paper presented at Asia-Pacific Economic Cooperation Symposium on Alternative Remittances Systems: Shaping the Remittances Market by shifting to Formal Systems, 3-4 June 2004 (Tokyo: Asian Development Bank Institute).

Passel, Jeffrey, 2003: *Mexican Immigration: A U.S. Perspective* (Washington, DC: Immigration Studies Program, The Urban Institute).

Passel, Jeffrey; D'Vera, Cohn, 2009: *Mexican Immigrants: How Many Come? How Many Leave?* (Washington, DC: Pew Hispanic Center).

Pearson, Elaine, 2002: *Human Traffic Human Rights: Redefining Victim Protection* (London: Anti-Slavery International).

Perera, Nadya Bhimani L., 2009: "Weighing the Options: The gendered representation of care in Sri Lanka and its impact on female agency in migration for work" (MA Thesis, International Institute of Social Studies of Erasmus University Rotterdam in The Hague, Poverty and Development Programme).

Pérez, Nancy Garcia, 2005: "Cruces en la frontera: Migración indocumentada y muertes en la frontera norte México-Estados Unidos", in: Memorias del Seminario Internacional sobre los Derechos Humanos de los Migrantes (México DF: Meéxico-Comisión Europea): 145-168.

Perrin, Delphine, 2009: "Immigration et création juridique au Maghreb. La fragmentation des mondes et des droits", in: Bensaâd, Ali (Ed.): *Le Maghreb à l'épreuve des migrations subsahariennes. Immigration sur émigration* (Paris: Karthala): 245-265.

Peterson, V. Spike, 1996: "The Politics of Identity in the Context of Globalization", in: *Women's Studies International Forum*, 19, 1-2: 5-15.

Peterson, V. Spike, 2003: *A Critical Rewriting of Global Political Economy: Integrating Reproductive, Productive and Virtual Economies* (New York: Routledge).

Phillips, Matthew W., 1998: "Gendered Work: an Analysis of Work in a Fijian Garment Factory", in: *Australian Geographer*, 29: 341-355.

Phizacklea, Annie (Ed.), 1983: *One Way Ticket: Migration and Female Labour* (London: Routledge & Kegan Paul).

Phongpaichit, Pasuk, 1983: *From Peasant Girls to Bangkok Masseuses* (Geneva: International Labour Organization).

Pineault, Éric, 2001: *Finance Capital and the Institutional Foundations of Capitalist Finance: Theoretical Elements from Marx to Minsky*, a Working Paper, Recherche du Canada en Mondialisation, Citoyenneté et Deĭmocratie (MCD). (Montréal: Université du Québec).

Piper, Nicola, 2008: "The 'Migration-Development Nexus' Revisited from a Rights Perspective"', in: *Journal of Human Rights*, 7, 3: 282-298.

Plant, Raymond, 2004: "Neo-liberalism and the Theory of the State: From *Wohlfahrstaat* to *Rechtstaat*", in: *The Political Quarterly*, 75, 1, Supplement: 24-37.

Pliez, Olivier, 2003: *Villes du Sahara. Urbanisation et urbanité dans le Fezzan libyen* (Paris: Centre Nationale des Recherches Scientifiques): 199.

Pliez, Olivier, 2004: "De l'immigration au transit? La Libye dans l'espace migratoire euro-africain", in: Pliez, Olivier (Ed.): *La nouvelle Libye. Sociétés, espaces et géopolitique au lendemain de l'embargo* (Paris: Karthala/Institut de Recherches et d'Etudes sur le Monde Arabe et Musulman): 138-155.

Pluymen, Manon; Minderhoud, Paul, 2002: "Access to Public Services as an Instrument of Migration Policy in the Netherlands", in: *Immigration, Asylum and Nationality Law*, 16, 4: 208-223.

Pogge, Thomas, 2005: "Recognised and Violated by International Law: the Human Rights of the Global Poor", in: *Leiden Journal of International Law,* 18, 4: 717-745.

Pollack, Mark A, 2004: "The New Institutionalism and European Integration", in: Wiener, Antje; Diez, Thomas (Eds.): *European Integration Theory* (Oxford/New York: Oxford University Press): 137-156.

Pollack, Mark A., 2005: "Theorizing EU Policy Making", in: Wallace, Helen; Wallace, William; Pollack, Mark A. (Eds.): *Policy-Making in the European Union* (Oxford: Oxford University Press): 13-48.

Pollard, Sidney, 1985: "Capital Exports, 1870-1914: Harmful or Beneficial?", in: *Economic History Review,* 2nd Series, 38, 4: 489-514.

Pollmann, Tessel; Seleky, Juan; Nienhuis, Bert, 1982: *Terug op de Molukken* [Back in the Moluccas] (Amsterdam: De Arbeiderspers).

Pollock, Jackie, 2007: *Collateral Damage: The Impact of Anti-Trafficking Policies on Human Rights of Migrant and Trafficked Persons* (Bangkok: Global Alliance Against Traffic in Women).

Portes, Alejandro, 1995: "Children of Immigrants: Segmented Assimilation and its Determinants", in: *The Economic Sociology of Immigration* (New York: Russell Sage Foundation): 248-279.

Portes, Alejandro, 2008: "Migration and Development: a Conceptual Review of Evidence", in: Castles, Stephen; Wise, Raùl Delgado (Eds.): *Migration and Development: Perspectives from the South* (Geneva: International Organization for Migration): 17-41.

Portes, Alejandro; Haller, William, 2005: "The Informal Economy", in: Smelser, Niel; Swedberg, Richard (Eds.): *Handbook of Economic Sociology* (New York: Russell Sage Foundation).

Portes, Alejandro; Rimbout, Rubén G., 1996: *Immigrant America* (2nd edition) (Berkeley/Los Angeles: University of California Press).

Posel, Deborah, 1991: *The Making of Apartheid 1948-1961: Conflict and Compromise* (Oxford: Clarendon Press).

Post, Dorothee; Niemann, Arne, 2007: "The Europeanisation of German Asylum Policy and the 'Germanisation' of European Asylum Policy: the Case of the 'Safe Third Country' Concept", Paper for the Conference of the European Union Studies Association, Montréal, Canada, 17-19 May (Pittsburgh PA: University Center for International Studies, University of Pittsburgh).

Poulin, Richard, 2003: "Globalization and the Sex Trade: Trafficking and the Commodification of Women and Children", in: *Canadian Women's Studies (Le Cahiers de Femme),* 22, 3-4: 38-43.

Pratt, Geraldine, 1997: "Stereotypes and Ambivalence: the Construction of Domestic Workers in Vancouver, British Columbia", in: *Gender, Place and Culture,* 4, 2: 159-78

Pratt, Geraldine, 1999: "From Registered Nurse to Registered Nanny: Discursive Geographies of Filipina Domestic Workers in Vancouver, BC", in: *Economic Geography,* 75: 215-236.

Punch, Samantha, 2002: "Youth Transitions and Interdependent Adult-Child Relations in Rural Bolivia", in: *Journal of Rural Studies,* 18,2: 123-133.

Raes, Stephan; Rath, Jan; Dreef, Marja; Kumcu, Adem; Reil, Flavia; Zorlu, Aslan, 2002: "Stitched Up: The Rise and Fall of the Turkish Garment Industry in Amsterdam", in: Rath, Jan. (Ed.): *Unravelling the Rag Trade: Immigrant Entrepreneurship in Seven World Cities* (Oxford: Berg Publishers): 89-112.

Raghuram, Parvati, 2009: "Which Migration, What Development? Unsettling the Edifice of Migration and Development", in: *Population, Space and Place,* 15, 2: 103-117.

Ramón, Consuelo, 2005: "La Política de Codesarrollo en la Unión Europea: ¿Hacia una Inflexión Significativa?", in: Abad, Luis V.; Aragall, Xavier; Aubarell, Gemma; Galán, Manuel Gómez; Joan, Lacomba; Íñigo Moré; Moreno, Luisa; Chorne, Consuelo Ramón (Eds): *Codesarrollo: Migraciones y Desarrollo Mundial* (Madrid: Centro de Investigación y Cooperación para el Desarrollo): 47-68.

Rao, Brinda, 1991: "Dominant Constructions of Women and Nature in Social Science Literature", Environmental Studies/Capitalism, Nature and Socialism, Pamphlet 2 (Santa Cruz CA: Center for Political Ecology).

Ravenstein, Ernest George, 1885: "The Laws of Migration", in: *Journal of the Statistical Society,* 46: 167-235.

Ravenstein, Ernest George, 1889: "The Laws of Migration: Second Paper", in: *Journal of the Royal Statistical Society,* 52: 241-305.

Rawls, John, 1971/1999: *The Theory of Justice,* revised edition (Cambridge, MA: Harvard University Press).

Rawls, John, 1974: "Reply to Alexander and Musgrave", in: *The Quarterly Journal of Economics,* 88, 4: 633-655.

Rawls, John, 1987/1999: "Preface for the French Edition of The Theory of Justice", in: Freeman, Samuel (Ed.): *John Rawls: Collected Papers* (Cambridge MA: Harvard University Press): 415-420.

Rawls, John, 1993: *Political Liberalism* (New York: Columbia University Press).

Rawls, John, 1999: *The Law of Peoples* (Cambridge MA: Harvard University Press).

Razavi, Shara, 2007: "The Political and Social Economy of Care in a Development Context Conceptual Issues, Research Questions and Policy Options", Gender and Development Programme Paper No. 3 (Geneva: United Nations Research Institute for Social Development).

Rein, Martin; Schön, Donald, 1977: "Problem-Setting in Policy Research", in: Weiss, Carol (Ed.): *Using Social Research in Policy-Making* (Lexington MA: Lexington Books): 235-251.

Rein, Martin; Schön, Donald, 1994: *Frame Reflection: Toward the Resolution of Intractable Policy Controversies* (New York: Basic Books).

Retaillé, Denis, 1986: "Le Kawar, problème géographique", in: *Cahiers géographiques de Rouen,* 26: 37-60.

Richmond, Anthony, 1994: *Global Apartheid: Refugees, Racism and the New World Order* (Oxford/New York/ Toronto: Oxford University Press).

Ricoy, Carlos, 1998: "Cumulative Causation", in: Kurz, Heinz D.; Salvadori, Neri (Eds.): *The Elgar Companion to Classical Economics A-K* (Cheltenham: Edward Elgar): 202-208.

Rijpma, Jorrit; Cremona, Marise, 2007: "The Extra-Territorialisation of EU Migration Policies and the Rule of Law", Working Papers Law No. 2007/01 (Brussels: European University Institute).

Rinsampessy, Djodjie, 2008: "Veranderen doe ik zelf" [Changing I do myself], in: Elias Rinsampessy (Ed.): *Tussen adat en integratie. Vijf generaties Molukkers worstelen en dansen op de Nederlandse Aarde* [Between Adat and Integration. Five Generations of Moluccans are Wrestling and Dancing on Dutch Soil] (Nijmegen: Stichting Muhabbat): 109-126.

Rinsampessy, Elias (Ed.), 2008: *Tussen adat en integratie. Vijf generaties Molukkers worstelen en dansen op de Nederlandse aarde* [Between Adat and Integration. Five Generations of Moluccans are Wrestling and Dancing on Dutch Soil] (Nijmegen: Stichting Muhabbat).

Risse, Thomas, 2004: "Social Constructivism and European Integration", in: Wiener, Antje; Diez, Thomas (Eds.): *European Integration Theory* (Oxford/New York: Oxford University Press): 159-175.

Risseeuw, Carla, 1989: *The Fish Don't Talk About the Water: Gender Transformation Power and Resistance Among Women in Sri Lanka* (Leiden/New York: Brill Academic Publishers).

Roach, Sister Marie Simone, 1987: *The Human Act of Caring: A Blueprint for the Health Professions* (Ottawa: Canadian Hospital Association Press).

Robin, Sophie; Barros, Lucile, 2000: "Review and Evaluation of the Measures Implemented", in: *Combating the Illegal Employment of Foreign Workers* (Paris: Organization for Economic Co-operation and Development): 81-100.

Robison, Richard, 2009: "Strange Bedfellows: Political Alliances in the Making of Neo-liberal Governance", in: Hout, Wil; Robison, Richard (Eds.): *Governance and the Depoliticisation of Development* (London: Routledge): 15-28.

Roces, Mina, 2009: "Prostitution, Women's Movements and the Victim Narrative in the Philippines", in: *Women's Studies International Forum*, 32, 4: 270-280.

Rodier, Claire, 2009: "Externalisation des frontières au sud de l'Europe. L'alliance Union européenne-Libye", in: Bensaâd, Ali (Ed.): *Le Maghreb à l'épreuve des migrations subsahariennes. Immigration sur émigration* (Paris: Karthala): 343-362.

Romaniszyn, Krystyna, 1996: "The Invisible Community: Undocumented Polish Workers in Athens", in: *New Community*, 22, 2: 321-334.

Roque, Maria-Àngels, 2003: *La Sociedad Civil en Marruecos. La Emergencia de Nuevos Actores* (Barcelona: Icaria).

Roth, Joshua Hotaka, 2002: *Brokered Homeland: Japanese Brazilian Migrants in Japan* (Ithaca: Cornell University Press).

Rother, Stefan, 2009a: "'Inside-Outside' or 'Outsiders by Choice'? Civil Society Strategies towards the 2nd Global Forum on Migration and Development in Manila", in: *Asien Aktuell*, 111 (April): 95-107.

Rother, Stefan, 2009b: "The Allure of Non-Binding Talks", in: *Development and Cooperation*, 36, 9: 331-333.

Rowthorn, Robert, Eric, 1995: "Capital Formation and Unemployment", in: *Oxford Review of Economic Policy*, 11, 1: 26-39.

Rowthorn, Robert, Eric, 2008: "The Fiscal Impact of Immigration on the Advanced Economies", *Oxford Review of Economic Policy*, 24, 3: 561-581

Roy, Arundhati, 2004: "Confronting Empire", in: Sen, Jai; Anand, Anita; Escobar, Arturo; Waterman, Peter (Eds.): *World Social Forum: Challenging Empires* (New Delhi: Viveka Foundation): 51-54.

Ruiz, Olivia, 2003: *La migración centroamericana en la frontera sur: Un perfil del riesgo en la migración indocumentada internacional* (Tijuana: El Colegio de la Frontera Norte).

Rupert, Mark; Solomon, Scott M., 2005: *Globalization and International Political Economy: The Politics of Alternative Futures* (Lanham, MD: Rowman & Littlefield).

Rusinovic, Katja; van der Leun, Joanne; Chessa, Weltevrede A.; Engbersen, Godfried; Vos, Jan, 2002: *Nieuwe vangnetten in de samenleving over problemen en dilemma's in de opvang van kwetsbare groepen* (Rotterdam: Erasmus Universiteit/RISBO).

Ryan, William (1971) *Blaming the Victim* (New York: Pantheon Books).

Sachs, Jeffrey David; McArthur, John W., 2005: "The Millennium Project: A Plan for Meeting the Millennium Development Goals", in: *Lancet*, 365, 9456: 347-353.

Saith, Ashawani, 1991: "Absorbing External Shocks: The Gulf Crisis, International Migration Linkages and the Indian Economy", Working Paper Series No. 107 (The Hague: International Institute of Social Studies of Erasmus University Rotterdam).

Saith, Ashwani, 2001: "Emigration Pressures and Structural Change: Case Study of the Philippines", International Migration Paper No. 19, Employment and Training Department (Geneva: International Labour Organization).

Sakanaka, Hidenori, 1989: *Kongo no Shutsunyukoku Gyosei no Arikata nitsuite* [Japanese Immigration Control Policy in the Future] (Tokyo: Nihon-kajo Shuppan Publisher).

Sakanaka, Hidenori, 2005: *Nyukan Senki* [Immigration Battle Diary] (Tokyo: Kodansha).

Sakata, Takashi (Ed.), 2007: *Shin Kyoiku-Kihon-Ho: Zenbun to Kaisetsu* [The New Basic-Law on Education: Full Text and Commentary] (Kyoiku Kaihatsu Kenkyu-Jo).

Sakuma, Takamasa, 2006: *Gaikokujin no Kodomo no Fushuugaku: Ibunka ni Hirakareta Kyouiku towa* [Out-of-School Foreign Children; What is Education Open to Different Culture?] (Tokyo: Keiso Shobou).

Samaddar, Ranabir, 1999: *The Marginal Nation. Transborder Migration from Bangladesh to West Bengal* (New Delhi: Sage Publications).

Samers, Micheal, 2004: "The 'Underground Economy', Immigration and Economic Development in the European Union: An Agnostic-sceptic Perspective", in: *International Journal of Economic Development*, 6, 2: 199-272.

Sasikumar S. K.; Hussain, Zakir, 2007: "Migration, Remittances and Development: Lessons from India", Research Studies No 083/2007 (New Delhi: V. V. Giri National Labour Institute, Ministry of Labour and Employment).

Sassen, Saskia, 1991: *The Global City: New York, London, Tokyo* (Princeton NJ: Princeton University Press).

Sassen, Saskia, 2004: "Local Actors in Global Politics", in: *Current Sociology*, 52,4: 649-670.

Saunders, Penelope; Soderlund, Gretchen, 2003: "Threat or Opportunity? Sexuality, Gender and the Ebb and Flow of Trafficking as Discourse", in: *Canadian Woman Studies (Le Cahiers de Femme)*, 22, 3-4: 16-24.

Schaffer, Kay; Smith, Sidonie, 2004: *Human Rights and Narrated Lives: The Ethics of Recognition* (London/New York: Palgrave).

Scheele, Judith, in press: "Tribus, États et fraude: la région frontalière algéro-malienne", in: *Études Rurales*, 183, special issue *La tribu dans le monde contemporain: pastoralisme nomade, État national et globalisation.*

Schiff, Maurice, 2006: "Brain Gain: Claims about its Size and Impact are Greatly Exaggerated", in: Özden, Çaglar; Schiff, Maurice. (Eds.), *International Migration, Remittances and the Brain Drain* (Washington, DC: World Bank/Palgrave Macmillan): 201-225.

Schinkel, Willem (Ed.), 2009: *Globalization & the State of the State* (Houndmills: Palgrave MacMillan).

Schinkel, Willem, 2005: *Aspects of Violence* (Rotterdam: University of Rotterdam).

Schmitter, Philippe C., 2004: "Neo-functionalism", in: Wiener, Antje; Diez, Thomas (Eds.): *European Integration Theory* (Oxford/New York: Oxford University Press): 45-74.

Schön, Donald; Rein, Martin, 1979: "Generative Metaphor: A Perspective on Problem-Setting in Social Policy", in: Ortony, Andrew (Ed.): *Metaphor and Thought* (Cambridge: Cambridge University Press): 254-283.

Schrover, Marlou; van der Leun, Joanne; Lucassen, Leo; Quispel, Chris (Eds.), 2008: *Illegal Migration and Gender in a Global and Historical Perspective* (Amsterdam: Amsterdam University Press Series).

Schumpeter, Joseph Alois, 1942: *Capitalism, Socialism and Democracy* (London: Allen & Unwin).

Schuster, Liza, 2005: "The Realities of a New Asylum Paradigm", Working Paper No. 20, Centre on Migration, Policy and Society (Oxford: University of Oxford).

Scott, James, 1985: *Weapons of the Weak: Everyday Forms of Peasant Resistance*. (New Haven CT: Yale University Press).

Scott, James, 1998: *Seeing like a State: How Certain Schemes to Improve the Human Condition have Failed* (New Haven CT: Yale University Press).

Secor, Anna J., 2003: "Belaboring Gender: the Spatial Practice of Work and the Politics of 'Making Do'", in: *Environment and Planning A*, 35, 12: 2209-2227.

Seekings, Jeremy; Nattrass, Nicoli, 2005: *Class, Race, and Inequality in South Africa* (New Haven CT/London: Yale University Press).

Seglow, Jonathan, 2005: "The Ethics of Immigration", in: *Political Studies Review*, 3: 317-334.

Seidman, Ann, 1985: *The Roots of Crisis in Southern Africa* (Trenton NJ: Africa World Press).

Seidman, Ann; Seidman Makgetla, Neva, 1980: *Outposts of Monopoly Capitalism: Southern Africa in the Changing Global Economy* (London: Zed Books).

Sellek, Yoko, 2001: *Migrant Labour in Japan* (Basingstoke: Palgrave).

Sen, Amartya, 2002: "Open and Closed Impartiality", in: *The Journal of Philosophy*, XCIX, 9 (September): 445-469.

Sen, Amartya, 2004: "Elements of a Theory of Human Rights", in: *Philosophy and Public Affairs*, 32, 4: 315-356.

Sen, Amartya, 2006: *Identity and Violence: The Illusion of Destiny* (London: Allen Lane).

Sen, Gita, 1996: "Gender, Markets and States: a Selective Review and Research Agenda", in: *World Development*, 24, 5: 821-829.

Sen, Samita, 1996: "Unsettling the Household: Act VI (of 1901) and the Regulation of Women Migrants in Colonial Bengal", in: *International Review of Social History*, 41, 135-156.

Sereny, Gita, 2003: "The Racism Within", in: Owen, Nicholas J. (Ed.): *Human Rights, Human Wrongs: the Oxford Amnesty Lectures* 2001 (Oxford/New York: Oxford University Press): 228-249.

Seshu, Meena; Bandhopadhyay, Nandinee, 2009: "How the Development Industry Imagines Sex Work", in: *Development*, 52, 1: 13-17.

Sharma, Nandita, 2003: "Travel Agency: A Critique of Anti-trafficking Campaigns", in: *Refuge*, 21,3: 53-65.

Shaw, Edward S., 1973: *Financial Deepening in Economic Development* (New York: Oxford University Press).

Sheffer, Gabriel (Ed.), 1986: *Modern Migrants in International Politics* (Kent: Croom Helm).

Shuto, Motoko, 2006: "Labour Migration and Human Security in East and Southeast Asia", in: Kleinschmidt, Harald (Ed.): *Migration, Regional Integration and Human Security: the Formation and Maintenance of Transnational Spaces* (Aldershot: Ashgate): 205-224.

Sidhu, Ravinder, 2006: *Universities and Globalization. To Market, To Market* (London: Lawrence Erlbaum Associates Publishers).

Silvey, Rachel, 2006: "Geographies of Gender and Migration: Spatializing Social Difference", in: *International Migration Review*, 40, 1: 64-81.

Simien, Evelyn M., 2007: "Doing Intersectionality Research: From Conceptual Issues to Practical Examples", in: *Politics & Gender*, 3, 2: 264-271.

Simkins, Charles, 1981: "Agricultural Production in the African Reserves of South Africa, 1918-1969", in: *Journal of Southern African Studies*, 7, 2: 256-283.

Simmel, Georg, 1950: *The Sociology of Georg Simmel* [Kurt Wolff, editor] (New York: Free Press).

Siracusa, Christina; Acacio, Kristel, 2004: "State Migrant-Exporting Schemes and their Implications for Rise in Illicit Migration: A Comparison of Spain and the Philippines", in: *Journal of International Migration and Integration*, 5, 3: 321-342.

Skilbrei, May-Len; Tveit, Marianne, 2007: *Facing Return: Perceptions of Repatriation among Nigerian Women in Prostitution in Norway* (Oslo: Fafo).

Skilbrei, May-Len; Tveit, Marianne, 2008: "Defining Trafficking Through Empirical Work. Blurred Boundaries and their Consequences", in: *Gender, Technology and Development*, 12,1: 9-30.

Skilbrei, May-Len; Tveit, Marianne; Brunovskis, Anette, 2006: *Afrikanske drømmer på europeiske gater. Nigerianske kvinner i prostitusjon i Norge* [African Dreams in European Streets: Nigerian Women in Prostitution in Norway] (Olso: Fafo).

Sklar, Holly (Ed.), 1980: *Trilateralism: the Trilateral Commission and Elite Planning for World Management* (Cambridge MA: South End Press).

Skogseth, Geir, 2006: Trafficking in Women - Fact-finding Trip to Nigeria (Abudja, Lagos and Benin City) 12-26 March 2006 (Oslo: Landinfo Norway)

Skrobanek, Siriporn; Boonpakdi, Nattaya; Janthakeero, Chutima, 1997: *The Traffic in Women: Human Realities of the International Sex Trade* (London/New York: Zed Books).

Sleegers, Fleur, 2007: *In Debat over Nederland: Veranderingen in het discours over de multiculturele samenleving en nationale identiteit* [Debate on the Netherlands. Changes in the Discourse on the Multicultural Society and National Identity] (Den Haag/Amsterdam: Wetenschappelijke Raad voor het Regeringsbeleid/Amsterdam University Press).

Smeets, Henk; Steijlen, Fridus, 2006: *In Nederland gebleven. De geschiedenis van Molukkers* 1951-2006 (Forced stay in the Netherlands. The History of the Moluccans 1951-2006) (Amsterdam/Utrecht: Bert Bakker/Moluks Historisch Museum).

Smelser, Neil J.; Swedberg, Richard, 1994: *The Handbook of economic Sociology* 2nd edition (Princeton NJ/Oxford: Princeton University Press): 403-425.

Smith, Andreas, 2003: "Europe's Invisible Migrants", in: Smith, Andreas (Ed.): *Europe's Invisible Migrants* (Amsterdam: Amsterdam University Press): 9-31.

Smith, Brian Clive, 2007: *Good Governance and Development* (New York: Palgrave Macmillan).

Smith, Lothar, 2007: *Tied to Migrants: Transnational Influences on the Economy of Accra, Ghana* (Leiden: Africa Studies Centre).

Smith, Michael Peter; Guarnizo, Luis Eduardo (Eds.), 1998: *Transnationalism from Below Comparative Urban and Community Research*, V 6. (New Brunswick NJ: Transaction Publishers).

Smith, Paul T., 1999: "Coastal Shrimp Aquaculture in Thailand: Key Issues for Research", in: *ACIAR Technical Reports*, 131 (Canberra: Australian Centre for International Agricultural Research).

Sousas Santos, Boaventura, 2007: "Beyond Abyssal Thinking: From Global Lines to Ecologies of Knowledge", in: *Review*, 30, 1: 45-90.

Soysal, Yasemin Nuhoglu, 1994: *Limits of Citizenship: Migrant and Postnational Membership in Europe* (Chicago: University of Chicago Press).

Spaan, Ernst; van Naerssen, Ton; Hillmann, Felicitas, 2005: "Shifts in the European Discourses on Migration and Development", in: *Asian and Pacific Migration Journal*, 14, 1-2: 35-69.

Spencer, Sarah, 2003: "Introduction", in: *The Political Quarterly*, 74, 1, Supplement: 1-24.

Spener, David, 2008: "Global Apartheid, *Coyotaje* and the Discourse of Clandestine Migration: Distinctions between Personal, Structural and Cultural Violence", in: *Migracio y Desarrollo* (First Semester): 115-40.

Spiga, Sassia, 2005: "Aménageurs et migrants dans les villes du Grand Sud Algérien", in: *Autrepart*, 36: 81-103.

Spivak, Gayatri Chakravorty, 2005: "Scattered Speculations on the Subaltern and the Popular", in: *Postcolonial Studies*, 8, 4: 475-486.

SPPNA, 2005: Report to Heads of State (Washington, DC: Security and Prosperity Partnership of NorthAmerica).

Srivastava, Ravi, 2006: "Worker Mobility and Poverty in India: Trends in the 1990s", in: John, Mary E.; Jha, Praveen Kumar; Jodhka, Surinder S. (Eds.): *Contested Transformations: Changing Economies and Identities in Contemporary India* (New Delhi: Tulika): 183-199.

Stalford, Helen, 2000a: "The Citizenship Status of Children in the European Union", in: *The International Journal of Children's Rights*, 8,2: 101-131.

Stalford, Helen, 2000b: "The Developing European Agenda on Children's Rights", in: *Journal of Social Welfare and Family Law (European Section)*, 22, 2: 229-236.

Stalford, Helen; Drywood, Eleanor, 2009: "Coming of Age? Children's Rights in the European Union", in: *Common Market Law Review*, 46,1: 143-172.

Staring, Richard, 1998: "Scenes from a Fake Marriage: Notes on the Flip-side of Embeddedness", in: Koser, Kalid; Lutz, Helma (Eds.): *The New Migration in Eu-*

rope: Social Constructions and Social Realities (London: MacMillan Press Ltd): 224-241.

Statistics South Africa, 2004: Census 2001: *Primary Tables South Africa, Census '96 and 2001 Compared* (Pretoria: Statistics South Africa).

Statistics South Africa, 2006: *Migration and Urbanisation in South Africa* (Pretoria: Statistics South Africa).

Steijlen, Fridus, 2004: "Molukkers in Nederland: geschiedenis van een transnationale relatie" [Moluccans in the Netherlands: a History of a Transnational Relation], in: *Migrantenstudies*, 20, 4: 238-251.

Stewart, Frances, 2002: "Horizontal Inequalities as a Source of Conflict", in: Osler, Fen Hamspon; Malone, David. (Eds.): *From Conflict Reaction to Conflict Prevention: Opportunities for the UN System* (Boulder, CO: Lynne Rienner): 105-136.

Stiglitz, Joseph Eugene, 2000: "Capital Market Liberalization, Economic Growth, and Instability", in: *World Development*, 28, 6: 1075-1086.

Stiglitz, Joseph Eugene 2007: Making Globalization Work (expanded edition) (New York: W.W. Norton).

Stiglitz, Joseph Eugene; Weiss, Andrew, 1981: "Credit Rationing in Markets with Imperfect Information", in: *American Economic Review*, 71, 3: 393-410.

Stockhammer, Engelbert, 2004: "Financialisation and the Slowdown of Accumulation" in: *Cambridge Journal of Economics*, 28: 719-741.

Strathern, Marilyn, 1988: *The Gender of the Gift: Problems with Women and Problems with Money in Melanesia* (Los Angeles: University Press of California).

Subramanian, Arvind, 2005: "The Globalization Guru", in: *Finance and Development*, 42, 3.

Sugimoto, Yoshio, 2003: *An Introduction to Japanese Society*, 2nd ed. (Cambridge: Cambridge University Press).

Suzuki, Nobue, 2003: "Transgressing 'Victims' Reading Narratives of Filipina Brides in Japan", in: *Critical Asian Studies*, 35, 3: 399-420.

Sweetman, Caroline (Ed.), 1998: *Gender and Migration* (New Jersey: Oxfam).

Takahashi, Toru, 2007: "Nihon no Gaikokujin Seisaku to Nyukan Shuyo Shisetsu" [Japanese Immigration Policy and Immigration Centers], in: Production Committee of Kabe no Namida (Eds.): *Kabe no Namida* [Tear dropping on the wall] (Tokyo: Gendaikikakushitsu Publishers).

Takii, Kazuhiro, 2003: *Bunmei-shi no naka no Meiji Kenpou: Kono Kuni no Katachi to Seiou Taikenn* [The Meiji Constitution in the History of Civilizations: The Shape of the Country reflecting its Exposure to Europe] (Japan: Kodansha): 93-95.

Tanaka, Yuki, 2002: *Japan's Comfort Women: Sexual Slavery and Prostitution during World War II and the US Occupation* (London: Routledge).

Task Force on Co-Development [Grupo de Trabajo sobre Codesarrollo], 2005: *Documento de Consenso: Aportaciones al Debate sobre Migración y Desarrollo* (Madrid: Consejo de Cooperación al Desarrollo, Ministerio de Asuntos Exteriores).

Taya, Chikako, 2000: *ODA to Ningen no Anzenhoshou* [ODA and Human Security] (Tokyo: Yuhikaku Publisher).

Teitel, Ruti G., 2003: "Transitional Justice Genealogy", in: *Harvard Human Rights Journal*, 16: 69-94.

Tempest, Sue; McKinlay, Alan; Starkey Ken, 2004: "Careering Alone: Careers and Social Capital in the Financial Services and Television Industries", in: *Human Relations*, 57, 12: 1523-1546.

Terrio, Susan J., 2008: "New Barbarians at the Gates of Paris? Prosecuting Undocumented Minors in the Juvenile Court - the Problem of the 'Petits Roumains'", in: *Anthropological Quarterly*, 81, 4: 873-901.

Terrón, Anna, 2004: *Migraciones y Relaciones con Países Terceros* (Barcelona: Center for International Relations and Development Studies).

Terry, Donald F.; Wilson, Steven R. (Eds), 2005: *Beyond Small Changes: Making Migrant Remittances Count* (Washington, DC: Inter-American Development Bank).

Testaì, Patrizia, 2008a: "From Metaphor of Slavery to Metaphor of Freedom: Article 18 and the Incorporation of Migrant Prostitutes into Italian Society" (PhD Dissertation, University of Nottingham, Department of History).

Testaì, Patrizia, 2008b: "Debt as a Route to Modern Slavery in the Discourse on 'Sex Trafficking': Myth or Reality?", in: *Human Security Journal*, 6: 68-77.

Thieme, Susan, 2008: "Living in Transition: How Kyrgyz Women Juggle Their Different Roles in a Multi-Local Setting", in: *Gender, Technology and Development*, 12, 3: 325-345.

Thomas, Caroline, 2000: *Global Governance, Development and Human Security: the Challenge of Poverty and Inequality* (London: Pluto).

Thompson, Leonard, 1985: *The Political Mythology of Apartheid* (New Haven CT: Yale University Press).

Thompson, Leonard, 1990: *A History of South Africa* (New Haven CT: Yale University Press).

Thongyou, Maniemai; Ayuwat, Dusadee, 2005: "Social Network of Laotian Migrant Workers in Thailand", Working Paper Series No. 80, South East Asia Research Centre (Hong Kong: City University of Hong Kong).

Tierney, Robert, 2007: "The Guest Labor System in Taiwan Labor Market Considerations: Wage Injustices, and the Politics of Foreign Labor Brokerage", in: *Critical Asian Studies*, 39, 2: 205-228.

Tilly, Charles, 1976: "Migration in Modern European History", Working Paper No. 145, Center for Research on Social Organization (Ann Arbor MI: University of Michigan).

Tilly, Charles (2006) *Why?* (Princeton NJ: Princeton University Press).

Tirado, Erubiel, 2005: "Frontera sur y seguridad nacional: El olvido intermitente", Paper for El Segundo Foro: Hacia una Política Migratoria Integral en la Frontera Sur de

México, Villahermosa, Tabasco, 1 July (México DF: Instituto Nacional de Migración [National Institute for Migration]).

Tirtosudamo, Riwanto, 2000: "Political Dimensions of International Migration: Indonesia and its Neighboring Countries", in: Sukamdi, Abdul Harris; Brownlee, Patrick, (Eds.): *Labour Migration in Indonesia: Policies and Practices* (Yogyakarta, Indonesia: Population Studies Center Gadjah Mada University).

Torpey, John, 2000: *The Invention of the Passport: Surveillance, Citizenship and the State* (Cambridge: Cambridge University Press).

Toyota, Mika, 2003: "Contested Chinese Identities among Ethnic Minorities in the China, Burma and Thai Borderlands", in: *Ethnic and Racial Studies*, 26, 2: 301-320.

Tremain, Rose, 2008: *The Road Home* (London: Vintage Books).

Trépanier, Monique, 2003: "Trafficking in Women for Purposes of Sexual Exploitation: A Matter of Consent?", in: *Canadian Woman Studies (Le Cahiers de Femme)*, 22, 3-4: 48-54.

Truong, Thanh-Dam, 1990: *Sex, Money, and Morality: Prostitution and Tourism in Southeast Asia* (London: Zed Books).

Truong, Thanh-Dam, 1996: "Gender, International Migration and Social Reproduction: Implications for Theory, Policy, Research and Networking", in: *Asian and Pacific Migration Journal*, 5,1: 27-53.

Truong, Thanh-Dam, 1998: "Sexual labour in Contemporary Capitalism", in: *Journal of Gender Studies*, 18, 1: 9-21.

Truong, Thanh-Dam, 2003: "Human Trafficking and Organized Crime", in: Viano, Emile C.; Magallanes, Jose; Bridel, Laurent (Eds.): *Transnational Organized Crime: Myth, Power, and Profit* (Durham NC: Carolina Academic Press): 53-72.

Truong, Thanh-Dam, 2005: "Human Security and Human Rights", in: Smith, Rhona; Van den Anker, Christine, (Eds): *The Essentials of Human Rights* (London: Hodder Arnold): 172-175.

Truong, Thanh-Dam, 2006: "Governance and Poverty in Sub-Saharan Africa: Rethinking Best Practices in Migration Management", in: *International Social Science Journal*, 58,190: 697-714.

Truong, Thanh-Dam, 2007: *Pauvreté, genre et traite des personnes en Afrique subsaharienne: repenser les meilleures pratiques en matière de gestion des migrations* (Paris: United Nations Educational, Scientific and Cultural Organization).

Truong, Thanh-Dam, 2009a: "Human Security and the Governmentality of Neo-liberal Mobility: A Feminist Perspective" in: Brauch, Hans Günter; Oswald Spring, Úrsula; Grin, John; Mesjasz, Czeslaw; Kameri-Mbote, Patricia; Behera, Navnita Chadha; Chourou, Béchir; Krummenacher, Heinz (Eds.): *Facing Global Environmental Change: Environmental, Human, Energy, Food, Health and Water Security Concepts*. Hexagon Series on Human and Environmental Security and Peace, vol. 4 (Berlin/Heidelberg/New York: Springer Verlag): 1183-1190.

Truong, Thanh-Dam, 2009b: *Feminist Knowledge and Human Security: Bringing Rifts through the Epistemology of Care*, Working Paper No. 481 (The Hague: Institute of Social Studies).

Truong, Thanh-Dam; Barajas, Cristina Sandoval Luz, 2006: *Gates to The Hague: Narratives on Dilemmas, Networks, and Turning Points in the Lives of Latin American Migrants*. A Project Report (2005-6) from the European Focal Point to the Human In/security in the Global City Networks Project coordinated by Chubu University (The Hague: International Institute of Social Studies of Erasmus University Rotterdam).

Truong, Thanh-Dam; Gasper, Des (Eds.), 2008: "Trans-Local Livelihoods and Connections: Embedding a Gender Perspective into Migration Studies", A special issue of *Gender, Technology and Development*, 12, 3: 285-507.

Tsuda, Takeyuki, 1999: "The Permanence of Temporary Migration: The Structural Embeddedness of Japanese-Brazilian Immigrant Workers in Japan" in: *The Journal of Asian Studies*, 58, 3: 687-722.

Tsuda, Takeyuki, 2003: *Strangers in the Ethnic Homeland: Japanese Brazilian Return Migration in Transnational Perspective* (New York: Columbia University Press).

Turner, Victor, 1967: *The Forest of Symbols: Aspects of Ndembu Ritual* (New York: Cornell University Press).

Tyner, James, 2000: "Global Cities and Circuits of Global Labor: The Case of Manila, Philippines", in: *The Professional Geographer*, 52, 1: 61-74.

Tyner, James, 1996: "Construction of Filipina Migrant Entertainers", in: *Gender, Place and Culture*, 33,1: 77-93.

United Kingdom Home Office, 2006: *Operational Guidance Note Nigeria* (London: UK Home Office).

United Kingdom Home Office, 2007: *The Accession: Immigration and Worker Authorisation Regulation* 2006, Statutory Instrument 2006 No. 3317 (London: UK Home Office).

United Kingdom House of Lords, 2008: "FRONTEX: *The EU External Borders Agency - Report with Evidence*, 9th Report of Session 2007-08 of the European Union Committee (London: The Stationery Office Limited).

United Nations, 2006: *International Migration and Development: Report of the Secretary-General*, A Preparatory document for the UN High Level Dialogue on International Migration and Development, September 2006 (New York: United Nations).

United Nations' Children's Fund (UNICEF), 2003: *Trafficking in Human Beings, Especially Women and Children in Africa* (Rome: Innocenti Centre)

United Nations Development Programme (UNDP), 2008: *Human Development Report 2007/8; Fighting Climate Change* (New York: Oxford University Press).

United Nations Development Programme (UNDP), 2009: *Human Development Report* 2009 (New York: Oxford University Press).

United Nations Development Programme (UNDP), 2009: *Overcoming Barriers: Human Mobility and Development, Human Development Report 2009* (Houndmills/ Basingstoke/Hampshire/New York: Palgrave Macmillan).

United Nations High Commissioner for Refugees (UNHCR), 1995: *The State of The World's Refugees 1995: In Search of Solutions* (Geneva: United Nations High Commissioner for Refugees).

United Nations High Commissioner for Refugees (UNHCR), 2003: *Framework for Durable Solutions for Refugees and Persons of Concern* (Geneva: United Nations High Commissioner for Refugees).

United Nations High Commissioner for Refugees (UNHCR), 2006: *The State of the World's Refugees 2006 - Human Displacement in the New Millennium* (Geneva: United Nations High Commissioner for Refugees).

United Nations High Commissioner for Refugees (UNHCR), 2007a: 2005 *UNHCR Statistical Yearbook: Trends in Displacement, Protection and Solutions* (Geneva: United Nations High Commissioner for Refugees).

United Nations High Commissioner for Refugees (UNHCR), 2007b: *Response to the European Commission's Green Paper on the Future Common European Asylum System* (Geneva: United Nations High Commissioner for Refugees).

United Nations High Commissioner for Refugees (UNHCR), 2009: *Global Trends: Refugees, Asylum-seekers, Returnees, Internally Displaced and Stateless Persons* (Geneva: United Nations High Commissioner for Refugees).

United Nations Office on Drugs and Crime (UNODC), 2005: *Transnational Organized Crime in the West African Region* (Vienna: United Nations Office on Drugs and Crime).

United Nations Office on Drugs and Crime (UNODC), 2006: *Measures to Combat Trafficking in Human Beings in Benin, Nigeria and Togo* (Vienna: United Nations Office on Drugs and Crime).

University for Peace, 2006: "*Capacity Building for Peace and Development: Roles of Migrant*", Final Report Expert Forum Migrant Conference 2006, 19-20 October (Toronto: University for Peace).

United States International Trade Commission (USITC), 2007: *U.S. Trade Balance by Partner* (Washington, DC: United States International Trade Commission).

Urzúa, Raúl, 2002: "International Migration, Social Science, and Public Policy", in: *International Social Science Journal*, 52, 165: 421-429.

Valenzuela, José Manuel, 2005: "Origen y antecedentes de las Maras", Paper for the Second Forum Hacia una política migratoria integral en la frontera sur de México, Villahermosa, Tabasco, 1 July (Tijuana: El Colegio de la Frontera Norte).

Van Amersfoort, Hans; van Niekerk, Mies, 2006: "Immigration as a Colonial Inheritance: Post-colonial Immigrants in the Netherlands, 1945-2002", in: *Journal of Ethnic and Migration Studies*, 32,3: 323-346.

Van Beckhoven, Anke P. M., 1991: *Van echt werk ga je zweten: een onderzoek naar de kwalitatieve aspecten van kinder- en jeugdarbeid* [Real Work Makes you Sweat: A Study of the Qualitative Aspects of Child and Youth Labour] (Voorburg: Directoraat-Generaal van de Arbeid van het Ministerie van Sociale Zaken en Werkgelegenheid).

Van Bueren, Geraldine, 1995: *The International Law on the Rights of the Child* (The Hague - Boston - London: Save the Children & Martinus Nijhoff Publishers).

Van de Berg, Carola; Boer, Hans de, 2000: "Nationaal Scholierenonderzoek 1999-2000: Inkomsten, bestedingspatronen en arbeid van scholieren uit het voortgezet onderwijs en uit groep 8 van het basisonderwijs" [Dutch National Pupil Survey 1999-2000: Income, spending-patterns, and labour of secondary school students and grade 8 students of primary education] (Utrecht: Nationaal Instituut voor Budgetvoorlichting)

Van der Leun, Joanne, 2003: *Looking for Loopholes. Processes of Incorporation of Illegal Immigrants in the Netherlands* (Amsterdam: Amsterdam University Press).

Van der Leun, Joanne, 2006: "Excluding Illegal Immigrants in the Netherlands: Between National Policies and Local Implementation", in: *West European Politics*, 29, 2: 310-326.

Van der Leun, Joanne; Kloosterman, Robert, 2006: "Going Underground: Immigration Policy Changes and Shifts in Modes of Provision of Undocumented Immigrants in Rotterdam", in: *Tijdschrift voor Economische en Sociale Geografie*, 97, 1: 59-68.

Van Dijk, Teun, 2001: "Multidisciplinary Critical Discourse Analysis: A Plea for Diversity", in: Wodak, Ruth; Meyer, Michael (Eds.): *Methods of Critical Discourse Analysis* (London: Sage): 95-120.

Van Dijk, Teun, 2009: "Critical Discourse Studies: A Sociocognitive Approach", in: Wodak, R.; Meyer, M. (Eds.): *Methods of Critical Discourse Analysis* (London: Sage): 62-86.

Van het Foort, Tijmen, 2008: "Veranderingen in de RMS-Politiek van 1950-2008", in: Rinsampessy, Elias (Ed.): *Tussen adat en integratie. Vijf generaties Molukkers worstelen en dansen op de Nederlandse Aarde* [Between Adat and Integration. Five Generations of Moluccans are Wrestling and Dancing on Dutch Soil] (Nijmegen: Stichting Muhabbat): 49-64.

Van Gennep, Arnold, 1960: *The Rites of Passage* (London: Routledge & Kegan Paul Ltd.).

Van Houtum, Henk, 2007: "The European Union as a Gated Community: the Two-faced Border and Immigration Regime of the EU", in: *Antipode*, 39, 2: 291-309.

Van Kalmthout, Anton, 2007: "Foreigners", in: Boone, Miranda; Moerings, Martin (Eds.): *Dutch Prisons* (The Hague: BJU Legal Publishers): 101-125.

Van Kalmthout, Anton; Hofstee van der Meulen, Femke; Dünkel, Frieder, 2007: "Comparative Overview, Conclusions and Recommendations", in: Van Kalmthout, Anton; Hofstee van der Meulen, Femeke; Dünkel, Frieder (Eds.): *Foreigners in European Prisons*, vol. 1 (Nijmegen: Wolf Legal Publishers): 7-88.

Van Leeuwen, Lizzy, 2008: *Ons Indisch Erfgoed. Zestig Jaar Strijd om Cultuur en Identiteit* [Indisch Heritage. Sixty Years of Struggle for Culture and Identity] (Amsterdam: Bert Bakker).

Van Meeteren, M.; van San, M.; Engbersen, Godfried, 2008: *"Zonder Papieren" Over de Positie van Irreguliere Migranten en de Rol van het Vreemdelingenbeleid in België* (Leuven: Acco).

Van Naerssen, Ton, 2008: "We are Bridging Cultures and Countries. Migrant Organisations and Development Cooperation in the Netherlands", in: van Naerssen, Ton; Spaan, Ernst; Zoomers, Annelies (Eds.): *Global Migration and Development* (London/New York: Routledge): 172-191.

Van Naerssen, Ton; Spaan, Ernst; Zoomers, Annelies (Eds.), 2008: *Global Migration and Development* (London/New York: Routledge).

Van Nieuwenhuyze, Inge, 2009: *Getting by in Europe's Urban Labour Markets: Senegambian Migrants' Strategies for Survival, Documentation and Mobility* (Amsterdam: Amsterdam University Press).

Van Parijs, Philippe, 2003: "Difference Principles", in: Freeman, Samuel (Ed.): *The Cambridge Companion to Rawls* (Cambridge: Cambridge University Press): 200-240.

Van Selm, Joanne, 2005: "European Refugee Policy: Is There Such a thing? New Issues in Refugee Research", Evaluation and Policy Analysis Unit Working Paper No. 115 (Geneva: United Nations High Commissioner for Refugees).

Van Selm Joanna; Besty Cooper, 2006: *The New 'Boat People': Ensuring Safety and Determining Status* (Washington, D.C.: Migration Policy Institute)

Van Wessel, Hans (Ed.), 2008: *Indische Sporen. Bronnen voor Lerarenopleiders* [Tracking "Indisch". Sources for Teachers Educators] (Nijmegen: Uitgeverij Vantilt).

Venet, Fabienne, 2006: *Informe breve sobre los antecedentes en la prestación de servicios a los migrantes* (México: Sin Fronteras, IAP).

Venet, Fabienne; Verduzco, Gustavo, 2007: *Modalidades de atención a la población migrante en riesgo y vulnerabilidad con un enfoque a mujeres y niñez* (México: El Colegio de México/Sin Fronteras).

Verkuyten, Maykel, 1999: *Etnische identiteit. Theoretische en empirische benaderingen* [Ethnic Identity. Theoretical and Empirical Approaches] (Amsterdam: Het Spinhuis).

Verkuyten, Maykel; van de Calseijde, Sofie; de Leur, Wieger, 1999: "Third Generation Moluccans in the Netherlands: the Nature of their Identity", in: *Journal of Ethnic and Migration Studies*, 25, 1: 63-79.

Vertovec, Steven, 1999: "Conceiving and Researching Transnationalism", in: *Ethnic and Racial Studies*, 22, 2: 447-462.

Vesta, Ellie, 2008: "The Paper Market: 'Borrowing' and 'Renting' of Identity Documents", Working Paper No. 3, Centre on Migration, Policy and Society (Oxford: University of Oxford).

Villalba, Maria Angela, 2002: *Philippines: Good Practices for the Protection of Filipino Women Migrant Workers in Vulnerable Jobs* (Geneva: International Labour Office).

Villareal, Magdalena M., 1992: "The Poverty of Practice: Power, Gender and Intervention from an Actor Oriented Perspective", in: Long, Ann; Long, Norman (Eds.): *Battlefields of Knowledge: The Interlocking of Theory and Practice in Social Research and Development* (London/New York: Routledge): 247-267.

Voutz, Hans; Rinsampessy, Elias, 2008: "Tussen adat en integratie, een analyse van de situatie van de Molukkers in Nederland" [Between Adat and Integration, an Analysis of the Situation of Moluccans in the Netherlands], in: Rinsampessy, Elias (Ed.): *Tussen adat en integratie. Vijf generaties Molukkers worstelen en dansen op de Nederlandse Aarde* [Between Adat and Integration. Five Generations of Moluccans are Wrestling and Dancing on Dutch Soil] (Nijmegen: Stichting Muhabbat): 11-31.

Walker, Eric Anderson, 1930: *The Frontier Tradition in South Africa* (London: Oxford University Press).

Walton-Roberts, Margaret, 2004: 'Globalization, National Autonomy and Non-Resident Indians.' *Contemporary South Asia*, 13, 1: pp. 53-69.

Waquant, Loïc, 1999: *Les Prisons de la Misère* (Paris: Editions Raisons d'Agir).

Webber, Frances, 2000: *Crimes of arrival: immigrants and asylum-seekers in the new Europe* (London: Statewatch).

Wee, Vivienne; Sim, Amy, 2004: "Transnational Networks in Female Labour Migration"; in: Ananta, Aris; Arifin, Evi Nurvidya (Eds.): *International Migration in Southeast Asia* (Singapore: Institute of Southeast Asian Studies).

Weinzierl, Ruth, 2008: *Human Rights at the EU's Common External Maritime Border: Recommendations to the EU Legislature* (Berlin: German Institute for Human Rights).

Weiss, Thomas George, 2000: "Governance, Good Governance and Global Governance: Conceptual and Actual Challenges", in: *Third World Quarterly*, 21, 5: 795-814.

Welbourne, Penelope, 2002: "Adoption and the Rights of Children in the UK", in: *The International Journal of Children's Rights*, 10, 3: 269-289.

Welch, Michael; Schuster, Liza, 2005: "Detention of Asylum Seekers in the US, UK, France, Germany and Italy: A Critical View of the Globalizing Culture of Control", in: *Criminal Justice*, 5, 4: 331-355.

Welsh, David, 1971: *The Roots of Segregation: Native Policy in Natal, 1845-1910* (Cape Town: Oxford University Press).

Wennerholm, Carolina; Zillen, Eva, 2003: *IOM Regional Counter-Trafficking Programme in the Western Balkans,*

SIDA Evaluation, (Stockholm: Swedish International Development Cooperation Agency, Department for Central and Eastern Europe).

Werthes, Sascha; Bosold, David, 2006: "Caught Between Pretension and Substantiveness - Ambiguities of Human Security as a Political Leitmotif", in: Debiel, Tobias; Werthes, Sascha (Eds.): *Human Security on Foreign Policy Agendas: Changes, Concepts and Cases*. INEF Report, 80/2006 (Duisburg: Institute for Development and Peace, University of Duisburg-Essen).

Wetenschappelijke Raad voor het Regeringsbeleid (WRR), 2007: *Identificatie met Nederland* [Identification with the Netherlands] (Amsterdam: Amsterdam University Press).

White, Ben, 2005: "Shifting Positions on Child Labor: The Views and Practice of Intergovernmental Organizations", in: Weston, Burns H. (Ed.): *Child Labor and Human Rights* (Boulder, CO: Lynne Rienner Publishers): 319-342.

Whitehead, Ann; Hashim, Iman, 2005: "Children and Migration: Background Paper for DfID Migration Team" (London: Department for International Development).

Whitehead, Ann; Hashim, Imam M.; Iversen, Vegard, 2007: *Child Migration, Child Agency, and Inter-generational Relations in Africa and South Asia* (Brighton: Development Research Centre on Migration, Globalisation & Poverty, Sussex University).

Whittaker, Andrea, 1999: "Women and Capitalist Transformation in a North-Eastern Thai Village", in: Jackson, Peter A.; Cook, Nerida (Eds.): *Gender and Sexualities in Modern Thailand* (Bangkok: Silk Worm Books): 43-62.

Willems, Wim, 2001: *De uittocht uit Indië* 1945-1995 [The Exodus from the Dutch Indies 1945-1995] (Amsterdam: Bert Bakker).

Willems, Wim, 2008: *Tjalie Robinson. Biografie van een Indo-schrijver* [Tjalie Robinson. Biography of an Indo-Writer] (Amsterdam: Bert Bakker).

Williams, Catharina Purwani, 2005:"Knowing One's Place': Gender, Mobility and Shifting Subjectivity in Eastern Indonesia", in: *Global Networks*, 5, 4: 401-441.

Williamson, Oliver Eaton, 2000: "The New Institutional Economics: Taking Stock, Looking Ahead", in: *Journal of Economic Literature*, XXXVIII, September: 595-613.

Wilson, Francis; Ramphele, Mamphela, 1989: *Uprooting Poverty: the South African Challenge: Report for the Second Carnegie Inquiry into Poverty and Development in Southern Africa* (New York: W.W. Norton).

Wilson, Monica; Thompson, Leonard, 1969: *The Oxford History of South Africa, Vol. 1, South Africa to* 1870 (Oxford: Clarendon Press).

Wolpe, Harold, 1972: "Capitalism and Cheap Labour-Power in South Africa: From Segregation to Apartheid", in: *Economy and Society*, 1, 4: 425-456.

Wong, Diana, 1996: "Foreign Domestic Workers in Singapore" in: *Asia Pacific Migration Journal* 5, 1:117-137.

World Bank, 1991: "Managing Development: The Governance Dimension", A discussion Paper (Washington, DC: The World Bank): 1-23.

World Bank, 1997: "Restraining Arbitrary State Action and Corruption", in: *World Development Report: The State in a Changing World* (Oxford: Oxford University Press): 99-109.

World Bank, 2005: *Global Economic Prospects, Economic Implications of Remittances and Migration* (Washington, DC: World Bank).

World Bank, 2006: *Global Economic Prospects 2006: Economic Implications of Remittances and Migration* (Washington, DC: World Bank).

World Bank, 2007: General Principles for International Remittance Services: Committee on Payment and Settlement Systems, Report No. 38821 (Washington, DC: The World Bank).

Yang, Guobin, 2000: "The Liminal Effects of Social Movements: Red Guards and the Transformation of Identity", in: *Sociological Forum*, 15, 3: 380-406.

Yang, Philip Q., 2000: "The 'Sojourner Hypothesis' Revisited", in: *Diaspora*, 9,2: 236-257.

Yaqub, Shahin, 2009: *Child Migrants with and without Parents: Census-based Estimates of Scale and Characteristics in Argentina, Chile and South Africa* (Florence: UNICEF- Innocenti Research Centre).

Yeoh, Brenda S.A.; Huang, Shirlena, 1998: "Negotiating Public Spaces: Strategies and Styles of Migrant Female Domestic Workers in Singapore" in: *Urban Studies* 35, 3: 583-602.

Yeoh, Brenda S. A; Willis, Katie D.; Abdul Khader Fakhri, S. M., 2003, "Introduction: Transnationalism and its Edges", in: *Ethnic and Racial Studies*, 26,2: 207-217.

Yoshida, Fumihiko, 2004: *Ningen no Anzenhoshou Senryaku* [Human Security Strategy] (Tokyo: Iwanami Shoten Publisher).

Young, Jock, 2007: *The Vertigo of Late Modernity* (London: Sage).

Young, Rita; de Vries, Zwaan, 2009: *Oorlog en overleven buiten Japanse kampen* [War and Survival Outside Japanese Camps] (Nijmegen: Uitgeverij Flanor).

Zeghbib, Hocine, 2009: "Droit et migrations au Maghreb: au cœur de la fabrique", in: Bensaâd, Ali (Ed.): *Le Maghreb à l'épreuve des migrations subsahariennes. Immigration sur émigration* (Paris: Karthala): 213-244.

Zieck, Marjoleine, 1997: *UNHCR and Voluntary Repatriation of Refugees: A Legal Analysis* (The Hague/Boston: Martinus Nijhoff).

Ziguras, Christopher, 2005: 'International Trade in Education Services: Governing the Liberalization and Regulation of Private Enterprise', in: Singh, Michael; Kenway, Jane; Appel, Micheal (Eds.) *Globalizing Education: perspectives from above and below* (New York: Peter Lang): 93-112.

Zoomers, Annelies, 2005: *Op zoek naar Eldorado: Over international migratie, sociale mobiliteit en ontwikkeling.* (Nijmegen: Radbouw Universiteit Nijmegen).

Zureik, Elia, 2001: "Constructing Palestine through Surveillance Practices", in: *British Journal of Middle Eastern Studies*, 28, 2: 205-227.

Biographies of Contributors

Michiel Baas (The Netherlands) is affiliated with the Amsterdam Institute for Social Science Research of the University of Amsterdam. His research master's dissertation dealt with Indian IT professionals who live and work in Bangalore, and explored how the local and global, traditional and modern, and the national and transnational interact and intersect in the fast-moving world of information technology. This study led to his PhD research, which looked into the lives of Indian overseas students in Australia, resulting in a dissertation titled *Imagined Mobility: Migration and Transnationalism among Indian Students in Australia* (2009), to appear in 2010 from Anthem Press, London. He has published on the lives of Indian students in Australia, their migration decisions, the intersection of migration and gender, love and arranged marriages in the IT industry, and related topics. He is currently working on a number of different topics related to the male middle class Indian in local/national/global/transnational settings.

Address: Dr. Michiel Baas, Amsterdam School for Social Science Research (ASSR), Universiteit van Amsterdam, Kloveniersburgwal 48, 1012 CX Amsterdam, The Netherlands.
Email: <Michiel.Baas@uva.nl>.
Website: <http://www.assr.nl>.

Amiya Kumar Bagchi (India) is Professor of Economics and Director/Founder of the Institute of Development Studies Kolkata, a multidisciplinary centre of excellence in the social sciences, which is affiliated with the University of Calcutta and promoted by the government of West Bengal. His research interests include finance, human development issues and other aspects of development, and the prospects of democracy in a globalizing world. He has been Visiting Professor at international academic institutions such as Cambridge University, Maison des Sciences de l'Homme (Paris), Cornell University, Curtin University (Perth, Western Australia), Naples University, and University of Bristol. Professional awards and honours include: First Chancellor of the newly reconstituted Tripura University (March 2008); D.Sc. *honoris causa* from North Bengal University (March 2008); Padma Shri from the Government of India (2005); Muzaffar Ahmad award for his book *Capital and Labour Redefined* (2004); honorary D.Litt. from the University of Kalyani (December 2002); doctorate *honoris causa* from Roskilde University, Denmark (2001).
He has authored/edited more than 250 academic articles and books (edited and monographs). Two of his most recent books are *Perilous Passage: Mankind and the Global Ascendancy of Capital* (Lanham, MD: Rowman & Littlefield, 2005; Oxford: Oxford University Press, 2006); and (co-edited with Gary Dymski): *Capture and Exclude: Developing Economies and the Poor in Global Finance* (New Delhi: Tulika Books, 2007).

Address: Prof. Dr. Amiya Kumar Bagchi, Calcutta University, Alipore Campus, 5th floor, 1 Reformatory Street, Kolkata 700027, India.
Email: <amiya.bagchi@gmail.com>.
Website: <http://idsk.edu.in>.

Alejandra Boni (Spain) holds a PhD in Human Rights from the University of Valencia. She is an Associate Professor at the Department of Projects Engineering and team leader of the Group for Studies on Development, International Cooperation and Ethics. She has been a visiting fellow at the International Institute of Social Studies of Erasmus University of Rotterdam and the Institute of Development Studies at the University of Sussex. She is special lecturer of the University of Nottingham. Currently, she is researching human development, capabilities and education. She has published in journals such as *Power and Education* (2009), *Higher Education* (2007), *Science and Engineering Ethics* (2008) and *European Journal of Engineering Education* (2008, 2009). She has also co-authored with Joan Lacomba, "The Role of Emigration in Foreign Aid Policies: The Case of Spain and Morocco", in: *International Migration*, 46, 1 (2008): 123-150.

Address: Dr. Alejandra Boni, Escuela Técnica Superior de Ingenieros Industriales, Universidad Politecnica de Valencia, Camino de Vera, s/n 46022 Valencia, Spain.
Email: <sandraboni@yahoo.es>.
Website: <http://www.upv.es/entidades/DPI/indexi.html>.

Julien Brachet (France) is researcher at the Institut de Recherche pour le Développement (IRD) and at the Université Paris 1 Panthéon-Sorbonne. He is currently Visiting Research Fellow at the International Migration Institute (University of Oxford). He obtained his PhD in geography at the University Paris 1 Panthéon-Sorbonne in 2007. His research focuses on mobility to and through the Central Sahara, particularly in northern Niger, where he studies migration networks, transport systems and trade between sub-Saharan and northern Africa. His current research focuses on shifting spatial boundaries and strategies that allow local people to adapt to a general context characterized by the growing severity of international policies regarding movement and migration. He has published several articles in French and English on these topics and a book: *Migrations transsahariennes. Vers un désert cosmopolite et morcelé (Niger)* (Paris: Éditions du Croquant, 2009).

Address: Dr. Julien Brachet, Institut de Recherche pour le Développement, UMR 201 "Développement & Sociétés", Université Paris 1 Panthéon-Sorbonne, 45 bis avenue de la Belle Gabrielle, 94736 Nogent sur Marne, France.
Email: <julien.brachet@ird.fr>.
Website: <http://www.ird.fr/>.

Dennis Broeders (The Netherlands) is a postdoctoral researcher at the Department of Sociology of the Erasmus University Rotterdam and a senior research fellow at the Dutch Scientific Council for Government Policy (WRR). The WRR is an independent strategic think tank for the Dutch government located under the Prime Minister's department. At the council he worked on reports to the Government on immigration and integration ("Netherlands as an Immigration Society", 2001), on decision-making procedures in an enlarged European Union (*Slagvaardigheid in de Europabrede Unie*, 2003) and on the working of social norms and values (*Waarden, normen en de last van het gedrag*, 2003). As a senior research fellow and project leader, he was responsible for the report "*Media Policy in the Digital Age*" (2005) and "*Identification with the Netherlands*" (*Identificatie met Nederland*, 2007). He is currently coordinator of the Policy, Information and Technology project group. In 2005, he joined the department of Sociology at the Erasmus University of Rotterdam as a researcher (part-time) to work on his PhD thesis on the development of internal surveillance on irregular migrants in the Netherlands and Germany and the EU-dimension of these policy developments. He obtained his doctorate in 2009 and remains affiliated with the Rotterdam department of Sociology as a postdoctoral researcher. Some of his publications include: "The Fight Against Illegal Migration", in: *American Behavioral Scientist*, 50,12: 1592-1609 (2007); "The New Digital Borders of Europe" in: *International Sociology*, 22, 1: 71-92 (2007); "The State versus the Alien: Immigration Control and Strategies of Irregular Immigrants", with Godfried Engbersen, in: *West European Politics*, 32, 5 (2009): 867-885; *Breaking Down Anonymity: Digital Surveillance of Irregular Migrants in Germany and the Netherlands* (Amsterdam: Amsterdam University Press).

Address: Dr. Dennis Broeders, Wetenschappelijke Raad voor het Regeringsbeleid (WRR), Lange Vijverberg 4-5, 2500 EA The Hague, The Netherlands.
Email: <broeders@wrr.nl>.
Website: <http://www.wrr.nl/index.jsp>.

Beatriz Campillo Carrete (México) has higher education qualifications in Public Administration and in Economics and received an MA in Development Studies from the International Institute of Social Studies of Erasmus University Rotterdam (ISS-EUR), The Netherlands. She has worked for the Mexican government; a research and capacity-building NGO in Mexico City; the Academic Program on Conflict Prevention and Negotiation of the National Autonomous University of Mexico (PAPCN-UNAM in Spanish), and collaborated with the Latin American Hydrologic International Program (IHP-LAC) of UNESCO. She has researched on Mexican NGO policy advocacy initiatives, return migration, Mexican labour institutions, and water and conflict. She has co-published (with Michael D. Layton, Ireri Ablanedo and Ana María Sánchez): "Mexico Case Study: Civil Society and the Struggle to Reduce Maternal Mortality", in: Gaventa, J.; McGee, R. (Eds.): *Citizen Action and National Policy Reform*, (New York: Palgrave McMillan, 2010); and edited "Conflicto y Cooperacion" [Conflict and Cooperation], in: ESPOL; et al. (Eds.): *Prevención de Conflictos y Cooperación en la Gestión de los Recursos Hídricos en América Latina* [Conflict Prevention and Cooperation in Water Management in Latin America] (Course Book, PCCP series, Montevideo: UNESCO-IHP LAC, 2006).

Email: <bcampilloc@yahoo.com.mx>.

Godfried Engbersen (The Netherlands) is professor of General Sociology at the Erasmus University of Rotterdam, The Netherlands. He studied sociology at the University of Leiden and has worked at the Universities of Leiden, Utrecht and Amsterdam. In spring 1996, he was a visiting professor at the Centre of Western European Studies at the University of California, Berkeley. He has written extensively on new forms of social inequality and urban marginality in advanced welfare states. He is the author of more than 15 books on social inequality, immigration, urban problems and the welfare state, including (with others): *Cultures of Unemployment: A Comparative Look at Long-term Unemployment and Urban Poverty* (Amsterdam: Amsterdam University Press (AUP), 2006). From 1997-2000, he was editor of the *Annual Dutch Report on Poverty and Social Exclusion* (AUP). He is a member of the *Amsterdam School for Social Science Research* (ASSR) and the IMISCOE-network, Dutch correspondent for the continuous Reporting System on Migration (SOPEMI) of the OECD, an elected member of the Royal Netherlands Academy of Sciences (KNAW) (since 2007) and of the Royal Holland Society of Sciences and Humanities (since 2002). From 2001-2009, he was an elected member of the Dutch Advisory Commission on Alien Affairs. From 2003-2006, he chaired the KNAW-committee on the Future of Dutch Sociology. He is currently working on the relationship between restrictive migration regimes and crime; local and transnational citizenship; and liquid migration from Central and Eastern Europe. He recently published *Fatale Remedies: De onbedoelde gevolgen van beleid en kennis* [Fatal Remedies. The Unintended Consequences of Social Policy and Knowledge] (Amsterdam: AUP, 2009); and (with Richard Black and others): *A Continent Moving West? EU Enlargement and Labour Migration from Central and Eastern Europe* (Amsterdam: AUP, 2010).

Address: Prof. Dr. Godfried Engbersen, Erasmus Universiteit Rotterdam, Faculteit der Sociale Wetenschappen, kamer M7-44 Postbus 1738 3000 DR Rotterdam, The Netherlands.
Email: <Engbersen@fsw.eur.nl>.
Website: <http://www.eur.nl/fsw/>.

Des Gasper (United Kingdom) is Professor of Human Development, Development Ethics and Public Policy, at the International Institute of Social Studies of Erasmus University Rotterdam (ISS-EUR), The Netherlands. Previous work includes: *Arguing Development Policy - Frames and Discourses*, with Raymond Apthorpe (London: Frank Cass, 1996); *The Ethics of Development - From Economism to Human Development* (Edinburgh: Edinburgh University Press, 2004; New Delhi: Sage India, 2005); "Living In Common and Deliberating In Common - Foundational Issues in Sustainable Human Development and Human Security", a special issue of *International Journal of Social Economics*, 2007, 34, 1&2: 5-126 (co-editor with P.B. Anand); *Trans-Local Livelihoods and Connections: Embedding a Gender Perspective into Migration Studies*, a special issue of *Gender, Technology and Development* 12, 3: 285-537 (2008) (co-editor with Thanh-Dam Truong); "Human Rights, Human Needs, Human Development, Human Security", in: Hayden, Patrick (Ed.): *Ashgate Research Companion to Ethics and International Relations* (Aldershot: Ashgate, 2009): 329-355; "How can Power Discourses be Changed?" (with M. Sinha), in: *Critical Policy Studies*, 3, 3-4 (2009): 290-308; *Development Ethics* (2010) (co-edited with Asuncion Lera St. Clair), (Aldershot: Ashgate, International Library of Essays in Public and Professional Ethics; "Movements of The 'We': International and Transnational Migration and the Capabilities Approach", co-author with Thanh-Dam Truong, *Journal of Human Development and Capabilities*, a special issue on human mobility, 11, 2 (2010): 339-357.

Address: Prof. Des Gasper, ISS, P.O. Box 29776, The Hague 2502 LT, The Netherlands.
Email: <gasper@iss.nl>.
Website: <http://www.iss.nl/iss/profile/AC1158>.

Tatsuo Harada (Japan): Professor of International Political Economy at the College of International Studies, Chubu University; research associate at the York Centre for International and Security Studies (YCISS), York University (2003); project director at the Chubu Centre for Human Security Studies (CHS) (2006-2008); head of Department of International Relations, Chubu University (2009). He won the second *NIRA Okita Commemorative Award for Policy Research* by the National Institute of Research Advancement as a contributor to the book: Yoichi, Mine; Sachiko, Hatanaka (Eds.): *Zouo kara Wakai he* [From Hatred to Accommodation] (Kyoto: Kyoto University Press, 2000). He focuses on post-development studies, human security and migration. Major publications in English include: "The Limits to Catching-up: OEM, Market Structure and Production Networks in East Asia", in: Hozumi, Toshihiko; Wohlmuth, Karl (Eds.): *Schumpeter and the Dynamics of Asian Development* (Hamburg: LIT, 2000); "Human Insecurity and Informalization: A Conceptual Sketch", in: Howell, Alison (Ed.): *Governance and Global (Dis)orders: Trends, Transformations, and Impasses* (Toronto: YCISS, 2004); (with Mushakoji, Kinhide): "Human Insecurity of Migrants in Japan", in: Mushakoji, Kinhide; Pasha, Mustapha Kamal (Eds.): *Human (In)Security in the Networks of Global Cities: the Final Report* (Kasugai: CHS, 2009).

Address: Prof. Tatsuo Harada, College of International Studies, Chubu University, 1200 Matsumoto, Kasugai, Aichi 487-8501, Japan.
Email: <tazz@isc.chubu.ac.jp>.
Website: <http://www.chubu.ac.jp/english/>.

Helen Hintjens (United Kingdom) is Senior Lecturer in Development and Social Justice at the International Institute of Social Studies of Erasmus University Rotterdam (ISS-EUR), The Netherlands. As well as working on immigration issues since the 1980's, and having published a number of articles on the subject, she has published on genocide and post-genocide politics and identities in Rwanda, as well as conflict and environment in the Great Lakes region. She is presently engaged in research on pro-asylum advocacy and on Roma and Traveller minority human rights issues in South Wales in an EU context. She is also conducting research on surveillance and exclusion of undocumented people, within the EU-funded COST network, *Living in Surveillance Societies* (LISS). Among her publications are: "Rwanda and Burundi" in: Herb, G.H.; Kaplan, D.H. (Eds.): *Nations and Nationalism: a Global Historical Overview* (vol. 4: 1989 to present, Santa Barbara: ABC-CLIO, 2008): 1668-1682; "Free Movement Activism", in Anderson, G.L.; Herr, K. (Eds.): *Encyclopaedia of Activism and Social Justice* (London: Sage, 2007): 585-587; "Citizenship under Siege in the Brave New Europe", in: *European Journal of Cultural Studies*, 10, 3: 409-414 (2007).

Address: Dr. Helen Hintjens, ISS, P.O. Box 29776, The Hague 2502 LT, The Netherlands.
Email: <hintjens@iss.nl>.
Website: <http://www.iss.nl/hintjens>.

Roy Huijsmans (The Netherlands) has worked in the education field in the Lao PDR, Malawi, Nepal, the Netherlands and Surinam. His research on children and young people's involvement in various forms of work in the European and South-East Asian context now extends to include migration and human trafficking. He is currently enrolled as a full-time PhD candidate at the Department of Geography, Durham University (United Kingdom) finalizing a thesis entitled: "Migrating Children, Households, and the Post-Socialist State: An Ethnographic Study of Migration and Non-migration by Children and Youth in an Ethnic Lao Village". Other projects include "Listening to Working School-Youth: A Child-centred Case-study of Employment Experiences of HAVO-students in Rural Eastern Netherlands", MA research paper, Institute of Social Studies: The Hague (2004); "Approaches to Lao Minors Working in Thailand", in: *Lao Development Journal: Juth Pakai* 8 (2007): 18-33; "Children Working Beyond their Localities: Lao Children Working in Thailand", in: *Childhood*, 15,3 (2008): 331-353. He completed an exchange programme in higher education (2005): "Gender, Development and Public Policy in Asia" funded by the EU-Asialink programme of the European Commission; and co-organized a European Alliance for Asian Studies international workshop on "Perspectives on Children's Active Engagement with Migration in South-East Asia" (Bangkok, 19-20 February 2009, together with the Institute of Population and Social Research of Mahidol University, Bangkok).

Address: Mr. Roy Huijsmans, Durham University, Department of Geography, Science Laboratories South Road, Dur-

ham, DH1 3LE, UK.
Email: <r.b.huijsmans@durham.ac.uk> and <r.b.huijsmans@gmail. com>.
Website: <http://www.dur.ac.uk/geography/>.

Kenji Kimura (Japan): Researcher for the Ministry of Foreign Affairs of Japan based in Jakarta, Indonesia. Researcher for the Centre for Human Security Studies, Chubu University, Japan (CHS) (2006-2008). His fields of specialization are International Relations, Southeast Asian Studies, Human Security and Migration. His major works in English are *"Human Trafficking in Indonesia: Rethinking the New Order's Impact on Exploitative Migration of Indonesian Women"* (M.A. thesis, Ohio University); *"Education and Human Insecurity of Brazilian Immigrant Children in Japan: The Case of Komaki City"* (paper to ISS conference on International migration, multi-local livelihoods and human security).

Address: Mr. Kenji Kimura, Setiabudi Residence unit 2511, Tower B, Jalan Setiabudi Selatan Raya Kav 1, Kuningan, HR Rasuna Said, Jakarta Selatan 12920, Indonesia.
Email: <kenchang@poiu.org>.

Karim Knio (Lebanon) is Lecturer in Politics, International Institute of Social Studies of Erasmus University Rotterdam (ISS-EUR), The Netherlands. He received his PhD from the University of Birmingham, UK. His research focuses on the political economy of governance, regionalism and trade with a focus on the Euro-Mediterranean region. He also has interests in Industrial Relations, EU democracy promotion programmes and Lebanese politics. Some of his recent publications include: "Investigating the Two Faces of Governance: The Case of the Euro-Mediterranean Development Bank", in: *Third World Quarterly*, 31,1 (2010): 105-121; "Conceptualizing Hezbollah's Transformation in Lebanon's Post-Cedar Revolution: Proxy Client or Structural Path Dependency?", in: Salih, M. (Ed.): *Interpreting Islamic Political Parties* (Basingstoke: Palgrave Macmillan, 2009): 259-268; "Social Forces and the Effects of (Post) -Washington Consensus Policy in Africa: Comparing Tunisia and South Africa" (with Hurt, S.; Ryner, M.), in: *The Roundtable: The Commonwealth Journal of International Affairs*, 98,402 (2009): 301-317; "Governance, Politics and the European Mediterranean Partnership (EMP): Problems of Implementation or Policy Design?", in: Hout, W.; Robison, R. (Eds.): *Governance and the Depoliticisation of Development* (London: Routledge, 2009): 77-91; "Is Political Stability Sustainable in Post 'Cedar Revolution' Lebanon?", in: *Mediterranean Politics*, 13,3 (2008): 445-451; "Leiden Economische Hervormingen tot meer Democratie?" (with De Vries, A.), in: *Idee*, 29,6: 40-43 (2008); "Theorising the State of Affairs in the Lebanese State: Is Lebanon a Failed State?", in: *Development Issues*, 8,2 (2006): 4-6; "Lebanon: Cedar Revolution or Neo Sectarian Partition?", in: *Mediterranean Politics*, 10,2 (2005): 225-231; *The EU Mediterranean Policy: Model or Muddle?* (New York: Palgrave Macmillan, 2010-forthcoming).

Address: Dr. Karim Knio ISS, P.O. Box 29776, The Hague 2502 LT, The Netherlands.
Email: <knio@iss.nl>.
Website: <http://www.iss.nl/knio>.

Yu Kojima (Japan) acquired her PhD degree in Development Studies from the International Institute of Social Studies of Erasmus University Rotterdam (ISS-EUR), The Netherlands. Her doctoral research was about trafficking in women and girls for domestic work and prostitution in Asia (Thailand, Cambodia, Laos and Sri Lanka). Prior to her PhD research, she served in the UNIFEM and UNDP South Pacific Regional Office based in Fiji. Her main responsibility was gender mainstreaming, CEDAW and VAW (violence against women) related projects in the region. Presently, she has been carrying out development-related research for human rights advocacy groups and development agencies on issues related to human trafficking and exploitative migration in Asia. Her most recent work and interest include trafficking/smuggling of Burmese migrant families into the fishery sector in southern Thailand, with particular focus on the agency of child migrants. Her main publications include *Women in Trafficking-Migration Continuum: From Perspective of Human Rights and Social Justice* (Maastricht: Shaker, 2007); "In the Business of Cultural Reproduction: Theoretical Implication of the Mail-Order Bride Phenomenon", 2001: *Women's Studies International Forum*, 24, 2: 199-210. She is also the co-author of *Priceless: Dynamics of Human Trafficking-Exploitative Migration in Asia* (Tokyo: Godo-Shupan, forthcoming) - the book series for development education purposes for schoolchildren in Japan.

Email: <yucita2004@yahoo.com>.

Richa Kumar (India) trained as a lawyer at NALSAR, University of Law, India, and recently completed a Masters programme at the International Institute of Social Studies of Erasmus University Rotterdam (ISS-EUR), The Netherlands, specializing in population, poverty and social development. Her dissertation on: *New Mobilities within Old Paradigms: Globalization, Citizenship and Migration Beyond the Nation State*, was nominated for the ISS Research Paper award for 2008. It focused on the case of the Morecambe Bay Cockle Pickers. She has worked on socio-legal issues including women and law, prison reform, law and gay rights, bonded labour and refugee rights (with UNHCR). She has also written a column for *The Hindu*, a secular Indian newspaper, as well as worked for Price Waterhouse Coopers. She has a special interest in refugee rights; and recently joined a number of NGOs in The Hague, including The Hague Process on Refugees and Migration.

Email: <richa.kumar@gmail.com>.

María Isabel de Lozano (México) is a sociologist who did graduate studies at the National Autonomous University of Mexico (UNAM), and the Leadership for Environment and Development Programme. She has worked in research projects related to migration, labour markets, workers' rights, childhood and public investment, rural development and environment, at El Colegio de Michoacán, El Colegio de México, the Mexican Institute of Social Studies, Centre for Research and Advanced Studies of the National Polytechnic Institute and as an independent researcher. She has evaluated some governmental social programmes in Mexico. From 1996-1997, she worked at the International Labour Rights Fund, a non-governmental organization based in Washington, DC. From 1997 to 2000, she collaborated with the Structural Adjustment Policies Participatory Review International Networking, on an appraisal of the impact of the Structural Adjustment Policies in Mexico. She was the coordinator of Civicus Index of Civil Society Projects in Mexico, an initiative launched by Civicus World Alliance for Citizen Participation. Since September 2008, she serves as the coordinator of Public Policies to Promote Civil Society Organizations with Alternativas y Capacidades, an NGO based in Mexico City.

Email: <marisaverduzco@gmail.com>.

Joan Lacomba (Spain) holds a PhD in Sociology; he is Professor of Social Work at the University of Valencia (Spain). His main research themes are migration and development, especially in Morocco. Some of his publications include: *Emergencia del islamismo en el Magreb: Las raíces sociopolíticas de los movimientos islamista,* (Madrid: Catarata, 2000); *El Islam inmigrado: Transformaciones y adaptaciones de las prácticas culturales y religiosas,* (Madrid: Ministerio de EducacioÌn, Cultura y Deporte, Secretaria General TeÌcnica, 2001);

Address: Prof. Dr. Joan Lacomba Facultat de Ciències Socials Universitat de València Edifici Departamental Occidental Av. Tarongers S/N 46022 València, Espanya.
Email: <joan.lacomba@uv.es>.
Website: <http://centros.uv.es/web/centros/sociales/castellano/>.

Wies Maas (The Netherlands) is a policy officer at The Hague Process on Refugees and Migration (THP) and freelance consultant on refugees, migration and development issues. Before working at THP, Maas worked as policy officer at the Dutch Ministry of Foreign Affairs for the international migration cluster (CIM). She worked on migration and development, circular migration, labour migration, diaspora organizations, brain drain and maintaining contacts with the academic world. Previously, Maas studied at the International Institute of Social Studies of Erasmus University Rotterdam (ISS-EUR), The Netherlands, where she obtained her Master's degree in Development Studies (Governance and Democracy). Her research paper (with distinction), which dealt with the Europeanization of immigration policies and refugee protection, won an ISS MA Research Paper Award. She was the founder and director of the foundation "Night of the Tips" (<www.nachtvandefooi.nl>), a development organization that aims to raise awareness and means within the Netherlands for development aid projects in developing countries. She also set up the Dutch branch of the European Youth Parliament. Some of her recent reports and publications include: *"Policy Options regarding Brain Drain",* A report written for the Ministry of Foreign Affairs (The Netherlands: The Hague, 2009); *"Does Europeanization undermine the Right to Seek Refugee Status? The Case of Frontex"*, (with Karim Knio), paper presented at the 50th Annual Convention of the International Studies Association (ISA, 15-18 February 2009, New York); *"Fleeing to Europe: Europeanization and the Right to Seek Refugee Status',* (ISS Working Paper No. 454, 2008); at: <http://biblio.iss.nl/opac/uploads/wp/wp454.pdf>.

Address: Ms. Wies Maas, P.O. Box 13074 2501 EB The Hague, The Netherlands.
Email: <wies.maas@gmail.com>.
Website: <http://www.thehagueprocess.org/>.

Yoichi Mine (Japan): Professor of Human Security, Development Studies and African Area Studies at Graduate School of Global Studies, Doshisha University, Kyoto; Visiting Professor at the Centre for Southeast Asian Studies, Kyoto University; and Visiting Fellow at JICA (Japan International Cooperation Agency) Research Institute, Tokyo. He studied at the Graduate School of Economics, Kyoto University, was Associate Professor at the Department of Political Science, University of Stellenbosch, South Africa, and has worked for Chubu and Osaka Universities in Japan. He has authored and edited several academic books in Japanese on development economics, African history and conflict resolution: *South Africa: The Road to a "Rainbow Nation",* (Tokyo: Iwanami Shoten, 1996); *Development Economics and Modern Africa,* Tokyo: Nihon Hyoron Sha, 1999 (awarded the 4th Okita Memorial Prize for International Development Research by FASID: Foundation for Advanced Studies on International Development, Tokyo); *From Hatred to Reconciliation: A Study of Regional Conflicts* (Kyoto: Kyoto University Press, 2000) for which he was awarded the 2nd Okita Commemorative Award for Policy Research by NIRA: National Institute for Research Advancement, Tokyo); *Sixty Chapters to Know South Africa* (Tokyo: Akashi Shoten, 2010); and *Learning from Africa* (Tokyo: Yuhikaku, 2010). His recent English publications include: "The Political Element in the Works of W. Arthur Lewis", in: *Developing Economies* 44, 3 (2006). He has also written extensively on human security issues and chairs the Japan Consortium for Human Security Education and Research.

Address: Prof. Dr. Yoichi Mine, Graduate School of Global Studies, Doshisha University, Hakuenkan bld., Karasuma-Hiagashi-iru, Imadegawa-dori, Kamigyo-ku, Kyoto, 602-8580, Japan.
Email: <kozam@kta.att.ne.jp>.
Website: <http://global-studies.doshisha.ac.jp/english/cur/cur4.html>.

Kinhide Mushakoji (Japan) is Director, Centre for Asia Pacific Partnership, Osaka University of Economics and Law (since 2003); he was Professor, Department of International Relations, Chubu University and Chubu Institute of Advanced Studies (2001-2004); Professor, Department of Global and Inter-cultural Studies, Ferris University (Yokohama) (1998-2000); Professor, Department of International Studies, Meiji-Gakuin University (1989-1998); Vice-Rector for Programmes, the United Nations University (1976-1989). Other areas of participation include Vice-President, International Movement Against All Forms of Discrimination and Racism (IMADR); Member of the Board: Asian Cultural

Forum on Development (ACFOD); President: Asia-Pacific Human Rights Information Centre (Human Rights Osaka); President: Osaka International Peace Centre (Peace Osaka). Among his many publications are "The Phenomenon of Xenophobia: in Relation to Racism and Racial Discrimination", UNESCO (Ed.): *Struggle against Discrimination* (Studies on Human Rights, 2004): 19-41; "Social Reproduction of Exclusion: Exploitative Migration and Human Insecurity", in: Bakker, Isabella; Gill, Stephen (Eds.): *Power, Production and Social Reproduction* (New York/UK: McMillan, 2003); "Engendering the Japanese 'Double Standard' Patriarchal Democracy: The Case of the 'Comfort Women' and Military Sexual Slavery", in: Kelly, Rita Mae; Bayes, Jane H.; Hawkesworth, Mary E.; Young, Brigitte (Eds.): *Gender, Globalization and Democratization* (Boulder, CO: Rowman & Littlefield, 2001): 205-222.

Address: Prof. Dr. Kinhide Mushakoji, 5-34-14, Yoyogi, Shibuya-ku, Tokyo 151-0053 Japan.
Email: <QWD00105@nifty.ne.jp>.
Website: <http://www.keiho-u.ac.jp/english/html/ins_pacific.html>.

Ton van Naerssen (The Netherlands) is Senior Research Fellow in Development Geography at the Faculty of Management Sciences, Radboud University Nijmegen, and freelance consultant. His major fields of interest include globalization processes, urban environment, international migration and civil society engagement in development. His research experiences are in Southeast Asia, but he also gained experience in Africa and Latin America. Among others, he co-edited books on: *Healthy Cities in Developing Countries* (Verlag fur Entwicklungspolitik Saarbrücken GmbH, 2002), *Asian Migrants and European Labour Markets* (London, Routledge: 2005), and *Global Migration and Development* (London: Routledge, 2008). He is member of the Nijmegen Urban Health Group (NUHG), the Migration and Development Research Group, the project advisory Committee of Oxfam/Novib and Board member of the Global Society Foundation (SMS), a migrant organization with its main office in The Netherlands.

Address: Mr. Ton van Naerssen, Department of Human Geography, Radboud University Nijmegen, Thomas van Aquinostraat 3, P.O. Box 9108, NL-6500 HK Nijmegen, The Netherlands.
Email: <t.vannaerssen@fm.ru.nl>.
Website: <http:// radboud.academia.edu/Departments/HumanGeography>.

Ahmed Pouri (The Netherlands) is Coordinator of Participating Refugees in Multicultural Europe (PRIME), a Hague-based NGO, which he helped establish in 1995 and which works to support refugees and undocumented people in The Netherlands. Originally a computer engineer and mathematician, Ahmed left Iran and has lived in the Netherlands since 1985. His vision of PRIME is to help refugees organize themselves. To facilitate this, PRIME regularly facilitates social events, special meetings for women, public debates, demonstrations and campaigns. PRIME aims to press for a more humane refugee policy in The Netherlands, and Ahmed consistently works to put pressure on Dutch Parliamentarians to amend immigration and asylum policies to make them more just. Most recently, the priority has been to struggle against the growth of racism in The Netherlands, and across Europe. PRIME has conducted research on the growing numbers of refugees imprisoned and detained in The Netherlands, and on the importance of rape being a potential basis for asylum claims. Ahmed has also sought to encourage the Dutch government to amend its policies towards Iran. PRIME has strong contacts with other similar organizations working across the EU, and is an affiliate of LOS, the Landelijke Ongedocumenteerde Stichting (National Association for the Undocumented). Ahmed Pouri has taken part in numerous initiatives to confront racism in the wider context of globalization, presenting a paper on this, for example, at the Netherlands Social Forum in 2004.

Address: Mr. Ahmed Pouri, Repelaerstraat 84, 2515 NA, The Hague, The Netherlands.
Email: <apouri@gmail.com>.
Website: <www.prime95.nl>.

Bernadette P. Resurreccion (Philippines) has PhD and MA degrees in Development Studies from the International Institute of Social Studies of Erasmus University Rotterdam (ISS-EUR), The Netherlands. She is an Associate Professor of Gender and Development Studies (GDS) at the Asian Institute of Technology in Thailand. Her teaching and research addressed the themes of gender, livelihoods, natural resource management and migration and their consequent policy processes in Southeast Asia, notably in the Philippines and the Mekong Region countries – Cambodia, Thailand and Vietnam. Selected publications include: (Ed.): *Gender and Natural Resource Management. Livelihoods, Interventions and Mobility* (UK: Earthscan); "Keeping the Peace is Not Enough: Human Security and Gender-based Violence During the Transitional Period in Timor Leste", in: *Sojourn* (2009); "Gender, Migration and Social Reproduction in the Mekong Region", in: *Asian and Pacific Migration Journal* (2009); "Reproducing Gender. Female Rural-Urban Migration in the Red River Delta", in: *Population, Space and Place* (2008); "Edging Women Out? Gender, Agency and Identity in Philippine Upland Development", in: *Development and Change* (2006); "Women in-between: Transnational and Rural-Urban Migration in the Mekong Region", in: *Gender, Technology and Development* (2005); "Gender and Migration in the Asia-Pacific Region": in: the *UNDP Asian Human Development Report* (in press).

Address: Dr. Bernadette P. Resurreccion, Asian Institute of Technology, P.O. Box 4, Klong Luang, Pathumthani 12120, Thailand.
Email: <babette@ait.ac.th>.
Website: <http://www.ait.ac.th/>.

Bernice Roldan (Philippines) received her MA in Development Studies from the International Institute of Social Studies of Erasmus University Rotterdam (ISS-EUR), The Netherlands. She currently works at Aflatoun (Child Savings International) in Amsterdam, and was previously at the Commission for Filipino Migrant Workers in Amsterdam, which coordinates RESPECT, a Europe-wide network of migrant domestic workers' organizations and support groups campaigning for the rights and welfare of migrants working in private households. In November 2009, she was a workshop facilitator at the Peoples' Global Action on Migration, Development and Human Rights, the civil society parallel process to the Global Forum on Migration and Development in Athens. In 2007 and 2009, she facilitated training and action research among Filipino migrant communities in Taiwan and the Netherlands on financial literacy and social entrepreneurship in the homeland. Her most recent published work is "One Size Doesn't Fit All: Tailoring Credit Programs along the Logic of the Poor", in: *An Exercise in Worldmaking: The Institute of Social Studies Best Student Essays of 2008/09* (The Hague: Institute of Social Studies, 2009).

Email: <berniceroldan@yahoo.com>.

Edsel E. Sajor (Philippines) is Associate Professor at the School of Environment, Resources and Development at the Asian Institute of Technology (AIT) in Bangkok, Thailand, where he teaches Urban Environment Management. He has PhD and MA degrees in Development Studies from the International Institute of Social Studies of Erasmus University Rotterdam (ISS-EUR), The Netherlands. His research and teaching interests include urban governance, peri-urban studies, land and water management, and environmental conflict resolution. In recent years, his range of research interests has expanded into the areas of biotechnology development and public policy in Asia. He has also managed a number of development action research studies and projects in Southeast Asia on environment, technology innovation and poverty alleviation, as part of AIT's outreach programme. Selected publications include: "Institutional and Development Issues in Integrated Water Resource Management of Saigon River", in: *Journal of Environment and Development* (2009); "Mixed Land Use and Equity in Water Governance in Peri-Urban Bangkok", in: *International Journal of Urban and Regional Research* (2007); "Promoting Waste Separation for Recycling and Local Governance in Thailand", in: *Habitat International* (2006); "Professionalization or Hybridization? Real Estate Brokers in Metro Cebu, Philippines during the Boom of the 90s", in: *Urban Studies* (2005).

Address: Dr. Edsel E. Sajor, P.O. Box 4, Klong Luang, Pathumthani 12120, Thailand.
Email: <esajor@ait.ac.th>.
Website: <http://www.ait.ac.th/>.

Amrita Sharma (India) has a Masters in Development Studies with a specialization in Governance and Democracy from the International Institute of Social Studies of the Erasmus University of Rotterdam (ISS-EUR), The Netherlands, and a Masters in Public Policy from Central European University, Budapest, with a specialization in international policy practice. She also has a postgraduate diploma in Rural Management from the Institute of Rural Management, Anand, Gujarat. She started her career with the International Water Management Institute - Tata water policy programme (ITP) in Anand, Gujarat and worked there for three years (2004-07). Her key research interests include seasonal and internal migration within India, and international migration management norms and policies. She has also published work on the changing agricultural demography of India. At present, she is working as a consultant for a constituency management team of a member of parliament in Delhi and for Aajeevika, an NGO working on seasonal migration management in western India.

Email: <a.sharma31@gmail.com>.

May-Len Skilbrei (Norway) is a senior researcher and research director at the Fafo Institute for Applied International Studies, Oslo. Before joining Fafo, she was a PhD research fellow at NOVA (Norwegian Social Research) and post-doctoral fellow at the Department of Criminology and Sociology of Law at the University of Oslo. She has also been a visiting scholar at Lancaster University, UK. She received her Dr. Polit. degree in sociology at the University of Oslo, and has worked on issues such as gender and unskilled labour, migration and gender, transnational prostitution and human trafficking, and published extensively on those issues in Norwegian. Her English publications include the articles "The Rise and Fall of the Norwegian Massage Parlours: Changes in the Norwegian Prostitution Setting in the 1990s", in: *Feminist Review*, 67: 63-77 (2001); (with M. Tveit): "Defining Trafficking Through Empirical Work. Blurred Boundaries and their Consequences", in: *Gender, Technology and Development* 12,1: 9-30 (2008); "Taking Trafficking to Court", in: Bernat, Frances (Ed.): *Human Sex Trafficking* (New York: Routledge, 2010); (with M. Tveit): *Facing Return. Perceptions of Repatriation among Nigerian Women in Prostitution in Norway*, Fafo-report 2007: 01 (Oslo: Fafo, 2007).

Address: Ms. May-Len Skilbrei, Fafo, P.O. Box 2947 Tøyen, N-0608 Oslo, Norway.
Email:<mls@fafo.no>
Website: <http://www.fafo.no/indexenglish.htm>.

Thanh-Dam Truong (The Netherlands) received her PhD from the University of Amsterdam. She is currently Associate Professor in Women, Gender and Development at the International Institute of Social Studies of the Erasmus University of Rotterdam (ISS-EUR). Her work has been translated into Dutch, French, Japanese, Indonesian, Thai and Spanish. Her book, *Sex, Money and Morality: Prostitution and Tourism in Southeast Asia* (published by Zed Books/ St. Martin Press, 1990), continues to be widely cited for its relevance and impacts. Her recent publications address the nexus of gender, migration and human security: *Poverty, Gender and Human Trafficking in Sub-Saharan Africa: Rethinking Best Practices in Migration Management* (UNESCO, Paris, 2006, translated into French in 2007); her contributions in the field of development ethics include: "One Humanity, Many Consciousnesses: Unresolved Issues in Nussbaum's Frontiers of Justice", in: *Development and Change* (2006); "Gender, Human Security and Global Connectivity", in: *Encyclopaedia on Globalisation and Human Security* (Santa Barbara, CA: Praeger, 2009); "Human Security and the Governmentality of Neo-liberal Mobility: A Feminist Perspective", in: Brauch, H.G.; et al. (Eds.): *Fac-*

ing Global Environmental Change: Environmental, Human, Energy, Food, Health and Water Security, (Berlin/Heidelberg, Germany: Springer, 2009); "Feminist knowledge and human security: bridging rifts through the epistemology of care" in: Young, B; Scherrer, C. (Eds.): Gender Knowledge and Knowledge Networks in International Political Economy (Baden-Baden: Nomos, 2010); co-edited volumes include: *Engendering Human Security* (London: Zed, 2006) (co-editors Amrita Chhachhi and Saskia Wieringa); *Trans-local Livelihoods and Connections: Embedding a Gender Perspective into Migration Studies*, a special issue of *Gender, Technology and Development* 12, 3 (2008): 285-537 (co-editor Des Gasper); "Gender, Poverty and Social Justice", in: Denemark, R.A (Ed.) *Compendium of the International Studies Association, Section: Feminist Theory and Gender Studies*, co-author Amrita Chhachhi (Hoboken, NJ: Wiley-Blackwell, 2010); "Development Ethics through the Lens of Caring, Gender and Human Security" (co-author Des Gasper), in: Esquith, S.L.; Gifford, F. (Eds.): *The Capabilities Approach: A Constructive Critique* (Pennsylvania: Pennsylvania State University Press, 2010); "Movements of The 'We': International and Transnational Migration and the Capabilities Approach", co-author Des Gasper, *Journal of Human Development and Capabilities*, a special issue on human mobility, 11, 2 (2010): 339-357.

Address: Dr. Thanh-Dam Truong, P.O. Box 29776, 2502 LT The Hague, The Netherlands
Email: <truong@iss.nl>.
Website: <http://www.iss.nl/truong>.

Marianne Tveit (Norway) is a researcher at the *Fafo Institute for Applied International Studies*, Oslo. She has a Cand. polit. degree in Media and Communication from the University of Oslo. Before joining Fafo, she worked as a journalist in the *Norwegian National Broadcasting Company* (NRK). As a researcher, she has worked mainly on issues related to female migration, transnational marriages, human trafficking and prostitution, and has published reports on those issues in both Norwegian and English. Her English publications include the reports: (with G. Tyldum and A. Brunovskis): *Taking Stock. A Review on Existing Research on Trafficking for Sexual Exploitation*, (Fafo-report 493); (with M-L. Skilbrei): *Facing Return. Perceptions of Repatriation among Nigerian Women in Prostitution in Norway*, (Fafo-report 2007): 01; (with G. Hasselknippe): *Against the Odds. How Palestinians Cope through Fiscal Crisis, Closure and Boycott*, (Fafo-report 2007):41; (with G. Tyldum): *Someone who Cares. A Study of Vulnerability and Risk in Marriage Migration from Russia and Thailand to Norway*, (Fafo-report 2008): 26; (with M-L Skilbrei): "Defining Trafficking Through Empirical Work. Blurred Boundaries and their Consequences", in: *Gender, Technology and Development*, 12,1: (2008): 9-30.

Address: Ms. Marianne Tveit, Fafo, P.O. Box 2947 Tøyen, N-0608 Oslo, Norway.
Email: <mtv@fafo.no>.
Website: <http://www.fafo.no/pers/bio/mtv.htm>.

Gustavo Verduzco Igartúa (México) received his PhD in sociology (1980) from the University of Texas, Austin, with a major in demography. He is Professor and Researcher at the Center for Sociological Studies, El Colegio de México. One of his main areas of expertise is the migration of Mexican workers to the United States and Canada. He is also expert in Civil Society Organizations. Some of his affiliations include: Mexican representative and member of the Executive Committee of the Consejo Latinoamericano de Ciencias Sociales (CLACSO) (2006-2009); Director of the Center for Sociological Studies at El Colegio de México (2000-2006); Member of the Mexican Academy of Sciences (since 1987); Member of the National Researchers System in Mexico, level III. He was invited to be a core member of the research team for the Binational Study on Migration between Mexico and the United States (1995-97), a commission created following a mandate of the presidents of the two countries. He has also conducted research on the Seasonal Agricultural Workers Programme that Mexico has with Canada since 1973. His publications include more than 70 articles or book chapters in Spanish (mainly), English and French. His most recent contribution is (with co-authors Jacqueline Butcher and Guadalupe Serna), "Findings, Challenges and Implications", in: Butcher, J. (Ed.): *Mexican Solidarity: Citizen Participation and Volunteering* (New York: Springer Books, 2010).

Address: Prof. Dr. Gustavo Verduzco Igartúa, El Colegio de México, A.C. Centro de Estudios Sociológicos (CES), Camino al Ajusco #20 Pedregal de Santa Teresa, Tlalpan, C.P. 10740 México, D.F.
Email: <gverduz@colmex.mx>.
Website: <http://ces.colmex.mx/index.html>.

Index

K

L

M